Globalization and Education

Integration and Contestation across Cultures

2nd Edition

Edited by
Nelly P. Stromquist and Karen Monkman

ROWMAN & LITTLEFIELD EDUCATION
A division of
ROWMAN & LITTLEFIELD
Lanham • Boulder • New York • Toronto • Plymouth, UK

Published by Rowman & Littlefield Education
A division of Rowman & Littlefield
4501 Forbes Boulevard, Suite 200, Lanham, Maryland 20706
www.rowman.com

10 Thornbury Road, Plymouth PL6 7PP, United Kingdom

British Library Cataloguing in Publication Information Available

Library of Congress Cataloging-in-Publication Data

Stromquist, Nelly P.
Globalization and education : integration and contestation across cultures / Nelly P. Stromquist and Karen Monkman.
p. cm.
Includes bibliographical references and index.
ISBN 978-1-4758-0527-7 (cloth : alk. paper) -- ISBN 978-1-4758-0528-4 (pbk. : alk. paper) -- ISBN 978-1-4758-0529-1 (electronic)
1. Education and globalization. 2. Education and globalization--Cross-cultural studies. I. Monkman, Karen. II. Title.
LC191.2.S77 2014
370.9--dc23
                                                                    2013049338

Printed in the United States of America

Contents

Preface

We are pleased to present the second edition of our book on globalization and education, an intellectual effort we can trace to 1997 when the two editors of this book selected "globalization" as the theme for the western regional conference of the Comparative and International Education Society. At that time, we felt that although the concept had attracted considerable interest in the academy and throughout most of the world, it had been examined primarily as an economic and technological phenomenon, seldom from an educational or cultural perspective.

During the years since, globalization has attracted the attention of educators across the globe who have in turn produced a large body of literature. The expanding interest in the intersection of education and globalization has brought up several new topics, including the salience of global policies with an education content (notably Education for All and the UN Millennium Development Goals), the expansion and differentiation of higher education, a greater emphasis on work-related training, and the use of information and communication technologies (ICTs).

PURPOSE, SCOPE, AND UNIQUE QUALITIES

We approach this book with the knowledge and experience gained over the fourteen years since its first edition. The contributors to this book comprise many of the original authors but also several new ones. They represent well-known scholars in the field of comparative education, but also represented are newer scholars. We have maintained the initial geographical coverage in terms of authors and, with the exception of the Caribbean, the countries and regions examined.

We offer here a collection of chapters that reflect that broad range of issues in accessible yet theoretically grounded detail. Authors who contributed to the first edition now expand on their data and reflection, demonstrating the dynamic nature of globalization and its wide range of consequences. This edition comprises important changes in content, deepening the treatment of key concepts and dimensions of what we have come to accept as globalization. It includes six chapters by authors new to the book. Most of the other chapters have been completely rewritten and the rest have been significantly revised and updated.

In terms of research methodologies, the reader will find essays that bring together the academic literature and a sharp analytical lens focused on several conceptual issues and levels of education. Also present is a chapter on qualitative methodologies especially suitable to the understanding of the intersection of globalization and education, as well as several chapters employing ethnographic techniques to comprehend taken-for-granted truths about current national educational policies and global initiatives.

The authors analyze phenomena on the global plane, in local spaces, and in the connections between the global and the local, distinguishing this book from others in the field, which tend to center on one issue (e.g., policy processes, labor, or international assessments), lack theoretical depth about the notion of globalization, or limit their focus to one geographical region. We consider that the integration of levels of education, scales of analysis (the global and the local), and the recognition of national diversity and context make this book unique.

While education is gaining widespread attention as a means to individual social mobility and national economic competitiveness, educators and policy-makers must continue to give globalization close scrutiny if we are to assess its impact on education in developing countries and on the interplay that is occurring between central and less developed countries. Consequences of globalization on the enormous expansion of higher education and global policies such as those seeking the provision of universal basic education need to be understood in their fullest implications. Innovations affecting the community college, the provision of distance education, restructured curricula, and the role of the university in the economy are emerging as powerful new agendas closely linked to globalization initiatives.

In fundamental ways, the forces of globalization challenge the previous approaches and theories of national development. In the minds of some observers, globalization is an exaggerated form of global capitalism; in the view of others, it is a wake-up call to look for alternative forms to the new social and cultural arrangements that are being both spontaneously and deliberately generated by globalization.

ORGANIZATION OF THE BOOK

This book is organized in three sections. The first addresses conceptual and methodological issues underlying such notions as globalization, internationalization, and multilateralism. The second presents empirical data from various countries and provides examples of shifts and transformations within a specific level or modality of the educational system. The third looks at the totality of educational changes taking the nation as the unit of analysis. These country-level case studies bring together in concrete and detailed ways the impacts of globalization at the multiple levels of the modalities of the education system.

We remind the reader that in this book we are not considering the popular media even though it is an important aspect of globalization. The absence of media chapters is not due to our lack of recognition of their importance but rather to the scope of the book, namely, concentrating on education, albeit defined in broad terms.

In the first section of this book—conceptual and methodological issues—the editors, Nelly P. Stromquist and Karen Monkman, begin with an essay defining globalization and assessing its implications for all levels of education. We find that two actors are imposing themselves on educational policy agendas: the market and the transnational corporation. The changes they are promoting affect not only the formal educational system but also the construction and restructuring of local cultures. The university, the educational level most affected by globalization, has seen enormous expansion accompanied by differentiation of institutions. At the same time, knowledge is being created at multiple sites, among which the university is only one. Globalization is promoting increased knowledge, a by-product of the constant and rapid exchange of information made possible by computer-mediated technologies. This new type of knowledge is likely to generate winners and losers at individual and national levels—even though the current discourse of globalization glosses over this possibility, preferring to talk instead of opportunities for persons and countries to develop their "comparative advantage."

Martin Carnoy's chapter brings together two key issues surrounding globalization: the impact of ICTs on the education system and the consequences of globalization upon the nation-state. On the question of ICTs, Carnoy finds that, despite improvements in hardware and software, ICTs' impact on student learning has been mixed, in part because of problems in computer access and teacher training. At the university level, impacts have been positive as research and teaching networks have expanded. The emergence of new forms of virtual education—for instance the massive open online courses—hold the promise of making knowledge accessible to large groups, including previously marginalized persons, but it remains to be seen to what extent massive open online courses enable certified knowledge at lower costs. While globalization has moved education policies toward privatization, there are signs of explicit decision-making to protect the quality of certain universities even though this occurs at the expense of poor students attending non-elite universities. Carnoy finds evidence that for the state some functions have been weakened and others strengthened, though in balance, he argues, countries still retain considerable decision-making space and pressures to move into unsuitable global policies can be successfully resisted.

Karen Mundy and Caroline Manion focus on global governance—specifically, the work of global institutions and transnational actors with educational mandates agendas—from a historical perspective, drawing on theories of global governance and international relations. They ask "how changes in world order and the international society of states over the last half-century have shaped existing institutions, and how global institutions have in turn developed new patterns and possibilities for global governance." Their chapter examines the "evolution of the international education for development regime alongside the United Nations mandate in education," calling to our attention the rise of the World Bank as the "preeminent global governor of this regime," and the "putative success of the 'education for all' movement over the last decade." The chapter examines also the involvement of nonstate actors and networks, including both powerful corporations and consulting firms as well as grassroots organizations. It concludes with a consideration of current shifting global patterns of geopolitical and economic power, and their implications for a future legitimate global governance in the area of education.

Monisha Bajaj's chapter shifts our focus to human rights, which, she posits, is the primary organizing force in global education policy discourse today. Three orientations—education *as* a human right, education *with* human rights, and education *for* human rights—frame her analysis of changes in international discussions and policy-making. She then presents a case study of the Right to Education Act in India, using the concepts of decoupling and loose coupling to understand the "intermediation of human rights education by ideology, context, constituency, and locale" in India, where "rights" talk informs understandings of quality. She concludes: "the use of rights talk to frame a particular vision of education, while contested, utilizes global discussions as a foundation but goes far beyond international agreements on the right to access primary schooling to entrench a far more comprehensive vision."

The chapter by Kathryn Moeller provides a stark example of transnational corporation engagement in education. Ostensibly seeking to improve gender conditions in developing countries, one such corporation, Nike, has endorsed the concept of "The Girl Effect," which targets adolescent girls and young women. This approach, based on the logic that girls are not only a vulnerable group but also a population that must be attended to before they become adult women and face more complex problems, at first sight has some merit. However, Moeller's ethnographic account shows that, while investing in young women in Brazil, Nike funds short-term education programs that essentially train girls for job preparation without helping them to problematize gender issues. Entering the terrain of national development, Nike reinforces narrow definitions of gender and, by focusing on poor girls, also fosters the racialization of gender. Through Moeller's case study, the de facto political role of transnational corporations in education is brought clearly into the open.

Noel Gough's chapter on curriculum, informed by narrative theory and poststructuralism, is guided by the question, *How does globalization work?* rather than, *What does it mean?* Based on his long experience as a curriculum specialist, Gough depicts how difficult and complex is the process of curricular renewal and the frequent reluctance to embrace the concept of individual and cultural differences. His interest in "what curriculum workers (teachers, administrators, academics, researchers) *do*, and *produce*, with the concept of globalization" takes shape in his exploration of the transnational curriculum conversations and deliberations related to global perspectives on school curricula—through which culturally inclusive curriculum is probed and examined—and of the internationalizing nature of the field of curriculum studies (i.e., ways in which local knowledge is globalized). His chapter raises many questions for readers to ponder.

Raising a voice from Africa, Catherine Odora Hoppers' chapter offers a sharp critique of the mirage of globalization as the new path to democracy and well-being. She finds that Western economic interests are omnipresent and that the Western notion of modernization not only prevails but its deployment further marginalizes different peoples and cultures, especially those in Africa. From her perspective, education conditions in Africa are defined by outsiders and education research often helps to legitimize the particular framing supported by international financial and development agencies. The conclusions of these agencies converge on identifying African governments as incapable of carrying out reforms and subsequent programs to improve education in their countries. Odora Hoppers presents accounts from several African countries showing the imposition of external education agendas. She calls for stronger affirmation of African values and perspectives in the shaping of education policies as well as in the production of knowledge that precedes them.

We close the first section of the book with a chapter focusing on qualitative methodologies deemed especially appropriate for the understanding of the complexities and nuances that can be found in globalization processes. The chapter by Lesley Bartlett and Frances Vavrus begins with a question: What new methodological approaches are required to examine globalization and education? They lay out a variety of frameworks related to globalization (influenced by anthropologist Tsing), sociocultural policy research, actor network theory, and the notion of policyscapes, as a grounding for their argument that a multi-sited, ethnographic approach is needed for nuanced, multi-faceted understandings of globalization. They describe the vertical case study approach as a methodology that captures the richness of these phenomena as they occur in multiple levels (vertical), multi-sites (horizontal), and across time (transversal). The interconnecting nature of global phenomena occurs in local contexts, within relationships or networks that stretch across space and time, and connects scales, places, and actors. The authors then present a case study of a learner-centered pedagogy in Tanzania to demonstrate the use and strengths of vertical case study research.

Part two of the book brings to the fore a discussion of the impact of globalization on various educational levels ranging from adult education to higher education. It also considers current developments in the community college model across national settings, and changes in vocational education in the changing global labor context.

Jan Currie and Lesley Vidovich focus their analysis of globalization's impact on university sectors in France, the Netherlands, and Australia. They look at how policy-makers are positioning Europe in the global marketplace of higher education, and how the three countries mentioned respond. The authors lay out a detailed analysis of university ranking systems and research assessment exercises, as they demonstrate elements of the neoliberal model of "best practice." This model influences responses within higher education, although there are differences in how and how much each country responds. Historical traditions and political economy shape what they adopt and how they adapt it. France, for example, has resisted some elements of neoliberalism, whereas the other two countries have more often emulated the world's leading universities. The dominance of English language higher education institutions in this global competition make for an uneven playing field.

Rosalind Raby considers the community college model of post-secondary education and its diffusion in many countries. She outlines the various forms it takes, and discusses why this model is of interest and how it is implicated in international development education. The latter—international development education—is motivated by privatization or humanitarian interests that are facilitated by globalization agendas. She finds similarity across structures and locations, yet unique local interpretations. Many forms of the community college focus on vocational and technical education for segments of the population without access to universities. She identifies five repercussions of globalization: financial, academic, cultural, applied, and philosophical.

Peter Kelly and Jane Kenway engage readers in examining the restructuring of gender, education (primarily vocational education and training), and work through young people's narratives in the era following the global financial crisis of 2008, and an analysis of a chef training program. Within this changing context, their research shows how young people, who are marginalized from and by education and labor markets, are discursively portrayed in negative terms as having low self esteem, self-defeating behaviors, and the like, and situates vocational education and training programs such as Jamie's Kitchen as key to their transformation. To be employable in the globalized labor markets, they argue, "the self … must think about, act on, and perform itself as an enterprise." The authors juxtapose this with text from "I am the 99 percent" which portrays youth as active, driven, hard-working, and able, but not having access.

Shirley Walters' chapter takes South Africa as its object of attention to discuss various aspects of adult education as they are being influenced by globalization trends, particularly economic globalization. Special attention is given to the national qualifications framework, a policy designed to recognize the knowledge and skills acquired through prior work experience—a strategy particularly relevant to South Africa, where the struggle against apartheid impeded the regular schooling of large populations. As the first country to try to integrate all levels of knowledge through its national qualifications framework, South Africa constitutes a rich site for examination of this policy, now in place in almost 150 countries. In the changing world of work created by globalization, many skills are used for a large variety of jobs, and workers themselves come increasingly from diverse cultural origins. The selection of criteria for the recognition of prior knowledge and skills proves to be a complex exercise, complicated by the fact that it is those in power who retain the final word on what is accepted. Global developments affecting the definition and status of adult education create new obstacles and possibilities for the adoption of lifelong learning strategies.

Section three of this book presents six case studies of particular countries. They comprise Japan, Mexico, Malaysia, Malawi, South Africa, and Australia. Through these case studies, we can see, in specific contexts, how globalization has engaged with particular educational policies, discourses, and practices.

Lynne Parmenter examines how globalization is interpreted, negotiated, and appropriated in Japanese schools and higher education. A shift in discourse from "anti-globalization" to "diverse globalizations" in Japan signals more acceptance of the influences from globalization, although tensions are clear: between the national and the global, between cultural homogeneity and a global orientation. The centralized structure—reflecting an entrenched system—resists change and has developed an incrementalist approach to educational reform in an effort to maintain stability and coherence. Parmenter demonstrates this in a look at how changes are made to courses of study and textbooks. She reveals a tension between the priorities of promoting global citizenship and recognizing diversity while also assuming homogeneity. In higher education, neoliberalism has welcomed market forces in shaping reforms. Internationalization efforts focus on attracting international students to Japan via the Global 30 initiative and situate Japan as a regional hub for higher education. Interestingly, however, this initiative is not driven by economic interests, but by a desire for full integration into the global education sphere.

Rosa Nidia Buenfil Burgos situates her analysis of Mexico within a broader discussion in which she problematizes the meanings of globalization, looking not at whether education has tended toward the universal or particular (or homogenization or heterogeneity), but a more complicated look at how "globalization travels throughout different social scopes, as it moves from the international recommendation, to the national policy, to the school-specific program (curriculum and syllabi), and finally to the classroom." She focuses on a policy called *Modernización Educativa* (Educational Modernization), 1988–2006, and its impact on teacher identity, the "revaluation" of the role of teachers, and the changing meanings of the notion of "quality." Buenfil sees "the particularity (local) overflowing and contaminating the universal (global)."

Centering on Malaysia—a country recognized as one of the few successful industrializing countries where "globalization of the economy" has been the basis for its growth—Molly Lee examines how globalization forces have affected the entire educational system of her country through an interplay of homogenization and particularization. As a result of the government's comprehensive review of Malaysia's education system, a set of eleven "shifts" is outlined relative to curriculum revisions, early childhood and secondary education expansion, improving resources for special education, upgrading and professionalizing the teaching force, administrative decentralization, ICT training, and encouraging private higher education. The particular forms of national response to challenges emanating from the global realm are formulated through the interplay of conflict and compromise. Implementation is then further shaped by local contexts, creating different practices for seemingly similar policies.

Nancy Kendall and Rachel Silver's contribution provides an in-depth look at the consequences of the massification of basic education in Malawi, a country seriously affected by external debt and subjected to stringent structural reforms imposed by international financial and development institutions. Weaving a narrative that juxtaposes economic opportunities and social status with formal schooling, Kendall and Silver demonstrate how parents, aware that government will not supply jobs and that the formal economy offers reduced possibility for well-being, opt for pursuing agricultural rather than academic skills for their children. The economic context of Malawi, characterized by the considerable importance of agricultural (tobacco) production, creates its own particular dynamics, promoting contestation from below (through parents and students) to global policies that are imposed from above and make little sense in their society. Not surprisingly, formal education enjoys low acceptance when it cannot meet expectations for a better life.

The chapter by Salim Vally and Carol Anne Spreen, the second in this book that centers on South Africa, probes the reach and outcomes of education policies that have encompassed and reflected elements of social justice. The call to be "internationally competitive," however, has produced a dominant discourse lodged in human capital theory, which assumes that socioeconomic development is contingent on the "productive" and instrumental role of education and training. The corollary to this belief is that unemployment, particularly youth unemployment, is seen as result of their lack of skills for the labor market. Vally and Spreen show how post-apartheid education policies around education and training relate directly to global trends fueled by neoliberalism. The policy and practice of limiting education to narrowly constructed objectives and economic rationales and the seduction of the global knowledge economy and corporate competitiveness has permeated major post-apartheid educational reforms, ignoring the broader purposes of education.

We close the book with a chapter on Australia by Jill Blackmore, who introduces the case of an industrialized country (as did Parmenter, discussing Japan) whose path may not be drastically different from less powerful countries in the developing world where structural and other policies associated with globalization affect both marginalized countries and individuals. Blackmore's chapter revisits the impact of globalization on higher education in Australia over the past ten years. She finds a solidification of neoliberal norms and practices as universities have adopted unambiguously the strategy of serving the market through scientific and technological products. Continuing her focus on gender dimensions of globalization, Blackmore finds that women in Australia—as in many other countries—have increased their participation as students in universities. However, women continue to occupy lower academic positions at the university and to have uneven participation across fields to study. They are increasingly located in teaching assignments and non-stable academic positions. The massive corporatization of these institutions has brought a competitive ethos that turns concerns with equity into preferences for efficiency. A number of government and institutional measures in recent years has dismantled equity and adopted the more neutral notion of diversity. The managerial university has created an opportunity for more women to enter mid-level administrative positions but, in the absence of efforts to resolve work-family tensions, these women find themselves in stressful positions. Thus, while women have become more visible in universities, the essential patriarchal arrangements remain uncontested.

CONTRIBUTION TO THE FIELD AND AUDIENCE

With this revised edition of the book, we raise a number of theoretical issues and bring a greater level of concreteness through reference to specific instances of the force of globalization as it affects education and the way selected countries have responded. The emerging terrains of convergence, dissonance, and conflict have helped us clarify the implications of globalization for education and knowledge in the twenty-first century.

This book will be particularly useful to researchers in the areas of globalization and education, global education policy, and the fields of comparative and international education, anthropology and sociology of education, women's/gender study programs, and other disciplinary intersections with education (political science, economics, cultural studies, etc.). We expect it to be required reading for graduate students in many programs and courses related to globalization, international development, comparative/international education, and disciplinary courses that focus on education; gender-related courses that are global or international in nature (e.g., gender and development, gender and education globally, and transnational gender studies) will also find it useful. Policy-makers, planners, and development workers have in this volume information on how others facing challenges similar to their own have dealt (or been unable to deal) with them; educators and others who seek to better understand how global forces are shaping their world will gain insight here.

ACKNOWLEDGMENTS

We wish to thank Nancy Evans, our editor at Rowman and Littlefield, for her warm and generous reception to the idea of a new edition of this book. Her encouragement and advice have been constant and most valuable. We also wish to thank our copy editors, Carlie Wall and Christopher Basso, for their authoritative assistance at various moments of production. Deep thanks go to all the contributors to this book who were willing to accept critique and produce even better versions; they are all very busy professionals but found time to respond to our calls. Finally, we want to thank Mallory Wessel and Brittany Young, graduate students at DePaul University, who helped us with logistics, research, and editing, and asked good questions that helped us to improve our process and product.

Abbreviations and Acronyms

ABE — adult basic education
ACE — American Council on Education
AERA — American Education Research Association
AHELO — Assessment of Higher Education Learning Outcomes
AI — Amnesty International
ANC — African National Congress
ARWU — Academic Ranking of World Universities
ASEAN — Association of South East Asian Nations
AWID — Association for Women's Rights in Development
BRIC — Brazil, Russia, India, and China
CAI — computer-assisted instruction
CARE — Cooperative for Assistance and Relief Everywhere
CBO — community-based organization
CEPAL — Economic Commission for Latin American and Caribbean
CERI — Centre for Educational Research and Innovation
CLA — collegiate learning assessment
CSR — corporate social responsibility
DAWN — Development Alternatives with Women for a New Era
EFA — Education for All
ESL — English as a second language
ETAN — European Technology Assessment Network
ETS — Educational Testing Services
EU — European Union
FDI — foreign direct investment
FPE — free primary education
FTZ — Free Trade Zone
GATS — General Agreement on Trade in Services
GCE — Global Campaign for Education
ICT — information and communication technology
IDOs — independent development organizations
IEA — International Association for the Evaluation of Educational Achievement
IMF — International Monetary Fund
ISO — International Organization of Standardization

LCP — learner-centered pedagogy
MDGs — Millennium Development Goals
MOOC — massive open online course
NAFSA — Association of International Educators
NAFTA — North American Free Trade Agreement
NGO — nongovernmental organization
NIC — newly industrializing country
NPA — new public administration
NQF — National Qualifications Framework
OAS — Organization of American States
OBE — outcomes-based education
ODA — official development assistance
OECD — Organization for Economic Cooperation and Development
PISA — Program for International Student Assessment
PPEALC — Principal Education Project for Latin American
PRSP — Poverty Reduction Strategy Paper
RPL — recognition of prior learning
SAP — Structural Adjustment Policy
STEM — Science, Technology, Engineering, and Mathematics
THE — Times Higher Education
TIMSS — Third International Math and Science Study
TNC — transnational corporation
TVET — technical vocational education and training
UDHR — Universal Declaration of Human Rights
VCS — vertical case study
VET — vocational education and training
VSHE — vocational schools of higher education
WBES — World Bank's Education Strategy
WCEFA — World Conference on Education for All
WEF — World Economic Forum
WFCP — World Federation of Colleges and Polytechnics
WTO — World Trade Organization

Part I

Conceptual and Methodological Issues

Chapter One

Defining Globalization and Assessing its Implications for Knowledge and Education, Revisited

Nelly P. Stromquist and Karen Monkman

GLOBALIZATION DEFINED

Globalization, a contemporary term well ingrained in people's consciousness, is a phenomenon that comprises multiple and drastic changes in all areas of social life, particularly economics, technology, and culture. Not surprisingly, its meaning varies depending on the angle that is emphasized when defining it. Globalization can be discussed in economic, political, and cultural terms. It can be found in neoliberal economic perspectives, critical theory, and postmodernity. While initially centering on convergence/divergence, homogenization/heterogeneity, and local/global issues (Stromquist and Monkman, 2000), it now is understood as a much more multi-faceted and complex dynamic (Held, McGrew, Goldblatt, and Perraton, 1999), one that is contingent, ambiguous, contradictory, and paradoxical. Despite its ability to capture in its unfolding changes the involvement of the entire world in one way or another, globalization remains an inexact term for the strong, and perhaps irreversible, changes in the economy, labor force, technologies, communication, cultural patterns, and political alliances that it is shaping in every nation.

As Harvey has nicely encapsulated, under contemporary capitalism we have a "time/space compression" (cited in Castells, 2010, p. 448). English is emerging as the global language and social/economic transactions are being formulated within what Castells (2010) calls the "network society," a rise in horizontal connections among related institutions and communities in diverse localities and dependent on computer-mediated technologies.

A useful definition of globalization is that offered by Gibson-Graham (2006): "a set of processes by which the world is rapidly being integrated into one economic space via increased international trade, the internationalization of production and financial markets, the internationalization of a commodity culture promoted by an increasingly networked global telecommunications system" (p. 120).

Globalization has many faces. In the area of economics, practices favoring free trade, private enterprise, foreign investment, and liberalized trade prevail. In the social area, new consumption patterns and lifestyles with consequences for family relations and social organization have arisen. At cultural levels, the flows of people, goods, information, and images reflect the influence of communication processes (Appadurai, 2002; Featherstone, 1990) and new identities and imaginaries are taking shape. At the political level, there is increased acceptance of pluralistic systems, multi-party democracy, free elections, independent judiciaries, and the call for human rights (Ghai, 1987; also see Bajaj, this volume). Some observers are skeptical that these practices and norms will alter the real economic order. For instance, González Casanova (1996) sees the term *globalization* as a rhetorical device for the reconversion of dependency, as it hides the effects of economic policies that are creating major social problems in many developing countries. As Amin (1996) notes, globalization affects not only trade but also the productive system, technology, financial markets, and many other aspects of social life. So far, because there are still people outside the modern economy, globalization has not affected the lives of every person in every country, but increasingly, it appears that ultimately all groups will be brought into conformity.

ESTABLISHED ACTORS IN THE GLOBAL ECONOMY

The unfolding dynamics of globalization have brought several major players into the economic and political decision-making process. The first of these is unquestionably the market; the others, the more tangible ones, are the transnational corporations (TNCs) with indisputable roles in the market and politics.

The Market

Today, with the demise of the centrally planned, socialist economies, great promise and reliance are placed on the role of the market to release creative energies and minimize inefficiencies. Through competition of firms, the market is expected to enable production to reach its highest volume and quality. Competitiveness, then, is a major principle in the globalized market.

Castells (2010) identifies sources of competitiveness in the global economy. They operate through four distinct processes: (1) the technological capacity of a country or the articulation of science, technology, management, and production; (2) access to large, integrated, affluent markets such as the European Union, North American Free Trade Agreement, or Japan; (3) a profitable differential between production costs at the production site and prices at the market of destination (including not just labor costs but land costs, taxes, and environmental regulations); and (4) the political capacity of national and supranational institutions to guide the growth strategy of those countries or areas under their jurisdiction (pp. 103–105). In this list, knowledge as technological capacity emerges as a key component in the attainment of competitiveness; as we will see later, knowledge might not be accessible to everyone.

The power exercised by markets does not benefit all. And this is the problematic situation, as no market self-regulatory apparatus exists. Financial markets behave in extremely speculative ways; not only do they not engage in productive investments but they have triggered currency devaluation of entire countries (e.g., Brazil, Mexico, Thailand, and Russia), with corresponding consequences in reduced national wealth and limited public spending. One million children in Asia were unable to return to school after the crisis in the late 1990s. And, we have seen the damaging consequences of this economic agenda on education and other social services, family well-being, and local and national economic infrastructures following the 2008 global economic crisis.

A feature of contemporary markets is their clustering in regional blocs to attain benefits of scale, coordinate production, and target specific populations. Three such blocs have emerged

(Europe, North America, and East Asia) and they are preparing themselves for increasing competition.[1] Together with the global market, we are seeing the creation of macroinstitutions to facilitate economic and political exchanges. Examples are the growing influence of the International Monetary Fund and the World Bank in numerous countries, the creation of the World Trade Organization and the General Agreement on Trade in Services, and the redefinition of the North Atlantic Treaty Organization to address sociopolitical problems within European countries. On the other hand, world institutions such as those needed for the creation of a new international economic order are not being fostered. Through structural adjustment programs, and subsequently the Poverty Reduction Strategy Papers, coordinated by the World Bank and the International Monetary Fund, the process of capital accumulation continues while impacting negatively on the process of distribution and reallocation of the social product (see Kendall and Silver, and Odora Hoppers, this volume) and shaping such distributions in ways that maintain existing hierarchies between and within nations. Neoliberalism, which can be defined as the economic doctrine that relies on market forces as the main adjudicator of social decisions, has solidified itself over the past twenty years.

Transnational Corporations

Some forty-three thousand large firms qualify today as TNCs (Vitali, Glattfelder, and Battiston, 2011). TNCs are both the primary agents and major beneficiaries of globalization (Ghai, 1987; Gibson-Graham, 1996). It is estimated that 70 percent of the world trade was controlled by the five hundred largest industrial firms in 2002 (Share the World Resources, 2013). Through access to highly mobile capital, TNCs have created global factories, relying on the cheapest combination of labor and skills for selected tasks. TNCs thus have generated increasingly integrated and interdependent systems of capital-labor flows across regions and between states. With the support of international financial institutions, TNCs can engage in substantial and speedy capital investment, technology transfer, financial exchanges, and increased trade.

The emergence of institutions that are less publicly accountable, such as TNCs, banks, and media conglomerates, has produced a society in transition with new philosophies about government (Independent Commission on Population and Quality of Life, 1996, p. 257). Blackmore (this volume) warns that, "Whereas the welfare state previously disciplined the market within its national boundaries, in a globalized context the corporate state now mediates transnational market relations in education …" (citing Rizvi and Lingard, 2010). A worrisome development is the recognition of TNCs in U.S. courts and in the discourse of UN documents as citizens and thus as having the same rights as "people" (Crookshanks, 2008; Development Alternatives with Women for a New Era [DAWN], 2013).

The emergence of TNCs as major players has implications for education. With business and profitability as the main referent, "social and public service interests are devalued" and "appropriate knowledge becomes increasingly narrowly defined" (Bhanji, 2008; Kempner, 1998, p. 455). At local levels, there is an increased presence of business in cooperation with the schools, determining what constitutes quality and what is needed.

Recently eyes have been on the Occupy Movement, the Arab Spring, and other global movements that seek to push back or limit the neoliberal agenda, limiting the economy's strong hand in shaping life chances (Hale, 2013). Whether there will be a long-term effect on economic structures, policies, or actors, and what it would look like, remains to be seen.

CULTURE

The impact of globalization on culture is universally felt. However, there are opposing viewpoints about current developments. While some observers see a tendency toward homogeneity of values and norms, others see an opportunity to rescue or even reinvent local identities.

Communication technologies such as cell phones and satellite television and the many modalities of Internet expression are accelerating cultural change faster than ever before. Advances in transportation and its decreasing costs are facilitating travel abroad, which fosters exposure to other ways of life. Through the mass media (television, film, radio, video), not only is English becoming the global language but there has developed a tendency, particularly among elites and middle classes all over the world, to adopt what might be termed an "American way of life."

For Cvetkovich and Kellner (1997), the cultural forces reflected in the global media influence roles, identities, and experiences. In their view, old identities and traditional ways of seeing and being in the world have been challenged, and new forms are being constructed out of the "multifarious and sometimes conflicting configurations of traditional, local, national, and now global forces of the present time" (p. 10). But they also argue that "although global forces can be oppressive and erode cultural traditions and identities they can also provide new material to rework one's identity and can empower people to revolt against traditional forms and styles to create new, more emancipatory ones" (p. 10). Nonetheless, globalization fosters a greater synchronization of demands as well as a greater similarity in taste and preference within the national markets. In a way, this homogeneity is necessary to ensure a more standardized, and thus easier to produce, supply of products and services such as leisure and foreign travel.

It is likely that globalization is creating forces that will divide people economically but it might also generate forces with the potential to offer new bases for solidarity (Kenway, 1997). While the world is becoming smaller and more homogeneous at some levels, in a variety of ways local cultures are making efforts to retain their identity and, in some cases, even to rediscover it. One such example concerns recent developments in Latin America. While for many years there raged a debate as to whether the indigenous question should be about social class or ethnicity, indigenous organizations have opted for the second position, which does not deny or ignore the exploitation indigenous peoples face but prefers to challenge it through an affirmation of ethnic identity (Stavenhagen, 1997). Some scholars argue that the renaissance of the local might be emerging as a defense against the impossibility of joining the global on favorable terms. In any case, efforts to recapture traditional identities and values come as unintended effects of globalization.

The prevailing values that are emerging bring a twist to traditional definitions. "Flexibility," for instance, means less the ability to accept cultural differences than the ability to adjust economically and adapt innovations in the production of goods and services. While there have been significant changes in production processes, which have moved into "post-Fordist" forms, current labor practices and work organization continue to have a hierarchical network structure. Large companies in central countries offer their workers reward systems based on seniority and cooperation with firm-based unions; but firms in developing countries, which Castells terms those "in the periphery of the network," treat labor as expendable and exchangeable, relying on temporary workers and part-time employees, among whom women and poorly educated youth are the majority. In other words, production forms seem to have changed more than the values and norms attached to the way production is organized.

Culture and Gender

An important dimension of culture regards the formation of masculinity and femininity. Institutions such as armies, bureaucracies, and even the stock market have served to export norms of violence, aggression, and domination that established masculinity as the dominant norm (Connell, 1998). In the globalization era, the mass media, including social media, function as a source of new ideas regarding gender equity but also serve to heighten messages that reproduce gender asymmetries.

The most positive feature of globalization for women has been their incorporation into the labor market, providing a potential source of economic independence. According to the Organization for Economic Cooperation and Development (OECD), this incorporation in the seven major national economies grew about 30 percent from 1970 to 1990, a growth that Castells calls a "massive incorporation of women in paid work" throughout the world (2010, p. 269). Yet, this incorporation has taken forms that have not been particularly advantageous to women. In Japan, the third major industrial power in the world, women still massively enter the labor force in their early twenties, stop working after marriage to raise their children, and return later to the labor force as part-timers. This structure of the occupational life cycle is reinforced by the Japanese tax codes, which make it more advantageous for women to contribute in a relatively small proportion to the family income than to add a second salary. While the strict labor participation pattern of Japan is not found to the same extent in the United States, the U.S. tax code also penalizes two-income families. Globally, more than 50 percent of immigrants, and 60 to 70 percent in some places, are women; many end up in low-status, low-wage jobs, often in gender-segregated and informal economies, and become more vulnerable to exploitation and sexual violence (UN Populations Fund, 2013). For some, children are left at home while mothers seek work in the global economy. With border restrictions and tightening migration policies, transnational family arrangements become more difficult, as fathers and mothers are often less able to return home and families are separated.

Part-time jobs represent about one-fifth of the jobs in OECD countries; under globalization, these types of jobs also have a tendency to increase. Women, more than men, favor flexible time and part-time work because it accommodates their needs to combine their childrearing tasks and their working lives. It should be obvious, however, that this "accommodation" tends to reproduce highly gendered social relations. Craske (1998) maintains that the neoliberal project that accompanies current globalization processes depends on women retaining their "traditional" family-oriented identities without undermining their availability for the labor market to provide low-wage competition.

Jaggar (2001) observes that neoliberal globalization promised that it would undermine local forms of patriarchy and would make women full participants in politics and the economy. In her view, as this form of globalization has undermined peace, democracy, and environmental health, while strengthening racism and ethnocentrism, it is hostile to women. She further observes that neither technological developments nor communication developments have altered policy-makers' disregard for the private sphere. Today, there is a visible struggle to secure more rights for women; these demands have emerged primarily from grassroots activism and constitute an example of globalization from below (Jaggar, 2001; Stromquist, 2007).

Through greater engagement by women's groups as well as by UN machinery, considerable attention is being paid to gender issues: domestic violence, women's access to property, sexual and reproductive rights, and employment, among others have moved to the forefront of social concerns. Women's movements are increasingly recognizing on a global scale that to advance the condition of women a multidimensional approach is required, one that includes not only cultural change but also reform in the financial, monetary, and trade systems (DAWN, 2013). However, schooling continues to be seen—by financial institutions, UN and bilateral agencies, and the women's movements in general—in uncritical ways. Stakeholders seek greater access by girls and women to formal education, but do not envisage the school system as a major venue for transformation through the provision of new knowledge and classroom experiences. It is assumed that increased access to education plays a transformative role in the creation of gender identities; this is, however, amply demonstrated as untrue by the visible reproduction of gender norms and practices in most countries. For example, a recent document prepared by UN Women (2013) on policies to be adopted following the UN Millennium Development Goals seeks to increase women's access to secondary education (and thus the goal goes beyond basic education). Yet, it is mute about the urgent need to train teachers in gender issues so that representations of femininity and masculinity, domestic violence and sexual harassment, and women's assignment to the private sphere may be challenged.

Transnational Cultural Space, Education, and a Sense of Belonging

Mobility is an emerging focus in studies of education and globalization; it also has implications culturally. Transnational mobility of people, technology, money, media, and ideas—or in Appadurai's (2002) terms: ethnoscapes, technoscapes, financescapes, mediascapes, and ideoscapes—contributes to reconfiguring social, political, and economic relations and global positions of influence, situating them on a global scale and within transnational spaces. Sassen (2012) argues that global power and processes are increasingly concentrated in "global cities," within which a "disproportionate share of the corporate economy … and the disadvantaged" (p. 1) are strategically situated. Such changes in the global configuration of social, economic, and political processes reconfigure the spaces within which education functions and how it seeks to shape societies. Several new trends are worth noting: transnational forms of education (the international baccalaureate, higher education), new identities, and the role of schooling in shaping character and a sense of global citizenship.

Brown and Lauder (2009) have examined the emergence of international systems of education and "international rather than state-certified forms of credential[ing]" (p. 130), as manifested in two examples: the International Baccalaureate (2013) program and in higher education. They argue that control of teachers and systems (e.g., through credentialing and accreditation) is increasingly situated beyond the nation state, shaped by the increasing power of the market, and results in a shift in the "character" (p. 131) of the students produced by these systems.

While this population is quite small, there are many more children being influenced by global media, curricula, testing regimes, etc., thereby promoting an orientation toward a broader context. The growth in "global education" curricula and programs, particularly in industrialized countries, reflects concerns about instilling in the next generation such a broader orientation, one in which children are more knowledgeable about the world and situate themselves within that broader world, understand global phenomena (such as environmental sustainability), and develop a respect for others and a sense of global responsibility. A global notion of citizenship, however, can also make diversity invisible, particularly as it relates to gender and minority groups (Arnot and Dillabough, 2000; Robertson, 2009). Teaching children to be citizens of the world confronts the reality that most formal education systems have a primarily national orientation and so, continue to produce citizens who reflect national identities. Parmenter (this volume) demonstrates this tension in the Japanese context, where the intended "global" orientation clashes with the concern for national cohesion.

KNOWLEDGE UNDER GLOBALIZATION

Rapid and sustained change is occurring in the ways we learn and do things. Boundaries in time and space are being crossed with great ease; people learn of events much quicker than ever before and they can go to distant places with great ease. A positive expectation about the new speed of information diffusion and human mobility is that the invisible hand of the market now also moves faster and with greater efficiency, which will both increase the satisfaction and welfare of consumers and exercise pressures for greater efficiency and thus knowledge among firms that wish to remain in the market.

Globalization increases interaction among people and this creates opportunities for new learning, but also for old learning. Among the new learning, we have now what is called the "cult of technology" and conversely the diminution of respect for spiritual and cultural values (Maugey, cited in Namer, 1999). Similarly, the prioritizing of STEM disciplines (science, technology, engineering, and mathematics) diminishes the perceived value of humanities and social sciences, and increases the focus on education-for-jobs thereby weakening broader notions of education-for-life. While some ideas indeed are being exchanged freely, it is a struggle to offer and disseminate ideas with weak connection to the market.

According to Giddens (1994), with the rise of multiple technologies and globalization dynamics, there are no permanent structures of knowledge or meaning today. The process of translation and adaptation calls for many changes and this in turn produces changes in intended as well as unintended ways. Giddens predicts the arrival of an era of reflexivity, caused by the growing proportion of people who are knowledge seekers. Because knowledge will be increasingly subject to revision, we might find "doubt" to be a feature of globalization. Giddens is perhaps only partly correct. Science and technology are fields that today receive much respect. But they are also fields whose "knowledge" is predicated on positivistic science with claims of certainty and precision. Such tendencies would generate an impetus for knowledge as certainty. In the social sciences, in fact, we are seeing a tendency toward the understanding of knowledge as precise, decontextualized, and thus fragmented. Such a trend is evident in the current attempts by agencies such as the World Bank to create "knowledge management systems" whose fundamental premise seems to be that knowledge can be reduced to a minimal and yet valid expression.

In a globalized world, as technology becomes its main motor, knowledge assumes a powerful role in production, making its possession essential for nations if they are successfully to pursue economic growth and competitiveness. This search for technological knowledge makes sense at one level, but at another perhaps sets countries on an impossible path. Often, one hears the assertion that workers can be transformed into owners of capital as knowledge can be put into their heads (Curry, 1997), an assertion predicated on the assumption that knowledge is more accessible than the other factors of production: land, capital, and technology (Friedman, 2005). But what this argument ignores is the great chasm that emerges between the poor and the international circuits of production, distribution, and access to knowledge.

In addition to the increased speed of circulation of knowledge, there has been a growth in the quantity, quality, and the density of knowledge embodied in the design, production, and marketing of even ordinary products (Curry, 1997). Consequently, knowledge is increasingly being embedded in technical capital. Countries that depend on natural resources extraction will likely build only minimal technical capital. Extrapolating from this trend, it follows that the knowledge composition of capital will be differentially distributed. If so, the fundamental relation between labor and capital may remain the same as before, even though the knowledge component of capital may be today far more sophisticated than in the past.

Current technological developments have contributed to a belief that technology can be used to dramatically improve learning in schools. The presumption that technology can have an independent effect—independent of how teachers are trained to use it and independent in design so as not to substitute for classroom activities normally carried out with paper and pencil—is endorsed even by such institutions as UNESCO (Kalman and Hernández, 2013). There have been major improvements in the development of software for educational purposes; problems remain in the areas of computer training and maintenance. Beyond schools, there is the hope that social media will generate political change, not unlike the beginnings of the Arab Spring in 2011. Through the social media, other voices can be heard and, concomitantly, other truths. It remains to be seen how much they can transform the world.

Several communication experts remark that there is a growing contrast between education and communication, the former being rigid, presenting materials in specific sequences, and retaining control in teachers, while communication is increasingly becoming non-linear, informal. Moreover, communication is becoming more visual and more reliant on multiple media. Sadly, however, communication today—especially among young people—appears overwhelmingly focused on bits of information, entertainment, and social networks rather than critical reflection. A major challenge will be to exploit the pedagogical opportunities created by multiple potential spaces and times.

It is not only technology that is shaping knowledge at present. Culture and politics also have an influence. An example pertains to changes in Islam and related educational policy changes. Milligan (2008) identifies two trends that are evident: one is influenced by fundamentalism, and the other by pragmatism. He argues that Muslim countries, particularly those in southeast Asia, are responding to global forces by formulating and/or accommodating local education policy in ways which seek "to sustain local cultural identities while preserving citizens' opportunities for effective participation in a globalizing economy" (p. 369). This takes the forms of "Muslim modernists [who tend] to view Islam as irrelevant—if not an actual impediment—to educational modernization" (p. 369) and also "calls to Islamise education" (p. 369) in several countries. In his case study of the Philippines, he finds active negotiation of knowledge—Islamic knowledge, and knowledge conveyed through Western forms of schooling—in a context where the dialectic of the global and the local shapes the policy dialogue. Milligan's detailed philosophical analysis of the arguments leads him to posit that in the Philippines they are more likely to take a more pragmatic path. Part of the influence on Muslim countries to determine their particular policy paths is the anti-Islamic sentiment coming from the West, much of which, Milligan comments, is uninformed and based on stereotypes. As with other situations involving negative stereotypes, responses often seek to conserve the traditional and accentuate difference.

GLOBALIZATION AND EDUCATION

Education is enjoying greater salience than it has in previous decades because the burgeoning global embrace of competitiveness has forced education to become intimately linked to technological and economic development. Education is now considered an undisputable pathway to increased social mobility and works in the global imaginary as key to economic competitiveness of countries. This is the case in advanced countries, where the income distance between a high school education and a college education continues to grow (OECD, 2012). The expansion of higher education has been the result of individual demand in most cases. Consequently, the expansion has led to greater differentiation so that those unable to qualify for the more established universities can enter the growing number of less selective or second-tier private institutions. Of concern, however, is that despite the considerable expansion of higher education, access still depends on social class. Because the poor have fewer possibilities of attending college and because the colleges they attend are likely to be of lower quality than those attended by their wealthier counterparts, higher levels of education in the population have not produced a more equal income distribution. This has been documented in the case of the United States (Carnoy, 2011).

The increasing importance of the global market has had several repercussions on formal schooling: First, criteria employed in firms for efficiency and productivity are being extended to schooling, sometimes in inappropriate fashion. Second, focus has shifted from child-centered curriculum to work preparation skills. This trend is evident in leading nations such as Japan, the United States, the United Kingdom, Germany, and Scandinavian countries, and in important new players such as China and Russia (Walters, 1998). Third, education is losing ground as a public good to become simply another marketable commodity (Benn, 2011). The state has become limited in its responsibility to schooling, often guaranteeing basic education but extracting in turn user fees from higher levels of public education, as any other service in the market. Fourth, teachers' autonomy, independence, and control over their work is being reduced while workplace knowledge and control find their way increasingly in hands of administrators (Compton and Weiner, 2008; McLaren, 1998).

In primary and secondary education today we see an almost unstoppable trend toward privatization and decentralization, both of which decrease the collective concern and bring heterogeneity of purpose and publics as unquestioned values. To serve the technological needs of the market better, new forms of flexible training in vocational and technical education are emerging through private offerings. Among the unintended consequences of these dynamics are (1) fields less connected to the market losing importance (e.g., history vis-a-vis math and science); (2) pedagogies less linked to the market also losing importance (e.g., classroom discussions based on critical theory as opposed to instrumental problem-solving tasks); (3) on a broader scale, issues of equality and equity concerning women and ethnic minorities are losing ground to the consideration of such issues as efficiency (often reduced to performance in math and reading tests).

Much is being made of the need for individuals to gain knowledge, and particularly technological knowledge, to move their countries into higher levels of economic competitiveness. But what is not taken into account in this argument are the contradictory demands that a technological society might make on its internal labor force. Individuals who will benefit from the new reality by virtue of their mastery of technological knowledge will likely transfer menial forms of service to others. Activities such as house cleaning, childcare, laundry, food preparation, and gardening will not only increasingly have to be conducted by these "others" but will possibly be subject to demands for higher quality. In other words, a "knowledge society" must count on a cadre of individuals whose knowledge is low enough to accept menial tasks or whose social conditions are such that they cannot claim the more dignified, higher paying tasks for themselves. Extrapolating these dynamics into the future, it might be said that schooling will be used to differentiate students in early phases and that, if this does not create a sufficient pool of local workers, migration will supply the missing labor. There is already evidence of migration of trained people from poor economies to wealthier countries (Kamat, Mir, and Mathew, 2004). Many such migrants lack access to jobs that use their skills, such as Peruvians with college degrees working in Chile as nannies, high-school graduates from Paraguay working in menial jobs in Argentina, women from various Caribbean and Latin American countries serving as maids in Europe and the United States, and Filipino women with college degrees working as maids in Kuwait. The "brain-drain" phenomenon occurs because the educated are the ones who will have the most facility in obtaining information and doing the paperwork needed for migration. But globalization welcomes them less for their higher levels of education than for their willingness to take on the low-skill jobs.

Higher Education

The adoption of the "knowledge society" promise has generated substantial expansion of universities and other institutions of higher education. But as the state has been modest in its educational investment, most of the growth has occurred through private education (i.e., with fee-paying students). Parallel to the universities' search for revenues, there has been an explosion in the number of international students, who are subject to intense recruitment. Because most international students pay their own tuition, special efforts concentrate on countries that can afford U.S. tuition payments, such as China and India. Not surprising, some 180,000 Chinese students went to overseas universities in 2007, and half of them were high school students. In the United States, international students generate revenues slightly above twenty billion dollars per year.

Across the world, more than 4.1 million higher education students attended college outside their country in 2010; this brings reputation, particularly in the United States and Europe. In 2008, a person with higher education in industrialized countries earned 58 percent more than a counterpart with only a secondary school degree (OECD, 2012). Despite the widening of access to higher education and its positive return, access remains affected by social class. Young people from families with low levels of education are less than half as likely to be enrolled as those with at least one parent with a tertiary degree (OECD, 2012).

Globalization with its sophisticated use of technology and increasing reliance on scientific inventions implies a crucial role for postsecondary education. TNCs have been making broad demands on universities for engagement in research and development, but it must be remembered that some of these companies are moving into their own direct involvement in research and development, portending a consequent reduction of the role of universities in technological development. In the field of microelectronics, the most definite globalization industry, this is certainly the case.

In a situation where universities will be linked more to the market and less to the pursuit of truth, it is likely that the definition and establishment of quality will become the prerogative of managerial rather than academic enterprise (Cowen, 1996; Currie and Vidovich, this volume). Universities have become more "client" or "customer" focused. This orientation is not necessarily deplorable because responsiveness to adult needs has always been a positive principle, but under globalization it is likely that the "client" will increasingly be powerful donors or contractual industrial clients and students from upper- and middle-class families, who might move the university toward reproducing distinctions of class or reducing its areas of knowledge to those research topics of interest to clients and donors (Simpson, 1998). The requirement to produce "consumer satisfaction" will place further emphasis on market-oriented effectiveness (Chaffee, 1998).

The university has long been a source of critical insights about its surrounding society. Dominant globalization ideologies, based on the success of the individual and the drive for competitiveness, have affected the university, placing its professors into a constant struggle to secure funds for research and to engage in research to the detriment of other crucial activities, which range from teaching to participating in community organizing. While a critical social science is essential to the understanding and reconstruction of society, critical educators at the university level find it difficult to introduce notions of solidarity and collective action. In addition, the salience of science and technology as a source of revenue and prestige has created a considerable split between university professors who do "hard" sciences and those who engage in "soft" disciplines. Fields crucial to the understanding of society such as sociology, women's studies, and cultural studies have made a "cultural turn," focusing on representation and discourse of the detriment of examining organizations and economic institutions (Fraser, 2008; Keating, 2013; Moghadam, 1999).

Entrepreneurial cultures now permeate university life in the prevailing "surveillance/appraisal" practices in British higher education and, in an emergent fashion, in the United States. In the United Kingdom, there is a well-established Research Assessment Exercise and a Teaching Quality Assessment program that not only appraises faculty performance but also reduces such performance to a few indicators (McNeil, 1999). As universities compete with each other, and intramural rivalries grow between schools or departments within these universities, this norm of competitive individualism has gradually limited attention to other areas of academic life that are not income-producing. Evaluations have an important role to play in universities, but as conceived in terms of marketability they are leading to distorted forms of academic performance.

Because the main beneficiaries of globalization are the TNCs as well as individuals with professional, technical, and managerial skills (Ghai, 1987), the university is becoming a highly contested terrain. One new form of contestation might be preemptive, via the creation of a highly differentiated postsecondary system, characterized by a small number of elite universities with highly competitive admissions on one side, compensated by an expanding range of other, more accessible, types of postsecondary education, including for-profit institutions.

This trend of affairs is now quite visible in Asia and Latin America, where universities are losing their monopoly over higher education. Many new institutions are emerging, usually simple in character and with no commitment to research. In Latin America today 85 percent of higher education institutions are not universities but a mixed bag of institutes and academies; at present 60 percent of the enrollment is still in universities, but this is likely to decline over time. Many students are also moving into private universities, many of which offer relaxed entrance requirements. In Colombia, Brazil, Chile, El Salvador, Guatemala, and Peru, more than 50 percent of the enrollment involves private institutions (UNESCO, 2009). The privatization of higher education offers several advantages to the proponents of a more competitive national economy. It reduces the financial burden of the government, satisfies aspirations for higher education of a large number of students (even though the prestige of their university may be much lower than that of the established universities), ensures that fields of study that are directly market-related will be offered in those institutions, and last, but of critical importance, contributes to the depoliticization of the university as students in private universities are readily inculcated by "careerist" as opposed to "critical" norms. For those concerned with the role of higher education in defining and supporting societal goals, the privatization of higher education puts it squarely in the productive sphere and weakens the principle of education as a public good, for its future marked class distinction will not permit all graduates to gather knowledge of similar type and quality or to reap similar rewards from postsecondary education.

Gender or women's studies in universities tend to be small programs serving a reduced number of students. But they are also crucial places in the production and transmission of critical knowledge. In the area of gender studies, globalization is also producing contradictory effects. With the greater circulation of information, some values, such as human rights, including the rights of women, are becoming increasingly accepted as topics to be examined within the academy. There is also a greater diffusion of gender studies in universities and much more contact among women-led nongovernmental organizations with each other and with academics in their national societies. Yet, as Blackmore (this volume) argues, globalization has affected the ties between feminists and the welfare state, and has weakened feminist work within the university.

Adult Education

Despite endorsement in principle of "lifelong learning," such as advanced during the VI International Conference on Adult Education (2009), attention to adult education in globalized times is minuscule. To be sure, the neglect of populations who never attended school or withdrew from it for whatever reason predates the advent of globalization, but its status has been further diminished by the current emphasis on the "knowledge society," which privileges formal education.

Grassroots movements, as reflected in their participation in annual World Social Forums held in various parts the world, are very active. While they give much attention to the environment and to the human rights of such groups as women, indigenous people, and immigrants, these movements also consider education among their priorities. In the history of many countries, adult education has played a transformative role in the hands of social movements. Nongovernmental organizations and grassroots groups are manifesting a strong voice in favor of adult education; unfortunately, their voice is not being sufficiently translated into concomitant government policies to attend their needs and aspirations.

THE STATE AND PUBLIC POLICY

Most discussions of the state under globalization highlight the relationship between the state and the market and are typified by very divergent views. Neoliberalism offers a negative view of the state in developing countries, characterizing it as corrupt, self-interested, and incompetent (Kendall, 2007; Mosley, Harrigan, and Toye, 1991). Measures of privatization, deregulation, decentralization, and integration into the global economy have, not surprisingly, coincided with a decrease in public expenditures (González Casanova, 1996). This decrease is in part fueled by ideology; in part it is caused by the new economic dynamics. With international pressure mounting for the free exchange of products (in an increasingly deregulated market), we see the reduction of taxes on imports and thus less revenue for the state. The challenge for many governments today concentrates on how to modify the tax structure to gain greater contributions from domestic sources. Guided by neoliberal ideology, which supports a reduced state, many governments today declare themselves to be facing serious financial austerity. Paradoxically, this self-declared limitation is occurring at a moment when the number of fabulously rich persons has increased in the world. The causes of fiscal contraction are not clear but statistics show that the poorest 5 percent in rich countries have an income higher than those of 68 percent of the world's population (Milanovic, 2010).

Neoliberal ideologies, in existence for almost three decades, have successfully fostered the practice of providing key services such as education and health care through the marketplace, making them available according to one's ability to pay. Associated government policies such as privatization heighten social class differences and make education an individual rather than collective right. Education, however, is a fundamental right and should thus be equal for everyone in terms of access and quality. But many of the actors now influential in global policies are less inclined to protect equality than to create an expanding cadre of workers to join the globalized and increasingly technological society.

There is an increasingly tight connection between powerful business, philanthropic, and policy-making networks that today constitute the new architecture of global governance (Ball, 2012). In influential ways these efforts shape economic and social policies (including education) through an array of legal, financial, and regulatory prescriptions affecting both advanced industrialized societies and low-income countries. Often business actors participate in educational networks because they want to explore further market opportunities (e.g., selling educational equipment and materials or offering continuous professional development, consulting, training, and management services). What makes their policy prescriptions problematic is that they are the product of non-elected bodies and that the networks they comprise are characterized by a lack of transparency. Under those conditions, it is not clear who holds the power to shape educational decisions and, consequently, who is accountable for policy decisions and policy failures. If decisions are being made by these informal networks, it must be asked, what are the implications for citizenship, democracy, and the relationship between citizens and political institutions? These informal networks, experts, and data are playing a major role in the transformation of education in Europe (Sum and Jessop, 2013); similar observations can be made about the United States (Ball, 2012).

Two institutions that have been gaining much traction in the promotion of education policies are the World Bank and OECD. The first continues to assert itself as a "knowledge bank" and expands this position through various strategies, including its recent Education Sector Strategy (Klees, Samoff, and Stromquist, 2012) and subsequent lending operations. OECD is asserting itself through the application in seventy countries of its Programme for International Student Assessment, which seeks to ascertain student achievement in math, science, and reading. According to Rizvi and Lingard (2010), "OECD has become the central agency in establishing the consensus of which it speaks" (p. 130; see also, Meyer and Benavot, 2013).

With neoliberalism and structural adjustment programs in many countries, there has been a considerable expansion of private investment from north to south and a simultaneous reduction in public-sector foreign aid programs (McGuire and Campos, 1997; see Mundy and Manion, this volume). State development policies have changed in nature and today seek to foster skills for economic production and to constrain dissent, while giving less time to modify or even consider structures of power and social inequalities. One important development concerns the amount of funds that now reach developing countries. According to the World Bank (2011), global remittances in 2010 amounted to $440 billion, of which $325 billion went to developing countries. This amount contrasts with the approximately $134 billion granted by Western countries in development assistance (OECD, 2012) and renders puny the support given by the World Bank through its non-interest loan branch (the International Development Agency), which in 2011 amounted to $16.3 billion (International Development Agency, 2013). In light of this, there is a strong mismatch between the influence of international agencies and the actual economic power they presently wield.

Significant trends in educational policy are evident. First, the state is altering the educational labor market in terms of supply by fostering private schools, enabling parental "choice" through voucher mechanisms, and demanding competitive performance of schools, and in terms of demand by redefining education as a commodity or a private rather than social good (Blackmore, 1997). Second, social expectations regarding educational policies have been transformed. Education used to be the state's greatest manifestation of social policy. An inspiring article by Weiler (1981) noted that the state uses education as a compensatory instrument of political legitimization, for in so doing it gains the good will of citizens without major changes in the economic and social structure. Today, such a strategy is no longer seen as relevant or crucial to state survival.

It can be asked, "What can education do for the state under globalization?" Education is being set up as a critical element in economic well-being and competitiveness, yet—as in the past—it continues to be one factor among several. With the globalization of labor, TNCs follow the cheapest bidder internationally; while the skills of the labor force are important usually lower levels of schooling are sufficient. For those countries able to generate high technical knowledge among its university graduates, retention of talent at the highest levels is seen as one of the main challenges of globalization for developing countries. Two factors operate against retention: one is the imitation factor that leads a professional in a low-income country to compare him or herself to others in the industrialized countries. For example, a Mexican CEO complains that he earns "merely" $450,000 while his counterpart in the United States earns $1 million per year. The other is the industrialized countries' ability to attract foreign knowledge producers on instant demand, as is seen in the current influx of microelectronics engineers.[2] Immigration policies in several industrialized countries grant preferential treatment to individuals with higher levels of education.

It also seems that the time and space for educational policies (and other types of policy) have been drastically altered. Those involved in policy-making observe that globalization is shortening times and budget cycles; thus, there has been an acceleration in the design cycles of such policies, with little time to reflect because responses are needed with greater urgency. While in the past the "horizon" of social policy was four to five years, today many programs arise and die in a twelve-month period; these programs also command fewer resources than in the past. Policy has moved from "strategic planning" to "continued responsiveness" in order to provide more market sensitivity. Policy formation in an increasing number of countries is accompanied by "ministerialization" (political appointments [i.e., minister and advisers]) rather than reliance on bureaucrats (i.e., regular and stable government officials).

WINNERS AND LOSERS

The prevailing discourse on globalization is still optimistic. By and large, many people see advantages to the new open, highly connected, competitive, far-reaching process of economic and cultural exchanges. On closer look, the tidal wave of globalization has impacted all countries to different degrees and in a mix of positive and negative directions.

Castells (2010) acknowledges that the global economy is deeply asymmetric. He clarifies that this asymmetry is not in the form of a single center with semi-peripheric and peripheric countries or the simplistic opposition of north and south, but rather more variegated and elusive. Nevertheless, a group of countries that corresponds approximately to membership in the OECD accounts for an overwhelming proportion of the world's technological capacity, capital, markets, and industrial production.[3]

At one level, the terrain under globalization is "a space of flows, an electronic space, a decentered space, a space in which frontiers and boundaries have become permeable" (Robinson, cited in McLaren, 1999, p. 11). But at another level, this space seems highly fixed. Amin (1996) contends that the center (i.e., the most powerful industrial nations) holds five monopolies: technology, world-wide financial markets, global natural resources (in terms of access), media and communications, and weapons of mass destruction. A crucial question is, Can we change the nature of these monopolies? A more specific question for us, as educators, is, Can education help break or at least weaken these monopolies?

Analyses of the distribution of wealth in countries conclude that globalization has not increased wages except in the United States. Wealth has grown tremendously and its allocation has been highly clustered. Within industrialized countries, "the new and wealthy class is the technological aristocracy and a cadre of business executives who work in the interests of corporate share price" (McLaren, 1998, p. 434). This has only increased after the 2008 global economic crisis. Economic growth no longer guarantees poverty alleviation or employment generation and both developed and developing regions must face high unemployment and a difficult job market, particularly among the youth.

Economic changes have altered the relations between human beings and the nature of their lives. Guided by this awareness, DAWN, one of the largest women-led nongovernmental organizations, maintains that:

> The first decade of the 21st century has been marked so far by two unprecedented critical events: the "war on terror" and the global financial crisis. In the wake of these two events, armed conflict, violence, terrorism, national security, migration and religion; and transnational capital, labour, and economies have come to preoccupy national and international, regional and national politics and given rise to public policies that have had an immediate effect on the lives of ordinary citizens. In their wake, issues of livelihoods, poverty, human rights, freedom of expression and mobility, identity and sexuality have come under pressure and been radically altered. (DAWN, n.d., para. 9.)

COUNTER-EFFORTS TO GLOBALIZATION

At present, capitalism is seen as the only economic model. In 1996, Gibson-Graham underscored that the discourse on globalization presents capitalism as an undefeatable force. After the 2008 economic crisis, however, scholars from the south and north alike questioned this as the only way (Faiola, 2008). These authors encourage us to deny the inevitability and reality of the power of TNCs over workers and communities and to explore ways in which we can render these TNCs accountable.

The challenge to seek different development paths and economic identities calls for the strengthening of the state. About 85 percent of total north-south private capital flows to only twelve developing countries. Clearly, state action (read nationwide and coordinated strategies) is needed to move developing countries to better economic positions.

The alternatives being proposed are few and need greater development. Over a decade ago, a UN Development Program Independent Commission argued that a new social contract is needed and that it must go beyond security, justice, and well-being to include an expanded citizenship with a sense of belonging, meaningful participation, and a stronger civil society. Amin, a well-known African scholar, calls for an "Alternative Humanist Project of Globalization," attentive to "disarmament; equitable access to the planet's resources; open, flexible economic relationships between the world's major regions; [and] correct management of global/national dialectics in the areas of communication, culture, and political policy" (1996, p. 6). In 1996, Cardoso, then the president of Brazil and a former student of development processes, called for an ethic of solidarity by the governments to create new associational forms between society and the state, which he sees as the best way to reduce the marginalization of the poor. The recent demands of Brazilians, however, for more funding for education and health care instead of support for FIFA and the Olympics, suggest that these new associational forms have not occurred.

People's actions such as the participatory budgeting processes occurring in many cities of the world provide a venue for decisions that foster social inclusion. Rebellious movements such as the Arab Spring and the Occupy movement may eventually produce stable ways for democratic participation in governance.

CONCLUSION

Though still not a precise concept, what we understand as "globalization" is bringing forth numerous and profound changes in the economic, cultural, and political life of nations. The current globalization context has made education salient, yet education remains very focused on its contribution to the labor force, less based on democratic decision-making, and, through the ethos of competition, less supportive of reflexivity on the directions of contemporary society.

In the fourteen years since we published the first edition of this book, we have seen a more systematic, pervasive, and stronger attack on public education all over the world. Neoliberalism has extended its economic features (deeper links between market and capital and between schooling and the labor force) to adopt cultural (new values, sensibilities, and relationships) and political features (new forms of governing—characterized by governance—and new subjectivities). These changes deeply affect how education is defined, whom it serves, and how it is assessed.

A dichotomous perspective of the effects of globalization, looking only at the extremes of the globalized and nonglobalized economies, might miss the important dynamics that occur in both global and local dimensions, and the interaction between the two levels. Local groups often reshape their local identities when they meet challenges related to globalization processes, but they do not have to abandon these identities to become entirely globally oriented. What was "local" becomes redefined as a modified form of "local" that can work in conjunction with the supralocal forces. It is in the way these forces mesh that hope for a positive transformation lies.

Today more than ever, there is a need to ask, "What purposes will education have in the globalization age?" Will it succumb to pressure to make us more productive and increase our ability to produce and consume, or will it be able to instill in all of us a democratic spirit which values the common good. This solidarity will have to recognize the different interests among men and women and among the dominant groups and disadvantaged groups; therefore, the new agreement will not be easy to achieve.

REFERENCES

Amin, Samir. 1996. The Future of Globalization. *Social Justice*, vol. 23, nos. 1–2, pp. 5–13.

Appadurai, Arjun. 2002. Disjuncture and Difference in the Global Cultural Economy. In Susanne Schech and Jane Haggis (eds.), *Development: A Cultural Studies Reader* (pp. 157–167). Oxford, England: Blackwell.

Arnot, Madeleine, and Jo-Anne Dillabough (eds.). 2000. *Challenging Democracy: International Perspectives on Gender, Education and Citizenship.* London and New York: RoutledgeFalmer.

Ball, Stephen. 2012. *Global Education Inc. New Policy Networks and the Neo-liberal Imaginary.* London: Routledge.

Bhanji, Zahra. 2008. Transnational Corporations in Education: Filling the Governance Gap through New Social Norms and Market Multilateralism? *Globalisation, Societies and Education*, vol. 6, no. 1, pp. 55–73.

Benn, Melissa. 2011. *School Wars: The Battle for Britain's Education.* London: Verso Books.

Blackmore, Jill. 1997. Level Playing Field? Feminist Observations on Global/Local Articulations of the Re-gendering and Restructuring of Educational Work. *International Review of Education*, vol. 43, nos. 5–6, pp. 439–61.

Brown, Phillip, and Hugh Lauder. 2009. Globalization, International Education, and the Formation of a Transnational Class? In Thomas S. Popkewitz and Fazal Rizvi (eds.), *Globalization and the Study of Education: 108th Yearbook of the National Society for the Study of Education, Part II* (pp. 130–147). Malden, MA: Wiley-Blackwell.

Carnoy, Martin. 2011. As Higher Education Expands, Is It Contributing to Greater Equality? *National Institute Economic Review*, vol. 215, no. 1, pp. R34–R47.

Castells, Manuel. 2009. *The Power of Identity*, 2nd edition. The Information Age, Economy, Society, and Culture, Vol. II. Malden, MA: Wiley & Sons.

_____. 2010. *The Rise of the Network Society*, 2nd edition. The Information Age, Economy, Society, and Culture, Vol. I. Malden, MA: Wiley and Sons.

Chaffee, Ellen. 1998. Listening to the People We Serve. In William Tierney (ed.), *The Responsive University. Restructuring for High Performance*. Baltimore: The Johns Hopkins University Press, pp. 5–31.

Compton, Mary F., and Lois Weiner (eds.). 2008. *The Global Assault on Teaching, Teachers, and Their Unions: Stories for Resistance*. New York: Palgrave Macmillan.

Connell, Robert. 1998. Masculinities and Globalization. *Men and Masculinities*, vol. 1, no. 1, pp. 3–23.

Cowen, Robert. 1996. Performativity, Post-Modernity and the University. *Comparative Education*, vol. 32, no. 2, pp. 245–58.

Craske, Nikki. 1998. Remasculinization and the Neoliberal State in Latin America. In Vicky Randall and Georgina Waylen (eds.), *Gender, Politics, and the State*. London: Routledge, pp. 100–20.

Crookshanks, John. 2008. Neoliberal Globalization: Threats to Women's Citizenship in Canada. Alberta: University of Alberta, unpublished document.

Curry, James. 1997. The Dialectic of Knowledge-in-Production: Value Creation in Late Capitalism and the Rise of Knowledge-Centered Production. *Electronic Journal of Sociology*, vol. 002-003. http://www.sociology.org/content/vol002.003/curry.html

Cvetkovich, Ann, and Douglas Kellner. 1997. *Articulating the Global and the Local: Globalization and Cultural Studies*. Boulder, CO: Westview.

Development Alternatives with Women for a New Era. 2013. From People's Rights to Corporate Privilege: A South Feminist Critique of the HLP Report on Post 2015 Development Agenda. www.dawnet.org/advocacy-appeals.php?signon=306&id=306

Eisenstein, Zillah. 1997. Women's Publics and the Search for New Democracies. *Feminist Review*, no. 57, pp. 140–67.

Faiola, Anthony. 2008. The End of American Capitalism? *The Washington Post*, Business section, October 10. http://articles.washingtonpost.com/2008-10-10/business/36925874_1_free-market-financial-system-capitalism

Featherstone, Mike. 1990. Global Culture(s): An Introduction. In Mike Featherstone (ed.), *Global Culture: Nationalism, Globalization and Modernity* (pp. 1–13). London: Sage.

Fraser, Nancy. 2008. *Scale of Justice: Reimagining Political Space in a Globalizing World*. New York: Columbia University Press and Polity Press.

Friedman, Thomas. 2005. *The World Is Flat: A Brief History of the Twenty-First Century*. New York: Farrar, Strauss and Giroux.

Ghai, Dharam. 1987. Economic Globalization, Institutional Change, and Human Security. In Staffan Lindberg and Arni Sverrisson (eds.), *Social Movements in Development. The Challenge of Globalization and Democratization*. Houndmills, UK: Macmillan Press, pp. 25–45.

Gibson-Graham, J.K. 1996. *The End of Capitalism (As We Knew It): A Feminist Critique of Political Economy*. Cambridge, Mass: Blackwell.

_____. 2006. *The End of Capitalism (As We Knew It): A Feminist Critique of Political Economy, With a New Introduction*. Minneapolis: University of Minnesota Press.

Giddens, Anthony. 1994. *Beyond Left and Right: The Future of Radical Politics*. Stanford: Stanford University Press.

González Casanova, Pablo. 1996. Globalism, Neoliberalism, and Democracy. *Social Justice*, vol. 23, nos. 1–2, pp. 39–48.

Hale, Sondra. 2013. Postcolonialism, Social Movements and Gender in a New World. Keynote, XV World Congress of Comparative Education Societies, Buenos Aires, June 24–28.

Held, David, Anthony McGrew, David Goldblatt, and Jonathan Perraton. 1999. *Global Transformations: Politics, Economics and Culture*. Stanford: Stanford University Press.

Independent Commission on Population and Quality of Life. 1996. *Caring for the Future. Making the Next Decades Provide a Life Worth Living*. Oxford: Oxford University Press.

International Baccalaureate. 2013. Mission Statement. http://ibo.org/mission/

International Conference on Adult Education. 2009. CONFINTEA VI. International Conference on Adult Education. Final Report. Paris: UNESCO.

Jaggar, Alison. 2001. Is Globalization Good for Women? *Comparative Literature*, vol. 53, no. 4, pp. 298–314.

Kalman, Judith, and Oscar Hernández. 2013. Frente a la pantalla. Educación de jóvenes y adultos en tiempos de la tecnología digital. Paper presented at the VII International Seminar on "As redes educativas e as tecnologias: transformações e subversões na atualidade," organized by Centro de Educação e Humanidades, Universidade do Estado do Rio de Janeiro, 3–6 July.

Kamara, Omar, and Karen Monkman. 2014. Internationally Recruited Teachers and Migration: Structures of Instability and Tenuous Settlement. In Jill P. Koyama and Mathu Subramanian (eds.), *Education in a World of Migration: Implications for Policy and Practice*. New York: Routledge.

Kamat, Sangeeta, Ali Mir, and Biju Mathew. 2004. Producing Hi-tech: Globalization, the State and Migrant Subjects. *Globalisation, Societies and Education,* vol. 2, no. 1, pp. 5–23.

Keating, Avril. 2013. New Modes of Governance in Europe: Mapping the Multiple Actors, Institutions, and Instruments in a Shifting Political Space. *British Journal of Sociology of Education*, vol. 34, no. 3, pp. 475–85.

Kempner, Ken. 1998. Post-Modernizing Education on the Periphery and in the Core. *International Review of Education*, vol. 44, nos. 5–6, pp. 441–60.

Kendall, Nancy. 2007. Education for All Meets Political Democratization: Free Primary Education and the Neoliberalization of the Malawian School and State. *Comparative Education Review*, vol. 51, no. 3, pp. 281–305.

Kenway, Jane. 1997. Education in the Age of Uncertainty: An Eagle's Eye-View. Paper commissioned by the Equity Section, Curriculum Division, Department for Education and Children's Services, South Australia, mimeo.

Klees, Steven, Joel Samoff, and Nelly P. Stromquist (ed.). 2012. T*he World Bank and Education: Critiques and Alternatives*. Rotterdam: Sense Publishers.

McGuire, James and Mauro Campos. 1997. Rethinking Development: Concept, Policies, and Contexts. *Workshop Proceedings*, June 3. Los Angeles: University of Southern California.

McLaren, Peter. 1998. Revolutionary Pedagogy in Post-Revolutionary Times. Rethinking the Political Economy of Critical Education. *Educational Theory*, vol. 48, no. 4, pp. 431–62.

_____. 1999. Traumatizing Capital: Oppositional Pedagogies in the Age of Consent. In Manuel Castells, Ramon Flecha, Paulo Freire, Henry Giroux, Donaldo Macedo, and Paul Willis (eds.), *Critical Education in the New Information Age* (pp. 1–36). Lanham, Maryland: Rowman and Littlefield.

Milanovic, Branko. 2010. *The Haves and the Have-Nots.* New York: Basic Books.

McNeil, Maureen.1999. The Challenges of a "New Equity Context" for British Education Approaching the Millennium. Paper presented at the international conference on Gender Equity Education organized by the Women's Research Program, May 13–15, Population Studies Center, National Taiwan University, Taipei.

Meyer, Heinz-Dieter and Aaron Benavot (eds.). 2013. *PISA, Power, and Policy: The Emergence of Global Governance*. Oxford: Symposium Books.

Milligan, Jeffrey Ayala. 2008. Islam and Education Policy Reform in the Southern Philippines. *Asia Pacific Journal of Education*, vol. 28, no. 4, pp. 369–81.

Moghadam, Valentine. 1999. Gender and the Global Economy. In Myra Ferree, Judith Lorber, and Beth Hess (eds.), *Revisioning Gender* (pp. 128–60). Thousand Oaks: Sage Publications.

Mosley, Paul, Jane Harrigan, and John Toye. 1991. *Aid and Power: The World Bank and Policy-Based Lending. Volume I: Analysis and Policy Proposals*. London: Routledge.

Namer, Claude. 1999 (August 10). Estamos en vías de una mundialización salvaje. *El Comercio*, p. C3.

Organization for Economic Cooperation and Development. 2012. Education at a Glance. Paris: OECD.

OECD. 2012. Development: Aid to Developing Countries Falls because of Global Recession. Newsroom, April 4. http://www.oecd.org/newsroom/developmentaidtodevelopingcountriesfallsbecauseofglobalrecession.htm

Rizvi, Fazal. 2009. Global Mobility and the Challenges of Educational Research and Policy. In Thomas S. Popkewitz and Fazal Rizvi (eds.), *Globalization and the Study of Education: 108th Yearbook of the National Society for the Study of Education, Part II* (pp. 268–89)*.* Malden, MA: Wiley-Blackwell.

Rizvi, Fazal, and Bob Lingard. 2010. *Globalizing Education Policy*. London: Routledge.

Robertson, Susan L. 2009. Globalization, Education Governance and Citizenship Regimes: New Democratic Deficits and Social Injustices. In William Ayres, Therese Quinn, and David Stovall (eds.), *Handbook of Social Justice in Education* (pp. 564–75). New York and London: Routledge.

Robertson, Susan L., Xavier Bonal, and Roger Dale. 2002. GATS and the Education Service Industry: The Politics of Scale and Global Reterritorialization. *Comparative Education Review*, vol. 46, no. 4, pp. 472–96.

Ruiz, Neil G., and Jill H. Wilson. 2013. A Balancing Act for H-1B Visas. Brookings Institution, April 18. http://www.brookings.edu/research/articles/2013/04/18-h1b-visa-immigration-ruiz-wilson

Sassen, Saskia. 2012. Cities: A Window into Larger and Smaller Worlds. *European Educational Research Journal*, vol. 11, no. 1, pp. 1–10.

Share the World's Resources. 2013. Multinational Corporations. http://www.stwr.org/multinational-corporations/key-facts.html

Simpson, Christopher (ed.). 1998. *Universities and Empire: Money and Politics in the Social Sciences During the Cold War*. New York: The New Press.

Stavenhagen, Rodolfo. 1997. Indigenous Organizations: Missing Rising Actors in Latin America. *CEPAL Review*, no. 62, pp. 63–75.

Stromquist, Nelly P. 2007. *Feminist Organizations and Social Transformation in Latin America.* Boulder, CO: Paradigm Publishers, 2007.

_____ and Karen Monkman. 2000. *Globalization and Education: Integration and Contestation across Cultures*. Lanham, MD: Rowman & Littlefield.

Sum, Ngai-Ling, and Bob Jessop. 2013. Competitiveness, the Knowledge-Based Economy, and Higher Education. *Journal of the Knowledge Economy*, vol. 4, no. 1, pp. 1–24.

Thomas, Jr., Landon, and Julia Werdigier. 2009. No Clear Accord on Stimulus by Top Industrial Nations. *New York Times*, business section webpage, March 14. http://www.nytimes.com/2009/03/15/business/15global.html?pagewanted=all&_r=0

UN Education Science and Cultural Organization. 2009. Trends in Higher Education. http://unesdoc.unesco.org/images/0018/001832/183219e.pdf

UN Population Fund. 2013. Migration: A World on the Move. Linking Population, Poverty and Development. http://www.unfpa.org/pds/migration.html

UN Women. 2013. *A Transformative Stand-Alone Goal on Achieving Gender Equality, Women's Rights and Women's Empowerment: Imperatives and Key Components*. New York: UN Women.

Vitali, Stefania, James B. Glattfelder, and Stefano Battiston. 2011. The Network of Global Corporate Control. *PLoS ONE*, vol. 6, no. 10. e25995. doi:10.1371/journal.pone.0025995

Walters, Shirley. 1998. *Globalization, Adult Education, and Training*. London: Zed Books.

Weiler, Hans. 1981. *Compensatory Legitimation in Educational Policy: Legalization, Expertise, and Participation in Comparative Perspective*. Stanford, CA: Institute for Research on Educational Finance and Governance, School of Education, Stanford University.

World Bank. 2011.

NOTES

1. Countries such as Mexico under the North American Free Trade Agreement have increased their production of goods enormously (even though that production also reflects the participation of foreign firms, firms posing as Mexican). Exports increased from $82 billion in 1993 to $160 billion in 1998, yet poverty and maldistribution have also increased. Some say the economic pie is getting bigger but this is difficult to accept given the constant growth of the informal sector and undocumented immigration to the United States.

2. Demand in the United States for H-1B visas has exploded, requiring the visa application period to close in just five days in 2013 because the cap of sixty-five thousand visas was reached (Ruiz and Wilson, 2013). H-1B visas are for workers (60 percent from India and 9 percent from China) to fill jobs when Americans cannot be found. Most are high tech jobs, although teachers are also recruited through this avenue (Kamara and Monkman, 2014; see also Kamat, Mir, and Mathew, 2004).

3. OECD plus the four newly industrialized countries of Asia represent about 73 percent of the world's manufacturing production. The G-20 (the nineteen leading industrial and developing nations and the European Union) represent about 85 percent of the world economy (Thomas and Werdigier, 2009, para. 2).

Chapter Two

Globalization, Educational Change, and the National State

Martin Carnoy

Globalization and information and communication technologies (ICTs) have changed the context in which national states and even school districts and individual universities make educational policy. Educational systems have always been the loci of political and social contestation (Carnoy and Levin, 1985). In the new context, this contestation is subject to new forces, which, in turn, are shaping educational politics, educational policies, and educational outcomes.

In this chapter, I outline the broad strokes of these new forces and how they appear to be affecting the political and policy dynamics of educational reform. I argue that the coming together of globalization and ICTs have greatly increased economic competition in the world economy, put increased emphasis on education as a key sector contributing to economic growth, and helped raise the economic returns to higher educated labor. They have also increased stress on national states to increase the quantity and especially the quality of their education systems. This has increased emphasis on measuring and comparing educational outcomes, made educational technology and its advocates key players in education reform, and placed political systems (states) directly in the crosshairs of conflicts over how to pay for such educational reforms, particularly because educational spending decisions play directly into conceptions of the public value of education and social preferences for equality.

By "globalization," I mean a global economy whose strategic, core activities, including innovation, finance, and corporate management, function on a planetary scale in real time[1] (Carnoy, Castells, Cohen, and Cardoso, 1993; Castells, 1997). And this globality became possible only because of the technological infrastructure provided by telecommunications, information systems, microelectronics machinery, and computer-based transportation. Today, as distinct from even a generation ago, capital, technology, management, information, and core markets are globalized.

A main base of globalization is information, and it, in turn, is highly knowledge-intensive. Internationalized and fast-growing information industries produce knowledge goods and services. Today, massive movements of capital depend on information, communications, and knowledge in global markets. And because knowledge is highly portable, it lends itself easily to globalization.

GLOBALIZED MARKETS

Globalization means increased competition among nations in a more closely intertwined international economy, a competition that is continuously enhanced by more rapid communication and computer technology and by a way of business thinking that is increasingly global rather than regional or national. Globalization also means relatively free trade, rather unregulated movement of finance capital, and the increased movement of innovative ideas (knowledge) and labor across national borders.

Major new players have emerged in the world economy, such as China, Korea, Taiwan, Brazil, and India. They are breaking the dominance of the United States, Europe, and Japan in manufacturing, although for the moment, firms (and universities) with their home base in the highly developed countries still have almost total control over the research and development of technical innovations.

The new dynamics of trade and investment, led by multinational corporations and transnational networks of firms, have increased the interdependence of labor markets (Bailey, Parisotto, and Renshaw, 1993). Some economists claim that the impact of trade on employment and wages in the United States is very positive (Krugman and Lawrence, 1994), but most believe that foreign trade has had a significant negative impact on the wages of less-educated workers and more recently, white-collar workers (Bardhan and Kroll, 2003; Bluestone, 1995). One estimate shows that between 1960 and 1990, skilled workers in the north benefited from the process of globalization, both in employment and wages, but unskilled workers lost out in the competition from developing countries. Demand for unskilled labor in the north fell by 20 percent, and wages declined (Wood, 1994). Others have shown that the potential of mobility for firms in the global economy provides management with extra bargaining power in obtaining concessions from the labor force in the north (Shaiken, 1993). Whereas indirect effects of globalization are not always visible, they do affect bargaining relations. They tend to reduce labor's share of economic surplus but simultaneously preserve jobs that cannot be easily exported, such as highly skilled jobs or those located in non-tradable services.

Thus, one of the main outcomes of such competition and cross-border movements is a worldwide demand for certain kinds of skills—namely language, mathematics reasoning, scientific logic, and programming—associated with higher levels of education. Globalized science-based technology firms are increasingly using scientists and engineers trained at least partially in newly industrializing countries' (NICs) universities to staff their innovation activities both in the developed countries and in the NICs themselves. At the same time, national states, particularly in the NICs of Asia, are increasing their scientific and technological higher education rapidly in the hope of capturing innovation rents as innovation continues to globalize.

But the impact on global skill formation does not end there. Developed countries' universities' science-technology training and research, almost entirely under the aegis of national state–sponsored research and development programs, are becoming increasingly internationalized, drawing heavily on first degree programs for graduate students in the NICs (Carnoy, 1998). The highly skilled scientists and engineers coming out of these graduate programs are available for globalized innovation, including innovation in enterprises owned and managed by NIC entrepreneurs and states.

Globalized demand for certain types of higher-level skills puts upward pressure on the payoffs to the higher educated around the world, particularly in those economies more closely tied into the globalization process. At the same time, as multinational firms expand into low-wage developing countries, globalization lowers demand for middle-skilled, higher-wage labor in the developed countries even as the output of high school and college graduates increases, lowering the pay of workers with secondary and even incomplete college education.

In the past generation, most countries have undergone rapid expansion of their primary and secondary education systems. This is not universally true, but thanks to a generalized ideology that basic education should be available to children as a right, even financial constraints in many debt-ridden countries, such as those in Latin America, did not prevent them from increasing access to basic and even secondary schooling (Castro and Carnoy, 1997). University education has also expanded, but given the bias of global demand for the higher educated, even in countries such as China and India, where transnational corporations have moved much of their manufacturing production and increased demand for middle-skilled workers, the tendency is still to push up rates of return to investment in higher education relative to the payoffs in investing in primary and secondary schooling. Estimated rates of return in countries such as Brazil, China, India, Russia (Carnoy, Loyalka, Dobryakova, Dossani, Froumin, Kuhns, Tilak and Wang, 2013), Argentina, Colombia, Singapore, Malaysia, Hong Kong, and the Republic of Korea, as well as in a number of the Organization for Economic Cooperation and Development (OECD) countries (Carnoy, 1995; Colclough, Kingdon, and Patrinos, 2010), show rates of return to university education as higher than to either secondary or primary.

Higher rates of return to higher education mean that those who get that education are benefited relatively more for their investment in education than those who stop at lower levels of schooling. In most countries, those who get to higher levels of schooling are also those from higher social class background. In addition, higher socioeconomic status (SES) students are those who get access to "better" schools and live in regions that are more likely to spend more per pupil for education, particularly in those schools attended by higher SES pupils. Competition for such higher-payoff education also increases as the payoff to higher education increases, because the stakes get higher. Higher SES parents become increasingly conscious of where their children attend school, what those schools are like, and whether they provide access to higher levels of education. Higher SES parents are also able to spend much more on out-of-school tutoring, which has become rampant in Asian countries (Bray, 2006). The total result is therefore that schooling becomes more stratified at lower levels rather than less stratified, especially under conditions of scarce public resources. National economic competition on a global scale gets translated into subnational competition in class access to educational resources.

In addition to raising the payoff to higher levels of education, globalization appears to have raised the rate of return for women's education. In many countries, rates of return for education for women were higher than for men early in the globalization era (Carnoy et al., 2013; Psacharopoulos, 1989; Ryoo, Carnoy, and Nam, 1993). The reasons for the increased participation of women in labor markets are complex, but two main factors have been the spread of feminist ideas and values and the increased demand for low-cost semiskilled labor in developing countries' electronics manufacturing and other assembly industries. The worldwide movement for women's rights has had the effect of legitimizing equal education for women, women's control over their fertility rates, women's increased participation in wage labor markets, and women's right to vote (Castells, 1997; Ramirez, Soysal, and Shanahan, 1997; Stromquist, 1995). The increased demand for low-cost labor and greater sense by women that they have the same rights as men have brought enormous numbers of married women into the labor market worldwide. This, in turn, has created increased demand for education by women at higher and higher education levels. So globalization is accentuating an already growing trend by women to obtain as much education as men, and, not infrequently, even more.

This does not mean that women receive wages equal to men's. That is hardly the case. Nor does it mean that women are obtaining higher education in fields that are most lucrative, such as engineering, business, or computer science. That is also far from true. Women are still vastly underrepresented in the most lucrative professions even in the most "feminized" countries, such as Sweden or the United States. But globalization seems gradually to be changing that, for both positive and negative reasons. The positive reasons are that flexible organization in business enterprise requires flexible labor, and women are as flexible as men, or even more so, and that information technology and telecommunications are spreading democratic ideas worldwide. The negative reason is that women are paid much less than men almost everywhere in the world, and it is profitable for firms to hire women and pay them lower wages. Yet, both sets of reasons gradually seem to be driving both the education and the price for women's labor up relative to men's. For example, the percentage of women in university science and engineering faculties is increasing worldwide. Although such increased professionalization of women may have costly effects on family life, it does serve to democratize societies and greatly raise the average level of schooling.

A third important aspect of globalization is the greater circulation of labor globally. Even if labor does not move nearly as much as goods and capital, immigration increased into the developed countries until the economic crisis of 2009, driven in part by low birth rates among ethnic Australians, Canadians, Western Europeans, and, to a lesser extent, Americans; hence the need for labor to do a wide variety of jobs, at both the low and high wage ends of the spectrum. At the same time, other than Luxembourg (37.3 percent), New Zealand (24.2 percent), Australia (23.6 percent), Switzerland (19.3 percent), Canada (17.4 percent), and the United States (10.4 percent), the foreign-born population in most developed countries is well below 10 percent, although it has increased in the past 10 years (NationMaster.com, 2013). These numbers belie the much larger percentage of first- and second-generation immigrants in the primary and secondary schools of these countries. For example, in Germany, 27 percent of the students taking the Programme for International Student Assessment (PISA) test in 2009 were first- and second-generation immigrants from eastern Europe, Russia, and Turkey (Stanat, Rauch, and Segeritz, 2010). In Australia, New Zealand, and Canada, most of the immigrants are from Asia, which has also changed the face of their school systems, probably raising international test scores. Increased multiculturalization of Eurocentric societies is therefore one important manifestation of globalization.

GLOBALIZATION, SCIENCE CULTURE, AND EDUCATIONAL MEASUREMENT

Globalization has also produced an increased emphasis on teaching science and mathematics and on educational measurement. The high value of information technology and other science-based industries has pushed countries to increase emphasis on science and mathematics education. This has been stimulated by the spread of a science and math culture (Schofer, Ramirez, and Meyer, 1997) and also the strong effort by many countries to attract foreign high-tech investment and build up domestic high-tech industries (Carnoy, 1998).

How much real improvement has taken place in science and math education is questionable, but the rhetoric surrounding the issue has increased greatly. Furthermore, there is a much greater focus in many countries on comparing performance in these subjects (as well as in reading) with student performance in other countries. With increased economic competition and the increased availability of information technology, data takes on greater value and increased use. Performance in real time is enhanced as an outcome; quantitative measurement appears easier, and its results have become increasingly the means of communication about performance.

An important element of such performance is linked to "efficiency." The application of this thinking, part and parcel of globalized thinking, to education takes the form of tracking the quantity and quality of education through data collection. The most recent expression of this is collecting data on student performance as a measure of the quality of education, largely with the intention of using such results to improve educational efficiency.

The new emphasis on measuring and comparing school outcomes across countries and within countries has not occurred spontaneously. Rather, it has been pushed by international organizations such as the International Association for Evaluation of Educational Achievement and the OECD, by the World Bank, the Inter-American Bank, and the Asian Development Bank, by nongovernmental organizations such as the Inter-American Dialogue, and by bilateral agencies such as the U.S. Agency for International Development. All these organizations share a globalized view of education and efficiency, which includes a highly quantitative view of progress. They also share an explicit understanding that "better" education can be measured and that better education translates directly into higher economic and social productivity. With more intensive economic competition among nation-states, the urgency of improving productivity is translated by these organizations into spreading the acceptance of inter- and intra-national comparisons on standardized tests of student knowledge (Hanushek and Kimko, 2000; Hanushek and Woessmann, 2008; OECD, 2011; UN Education Science and Cultural Organization, 2005). The World Bank and other international and bilateral lenders have also pushed this new emphasis on test score measures of the quality of education through direct monetary incentives of additional foreign assistance for those developing countries that participate in international tests and develop national testing regimes.[2]

Nations' average international test performance is playing an increasing role in the way the public in those countries view themselves educationally. The two major players in the international testing universe are the International Association of the Evaluation of Educational Achievement, which began testing internationally in the 1960s and now produces the Trends in International Mathematics and Science Survey (TIMSS), and the OECD, which runs the PISA. Their impact on national educational policy is steadily increasing, and so is the number of countries that participate in one or the other, or both. For example, according to one Irish analyst,

> Over the past two decades, the fortunes of the Irish economy have undergone major fluctuations. Inevitably, this economic volatility has impacted on the level and quality of educational provision in the country. At the same time, the results of PISA 2009 for Ireland, although open to a variety of interpretations, resulted in a drop down the PISA league tables and generated something of a "PISA shock." This has been a key catalyst for a range of educational reforms, many of which are contained in the National Literacy and Numeracy Strategy (in 2011). (Wall and Looney, 2013)

The policy impact of the tests is growing despite frequently different messages given by the results in the PISA and the TIMSS. Finnish students do extraordinarily well on the PISA mathematics tests and only moderately well on the TIMSS—about the same as students in the United States, whereas U.S. students do relatively poorly on the PISA mathematics test. Russian students do poorly on the PISA math and very well on the TIMSS test. Students in the United Kingdom have shown a large decline on the PISA mathematics test in 2000–2009, whereas English students have done significantly better on the TIMSS test in the same period (1999–2011). Furthermore, the policy influence of the tests is increasing even though the test data and the surveys of students and school personnel that accompany them provide little information that can be used to explain why some countries' students perform better than others. An OECD study (2011) commissioned by the U.S. Secretary of Education, Arne Duncan, claimed that U.S. education could learn many lessons from specific countries and regions that scored high on the PISA test, but could find no evidence that the factors cited were actually responsible for the high scores. Moreover, the study claimed that U.S. students made little or no progress over the past ten years, when PISA results themselves suggest that lower social class students had made substantial gains in both mathematics and reading, even when compared to gains in high scoring countries such as Finland, Canada, and Korea (Carnoy and Rothstein, 2013).

The use of student tests in the global conception of measurement and efficiency is, however, currently rather confused. This is due largely to the push by international organizations such as the World Bank and Inter-American Bank for comparative data to reform systems in keeping with system efficiency, mainly in financial terms. The OECD has been at the forefront of two major interpretations of international test results—namely that students' social class is not the main barrier to high test scores (after all, Chinese students wherever they live, Korean students, and Japanese students perform much better on these tests no matter their social class than do students in, say, the United States or Germany), and that more spending on education is not an important factor in explaining how much students learn.

The implication is that spending more resources on low-income students or focusing on efforts that reduce poverty is not a fruitful direction for policy-makers to take when thinking about how to improve students' learning outcomes. Yet, recent studies have shown precisely the opposite. Researchers have now shown that a nation's income inequality has a negative relation to its *average* student performance on these international tests even when controlling for income per capita (Adamson, 2010; Chiu and Khoo, 2005). Some cross-country studies indicate little relation between spending per student and average test score (Woessmann, 2000, using 1995 TIMSS data), but another study by the same author shows a positive relation (Fuchs and Woessmann, 2004, using PISA data). One of the main problems with such studies is that they do not account for the large private expenditures on out-of-school courses and tutoring in Asian countries (Bray, 2006), where the total spending per student including these unmeasured expenditures may be more than double the public spending per student, or for the differential spending among countries on early childhood education. For example, in Scandinavia and France almost all children spend many hours per day in high-quality, expensive early childhood centers from two or three years old until they enter regular schooling. Were these two types of spending included in the international estimates of the relation of educational spending per student to test performance, they would surely produce very different results.

More recent research in Chile on 2008 legislation that increased the amount of public spending that low-income children received by 50 percent shows that the additional spending per pupil in first to fourth grade had a reasonably large average causal impact (0.2 standard deviations in national test scores). The results of the study suggest that more spending on low-income children does make a difference in student learning—at least part of the effect was through increasing the capacity of schools with large numbers of such low-income students to purchase more and higher quality inputs.[3]

Although articulated and justified in terms of their potential contribution of making education more efficient in terms of improving education, international tests are not necessarily consistent with measures needed for improving schooling. PISA, for example, is not linked to national curriculum standards. Rather, it is a measure of knowledge that experts believe makes youth more functional economically and socially in the current knowledge environment. It is true that cross-nationally PISA results are highly correlated with other test results, but its mathematics portion, for example, would not serve well for writing a mathematics curriculum. That said, when results of PISA or TIMSS are compared for similar social class groups across countries and across time, they do provide information on how one country's educational system may be performing compared to other countries, and may provide clues on how educational systems are serving lower and higher social class groups. But much more research would be needed to discover what is going right or wrong in educational systems.

Furthermore, other ways of using testing are linked more directly to school improvement. In the best of cases, school personnel participate in designing and applying the tests, and the tests are directly linked to knowledge transmission goals set either at the national or regional level. Important aspects of school efficiency can certainly be understood through such tests, but efficiency here is less concerned with resource allocation per se than with process and use of resources. In Chile, for example, national testing of fourth- and eighth-grade students was originally, in the 1980s, used simply as a way to stimulate competition among private and public schools competing for students and the voucher funds attached to each student. Available evidence suggests that this use of tests had no positive effect on student achievement. However, in the 1990s, the use of national testing linked to central government school improvement programs did apparently increase test scores in lower-scoring schools catering to low-income students.

Global notions of efficiency and measurement can have a positive effect on educational output, and improving educational quality may have an effect on economic productivity. For these links to play out, however, policy-makers first have to pass notions of measurement through local filters and have as their specific purpose school improvement even if school improvement requires more resources, which is likely the case in most developing societies. The distinction between this type of application of measurement to raising efficiency and the use of testing to develop national policies for resource use with the intention of avoiding discussions of public resources available for education is subtle and is mainly rooted in how the state, rather than international organizations, interprets the role of measurement in conditioning educational change. In addition, higher test scores must be linked to an improved quality of life for students scoring higher on tests. Although we would all like to believe that better schools will result in better economic and social opportunities for graduates, this may not be the case in highly unequal societies that can only absorb a small percentage of these higher-quality graduates into higher-paying jobs. The success of any education policy in promoting economic growth and social mobility depends on national state economic and social policies. In the following, the crucial role of national states in the crosswinds of international agency definitions of educational excellence and its relation to economic growth and social mobility is discussed.

GLOBALIZATION AND THE ROLE OF EDUCATIONAL TECHNOLOGY IN REFORM

The ICT revolution that has helped shape globalization is also gradually influencing education in three ways. First, computers in classrooms are being used increasingly—albeit still in limited ways—to supplement regular classroom teaching. Computers in the classroom have had much less influence in education processes than expected, even after thirty years. Second, the worldwide growth of the Internet has made possible virtual instruction on a global scale and this has been particularly important in post-secondary education. Third, the increased use of testing to measure student performance has made available vast amounts of information to schools and even to teachers on how well their students are learning the material being taught. ICT allows teachers to follow systematically student progress and communicate that progress to parents and students. It allows principals to evaluate teachers, hold them accountable, and assist teachers to improve. It also gives higher-level administrators information that—if they know how to use it—helps them make better management decisions. Again, the use of ICT in educational management is still struggling through a long incipient stage.

The driving force behind the incorporation of ICT into education is ostensibly to improve student learning and to prepare youth for a global economy in which education contributes to higher productivity. As argued earlier in this chapter, there are strong underlying economic growth motives here, fostered by increased competition in the global economy. Allegedly, nations that have higher scoring students will perform better economically. Nations with students versed in the use of computers and the Internet will be more productive. There is a second type of economic driver for the use of ICT in education—one that also motivated the use of educational radio and television a generation earlier: with ICT, the argument goes, it is possible to deliver reasonably high-quality teaching to large numbers of students at low cost.

With the development of portable communications and the melding of portable communication and information software, the possibility that ICT will become ubiquitous even in very-low-income societies is no longer a dream (Negroponte, 1996). Even so, actual differences exist in access to ICT for different income groups. This is known as the digital divide and it, too, is an important feature of the information revolution.

ICT and Student Achievement in Schools

Given the importance of ICT skills and perhaps the even greater importance of improving academic achievement for increasing productivity in a knowledge economy, formal education's role in producing ICT knowledge and the role of ICT in raising student achievement in school are both crucial issues in the ICT/knowledge economy nexus. The issue may be even more crucial when it comes to social and economic equity, as part of the digital divide is also evident in education systems. Children from lower-income families live in poorer communities with less access to ICT and attend schools that are also likely to have less access to ICT hardware, software, and Internet. Although some developing countries have tried to close this gap—Chile, for example, with its ENLACES program—there are real questions whether simply putting hardware, Internet access, and some educational software into schools is enough to close the digital divide significantly, and whether ICT distribution programs such as ENLACES have a significant effect on children's learning. There is a serious problem in schools even in developed countries of teacher and management capacity to implement ICT to improve student learning. Teacher capacity is not distributed equally across schools serving lower and higher social class students. Thus, even if all students were given equal access to ICT hardware and software, using those new inputs to their optimal levels depends on the quality of teacher and management ICT education-related skills available to students in each school.

In this section, the main concern is the nexus between globalization and the role of ICT in education. We can assume that when students are exposed more to computers and using them for various activities, it would be easier to train them as adults to use computers in work situations. Equipping schools with computers and Internet in low-income countries and in low-income areas within countries can therefore play an important role in reducing the digital divide in these terms (Claro, 2010).

It is also fair to say that the evidence for the positive impact on learning of ICT, including Internet, in classrooms is at best mixed (see, for example, Kulik, 1994; Wenglinsky, 1998 for the United States; and Claro, 2010; Sunkel, Trucco, and Moller, 2011; Venezky and Davis, 2002, for international reviews). Contrary to idealistic notions of enhancing students' problem-solving skills through ICT in schools, there is little or no evidence that this occurs. On the other hand, some evidence suggests that ICT may be rather effective in increasing student performance on standardized tests by employing computer-assisted instruction (CAI), especially in conjunction with teacher-student interaction around imaginative drill and practice software.

Such findings can provide insights into why ICT has had relatively little impact on higher-order student learning and into its continued use in schools mainly as a mechanism to raise student test scores through drill and practice (generally known as CAI) software. One reason is that CAI requires much lower levels of teacher training, particularly training in ICT applications. Even in high-income countries, most classroom teachers have relatively unsophisticated computer knowledge. Yet, without better-trained teachers, ICT is probably ineffective in teaching higher-level skills. Thus, school system administrators do not even try to use ICT for higher-order activities. The second reason is the increased emphasis on student test performance in the global economic and educational environment. With pressure from international lending and testing agencies to use student test scores as a major measure of nations' capacity for economic development and of their educational systems' quality, it is logical that the role of ICT in classrooms would be increasingly shaped by its potential enhancement of student performance on tests.

ICT and Higher Education

The ICT equation is different in higher education. The absence of computer skills we observe in primary and secondary education is much less of a problem at the university level. To a much greater extent than in lower levels of education, university teachers use e-mail as a major form of communicating with colleagues and, increasingly, with students. Many courses are posted on the Web, and, also increasingly, teacher assignments and student work is Web-based. Research and teaching networks have been greatly extended. For professors at many universities, these networks are worldwide. These represent important widespread changes in work processes in universities. The fact that teachers (and students) in higher education have greater ICT skills means that higher education is characterized by greater use of ICT and work processes are more likely to be affected by ICT. This seems to confirm that the main barrier to changing work processes in lower levels of schooling through ICT is lack of ICT skills.

However, there is still an apparent contradiction between the spread of ICT-driven work changes, such as e-mail and Web-facilitated teaching and learning, and the continued persistence (and glorification) of very traditional teaching and learning. This raises an important point about barriers to ICT use in education that go beyond teacher ICT skills. Is there something inherently different about the production of academic skills (cognitive learning) that puts limits on ICT use—even as a catalyst—in improving educational delivery? If we consider high-quality higher education as a model for lower levels of education (if we could afford to spend as much per student on lower levels as we do on university), then we probably still believe that the "best" learning takes place where a professor (teacher) is able to have direct personal interaction with students over a period of time to analyze and discuss subject matter that the professor (teacher) judges to be important. The "best" professors are usually those that have greatest intellectual command over the subject matter, often introducing students to an unusual and original way to view the subject matter.

Nevertheless, "distance" education using Internet-based teaching/learning platforms are spreading. University of Phoenix[4] in the United States and the Open University of Cataluña

(UOC) are good examples of such "virtual" universities. In both cases, students take Web-based courses developed by the university specifically for students who cannot come regularly to classes at a fixed site. Students do the course work according to their schedules. They send their completed assignments electronically to the university where they are graded by professors and their assistants. At UOC, students are assigned a tutor professor to guide them through their coursework toward the degree and a consulting professor (hired from other universities) to oversee the tutor professors in each course. UOC also has a few interactive virtual seminars available to advanced students.

One of the hoped-for features of virtual universities would be lower costs per student while simultaneously achieving equal or better academic results than traditional higher education. In terms of making low-cost, high-quality university education available to the mass of lower-income students, this would be ideal, if it were true. From the institutional side, however, costs per student at Phoenix online seem to be about the same as or higher than in large state universities, and costs at the UOC are also no lower than and may be higher than in traditional Catalan and Spanish universities. With one consultant professor for every ten students at UOC, this is likely to be the case. The main saving is in private costs, as students attending UOC or Phoenix are bound to be working full-time while taking online courses for credit. The savings in income foregone can be used to pay the relatively high tuition rates at Phoenix, or can be simply passed on directly to students by charging low tuition, such as at UOC.

The newest form of virtual higher education and the most recent expression of the combined impact of globalization and ICT on education is the massive open online course (MOOC). In theory, MOOCs could make available to a global student clientele courses taught by experts in particular subjects from the very best universities in the world using effective lecture techniques, high-level curricula, and well organized evaluation activities (problem sets, tests, etc.). For students who are academically able and disciplined enough to work independently in such courses, they could create the possibility of much higher standards of knowledge transmission worldwide. It is argued that they could also boost the quality of second tier higher education institutions by giving students there the opportunity to study with the very best professors in the world at a distance. However, the main objective of using MOOCs in second-tier institutions is likely to be to lower costs per student, not to raise quality. As discussed in the following, states are under pressure to decrease the costs of higher education expansion. MOOCs will certainly play a role in accomplishing that goal without necessarily raising higher educational quality.

Is this the future of universities in a world where university degrees are needed to get good jobs, and many people already in full-time jobs would benefit from a university degree? Virtual universities and virtual courses require much more analysis by researchers, not only in terms of what students learn (the limited studies done to date at UOC suggest that they learn the material just as well as students in traditional universities), but how employers regard the degrees from such universities, and the relative pay of students graduating with virtual university degrees. Surprisingly, little is known about the economic value of distance university degrees, even though institutions such as the U.K.'s Open University and its spin-offs around the world have been in existence for many years. The main benefit to individuals and to society is probably that people can work while "attending" university, thereby reducing the cost of attaining a degree.

ICT and Educational Management

We should also see globalization's impact on the spread of testing reflected in more use of ICT employing test data in the management of schools and school systems. The World Bank and other international agencies have been pushing (and lending money to) countries to develop school accountability systems built around ICT. Educational administrators need to have basic information on student and teacher flows, probably also of school supplies, and how much the system is spending on various inputs, in order to make the most basic resource allocation decisions. Undoubtedly, ICT has played an important role in improving data collection in educational systems. It has also made these data more widely available to school personnel, parents, and the public at large through central administration websites, and in some countries through direct access to central or district databases by school personnel.

These rudimentary data collection functions are expanded in some countries and regions by more sophisticated quality control data, namely student evaluation data. Brazil, Chile, and Mexico have test data on entire school populations in various grades and the governments make school level results available publicly, but it is remarkable how few inroads student data analysis using ICTs have made into states, municipalities, and schools in these three countries. As in the case of ICTs for learning, the main barrier seems to be the human capacity to implement ICTs for educational management. Yet, in the future these barriers should gradually come down and, for better or worse, top down data-driven accountability systems will be used increasingly to try to raise productivity in schools.

THE ROLE OF THE NATIONAL STATE IN A GLOBALIZED EDUCATION ENVIRONMENT

Is the power of the national state diminished by globalization? Yes and no. Yes, because increasing global economic competition makes the national state focus on economic policies that improve global competitiveness, at the expense of policies that stabilize the current configuration of the domestic economy or possibly social cohesion (Castells, 1997). Yes, because the national state is compelled to make the national economy attractive for the mass of capital that moves globally in the rate of flows, and that may mean a reduction of public spending and the introduction of monetary policy that favors financial interests rather than workers and consumers (Castells, 1997).

But no, because ultimately national states still greatly influence the territorial and temporal space in which most people acquire their capacity to operate globally and where capital has to invest. National states are largely responsible for the political climate in which businesses conduct their activities and individuals organize their social lives. Some analysts have called this underlying context for social and economic interaction "social capital" (Coleman, 1988). Others have focused on trust (Fukuyama, 1995). National public policy has an enormous influence on social capital and trust. Even the World Bank, supposedly a global institution, has rediscovered the national state as crucial to national economic and social development (World Bank, 1997). It makes a major difference to a nation's economic possibilities when the national state is capable of formulating coherent economic and social policies and carrying them out. It makes a major difference if the national state can reduce corruption and establish trust, and it is difficult to imagine achieving greater social capital in most places without a well-organized state.

Ultimately, the state is concerned with its own reproduction. To reproduce its political power, the state bureaucracy seeks political legitimacy even when it is a non-democratic regime. In the past and now even more in a globalized knowledge economy, achieving political legitimacy includes providing education to the mass of a nation's population. More recently, state legitimacy includes improving the quality of that mass education, particularly in terms of student scores on international and national assessments. It has also come to include greatly expanding higher education and, in the larger economies, investing in a prime symbol of knowledge economy prestige, the "world-class" university (Altbach, Reisberg, and Rumbley, 2009).

As noted, the tendency for the state in the new competitive global environment is to focus on education policies that enhance its economy's global competitiveness. We noted that an important influence of globalization is to increase the relative value of higher educated labor (or decrease the value of less educated labor). Thus, the private rates of return to higher education are rising in most countries and, in many, now exceed the payoff to lower levels of schooling. We need to remember that when the payoffs to higher education rise, this increases the demand not only for places in higher education, but also for lower levels of education and for increased *quality* of lower levels of schooling so students can better compete for university places. The state's legitimacy is entwined with its capacity to expand and improve the educational system as a whole.

Yet, there are both objective and ideological financial constraints surrounding this expansion. Increased competition in the global economy has made it more difficult for both developed and developing nations to raise revenue through increased taxation, particularly on corporate profits and individual income, because governments fear the flight of capital or not being able to attract capital investment. Further, many of the world's governments have low capacity to collect income taxes, so rely on excise taxes (VAT, import tariffs, export taxes). Finally, governments are under pressure from international financial institutions, such as the International Monetary Fund and the World Bank, to keep public spending low. A major part of the International Monetary Fund package for countries preparing themselves for "sound" economic growth is to reduce the size of public deficits and shift national resources from government control to the private sector. This, in turn, means keeping public spending low relative to the size of the private sector.

The main argument for providing free public education at low cost, even under conditions of highly restricted public access, has been that there are large "externalities," or social value, associated with the graduates of these universities. The social value of education includes the positive effects of an educated population on civil society, tolerance for dissenting views, political stability, strengthened democracy, treatment of women and minority groups, and overall economic productivity—more educated people tend to make their coworkers more productive as well. It is therefore generally agreed that primary and basic secondary education should be heavily subsidized if not altogether free, so that no child in the society would be prevented from accessing those levels. Even at the university level and even when university graduates generally belong to a privileged socioeconomic group, the case has been made politically for publicly financing such students to earn higher incomes at public expense. The contention is that high social class individuals increasing their human capital at public expense also increase everyone else's well-being by becoming good doctors, good engineers, and good leaders. These large benefits, it could be claimed, accrue to the society as a whole, not just to the graduates themselves. One of the main arguments used for investing much larger amounts per student in elite or "world class" institutions is that their graduates and the research done there will have large "spillover" effects for society as a whole.

Equity has played a role in the debate as well: lower social class families may face especially large financial, informational, or other barriers to entry into secondary and higher education. If a society values fairness and places social and political value on ensuring desired levels of equity, the public aspect of education would include financing it in ways that remove such barriers. This equity argument has been extended to make education as a whole—including higher education—a human right, situating it completely in the public space, available for all at public expense.[5] Again, social preferences for equity are mediated through the state, and depending on power relations in the state, the state can interpret how education is to be financed as a public or private good.

Globalization and the Shift to Education as a Private Good

Given this framework, globalization—particularly the economic competition and accompanying ideology of that competition—has had an important influence on the objective and ideological financial conditions surrounding educational expansion. These conditions have allowed/promoted states to "privatize" educational financing, particularly in higher education.

It is worth dividing the shift toward viewing education more as a private good into two parts. The first part concerns the financing of education. States vary greatly in how they finance educational expansion (James, 1993). Recent trends have varied as well, with some African nations eliminating fees in public schools but also allowing the expansion of private, fee-based schools; some Latin American countries such as Brazil greatly expanding public secondary education; and others, such as Chile, allowing private subsidized schools to charge fees on top of the public subsidy but more recently, increasing by 50 percent the amount of funding for schools serving low-income students. The tendency worldwide in higher education has been for states to turn increasingly to the privatization of higher education financing through cost-sharing (tuition) in public universities and the expansion of private higher education institutions to handle increased enrollment (Altbach and Levy, 2005; Altbach, Reisberg, and Rumbley, 2009; World Bank, 2000).

These state decisions concerning financing are couched in the overall debate about education as a public versus private good in the context of financial "constraints" on the public sector in its need to expand education and improve its quality. There is little doubt, for example, that the Chilean state based its decision in the 1990s to allow publicly financed, privately run primary and secondary schools to charge fees (South Africa does the same) in anticipation of the large amount of revenue such a policy would generate. The clearest example, however, is the more general shift to tuition-financed higher education expansion (even in developed countries). Rising private rates of return to higher education not only pressure national states to expand higher education through the increasing demand of their population to access universities, these higher payoffs also allow states to shift the costs of financing higher education to families. Rising private payoffs to higher education shift the public's perception of the private and public value of higher education. When university graduates earn much more than the rest of the population, and college graduates are likely to be children of the more educated and higher income groups in society, those with little access to higher education can reasonably ask whether the public benefit to them is high enough to justify subsidizing these more elite groups. The state can de-emphasize the social benefits of education in justifying investments in higher education and can simultaneously persuade families to bear direct "user taxes" in the form of tuition and other costs to pay for that education. The cost to the state in the form of political legitimacy for making families pay directly for education is much lower when private payoffs to education are high.

The second part of the shift toward education as a private good is based on the notion that private provision (management) of education is more effective (students are able to learn more) and more efficient (students are able to learn as much at lower cost) than publicly provided education. A large body of evidence suggests that generally, privately run schools and universities are *not* more effective than their publicly run counterparts (with similar students) and are more efficient only because they can select their students (in the case of primary and secondary schools) or are able to cut costs because they deliver a lower quality product—they deliver less quality for a lower quality/cost ratio (Carnoy and Carrasco, 2013; Levin and Belfield, 2002; McEwan and Carnoy, 2000). There are exceptions to these findings (in Bangladesh and Pakistan, for example), but it is difficult to make a persuasive general case for privatizing the delivery of education on either effectiveness or efficiency grounds. Yet, international agencies such as the World Bank have consistently pushed this policy, both on financial but mainly ideological grounds, claiming privately run schools are more market-sensitive and responsive to parents' needs (Patrinos, 2000).

Thus, in a globalized economy global social constructions (often accompanied by a financial "stick" of international funding) can have a major influence on nation-states' choices in financing and shaping their higher education systems (Meyer, Ramirez, Frank, and Shofer, 2005). This shift and other aspects of (higher) education expansion in developing countries have been linked to a neoliberal hegemonic globalization of economy and culture (Marginson and Ordorika, 2010).

The cost in terms of producing both adequate public outcomes of education and of reaching goals of quality and equity may be high if the state goes along with this neoliberal conception of the balance between education as a private and public good at the primary and secondary level. Many years of management privatization in Chile and more recent experiences with charter schools in the United States suggest that shifting to privately managed schools contributes to even higher levels of school social class stratification in what were already highly stratified school systems (Bifulco and Ladd, 2006; McEwan and Carnoy, 1998; OECD, 2004). Such stratification does not bode well for developing cohesive, tolerant, democratic societies. Neither does it make improving school quality any easier. Evidence suggests that more unequal societies (read: more highly socially stratified school systems) have lower average student achievement even at similar levels of gross domestic product per capita. The bottom line is that the competition for higher social class schools is lower social class schools—if the bottom of the system is of low quality, so will be the top of the system. Making schools privately managed does not solve this problem, and it may exacerbate it.

Higher Education as a Public and Private Good

The story in higher education is not so much different, except that in most societies, only a minority of students currently attends higher education institutions. Higher education students in these societies are considered more privileged, so as has been noted, when the private payoffs are high to higher education graduates, it is easier for the state to argue that heavily subsidizing those students overburdens the public budget to help make the advantaged even more advantaged. The state can also soften "user taxes" for university education with affirmative action programs, such as those in India and Brazil, which help legitimize the state with lower income groups without unduly increasing the cost of providing largely privately financed higher education in those two countries (Carnoy et al., 2013).

Thus, when the state decides to charge tuition at public higher education institutions or to allow the expansion of private higher education institutions, the main issue, it could be argued, is not whether higher education is a "private" versus a "public" good. It is rather whether large subsidies at public expense to students for higher education substantially benefit society as a whole and whether these public subsidies are distributed equitably or not among different social class groups. Assume that in practice only a small fraction of a nation's citizens have access to a "public" good and this fraction comes from essentially the same social class group in generation after generation. The case made by this group for public subsidies is that much general social good comes from educating them. Yet, it could just as easily be claimed that a certain class of citizens has appropriated public revenues for its private use, deploying their political power to justify the level of subsidy they receive.

In terms of societies' preferences for equity—an important part of the public-private debate—the state's shift from a more public to a more private definition of (mainly higher) education may (ironically) be producing more rather than less fairness in the way the state distributes its resources. Because social preferences for equity are associated with the provision of education, the state's distribution of public resources going to higher education among different social class groups should therefore be included in its definition as a public/private good. However, it is likely that lower social class groups are less concerned with the distribution of public resources than with their own potential access to higher education and the perceived financial barriers they face from this shift to private higher education. Lower social class groups may prefer free, publicly financed higher education even if, given financial constraints on the state, this means greater subsidies for the rich at the expense of the poor.

In Brazil, for example, about 75 percent of all students enrolled in higher education attend private institutions and pay full tuition (except for a small percentage of partially publicly financed lower social class students in private universities). The 25 percent of students in public universities, a number of them elite institutions, pay no tuition. The average social class of the students attending private institutions is somewhat higher than in public institutions, but in both, the majority of students come from families in the top 20 percent of income earners. As it is, in 2007, 50 percent of all public spending on higher education in Brazil went to that top 20 percent of income group and only 12 percent to the bottom 40 percent. The distribution of funds would have been even more unequal had a higher fraction of students attended public institutions (Carnoy et al., 2013, Chapter 8).

Keep in mind this distribution of public funds view of how "public" the higher education system is. Now consider the impact of increased global economic competition when it comes to the rush to develop "world-class" universities. If states are constrained financially in expanding higher education enrollment, one way they stretch their available funds is to privatize costs. A second way is to absorb most of the increased enrollment in low-cost, low-quality institutions and to provide incentives for those institutions to reduce costs per student even further. This is precisely what many countries, including the United States, Brazil, and China, are doing (Carnoy et al., 2013). At the same time, expensive elite universities (world class, attended, on average, by much higher social class students) receive increasing levels of resources, in Brazil and China almost entirely at public expense. This increasing differentiation is a key feature of state strategies to make themselves more competitive in the global knowledge economy. This strategy is argued to produce very high social benefits because of the new knowledge that such elite institutions are likely to produce. But students who graduate from world-class universities also reap very high private benefits. Thus, increasing differentiation may indeed be producing greater social inequality even accounting for high externalities.

SUMMING UP

National education has been significantly affected by globalization even though we may not necessarily observe these effects in most of the world's classrooms. The effects are expressed through changes in the payoffs to different levels of education and the implication that has for the value attached to different levels and kinds of knowledge in each society. They are also expressed through the educational policies implemented at the national level in the context of a globalized economy. The main theme of the global economy is increased competition, with education as an important symbol of nations' capacity compete. This brings with it increased emphasis on measurement of educational output and the use of measures to evaluate national educational quality. It also brings with it an emphasis on efficiency, which has meant increased pressure to lower the costs of education, particularly of higher education, and to increase output per unit of school input. One of the main instruments being used in attempting to meet the pressures of completion is ICT, although the successful inroads that ICT has made in education have been surprisingly small.

All of these effects of globalization on education are passed through the policy structures of national states, so it is these states that ultimately decide how globalization affects national education. I would argue that there is much more political and even financial space for the national state to condition the way globalization is brought into education than is usually admitted. Testing and standards are a good example of this space, and ICT is another. States can provide schooling access more equally, improve the quality of education for the poor, and produce knowledge more effectively and more equally for all within a globalized economy. There are many examples of successful efforts to shift resources to the poor and of making public educational systems more effective for everyone. Indeed there is evidence that the U.S. educational system, several Latin American systems, and the German and Polish educational systems have improved quality substantially in the past ten years and that they have done so without more privatization (Carnoy and Rothstein, 2013). That many states choose to adopt education policies that lower costs without improving quality (particularly in higher levels of education) is at least partly the result of caving in to poor politics in the face of new competitive pressures and new, globalized thinking. Although it is difficult to counter strong, worldwide ideological trends and, indeed, the objective reality of financial globalization, states can choose to emphasize more productive, more equal, and more effective public education even in the highly competitive global economic environment. Indeed, should they do so, they are much more likely to make their societies better off economically, socially, and politically.

REFERENCES

Adamson, Frank. 2010. How Does Context Matter: Comparing Achievement Scores, Opportunities to Learn, and Teacher Preparation Across Socio-Economic Quintiles in TIMSS and PISA. Unpublished Ph.D. dissertation, Stanford University School of Education.

Altbach, Philip, and Daniel Levy (eds.). 2005. *Private Higher Education: A Global Revolution*. Chestnut Hill, MA: Center for International Higher Education, and Rotterdam: Sense Publishers.

Altbach, Philip, Liz Reisberg, and Laura Rumbley. 2009. *Trends in Global Higher Education: Tracking an Academic Revolution*. Chestnut Hill, MA: Boston College Center for International Higher Education.

Bailey, Paul, Aurelio Parisotto, and Geoffrey Renshaw (eds.). 1993. *Multinationals and Employment*. Geneva: International Labour Office.

Bardhan, Ashok, and Cynthia Kroll. 2003. The New Wave of Outsourcing. Research Report. Fisher Center for Real Estate and Urban Economics, Fall.

Bifulco, Robert, and Helen Ladd. 2006. The Impact of Charter Schools on Student Achievement: Evidence from North Carolina. *Education Finance and Policy*, vol. 6, pp. 50–90.

Bluestone, Barry. 1995. The Inequality Express. *The American Prospect*, no. 24, pp. 81–95.

Bray, Mark. 2006. Private Supplementary Tutoring: Comparative Perspectives on Patterns and Implications. *Compare*, vol. 36, no. 4, pp. 515–30.

Carnoy, Martin. 1995. Rates of Return to Education. In Martin Carnoy (ed.), *International Encyclopedia of the Economics of Education*, 2nd edition (pp. 364–69). Cambridge, UK: Pergamon.

———. 1998. The Globalization of Innovation, Nationalist Competition, and the Inter-nationalization of Scientific Training. *Competition and Change*, vol. 3, pp. 237–62.

——— and Henry M. Levin. 1985. *Schooling and Work in the Democratic State*. Stanford, CA: Stanford University Press.

Carnoy, Martin, Manuel Castells, Stephen S. Cohen, and Fernando Henrique Cardoso. 1993. *The New Global Economy in the Information Age*. University Park: Pennsylvania State University Press.

Carnoy, Martin, and Richard Rothstein, 2013. *What Do International Tests Really Show About U.S. Student Performance?* Washington, DC: Economic Policy Institute.

Carnoy, Martin, Prashant Loyalka, Maria Dobryakova, Rafio Dossani, Isak Froumin, Katherine Kuhns, Jandhyala B.G. Tilak, and Rong Wang. 2013. *University Expansion in a Changing Global Economy: Triumph of the BRICs?* Stanford, CA: Stanford University Press.

Carnoy, Martin, and Rafael Carrasco. 2013. Achievement Gains in Brazilian Universities: The Case of Engineering and Computer Science Programs. Stanford University School of Education (mimeo).

Castells, Manuel. 1997. *The Power of Identity.* London: Blackwell.

Castro, Claudio de Moura, and Martin Carnoy. 1997. *La Reforma Educativa en America Latina.* Washington, DC: Inter-American Development Bank, Department of Social Programs and Sustainable Development.

Chiu, Ming Ming, and Lawrence Khoo. 2005. Effects of Resources, Inequality, and Privilege Bias on Achievement: Country, School, and Student Level Analyses. *American Educational Research Journal*, vol. 42, no. 4, pp. 575–603.

Claro, Magdalena. 2010. Impacto de las Tecnologías Digitales en el Aprendizaje de Estudiantes. Estado del Arte. Documento de Proyecto. Proyecto @LIS2, Componente Educación, División de Desarrollo Social CEPAL.

Colclough, Christopher, Geeta Kingdon, and Harry Patrinos. 2010. The Changing Pattern of Wage Returns to Education and its Implications. *Development Policy Review*, vol. 28, no. 6, pp. 733–47.

Coleman, James. 1988. Social Capital in the Creation of Human Capital. *American Journal of Sociology*, vol. 94, supplement, pp. S95–S120.

Fuchs, Thomas, and Ludgar Woessmann. 2004. What Accounts for International Differences in Student Performance: A Re-examination Using PISA Data. Center for Economic Studies, Munich, Germany, CESifo Working Paper No. 1235.

Fukuyama, Francis. 1995. *Trust.* New York: Free Press.

Hanushek, Eric, and Dennis Kimko. 2000. Schooling, Labor-Force Quality, and the Growth of Nations. *The American Economic Review*, vol. 90, no. 5, pp. 1184–208.

——— and Ludgar Woessmann. 2008. The Role of Cognitive Skills in Economic Development. *Journal of Economic Literature*, vol. 46, no. 3, pp. 607–68.

James, Estelle. 1993. Why Do Different Countries Choose a Different Public-Private Mix of Educational Services? *The Journal of Human Resources*, vol. 28, no. 3, pp. 571–92.

Krugman, Paul, and Robert Z. Lawrence. 1994. Trade, Jobs, and Wages. *Scientific American*, April, pp. 44–49.

Kulik, James. 1994. Meta-Analytic Studies of Findings on Computer-Based Instruction. In Eva L. Baker and Harry O'Neil, Jr. (eds.), *Technology Assessment in Education and Training* (pp. 9–33). Hillsdale: Erlbaum.

Levin, Henry, and Clive Belfield, 2002. The Effects of Competition Between Schools on Educational Outcomes: A Review for the United States. *Review of Educational Research*, vol. 72, no. 2, pp. 279–341.

Marginson, Simon, and Imanol Ordorika. 2010. "El Central Volumen de la Fuerza." (The Hegemonic Global Pattern in the Reorganization of Elite Higher Education and Research). In Diana Rhoten and Craig Calhoun (eds.), *The Transformation of "Public" Research Universities: Shaping an International and Interdisciplinary Research Agenda for the Social Sciences.* New York: Social Science Research Council.

McEwan, Patrick, and Martin Carnoy. 1998. Competition and Sorting in Chile's Voucher System. Stanford University, School of Education (mimeo).

———. 2000. The Effectiveness and Efficiency of Private Schools in Chile's Voucher System. *Educational Evaluation and Policy Analysis*, vol. 22, no. 3, pp. 213–39.

Meyer, John, Francisco Ramirez, David J. Frank, and Evan Shofer. 2005. Higher Education as an Institution. Stanford University (mimeo).

NationMaster.com. 2013. Foreign Population (Most Recent) by Country. www.nationmaster.com/graph/imm_for-immigration-foreign-population

Negroponte, Nicholas. 1996. *Being Digital.* New York: Vintage Books.

Organization for Economic Cooperation and Development. 2004. *Reviews of National Policies for Education: Chile 2004.* Paris: OECD.

———. 2011. Lessons from PISA for the United States, Strong Performers and Successful Reformers in Education. Paris: OECD.

Patrinos, Harry. 2000. Market Forces in Education. *European Journal of Education*, vol. 35, no. 1, pp. 61–80.

Psacharopoulos, George. 1989. Time Trends of the Returns to Education: Cross-National Evidence. *Economics of Education Review*, vol. 8, no. 3, pp. 225–39.

Ramirez, Francisco, Yasemin Soysal, and Suzanne Shanahan. 1997. The Changing Logic of Political Citizenship: Cross National Acquisition of Women's Suffrage Rights, 1890 to 1990. *American Sociological Review*, vol. 62, no. 5, pp. 735–45.

Ryoo, Jai-Kyung, Martin Carnoy, and Young-Sook Nam. 1993. Rates of Return to Education in Korea. *Economics of Education Review*, vol. 12, no. 1, pp. 71–80.

Schofer, Evan, Francisco Ramirez, and John Meyer. 1997. Effects of Science on Economic Development. Paper presented at the annual meetings of the American Sociological Association, Toronto.

Shaiken, Harley. 1993. Beyond Lean Production. *Stanford Law & Policy Review*, vol. 5, no. 1, pp. 41–52.

Stanat, Petra, Dominique Rauch, and Michael Segeritz. 2010. Schülerinnen und Schuler mit Migrationshintergrund. In Eckhard Klieme, Cordula Artelt, Johannes Hartig, Nina Jude, Olaf Köller, Manfred Prenzel, Wolfgang Schneider, and Petra Stanat (eds.), *PISA 2009. Bilanz nach einem Jahrzehnt* (pp. 200–30). Munster, Germany: Waxmann.

Stromquist, Nelly P. 1995. Romancing the State: Gender and Power in Education. *Comparative Education Review*, vol. 39, no. 4, pp. 423–54.

Sunkel, Guillermo, Daniela Trucco, and Sebastian Moller. 2011. Aprender y Enseñar con las Tecnologías de la Información y las Comunicaciones in América Latina: Potenciales Beneficios. Document 169. Santiago, Chile: CEPAL.

Tobin, James. 1970. On Limiting the Domain of Inequality. *Journal of Law and Economics*, vol. 13, no. 2, pp. 263–77.

UN Education Science and Cultural Organization. 2005. World Education Report 2005. Paris: UNESCO.

Venezky, Richard, and Cassandra Davis. 2002. Quo Vademus? The Transformation of Schooling in a Networked World. Paris: OECD/CERI, Version 8c, March 6.

Wall, Eugene, and Anne Looney. 2013. Ireland's Education Reform Agenda; Austerity Meets Assessment. Presentation at the American Educational Research Association, San Francisco, April 24–28.

Wenglinsky, Harold. 1998. Does It Compute? The Relationship Between Educational Technology and Student Achievement in Mathematics. Educational Testing Services (ETS) Policy Information Report.

Woessmann, Ludgar. 2000. Schooling Resources, Educational Institutions, and Student Performance: The International Evidence. Working Paper No. 983. Kiel Institute of World Economics.

Wood, Adrian. 1994. *North-South Trade, Employment and Inequality.* Oxford: Clarendon.

World Bank. 1997. *World Development Report: The State in a Changing World.* New York: Oxford University Press and World Bank.

———. 2000. *Higher Education in Developing Countries: Peril and Promise.* Published for the Task Force on Higher Education and Society. Washington, DC: World Bank.

NOTES

1. Real time is, in entertainment parlance, "live," meaning that information is exchanged or communicated as it is produced.

2. Based on unpublished research findings by Rie Kijima, a Ph.D. candidate in the Graduate School of Education at Stanford University.

3. These results are from unpublished research in progress by Rafael Carrasco, a Ph.D. candidate at Stanford Graduate School of Education, Stanford University.

4. The University of Phoenix, founded in 1976, is the nation's largest private institution of higher learning. As of May 31, 2004, over one hundred thousand students attend classes in any one of hundreds of campuses and learning centers located in more than twenty states, Puerto Rico, and Canada. Additionally, over 109,000 students attend via the Internet through the University's online campus. This is by far the fastest growing part of Phoenix's business. See http://www.university-of-phoenix-adult-education.com

5. Tobin (1970) has argued, for example, that societies may choose to provide basic education to all in the spirit of commodity egalitarianism.

Chapter Three

Globalization and Global Governance in Education

Karen Mundy and Caroline Manion

The terms "global governance" and "globalization" have come into frequent use over the past two decades. They are, in a conceptual sense, conjoined twins. "Globalization"—which we take to refer not only to the intensification of global economic integration but also the increasing volume and rapidity of flows of people, ideas, and culture across the traditional territorial boundaries of the nation-state—is typically used as a catch-all for describing the erosion of our ability to govern human societies effectively and fairly. "Global governance" has both an aspirational and analytical inflection, referencing the possibility of more just and democratic ordering of an increasingly integrated world, as captured in the two following quotes:

> The very language of global governance conjures up the possibility and the desirability of effecting progressive change in global life through the establishment of a normative consensus—a collective purpose. ... (Barnett and Duvall, 2005, p. 1)

> The idea that societies are capable of democratic self-control and self-realization has until now been credibly realized only in the context of the nation-state. ... What would a political response to the challenges of a postnational constellation look like? (Habermas, 2001, p. 61)

This chapter looks at global governance in education: the work of global institutions and transnational actors with educational mandates. It does so from an historical perspective and draws on theories of global governance and international relations. The chapter asks how changes in world order and the international society of states over the last half-century have shaped existing institutions, and how global institutions have in turn developed new patterns and possibilities for global governance. The chapter explores the origins of the international education for development regime alongside the United Nations mandate in education, highlighting the emergence of the World Bank as the preeminent global governor of this regime, and the putative success of the "education for all" movement over the last decade. It also considers other sources of global governance in education: nonstate actors and networks, the private sector, and emerging world powers. The chapter concludes with a consideration of current shifts in global patterns of geopolitical and economic power, and their implications for education's global governance.

GLOBAL GOVERNANCE AND GLOBALIZATION: RECONCEPTUALIZING INTERNATIONAL RELATIONS

Over the past decade, the theme of global governance has gained enormous traction in the fields of political science and international relations. After many decades in which global-level policy processes were seen as driven primarily by nation-states, changes both in international political economy related to globalization, and shifts within the discipline of international relations, led to this rising reconceptualization.

For much of the period between 1950 and the end of the Cold War, research on the formal architecture of the world polity evolved from three dominant paradigms or worldviews: realism, liberalism, and critical theories. *Realist* views emphasized a world order shaped fundamentally by the relationships of sovereign, territorially distinct nation-states, each focused on maximizing their own interests and power. Realism's main concern was the achievement of peace through the balancing of state power and interests. In the realist view, international organizations were likely to be used by the more powerful to coerce the less powerful (Holsti, 1985; McKinlay and Little, 1986). The idea that international institutions might play an independent role in socializing or civilizing the behavior of states was anathema to the realist view of how international relations worked (Gilpin, 1981; Morgenthau, 1967).

Liberal views accorded a stronger place for international organizations and international cooperation in their conceptualization of a world polity, and brought into fashion detailed empirical studies of the growth of formal mechanisms for international coordination and the construction of international regimes of actors around specific issue arenas. Building on notions of internationalism (Jones, 2000), liberal scholarship adopted a highly rationalistic and state-centric frame: governments, liberal scholars argued, cooperate on matters of common strategic or instrumental interests, particularly when they hold common values or when they face uncertainty (Keohane, 2004; Keohane and Nye, 1977).

Critical and *neo-Marxist* views critiqued both the liberal and the realist views of the world polity, arguing that the fundamental organizational unit of the world polity was not the nation-state but an expansionary capitalist system, within which nation-states held either core positions, or more peripheral and dependent positions. The wealth of the capitalist centers had been built on territorial imperialism pre-1945, and continued in the post-1945 world through the extraction of profit from countries in the periphery (Wallerstein, 1984). Critical scholarship has tended to be highly skeptical of any form of international cooperation, and particularly of the liberal humanism espoused by many international organizations, including the United Nations (Cox, 1981; Murphy, 1994). However, many neo-Marxist as well as social democratic scholars (sometimes termed "compensatory liberalism"; see McKinlay and Little, 1986) posited that structural contradictions between the liberal promises of progress, freedom, and citizenship and the enduring inequalities produced by a capitalist world order would ultimately yield popular calls for reform of the world polity and its international organizations (Cox, 1981; Held, 1995; Lumsdaine, 1993; Murphy, 1994; Ruggie, 1982). Thus, critical scholars and left-leaning liberal scholars held out the analytical possibility of a thicker and more equity-focused, social democratic polity on a world-scale. Some studied the possibilities for a just, inter-civilizational world order (Falk, 1975; Galtung, 1980).

After 1990, the field of international relations (IR) began an important movement away from this tripartite inter-paradigm debate about world order, toward a newly reconstructed debate about "global governance." Why did this occur? Most accounts focus on three interrelated factors. First, after decades in which bi-polar power politics dominated IR, the end of the Cold War opened up the field of international relations and made the practical potential for international cooperation seem less limited (Price and Reus-Smit, 1998, p. 265). The fact that the relatively peaceful collapse of the Soviet Union had been unanticipated in either liberal or realist IR scholarship seemed to beg the need for a new approach that could account for major historical shifts in the world system.

Second, serious attention to the concept of global governance among IR theorists was spurred forward by an apparent transformation of state capacities and state sovereignty through processes of "globalization." The rising magnitude of interregional and deterritorialized flows of all kinds of social interaction suggested that states no longer were the sole or most significant building blocs of the global order (Ruggie, 1994). Processes of economic integration and liberalization not only undermined the sovereignty and capacity of the post-war Keynesian welfare state; they also created new forms of transnational private authority (both corporate and nongovernmental) whose roles had not been adequately captured in realist, liberal, or neo-Marxist paradigms (Biersteker and Hall, 2002).

Finally, new attention to global governance was predicated upon the development of "constructivist" scholarship, which stepped into the gaps in IR scholarship created by globalization and the end of the Cold War (Price and Reus-Smitt, 1998; Ruggie, 1982, 1998a, b). These scholars argued that shared normative or ideational structures and processes had always mattered at least as much as material interests of states in the world polity, primarily because systems of meaning define how actors interpret and work on their material environment (Finnemore, 1996a, b; Price and Reus-Smit, 1998, p. 266; Ruggie, 1982). A steady stream of careful empirical case studies showed, for example, that state behavior in armed conflicts had changed significantly over the course of the twentieth century (e.g., through the Geneva conventions, the banning of chemical weapons, as well as the more recent ban on landmines) (Finnemore, 1996a; Price and Reus-Smit, 1998). Such changes could not be attributed solely to a change in the material/strategic interests of states; instead they depended on the ability of nonstate actors to make normative claims that states later adopted in order to preserve domestic and international legitimacy (Barnett and Finnemore, 2004; Finnemore and Sikkink, 1998; Keck and Sikkink, 1998). Constructivist scholarship argued that states and their interests are historically constructed within an overall system of norms and expectations, and showed that actors other than states could wield substantial transnational authority, often using norms and ideas as tools of power (Biersteker and Weber, 1996; Finnemore and Sikkink, 1998; Ruggie, 1998a). By emphasizing examples of norm-driven change in the international system, empirical research by constructivists opened the way to a new discussion about global governance that would have seemed purely idealistic a decade earlier.

The term "global governance" came first to the fore through Rosenau's now classic re-framing of world order as a system of "governance without government," highlighting the fact that systems of rules and regulatory mechanisms had emerged at the international level, even though such rules lacked the formal, coercive basis of legitimated political authority traditionally associated with nation-states (Rosenau, 1992). The term was further elaborated by the UN-endorsed 1995 report of the Commission on Global Governance, which offered the following definition:

> Governance is the sum of the many ways individuals and institutions, public and private, manage their common affairs. It is a continuing process through which conflicting or diverse interests may be accommodated and cooperative action may be taken. It includes formal institutions and regimes empowered to enforce compliance, as well as informal arrangements that people and institutions have either agreed to or perceive to be in their interest. ... At the global level, governance has been viewed primarily as intergovernmental relationships, but it must now be understood as also involving nongovernmental organizations, citizens' movements, multinational corporations, and the global capital market. Interacting with these are the global mass media of dramatically enlarged influence. (Commission on Global Governance, 1995)

As is apparent from this definition, the concept of global governance draws from an expanding literature about "governance" from the policy sciences, where the notion of governance is used both normatively—to draw attention to the value of public/private partnerships and less state-driven action—and analytically—to describe the increasingly disaggregated nature of public action in the context of globalization (Dale, 2004; Reinicke, 1989; Smouts, 1998). The term "global governance" is thus typically used to capture the fact that the global polity is an evolving set of processes and interactions (rather than a fixed rule system and administrative hierarchy) that by definition involves heterogeneous private and public actors at multiple levels or scales of action: local, national, international, and transnational (Higgot, 2000; Jessop, 2005).

The term "global governance" is not meant to imply that previous relations of power and inequality have vanished. Instead, recent work on global governance prompts us to look for power in new places: in transnational networks and coalitions of actors, and not only in traditional bastions of geopolitical power. Conceptualizing international relations through the lens of global governance focuses attention on "efforts to bring more orderly and reliable responses to social and political issues that go beyond the capacity of nations states to address individually" and thus on creating the opportunity for "a standard setting reflection for building a better world" (Smouts, 1998, p. 88; see also Weiss and Gordenker, 1996). But more importantly, it encourages us to explore the role played by an increasingly complex web of private sector and civil society actors, interacting with states and official international institutions, in shaping the prospects for just and equitable governance at the world scale.

GLOBAL GOVERNANCE IN EDUCATION: ORIGINS AND EVOLUTION

Education has long been deeply implicated in processes of internationalization and economic integration. Formal schooling, for example, was among the most significant of the cultural exports of colonial powers, leading to sustained (if unequal) cultural links between colonial and postcolonial nations and the widespread institutionalization of educational systems as part of the common apparatus of the nation-state. The period after World War II saw the proliferation of international organizations and agreements that helped to define shared norms about educational rights and educational development (see Bajaj, this volume). The activities of a host of international actors fed the institutionalization of rather similar-looking systems of public education.

Initially designed for the elite, by the early twentieth century schooling in the west (at least at the primary level) was increasingly being offered to all citizens, typically in systems run and funded by nation-states. So widespread had the institution of schooling and its imagined role in shaping national trajectories become (see Anderson, 1991), that by the middle of the twentieth century the international community promised to uphold a "universal" right to education, first through the creation of the UN Education Science and Cultural Organization (UNESCO) in 1944, and secondly through Article 26 of the 1948 Universal Declaration of Human Rights, which states:

> Everyone has the right to education. Education shall be free, at least in the elementary and fundamental stages. Elementary education shall be compulsory. Technical and professional education shall be made generally available and higher education shall be equally accessible to all on the basis of merit. (UN General Assembly, n.d.)

The first and largest international regime to emerge from this post–World War II commitment to education focused on educational development in postcolonial societies (Mundy, 2006,

2010). Initially centered at UNESCO, the notion that education could be used as an important tool for national development in postcolonial societies was quickly taken up in the work of newly formed bilateral aid agencies across the Western world during the 1950s and 1960s (e.g., U.S. Agency for International Development, Canadian International Development Agency, Swedish International Development Cooperation Agency, U.K. Department for International Development, etc.). This new educational development regime was fed both by Cold War interstate competition and by the evolution of redistributive claims for education modeled within Western welfare states, whose governments promoted commitment to universality and public provision of education as an alternative to the direct redistribution of wealth promised by socialism. However, the Cold War made Western governments increasingly unwilling to provide funding for educational development through multilateral institutions like UNESCO, where eastern bloc countries held important roles in governance. Instead, they preferred bilateral flows of educational aid that could be organized primarily around the geopolitical and economic objectives of donor nations. Thus though rich country aid for educational development grew quickly, more than three-fourths of all flows of foreign assistance to education went through bilateral channels (Mundy, 2010). Educational development interventions remained deeply fragmented and uncoordinated, with bilateral aid for education focused predominantly on programs of post-primary training, foreign scholarships, and tertiary level institution-building, and heavily tied to technical assistance from the donor countries (King, 1991; Mundy, 2006).

International organizations played a financially smaller, yet increasingly powerful role within the educational aid regime, helping to structure a normative understanding of what educational development should be: answering questions about levels, inputs, processes, and results, and thereby providing operating instructions to bilateral donor governments and recipient governments alike (Chabbott, 2003; Jones, 1988, 1992; Jones and Coleman, 2005; McNeely, 1995; McNeely and Cha, 1994; Mundy, 1998, 2002). UNESCO, which holds the formal UN mandate for education, kicked things off with ambitious regional conferences and targets for educational expansion and adult literacy in the late 1960s and 1970s (Chabbott, 2003). However, Western governments failed to fund UNESCO at levels sufficient to allow it to play a global coordinating role, and intense politicization limited its influence and capabilities in the 1970s and 1980s (Imber, 1989; Jones, 1988; Mundy, 1998, 1999; Preston, Herman, and Schiller, 1989; Sack, 1986; Sewell, 1975). UNESCO's weakness created space for other, more entrepreneurial UN organizations to become active in educational development. The UN Children's Fund developed its own distinctive approach to educational development during the 1960s, targeting marginalized children and after 1980 developing programs such as its "child friendly schools" initiative that link education to children's rights (Black, 1996; Fuchs, 2007; Jolly, 1991; Phillips, 1987).

By the 1980s, the World Bank had emerged as not only the single largest source of international finance for educational development, but also as an influential thought leader responsible for reframing educational development around a focus on strategic investments in human capital for purposes of economic growth, and promoting the increased use of market-like mechanisms to ensure educational efficiency (Alexander, 2001; Jones, 1992; Jones and Coleman, 2005; Mundy, 2002; Resnik, 2006). While the World Bank's fixed capital base provides it with some autonomy, the historical record suggests that its agenda has been strongly influenced by the policy preferences of northern countries, which hold the largest number of voting shares in the organization. In particular the United States, which holds the power of veto and appoints the World Bank's president, has pushed the World Bank to focus on economic growth and private sector development (Woods, 2000). During the 1980s, the

World Bank was influential in designing a reform agenda for countries facing debt crises due to the loss of cheap international credit. The World Bank emerged at the "center of a neo-classical resurgence" in development economics, more responsible than perhaps any other organization for elaborating what has come to be called the "Washington consensus" agenda for low and middle income countries (Miller-Adams, 1999). Around the world, governments were advised to restructure their education sectors by lowering subsidies to tertiary-level education and introducing user fees at this level, and encouraging efficiency-driven reforms in kindergarten to grade twelve–level schooling through the use of contract teachers, lowering of repetition rates, and parental "participation" in school level costs (Alexander, 2001; Hinchcliffe 1993; Independent Evaluation Group, 2011; Psacharopoulos, 1986; World Bank, 1988, 1995). Paradoxically, the era of structural adjustment contributed to substantial increases in World Bank lending activity in education, especially for primary schooling (Mundy, 2002).

In addition to the "education for development regime," a second arena for educational multilateralism emerged around what might be described as shared problem solving among predominantly Western states after World War II. Initially, the idea of information sharing and standard setting in education was mandated to UNESCO, which embodied the liberal internationalist ideal of creating equality of opportunity through enhanced provision of education. Later, however, scientific contest between the Soviet Union and the United States helped to produce a strong strategic interest in information sharing and standard setting in a uniquely Western "club," stimulating the first education work undertaken by the Organization for Economic Cooperation and Development (OECD). Resnik has shown how the voluntary membership in intergovernmental organizations like the OECD taught member governments to "think" about the relationship between education and the economy in new ways—in terms of investment in human capital for greater economic growth, rather than as a social service (Resnik, 2006).

Building upon the foundation of voluntary collaboration and mutual problem solving, from the 1970s onward the OECD was able to encourage governments to fund new joint ventures—including the creation of standardized performance benchmarks of education systems, and somewhat later, the development of voluntary programs of international assessment and cross-national comparison among Western educational systems, which members opted into and paid for themselves (Papadopoulos, 1994). Such activities spread rapidly, with many non-OECD nations joining in the Program for International Student Assessment. Many scholars have argued that the OECD and these new programs have helped to produce more uniform, neoliberal national policies for education, modeling a new approach to doing education policy "by numbers" and with a focus on economic efficiency, in ways that limited more direct engagement of citizens in educational decision-making (Dale and Robertson, 2002; Henry, Lingard, Rizvi, and Taylor, 2001; Seller and Lingard, 2013). However, it would be wrong to conceptualize the OECD as holding uncontested or unmediated power over educational policies. As much recent scholarship suggests, the OECD's policy recommendations are mediated in important ways by national politics and strong local policy coalitions to produce enormous variation in the uptake of specific policies (Bieber and Martens, 2011; Martens and Jakobi, 2010; Martens and Wolf, 2009). Furthermore, when compared to the World Bank, the OECD has often taken a stronger stance on equity issues in education that appears at times to be more closely aligned to social democracy than neoliberalism—for example, in its championing of the educational systems of Finland and Canada as models for high equity systems, and in its work on early childhood education and the education of migrant populations (Mahon, 2010; Mahon and McBride, 2008; Nusche, 2009; OECD, 2006, 2012). In an important way, it has also provided the public with information about quality and equity within education systems that were previously unavailable. At the same time, the pattern of voluntary engagement in international benchmarking established by the OECD is spreading rapidly to other regional organizations, such as the European Union, where joint educational initiatives have grown substantially (Grek, 2013; Lawn and Grek, 2012). Comparison and benchmarking educational systems has become a widespread device for governing national educational systems.

Overall, the second half of the twentieth century saw the thickening of global educational governance. But global institutions and the educational flows and activities they unleashed did not form a coherent and cohesive platform for international engagement. While shaped by a set of redistributive or compensatory (liberal) norms, as mandated for educational multilateralism at the time of the construction of the United Nations, and reinforced by the deepening of the welfare state model after 1945, global educational governance was significantly driven by (realist) economic and geopolitical self-interests of the sovereign nation-states who make up the membership of most intergovernmental organizations. Education's global institutions were quite diverse, including significant bilateral aid programs, the multilateral agencies under the United Nations and the international financial institutions, and regional "clubs" such as the OECD—who worked separately and with limited cross-coordination. Furthermore, these organizations were increasingly torn between a more rights-focused agenda and the strengthening of ties between education and notions of economic development, and adjustment to a more competitive global economy.

THE NEW MILLENNIUM: A DECADE OF GLOBAL CONSENSUS ON EDUCATION?

Over the last fifteen years, the global governance of education has changed substantially. After three decades of rapid yet uneven economic globalization, heightened mobility (for some), and the end of the Cold War, both the nature of governments' strategic interests and their ability to control and contain flows of educational services have changed. The density of international organizations and transnational private authority has increased, and there is rising evidence of experimentation with educational multilateralism across such institutions as the OECD, the G-8, the World Bank, the European Union, and the World Trade Organization. Yet many of the earlier tensions and contradictions in international educational governance have remained.

Without the pressure of the Cold War, and in the context of a world order dominated by the West, the turn of the millennium saw a new consensus about international development emerge. As captured in the UN Millennium Development Declaration and Millennium Development Goals (UN, 2000), this new consensus bridged the neoliberal and pro-economic approaches to globalization and development endorsed by the International Monetary Fund and the World Bank in the 1980s-1990s, and the equity and rights-based approaches adopted by various UN organizations, the European Union, and other governments (Held, 2005; Noel, 2005; Therien 2002, 2005). The origins of this rapprochement can also be located both in the need to respond to rising international protests against globalization and structural adjustment programs, and to the aftermath of the east Asian economic crisis of the late 1990s (Klein, 2001; Mundy and Murphy, 2001; Stiglitz, 2003). Ruggie describes this new global compact as encompassing:

> the centrality of governance, the rule of law, education, and health to economic success; the positive role of investment, including skills and technologies embodied in foreign direct investment; the need for further debt relief and other forms of development assistance for poor countries; the urgency of lowering trade barriers imposed on developing country exports by agricultural subsidies and other non-tariff barriers in the rich countries; the protectionist potential posed by

pursuing social and environmental objectives through linkages to trade agreements; and the need for governments and international institutions alike to forge partnerships with the private sector and a wide range of civil society actors. (Ruggie, 2003, p. 305)

Education was elevated to a position of importance within the new development compact, in part because it straddles both equity and productivity agendas for globalization, with its links to economic growth, democratic citizenship rights, and effective governance. Two of the Millennium Development Goals addressed education, resulting in an unprecedented level of attention to primary education within the international development regime that contrasts sharply with the failure of the international community's efforts to tackle basic education after the World Conference on Education for All in Jomtien, Thailand, in 1990 (Chabbott, 2003; Torres, 2000) and the precipitous decline in overall flows of aid to education in the 1990s (Mundy, 2010). Bilateral aid donors began to pool their funding and directly support the recurrent costs of primary education in developing countries, leading to a sharp rise of bilateral aid for basic education between 2002 and 2008 (Mundy, 2010). While an advance on previous efforts, many critics have decried this new consensus for its focus on expanding access to elementary schooling (see Bajaj, and Kendall and Silver, this volume), its minimalist concept of the purpose of education (Unterhalter, 2007), and the "tough political reforms" advocated, which include decreases in the unit costs of schooling, decentralization of educational systems, inclusion of private providers, the introduction of standardized testing regimes, and the introduction of performance incentives for teachers (Rose, 2003; UN Millennium Project, 2004, 2005; World Bank, 2004a, b, c).

The International Monetary Fund and the World Bank have played what many regard as a paradoxical role in this new consensus on the importance of getting all children into school. Long criticized for undermining the right to education, both institutions became more attentive to poverty-focused development after 2000 (Tarabini and Jacovkis, 2012; Vetterlain, 2012). While maintaining their earlier emphasis on incentives, privatization, and strategic investing in education for economic growth, the World Bank nonetheless signaled its alignment with the new consensus by shifting its stance on primary level school fees, and providing the home, technical support, and initial financing for the first global pooled fund for education, the Global Partnership for Education (previously the Education for All Fast Track Initiative) (Bruns, Mingat, and Rakotomalala, 2003; Mundy, 2010; Vavrus and Kwauk, 2012). It became one of the largest external funders of primary school expansion across Africa and the donor whose resources were most likely to target low-income countries (Easterly and Pfutze, 2008; UNESCO, 2008). Yet the policy reforms that it markets through its financing and technical assistance to borrowing governments were not driven by a commitment to human rights but by a notion of efficient investment in human capital, and inflected by a classical liberal stance that remains skeptical about the role of governments in delivering public services, preferring instead to provide individuals access to competitive suppliers of social services.

An important aspect of this new era of global educational governance has been the rise of nonstate actors as significant players on the global stage. As Mundy and Murphy (2001) and others have shown, transnational advocacy networks on such issues as human rights, debt relief, official development assistance reform, and anti-globalization have frequently taken up the issue of the universal right to education as one part of their broader advocacy efforts. Transnational advocates played substantive roles in pressing OECD governments to support a global debt relief initiative (the Highly Indebted Poor Country Initiative), which provided the fiscal space for many governments to rapidly expand access to primary schooling (Hinchcliffe, 2004). They have played a critical role in stimulating public awareness of gender equity in education, often working in concert with UN-based organizations. Transnational advocates have been active too in protesting the inclusion of educational services in the liberalization supported by the World Trade Organization's General Agreement on Trade in Services, where according to Verger, they shaped the degree to which policies promoting the liberalization of international trade in educational services have been adopted by nations (Verger, 2010). There are also many instances in which national civil society has effectively utilized the global framing of education as a human right to protest the educational policies of their home governments: in Chile, for example during the 2011 student-led movement for equitable access to higher education and the 2013 movement for social equity in Brazil. Verger and Novelli (2012) provide similar examples in their study of national education coalitions in low- and middle-income countries.

One important transnational advocacy networks operating in education is the Global Campaign for Education, an organization initiated by OXFAM International, ActionAid, and the international association of teachers unions (Education International), which now counts among its membership a large number of national civil society Education For All coalitions around the world, as well as some of the largest international nongovernmental organizations involved in education (OXFAM, CARE, ActionAid, Global March) (Mundy, 2012; Verger and Novelli, 2012). As an illustration of the powerful role played by the Global Campaign for Education and transnational civil society, the successful campaign against primary school user charges in Tanzania is often cited. In this case, research on the impact of user fees generated by Tanzanian civil society organizations was used by U.S. nongovernmental organizations to press the U.S. government to halt funding to the World Bank if it imposed any form of user fees as part of its loan conditions. The World Bank subsequently removed this loan condition and the Government of Tanzania declared free primary education. The Tanzania experience in turn stimulated a number of other African governments to remove user fees in education and declare universal free primary education (Alonso i Terme, 2002; Mundy, Hagerty, Cherry, Maclure and Sirasubramaniam, 2007; Sumra, 2005; Tanzania Education Network/Mtandao wa Elimu Tanzania, 2006).

Perhaps in tension with the rising consensus about basic education as a global public good worthy of official intergovernmental action, has been the rise of transnational actors engaged in expanding the market for educational services. The creation of the World Trade Organization and its General Agreement on Trade in Services, alongside the rapid expansion of demand for certain kinds of educational services (particularly technology training and higher education) have opened new opportunities for cross-border provision by transnational corporations and higher education institutions, who in turn press for liberalized access to educational markets (Bhanji, 2008, 2012; Heyneman, 2001; Verger, 2010). Robertson, Bonal, and Dale (2012) and Marginson (2013), among others, have noted how the efforts to liberalize higher education dovetails with a new emphasis on international ranking and quality assurance in higher education, spearheaded and supported by both international organizations and private actors (see also Robertson, Mundy, Verger, and Menashy, 2012). Bhanji has documented the role played in particular by software corporations in shaping a new global market place of education and training services (2008, 2012). Less well known is the development of a significant transnational network promoting low-fee private schooling as an alternative to publicly provided education, which brings together new players, including among others the Pearson corporation (a leading provider of educational services and materials), the Omidyar Foundation, and the private sector arm of the World Bank, the International Finance Corporation (Ball, 2012; Mundy and Menashy, 2012; Nambissan and Ball, 2012; Robertson, Mundy, Verger, and Menashy, 2012; Verger, 2012), and which promote the expansion of private education in many parts of the world. In Africa, it is contributing to serve rural communities, mostly through low-quality education services provided by small-scale entrepreneurs. Going forward, the rise of new, technologically enabled educational services—think for example of the massive open online courses (see Carnoy, this volume)—will no doubt intensify the opportunities for for-profit entrepreneurship in trans-border educational services, deepening the challenges to territorially based education systems

One area in which there has been limited research or analysis is the potential role emergent world powers might play in the construction of global collective action on issues such education. Since 2000, several of the most powerful emergent economies have established bilateral programs of foreign aid for education—including among others, China, Russia, Brazil, Turkey, India, South Africa, and South Korea, as well as some countries in the Middle East. Many of these emergent powers are also longstanding members of the major multilateral organizations engaged in education, where they have been active in calling for governance reforms to reflect the changing balance of power between Western and non-Western nations. These rising powers are primarily focused on expanding their spheres of geopolitical influence on a bilateral basis. Characterized by sharply differing national approaches to economic and social development, they share a limited appetite for international regimes that constrain national sovereignty (including in such putatively domestic spheres as education). The growing voice of emergent economies in global decision-making is illustrated by the development of the Group of 20 (G-20), which has now replaced the G-8 as key global summit on world financial and economic matters. As Kumar explains, emergent economic powers have insisted that the G-20 officially adopt "international development" as a specific area of attention, despite the preference among Western industrialized governments that the G-20 concentrate primarily on global financial and economic governance (Kumar, 2010). However, the only reference to education in recent G-20 communiques refers to education for economic development and skills formation, reflecting a focus on working together to advance science, technology, and skills to advance their own economic competitiveness. Furthermore, the tendency of emerging powers to tie foreign aid to their own economic self-interest—particularly in resource-rich African countries—suggests that they may contribute more to the erosion of the existing "global compact" than to its amplification (Bracht, 2013; Brautigam, 2010; Cammack, 2012; Gu, Humphrey, and Messner, 2008; Nordveit, 2011; Rodrik 2013; Woods, 2008).

CONCLUSION: A POST-2015 AND A POST-WESTERN WORLD: WHITHER THE FUTURE OF GLOBAL GOVERNANCE IN EDUCATION?

This chapter has provided a broad overview of the changing shape of global level governance in education. In broad strokes, it has argued that an initial consensus about the importance of national educational systems at the end of World War II led to a complex and fragmented regime of bilateral aid and international institutions with educational mandates, organized primarily around relationships between Western and postcolonial countries. At the same time, a second constellation of actors grew up around the "problem-solving" multilateralism of the OECD, which led to the growth of powerful instruments for international comparison and benchmarking of educational systems joined voluntarily by many governments. More recent shifts in the global governance of education include an increasingly visible role for transnational civil society, the rise of new economic powers with their own conceptualization of international educational relations, and the rise of private sector networks in education, with the capability in particular of leveraging new technologies to weave together trans-border delivery of educational services.

The chapter has also advanced the value of utilizing a "global governance" lens when looking at international and transnational relations in education. Until quite recently, debates about the educational dynamics of the world political system have focused primarily on the unequal power wielded by states due to their economic or geopolitical location in the world. A global governance frame can help us to extend this conceptualization, signaling the importance of understanding not only shifts in the balance of power across states, but the significance of norms and ideas in structuring state preferences, and the heightened and potentially powerful roles played by international organizations and transnational nonstate actors in shaping global norms and consensus. A global governance approach is not blind to issues of power and injustice: it fits with other accounts of global education politics by recognizing the widening role played by forms of policy-making that are distant from citizen deliberation. Yet a global governance lens also complicates previous notions of power with its new interest in understanding how networks and coalitions of actors can shape real and surprising changes in the world of education. Perhaps most importantly, a global governance lens prompts us to engage with normative questions about the future of education and its delivery in a changing world order, including the fundamental question of which actors and processes are shaping the educational dimensions of our changing world polity.

REFERENCES

Alexander, Nancy C. 2001. Paying for Education: How the World Bank and IMF Influence Education in Developing Countries. *Peabody Journal of Education*, vol. 76, nos. 3–4, pp. 285–338.

Alonso i Terme, Rosa. 2002. The Elimination of User Fees for Primary Education in Tanzania: A Case Study in the Political Economy of Pro-poor Policies. Joint Donor Staff Training Activity: Partnership for Poverty Reduction, Module 1. Washington, DC: World Bank.

Anderson, Benedict R. 1991. *Imagined Communities: Reflections on the Origin and Spread of Nationalism* (Revised and extended edition). London: Verso.

Ball, Stephen. 2012. *Global Education Inc.: New Policy Networks and the Neo-liberal Imaginary*. London: Routledge.

Barnett, Michael, and Raymond Duvall (eds.). 2005. *Power and Global Governance*. Cambridge: Cambridge University Press.

Barnett, Michael, and Martha Finnemore. 2004. *Rule for the World: International Organizations and Global Politics*. Ithaca, NY: Cornell University Press.

Bhanji, Zahra. 2008. Transnational Corporations in Education: Filling the Governance Gap Through New Social Norms and Market Multilateralism? *Globalisation, Societies and Education*, vol. 6, no. 1, pp. 55–73.

———. 2012. Transnational Private Authority in Education Policy in Jordan and South Africa: The Case of Microsoft Corporation. *Comparative Education Review*, vol. 56, no. 2, pp. 300–19.

Bieber, Tonia, and Kerstin Martens. 2011. The OECD PISA Study as a Soft Power in Education? Lessons from Switzerland and the US. *European Journal of Education*, vol. 46, no. 1, pp. 101–16.

Biersteker, Thomas J., and Cynthia Weber. 1996. *State Sovereignty as a Social Construct*. Cambridge: Cambridge University Press.

Biersteker, Thomas J., and Rodney Bruce Hall. 2002. Private Authority as Global Governance. In Rodney B. Hall and Thomas J. Biersteker (eds.), *The Emergence of Private Authority in Global Governance* (pp. 203–22). Cambridge: Cambridge University Press.

Black, Maggie. 1996. *Children First: The Story of UNICEF Past and Present*. New York: Oxford University Press.

Bracht, Caroline. 2013. Will the BRICS Deliver a More Just World Order? *Guardian Weekly*, May 8. http://www.guardian.co.uk/global-development-professionals-network/2013/may/08/brics-development-bank.

Brautigam, Deborah. 2010. China, Africa and the International Aid Architecture. Working Paper No. 107. Abidjan, Cote d'Ivoire: African Development Bank Group.

Bruns, Barbara, Alain Mingat, and Ramahatra Rakotomalala. 2003. *A Chance for Every Child: Achieving Universal Primary Education by 2015*. Washington, DC: World Bank.

Cammack, Paul. 2012. The G20, the Crisis, and the Rise of Global Developmental Liberalism. *Third World Quarterly*, vol. 33, no. 1, pp. 1–16.

Chabbott, Colette. 2003. *Constructing Education for Development: International Organizations and Education for All*. New York: Routledge/Falmer.

Commission on Global Governance. 1995. *Our Global Neighborhood: Report of the Commission on Global Governance*. Oxford: Oxford University Press.

Cox, Robert W. 1981. Social Forces, States and World Orders: Beyond International Relations. *Millennium: Journal of International Studies*, vol. 10, no. 2, pp. 126–55.

Dale, Roger. 2004. Forms of Governance, Governmentality and the EU's Open Method of Coordination. In Wendy Larner and William Walters (eds.), *Global Governmentality: Governing International Spaces* (pp. 174–94). London: Routledge.

_____ and Susan Robertson. 2002. The Varying Effects of Regional Organizations as Subjects of Globalization of Education. *Comparative Education Review*, vol. 46, no. 1, pp. 10–36.

Easterly, William, and Tobias Pfutze. 2008. Where Does the Money Go? Best and Worst Practices in Foreign Aid. *The Journal of Economic Perspectives*, vol. 22, no. 2, pp. 29–52.

Falk, Richard A. 1975. *A Study of Future Worlds*. New York: Free Press.

Finnemore, Martha. 1996a. *National Interests in International Society*. Ithaca, NY: Cornell University Press.

_____. 1996b. Norms, Culture and World Politics: Insights from Sociology's Institutionalism. *International Organization*, vol. 50, no. 2, pp. 325–47.

_____ and Kathryn Sikkink. 1998. International Norm Dynamics and Political Change. *International Organisation*, vol. 52, no. 4, pp. 887–917.

Fuchs, Eckhardt. 2007. Children's Rights and Global Civil Society. *Comparative Education*, vol. 43, no. 3, pp. 393–412.

Galtung, Johan. 1980. *The True Worlds: A Transnational Perspective*. New York: The Free Press.

Gilpin, Robert. 1981. *War and Change in World Politics*. Cambridge: Cambridge University Press.

Grek, Sotiria. 2013. Expert Moves: International Comparative Testing and the Rise of Expertocracy. *Journal of Education Policy*. DOI:10.1080/02680939.2012.758825

Gu, Jing, John Humphrey, and Dirk Messner. 2008. Global Governance and Developing countries: The Implications of the Rise of China. *World Development*, vol. 36, no. 2, pp. 274–92.

Habermas, Jurgen. 2001. *The Postnational Constellation: Political Essays*. Cambridge, MA: MIT Press.

Held, David. 1995. *Democracy and the Global Order: From the Modern State to Cosmopolitan Governance*. Stanford: Stanford University Press.

_____. 2005. At the Global Crossroads: The End of the Washington Consensus and the Rise of Global Social Democracy. *Globalizations*, vol. 2, no. 1, pp. 95–113.

Henry, Miriam, Bob Lingard, Fazal Rizvi, and Sandra Taylor. 2001. The OECD and Educational Politics in a Changing World. In Miriam Henry, Bob Lingard, Fazal Rizvi and Sandra Taylor (eds.), *The OECD, Globalisation and Education Policy* (pp. 157–75). Oxford: Pergamon Press.

Heyneman, Stephen. 2001. The Growing International Commercial Market for Educational Goods and Services. *International Journal of Educational Development*, vol. 21, no. 4, pp. 345–59.

Higgott, Richard. 2000. Contested Globalization: The Changing Context and Normative Challenges. *Review of International Studies*, vol. 26, no. 5, pp. 131–53.

Hinchliffe, Keith. 1993. Neo-liberal Prescriptions for Education Finance: Unfortunately Necessary or Inherently Desirable? *International Journal of Educational Development*, vol. 13, no. 2, pp. 183–87.

_____. 2004. Notes on the HIPC Debt Initiative on Education and Health Public Expenditure in African Countries. Africa Region Human Development Working Paper. Washington, DC: World Bank.

Holsti, Kalevi Jaakko. 1985. *The Dividing Discipline: Hegemony and Diversity in International Theory*. London: Allen and Unwin.

Independent Evaluation Group. 2011. *A Portfolio Note: World Bank Support to Education Since 2001*. Washington, DC: The World Bank Group.

Imber, Mark F. 1989. *The USA, ILO, UNESCO and IAEA: Politicization and Withdrawal in the Specialized Agencies*. London: Macmillan.

Jessop, Bob. 2005. Multi-level Governance and Multi-level Metagovernance: Changes in the European Union as Integral Movements in the Transformation and Reorientation of Contemporary Statehood. In Friedrich V. Kratochwil and Edward D. Mansfield (eds.), *International Organization and Global Governance: A Reader* (pp. 355–67). New York: Pearson Longman.

Jolly, Richard. 1991. Adjustment with a Human Face: A UNICEF Record and Perspective on the 1980s. *World Development*, vol. 19, no. 12, pp. 1807–21.

Jones, Phillip W. 1988. *International Policies for Third World Education: UNESCO, Literacy and Development*. London and New York: Routledge.

Jones, Phillip W. 1992. *World Bank Financing of Education: Lending, Learning and Development*. London: Routledge.

_____. 2000. Globalization and Internationalism: Democratic Prospects for World Education. In Nelly P. Stromquist and Karen Monkman (eds.), *Globalization and Education: Integration and Contestation Across Cultures* (pp. 27–42). Lanham, MD: Rowman and Littlefield.

_____ and David Coleman. 2005. *The United Nations and Education: Multilateralism and Globalisation*. New York: Routledge Falmer.

Keck, Margaret E. and Kathryn Sikkink. 1998. *Activists Beyond Borders*. Ithaca, NY: Cornell University Press.

Keohane, Robert Owen. 2004. Theory and International Institutions. http://www.isn.ethz.ch/Digital-Library/Video/Detail/?ots591=966c9813-6e74-4e0b-b884-8ed9f3f0978c&lng=en&id=160768.

_____ and Joseph S. Nye. 1977. *Power and Interdependence: World Politics in Transition*. Boston: Little Brown.

King, Kenneth. 1991. *Aid and Education in the Developing World: The Role of Donor Agencies in Educational Analysis*. Essex, UK: Longman.

Klein, Naomi. 2001. Reclaiming the Commons. *New Left Review*, http://newleftreview.org/II/9/naomi-klein-reclaiming-the-commons.

Kumar, Rajiv. 2010. A Development Agenda for the G20. *Policy brief prepared for the European Think-Tank for Global Action (FRIDE)*, http://www.fride.org/download/PB_G20_6_eng_A_development_agenda_for_the_G20.pdf.

Lawn, Martin, and Sotiria Grek. 2012. *Europeanizing Education: Governing a New Policy Space*. Oxford, UK: Symposium Books.

Lumsdaine, David Halloran. 1993. *Moral Vision in International Politics: The Foreign Aid Regime 1949-1989*. Princeton, NJ: Princeton University Press.

Mahon, Rianne. 2010. After Neoliberalism? The OECD, the World Bank and the Child. *Global Social Policy,* vol. 10, no. 2, pp. 172–92.

_____ and Stephen McBride. 2008. *The OECD and Transnational Governance*. Vancouver: University of British Columbia Press.

Marginson, Simon. 2013. The Impossibility of Capitalist Markets in Higher Education. *Journal of Education Policy*, vol. 28, no. 3, pp. 353–70.

Martens, Kerstin, and Anja P. Jakobi. 2010. *Mechanisms of OECD Governance: International Incentives for National Policy-making*. Oxford: Oxford University Press.

_____ and Klaus Dieter Wolf. 2009. Boomerangs and Trojan horses: The Unintended Consequences of Internationalising Education Policy through the EU and the OECD. In Alberto Amaral, Guy Neave, Christine Musselin, and Peter Maassen (eds.), *European Integration and the Governance of Higher Education and Research* (pp. 81–107). London and New York: Springer.

McKinlay, Robert, and Richard Little. 1986. *Global Problems and World Order*. London: Frances Pinter Ltd.

McNeely, Connie L. 1995. Prescribing National Education Policies: The Role of International Organizations *Comparative Education Review*, vol. 39, no. 4, pp. 483–507.

_____ and Yun-Kyung Cha. 1994. Worldwide Educational Convergence Through International Organizations: Avenues for Research. *Education Policy Analysis Archives*, vol. 2, no. 14. http://epaa.asu.edu/ojs/article/view/677/799.

Miller-Adams, Michelle. 1999. *The World Bank: New Agendas in a Changing World*. New York: Routledge.

Morgenthau, Hans J. 1967. *Politics Among Nations*. New York: Knopf.

Mundy, Karen. 1998. Educational Multilateralism and World (Dis)order. *Comparative Education Review*, vol. 42, no. 4, pp. 448–78.

_____. 1999. UNESCO and the Limits of the Possible. *International Journal of Educational Development*, vol. 19, no. 1, pp. 27–52.

_____. 2002. Education in a Reformed World Bank. *International Journal of Educational Development*, vol. 22, no. 5, pp. 483–508.

_____. 2006. Education for All in the New Development Compact. *International Review of Education*, vol. 52, no. 1, pp. 23–48.

_____. 2010. Education for All and the Global Governors. In Deborah Avant, Martha Finnemore, and Susan K. Sell (eds.), *Who Governs the Globe?* (pp. 333–55). Cambridge: Cambridge University Press.

_____. 2012. The Global Campaign for Education and the Realization of "Education for All." In Antoni Verger and Mario Novelli (eds.), *Campaigning for "Education For All": Histories, Strategies and Outcomes of Transnational Social Movements in Education* (pp. 23–36). Rotterdam: Sense.

_____ and Lynn Murphy. 2001. Transnational Advocacy, Global Civil Society: Emerging Evidence from the Field of Education. *Comparative Education Review*, vol. 45, no. 1, pp. 85–126.

_____, Megan Haggerty, Suzanne Cherry, Richard Maclure, and Malini Sivasubramaniam. 2007. Basic Education, Civil Society Participation and the New Aid Architecture: Lessons from Burkina Faso, Kenya, Mali and Tanzania. Haki Elimu Working Paper 07.3. Dar es Salaam: Haki Elimu.

_____ and Francine Menashy. 2012. Investing in Private Education for Poverty Alleviation: The Case of the World Bank's International Finance Corporation. *International Journal of Educational Development*. http://dx.doi.org/10.1016/j.ijedudev.2012.06.005.

Murphy, Craig, N. 1994. *International Organization and Industrial Change: Global Governance Since 1850*. Cambridge: Polity Press.

Nambissan, Geetha B., and Stephen J. Ball. 2010. Advocacy Networks, Choice and Private Schooling of the Poor in India. *Global Networks*, vol. 10, no. 3, pp. 324–43.

Noel, Alain. 2005. The New Politics of Global Poverty. Paper presented at Social Justice in a Changing World, 10-12 March, at Bremen, Germany. http://www.uni-bielefeld.de/soz/personen/Leisering/pdf/Noel%20globale%20Armut.pdf.

Nordveit, Bjorn H. 2011. An Emerging Donor in Education and Development: A Case Study of China in Cameroon. *International Journal of Educational Development*, vol. 31, no. 2, pp. 99–108.

Nusche, Deborah. 2009. What Works in Migrant Education: A Review of Evidence and Policy Options. OECD Working Paper No. 22. Paris: OECD.

Organization for Economic Cooperation and Development. 2006. Where Immigrant Children Succeed. A Comparative Review of Performance and Engagement in PISA 2003. Paris: OECD.

_____. 2012. Equity and Quality in Education: Supporting Disadvantaged Students and Schools. Paris: OECD.

Papadopoulos, George. 1994. *Education 1960-1990: The OECD Perspective*. Paris: OECD.

Phillips, Herbert Moore 1987. *UNICEF and Education: A Historical Perspective*. New York: UNICEF.

Preston, William, Jr., Edward S. Herman, and Herbert I. Schiller. 1989. *Hope and Folly: The United States and UNESCO, 1945-1985*. Minneapolis: University of Minnesota Press.

Price, Richard, and Christian Reus-Smit. 1998. Dangerous Liaisons: Critical International Theory and Constructivism. *European Journal of International Relations*, vol. 4, no. 3, pp. 259–94.

Psacharopoulos, George. 1986. *Financing Education in Developing Countries: An Exploration of Policy Options*. Washington, DC: World Bank.

Reinicke, Wolfgang. 1989. *Global Public Policy: Governing without Government?* Washington, DC: Brookings Institute.

Resnik, Julia. 2006. Bringing International Organizations Back In: The "Education-Economic Growth" Black Box and its Contribution to the World Education Culture. *Comparative Education Review*, vol. 50, no. 2, pp. 173–95.

Robertson, Susan L., Karen Mundy, Antoni Verger, and Francine Menashy (eds.). 2012. *Public Private Partnerships in Education: New Actors and Modes of Governance in a Globalizing World*. Cheltenham, Gloucestershire: Edward Elgar Publishing.

Robertson, Susan L., Xavier Bonal, and Roger Dale (eds.). 2012. *WTO/GATS and the Education Se rvice Industry: Global Strategy— Local Responses* . London: Routledge.

Rodrik, Dani. 2013. Leaderless Global Governance. *Project Syndicate: A World of Ideas*, http://www.project-syndicate.org/commentary/leaderless-global-governance.

Rose, Pauline. 2003. The Education Fast Track Initiative. Report prepared for ActionAid on behalf of the Global Campaign for Education. London: ActionAid.

Rosenau, James N. 1992. Governance, Order and Change in World Politics. In James N. Rosenau and Ernst Otto Czempiel (eds.), *Governance Without Government: Ord er and Change in World Politics* (pp. 1–29). Cambridge: Cambridge University Press.

Ruggie, John Girard. 1982. International Regimes, Transactions, and Change: Embedded Liberalism in the Postwar Economic Order. *International Organization*, vol. 36, no. 2, pp. 379–415.

_____. 1994. At Home Abroad, Abroad at Home: International Liberalisation and Domestic Stability in the New World Economy. *Millennium: Journal of International Studies*, vol. 24, no. 3, pp. 507–26.

_____. 1998a. *Constructing the World Polity: Essays on International Institutionalization*. New York: Routledge.

_____. 1998b. What Makes the World Hang Together? Neo-utilitarianism and the Social Constructivist Challenge. *International Organization*, vol. 52, no. 4, pp. 855–85.

_____. 2003. The United Nations and Globalization: Patterns and Limits of Institutional Adaptation. *Global Governance*, vol. 9, no. 3, pp. 301–21.

Sack, Richard. 1986. UNESCO: From Inherent Contradictions to Open Crisis. *Comparative Education Review*, vol. 30, no. 1, pp. 112–19.

Seller, Sam, and Bob Lingard. 2013. The OECD and Global Governance in Education. *Journal of Education Policy*. DOI:10.1080/02680939.2013.779791

Sewell, James P. 1975. *UNESCO and World Politics: Engaging in International Relations*. Princeton, NJ: Princeton University Press.

Smouts, Marie-Claude. 1998. The Proper Use of Governance in International Relations. *International Social Science Journal*, vol. 50, no. 155, pp. 81–89.

Stiglitz, Joseph. 2003. *Globalization and Its Discontents*. New York: W.W. Norton.

Sumra, Suleman. 2005. Commonwealth Education Fund Global Midterm Review: Tanzania Programme Report. London: Commonwealth Education Fund.

Tanzania Education Network/Mtandao wa Elimu Tanzania. 2006. *Strengthening Education in Tanzania: CSO Contributions to the Education Sector Review 2006*. Dar es Salaam: TEN/MET.

Tarabini, Aina, and Judith Jacovkis. 2012. The Poverty Reduction Strategy Papers: An Analysis of a Hegemonic Link Between Education and Poverty. *International Journal of Educational Development*, vol. 32, no. 4, pp. 507–16.

Therien, Jean-Philippe. 2002. Multilateral Institutions and the Poverty Debate. *International Journal*, vol. 57, no. 2, pp. 233–52.

_____. 2005. The Politics of International Development: Towards a New Grand Compromise? *Economic Policy and Law: Journal of Trade and Environmental Studies* http://www.ecolomics-international.org/epal_2004_5_therien_towards_new_grand_compromise....pdf.

Torres, Rose-Marie. 2000. *One decade of Education for All: The Challenge Ahead*. Buenos Aires: International Institute of Educational Planning.

UN Education Science and Cultural Organization. 2008. *Education for All Global Monitoring Report: Education for all by 2015, Will We Make It?* Paris: UNESCO.

United Nations. 2000. United Nations Millennium Declaration. New York: United Nations. http://www.un.org/millennium/declaration/ares552e.htm.

United Nations General Assembly. n.d. Article 26, *Universal Declaration of Human Rights*, 1948. http://www.un.org/Overview/rights.html

United Nations Millennium Project. 2004. Interim Report on Achieving the Millennium Development Goal of Universal Primary Education. *Report of the Millennium Development Project*, http://www.unmillenniumproject.org.

_____. 2005. Toward Universal Primary Education: Investments, Incentives and Institutions. *Report from the Task Force on Education and Gender Equality*, http://www.unmillenniumproject.org/.

Unterhalter, Elaine. 2007. *Gender, Schooling and Global Social Justice*. London: Routledge.

Vavrus, Frances, and Christina Kwauk. 2012. The New Abolitionists? The World Bank and the "Boldness" of Global School Fee Elimination Reforms. *Discourse: Studies in the Cultural Politics of Education*. DOI:10.1080/01596306.2012.717189

Verger, Antoni. 2010. *WTO/GATS and the Global Politics of Higher Education*. London and New York: Routledge.

_____. 2012. Framing and Selling Global Education Policy: The Promotion of PPPs in Education in Low-Income Countries. *Journal of Education Policy*, vol. 27, no. 1, pp. 109–30.

_____ and Mario Novelli. 2012. *Campaigning for "Education for All": Histories, Strategies and Outcomes of Transnational Social Movements in Education*. Rotterdam: Sense.

Vetterlain, Antje. 2012. Seeing Like the World Bank on Poverty. *New Political Economy*, vol. 17, no. 1, pp. 35–58.

Wallerstein, Immanuel. 1984. *The Politics of the World Economy: The States, the Movements and the Civilizations*. Cambridge, MA: Cambridge University Press.

Weiss, Thomas G and Leon Gordenker (eds.). 1996. *NGOs, the UN, and Global Governance*. Boulder, CO: Lynne Rienner.

Woods, Ngaire. 2000. The Challenge of Good Governance for the IMF and the World Bank Themselves. *World Development*, vol. 28, no. 5, pp. 823–41.

_____. 2008. Whose Aid, Whose Influence? China, Emerging Donors and the Silent Revolution in Development Assistance. *International Affairs*, vol. 84, no. 6, pp. 1–17.

World Bank. 1988. *Education in Sub-Saharan Africa: Policies for Adjustment, Revitalization and Expansion*. Washington, DC: World Bank.

_____. 1995. *Priorities and Strategies for Education*. Washington, DC: World Bank.

_____. 2004a. Education for All (EFA)—Fast Track Initiative News August, September, October. Washington, DC: World Bank.

_____. 2004b. Aid Effectiveness and Financing Modalities. http://siteresources.worldbank.org/DEVCOMMINT/Documentation/20264307/DC2004-0012(E)%20Aid%20Eff%20Add1.pdf

_____. 2004c. Education for All (EFA)—Fast Track Initiative: Progress report. Washington, DC: World Bank.

Chapter Four

The Productive Plasticity of Rights: Globalization, Education, and Human Rights

Monisha Bajaj

Globalization, education, and, in the last sixty-five years, human rights, interact in complex ways not reducible to a singular, linear argument.[1] In this chapter, I examine the ways in which the contemporary forces of globalization and human rights are refracted differentially in educational policy discussions, textbook revisions, teacher education, and in the everyday life of schools. For better and worse, as I will argue, rights frameworks have become the primary organizing force for diverse actors from international organizations to lawyers, educational scholars, and policy-makers at national and local levels. In particular, I examine what I believe to be the productive plasticity of rights discourse. Culminating with a case study of the Right to Education (RTE) Act in India, I look at how "human rights" concepts often assume different meanings, uses, and definitions. I also consider that the international currency and discursive popularity of these frameworks can be and are utilized by local actors strategically and usefully, even if in ways whose ends are not at-the-moment determined, in promoting greater access to quality education.

One of the most common shifts in international educational policy discourse is the assertion of rights-based claims that education, in and of itself, is an entitlement alongside the decades-old conditional and cost-benefit analyses of schooling—namely, human capital theory and rate of return analyses (Gillis, Radelet, Snodgrass, Roemer and Perkins, 2001; Psacharopoulos, 1996; Schultz, 1961, 1980). Rights-based approaches emphasize marginalized and hard-to-reach populations, such as ethnic minorities, certain religious groups, and disabled children, viewing their access to schooling as a fundamental component of their guarantees as citizens and human beings (UN Education Science and Cultural Organization [UNESCO], 2010). International documents increasingly count out-of-school children in global, rather than purely national, terms, highlighting the efforts toward international partnership for Education for All launched through the 1990 (Jomtien) and 2000 (Dakar) summits and subsequent meetings (see Mundy and Manion's chapter in this volume).

This chapter explores three lines of inquiry operating on different registers and levels of specificity. My first line of inquiry examines how globalization is affecting human rights. There has been a global diffusion of ideas related to democracy and human rights—often with different operational meanings—within donor agencies, international organizations, national governments, and local bodies. With more institutions and actors paying attention to human rights, it is important to explore how such concepts are engaged despite gaps between advocacy and implementation. My second line of inquiry, then, explores differing deployments of human rights and education under contemporary conditions of globalization. These are education *as* a human right (entitlement claims), education *with* rights (equality and dignity claims), and education *for* human rights (exploring matters such as curriculum and teacher training).[2] My third line of inquiry interrogates some of the strategic and contingent uses of "rights talk" utilized by actors at the local, national, and international levels as a means of highlighting the plasticity, malleability, or pluriform character of this discourse, terms I use to emphasize the capaciousness and possibility of rights talk such as it is, not to dismiss the framework for relativism.[3] The case study of India's national adoption of a "Right to Education" bill in 2009 and debates surrounding its implementation will further illuminate some of the ways in which local policy actors operating within the landscape of the globalization of human rights have engaged rights talk to promote greater social equity.

Various approaches have been applied to the study of globalization and education in the field of international and comparative education. Resisting the claim that school systems are converging beyond the discursive level, this chapter is premised on postcolonial and "cultural-ist" perspectives that "local actors borrow from multiple models in the global flow of educational ideas" (Spring, 2008, p. 336; see also Anderson-Levitt, 2003; Crossley and Tikly, 2004; Little, 2003; Steiner-Khamsi, 2004; Stromquist, 2002). This chapter draws on an approach to globalization and education that gives primacy to networks and flows, akin to Arjun Appadurai's concept of *scapes* in terms of the movement of ideas, knowledge, and information. It also draws on the work of rights scholars broadly, even if not specifically concerned with educational rights (Baxi, 1998; Dembour, 2010; Madhok, 2010; Merry, 2003). In this view then, rights talk and rights "scapes"[4]—here the scapes created by the shifting intersections of globalization, education, and human rights—are neither wholly liberating nor oppressive; rather, they provide a site in which to explore the creation of new forms of citizenship, as well as the unique limitations and possibilities for the exercise of human agency.

GLOBALIZATION AND HUMAN RIGHTS

Despite scholarly debates about the historic origins of human rights (from ancient Persia, to various religious scriptures, to the European Enlightenment and the French Revolution), the modern rise of human rights in the post–World War II era can be traced to the establishment of the United Nations in 1945 and the adoption of the Universal Declaration of Human Rights in 1948. While further documents, treaties, declarations, and conventions expounded on different categories of rights (e.g., related to race, gender, torture, the rights of children) in subsequent decades, the period of the Cold War (1947–1991) divided human rights supporters among those giving primacy to civil and political rights and aligned with the United States and western Europe, and those who favored economic and social rights and tended to align more with the Soviet Bloc.

After the fall of the Soviet Union in 1991, international consensus shifted toward the importance of human rights, particularly civil and political rights, and several milestones related to the global rise of human rights occurred at the United Nations World Conference on Human Rights held in Vienna soon after (1993). The first international conference on human rights was held by the United Nations in Tehran in 1968 to assess progress related to the Universal Declaration of Human Rights, and the second international conference was held in Vienna in 1993, arguably at a very distinct historical moment given the shifting balance of power globally. For the purpose of this discussion on education, globalization, and human rights, three outcomes of the Vienna conference were notable: (1) despite the fall of the Soviet

Union, the Vienna conference recommended the development of indicators for assessing the progress of nations toward the fulfillment of obligations outlined in the International Covenant on Economic, Social and Cultural Rights (including on education as outlined in Articles 13 and 14); (2) the Vienna conference created the post of the UN High Commissioner for Human Rights, an office charged with education and public information related to human rights; and (3) the Vienna Declaration and Program of Action (adopted by consensus by the representatives of the 171 countries present) asserted that human rights education (HRE) be a task that member states engage in, calling on "all States and institutions to include human rights, humanitarian law, democracy and rule of law as subjects in the curricula of all learning institutions in formal and non-formal settings" (UN, 2013, para 1). Arguably, the global attention and commitment to human rights in Vienna (and subsequently) increased the diffusion of ideas related to democracy and rights, particularly as it corresponded with changes in information and communication technology underway in the mid- to late 1990s.

The more than two decades since the Vienna Conference have been marked by an increasing emphasis on human rights–based approaches to development, foreign aid, and international engagement. While the gap between policy and implementation is important to consider, the discursive shift toward human rights–based approaches is evidenced in international documents, compacts, declarations, and meetings. Institution-wide initiatives, such as the United Nations' mainstreaming of human rights since 1997 and subsequent development of an inter-agency "Common Understanding of a Human Rights-Based Approach to Development (2003),"[5] suggest the power of global parlance to influence transformations within institutions involved in global governance, aid, and development. Since the late 1990s, the World Bank has issued various reports on human rights that have "explored the ways in which structural and distributional inequalities can hinder development" (World Bank, 2012, para 3). Rights-based approaches to development undergird shifts in the policy and practice of many bilateral and multilateral aid agencies as well, including those of Germany, the United Kingdom, and others, who find that "A human rights-based approach to development cooperation promotes non-discrimination and equality of opportunity, participation and empowerment, transparency and accountability. … The German government promotes a form of development cooperation which views the people as agents of their own development" (German Federal Ministry for Cooperation and Development, 2013, para 1). Having charted the global rise and diffusion of human rights, the following section focuses squarely on how human rights concepts have influenced international discussions and policy-making related to education, delineating three relationships: (1) education *as a* human right, (2) education *with* human rights, and (3) education *for* human rights.

EDUCATION AND HUMAN RIGHTS

Education *as a* Human Right

From the vantage point of the Global South, in the years after independence from colonial rule, access to schooling shifted from an elite concern to part of broader national visions for advancing integration and social cohesion (however slowly and partially realized) (Meyer, Ramirez, and Soysal, 1992). Post–World War II, as the process of decolonization began in parts of Asia and Africa, and with the emergence of institutions such as the World Bank and the United Nations, seminal instruments such as the Universal Declaration of Human Rights (1948) announced the right to education for all children. Governments were conceived as the primary guarantors of rights. The deepening of western schooling in newly independent nations corresponded with international calls for equitable and broad access to schooling regardless of whether rights justifications were utilized locally for such decisions (Boli, Meyer, and Ramirez, 1985; Fuller, 1991).

In industrialized countries, educational access and equity also expanded in the post–World War II period. For example, in the United States, the Supreme Court's *Brown v. Board of Education* decision (1954) desegregated schools and led to greater calls for racial equity in education despite the lingering and continuing practices of unequal school funding (rooted in financing through property taxes) (Orfield and Eaton, 1997). Assimilationist education practices toward indigenous groups that stripped communities of their linguistic and cultural heritage in places such as Australia and the United States were discontinued amidst increasingly global discussions of civil and human rights (Deyhle and Swisher, 1997; Sumida Huaman, 2011).

Positing access to schooling as a human right has provided rights-bearers the ability, at least in theory, to hold governments accountable. Efforts toward educational rights, which require involvement on global scales, were advanced most notably through the Education for All Declarations adopted in Jomtien[6] and Dakar, and codified through the Millennium Development Goals (2000). Rights frameworks also facilitate the agency of children and their families in demanding their right to schooling as opposed to being passive beneficiaries or targets of interventions (typically framed in larger efficiency terms rooted in arguments for economic development) (McCowan, 2013; Robeyns, 2006).

Critiques of the rights framework in education often focus on the limited entitlement offered by international declarations and meetings: "access to primary schooling," rather than a more comprehensive vision of rights to further secondary and tertiary education, food, work, social security, etc. Additionally, the inordinate focus on *access*, at least in the Millennium Development Goals, has also been critiqued for its myopia to questions of overcrowding, lack of resources in schools, and consequent poor quality education that does not benefit children (and may actually put them at heightened risk, particularly girls, as they attend crowded schools with limited adult supervision) (Mirembe and Davies, 2001).

Still, the contemporary framing of access to education as a human right demonstrates the potential of globalization to diffuse ideas and frameworks internationally. International organizations, such as the UN Children's Fund (UNICEF), have declared and promoted the view that, "Education is not a static commodity to be considered in isolation from its greater context; it is an ongoing process and holds its own inherent value as a human right" (UNICEF, 2007, p. xii). Since the initial codification of the right to education in the Universal Declaration of Human Rights in 1948 when a small minority of the world's children had access to schooling, the rise of globalization and, with it, increased international attention on educational access, has resulted in the majority of children across the globe attending school with considerable consensus on the need for attaining universal primary enrollment. Less discussed, however, are questions of ensuring students' rights once they reach schools.

Education *with* Human Rights

The importance of education of high quality, with dignity, and as part of a process in which families and communities can effectively participate in schooling, is increasingly a focus of attention in international and national policy forums. Access to crumbling and overcrowded primary schools is surely a poor realization of the right to education. Nonetheless, despite the growing recognition of the limits of policy focus on access, donor funding has inordinately been earmarked for primary education and removing access-related barriers (Jones, 2007). Only recently has literature begun to expand its focus from school "drop-outs" (where the blame is placed on children and families) to "push-outs," or children and families who opt out of formal education due to school-level factors such as discrimination, corporal punishment, poor quality, absentee teachers, among other reasons (Reddy and Sinha, 2010).

In elaborating a more holistic vision of educational rights, the former UN Special Rapporteur for the Right to Education, Katarina Tomasevski, elaborated four "A's" that must be considered and acted upon in education. The four include: Availability, namely, that education is free, government-supported, and that both the "hardware" (adequate school facilities, etc.) and "software" (curricular materials, trained teachers, etc.) of education are provided; Accessibility, namely that schools are open to members of different social groups without discrimination and that efforts are made to ensure that marginalized and hard-to-reach populations are included in government education; Acceptability, in that the curriculum is relevant (culturally, linguistically, and in terms of level), of high quality, and in safe locales staffed with professional teachers; and Adaptability, namely, that education can adjust to the needs of families and communities in order to suit local conditions and realities, and lessen social inequalities (Tomasevski, 2006).

Education with human rights is promoted within global networks that diffuse ideas, curricula, and school-level policies. Many of these initiatives emerged in response to the numerous reports across the globe of abuses within schools ranging from corporal punishment, teacher absenteeism, sexual abuse, and violence or bullying. In order to make schools places where students can learn with dignity and safety, attention has been paid toward developing indicators and standards for "Child-Friendly Schools," UNICEF's flagship initiative of thousands of schools in over fifty-six countries (UNICEF, 2009). Since 1953, UNESCO has had a network of educational institutions (now numbering nine thousand) that form its Associated Schools Project Network in which rights-based curriculum and approaches are shared through a global network of schools (UNESCO, n.d.). Amnesty International has also published guidelines for human rights–friendly schools that lay out the processes, content, pedagogy, structures, and policies that frame how schools can operate with the principles of equality, dignity, respect, non-discrimination, and participation (Amnesty International, 2009). Schools globally have been identified and selected as human rights–friendly schools in order to advance Amnesty International's vision. One component of child- and rights-friendly schools—whether connected to UNICEF, UNESCO, or Amnesty International—is curricular content and pedagogy oriented toward teaching for human rights, as discussed in the following section.

Education *for* Human Rights

Over the past four decades, HRE has become a greater part of international discussions of educational policy, national textbook reform, and the work of nongovernmental organizations (NGOs) (Bajaj, 2011; Meyer, Bromley-Martin, and Ramirez, 2010; Ramirez, Suarez, and Meyer, 2007). While there are many variants of HRE, there is broad agreement about certain core components. First, most scholars and practitioners agree that HRE must include both *content* and *process* related to human rights (Flowers, 2003; Tibbitts, 2002). Indeed, Tibbitts (2005) finds that "nearly all formal literature associated with HRE will mention the importance of using participatory methods" for effectively teaching about human rights (p. 107). Second, most literature discusses the need for HRE to include goals related to cognitive (content), attitudinal or emotive (values/skills), and action-oriented components (Bajaj, 2011).

As HRE figured more prominently in intergovernmental discussions, the United Nations declared 1995–2004 the International Decade for Human Rights Education (which, in 2005, became the ongoing UN World Program for Human Rights Education, housed within the United Nation's Office of the High Commissioner for Human Rights). The UN General

Assembly also declared 2009 the International Year of Human Rights Learning and subsequently adopted the UN Declaration on Human Rights Education and Training in 2011. Since 1999, the NGO Human Rights Education Associates has operated an online list-serve of over eight thousand members from 190 countries—a global network that consists of academics, educators, human rights activists, and government officials at all levels (Human Rights Education Associates, n.d.).

Despite the highly favorable and prescriptive literature on education for human rights, some scholars of globalization and education have asserted that by the time human rights content gets incorporated into textbooks, HRE may be altered such that it loses its activist-oriented focus to the extent that human rights are presented in a manner delinked from the struggles that have achieved such rights (Bajaj, 2011; Cardenas, 2005). Indeed, these processes of adaptation can generate greater variation among HRE initiatives; just as pressure from above depoliticizes HRE, pressure from below can deepen the connection of HRE to social justice struggles. In discussing the disconnection of HRE from its discursive convergence to "decoupled" practice, the work of neoinstitutionalist scholars in international and comparative education on issues of human rights in education, and HRE, proves insightful as do perspectives from the fields of law and political science on the various meanings and uses of rights.

CONCEPTUAL PERSPECTIVES ON HUMAN RIGHTS AND THE GLOBALIZATION OF EDUCATION

Neoinstitutional Theory and Human Rights in Education

The diffusion of educational reforms has concerned scholars of international and comparative education as a key component of increased globalization in recent decades (e.g., Ramirez, Suarez, and Meyer, 2007; Taylor, 2009). Specifically, the role of human rights principles and HRE has been discussed as a core component of a "world society" through the convergence toward similar curricular reforms among nation-states (Meyer, Bromley-Martin, and Ramirez, 2010; Ramirez, Suarez, and Meyer, 2007). In explaining the rise of human rights frameworks in education globally and HRE in international textbooks, neoinstitutionalist scholars have linked the influence of processes of globalization on the formation of a world society that valorizes individual rights (Ramirez, Suarez, and Meyer, 2007). Scholars have pointed to the rise in human rights content in textbooks across the globe, prioritizing individual agency as a rights bearer in an international system over one's status as a national citizen (Meyer, Bromley-Martin, and Ramirez, 2010; Ramirez, Suarez, and Meyer, 2007; Suarez, 2007). Various explanatory factors are given for this reframing including the rise of the human rights movement after World War II, increasing global connections at the international level, the circulation of fashionable reforms that states feel compelled to adopt (at least nominally), among others.

The concepts of decoupling and loose coupling are particularly useful in understanding the intermediation of HRE by ideology, context, constituency, and locale. The term "decoupling," as it emerged in new institutional theory, refers to the existence of discrepancies between formal policies and actual practice and local adaptation of these norms to diverse ends (Meyer and Rowan, 1978). The term has been applied to organizational studies as well as practices in schools, agencies, and other entities. A world society perspective on decoupling and human rights holds that even though nations may sign treaties or agree to adopt HRE because it is the "expected, rational, and legitimate" thing for countries to do (Bromley, 2009, p. 40), the level of commitment of governments to enact these agreements varies (Ramirez and Wotipka,

2007). The case study of the RTE Act in India, that follows the subsequent section on the diverse meanings and uses of rights, offers a productive example of the tensions between the globalization of rights-talk and strategic decoupling by local policy actors to advance agendas that are beyond the scope of the human rights framework.

Differing Meanings and Uses of Rights

Scholars of neoinstitutional theory identify decoupling as a process of adaptation and change broadly, whereas legal scholars of human rights have increasingly noted the different meanings and uses of "human rights" by different groups with diverse orientations (Baxi, 1998, 2006; Dembour, 2010). For example, legal scholar Upendra Baxi terms the different "languages and logics of human rights," that vary from the discourse of international covenants, to the use of rights language as a part of corporate social responsibility, and to the use of human rights to frame the struggles of historically disadvantaged groups (Baxi, 2006, p. 119). He further distinguishes between "modern" and "contemporary" forms of human rights; the former having been used as a force of exclusion with a state-centric and Eurocentric slant, while the latter are "increasingly inclusive and often marked by intense negotiation between NGOs and governments" (Baxi, 1998, p. 135).

Legal scholar Marie-Bénédicte Dembour distinguishes between four schools of thought regarding the rise of human rights in global parlance and governance. The four schools suggest different ways that scholars and activists perceive the provenance and nature of rights, indicating their position toward and advocacy based on them. The first school, natural rights scholars, "conceive[s] of human rights as given," drawing on nature or God as the source of rights (Dembour, 2010, p. 1). The second group, "deliberative scholars," views human rights as "agreed upon" as the best system and sees legal recognition and human rights law as the central aim of the human rights project. The third group, "protest scholars," sees human rights as fought for and won through collective struggle, focusing on lessening the gap between guarantees and actual social conditions faced by marginalized groups. The fourth group, which she terms "discourse scholars," views human rights skeptically and identifies their prominence as arising simply because rights are talked about, but not necessarily real beyond the discursive level. Dembour and Baxi advance critical legal scholarship that seeks to define more explicitly the different uses (and arguably, misuses) of human rights language at different levels and in different venues (see also Mutua, 2002). The differential uses of rights talk also apply to how rights-based frameworks enter into global educational discussions and what becomes codified in curriculum to be included in HRE endeavors.

The conceptualization of different forms and meanings of human rights offers a framework in which to better understand how local, national, and global actors leverage different networks and ideas within a larger framework of similar sounding "rights talk" to advance a variety of agendas. Political scientists have explored how governments and nongovernmental actors converge around similar discourses, such as those pertaining to human rights, through theories of "norm diffusion." Finnemore (1996) attributes significant norm diffusion related to perspectives on poverty alleviation to the work of international organizations, such as the World Bank, that influences local discourses in a variety of national contexts. Further elaborating, Finnemore and Sikkink (1998) find that "norm entrepreneurs," be they institutions such as international organizations or NGOs, or individuals, can spread norms in diverse ways.

Political scientists Keck and Sikkink (1998) further explore how networks of individuals come together to advance certain ideas with an emphasis on the global spread of human rights. The global linkages at the level of governments through international meetings and through the United Nations is paralleled by the greater contact between civil society groups through dense global networks, leading toward what Keck and Sikkink term the "boomerang effect." For example, local- and national-level officials are influenced by global transnational advocacy networks—that local NGOs are often part of—that then have an impact on policy changes, creating multi-directional flows of ideas and reforms. Although rights talk may be co-opted and used differentially, the fact that national- and local-level policy actors, as well as local social movements and NGOs, are utilizing the same language allows for unforeseen pressures to be placed on policy decisions from above, below, and in the circular way that these networks operate. The case of India's RTE Act also sheds light on how globalization influences educational policy and practice through the strategic use of the global currency of "rights talk" that demonstrates how human rights norms are indigenized in national policy.

Case Study: India's Right to Education Act

The use of rights talk to frame a particular vision of quality education in India utilizes global discussions as a springboard but goes far beyond international agreements on the right to access primary schooling to offer a far more comprehensive vision for children. While such legislation is contested locally, it demonstrates the strategic use of rights language and "rights scapes" to frame an agenda that has deep roots in progressive education circles in India.

The Indian Constitution (1950), in hindsight, is deeply and subtly innovative in codifying a transformative agenda into the very blueprint of governance. India, of course, is a vast and socially, culturally, and linguistically diverse nation state, that had a mere 16.9 percent literacy rate and a weak state at the time of independence in 1947. The Constitution was sold by its framers, the Dalit[7] icon and lawyer B.R. Ambedkar and Fabian socialist Jawaharlal Nehru, as reflecting Western best practices, and indeed can be seen as part of a deep century-long intellectual engagement with the Western enlightenment tradition. Yet, in practice, the document codifies a revolutionary social agenda; an agenda that has had all the contradictions, successes, and limitations that such an agenda—radical social transformation through the formal procedures of government as opposed to revolution preceding the formation of government—would entail. In this context, the right to education was identified in the original framing of the Indian Constitution (1950) as a "directive principle," distinguished from the fundamental rights enshrined in that document. Access to schooling was made a priority, but not a right, for all Indians (Premi, 2002).

Rights language has also been used strategically to frame progressive education agendas in India since the 1960s. After the first Prime Minister Nehru's tenure (1947–1964), enrollment rates grew throughout the 1970s and 1980s. Schooling was a state responsibility in the years following independence, but in 1976, a constitutional amendment made education a "concurrent" responsibility of states and the central or national government (Bajaj, 2011). In 1986, the National Policy on Education was adopted, which resulted in various initiatives that sought to utilize technology and equip all schools with the basic classroom materials needed for teaching (e.g., Operation Blackboard). The National Literacy Mission was also launched to combat adult illiteracy, particularly of women, nationwide. Some states in India had been providing "mid-day meals" to children at schools since the 1960s, though nationwide adoption of the program commenced only after a landmark 2001 Supreme Court decision provided a legal entitlement to the right to food in primary schools (Asia-Pacific Human Rights Network, 2002).

India liberalized trade and made formal decisions to integrate firmly into the global economy in the mid-1980s, and decisively in 1991. Concomitant with this massive sea change in Indian governance, educational policy moved into greater alignment with the "rights talk" in global educational discussions of the time. For example, in 1978 the National Curricular Framework for Teacher Education framed the purpose of teacher education "to develop Gandhian values of education such as non-violence, truthfulness, self-discipline, self-reliance, [and] dignity of labor [to achieve] the goals of building up a democratic, secular, and socialist society" (as cited in Bajaj, 2011, p. 44). Whereas, an excerpt from the updated Curricular Framework in 1998, soon after India's greater integration into the global market, demonstrates increasing convergence toward global educational priorities at that moment: "[The objectives of teacher education are] ... to sensitize teachers towards the promotion of social cohesion, international understanding and protection of human rights and child rights; [and] to sensitize teachers and teacher educators about emerging issues such as environment, ecology, population, gender equality, etc." (as cited in Bajaj, 2011, p. 44). More recent versions of these frameworks have included language related to learner-centered and critical pedagogies, peace, democracy, and citizenship. The global influence of rights talk in Indian educational policy can be seen in how policies are enacted as well as how they are framed.

Drawing on international agreement around accomplishing universal primary enrollment, notably the consensus achieved in the Millennium Development Goals and Education for All conferences (1990 and 2000), India launched its domestic *Sarva Shiksha Abhiyan* program, first announced in 2000, to eradicate all obstacles to primary school access (Iyengar, 2010). Significant activities under this campaign have included teacher training, district resource centers, free materials and supplies to marginalized children, construction of new classrooms, and, in some states, the recruitment of para-professional teachers (UNESCO, 2004). In 2010, the RTE Act came into force after several years of discussion and debate, shifting education from a non-binding "directive principle" to an enforceable "fundamental right" in Indian constitutional law and providing all children aged six to fourteen the right to a free and compulsory education in a school within one to three kilometers of their home. There are several provisions in the RTE Act that deepen the legal claims individuals and families can make on the government, and a considerable onus is placed on state governments to increase spending in order to be compliant.

While many of the provisions of the RTE Act mirror global discussions on quality education, such as education for disabled and minoritized children, there are other more controversial aspects of the Act that have not gone unnoticed. Those charged with drafting the legislation—members of civil society who had long been active in educational NGOs and movements as well as policy-makers—drew on human rights language to include a variety of measures, some of which are beyond the scope of conventional educational rights reforms. The most controversial aspect of the RTE Act has been the mandate that private schools (many of which are for-profit endeavors in India) set aside 25 percent of their seats for non–fee-paying children from "weaker sections of society," justified on the grounds that 25 percent of the population comes from various marginalized and low-income backgrounds, and that the government frequently provides land and other resources to private institutions, which renders these institutions, functionally speaking, not wholly private. These students are determined eligible by their families' annual income in relation to the poverty line, and the government is to reimburse private schools for part of the fees of these children. Affluent families who compete (and often pay large "donations") to secure a spot in such schools for their children and who will now be displaced by the policy have not accepted this change silently, especially as many worry that their fees will go up to accommodate the lesser fees the government may pay for the 25 percent of students. The opinion pages in Indian (and international) papers and online blogs, which cater to a privileged middle class audience, have been a site of heated and tilted debates couched in arguments of financing, efficiency, and sometimes straight prejudice. For example, commentators ranging from the libertarian Cato Institute to a magazine noted for its investigative journalism and exposés on various corruption scandals have noted the following:

> India has just enacted a Right to Education Act, guaranteeing every child in the six to 14 age group the right to free, compulsory education. The new law is essentially socialist: it seeks to ensure that, as far as possible, state governments provide free government schooling to all children. But it also obliges private schools to reserve a quarter of their seats for poor and low-caste children. ... [Many] view the 25 per cent reservation as a way of hammering elite schools rather than empowering students through school choice. (Aiyar, n.d., paras 1-2)

> Now the new RTE Act with its rather absurd reservation of 25 percent seats in all schools has been heralded as the panacea for all ills. However, in a state like Delhi around 9000 poor children will benefit from this; for the rest, the poorly run government schools will have to do as nothing pertains to their upgradation in the new bill. ... Needless to say, the schools are up in arms and wondering where the missing numbers would come from. The option that jumps to mind is the increase of fees thus passing the burden to parents of "rich" children. This is terribly unfair as many middle class parents scrap[e] the barrel to send their children to a good school. (Bakshi, 2012, paras 3-4)

> Private schools have been opposing the idea of RTE and its implementation for long now. The Karnataka Unaided Schools Management Association (KUSMA), an organisation of private schools, has been fiercely opposing the idea since its inception. KUSMA president GS Sharma had to quit on 18 July after his remark that students gaining admission into private schools under RTE were like "sewage flowing into clean water." In the case of Oxford English School (OES), a member of KUSMA, parents [of poor children] allege that the school management cut off their children's hair to humiliate and ostracise them. According to the parents, the school has been systematically discriminating against them from the beginning. Even to get the RTE form, parents claim they had to resort to protest. In a class of 40 students of Standard [grade] I at OES, eight children were admitted under RTE. "They were made to sit on the last bench, their names were not included in the attendance register and no books were provided to them. They were not given neck-ties, belts, or even homework. And on top of that, the teachers used to check their [lunch] boxes—asking them if they'd brought the previous day's leftover 'since you're from poor families,'" says Geeta, mother of one of the victims. (Khan, 2012, paras. 2-3)

Some commentators and officials were of course favorable to the decision, and the RTE Act was upheld by the Supreme Court in 2012 despite a legal challenge by dozens of private schools. The Act exempts religious schools, and, not surprisingly, many elite private schools are seeking to affiliate with religious organizations (or emphasize long-dormant connections) suggesting that strategic avoidance of rights legislation is as vibrant as its utilization.

The story of India's RTE and the 25 percent set-asides further illuminates the tensions between the global proliferation of rights-talk and local decoupling. The committee charged with drafting the legislation sought to secure a provision that considered two opposing positions that held sway in India for decades. On the one hand, a vibrant, yet marginalized, sector of government officials, educators, and activists have been lobbying for a "Common School System" since the position was first articulated in the Kothari Commission report in 1966. In this view, all children would be able to attend any neighborhood school—public or private— regardless of their background, ability to pay fees, or other factors. Opponents, on the other hand, argued that the state could not mandate anything that pertains to private schools and must only concern itself with government-run schools. Vinod Raina, a key protagonist in the drafting of the RTE Act, has written,

The inclusion versus quality (merit) argument has gone on for long in this country. While we bemoan the fact that our children are nearly at the bottom of PISA tests in terms of learning outcomes, even though such tests are and will remain controversial, we should also pay attention to the fact that children from countries that are at the top of these tests, like Finland, Sweden, Denmark and even Singapore have been practicing inclusive classrooms for years now. They have demonstrated that rather than a burden on quality, inclusion helps improve quality. Time we gave up our colonial time biases that poor and disadvantaged children will "pollute" our smartly dressed children in classrooms and as parents and teachers, learn the lessons of inclusion. It is the endowed parents who have problems with inclusion, not the children. (Raina, 2012, para. 8)

Other somewhat controversial aspects of the RTE Act demonstrate how policy actors, in this case nongovernmental and governmental members that comprised the Central Advisory Board for Education drafting group, understand and localize what quality education means. The Act mandates that all schools must have libraries that include newspapers, magazines, and books; stipulates that 50 percent of School Management committees be comprised of women with adequate representation of low-income parents; bans teachers from offering private lessons for which they charge tuition that often supplement teachers' income in after-school settings; and prohibits any high-stakes testing at the primary/elementary level. As such, the use of rights talk to frame a particular vision of education, while contested, utilizes global discussions as a foundation but goes far beyond international agreements on the right to access primary schooling to entrench a far more comprehensive framework for Indian children.

CONCLUDING THOUGHTS

The impact of globalization and the framing of rights language in education policy is a complex and multifaceted phenomenon. Certainly, rights-based claims to education have their critiques, particularly from international and comparative education scholars writing from a capabilities perspective (Unterhalter, 2003). Ingrid Robeyns finds that, despite its justice orientation, the rights framework "sounds overtly rhetorical" with governments adopting guarantees while millions of children still languish out of school (2006, p. 76). Similarly, she notes that the reduction of the right to education to merely a legal right standing alone, without any connection to a moral imperative or comprehensive plan for implementation, risks confining the right to political discourse. Next, Robeyns offers an equity argument that a government, once a right to education is in place, may not go beyond "its duties in terms of the rights-based policies, to undertake action to ensure that every child can fully and equally enjoy her right to education" (2006, p. 77). Where cultural or social impediments to educational access exist, significant racial, caste, religious, or gender gaps may still persist if rights are limited to laws on paper to be enacted by governments and absent engagement with unequal social structures and hierarchies.

Rights-based arguments for educational access, quality, and equity have rivaled the efficiency and rate of return arguments of decades past (and present) in calling for the expansion of education worldwide. Many nations will not meet the targets set forth in the Education for All and Millennium Development Goals agreements. While intergovernmental agencies, NGOs, and research institutes begin discussing strategies and responses post-2015, questions remain about what rights and justice claims do for families and communities. India's pioneering RTE Act offers one example of domestic legislation that allows parents to sue the government for violations of the provisions related to accessible schooling, absentee teachers, and availability of resources for disabled children. The tests of such legislative measures are their implementation, enforcement, and their ability to sanction violations. Further questions, which suggest the limits and depth of rights talk and claims, include the following:

- To what extent are rights-based claims for education sufficient for ensuring quality and accountability in the provision of state-sponsored schooling for children of all social groups?
- In what ways will the strategic use of rights talk advance or limit the localization of human rights in educational policy and practice?
- How and in what ways will declarations and policy mandates related to education for human rights influence curricula, teacher training, and pedagogy on the ground in the Global South?
- How do cultural and social practices interact with rights proclamations in the formation of "vernacular" rights movements and practices (Levitt and Merry, 2009)?

In today's version of globalization, rights frameworks have become the primary organizing force for diverse actors from international organizations, lawyers, educational scholars, and policy-makers at national and local levels. Yet, human rights concepts often assume different meanings, uses, and definitions, and indeed are used strategically, to varying ends, by these actors. The case of the RTE Act in India suggests the productive plasticity of rights talk and demonstrates how "human rights" concepts are strategically engaged due to their international currency and discursive popularity. As such, the use of rights talk, while contested, draws on, but goes far beyond international agreements on the right to access primary schooling to posit a far more wide-ranging vision of educational access and quality for Indian children. Certainly, the extent of success and depth of these claims in promoting greater access to quality education over longer periods of time requires further study. Widening gaps in social and economic inequalities between the "North" and "South" and within nations of the Global South, not to mention the limits of social struggles deploying rights claims suggested previously, may yet belie the imperative to understand schooling as a force for social justice and equity. These topics and many more should concern scholars of globalization and education in the years ahead.

Acknowledgments

This chapter benefited from advice offered by Indian education scholar Dhir Jhingran and the extensive comments provided by legal scholar Bikku Kuruvila.

REFERENCES

Aiyar, Swaminathan. n.d. A Right to Schooling, but Not to Education. Commentary, Cato Institute. http://www.cato.org/publications/commentary/right-schooling-not-education

Amnesty International. 2009. *Guidelines for Human Rights Friendly Schools*. London: Amnesty International.

Anderson-Levitt, Kathryn. 2003. A World Culture of Schooling? In Kathryn Anderson-Levitt (ed.), *Local Meanings, Global Schooling: Anthropology and World Culture Theory* (pp. 1–26). New York: Palgrave MacMillan.

Asia-Pacific Human Rights Network. 2002. Right to Food: The Indian Experience. *Human Rights Features*. http://www.hrdc.net/sahrdc/hrfeatures/HRF58.htm

Bajaj, Monisha. 2011. *Schooling for Social Change: The Rise and Impact of Human Rights Education in India*. New York: Continuum Publishing.

_____ and Bikku Kuruvila. 2012. Rights and Resistance: The Limits and Promise of Human Rights Education in India. In Dip Kapoor, Bijoy P. Barua and Al-Karim Datoo (eds.), *Globalization, Culture, and Education in South Asia: Critical Excursions* (pp. 123–38). New York: Palgrave.

Bakshi, Anouradha. 2012. Right to Education … Passing the Buck. Project Why, April 27. http://project-why.blogspot.in/2012/04/right-to-education-passing-buck.html.

Baxi, Upendra. 1998. Voices of Suffering and the Future of Human Rights. *Transnational Law and Contemporary Problems*, vol. 8, pp. 125–70.

———. 2006. Human Rights and Human Rights Education: Arriving at the Truth. In *Human Rights Learning: A People's Report* (pp. 117–36). New York: People's Movement for Human Rights Learning.

Boli, John, John Meyer, and Francisco Ramirez. 1985. Explaining the Origins and Expansion of Mass Education. *Comparative Education Review*, vol. 29, no. 2, pp. 145–70.

Bromley, Patricia. 2009. Cosmopolitanism in Civic Education: Exploring Cross-National Trends, 1970-2008. *Current Issues in Comparative Education*, vol.12, no. 1, pp. 33–44.

Cardenas, Sonia. 2005. Constructing Rights? Human Rights Education and the State. *International Political Science Review*, vol. 26, no. 4, pp. 363–79.

Chatterjee, Partha. 2011. *Lineages of Political Society: Studies in Postcolonial Democracy*. New York: Columbia University Press.

Crossley, Michael, and Leon Tikly. 2004. Postcolonial Perspectives and Comparative and International Research in Education: A Critical Introduction. *Comparative Education*, vol. 40, no. 2, pp. 147–56.

Dembour, Marie-Bénédicte. 2010. What Are Human Rights? Four Schools of Thought. *Human Rights Quarterly*, vol. 32, no. 1, pp. 1–20.

Deyhle, Donna, and Karen Swisher. 1997. Research in American Indian and Alaska Native Education: From Assimilation to Self-determination. *Review of Research in Education*, vol. 22, pp. 113–94.

Finnemore, Martha. 1996. *National Interests in International Society*. Ithaca: Cornell University Press.

——— and Kathryn Sikkink. 1998. International Norm Dynamics and Political Change. *International Organization*, vol. 52, no. 4, pp. 887–917.

Flowers, Nancy. 2003. *What Is Human Rights Education?* Hamburg: Bertelsmann Verlag. http://www.hrea.org/erc/Library/curriculum_methodology/flowers03.pdf

Fuller, Bruce. 1991. *Growing up Modern*. New York and London: Routledge.

German Federal Ministry for Economic Development and Cooperation. 2013. The Importance of Human Rights in German Development Policy. http://www.bmz.de/en/what_we_do/issues/HumanRights/allgemeine_menschenrechte/deutsche_entwicklungspolitik/index.html

Gillis, Malcolm, Steven Radelet, Donald Snodgrass, Michael Roemer, and Dwight Perkins. 2001. *Economics of Development*, 5th edition. New York: W.W. Norton.

Human Rights Education Associates. n.d. The Global Human Rights Education List. Human Rights Education Associates, http://www.hrea.org/lists/hr-education/

Iyengar, Radhika. 2010. Different Implementation Approaches to a Common Goal: Education for All in the Indian Context. *Society of International Education Journal*, vol. 7, no. 1, pp. 63–91.

Jones, Phillip W. 2007. *World Bank Financing of Education: Lending, Learning and Development*. New York: Routledge.

Kaviraj, Sudipta. 2012. *The Enchantment of Democracy and India: Politics and Ideas*. Hyderabad: Orient Blackswan.

Keck, Margaret, and Kathryn Sikkink. 1998. *Activists Beyond Borders*. Ithaca: Cornell University Press.

Khan, Imran. 2012. No Way to Teach a Lesson in Class. *Tehelka*, August 4. http://tehelka.com/no-way-to-teach-a-lesson-in-class/

Levitt, Peggy, and Sally Merry. 2009. Vernacularization on the Ground: Local Uses of Global Women's Rights in Peru, China, India and the United States. *Global Networks*, vol. 9, no. 4, pp. 441–61.

Little, Angela. 2003. Extended Review: Clash of Civilisations: Threat or Opportunity? *Comparative Education*, vol. 39, no. 3, pp. 391–94.

McCowan, Tristan. 2013. *Education as a Human Right: Principles for a Universal Entitlement to Learning*. London: Bloomsbury.

Madhok, Sumi. 2010. Rights Talk and the Feminist Movement in India. In Mina Roces and Louise Edwards (eds.), *Women's Movements in Asia: Feminisms and Transnational Activism* (pp. 224–40). New York: Routledge,

Merry, Sally. 2003. Rights Talk and the Experience of Law: Implementing Women's Human Rights to Protection from Violence. *Human Rights Quarterly*, vol. 25, no. 2, pp. 343–81.

Meyer, John W., and Brian Rowan. 1978. The Structure of Educational Organizations. In John W. Meyer, Brian Rowan and W. Richard Scott (eds.), *Organizations and Environments* (pp. 78–109). San Francisco: Jossey Bass.

Meyer, John W., Francisco O. Ramirez, and Yasemin Nuholu Soysal. 1992. World Expansion of Mass Education, 1870-1980. *Sociology of Education*, vol. 65, no. 2, pp. 128–49.

Meyer, John W., Patricia Bromley-Martin, and Francisco O. Ramirez. 2010. Human Rights in Social Science Textbooks: Cross-National Analyses, 1970-2008. *Sociology of Education*, vol. 83, no. 2, pp. 111–34.

Mirembe, Robina, and Lynn Davies. 2001. Is Schooling a Risk? Gender, Power Relations, and School Culture in Uganda. *Gender and Education*, vol.13, no. 4, pp. 401–16.

Mutua, Makau. 2002. *Human Rights: A Political and Cultural Critique*. Philadelphia: University of Pennsylvania Press.

Orfield, Gary, and Susan E. Eaton. 1997. *Dismantling Desegregation: The Quiet Reversal of Brown V. Board of Education*. New York: New Press.

Premi, Mahendra. 2002. India's Literacy Panorama. *Seminar on Progress of Literacy in India*. http://www.educationforallinindia.com/page172.html.

Psacharopoulos, George. 1996. *Human Capital Underdevelopment: The Worst Aspects*. Washington, DC: The World Bank.

Raina, Vinod. 2012. On RTE, Set the Record Straight. *The Indian Express*, May 25. http://www.indianexpress.com/news/on-rte-set-the-record-straight/953538/0.

Ramirez, Francisco, David Suarez, and John Meyer. 2007. The Worldwide Rise of Human Rights Education. In Aaron Benavot, Cecilia Braslavsky, and Nhung Truong (eds.), *School Knowledge in Comparative and Historical Perspective* (pp. 35–52). Dordrecht: Springer.

Ramirez, Francisco, and Christine Min Wotipka. 2007. World Society and Human Rights: An Event History Analysis of the Convention on All Forms of Discrimination against Women. In Frank Dobbin, Beth Simmons, and Geoffrey Garrett (eds.), *The Global Diffusion of Markets and Democracy* (pp. 303–43). Cambridge: Cambridge University Press.

Reddy, Anugula N., and Shantha Sinha. 2010. School Dropouts or Pushouts? Overcoming Barriers for the Right to Education. Research Monograph No. 40, CREATE Pathways to Access. New Delhi: National University of Educational Planning and Administration.

Robeyns, Ingrid. 2006. Three Models of Education: Rights, Capabilities and Human Capital. *Theory and Research in Education*, vol. 4, no. 1, pp. 69–84.

Schultz, Theodore. 1961. Investment in Human Capital. *American Economic Review*, vol. 51, no. 1, pp. 1–17.

———. 1980. Nobel Lecture: The Economics of Being Poor. *The Journal of Political Economy*, vol. 88, no. 4, pp. 639–51.

Spring, Joel. 2008. Research on Globalization and Education. *Review of Educational Research*, vol. 78, no. 2, pp. 330–63.

Steiner-Khamsi, Gita (ed.). 2004. *The Global Politics of Education Borrowing*. New York: Teachers College Press.

Stromquist, Nelly P. 2002. *Education in a Globalized World: The Connectivity of Economic Power, Technology and Power*. Lanham, MD: Rowman & Littlefield.

Suarez, David. 2007. Education Professionals and the Construction of Human Rights Education. *Comparative Education Review*, vol. 51, no. 1, pp. 48–70.

Subrahmanian, Ramya. 2003. Gender Equality in Education: Definitions and Measurements. Background Paper for UNESCO Global Monitoring Report 2003. Paris: UNESCO.

Sumida Huaman, Elizabeth. 2011. Transforming Education, Transforming Society: The Co-Construction of Critical Peace Education and Indigenous Education. *Journal of Peace Education*, vol. 8, no. 3, pp. 243–58.

Taylor, Aleesha. 2009. Questioning Participation. In Frances Vavrus and Lesley Bartlett (eds.), *Critical Approaches to Comparative Education* (pp. 75–92). New York: Palgrave Macmillan.

Tibbitts, Felisa. 2002. Understanding What We Do: Emerging Models for Human Rights Education. *International Review of Education*, vol. 48, nos. 3-4, pp. 159–71.

———. 2005. Transformative Learning and Human Rights Education: Taking a Closer Look. *Intercultural Education*, vol. 16, no. 2, pp. 107–13.

Tomasevski, Katarina. 2006. *Human Rights Obligations in Education: The 4-a Scheme*. Nijmegen, Netherlands: Wolf Legal Publishers.

United Nations. 2013. Outcomes of Human Rights. United Nations. http://www.un.org/en/development/devagenda/humanrights.shtml

UN Education Science and Cultural Organization. n.d. Associated Schools Project Network. UNESCO. http://www.unesco.org/new/en/education/networks/global-networks/aspnet/

———. 2004. *Para Teachers in India: A Review*. Paris: UNESCO.

———. 2010. *2010 Global Monitoring Report: Reaching the Marginalized*. Paris: UNESCO.

UN Children's Fund. 2007. *A Human Rights-Based Approach to Education for All*. New York: UNICEF.

———. 2009. Child Friendly Schools Manual. New York: UNICEF.

Unterhalter, Elaine. 2003. Education, Capabilities and Social Justice. Background Paper for the EFA Global Monitoring Report 2003/4. Paris: UNESCO.

World Bank. 2012. Human Rights. World Bank. http://web.worldbank.org/WBSITE/EXTERNAL/EXTSITE-TOOLS/0,,contentMDK:20749693~pagePK:98400~piPK:98424~theSitePK:95474,00.html

NOTES

1. For example, the relationship between colonial modernity and education is a nodal point of reference that has been theorized extensively in an Indian context by historians and political theorists such as those of the Subaltern Studies school (see Chatterjee, 2011, and also Kaviraj, 2012).

2. These distinctions are reminiscent of Ramya Subrahmanian's (2003) discussions of gender and education, which she conceptualizes in three ways: (1) girls' right to education (access), (2) rights within education (schools that are safe and welcome for girls), and (3) rights through education (related broadly to greater gender justice).

3. I use the term "rights talk" here and elsewhere (Bajaj and Kuruvila, 2012) to connote the way that human rights language has permeated international-, national-, and local-level discourses and operations. As anthropologist Sally Merry notes, in terms of social movements, "From civil rights to human rights, rights talk remains a dominant

framework for contemporary social justice movements" (2003, p. 344). Other studies have discussed "rights talk" as an organizing framework to situate demands on the state (or other entities) in rights-based terms. Here I use rights talk in a slightly more diffuse way given its prominence in educational policy discussions, often with vague or diverse meanings attached to which rights are being referenced in a given situation or context. This is similar to the way that legal scholar Upendra Baxi identifies the manipulation of rights talk that "code[s] for power and hierarchy" (1998, p. 129).

4. For example, Sumi Madhok's (2010) work on "rights scapes" offers a useful framework for analyzing how local actors engage with globally circulating discourses: "Emergent 'rights scapes' provide fertile opportunities for investigating how rights actually operate when coupled alongside strong claims for social justice and the new subjectivities and forms of subjection these create" (Madhok, 2010, p. 236).

5. The United Nation's "Common Understanding" adheres to normative concepts within human rights related to their inalienability, indivisibility, interdependence, and universality; the United Nation's approach further stipulates that rights-based development programs enhance participation, inclusion, non-discrimination, empowerment, and accountability (UNICEF, 2007).

6. The Children's Rights Convention adopted by the United Nations in 1989 also provided a contemporary framework for the discussion of the right to education for the first World Conference on Education for All at Jomtien in 1990.

7. Dalits (literally translated as "broken people" and formerly called "untouchables") constitute 16 percent of India's population.

Chapter Five

"The Girl Effect": U.S. Transnational Corporate Investment in Girls' Education

Kathryn Moeller

In the midst of the deepening global financial crisis, the World Economic Forum held a plenary session titled "The Girl Effect on Development" on January 31, 2009, at its Annual Meeting in Davos, Switzerland (World Economic Forum, 2009). It was the first session on girls in the organization's history, and it was the fourth most attended event during the meeting (World Bank, 2009). As articulated by moderator Dr. Helene Gayle, executive director of CARE, the goal was to address the "unique needs, challenges, and the opportunities" that come from investing in girls (World Economic Forum, 2009). The panel included individuals from powerful institutions, including Nike, Inc., a Fortune 500 U.S. transnational corporation; the Bill and Melinda Gates Foundation, the largest private foundation in the world; two multilateral agencies, the World Bank and the United Nations Children's Fund; CARE, a transnational nongovernmental organization (NGO); the Grameen Bank, a Nobel Prize–winning transnational NGO; and the Ministry of Trade of Indonesia. While not on the panel, Maria Eitel, the president and CEO of the Nike Foundation and vice president of Nike, Inc., and her team at the Nike Foundation were primary organizers along with the UN Foundation and the NoVo Foundation.

During the session, the panel focused on the "potential multi-trillion-dollar impact of girls on national economies, the economic cost of not investing, and the impact of these investments on developed economies" (Nike, Inc., 2009). Panelist Ngozi Okonjo-Iweala, then managing director of the World Bank, riffed on the World Bank's catchphrase for its Gender Action Plan in her remarks: "Investing in women is smart economics, and investing in girls, catching them upstream, is even smarter economics. If you invest in girls, if you educate girls, if you get girls into jobs, you solve so many problems, the population problem, the climate change problem, poverty" (World Economic Forum, 2009). The panelists' statements were attributed to "The Girl Effect."

DEFINING "THE GIRL EFFECT"

The Nike Foundation defines The Girl Effect as "the unique potential of 250 million adolescent girls to end poverty for themselves and the world" (Nike Inc., 2011). It is a brand of the Nike Foundation—the philanthropic arm of Nike, Inc., the world's largest maker of sporting goods and apparel. It brands particular adolescent girls—poor, of color, and in the Global

South—with the potential to end poverty in the new millennium. This purported potential is predicated on what the foundation identifies as "the ability of adolescent girls in developing countries to bring unprecedented economic and social change to their families, communities, and countries" (Nike, Inc., 2008). This ability supposedly generates a "ripple effect" (Nike Foundation, 2008, p. 3) across multiple development indicators, including alleviating poverty, promoting economic growth, reducing fertility rates and population growth, controlling the spread of HIV/AIDS, and conserving environmental resources.

The Nike Foundation launched the brand in 2008 with the financial support of the NoVo Foundation, three years after Nike, Inc., transformed the foundation to focus exclusively on adolescent girls. The brand was developed through a collaboration between the Nike Foundation's in-house creative team and Nike, Inc.'s longtime Portland-based advertising firm, Weiden + Kennedy. Using this brand, the corporation and its foundation promote global investment in adolescent girls through institutional partnerships with organizations such as those represented on the "The Girl Effect on Development" panel at the World Economic Forum (2009).

SIGNIFICANCE OF TRANSNATIONAL CORPORATE INVESTMENT IN GIRLS' EDUCATION

Since the beginning of the new millennium, U.S. transnational corporations have significantly expanded their influence over programs and policies in the field of gender, education, and development. They have done so through the increasingly entangled discourses of gender equality, ending poverty, economic growth, and corporate social responsibility. The corporations and corporate foundations include but are not limited to Becton Dickenson, Chevron, Cisco Systems, ExxonMobil, Gap, Inc., General Electric, Gucci, Intel Corporation, J.P. Morgan Chase, Johnson & Johnson, Microsoft Corporation, Nike, Inc., Standard Chartered Bank, and Starbucks Corporation.

These corporations are building on decades of empirical evidence, particularly from an economic and population perspective, that investing in girls' education generates a high rate of return for development (Herz and Sperling, 2004; King and Hill, 1993; Psacharopoulos and Patrinos, 2002; Summers, 1992; Tembon and Fort, 2008). Over the past decade, this evidence has increasingly circulated through an ever transforming and continually expanding constellation of international agencies, NGOs, global forums, universities, and, most recently, corporations and corporate foundations. New networks and platforms for knowledge sharing and resource mobilization, such as the "The Girl Effect on Development" panel at the World Economic Forum, have emerged from this constellation. They have facilitated what Peck (2011) identifies as "fast policy integration" or "the (still uneven) globalization of prevailing rationalities and practices in poverty management" (p. 166). Through this "fast policy regime," forms of knowledge and expertise on gender are deeply reductionist and, thus, depoliticizing (Ferguson, 1994; Peck, 2011, p. 177). The focus on gender equality in these discourses, as reflected in the World Bank's catch phrase "Gender Equality is Smart Economics," functions as code for a strategic focus on girls and women as a population. This focus is frequently divorced from understandings of gender as a social construction and as a structuring relation of power.

Corporations have incorporated these rationales to make even stronger claims for the purposes of development, and to design programs and policies that position girls as a resource for development. Maria Eitel (2010), the current president of the Nike Foundation, illuminates this when she says, "I'll never get tired of saying it: Girls are the world's greatest untapped resource for economic growth and prosperity" (para. 7). Using this approach, these corporate-funded programs employ an instrumental logic that focuses on the return on their investment, educating girls as means rather than as ends in and of themselves (Unterhalter, 2007). Yet, this return is the result of inequitable sociocultural and political-economic conditions that make poor girls of color or, more specifically, the racialized trope of "Third World girl" disproportionately responsible for the well-being and futures of others, such that their education generates a ripple effect across multiple development indicators from the scale of the family to the world (Moeller, forthcoming-a). Through their approach, these corporations risk maintaining, if not potentially exacerbating, unequal relations of power across multiple axes of difference—gender, racial, class, religious, and geographic—by perpetuating traditionally inequitable roles of social reproduction (Moeller, forthcoming-a).

Moreover, in our historical context of ongoing economic crises, people and communities rising up across the globe have revealed the fundamental misalignment of corporate power in our global economy. Three decades of *de*regulation and *re*regulation in favor of corporations in the United States and globally has led to corporations becoming disproportionately powerful in fundamental aspects of our lives from finance to housing to health care to education. This study on corporate development in girls' education is important for understanding one of the ways corporations are extending their power and influence in education. It theoretically and politically conceptualizes corporations as educational actors, and empirically demonstrates how girls, educators, and classrooms become part of the corporate domain. This represents an expanded theoretical and empirical understanding of corporations in education. The utility of this conceptualization extends beyond girls' education to illuminate the expansion of corporate philanthropy in education (Ball, 2012; van Fleet, 2011), public-private partnerships (Robertson, Mundy, and Verger, 2012), the private supplemental services industry in education (Acosta, Good, Burch, and Stewart 2013; Burch, 2009; Good et al., forthcoming; Koyama, 2010), and classroom technology throughout the world provided by US corporations (Bhanji, 2012). In doing so, it reveals a new spatiopolitical understanding of the corporation. While the classroom would normally not be understood as part of a corporate geography, this study reveals that we must examine new spheres of corporate influence to understand how it affects the provision of education and to consider how unequal social and institutional actors negotiate corporate practices and policies on multiple spatial scales (Ball, 2012).

METHODOLOGY

This chapter is part of a broader study investigating U.S. transnational corporate investment in girls' education. It seeks to understand why U.S. corporations are investing in girls' education in the Global South, the logic they employ, and the intended and unintended consequences of their practices. To investigate this phenomenon, this study examined Nike, Inc., and the Nike Foundation's philanthropic investments in The Girl Effect. It is based on two years (2009–2010) of ethnographic fieldwork on Nike, Inc., the Nike Foundation, and their relationships with institutions in the United States and Brazil, including two transnational NGOs in Brazil, the World Bank in Washington, DC, and the Clinton Global Initiative in New York City.

In 2008, I visited the Nike, Inc. and Nike Foundation headquarters on two occasions for formal interviews. I continued to interview a select group of these employees and relevant new employees in 2010 and 2012, as turnover rates are high at the foundation. Moreover, I conducted interviews with former foundation employees, consultants, and other institutional partners between 2007 and 2012. I recorded all of my interviews with employees of the Nike

Foundation and Nike, Inc., using extensive field notes and audio recordings. The one exception was my first interview at the Nike Foundation, which the foundation recorded for itself. I also conducted ongoing participant observation and interviews at an NGO (2009–2010) in Brazil. To ensure the protection of human subjects, I will not be revealing the particular NGO this article focuses on or its location in Brazil. I only refer to it as the NGO and its educational program for adolescent girls as an "economic empowerment" program.

The fieldwork focused on The Girl Effect as its object of analysis. It was therefore a conscious theoretical decision not to study the girls in the NGO programs as the objects of analysis. Rather, the research shifted the gaze from the girls to the "development apparatus" (Ferguson, 1994, p. 23) that operates around them and claims to intervene on their behalf. To study The Girl Effect is to empirically understand how the processes of neoliberal globalization, corporatization, and the racialized Othering of girls are articulated through the practices and policies of girls' education operating on multiple spatial scales. In doing so, the study employs Hart's (2002) understanding that "globalization—*both* in the sense of intensified processes of spatial interconnection associated with capitalist restructuring *and* of discourses through which knowledge is produced—is deeply infused with the exercise of power" (p. 12, emphasis in original). Understanding the uneven power relations that constitute The Girl Effect necessitates observing the negotiation of The Girl Effect's logic and its effects across institutions and on different scales. The research carefully examined how these negotiations occurred in a particular constellation of the Nike Foundation's investments in Brazil in order to shed light on its broader practices and their effects.

In this way, the study's design is informed by recent multi-sited, critical ethnographies of corporations, development, and globalization. Each site functions as a strategic "fieldwork node" (Roy, 2003, p. 36). In contrast to traditional conceptions of sites as bounded localities, these nodes are unbounded. They operate as what Goldman (2005) calls "sites of encounter" in his ethnography of the World Bank (p. 24). They are constituted through interconnected, yet unequal relationships and exchanges of money, knowledge, resources, and labor between diverse institutions and individuals, many of whom will never have direct contact with one another.

The study's analysis seeks to understand how the Nike Foundation's investments in The Girl Effect are created, transformed, and experienced through practice and through spatial connections to regional, national, and transnational arenas. By carefully examining a particular constellation of the Nike Foundation's investments in Brazil, the analysis works to elucidate its broader investment logic, its practices, and, ultimately, its intended and unintended effects (Hart, 2002). It is by analyzing how these relations are produced and transformed in practice in a specific constellation that a particular part of the Nike Foundation's investment strategy and practice can elucidate a broader whole. While it is not expected that the experiences of Nike, Inc., its foundation, and their institutional partners in any specific geography will be exactly replicated by another set of institutions focused on The Girl Effect or by other corporations or corporate foundations investing in girls' education, this study places these investments within a larger constellation of discourse and practice in order to understand this emergent phenomenon.

Based on this analysis, this chapter proposes that The Girl Effect functions through a gendered and racialized logic of neoliberalism (Moeller, forthcoming-a). It is based on the relationship between the presumed reproductive capacity and imagined future economic potential of particular girls, or, more specifically, those who occupy the racialized subject position of "Third World girl." It "attempts to 'push back' childbearing and marriage in order to 'unleash' their future economic potential. This intimate relationship between sexuality and

economics enables the production of the returns—real or imagined—these corporate investments purportedly create on multiple spatial scales" (Moeller, forthcoming-a). Girls' education becomes the means for achieving this. As a result, when The Girl Effect's neoliberal logic
is materialized through practice, it shapes the population served by the corporate funded
programs, their curriculum and pedagogy, and the social and institutional relations of girls'
education.

HISTORY OF INVESTING IN GIRLS' EDUCATION

A powerful globalized discourse emerged in the 1980s and early 1990s on the benefits of
investing in girls' education in the Global South as a development solution (World Bank 1995;
for critiques of this narrow framing of gender issues, see Cortina and Stromquist, 2000;
Heward and Bunwaree, 1999; Vavrus, 2003). It developed, first, as a handmaiden easing the
pain of the World Bank and the International Monetary Fund's devastating structural adjustment programs in the Global South during the 1980s and early 1990s. Second, it emerged as
the fruit of Western, liberal feminism's progressively more strident efforts to ensure equality
of opportunity for girls and women in education, the labor market, and the development
process. Third, its power and legitimacy grew from its correspondence to the calls for girls'
and women's access to schooling in the Global South and the authentic desires of girls and
women for education and economic security as a population historically excluded from
schooling and disproportionately bearing the costs of the austerity policies.

The convergence of these multiple factors in the early 1990s produced a racialized and
gendered (neo)liberalism—a fresh liberal face on beleaguered neoliberal values—representing
the simultaneous resurgence of liberalism and the furtive, yet dogmatic persistence of neoliberalism. The promotion of the liberal political ideals of equality and human rights for girls and
women was critical to the reconstitution and re-legitimization of the neoliberal agenda after
the devastating decade in the 1980s. Yet, below these liberal values lie a persistent set of
political economic practices that promote the "Third World girl" as an autonomous actor and
the market as the guarantor of socioeconomic well-being in the wake of the rollback of the
welfare state. It imagines her to be responsible for and to possess the agency necessary to
solve the structural problems of poverty and the contradictions of economic development even
as neoliberal practices and policies have created and/or exacerbated conditions of vulnerability
for girls, women, and the poor over the past three decades.

Over time, the idea of investing in girls' education began to function as a natural, seemingly obvious solution to ending poverty, or, in the language of Gramsci (1971), as "common
sense." As he describes, "it is the diffuse, unco-ordinated features of a generic form of thought
common to a particular period and a particular popular environment" (p. 330). It is "not
something rigid and immobile, but is continually transforming itself, enriching itself with
scientific ideas and with philosophical opinions which have entered ordinary life" (Gramsci,
1971, p. 326). The notion of investing in girls' education has come to function as a natural,
seemingly obvious solution to poverty alleviation in this historical moment. As such, a broad
set of individual and institutional actors with diverse and, perhaps, contradictory rationales
coalesced around it from multilaterals to NGOs. Beginning in the new millennium, corporations capitalized on this "common sense" idea as they sought to find a non-controversial way
to enter the business of development.

ON CORPORATE SOCIAL RESPONSIBILITY

Since the beginning of the new millennium, corporations and their foundations have rapidly expanded their efforts in the area of development through the discourse of corporate social responsibility (CSR). Simply put, CSR is predicated on "doing well by doing good." Consent for "doing well" is constructed through the other half of the mantra—"by doing good." Corporate investments in development, including the areas of education, health, finance, and the environment, suture them together. This occurs as corporations fund, advocate, design, implement, and brand programs and policies in the field. It enables "doing well" and "doing good" to occur in concert rather than in conflict with one another. As such, responsibility has become a corporate word. It is heralded with such frequency that it is difficult to remember a moment when corporations were not engaged in the performance of being responsible. Yet, this has not always been the case.

In the wake of the anti-sweatshop and anti-globalization movements at the end of the twentieth century, corporations were pressured to respond to the demands of critics concerned with their socially, morally, economically, and environmentally deleterious practices (Browne and Milgram, 2009; Dolan and Rajak, 2011; Rajak, 2011; Schwittay, 2006). This cultural crisis of corporate capitalism was defined by mounting social, political, and economic pressures for corporations to remain accountable to labor, consumers, local communities, governments, and the environment.

While corporations have long been principal architects and beneficiaries of development, since the beginning of the new millennium they have become increasingly influential in funding, advocating, designing, implementing, and branding programs and policies in the field. Powerful globalized forums like the World Economic Forum, the Clinton Global Initiative, the UN Global Compact, and the World Bank Private Sector Leaders Forum have been critical to extending corporate influence in the business of development. As recent critical ethnographies of corporations (Rajak, 2011; Schwittay, 2006) have shown, increasing involvement of corporations and their foundations in development was a powerful mechanism for responding to and recuperating from both external and internal criticism of corporate practices. And, thus, it was important for revising their tarnished images and securing their "social licenses to operate" and, correspondingly, their financial bottom-lines. As such, these development efforts were critical to the restoration of corporate hegemony at the beginning of the new millennium, thereby extending corporations' legitimacy, authority, and reach without having to deal with the fundamental contradictions in their business practices and in capitalism itself. For corporate executives (Fiorina, 2007) and other proponents (McElhaney, 2008), CSR is not merely an altruistic endeavor; rather, it contributes to the corporation's financial bottom line (Muirhead, 1999) by fortifying existing market share, opening new markets, and producing potential new consumers and workers.

By the beginning of the new millennium, broad consent for CSR made the critiques of sweatshops and globalization from the 1990s almost passé. Moreover, the institutionalization of CSR through corporate development enabled corporations to dedicate themselves to ending poverty and promoting social and economic development. They signed moral compacts, and they promised to dedicate themselves to supporting the Millennium Development Goals. They also channeled their influence through platforms within development institutions, and, lastly, they became large-scale donors of NGOs such as the ones I studied in Brazil. In short, they rapidly positioned themselves at the forefront of development (Rajak, 2011) and, more specifically, international education development (Bhanji, 2012; Schwittay, 2006; van Fleet, 2011).

THE CASE OF NIKE, INC.

Beginning in the early 1990s, Nike emerged as the quintessential target of the anti-sweatshop and anti-globalization movements (Locke, 2003). Criticism focused on the corporation's well-documented abusive practices against its predominantly young, uneducated, poor female labor force in the Global South. To respond to tarnishing accusations against it, including media exposés on child labor, then CEO Phil Knight publically stated in 1998, "Nike product has become synonymous with slave wages, forced overtime, and arbitrary abuse" (Knight, 1998). Despite Knight's claims to transform the corporation's practices over a decade ago, accusations of abusive labor problems persist in its contract factories, as reflected in recent, well-publicized worker strikes in Cambodia, Honduras, and Indonesia (Barber, 2013; Casey and Pura, 2008; Hookway and Nguyen, 2008). Nevertheless, since this moment of crisis, the corporation has focused on remaking itself as socially responsible. Yet, as critical ethnographies of corporations (Rajak, 2011; Schwittay, 2006) have shown, the increasing involvement of corporations and their foundations in the business of ending poverty has been a powerful mechanism for recuperating from external and internal criticism. It secures their "social licenses to operate" and their financial bottom-lines without having to deal with the fundamental contradictions in their business practices and in capitalism itself. The Girl Effect is a product of this constellation of forces. Its logic has come to influence how development institutions and other corporations understand girls in the Global South and how they structure educational interventions in their name. To illustrate this, the remainder of the chapter focuses on an NGO in Brazil where I conducted participant observation for nine months.

INVESTING IN "THE GIRL EFFECT" IN BRAZIL

Based on its grant contract with the Nike Foundation, the NGO was required to educate adolescent girls in Brazil over three years (2008–2011) through its nonformal, extracurricular educational program. While the Nike Foundation targets adolescent girls as a population, the NGO used the term *jovens mulheres*, translated as young women, when referring to the participants in their program. This chapter therefore refers to the participants as young women. The participants in this five-month course were poor, predominantly Afro-Brazilian and mixed race young women, ages sixteen to twenty-four from *favelas* (poor communities) on the periphery of the city. While some had already graduated, the majority of them concurrently attended secondary school and participated in the program every morning or afternoon depending on their school schedule. For the young women who had previously left school, one of the NGO requirements was that they re-enroll in school. Staff members worked, in most cases quite successfully, to find them spots in local public high schools.

Through its program, the NGO aimed to empower the young women to enter the formal labor market or pursue entrepreneurial activities.[1] As explained by one senior staff member, Susanna, during a recruitment event at a local high school, "The course objective is qualification for the labor market with the way of being the market looks for. It prepares you with the profile that companies are looking for." She further explained, "We develop abilities that the labor market looks for like teamwork, discipline, respect." She described the commitment to the students: "The program has two principle courses: technical administration and entrepreneurship. It is a five-month long, intensive course, Monday through Friday, from 8 am to 1 pm or 1 pm to 5 pm."

In this time-intensive program, their primary coursework focused on two areas: training to become administrative assistants and entrepreneurship. In addition, they learned basic computer skills, reviewed their mathematic skills, practiced their writing and reading, and focused on their legal, gender, and human rights. The program was largely unsuccessful in finding them positions either before or after graduating with their certificates. When it was, with a few exceptions, it channeled them into insecure, low-wage, employment in businesses, often in telecommunications centers, supermarkets, and bus companies.

As a result of the NGO's anxiety to successfully prove The Girl Effect, this study's research findings demonstrate that the program's population target and its curriculum and pedagogy reflected, to a large degree, The Girl Effect's logic as the perceived success or failure of the educational intervention mirrored this logic. The remainder of the chapter draws on four ethnographic moments to illuminate how this logic materialized in practice.

"Third World Potential"[2]

In order to meet the program's goal of educating one hundred adolescent girls during its second session, I accompanied Susanna, a senior staff member, to recruit adolescent girls over four months. We would walk around the neighboring communities, hanging program posters in the windows of beauty parlors and Internet cafes, and leaving small white flyers on the desks of other local NGOs. The participant profile was written on the flyers: "Female sex, sixteen to twenty-four years old, likes sports, and interested in entering the labor market or becoming an entrepreneur."

One late afternoon, we visited a nearby neighborhood association. When we entered, Susanna asked the president if she knew of any adolescent girls from their neighborhood who might be eligible for the program.[3] The president thought for a moment before asking about the ages of the participants for whom we were looking. Susanna stated, "Between sixteen and twenty-four years old." The president thought for a moment before explaining, "I know lots of girls, but they are all pregnant." I anticipated Susanna would include them in program recruitment; she did not, however, despite the presence of mothers in the program. Before leaving the office, the older woman asked us, "Do you have a program for adults?" Susanna responded, "No, just young women." The woman further stated, "I am unemployed." Susanna asked, "What type of work do you do?" "Cook," Then she briefly paused, stating with more confidence, "I am a cook." Susanna noticed the woman's discomfort so she explained why she was asking, stating "I ask because I might know of an opening." As the conversation ended, Susanna handed the president a new poster and a set of small, white informational flyers before we left the office.

We never found the one hundred participants necessary to meet the NGO's required numbers. So the program began with approximately seventy participants. However, we did find a multitude of other individuals along the way who were interested in the program and in need of educational training. These included pregnant young women, older women, and young men. It was striking how our search excluded all those outside of the population category, despite its failure to sufficiently populate the program.

The search illuminates how The Girl Effect is predicated on what I identify as girls' perceived "Third World potential" (Moeller, forthcoming-a). I define it as "the imagined potential of their particular body's difference to either reproduce or end poverty in our particular historical moment" (Moeller, forthcoming-a). It is predicated on "the assumption that they are already responsible for more than themselves, and that investments in their education and training are simply enabling them to unleash this potential across multiple scales" (Moeller, forthcoming-a). Through this concept, the "Third World girl" is "simultaneously the potential "answer" for development and its universal victim of oppression in need of saving.

Through its partnership with the Nike Foundation, the program sought out a population with this potential; it is defined by the possibility of delaying pregnancy and marriage in order to unleash their economic potential. Yet, if this potential was perceived as foreclosed or nonexistent, as it was in the case of the pregnant young women, older women, and young men that were encountered on the search, they were not recruited. This occurred despite the desperate need of the NGO to populate its program and the very real diversity of educational needs and desires in the community where the program operated. Within the logic of The Girl Effect, pregnant young women have already lost their potential to end poverty. The educational intervention must mold them during the temporal moment of adolescence prior to becoming mothers in order to ensure their success in ending poverty.

Correspondingly, the rationale for older female adults is similar as they are "imagined to no longer hold the potential to end poverty" (Moeller, forthcoming-a). They have already moved into their "adult roles as wife, mother, worker, and citizen" (Levine, Lloyd, Greene, and Grown, 2008, p. 10), as described in "Girls Count: A Global Investment & Action Agenda," a report funded by the Nike Foundation. Under this conceptualization, the temporal moment for intervention has passed (Moeller, forthcoming-a). Moreover, young men neither hold the reproductive capacity nor the presumed social potential to end poverty, and adult males are excluded for the same reasons. Yet, I was approached by numerous young men or their parents with interest in the program either during recruitment or at the program site. Nevertheless, this program and the other NGO program in the Economic Empowerment Portfolio in Brazil only recruited adolescent girls even though they had each had previously worked with young men and women and would later return to also working with young men after their grants ended.

Moreover, despite the official color-blind nature of the Nike Foundation's use of the category of adolescent girl, the search for girls in Brazil was highly racialized. It "mapped onto the "racial formation" (Omi and Winant, 1994) of this Brazilian city where the spatialized distribution of opportunity occurs along highly racialized and classed lines" (Moeller, forthcoming-a). Recruitment of girls only took place in *favelas*, poorer communities where residents are majority Afro-Brazilian, mixed race, and darker skinned (Moeller, forthcoming-a). The search for adolescent girls for the program therefore also reveals the racialized constitution of the category of adolescent girl in The Girl Effect and, correspondingly, the racialized nature of the "Third World potential" that the subject position is imagined to possess.

"Pushing Back" Pregnancy[4]

Toward the end of my fieldwork, during a long, late afternoon staff meeting, I observed how the Nike Foundation's goal of pushing back pregnancy materialized in practice. As the previous conversation faded, Susanna gently shook her head, saying "I have something sad. Again, there is a girl in the program who is pregnant. We didn't meet our goal, our indicator." Turning to another staff members, she asked, "How many months is she?" "Three months," the staff member replied. Susanna quietly stated, "And after the gender class."

This story reflects how The Girl Effect's logic resulted in a strong focus on pushing back the age of pregnancy and marriage. At the time of the study, one of the Nike Foundation's three "universal indicators" for understanding adolescent girls around the world was "age of first birth" or "age of pregnancy." Within the Nike Foundation's strategic vision during this period of time, these "universal indicators," measured through a pre- and post-questionnaire, served as "proxy measures" for the "ultimate measures" of "income rates" and "accumulated assets," including both financial assets and material goods. As described by a senior manager of the Nike Foundation, these measures were part of positioning The Girl Effect as "an economic equation." This led to ongoing pedagogical and curricular interventions through the program to regulate the participants' heterosexual practices, including ongoing explicit conversations with the young women by senior staff members on the program's goal of delaying their first sexual encounters and "pushing back" the age of pregnancy. Fear of programmatic "failure" loomed large for the NGO, so ensuring the adolescent girls did not get pregnant was part of guaranteeing they proved The Girl Effect, which was the ultimate measure of the program's broader success. Yet, as Susanna alluded, in this instance the pedagogical and curricular interventions through the gender class and everyday classroom interactions had failed.

While the course should have provided a space for addressing gender and sexuality with the young women, the broader focus on "pushing back" pregnancy in the program marginalized other important aspects of gender and sexuality. These included conversations on healthy, safe sexual relationships regardless of sexual orientation and the rights of parenthood, its responsibilities, and the challenges it presents. Moreover, as gender and sexuality are "co-formed" (Bacchetta, 2007) with other axes of difference, including race, class, and place, the program did not adequately or explicitly address the particular experiences of being poor, young black women or women of color living in *favelas* on the periphery of city. As Susanna explained when I asked about why the program did not discuss race with the young women, "We focus on gender not race." Importantly, it did not directly address the ways their racialized positioning would impact their trajectories and experiences in the systems of higher education and the labor market.

Economically Empowering Girls

The Girl Effect's focus on economic empowerment led to channeling the girls into insecure, low-wage employment rather than addressing the core educational inequities they face. At the very beginning of the program, the girls went around the room telling us their professional goals despite the multiple constraints on their lives—one wanted to be a pharmacist, another a doctor, another a veterinarian, and so on. Yet, by the end of the six-month program, the highlight of which was a course training them to become administrative assistants, the same group of girls went around the same room telling a visitor from the United States what they wanted to be. The majority of the group wanted to be administrative assistants. It was striking. The visitor actually turned to me, quite startled, and asked, why do they all want to be administrative assistants? This shift in focus seems linked to their experience in the program; it might be that the young women reworked their goals to fit the program's.

In this case, their professional desires or imaginations of what they could be were diminished even though the program was supposedly opening opportunities for them. This ethnographic moment illuminates that because the program needed to prove they were economically empowering the girls, they focused on immediately channeling them into insecure, low-wage employment in call centers, supermarkets, or bus companies rather than addressing core educational inequities in their lives that result in challenges completing secondary education and pursing higher education to begin the professional lives they desired. As a result, the program had the effect of diminishing their possibilities rather than enlarging them, even though the program was largely unsuccessful in placing the majority of the participants in jobs before or after graduation. While the skills the program taught them, such as learning how to write a letter, answer the phone, or create a spreadsheet, are indeed useful skills, they did not address their primary educational challenges.

If the program had been focused on actually transforming their futures, it could have potentially worked with the participants to pass the rigorous, highly competitive national exam to enter the high-quality, free public university system in Brazil to pursue the stable professional jobs they desired and that their middle class and wealthy counterparts will have access to. However, passing the exam requires a solid educational foundation and extensive tutoring, and these classes, which are mostly private, were well beyond their means. Whereas scholars have demonstrated the persistence of these structural educational challenges in Brazil (Plank, 1996) despite the implementation of affirmative action policies earlier in the decade (Htun, 2004; McCowan, 2007), the program could have tailored its resources to address significant educational barriers along racial and class lines in the Brazilian context.

Shifting the Burden of Development onto Girls

Lastly, The Girl Effect's logic of shifting the burden of development onto girls was communicated to the program participants. During group selection interviews, one of the girls asked why there were only adolescent girls in the program. Carolina, a staff member, explained that they had decided to focus only on girls because when you invest in girls and women, everyone else wins. To illustrate this, she asked them, "If you go to the beach for the day, and the others do not have money, who pays?" The girls all responded, "the woman," nodding their heads that women pay for themselves, their children, and men. One of the girls stated, "The woman pays for transportation and lunch." Carolina asked, "And who wins? The woman and everyone around her," she explained.

Educators and NGO staff members communicated The Girl Effect's logic of responsibility to the girls in the program, thereby reinforcing what critical development theorist Chant (2006) calls the "feminization of responsibility and obligation" (p. 206) beginning at the scale of girl. In everyday classroom interactions and program activities, the idea of girls and women being responsible for the lives of others far beyond themselves was communicated to the participants.

Yet, this logic did not go without contestation. Over time, a number of staff members began to question how it positioned the girls. On one occasion a senior staff member, Marcela, commented to me during a conversation, "Sometimes I think, we are asking too much of them. So they will do what their mothers and grandmothers did." Late in my fieldwork, she shared this idea during a staff meeting. We were all engaged in conversation when she stated, "They are not all going to be leaders or change the reality in their communities. What do you ask of your child?" A junior staff member remarked, "To be someone in life." Marcela continued, "The girls first need to take care of their own lives and their education. We need to stop with this idea," she paused, "that they are going to take care of the streets."

If particular girls and women are more responsible, it is based on a particular set of historically produced, political economic and sociocultural conditions that make it so. It is not that they are naturally more responsible or selfless than other girls, women, or men. As Leonardo (2004) states, "To borrow a phrase from radical feminism, we can say that the 'personal is structural'" (p. 13). Therefore, if they are, it is because they are structurally positioned to be so (Moeller, forthcoming-a).

CONCLUSION

Investing in girls' education is at the top of the global development agenda of many international agencies. Yet, as this study reveals, an instrumental logic linked to job preparation and economic growth dominates this discourse, and corporations are capitalizing on this for purposes beyond educating girls. This chapter has not investigated whether the purported benefits of educating girls are true or untrue, or whether corporations are successful in generating these outcomes through their programs. Rather, it has sought to intervene in this dominant global discourse by providing empirical evidence regarding the effects of corporate programs and policies that employ this logic. It has done so by examining the unintended consequences of investing in The Girl Effect and, more specifically, the effects of its logic on educational practice in a specific ethnographic context in Brazil in an effort to illuminate a broader phenomenon. In this way, the study contributes to the ongoing efforts in the field of gender, education, and development to ensure educational programs and policies employ discursive, curricular, and pedagogic practices that seek to transform the persistently inequitable sociocultural and political-economic conditions that make poor girls and women of color disproportionately responsible for the well-being and futures of others.

Through instrumental programs and polices in girls' education, corporations are extending their power and influence over new bodies, institutions, and geographies. Yet, they are doing so without accountability to the girls, women, and communities they are supposedly serving and without addressing fundamental contradictions in their corporate business practices that often create or exacerbate conditions of vulnerability for girls and women, as the case of Nike, Inc.'s ongoing labor problems demonstrates. These contradictions in corporate social responsibility need to be further examined and addressed by those concerned with the misalignment of corporate power globally.

As an example of this, transnational women's and feminist organizations intensely responded to the most recent report by the UN Secretary-General's High-Level Panel (HLP) of Eminent Persons on the "Post 2015 Development Agenda" (UN, 2013). They were concerned with two aspects of particular relevance. First, they targeted the "privileged role the HLP report gives to the business and corporate sector in driving development" in contrast to "a very weak framework to hold corporations accountable" (Association for Women's Rights in Development, 2013, para. 16). The Centre for Economic and Social Rights (2013), in particular, critiqued the United Nation's facilitation of this by giving "undue prominence to an outdated vision of market/business-led development" (para. 12). Second, they noted that while gender equality was "more comprehensively addressed than under the current MDGs, it is still framed in a reductive and instrumental" (Centre for Economic and Social Rights, 2013, para. 8). The interrelationship between this framing of gender equality and the simultaneous prioritization of business for development by the United Nations and other international organizations facilitates the expanding power and influence of corporations in development, as this chapter has sought to illuminate.

The results of this study also have implications for more broadly understanding increasing corporate influence in education throughout the world. They necessitate that we begin to ask more forceful questions about how corporations are influencing the curriculum and pedagogy of schools and the lives, educations, and futures of young people globally. The movement of corporations into the sphere of education is occurring under and through the guise of benevolence. While some of the intentions and actions may indeed be benevolent, it is necessary to understand the intended and unintended consequences of these endeavors. The expansion of corporate power in education is closely related to the concomitant shrinking of public commitment to education and decreasing public regulation in education in many countries, including the United States, and as this occurs, marginalized individuals and communities are the first ones to be affected. As such, corporate influence in diverse areas of policy and practice in education must be more carefully studied and regulated in order to ensure educational equity for all.

Acknowledgments

The research and writing of this chapter was supported by a postdoctoral fellowship at the Haas Institute for a Fair and Inclusive Society at the University of California, Berkeley, and grants from the National Science Foundation, Fulbright-Hays, and the National Academy of Education/Spencer Foundation. I am grateful to Miguel Zamora, Patricia Baquedano-López, Ananya Roy, Zeus Leonardo, Paola Bacchetta, Cecilia Lucas, Hiba Bou Akar, Rebecca Alexandra, Emily Gleason, Erica Boas, Susan Woolley, and Genevieve Negron-Gonzales for supporting this study and for their feedback on this chapter. I would also like to thank the individuals and institutions that participated in my study for their generosity, time, and insights. All errors in the chapter are my own.

REFERENCES

Association for Women's Rights in Development. 2013. Some Reactions To The HLP Report On The Post-2015 Agenda From A Women's Rights Perspective, June 21. http://www.awid.org/eng/News-Analysis/Special-Focus-Post-2015-Development-Agenda/AWID-Analysis-and-Publications/AWID-Analysis-and-Publications/Some-Reactions-To-The-HLP-Report-On-The-Post-2015-Agenda-from-a-Women-s-Rights-Perspective

Acosta, Rodolfo, Annalee Good, Patricia Burch, and Mary Stewart. 2013. Devil is in the Details: Examining Equity Mechanisms in Supplemental Educational Services. In Gail Sunderman (ed.), *Charting Reform, Achieving Equity in a Diverse Nation*. Charlotte, NC: Information Age.

Bacchetta, Paola. 2007. Openings: Reflections on Transnational Feminist Alliances. Paper presented at the Conference Genre et Mondialisation, Ministère de la Recherche, Paris, France, March 23.

Ball, Stephen J. 2012. *Global Education Inc.: New Policy Networks and the Neoliberal Imaginary*. New York and London: Routledge.

Barber, Elizabeth. 2013. Some 300 Nike Workers Fired after Protest. *The Christian Science Monitor*, June 12. http://www.csmonitor.com/World/Asia-Pacific/2013/0612/Some-300-Cambodian-Nike-workers-fired-after-protests

Bhanji, Zahra. 2012. Transnational Private Authority in Education Policy in Jordan and South Africa: The Case of Microsoft Corporation. *Comparative Education Review*, vol. 56, no 2, pp. 300–19.

Browne, Katherine E., and B. Lynne Milgram (eds.). 2009. *Economics and Morality: Anthropological Approaches*. Lanham, MD: Altamira.

Burch, Patricia. 2009. *Hidden Markets: The New Education Privatization*. New York: Routledge.

Casey, Nicholas, and Raphael Pura. 2008. Nike Addresses Abuse Complaints at Malaysia Plant. *The Wall Street Journal*, August 4. http://online.wsj.com/article/SB12177920 4898108093.html

Centre for Economic and Social Rights. 2013. High Level Panel Recommendations Fall Short of the Human Rights Litmus Test, June 5. http://www.cesr.org/article.php?id=1484

Chant, Sylvia. 2006. Re-thinking the "Feminization of Poverty" in Relation to Aggregate Gender Indices. *Journal of Human Development*, vol. 7, no. 2, pp. 201–20.

Cortina, Regina, and Nelly P. Stromquist (eds.). 2000. *Distant Alliances: Promoting Education for Girls and Women in Latin America*. New York: Routledge Falmer.

Dolan, Catherine, and Dinah Rajak. 2011. Introduction: Ethnographies of Corporate Ethicizing. *Focaal*, vol. 2011, no. 60, pp. 3–8.

Eitel, Maria. 2010. "Day One at Davos: Girls, Economies, and Green Innovation." *Huffington Post*, January 28. http://www.huffingtonpost.com/maria-eitel/day-1-at-davos-girls-econ_b_440715.html

Ferguson, James. 1994. *The Anti-Politics Machine: "Development," Depoliticization, and Bureaucratic Power in Lesotho*. Minneapolis, MN: University of Minnesota Press.

Fiorina, Carley. 2007. Middle East World Economic Forum 2007, May 18. http://www.youtube.com/watch?v=Odw2oQLaMQ8

Goldman, Michael. 2005. *Imperial Nature: The World Bank and Struggle for Social Justice in the Age of Globalization*. New Haven, CT: Yale University Press.

Good, Annalee, Patricia Burch, Mary Stewart, Rodolfo Acosta, and Carolyn Heinrich. Forthcoming. Instruction Matters: Lessons From a Mixed-Method Evaluation of Out-of-School Time Tutoring Under No Child Left Behind. *Teachers College Record*.

Gramsci, Antonio. 1971. *Selections from Prison Notebooks*, edited by Quentin Hoare and Geoffrey Nowell Smith. London: Lawrence and Wishart.

Hart, Gillian. 2002. *Disabling Globalization: Places of Power in Post-Apartheid South Africa*. Berkeley: University of California Press.

Herz, Barbara, and Gene Sperling. 2004. *What Works in Girls' Education: Evidence and Policies from the Developing World*. Washington, DC: Council on Foreign Relations.

Heward, Christine, and Shelia Bunwaree. 1999. *Gender, Education and Development: Beyond Access to Empowerment*. London: Zed Books.

Hookway, James, and Anh Thu Nguyen. 2008. Vietnam Workers Strike: Factory Employees Seek Higher Wages. *The Wall Street Journal*, April 2. http://online.wsj.com/article/SB120704094273579965.html?mod=rss_whats_news_us&apl=y&r=127522

Htun, Mala. 2004. From "Racial Democracy" to Affirmative Action: Changing State Policy on Race in Brazil. *Latin American Research Review*, vol. 39, no. 1, pp. 60–89.

King, Elizabeth M., and M. Anne Hill. 1993. *Women's Education in Developing Countries: Barriers, Benefits, and Policies*. Published for the World Bank. Baltimore, MD: The Johns Hopkins University Press.

Knight, Phillip H. 1998. "Nike in the Global Economy." National Press Club, May 12. http://press.org/news-multimedia/videos/cspan/105477-1

Koyama, Jill. 2010. *Making Failure Pay: For-Profit Tutoring, High-Stakes Testing, and Public Schools*. Chicago: University of Chicago

Leonardo, Zeus. 2004. Critical Social Theory and Transformative Knowledge: The Functions of Criticism in Quality Education. *Educational Researcher*, vol. 33, no. 6, pp. 11–18.

Levine, Ruth, Cynthia Lloyd, Margaret Greene, and Caren Grown. 2008. Girls Count: A Global Investment & Action Agenda. Washington, DC: Center for Global Development.

Locke, Richard M. 2003. The Promise and Perils of Globalization: The Case of Nike. In Richard Schmalensee & Thomas A. Kochan (eds.), *Management: Inventing and Delivering Its Future* (pp. 39–70). Cambridge: Massachusetts Institute of Technology Press.

McElhaney, Kellie. 2008. *Just Good Business: The Strategic Guide to Aligning Corporate Responsibility and Brand*, Maximizing Business Value by Sharing Your Company's CSR Story. Williston, VT: Berrett-Koehler.

McCowan, Tristan. 2007. Expansion Without Equity: An Analysis of Current Policy on Access to Higher Education in Brazil. *Higher Education*, vol. 53, no. 5, pp. 579–98.

Moeller, Kathryn. Forthcoming-a. Searching for Adolescent Girls in Brazil: The Transnational Politics of Poverty in "The Girl Effect." *Feminist Studies*.

_____. Forthcoming-b. Proving "The Girl Effect": Corporate Knowledge Production and Educational Intervention. *International Journal of Education Development*.

Muirhead, Sophia A. 1999. *Corporate Contributions: The View from 50 Years*. New York: The Conference Board.

Nike Foundation. 2008. *The Girl Effect Media Kit.* http://www.nikefoundation.com/files/ The_Girl_Effect_Media_Kit.pdf.

Nike, Inc. 2008. Nike Foundation and Buffetts Join to Invest $100 Million in Adolescent Girls. Nike, Inc. Press Release. http://nikeinc.com/nike-foundation/news/nike-foundation-and-buffetts-join-to-invest-100-million-in-girls

_____. 2009. World Economic Forum Gives Adolescent Girls a Voice Globally. Nike, Inc. Press Release, January 30. http://nikeinc.com/nike-foundation/news/world-economic-forum-gives-adolescent-girls-a-voice-globally

_____. 2011. The Girl Effect. http://nikeinc.com/pages/the-girl-effect

Omi, Michael, and Howard A. Winant. 1994. *Racial Formation in the United States: From the 1960s to the 1990s*. London and New York City: Routledge.

Peck, Jamie. 2011. Global Policy Models, Globalizing Poverty Management: International Convergence or Fast Policy Integration? *Geography Compass*, vol. 5, no. 4, pp. 165–81.

Plank, David N. 1996. *The Means of Our Salvation: Public Education in Brazil, 1930-1995*. Boulder, CO: Westview Press.

Psacharopoulos, George, and Harry Patrinos. 2002. Returns to Investment in Education: A Further Update. World Bank Policy Research Working Paper 2881. Washington, DC: World Bank.

Rajak, Dinah. 2011. *In Good Company: An Anatomy of Corporate Social Responsibility*. Palo Alto, CA: Stanford University Press.

Robertson, Susan L., Karen Mundy, and Antoni Verger (eds.). 2012. *Public Private Partnerships in Education: New Actors and Modes of Governance in a Globalizing World*. Northampton: Edward Elgar Publishing.

Roy, Ananya. 2003. *City Requiem, Calcutta: Gender and the Politics of Poverty*. Minneapolis: University of Minnesota Press.

Schwittay, Anke. 2006. *Digital Citizens, Inc.: Producing Corporate Ethics, Flexible Networks and Mobile Entrepreneurs in the Global Marketplace*. Ph.D. Dissertation, University of California, Berkeley.

Summers, Lawrence. 1992. The Most Influential Investment. *Scientific American*, vol. 267, no. 2, p. 132.

Tembom, Mercy, and Lucia Fort. 2008. *Girls Education in the 21st Century: Gender Equality, Empowerment and Economic Growth*. Washington, DC: The International Bank for Reconstruction and Development/The World Bank.

Unterhalter, Elaine. 2007. *Gender, Schooling and Global Social Justice*. London and New York: Routledge.

United Nations. 2013. *A New Global Partnership: Eradicate Poverty and Transform Economies through Sustainable Develomment*. New York: United Nations Publications. http://www.un.org/sg/management/pdf/HLP_P2015_Report.pdf

van Fleet, Justin. 2011. A Global Education Challenge: Harnessing Corporate Philanthropy to Educate the World's Poor. Center for Universal Education, Working Paper 4. Washington, DC: The Brookings Institution.

Vavrus, Frances. 2003. *Desire and Decline: Schooling amid Crisis in Tanzania*. New York: Peter Lang.

World Bank. 1995. *Priorities and Strategies for Education: A World Bank Review.* Washington, DC: The International Bank for Reconstruction and Development/The World Bank.

_____. 2009. Adolescent Girls in Focus at the World Economic Forum. Gender and Development website. http://go.worldbank.org/QWPUUOPVY0

World Economic Forum. 2009. Davos Annual Meeting 2009—The Girl Effect on Development. http://www.youtube.com/watch?v=CQc7NZPjqBA

NOTES

1. The data presented in the rest of this section is drawn from Moeller (forthcoming-a).

2. This section is drawn from Moeller (forthcoming-a).

3. See Moeller (forthcoming-a) for more detail about who qualified for the program and how it complicates the universalized category of adolescent girl.

4. This section is drawn from Moeller (forthcoming-b).

Chapter Six

Globalization and Curriculum Inquiry: Performing Transnational Imaginaries

Noel Gough

The act of curriculum inquiry, for me, usually begins from a position informed by narrative theory and poststructuralism, one corollary of which is that I rarely feel any obligation to start a chapter by providing stipulative definitions. In this chapter, globalization is not a subject and/or object to be constrained by definition, but a focus for speculation—for generating rather than prescribing meanings. To paraphrase Deleuze and Guattari's (1977, p. 109) orientation to the subject of desire, the question posed by globalization is not "What does it mean?" but rather "How does it work?" I am interested in what curriculum workers (teachers, administrators, academics, researchers) *do* and *produce*, with the concept of globalization, and in working toward a defensible position on the concepts we create through our curriculum practices.

In the first version of this chapter (Gough, 2000), I quoted Henry and Taylor's (1997, p. 47) identification of two aspects of globalization—"the facts concerning transnational processes and communication" and "an increasing awareness of this reality"—and, as previously, I continue to focus here on the latter. There is, of course, no unitary "reality" of globalization, and I suggested that whatever "awareness" of globalization might then have been "increasing" was a somewhat inchoate apprehension of complex, multiple, proliferating, and immanent realities, overlaid (and further complexified) by our own reflexive "awareness" of the need to be—and to be *seen* to be—aware that globalization was, indeed, worthy of our attention. At that time I was drawn toward attending to those traces of globalization that Wilson and Dissanayake (1996) describe as a "transnational imaginary," namely, "the *as-yet-unfigured* horizon of contemporary cultural production by which national spaces/identities of political allegiance and economic regulation are being undone and imagined communities of modernity are being reshaped at the macropolitical (global) and micropolitical (cultural) levels of everyday existence" (p. 6, emphasis in original).

For those of us who identified ourselves as "reconceptualist" curriculum scholars in the wake of Schwab's (1969) immensely influential paper on curriculum as a discipline of "the practical,"[1] a key imaginary informing curriculum inquiry during the 1990s was Pinar, Reynolds, Slattery, and Taubman's (1995, p. 848) foreshadowing of the "*as-yet-unfigured* horizon" of curriculum inquiry in terms of generating and sustaining "complicated conversations":

Curriculum is an extraordinarily complicated conversation. Curriculum as institutionalized text is a formalized and abstract version of conversation, a term we usually use to refer to those open-ended, highly personal, and interest-driven events in which persons encounter each other. That curriculum has become so formalized and distant from the everyday sense of conversation is a profound indication of its institutionalization and bureaucratization. Instead of employing others' conversations to enrich our own, we "instruct" students to participate in others'—i.e. textbook authors'—conversations, employing others' terms to others' ends. Such social alienation is an inevitable consequence of curriculum identified with the academic disciplines as they themselves have been institutionalized and bureaucratized over the past one hundred years. Over the past twenty years the [reconceptualized] American curriculum field has attempted to "take back" curriculum from the bureaucrats, to make the curriculum field itself a conversation, and in so doing, work to understand curriculum.

More recently Pinar (with the encouragement and support of many colleagues worldwide, myself among them) has deliberately sought to make participation in the complicated conversations that constitute curriculum work more culturally inclusive by establishing the International Association for the Advancement of Curriculum Studies (IAACS) in 2000. Through its triennial conferences, online journal, *Transnational Curriculum Inquiry* (*TCI*) and associated publications (see, for example, Pinar, 2003; Trueit, Doll, Wang, and Pinar, 2003), IAACS has provided a number of forums for such conversations, which now have additional layers of complication and complexity by virtue of being conducted transnationally, transculturally and, at least to some extent, translinguistically. [2] The focus and scope of these transnational curriculum conversations and deliberations is captured in the following statement about *TCI* from its editorial policies web page:

> although much curriculum work continues to take place within national borders (often informed by governmental policies and priorities), processes of economic globalisation are blurring nation-state boundaries and destabilising national authority in curriculum decision making. Thus, *TCI* encourages contributions that examine the impact of globalisation on curriculum work in relation to national and international debates on such matters as human rights, social justice, democratisation, national, ethnic and religious identities, issues of gender and racial justice, the concerns of indigenous peoples, and poverty and social exclusion. A specific aim of *TCI* is to examine the interrelationships between local, national, regional and global spheres of curriculum work.

The work represented in *TCI*, together with the publications cited previously, constitutes efforts through the past decade to deliberately *configure* transnational imaginaries for curriculum inquiry that I characterized in the previous version of this chapter as *as-yet-unfigured*. As a result, this chapter differs somewhat from its predecessor, not least because I have been personally involved in the work of IAACS (as founding editor of *TCI*) and have also had experiences of working transnationally that have profoundly influenced the ethical standpoints from which I perform transnational curriculum work. One continuity between the two chapters is the persistence of economic restructuring—driven by the need for Australia to respond to international economic and technological trends—as the master discourse informing policy decisions at all levels of education. This discourse persisted through the 2000s and reached its zenith (or, depending upon one's standpoint, its nadir) in 2009, when the Australian Labor federal government took office proclaiming an "education revolution" that featured calls for a knowledge economy to be achieved through a national curriculum that focused on "the basics" and an expanded testing and accountability system. Australia, like a majority of Organization for Economic Cooperation and Development nations (and many other countries aspiring to a similar economic status) thus continues to participate in what Luke (2011) describes as a move toward a global curriculum settlement around educational basics and "new economy" competences that focuses almost exclusively on the measurable production of human capital. It pushes for interoperability and equity of exchange, but in so doing, it simply excludes other goals of democratic education—debates and learnings about civics, civility, language, and culture; about diverse and common cultural touch-stones; and about learning to live together—and it altogether ignores Indigenous lessons about the stewardship of cultures, the land, and the planet (p. 375).

In the previous version of this chapter, I focused on three facets of globalization in curriculum discourse, namely, (1) the sedimented history of global perspectives in school curricula, (2) popular expectations that globalizing technologies such as the Internet will transform schools and their curricula, and (3) the "internationalization" of the field of curriculum studies itself. In the remainder of this chapter, I will revisit the first and third of these foci of my previous inquiries, but extend my discussion of them in the light of more recent work and experiences. I have omitted further discussion of the transformative effects of the Internet and other globalizing technologies on schools and their curricula for two reasons: first, the literature of curriculum and schooling now seems to me to be saturated by references to the "digital revolution" to which I have little to add; second, these matters have ceased to be significant objects of my own inquiries. Rather, my attention has been focused more specifically on the effects of digitalization, the Internet, open access initiatives, trends toward multidisciplinary scholarship and related issues of academic "gatekeeping" on the activities and products of transnational curriculum workers (see Gough, 2012).

GLOBALIZATION IN THE CURRICULUM

The move that Luke describes has meant that many of the school curriculum programs and resources that dealt with global issues and concerns—such as the initiatives in development education, peace studies, and environmental education that I previously argued were part of the sedimented history of global perspectives in school curricula—have been marginalized or removed from school programs under pressure to privilege "the basics." However, it is not difficult to argue that world history during the past decade has provided ample incentives for education that focuses on "learning to live together." For example, the *World Yearbook of Education 2011* (Yates and Grumet, 2011a) brings a range of international contributors together to analyze and reflect on the ways in which curricula in their respective nations during the past decade have been shaped by events in the wider world.

The attacks by al-Qaeda upon the United States on September 11, 2001, are a significant point of reference for the editors and some contributing authors in the *Yearbook*. Thus, in the series editors' introduction we read, "Ten years on from 9/11, the idea of the world is in flux" (p. xvi), and Yates and Grumet's (2011b, p. 8) introductory chapter, "Curriculum In Today's World," recounts that they had originally intended to title the *Yearbook* "Curriculum in Vulnerable Times," noting in particular the association of the term *vulnerable* with the United States' awareness of its changed relationship with "the post-9/11 world." Some of the curriculum implications of al-Qaeda's attacks are examined in a chapter by Stoddard, Hess, and Mason Hammer, "The Challenges of Writing 'First Draft History': The Evolution of the 9/11 Attacks and their Aftermath in School Textbooks in the United States." I was not surprised by Stoddard, Hess, and Mason Hammer's U.S.-centrism but I was deeply disappointed that Yates and Grumet—curriculum scholars for whom I have the utmost respect—should be so lacking in cross-cultural sensitivity that they recognize September 11 as a significant anniversary only of events that took place in the United States in 2001. Referring to "9/11" or "September 11" without including the year 2001 tacitly participates in a form of U.S.-centrism and intellectual colonization signified by the privileging of an unmarked category (we see something similar in the informational domains of the Internet: U.S. addresses are unmarked, but every other country's is identified by the final term: au for Australia, sg for Singapore, za for South Africa, etc.). For Chileans, and many other people in nations that have suffered from U.S. political interventions, "9/11" is September 11, 1973, the day that Salvador Allende, then President of Chile (and the first Marxist leader of a nation to be democratically elected), was assassinated during the U.S.-backed military coup that unleashed the seventeen-year rule of the Pinochet regime during which it brutally and systematically violated civil liberties and human rights.

Culturally Inclusive Curriculum

Cultural inclusivity as a driver of change in schools and universities follows in part from the growth of export markets in educational services. In many Australian universities, "internationalization" is a code word for optimizing the institution's position in the global higher education market by increasing the enrollment of full-fee-paying overseas students, exporting coursework, establishing offshore and/or virtual campuses, and increasing student and staff participation in overseas exchanges. Market forces have made internationalization a user-friendly term among the senior executives of universities, attracting support for policies and programs that should already be in place in response to social and cultural diversity. Unfortunately, many academics and administrators still see cultural diversity as a difficulty—as a problem for someone else to solve—rather than as an invaluable social, cultural, economic, and educational resource. Thus, the challenges of internationalizing curricula reside, at least in part, in realizing the opportunities that policy imperatives provide for initiating and sustaining desirable changes in content, teaching methods, resources, and attitudes.

In the West, especially in nations such as the United States and Australia where there has been a resurgence of rightwing political power, cultural inclusivity often is criticized as (and/or co-opted by) "political correctness." In addition, many attempts to produce culturally inclusive curricula result in shallow or token multiculturalism that promotes cultural stereotypes by focusing on exotic cultural practices. The practical challenge is how to *perform* an ethics of inclusion rather than a politics of exclusion. For example, I argue that it is indefensible to teach any discipline solely from a U.S./Eurocentric standpoint, but many university and school teachers remain oblivious to how other civilizational perspectives on knowledge and knowledge production (such as Islam, Confucianism, Tantra, indigenous peoples, etc.) are treated in courses and texts—if they are treated at all. We Western professors are faced with the difficult task of attempting to decolonize the spaces of academic discourse that we access from our own privileged positions.

For much of my academic career I—like many of my colleagues—have struggled with the difficulties and complexities of reading, representing, and narrating cultural difference without fearing or fetishizing it, and of performing modes of inquiry that respond constructively to the effects of difference in mediating educational change. But I have become much more aware of the limits of my understandings in recent years, especially since 1998 when I began to participate in a number of research and teaching activities in southern Africa (see, for example, Gough, 2001, 2008; Gough and Gough, 2004).

My many years of living and working in Australia, Europe, and North America did not prepare me for the visibility and viciousness of the racism, sexism, patriarchy, homophobia, class and language biases, and ethnic nationalism that constitute everyday life for most South Africans. I expected the effects of institutionalized racism to persist, but I was surprised by the continued normalization of other forms of discrimination, such as the pervasive hostility toward women. Despite decades of schooling for girls, men's subjugation of women prevails in South Africa regardless of race and ethnicity (see Meier, 2002). Sexual harassment of women teachers is rife and, according to one study, schoolteachers perpetrate one-third of the reported rapes of girls under the age of fifteen (Galloway, 2002). Traces of gender discrimination appear in some unexpected places. For example, the faculty of education staff lounge at one prestigious (formerly whites-only) university in the Western Cape superficially epitomizes academic civility. It is a spacious, light-filled, tastefully furnished room in which faculty members gather at appointed times for morning or afternoon tea and polite conversation. But it was here that I overheard the predominantly white male professoriate exchanging "jokes" about wife beating (the "wife-beating Boer" is a stereotypical figure among Afrikaners, but violence against women is also endemic in black communities).

A visit to South Africa in August-September 2001 troubled me more than previous ones. At the time I left Australia, the so-called "*Tampa* affair" was headline news. A Norwegian cargo ship (the *Tampa*) had rescued more than three hundred asylum seekers, mainly from Afghanistan, when their boat capsized, but the Australian federal government, led by Prime Minister John Howard and Immigration Minister Phillip Ruddock, refused to accept them. My thoughts about the politics of difference informing the government's (in)actions in this situation were inflected by my previous experiences in Africa. I wondered if Howard's and Ruddock's responses would have been different if the *Tampa* had rescued white farmers fleeing from Zimbabwe rather than refugees from middle-eastern conflicts.

The UN World Conference Against Racism, Racial Discrimination, Xenophobia and Related Intolerance began in Durban on the day that I arrived in South Africa. My research methodology seminars and consultations with doctoral students at the University of Durban-Westville were interspersed with daily news of the conference's controversial proceedings, such as the protests that accompanied the United States' early withdrawal of its already low-level delegation. On this visit, I worked more closely than previously on problems and issues in students' own workplaces, many of which gave new meaning to questions of diversity, difference, and inclusion. A majority of the students were researching educational aspects of the HIV/AIDS pandemic, which accounts for more than 40 percent of all deaths in KwaZulu-Natal province. For example, one student was analyzing trends in the impact of HIV/AIDS on teacher attrition. Another was interpreting the educational experiences of AIDS orphans through life history research. We all struggled with questions about what an "inclusive" curriculum could possibly be in classrooms where up to 20 percent of learners were terminally ill with HIV/AIDS.

I was still in Durban on Tuesday September 11, 2001, and during the next few days I observed some of the different ways in which various constituents of multicultural South Africa reacted to the attacks on the World Trade Center and the Pentagon and to the U.S. government's response. For example, Cape Town's broadsheet, *The Cape Times*, devoted twelve pages to detailed descriptions and global economic analyses, whereas the tabloid *The Sowetan* (South Africa's biggest selling daily newspaper) had just three pages, most of which were filled with photographs. From page 4, *The Sowetan* was business-as-usual, which for most South Africans consists of everyday struggles for (and threats to) existence—HIV/AIDS, violent crime, access to safe drinking water, adequate sanitation and housing, and the seemingly endless work of repairing the social and economic fabric torn by decades of apartheid.

Many of the South Africans with whom I interacted in Durban, Cape Town, and Johannesburg in the following days paid little attention to the attacks. I was not surprised by their relative indifference, because few people who call the African continent home are ever very far away from terrors of a much greater durability and magnitude. For example, if we assume that annual deaths are evenly spread then, on September 11, 2001, 24,000 people died from hunger, 6,020 children were killed by diarrhea, and 2,700 children died from measles (see New Internationalist Collective, 2001, pp. 18–19). Sub-Saharan Africa suffers around three million deaths per year from malaria, a similar magnitude to deaths from HIV/AIDS but with two significant differences: most malaria deaths are children under age five, and malaria, unlike AIDS, can be cured or its effects significantly reduced to non–life-threatening status. Extrapolating from these figures, I conservatively estimate that if the United States suffered from the same enduring "terrors" as, say, sub-Saharan Africa, then its death toll would be equivalent to the events of September 11, 2001, being repeated *at least twice per week* for the foreseeable future.

When I returned to Australia on September 14, 2001, I found myself becoming increasingly irritable and impatient with what I saw as excessive public and media interest in the attacks on the Untied States. But I quickly realized that my irritation was not with others but with myself—with my frustration at the powerlessness I and my South African colleagues and students had felt in our deliberations about how best to do educational research in the circumstances they/we faced. What social, cultural, and educational norms do we need to disrupt to make the enduring terrors of HIV/AIDS and child rape seem as shocking and horrifying and unendurable as the loss of 2,988 lives in the United States on September 11, 2001? How might we as educators reduce the ignorance of "educated" citizens in nations such as Australia and the United States that helps to produce more than thirty thousand deaths per day from starvation, diarrhea, and preventable diseases such as malaria in the majority world?[3]

GLOBALIZATION LOCAL KNOWLEDGE TRADITIONS: THE "INTERNATIONALIZATION" OF CURRICULUM STUDIES

In the previous version of this chapter, I introduced the issue of the "internationalization" of curriculum studies by quoting the then-current guide for authors intending to submit manuscripts to the *Journal of Curriculum Studies*:

> All authors are asked to take account of the diverse audience of *Journal of Curriculum Studies.* Clearly explain or avoid the use of terms that might be meaningful only to a local or national audience. However, note also that *Journal of Curriculum Studies* does not aspire to be international in the ways that McDonald's restaurants or Hilton Hotels are "international"; we much prefer papers that, where appropriate, reflect the particularities of each higher education system.

This advice expresses a view of global/local relations that seems to resist "globalization"—understood as economic integration achieved through "free trade" in a deregulated global marketplace—while affirming "internationalism" (in the sense of promoting global peace, social justice, and well-being through intergovernmental cooperation and transnational social movements, agencies, and communities—such as the international community of curriculum scholars that produces and reads *Journal of Curriculum Studies*). (See Jones, 2000, for a discussion of the distinctions that may be made between globalization and internationalism.) My chapter sought to refine and amplify some of the tacit assumptions underlying this advice to authors, by considering ways in which diverse local knowledge traditions—as are still represented in at least some local and national curriculum policies and syllabuses, as well as in some "indigenous" approaches to curriculum studies per se—can be sustained and amplified transnationally while resisting the forms of cultural homogenization for which McDonald's and Hilton Hotels are emblematic.

The literature that I then found most useful in thinking about globalization and internationalization in relation to local knowledge production was, broadly speaking, that which Harding

(1998) calls post-Kuhnian and postcolonial science and technology studies, and more particularly the work of Turnbull (1997, 2000). Turnbull argues that all knowledge traditions are spatial in that they link people, sites, and skills. His approach is thus to recognize knowledge systems (including Western science) as sets of local practices so that it becomes possible to "decenter" them and develop a framework within which different knowledge traditions can be equitably compared rather than absorbed into an imperialist archive. The purpose of Turnbull's emphasis on analyzing knowledge systems comparatively in terms of spatiality and performance is to find ways in which diverse knowledge traditions can coexist rather than one displacing others. He argues that nourishing such diversity is dependent on the creation of "a third space, an interstitial space" in which local knowledge traditions can be "reframed, decentred and the social organisation of trust can be negotiated." The production of such a space is "crucially dependent" on "the re-inclusion of the performative side of knowledge":

> Knowledge, in so far as it is portrayed as essentially a form of representation, will tend towards universal homogenous information at the expense of local knowledge traditions. If knowledge is recognised as both representational and performative it will be possible to create a space in which knowledge traditions can be performed together. (Turnbull, 1997, pp. 560–61)

I still have no quarrel with Turnbull's analysis, and I continue to resist the homogenizing effects of globalization and internationalization in the field of curriculum studies by emphasizing the performative rather than the representational aspects of curriculum inquiry. That is, I still understand the "internationalization" of curriculum studies as a process of creating transnational "spaces" in which local knowledge traditions in curriculum inquiry can be performed together, rather than an attempt to translate local representations of curriculum into a universalized discourse. In the past decade, those of us who have been explicitly engaged in projects of internationalizing curriculum inquiry have addressed questions of *how* local knowledge traditions in curriculum inquiry can be performed together in a variety of ways.

For example, Pinar (2005) formulates his guiding question as follows: how do we provide opportunities for "complicated conversation" and "intellectual breakthrough" in the internationalization of curriculum studies? Pinar (2005) explores this question through three concepts that structure Axelrod's (1979) sociological study of intellectual breakthrough, namely, *thinking*, *individuality*, and *community*, and has conducted inquiries in Mexico (Pinar, 2011b), Brazil (Pinar, 2011a), South Africa (Pinar, 2010), and the United States (Pinar, 2013) that use these concepts to structure planned sequences of transnational curriculum conversations. However, my personal experiences of research, consultancy, and teaching in various nations/ regions—including Australia, China, Europe, Iran, New Zealand, and southern Africa—during the past decade and more have served to deepen my conviction that the "complicated conversation" to which Pinar refers is not yet complicated enough in the disciplines within which I work (principally curriculum studies, research methodology, environmental education, and science education). The international discourses of these disciplines are "complicated" complex, and diverse only within Western registers of difference in the sign systems of disciplined inquiry, principally because they remain dominated by scholars who work in Eurocentric scholarly traditions.

I have found Deleuze and Guattari's (1987) "geophilosophy"—a new critical language for analyzing thinking as flows or movements across space—particularly helpful in thinking about the unavoidable concept of *difference* (within and between nations/regions/cultures) and the opportunities and dilemmas for curriculum scholars that difference produces. Pinar (2005) alludes to the productivity of difference in his description of one of the phases of his research on the internationalization of curriculum studies:

One potential function of "internationalization"—being called by a foreigner to reflect upon one's own nationally and/or regionally-distinctive field, including one's own situatedness within it—is the dislocation of the native scholar-participant from his or her embeddedness in his or her local or domestic field. This opportunity for dislocation is occasioned by the call to study one's locality in conversation with foreigners in a foreign setting. Such dislocation functions to interpellate the individual scholar as a "stranger," certainly to foreigners and, to a lesser and relative extent, to one's fellow citizens. (pp. 13–14)

Here the concept of difference is marked by other concepts such as "native" and "foreigner," and I will now demonstrate how Deleuze and Guattari's approach differs from that of analytical philosophers by focusing more sharply on the concept of "foreigner." For Deleuze and Guattari (1994, p. 5), the philosopher's task is not to construe the concept of "foreigner" as an object of "contemplation, reflection and communication" but, rather, to ask how the concept of "foreigner" is (or can be) created. However, before I outline (my interpretation of) Deleuze and Guattari's response to this question, I suggest that their philosophy of concept creation might be more intelligible if we can first imagine some possible circumstances in which the concept of "foreigner" is *not* (and perhaps *cannot* be) created.

Le Guin (2000) imagines such circumstances in *The Telling*, a novel in her series of so-called "Hainish" stories. The common background for this series supposes that, at least half a million years ago, intelligent humanoids from the planet Hain spread across the galaxy and settled on nearly a hundred habitable worlds, including Terra (Earth), which were then left alone for many millennia. Le Guin's stories imagine that communication and travel between the worlds has resumed and that a loose interplanetary federation, the Ekumen, coordinates the exchange of goods and knowledge among the myriad of diverse cultures, religions, philosophies, sciences, and forms of governance that have evolved separately on the various planets. Representatives of the Ekumen travel to each planet when it is rediscovered and invite peoples of Hainish descent to participate in the federation, if they wish.

In *The Telling*, Sutty is a Terran Observer for the Ekumen, a language and literature specialist who travels to the planet Aka to continue studies initiated by the first Observers to make contact with the Akan people some seventy years earlier. Aka is a world with only one continent, so all of its peoples live on just one landmass. In the following passage, Sutty meditates on the significance of this difference from Terra—and its implications for the politics of identity—and, related to this, her conviction that traditional Akan spirituality is not a "religion":

religion as an institution demanding belief and claiming authority, religion as a community shaped by a knowledge of foreign deities or competing institutions, had never existed on Aka. Until, perhaps, the present time.

Aka's habitable lands were a single huge continent with an immensely long archipelago of its eastern coast. … Undivided by oceans, the Akans were physically all of one type with slight local variations. All the Observers had remarked on this, all had pointed out the ethnic homogeneity … but none of them had quite realised that among Akans *there were no foreigners*. There had never been any foreigners, until the ships from the Ekumen landed.

It was a simple fact, but one remarkably difficult for the Terran mind to comprehend. No aliens. No others, in the deadly sense of otherness that existed on Terra, the implacable division between tribes, the arbitrary and impassable borders, the ethnic hatreds cherished over centuries and millennia. "The people" here meant not *my* people, but people—everybody, humanity. "Barbarian" didn't mean an incomprehensible outlander, but an uneducated person. On Aka, all competition was familial. All wars were civil wars. (Le Guin, 2000, pp. 98–99)

We hardly need to be reminded of just how deadly our sense of otherness can be. The breadth of new antiterrorist legislation in nations such as Australia and the United States—coupled in Australia with the federal government's paranoid approach to "border protection" and treatment of asylum seekers that amounts to institutionalized racism—is eroding the foundations of respect for human rights in these countries and worldwide. *The Telling* is testimony to the *possibility* of thinking what many humans think is unthinkable, such as imagining a world without "foreigners." What would social and educational policy look like if we too assumed that "the people" meant "everybody, humanity"? Le Guin demonstrates that it is possible to think differently about identity and community, and related questions of inclusion and exclusion, without ever underestimating the immense difficulty of doing so, and the even greater difficulty of bringing new imaginaries into effect. Deleuze and Guattari (1994) show us how to perform philosophy in ways that can produce similar effects to Le Guin's storytelling arts, that is, to create a perspective through which the world takes on a new significance: "The task of philosophy when it creates concepts … is always to extract an event from things and beings, always to give them a new event: space, time, matter, thought, the possible as events" (p. 33).

For Deleuze and Guattari (1994, pp. 35–36), *doing* philosophy means creating concepts on planes of immanence: "Philosophy is a constructivism, and constructivism has two qualitatively different aspects: the creation of concepts and the laying out of a plane." Every concept is a finite multiplicity. For example, our concept of "foreigner" involves many other concepts, such as ethnic/racial difference and territorial divisibility. Neither singular nor universal concepts are possible because every concept has a "history" and a "becoming"—a history of its traversal of previous constellations of concepts, and a becoming as it joins with other concepts within similar or contiguous fields of problems.

As I interpret Deleuze and Guattari (1994, p. 37), the proposition that every concept has a history and a becoming is not only a matter of concepts developing within various and changing social and historical contexts but also recognizes that concepts have *acontextual* and *atemporal* features. Every concept inaugurates the plane of immanence of the concept, which is "neither a concept nor the concept of all concepts" but, rather, is a preconceptual field presupposed within the concept, "not in the way that one concept may refer to others but in the way that concepts themselves refer to nonconceptual understanding" (Deleuze and Guattari, 1994, p. 40). Deleuze and Guattari (1994, p. 37, my emphasis) argue that the "plane of immanence is not a concept that is or can be thought but rather *the image thought gives itself of what it means to think, to make use of thought, to find one's bearings in thought*." For example: "in Descartes [the plane of immanence] is a matter of a subjective understanding implicitly presupposed by the 'I think' as first concept; in Plato it is the virtual image of an already-thought that doubles every actual concept" (Deleuze and Guattari, 1994, pp. 40–41). The plane of immanence is inaugurated within the concept (that which is created) but it is clearly distinct from the concept (because it expresses the uncreated, that which "thought just does"). The plane of immanence thus expresses the nonconceptual that is *both* internal to *and* "outside" the concept. Deleuze and Guattari (1994, p. 36) characterize this complex and paradoxical relationship as follows: "concepts are events, but the plane is the horizon of events, the reservoir or reserve of purely conceptual events." By way of example, MacKenzie (1996) suggests:

> "the present happens" because there is a "past-becoming-future horizon" presupposed within it. Without a presupposed limitless expanse of time we could not talk of the present. In the same way, without the presupposed plane of immanence concepts would never "happen." Moreover, as the present would never change without the existence of an "eternal horizon" presupposed within it, without the institution of the plane—that which thought "just does"—concepts would never

change. The fact that concepts institute this "unthinkable" plane at their core engenders the movement of concepts; their history and becoming. (p. 1236)

In a similar way, we could say that the concept of "foreigner" happens for us because there is
an "us-becoming-other" horizon presupposed within it. Neither the concept nor the preconceptual field happened for the Akans until they created it to make sense of the existence of the
Ekumen.

Deleuze and Guattari's geophilosophy enlarges the field of concepts and signs that we can
deploy to account for difference, which in turn multiplies the possibilities for analyses, critiques, and interventions. Such a broadening of our repertoires of representation and performance might be particularly useful when we encounter *remarkable* difference (difference that
puzzles, provokes, surprises, or shocks us)—as we almost certainly will as transnational
curriculum conversations become more widespread, inclusive, and complicated/complex.
Gottlieb (2002) provides one example of such remarkable difference in her ethnographic study
of the Beng villagers in Africa's Ivory Coast. She focuses on the Beng belief that children are
reincarnated souls from whom their parents must learn lessons of the afterlife. Mediated by
local seers, Beng parents understand education to be a listening process through which they
discover their child's hidden knowledge and capture the essence and destiny of his or her soul.
Parents assume that their children are maximally multilingual at birth, because they knew all
languages in the afterlife, but that they lose this multilingual capacity around the age of three.
If we can say that the Beng people have a concept of "language education," then (in our terms)
it is a reactualization process of selecting the "right" channels that will be useful for communicating with others in this new life; it is a process of *forgetting* many languages, not "learning"
one.

How should we (the "we" who belong to international organizations such as IAACS or
who otherwise work transnationally) respond to such a remarkable difference between concepts of education? Some might seek to "explain" the difference in terms of social and
historical contexts. Some will invoke cultural relativism. I must admit that my first response
was to welcome the Beng as a resource for teaching in my curriculum studies courses, using
their understanding of learning-as-forgetting as a defamiliarization strategy. Defamiliarization
(often rendered as "to make the familiar strange, and the strange familiar"[4]) assumes that the
tactic of surprise may serve to diminish distortions and help us to recognize our own precon-
ceptions, and it is a recurrent feature of artistic manifestos and of creative brainstorming
sessions in many fields (that is, defamiliarization is potentially a tool for intellectual breakthrough).

But these sorts of responses do nothing in this world for Beng children. One of the apparent
consequences of Beng parents' belief that children are reincarnated souls is that they pay scant
attention to their children's material needs (the Beng do not fear the afterlife) and infant
mortality rates are horrendous even by African norms: fewer than 20 percent of Beng children
survive beyond the age of five years.

Deleuze and Guattari's geophilosophy cannot tell us precisely how we might resolve the
dilemmas produced by this encounter with difference, but I am prepared to argue that they
offer a more ethically defensible approach to seeking such a resolution than conventional
Western philosophies that repress difference in the name of what is "right" (and righteous).
For Deleuze and Guattari (1994): "Philosophy does not consist in knowing and is not inspired
by truth. Rather, it is categories like Interesting, Remarkable, or Important that determine its
success or failure" (p. 82). Their philosophy is a creative and hopeful practice whose purpose
is not to be "right" in an abstract or universal sense but to contribute to the quality of "real"
lives. Deleuze (1994, p. xx) insists that concepts "should intervene to resolve local situations"

and consistently argues that (Western) philosophy has been aligned too closely with dominant interests in promoting identity and sameness and marginalizing difference:

> The history of philosophy has always been the agent of power in philosophy, and even in thought. It has played the repressor's role. … Philosophy is shot through with the project of becoming the official language of a Pure State. The exercise of thought thus conforms to the goals of the real State, to the dominant meanings and to the requirements of the established order. (Deleuze and Parnet, 1987, p. 13)

Thus, if philosophy is to succeed in doing important things (such as reducing infant mortality rates), it must also seek to do interesting and remarkable things by creating novelty and difference. If we think it is important *both* to save Beng children's lives *and* to conserve Beng cultural traditions, we need to invent ways in which our different knowledge traditions can coexist rather than displacing "theirs" by "ours." Imagining that the Beng, too, create concepts on planes of immanence respects our differences and offers us an ethically defensible reper-toire of dispositions and conceptual tools that we might be able to use in building a space created through the process that Turnbull (2000, p. 228) describes as "negotiation between spaces, where contrasting rationalities can work together but without the notion of a single transcendent reality" (p. 228). Elsewhere, Turnbull (1997, p. 560; also see Gough, 2003) refers to the space he envisages as "a third space, an interstitial space." In Deleuze's (1987, p. 8) thought, the dynamics of becoming are such that any given multiplicity, such as the constella-tion of concepts that structure the Beng view of learning, "changes in nature as it expands its connections." This gives me hope that a new multiplicity, created in a "third space" in which Beng people negotiate with others, might include (say) a concept of children as reincarnated souls that is *not* incommensurate with caring for their health.

The idea of a presupposed plane of immanence generates many other new questions and possibilities for complicated conversation around concepts such as "intellectual breakthrough" in the internationalization of curriculum studies, and the many other concepts that constitute its multiplicity, including those that Axelrod (1979) identifies: "thinking," "individuality," and "community." We can ask questions such as: what preconceptual fields are presupposed within the concept of intellectual breakthrough in different nations/cultures? What are the acontextual and atemporal features of intellectual breakthrough in different nations/cultures? What presupposed horizon of events permits concepts such as "thinking," "individuality," and "community" to "happen" when and where they do?

Zdebik (2003) offers a way to think metaphorically about the relationship between con-cepts and planes that might be useful for some purposes:

> In order to describe the plane of immanence, Deleuze and Guattari must simultaneously describe the concept. The plane of immanence and the concept mutually define each other. It is as if the plane of immanence is an invisible mental landscape that can only be seen through the concepts occupying it. It is a place that becomes noticeable through the objects that occupy this space. It is like cities that appear to an airplane flying over dark continents when, after night has fallen, the lights come on.
>
> From the height of this plane we can map out the geography of the plane of immanence, because geography [quoting Deleuze and Guattari, 1994, p. 96] "is not merely physical and human but mental, like a landscape." (Zdebik, 2003, p. 142)

What other generative metaphors might help us to reveal the "invisible mental landscapes" of curriculum studies and stories in various nations/regions? What "invisible mental landscapes" do (or might) curriculum scholars and/or environmental educators and/or philosophers of education who work transnationally share? These are significant questions because, as Deleuze and Guattari (1994) argue, modes of intellectual inquiry need to account for the planes of immanence upon which they operate. Following this line of argument, Curthoys (2001) suggests that "conceptual thinking needs to retain a multifarious 'sense' of what it is doing, the kinds of problems it addresses and the cultural context it seeks to influence and is influenced by." Curthoys' perspective is particularly useful for my purposes because he deploys terms and tropes that resonate with IAACS's mission to support complicated scholarly conversations across national and regional borders:

> The plane of immanence is the complex ongoing conversation, the dilemma, the received history of fraught questions that one intuitively recognises as a formative background for one's own critical enunciations. In other words, the plane of immanence is the admission that thought is not simply a contemplative relation to a secure object of knowledge, nor a solution to a problem, but rather an affirmation of all that is problematic and historically negotiated. As an historically inflected thinking, the plane of immanence turns one's focus towards the cultural competency required for addressing a set of issues and the historically productive conditions of transformative thinking.[5]

Seeking the "productive conditions of transformative thinking" clearly resonates with Pinar's (2005) question of how to provide opportunities for "intellectual breakthrough" in the internationalization of curriculum studies. Furthermore, the preamble to the IAACS Constitution states that: "at this historical moment and for the foreseeable future, curriculum inquiry occurs within national borders, often informed by governmental policies and priorities, responsive to national situations. Curriculum study is, therefore, nationally distinctive" (http://iaacs.ca). If we restate this assertion in Deleuze and Guattari's terms, we could say that curriculum inquiry presently operates on numerous nationally distinctive "planes of immanence" (or, in Zdebik's terms, "invisible mental landscapes"). If we also agree with the founders of the IAACS who "do not dream of a worldwide field of curriculum studies mirroring the standardization and uniformity the larger phenomenon of globalization threatens" (http://iaacs.ca), then it follows that the internationalization of curriculum studies should not create concepts that inaugurate a single transnational plane of immanence (or posit a single "invisible mental landscape" in which transnational curriculum inquiry takes place) but, rather, will be a continuous process enacted by curriculum scholars worldwide who have the capacities and competencies to *change planes*. In this context, "changing planes" refers both to movements between one plane of immanence and another, and/or to transformations of one's own plane (Gough, 2007, 2009).

NOT A CONCLUSION

I share Kappeler's (1986) perspective on concluding an essay:

> I do not really wish to conclude and sum up, rounding of the argument so as to dump it in a nutshell on the reader. A lot more could be said about any of the topics I have touched upon. ... I have meant to ask the questions, to break the frame. ... The point is not a set of answers, but making possible a different practice. (p. 212)

Accordingly, I ask only that readers contemplate the different practices for transnational curriculum inquiry that the imaginaries performed previously might generate.

REFERENCES

Axelrod, Charles David. 1979. *Studies in Intellectual Breakthrough*. Amherst, MA: The University of Massachusetts Press.

Curthoys, Ned. 2001. Future Directions for Rhetoric—Invention and Ethos in Public Critique. *Australian Humanities Review,* April. http://www.australianhumanitiesreview.org/archive/Issue-April-2001/curthoys.html

Deleuze, Gilles. 1994. *Difference and Repetition* (Paul Patton, trans.). New York: Columbia University Press.

_____, and Félix Guattari. 1977. *Anti-Oedipus: Capitalism and Schizophrenia* (Robert Hurley, Mark Seem, and Helen R. Lane, trans.). New York: The Viking Press.

_____, and Félix Guattari . 1987. *A Thousand Plateaus: Capitalism and Schizophrenia* (Brian Massumi, trans.). Minneapolis: University of Minnesota Press.

_____, and Félix Guattari . 1994. *What is Philosophy?* (Graham Burchell and Hugh Tomlinson, trans.). London: Verso.

_____, and Claire Parnet. 1987. *Dialogues* (Hugh Tomlinson and Barbara Habberjam, trans.). New York: Columbia University Press.

Galloway, Michelle Rotchford. 2002. Rape in Schools a "Substantial Public Health Problem" in South Africa. *Medical Research Council of South Africa AIDS Bulletin*, vol. 11, no. 1, pp. 4–5.

Gottlieb, Alma. 2002. Deconstructing the Notion of Education: A View from West Africa. In Liora Bresler and Alexander Ardichvili (eds.), *Research in International Education: Experience, Theory, and Practice* (pp. 83–101). New York: Peter Lang.

Gough, Annette, and Noel Gough. 2004. Environmental Education Research in Southern Africa: Dilemmas of Interpretation. *Environmental Education Research*, vol. 10, no. 3, pp. 409–24.

Gough, Noel. 2000. Globalization and Curriculum Inquiry: Locating, Representing, and Performing a Transnational Imaginary. In Nelly P. Stromquist and Karen Monkman (eds.), *Globalization and Education: Integration and Contestation across Cultures* (pp. 77–98). Lanham, MD: Rowman & Littlefield Publishers Inc.

_____. 2001. Learning from *Disgrace*: A Troubling Narrative for South African Curriculum Work. *Perspectives in Education*, vol. 19, no. 1, pp. 107–26.

_____. 2003. Thinking Globally in Environmental Education: Implications for Internationalizing Curriculum Inquiry. In William F. Pinar (ed.), *International Handbook of Curriculum Research* (pp. 53–72). Mahwah NJ: Lawrence Erlbaum Associates.

_____. 2007. Changing Planes: Rhizosemiotic Play in Transnational Curriculum Inquiry. *Studies in Philosophy and Education*, vol. 26, no. 3, pp. 279–94.

_____. 2008. Narrative Experiments and Imaginative Inquiry. *South African Journal of Education*, vol. 28, no. 3, pp. 335–49.

_____. 2009. Becoming Transnational: Rhizosemiosis, Complicated Conversation, and Curriculum Inquiry. In Marcia McKenzie, Heesoon Bai, Paul Hart, and Bob Jickling (eds.), *Fields of Green: Restorying Culture, Environment, and Education* (pp. 67–83). Cresskill, NJ: Hampton Press.

_____. 2012. W(h)ither Gatekeeping? Academic Publishing and Peer Review in Complex Networked Systems. *ACCESS: Critical Perspectives on Communication, Cultural & Policy Studies*, vol. 31, no. 1, pp. 35–41.

Harding, Sandra. 1998. Multiculturalism, Postcolonialism, Feminism: Do They Require New Research Epistemologies? *Australian Educational Researcher*, vol. 25, no. 1, pp. 37–51.

Henry, Miriam, and Sandra Taylor. 1997. Globalisation and National Schooling Policy in Australia. In Bob Lingard and Paige Porter (eds.), *A National Approach to Schooling in Australia? Essays on the Development of National Policies in Schools Education* (pp. 45–59). Canberra: Australian College of Education.

Jones, Phillip W. 2000. Globalization and Internationalism: Democratic Prospects for World Education. In Nelly P. Stromquist and Karen Monkman (eds.), *Globalization and Education: Integration and Contestation across Cultures* (pp. 27–42). Lanham MD: Rowman & Littlefield.

Kappeler, Susanne. 1986. *The Pornography of Representation*. Cambridge, MA: Polity Press.

Le Guin, Ursula K. 2000. *The Telling*. New York: Harcourt.

Luke, Allan. 2011. Generalizing Across Borders: Policy and the Limits of Educational Science. *Educational Researcher*, vol. 40, no. 8, pp. 367–77.

MacKenzie, Iain. 1996. Deleuze and Guattari's Poststructuralist Philosophy. In Patrick Dunleavy and James Stanyer (eds.), *Contemporary Political Studies 1996* (pp. 1234–41). Exeter: Political Studies Association.

Meier, Eileen. 2002. Child Rape in South Africa. *Pediatric Nursing*, vol. 28, no. 5, pp. 532–35.

New Internationalist Collective. 2001. Twin Terrors: The Facts. *New Internationalist*, vol. 340 (November), pp. 18-19.

Pinar, William F. (ed.). 1975. *Curriculum Theorizing: the Reconceptualists*. Berkeley, CA: McCutchan.

_____. (ed.). 2003. *International Handbook of Curriculum Research*. Mahwah, NJ: Lawrence Erlbaum Associates.

_____. 2005. Complicated Conversation: Occasions for "Intellectual Breakthrough" in the Internationalization of Curriculum Studies. *Journal of Curriculum Studies* [Taiwan], vol. 1, no. 1, pp. 1–26.

_____. (ed.). 2010. *Curriculum Studies in South Africa: Intellectual Histories, Present Circumstances*. New York: Palgrave Macmillan.

_____. (ed.). 2011a. *Curriculum Studies in Brazil: Intellectual Histories, Present Circumstances*. New York: Palgrave Macmillan.

_____. (ed.). 2011b. *Curriculum Studies in Mexico: Intellectual Histories, Present Circumstances*. New York: Palgrave Macmillan.

_____. (ed.). 2013. *Curriculum Studies in the United States: Present Circumstances, Intellectual Histories*. New York: Palgrave Macmillan.

_____, William M. Reynolds, Patrick Slattery, and Peter Taubman. 1995. *Understanding Curriculum: An Introduction to the Study of Historical and Contemporary Curriculum Discourses*. New York: Peter Lang.

Schwab, Joseph J. 1969. The Practical: A Language for Curriculum. *School Review*, vol. 78, no. 1, pp. 1–23.

Shklovsky, Victor. 1965. Art as Technique (1917). In Lee T. Lemon and Marion J. Reis (eds. and trans.), *Russian Formalist Criticism: Four Essays* (pp. 3–24). Lincoln: University of Nebraska Press.

Trueit, Donna, William E. Doll, Hongyu Wang, and William F. Pinar (eds.). 2003. *The Internationalization of Curriculum Studies: Selected Proceedings from the LSU [Louisiana State University] Conference 2000*. New York: Peter Lang.

Turnbull, David. 1997. Reframing Science and Other Local Knowledge Traditions. *Futures*, vol. 29, no. 6, pp. 551–62.

_____. 2000. *Masons, Tricksters and Cartographers: Comparative Studies in the Sociology of Scientific and Indigenous Knowledge*. Amsterdam: Harwood Academic Publishers.

Wilson, Rob, and Wimal Dissanayake (eds.). 1996. *Global/Local: Cultural Production and the Transnational Imaginary*. Durham and London: Duke University Press.

Yates, Lyn, and Madeleine Grumet (eds.). 2011a. *World Yearbook of Education 2011—Curriculum in Today's World: Configuring Knowledge, Identities, Work and Politics*. Abingdon and New York: Routledge.

_____ and Madeleine Grumet. 2011b. Curriculum in Today's World: Configuring Knowledge, Identities, Work and Politics. In Lyn Yates & Madeleine Grumet (eds.), *World Yearbook of Education 2011—Curriculum in Today's World: Configuring Knowledge, Identities, Work and Politics* (pp. 3–13). Abingdon and New York: Routledge.

Zdebik, Jakub. 2003. The Archipelago and the Diagram. *Journal for the Arts, Sciences, and Technology*, vol. 1, no. 2, pp. 141–46.

NOTES

1. Reconceptualist curriculum scholars shifted the emphasis of curriculum studies from theorizing curriculum *development* toward generating theoretical frames for *understanding* curriculum (see Pinar, 1975).

2. *TCI* has published and reviewed articles written in Chinese, Portuguese, French, and Turkish (see http://ojs.library.ubc.ca/index.php/tci/issue/archive); (accessed 19 January 2014).

3. I prefer the term "majority world" to the largely inaccurate, outdated, and/or non-descriptive terms "developing" nations, "Third World," and global "South." Since the early 1990s, the communications cooperative New Internationalist (www.newint.org) has used "majority world" to describe this global community by reference to what it is, rather than what it lacks, and also to draw attention to the disproportionate impact that the Group of Eight countries—which represent a relatively small fraction of humankind—have on the majority of the world's peoples.

4. This phrase has been attributed to the German poet Novalis (1772–1801, aka Friedrich von Hardenberg). The concept of defamiliarization is found among other Romantic theorists such as Wordsworth and Coleridge and is also closely associated with Surrealism. Russian formalist Victor Shklovsky (1917/1965) introduced the concept of *ostranenive* (literally "making strange") to literary theory.

5. Seeking the "productive conditions of transformative thinking" clearly resonates with Pinar's (2005) question of how to provide opportunities for "intellectual breakthrough" in the internationalization of curriculum studies.

Chapter Seven

Globalization and the Social Construction of Reality: Affirming or Unmasking the "Inevitable"?

Catherine A. Odora Hoppers

My intention in this article is to invite the reader into my world and share what concerns me deeply, and what we are doing about it—to bring the reader to look with me and perhaps see what I have seen, and experience what many continue to experience.

From hanging onto those traditions that curse emotion and intuition, the citizens are raising their heads to ventilations and to the partially opened windows of the laboratory, and filling the rooms with an incessant din: WE ALSO MATTER! Anita Roddick (2001) has stated that progress, development, and an end to poverty have been cited as the pot of gold at the end of the globalization rainbow. Yet time and time again, the needs, the aspirations, and varying cultures of the developing world are blatantly ignored to open up new opportunities for the developed world and the firms they back, to exploit relationships in the south. Apart from the indignity suffered and being suffered in this appalling game, the environment is also suffering, creating a time bomb that will explode with catastrophic results.

Nodding appreciatively at Hazel Henderson (1996), it can be said that we need to adopt the voice of metaphysics in order to look into the planetary cupboard with a transdisciplinary lens, and see how economics has become a substitute for thought. We need human-centered perspectives, and organically based thought, emerging from the exercise of sympathy and empathy, if we are to diagnose and create an adequate prognosis out of the Midas curse that continues to bedevil us and go beyond.

PUTTING A FORENSIC EYE ON GLOBALIZATION

It is possible today to think of globalization in terms of intensifying information and technology networks, corporate mergers, transnational capital, and a proliferation of group-level interactions that range from intense professional networks using the Internet, to chat groups and online education, trade, and exchange. To some, this technology-driven superhighway system represents the ultimate level of human communication. Where human contact has failed, apparently the Web will succeed. Where national state systems have failed to bring peace, maybe transnational capital and globalization will succeed. Ostensibly, the temptation is to extend the optimism to issues that have so easily fallen through the cracks of capitalist forms of organization: gender and indigenous perspectives.

If globalization denotes something extensive, comprehensive, inclusive, universal, and "indiscriminate," then indeed, we should all be beside ourselves with joy and bliss at its heralding, for, at last, our journey in search of justice, peace, human rights, equity, and equality should all surely be at its end. Memory, hard and usually quite painful, however, warns us to meet globalization processes at best halfway, at worst to be wary of the nature of the beast.

This chapter therefore sets out the parameters for a cautionary and critical approach to indulging in the globalization mania by invoking, from an African perspective, crucial tenets of reality that preceded and that continue to undergird this phenomenon. In terms of education, the chapter focuses on a critique at the level of the model of education, rather than details of everyday practice. It argues that globalization is essentially about affirming the locus of the creation and policing of rules by which verbal speech and written statements are made meaningful as being geographically located in the northwest Atlantic. It is also this corpus of geopolitically situated "reality creation and maintenance" mechanisms that requires for its survival a consistent stifling of debates on alternative models.

For educationists especially, positive or potentially positive aspects of globalization are quickly complicated by the role of education in what Berger and Luckmann (1967, p. 124) articulate as the "maintenance of the symbolic universe," especially in a context in which diversity, and the right to "be," is rhetorically being affirmed but is continually under threat from the unresolved issues of Western hegemony. It is maintained that globalization is part of a subtle, calculated technology of subjection (Giddens, 1995) that consolidates and cements the gains of historical direct violence of colonial conquest, the structural violence of global economic relations, and the cultural or epistemic violence of discourses of concealment (Galtung, 1996; Odora Hoppers, 1998b).

The Problem: The West and the "Other"

As globalization penetrates the big and small spaces of human life with a vengeance, and amnesia sets in undisturbed, reminders of the tenets undergirding the relations in this "global family" get harder to subject to rigorous scrutiny. On the other hand, it gets harder to simply wish away. With talk of the information superhighway, global competitiveness, and untrammeled penetration of the structural adjustment programs in the poor countries, the social contract on a global scale remains the political scientist's emphasis upon regime formation, treaties, and international coalition formation (Bergesen, 1994), within which education sits blissfully as the tool for national development. Everywhere in "structurally adjusting" Africa, there is talk of reforming education, a reform talk that is a euphemism for tailoring education policy to fit with the requirements of neoliberalism.

In attempting to unmask these discourses, practices, and assumptions for whatever they are worth, it needs to be stated that for the vast majority of the countries as they exist today, the international system continues to reaffirm and reproduce the inequities that are so necessary for that limited and provincial version of progress and understanding of development not only to be writ larger, but to be thoroughly assimilated and routinized on a world scale. In most discourses surrounding global development, there is a total obfuscation of the fundamental element of force and power and especially the political and economic dominance of the European core (read Western powers) over the rest of the world (Bergesen, 1994).

The core struggle as captured, interestingly enough, in Huntington's thesis, is that at the end of the twentieth century, the concept of universal civilization helped justify Western cultural dominance over other societies and the need for those societies to ape Western practices and institutions. Universalism, he states, is the "ideology of the West in confrontation with non-Western cultures" (Huntington, 1996, p. 66).

The West is attempting, and will continue to attempt, to sustain its pre-eminent position and defend its interests by defining those interests as the interests of the "world community." That phrase has become the euphemistic collective noun replacing the "Free World" to give global legitimacy to actions reflecting the interests of the United States and the other Western powers. The West is, for instance, attempting to integrate the economies of non-Western societies into a global economic system that it dominates. Through the International Monetary Fund (IMF) and other international economic institutions, the West promotes its economic interests and imposes on other nations the economic policies it thinks appropriate (Huntington, 1996).

The imposition is also accompanied by a near schizophrenic urge to monitor and keep the barbarians in check. In an article in *Le Monde Diplomatique*, Phillippe Rivière (1999) reviews the immense U.S.$26.7 billion annual intelligence budget the United States alone at that time maintained, which, in conjunction with global technology and other Western powers, enables them to tap into, scrutinize, sort, select, and analyze hundreds of thousands the world's telephones, faxes, and electronic mail as a matter of routine. This definitely has more to do with surveillance than with protecting individual liberties.

Put in another way, it can be argued that what lingers on is apparently patriarchy's problem with alien men, the "Other" of which Miller (1991) has written. Knowing well that conquest and violence has characterized the history of the relationship between the West and other parts of the Third World, one is forced to reflect on the tension—both latent and overt—on the part of the conqueror, as to what exactly to do with the conquered.

> From its inception, patriarchy had a fundamental problem: how to deal with men not covered by the bonds of filial relationship. Patriarchy had defined humanity in terms of genealogical descent, and society in terms of relationships between the descendants of common ancestors. Persons with the same genealogical heritage were protected by a set of reciprocal rights, obligations and duties, constituting a covenant of kinship. Conversely, in patriarchal terms, non-kins were non-persons. They lacked genealogical pedigree and protection. They were aliens from rival lineages. They were outside the covenant of kinship. (Miller, 1991, p. 121)

The problem for patriarchy then was, what to do with the conquered lineage?

The *first* practice that developed was for the triumphant lineage to *kill all the members of the defeated lineage*: men, women, and children. This was to ensure double death: death of the individual members, and death of the lineage itself, with their descent line permanently cut. The dead lineage had a history but no future. For while the conquered men's potential to contribute to the wealth of the lineage could not be overlooked, their potential for disrupting the structure of power was real. The *second* practice in the ancient world was to *make eunuchs of male captives*. The original eunuch was a captive whose death sentence had been commuted. The male captive's life could be spared if his manhood was disposed of. Castration of all the vanquished males would achieve the same outcome as killing all the captives, or the men, in that it achieved the genealogical death of the defeated lineage while allowing the vanquished men to live. The *third* method was *slavery*. Patterson (cited in Miller, 1991, p. 127) defines slavery as the permanent, violent domination of natally alienated and (and thus) dishonored persons. The permanent loss of connection with one's lineage dishonored the individuals so affected and made them powerless and defenseless in lineage society. They were socially dead. The institution of slavery itself was based on two principles: marginality and integration. Slavery was institutionalized marginality, and at the same time slavery was institutionalized reintegration of natally alienated persons into the lineage system (Miller, 1991, pp. 130–34).

Miller's analysis is valuable for the insights it provides in understanding the annihilation strategies used in the period following the colonial conquest of Africa, in modernization, and in globalization strategies.

Reification of Development Models of Old

Plainly put, globalization silences the debates over development models, over the notion of the Third World by routinizing Western hegemony and dressing it up as a new ubiquitous force in global development. The tolerated conception of development is the one in which non-Western societies are carefully theoretically incorporated into the supposedly linear progress developmental paradigm. Essentially a discourse of power and subjugation, it is constituted in a context of present global relations as a recipe for social change, stating as matter of fact, what was once a matter of debate.

> The central thesis of developmentalism is that social change occurs according to a pre-established pattern, the logic and direction of which are known. Privileged knowledge of the direction of change is claimed by those who declare themselves furthest advanced along its course. Developmentalism is the truth from the point of view of the center of power; it is the theorization (or rather ideologization) of its own path of development, and the comparative method elaborates this perspective. (Pieterse, 1991, p. 2)

Global space is transformed into a time sequence, with Europeans as the only contemporaries, the sole inhabitants of modernity—a perspective that served very successfully as a manual for imperial management of societies—at different evolutionary stages. Europe (now read the "West" or the "North") defines the world and gives names to phenomena in the genesis of the new world society brought forth in the wake of European expansion and conquest, industrial revolution, and, now, the advance of the world market. The naming process itself was an extension of the process of conquest, making becoming "modern" mean becoming Western. The convergence between development methods, modernization, and the tenets of this democracy lies in the fact that social engineering from above ensures the political containment of the dispossessed.

The rule of market forces now in force further heightens the false understanding that the principal social objectives of all countries are consumption and accumulation, twin objectives to be enforced through the two complementary strategies of the *carrot of consumerism*— through which a system of total demand is created—and the *competitive stick* of enforced economic participation. In this second strategy, the resources and social structures that give independence or relief from the market are ruthlessly assaulted or sequestered; families and communities are ruptured, water and biomass expropriated in the name of economic progress and efficiency.

> In a bizarre and profoundly irrational piece of sophistry, it is often claimed that those who are impoverished and immiserized by the forces of "development" are actually (or will imminently be) its beneficiaries through some "trickle down" process whereby some portion of the resources taken from them will be returned in more modern form. (Ekins, 1992, p. 205)

EDUCATION AND THE DIFFUSION OF CULTURAL ORIENTATIONS IN AFRICA

Globalization is given further legitimacy through prescriptive action by groups or bodies operating at the international level. On the subject of prescriptive action, McNeely (1995) has argued that international organizations facilitate the process of diffusing cultural themes developed primarily in the West, and apply pressure for these to be adopted worldwide as "universal" values. Development and education experts, McNeely argues, are part of an epistemic community already thoroughly imbued with the substantive ideology of this universalism, and are generally the foot soldiers in facilitating the symbolic and actual establishment of the universalist claims throughout the world. They are also responsible for constructing the requisite policy domains under the pretense that they are "neutral," "skilled" persons.

At the level of objectives of education, the fundamentally unresolved problems with the nature and philosophical basis underpinning education in Africa give education a different flavor once globalization becomes a norm. Fägerlind and Saha have stated that education plays key roles in the development of an individual and society. In its skills and human capital formation role, education provides a learner with new skills and knowledge that should enable her/him to function in a modern society. In its liberation role, education has been conceived as a tool for illuminating the structures of oppression and equipping the learners with the means to alter those oppressive structures in society (Fägerlind and Saha, 1989). However, there is a third role of education, which is the transmission of the normative heritage of a people from one generation to the next. A people's culture, wa Thiong'o wrote, is the carrier of values evolved by that community in the course of their economic and political life. The values they hold are the basis of their world outlook, the basis of their collective and individual image of self, their identity as a people who look at themselves and to their relationship to the universe in a certain way (wa Thiong'o, 1981).

In the context of Africa, the two last roles of education—that of liberation, and that of transmission of the normative heritage of a people—are not only being rendered irrelevant, but more accurately, being buried alive. It is quite evident that by transmitting judiciously the normative heritage of only one culture, the Western, and transposing it onto *all* other people, education, as presently constituted, becomes a key carrier of a most insidious cultural and epistemic violence. As people's thoughts and cognition are shaped to enhance maximal congruency with the values and practices of Western society, and as this process is routinized and made to appear quite normal, discourses are formed to legitimize this normalcy, and any attempt to create or contemplate another discourse is quickly rendered as an anomaly.

Reward motivates further compliance, and it is of no surprise at all that in a study by Lewin, Little, and Colclough (1982) examining twenty-nine national education plans for the twenty-nine-year period from 1966 to 1985, all these plans were found to uniformly express the major role of education in development, and all of them emphasized the role of education in labor force development and nation-building—all of which are consistent with "world cultural values" represented by UN Education Science and Cultural Organization and World Bank education policies. The two organizations have also been primal technical agencies that have "assisted" in the drafting of those plans, emphasizing the dissemination and the modalities for disseminating "world accounts" (McNeely, 1995).

Ki-Zerbo (1996) provides a refreshing African rejoinder to this gleeful process by arguing that as a system within a system, among other systems, education is closely linked with the functioning of the other sub-systems, and is, in fact, the strategic pillar to the success of the other systems. Education, he states, is key to the preservation of the status quo, and in a situation of structural violence, education policy and practice become the main egalitarian mask and smokescreen for the massive violence being carried out in the other systems. In

Africa, as the education sub-system is exogenous, it is organic by implantation, which means that its lifecycle is closely guarded by the implanter. This makes education carry a "double mask," one of its relationship and link with the other sub-systems such as the economy and Western ideology with which it has a dialectical relationship of mutual influence, and the other which is the mask of the dominating power.

Education in the African context, he states, is not just for the production of the "new self," but also for the reproduction of the social, economic, political, and cultural structures. The drama (comic and tragic) of reproduction in the African context, and one for which education earns itself the trophy of being the chief conduit of structural violence is that the reproduction is not of own society, but of an-other society. The structural violence of the educational policy at the systemic level is in reproducing not just "an-other society," but also in reproducing the violences of the other sub-systems into the conquered societies via its monopoly of, and influence over, the mind space of the young (and old) of the conquered societies (Odora Hoppers, 1998a).

For women in non-Western contexts, for instance, the education system of the Western type carries the *double violation* in that such an education is not only reproducing "an-other society" in general, but also, in most precolonial societies where women had the sacred role as mediator between the transcendent and humankind, the new mode of social reproduction now ensures that the space for social and cultural reproduction from an endogenous point of view is abrogated and supplanted by *something else* (Odora, 1993). As school is at once the site for reproduction, formation, and *deformation*, control of the mind space of the young is the main battlefield, making education become the most critical sub-system and key to the sustenance of the structural violence, from its privileged site for legitimizing alienation from "self," and bondage and drugged identity with the prescribed "other-ness" (Ki-Zerbo, 1996).

Geopolitics and the Demarcation of What Is a "Problem" in Education in Africa

Another area in which reality is steadily being obscured is in the agenda-setting and the demarcation of what constitutes a "problem" in education in Africa. For Africa, the interventions through donor conditionalities that persisted since the 1980s have gone to such an extent that a new de facto dependency has been institutionalized as part of what Ninsin refers to as the big game involving a new colonialism, which finds its greatest advantages in the nominal independence of the countries of the continent (Ninsin, 1988, cited in Mohan, 1994, p. 526). In the new geo-political terrain in place over Africa, Mohan states, the control exerted over African states is achieved without direct imposition of political power as of old. The new form of coercion for achieving consensus amenable to Western control is executed by supranational political agents working at "arm's length," relying now on more subtle means centered upon the *creation and dissemination of knowledge*; that is to say, abstract knowledge is used explicitly to create consensus for more concrete policy intervention (Mohan, 1994).

The area of research that informs policy has especially been identified by scholars as one such site in which hegemonic thought, visions, and meaning are constructed, and in which manufacture of consensus in present-day Africa most effectively occurs. With the World Bank strongly leading the crew in establishing consensus for its (and the West's) neoliberal agenda, Samoff's studies reveal a new game of mind and policy control and manipulation, in which wealthy lender agencies set the research agendas and then base their policy discourses on this self-funded and "objective" research (Samoff, 1992a). The World Bank is undoubtedly selective, not only in the way in which it deploys its statistical evidence in support of its own analysis, but also in the choice of "successes" and "failures" as examples to support arguments about the effectiveness of structural adjustment programs (Loxley and Seddon, 1994, p. 489).

According to Samoff, it is no longer a world in which policy-makers rationally survey a wide range of literature before making policy decisions. Indeed, the convergence in the relationship between research, funding, and policy does not begin at the point of funding, but further upstream and deeper at the level of meta-theoretical assumptions (Samoff, 1992a). Beginning with a definition of what is deemed wrong with Africa, one set of such pervasive assumptions on governance is that African countries are somehow in such a disarray that the state cannot fulfill its developmental role; therefore, the Western transnationals and technical expertise should of necessity be called upon to fill this void (Samoff, 1992a). A sweeping generalization of what is worst in Africa becomes a strategic indulgence, with a strong tendency to stress the "internal" problems and to blame the victims of the crisis—all too often by resorting to sociocultural explanations which suggest an intrinsic incapacity (Loxley and Seddon, 1994).

Geopolitics of sameness in the context of educational development is revealed in the striking uniformity and commonality of assumptions, the type of diagnosis, the content of prescriptions, and directions in the recommendations for action that nearly all bilateral and multilateral donors make to all their recipient countries. As if propelled by some higher order, all of them push for cost-effectiveness and efficient management, numerical enrollment and retention, information and management, and all of them say that there is a "lack of capacity" for policy implementation at all levels. It should be recalled that such has been the historic preoccupation of Western intervention in Africa since independence. Thus it is interesting indeed that even after massive investments in training have been made by the recipient countries (following their very advice), the diagnosis seems to remain like the stylus on a damaged vinyl record, *constant*: it is a perpetual problem of incapacity (see Samoff, 1992b).

African education systems are, by ascription, labeled as having "deteriorated" in recent years, and quality of education—not just quantity—is the matter at stake. Quality is then dwelt on without considering the cultural relativity of such a concept, and especially without humility as to the fact that international standards of educational quality are conditioned by international technological, economic, and political relationships that are defined by the cultures of the powerful nations. It ignores that the framework of technical rationality within which the mainstream research that informs such interventions is itself a product of Western culture.

Thus it can be stated that geopolitical reasoning works by the active suppression of complex geographical reality of places in favor of controllable geographical abstractions. In this frame, "research has shown" that all sub-Saharan African countries have similar characteristics. The Third World is then affirmed with paternalism as a bloodless universality without aspirations, without dreams, without visions, without competencies (Naipul, cited in Mohan, 1994, p. 525).

From this perspective of authority, various "cures" to the "common for all" ailments are prescribed en masse as has happened with the structural adjustment programs (SAPs). In fact they are not only prescribed, but in no time at all they become disseminated as the official descriptors in the discourse of all bilateral donors, and thereafter as the legitimate basis for new conditionalities. At the level of governance, the universalizing of Western liberal democracy under the influential diatribe of "good governance" is quickly routinized, the hegemony of the market is endorsed and disseminated, and decentralization to the advantage of privatization is legitimized (Mohan, 1994).

The agencies say the recipient countries should "own" their agenda now, but almost all the donors along with their activities remain opaque and most inaccessible to scrutiny by national governments of recipient countries. They say "transparency" is the key to good governance, but continue to insulate themselves and the premise of their diagnosis from any review by experts within the countries they support. They all want less government, privatization, increased school fees, and even "community participation" (Samoff, 1992b), but with no discussion as to other forms of learning—other than the Western one—that are also worth investing in, and which are important to a growing child in Africa.

It can be stated therefore that in the main, unlike in the colonial period in which political power was imposed in the form of an imperial state, consensus for intervention is achieved today via active supranational *political* agents relying on more subtle means centered around the creation and dissemination of knowledge. It is the task of these seemingly neutral, and innocently technical institutions and intellectuals of statecraft (Mohan, 1994) to produce, transmit, and especially to stabilize various development "truths," and ensure that they are posited and partaken as "universal." The locus of the creation of the rules by which verbal speech and written statements are made meaningful continues, as in the colonial era, to have a distinctly geographical nature, and they entail modes and techniques of suppression of complex social, cultural, and geographical realities whenever these attempt to emerge, and a permanent stranglehold on those that are already in existence (Loxley and Seddon, 1994).

STRUCTURAL ADJUSTMENT PROGRAMS AND THE REDEFINITION OF POLITICS AND GOVERNANCE IN AFRICA

Globalization had a "John the Baptist" of its own: the structural adjustment programs and their successor, the Poverty Reduction Strategies Papers (PRSPs). Many African countries have been implementing these economic austerity strategies for more than twenty years. The process has involved a shift in aid programs with accompanying macroeconomic conditionalities (Havnevik and van Arkadie, 1996). It is also no longer any secret that donors are steadily shifting their ground, pushing conditionality beyond narrowly defined economic policy into institutional arrangements, ownership, privatization, changes in public service delivery systems, and political practice. This last especially brings into question the issue of the political sovereignty of African countries, "indirect rule" through aid, and a call for a second liberation in Africa (Fundanga, 1996; Havnevik and van Arkadie, 1996; Mkandawire, 1996; Olukoshi, 1996).

The ensuing culture of surface partnership and structural subservience implies that government officials are not only subservient to often paternalistic donor officials, but political leaders are held accountable for policies designed elsewhere. It is also clear that African countries continue to have very little influence over their own development agenda. Within national systems, adjustment-oriented "reforms" are promoted by manipulation through establishing alliances with ministers of finance to "get it moving." In the meantime, power in the recipient bureaucracies has shifted to the technocrats, recruited by external donors and placed in small units within key ministries with responsibility for the coordination and promotion of the adjustment programs.

Alongside calls for more democracy and transparency, critical decisions have been appropriated in the confidential milieu of donor-recipient negotiations. In the meantime, both the projects of nation-building and democratization are threatened by economic austerity measures that weaken the capacity of the state to respond in a political way to the many demands on it, and by riding roughshod over public opinion. It is the "anti-popular" content and political form—the foreign imposition and non-transparency of policy-making institutions—that have provoked the most negative response. African scholars argue that it is not in the SAPs and PRSPs, but in resistance to them that democratic forces have been bred (Fundanga, 1996; Mkandawire, 1996; Olukoshi, 1996). It is no surprise that the governments that the World

Bank has peddled as strong adjusters—Rawling's Ghana, Babangida's Nigeria, and Museveni's Uganda—have been essentially military regimes (Mkandawire, 1996).

SAPs are not only about the liberalization of domestic markets, but also about submission to the logic of global markets. The effect of exigencies of global financial liberalization has been to strengthen the structural predominance of the entrepreneurial class by making the threat of capital flight a sword of Damocles hanging over policy-makers. In the process, "market" has become reified into a neutral, apolitical, and ahistorical institution (Kiren Aziz Chaudry, 1993, in Mkandawire, 1996, p. 36). It is fetishized so as to acquire such human attributes as "anger," "disappointment," "displeasure," or "nervousness." In this fetishization of social arrangements, it is the "market" that insists on the devolution of power to the central banks to allay the markets' suspicion that the government may not be seriously committed to orthodox market policies (Mkandawire, 1996).

A dramatic deprofessionalization of public administration is also taking place with the emergence of the technocratic elite aligned to the external constituencies. These insulated international technocracies, ensconced in key ministries, wield enormous power. This aggravates further the tension between the practice of generating this cadre, and the pressure on governments to become more transparent. The professional arrogance of these elites is fanned further by the heaps of praise accorded to them as the national salvation, in sharp contrast to the denigration that the domestic politicians and interest groups suffer at the hands of international financial institutions. On the other hand, the technocrats narrow the choices of the politicians by either being part of a transnational technocratic alliance or by identifying themselves with particular international models of crisis management such as orthodox SAPs and PRSPs.

Politics is reduced to serving this technocratically defined "welfare function" instead of the technocrats devising the instruments necessary to meet a democratically specified "social welfare program." Mkandawire (1996) argues that SAPs have introduced a truncated democracy whose area of competence is severely restricted. It is a choice-less democracy, on an inflexible take-it-or-leave-it basis in which the silent compulsions of market forces reign unchallenged by human will and collective action (Olukoshi, 1996).

Holders of African debt, organized into the Paris and London Clubs, Olukoshi states, are treated to the same take-it-or-leave-it principle. Buffeted from all sides by pressures requiring them to reach agreements with the World Bank and the IMF, African governments caved in one by one. They feel that they have lost control over the key aspects of economic decision-making. Not only that, African governments are required to submit themselves regularly to monitoring missions from Washington. The gradual erosion of national sovereignty has only deepened with the almost complete takeover of the policy terrain by multilateral donors, with state officials reduced to mere implementers of the preferences that emanate, one way or the other, from the Bretton Woods twins.

At another level, the requirements for meeting the demands of donor conditionality increasingly mean that public officials account more to the World Bank and the International Monetary Fund than to the people. Public officials, moreover, spend disproportionate amounts of time preparing reports, one after another for the World Bank, the IMF, a host of bilateral donors, and the Paris and London Clubs. This is in addition to time spent with a variety of evaluation/monitoring missions and in undertaking missions to the Bretton Woods institutions, the Paris and London Clubs, and with other donors to negotiate/justify (further) financing. The sum total of all of this is that governmental effectiveness is severely impaired (Olukoshi, 1996).

THE STIGMATIZED STATE AND EDUCATION POLICY [1]

Olukoshi argues that the collapse of the former Soviet bloc, it would appear, has coalesced into a neoliberal triumphantism to create the impression of an inexorable march by all human-kind toward "free" market policies and ideas. State policies and agencies are treated as the primary obstacle to the economic development of the continent. The critique of the postcoloni-al state built into the structural adjustment model situates the public in opposition to the private, the rural to the urban, the formal to the informal, and agriculture to industry in a one-sided manner. This is further developed by a copious borrowing from American behavioral political science writing on Africa tailored to the objectives of neoliberalism in Africa. For its part, the World Bank and its allied political economists perfected a set of referents with regards to the state. Some of these include descriptors such as prebendal, crony, neo-patrimo-nial, over-extended, lame leviathan, kleptocratic, parasitical, predatory, weak, soft, and rentier. All of these are denigrating terms (Olukoshi, 1996).

In other words, from being the cornerstone of development in the pre-adjustment period, the state, which a priori is defined as deficient, is now seen as the millstone holding back a system of market-led development. Where the state is to be mercilessly retrenched and put in its rightful place, the market is to be unbound and allowed to flower unrestrained (Olukoshi, 1996).

To reiterate here, application of conditionality is the primary means by which the multilat-eral donors who designed the adjustment framework seek to ensure that African states adopt and implement their reform program. As African governments can only expect to receive donor funds and support if they agree to adopt and implement policy reforms prescribed by the Bretton Woods institutions, this means that the IMF and the World Bank are well positioned to compel adoption of their favored policy options. The effectiveness of the leverage exercised over African countries is further reinforced by a system of cross-conditionality whereby bilateral donors agree to do business with governments only when they (the African govern-ments) have made their peace with the World Bank, and could produce a clean bill of health from the IMF.

Policy formulation experiences in Africa confirm the extensive presence of external donor agencies in the formulation of the policy documents, and that all the education reforms being undertaken are impelled by the structural adjustment process. Ghana is interesting in that policy formulation and reform in education took a glaring swing in 1983 when the military regime veered away from its policies self-reliance and undertook extensive adjustment pro-grams with the support from the IMF and the World Bank (Fobih, Koomson, and Godwyll, 1996). In Guinea, following the launching of the SAP in 1986, the state was removed from the productive sectors of the economy. At the end of 1988, with the support of the World Bank and other donors, the government began two projects: Education I and II. By the end of the second project in 1989, as preparations for the SAP in education were already underway, a reasoning had been consolidated in the context of these projects to the effect that "experience" in "other countries" had shown that a coherent policy framework linked to macro adjustment programs can lead to changes in the education sector that have a profound effect on the nation's schooling. In the context of an adjustment package financed by several funding agencies (the French bilateral development agency, U.S. Agency for International Develop-ment, IMF, World Bank, and others), a policy declaration in Guinea was approved in 1989 that provided the basis for a multi-agency financed education sector adjustment program. When the policy document was ready, it had to be approved by donors; when the sectoral adjustment was all in place, the Guinean government, through the Minister of Finance, af-firmed their acquisition of the necessary concepts as required by the agencies. The minister addressed a special letter to the president of the World Bank, presenting "the relationship between the macro economic reforms to the proposed reform of the education sector" (Kamano, 1996).

The story of Uganda's involvement with the IMF and the World Bank began in 1987 when the then one-year-old government decided to abandon its policy of self-reliance in favor of the market economy espoused by the Bretton Woods institutions. The SAP that followed came amidst protests from civil society as to the negative effects that such a program would have on education, health, water and sanitation, child welfare, and other protection programs (wa Irumba, 1996). In 1987, an Education Policy Review Commission supported by the World Bank was appointed and a secretariat was set up. In terms of consultations, it is evident that despite what has been dubbed the "most extensive consultations ever," the Education Policy Review Commission held consultations only in urban areas. Rural communities, marginalized urban communities, and security agencies like the police force, the army, and the prisons department were not asked their views. The impressive list of 496 memoranda and resource papers does not show any involvement of the marginalized groups, but rather, that of an educated elite.

In Benin, it was well recognized that many problems in education are symptoms produced by complex combinations of factors, and cannot be fixed with simple, single-factor solutions. For this, the legacy of colonialism was spelled out in detail in the country report. Academic institutions were identified as being bastions of colonial conservatism. An elitist policy uses academic exams as the basis of selection. The whole educational system is identified as being an alienating one (Debourou, 1996). But when agencies came around to affect an educational reform, only enrollment was picked upon as a problem, with issues restricted to internal efficiency of the education system itself, to planning problems, teacher qualifications, and the issue of quality (however defined). In the UNDP/UNESCO Education Policy Analysis project, managed by a Beninese but with "qualified" external expert assistance, there is no reference to designing the kind of reform policies that would address the factors related to colonialism.

RECONSTRUCTING REALITY: RECOVERING THE BASIS OF HUMANITY

As we move further into the twenty-first century, we take stock and look to the new millennium with both expectation and uncertainty. We grope to find a new foundation upon which to recover our sense of humanness. We seek to discover and to foster tools that shall enable us to mature, and muster courage and faith enough to cultivate the capacity to love (Fromm, 1975). We seek new directions in dealing with diversity: from a view of diversity as a tool for containment to diversity as a basis for human relations of respect. We seek to build bridges and affirm the value of holism in thought and practice. We commit to a new understanding of human rights: the right to know, the right to do, the right to be and become, and the right to live together (*Delors Report*, 1996, cited in Odora Hoppers, 1998a).

We seek an education that can enable people to bring to the field rich collective experiences and abilities, and which can permit these to be given place and name in the scheme of things. It is an education that builds capacities, fosters resistance and the creation of alternative models, as well as facilitates the unshaping of old roles. It is an education that can permit each human being to participate in naming the world on terms that they can understand (Odora Hoppers, 1998a).

Embodied in the African philosophy of *Ubuntu*, a new universalism promises to emerge that seeks to affirm a concept of development in which fear is replaced by joy, insecurity by confidence, and materialism by spiritual values. *Ubuntu* ("I am because we are") is humaneness, care, understanding, and empathy. It is the ethic and interaction that occurs in the African extended family. The *ubuntu* concept is found in proverbs from many African societies and communities such as "the stomach of the traveler is small" (Zulu), "a home is a real one if people visit it" (Zulu), "a bird builds its nest with another bird's feathers" (Xhosa), and "the hands wash each other" (Xhosa). All these proverbs demonstrate an innate encouragement that sharing is good, and *a person is only a person because of other people* (Boon, 1996). It is this philosophy that differentiates African society fundamentally from European and Western societies, which seek competition even unto death, exploitation till decimation, and which have great difficulty in founding relationships with "others" except through conquest.

As we take stock and move to recover our sense of humanness and basis for practice, as we muster that courage to love, the one moral and ethical summons before us is to work tirelessly to help restore humanity to others so systematically separated from their own selves. This task is about recognizing and confronting the forms of epistemic violence of global proportions that has had unprecedented success in not just cultivating a sense of alienness, but also in decapitating peoples from their capacity to use their human powers to the fullest. But at another level, the task is also about understanding the fact that epistemic violence is not only diffuse but also extremely productive.

Taking Cues from Post-Modernist and Feminist Critiques

Rust (1991) states that as a critical discourse, postmodernism underscores contingency of meaning and challenges the major tenets of modern scientific and rational knowledge. For its part, globalization compels us to revisit two aspects of the postmodernism discourse and debate that are extremely relevant for the setting of new foundations for educational thought in the twenty-first century. These are the critique on the totalitarian nature of metanarratives, and the problem of the "Other" (Rust, 1991). The issue of "Othering" is in large part associated with the notion of a culture of inner and outer imperialism, an imperialism that though taken very much for granted by devoted moderns, no longer goes unchallenged. Whereas self-determination and numerous liberation movements have adequately challenged "outer imperialism" with a substantial degree of success, the entire terrain of "inner imperialism" has not been seriously confronted. Thus, the fact that the core industrialized powers now aim at the control of thought of all "Others" by locking the spaces of their cognitive thought in what Jean-François Lyotard (in Rust, 1991, p. 615) called "totalitarian and logocentric systems of thought" should be posited as a big part of the problem.

It is also at this point that the feminist sciences provide crucial theoretical and conceptual devices. At the core of a feminist dialectic is a sociology of knowledge, a conception that the world is known from the varied vantage points of actors differently situated in the social structure. This view, that knowledge is anchored in and patterned by the knower's structurally situated vantage point, leads one to the position that knowledge is itself the key problematic. This is particularly because people's perceptions of social reality are always partial and interest-based. Feminist sociology therefore seeks to understand how people come to their views of social reality, how they justify those views in the face of seemingly contradictory opinions and evidence, how they act on those views, condone their own behavior, or reconcile themselves to their social situation according to those views (Lengerman and Niebrugge-Brantley, 1988). Because women's experiences and knowledge, like those of Africans, have been obscured in the male bias of Western academe including development theory and practice, the task is not just to add women or African experiences into the known equation but to work with new epistemologies and methodologies. This implies an open challenge to current knowledge production, a challenge to displace the neutral male subject of Western science, and dissolve the division between research and practice (Harcourt, 1994).

As Foucault (1994) has posited, there is a need to develop new perspectives on society, knowledge, discourse, and power that can equip us with such tools of analysis that are capable of discerning that slippery interface between modern forms of power and knowledge, rationality and institutions that has served to create new forms of domination that Hegelian and Marxist philosophies have been unable to grasp, "recognizing that systematizing methods produce reductive social and historical analyses, and that knowledge is perspectival in nature, requiring multiple viewpoints to interpret a heterogeneous reality" (Best and Kellner, 1994, pp. 34–35).

We should begin to ask: How can we attain that much-rhetoricized goal of attaining a plurality of history of diversity in histories and render these capable of contesting for space in the face of the totalizing metanarratives of Westernization, of modernization, of industrialization with all that these narratives have entailed? How, indeed, are we going to foreground the material context of subject construction that undergirds the global practices and discourses today?

In short, we need to critically revisit that process by which individuals and nationalities as "subjects" get "subjected" to someone else through control and dependence, tied to their own identity by a *conscience* or self-knowledge. The formation of ideology has to begin with the development of a true conscience which is, in the first place, free from the dominating presence of institutions and structures and, in the second, one which is capable of undertaking transformative goals even in the absence of some large-scale uprising or massive revolution.

> If Foucault is right that power is irreducibly plural, that it thrives at the local and capillary levels of society and is only subsequently taken up by larger institutional structures, then it follows that a change only in the form of the state, modes of production or class composition of society fails to address autonomous trajectories of power. Thus the key to micrological strategies ... is that since power is decentered and plural, and so in turn must be forms of political struggle. A Foucauldian post-modern politics, therefore, attempts to break with unifying and totalizing strategies, to cultivate multiple forms of resistance, to destroy the prisons of received identities and discourses of exclusion. (Best and Kellner, 1994, pp. 56–57)

The political task of genealogy, therefore, is to recover the autonomous discourses, knowledges, and voices suppressed through totalizing narratives. As Best and Kellner (1994) also argue, the subjugated voices of history speak through hidden forms of domination, and to admit their speech is necessarily to revise one's conception of what and where power is. The task of genealogy then becomes that of problemmatizing the present and exposing the operations of power and domination, working behind the neutral or beneficent facades. Writes Foucault: "It seems to me that the real political task in a society such as ours is to criticize the working of institutions which appear to be both neutral and independent; to criticize them in such a manner that the political violence which has always exercised itself obscurely through them will be unmasked, so that we can fight them" (Foucault, 1994, p. 171).

If "truth" is best understood not as correspondence or correctness of assertion, but as the absence of concealment, then the task of the critical social cartographers is to focus attention to the small and previously hidden narratives, and on making the *invisible visible*. It becomes our responsibility to track omissions and understand mechanisms of power tied to the deletion of certain practical and intellectual work (Paulston and Liebman, 1993). Engaging in remaking the maps would reveal both acknowledged and perceived social inclusions while leaving space for further inclusions of social groups and ideas.

To be human is to be born into a world that pulls out and pushes back the potentials inside us. I push and pull back trying to find or shape a part of the world … that supports my inborn potential. … Sometimes the world supports me. Sometimes it crushes part of me. … What kind of a dance can I do with a culture that loads me with sludge and does not recognize my inner shine? All I can think to do is to tune into whatever I know of the light and love of the universe, without denying the existence of my own failures. (Meadows, 2000, pp. 67, 69)

Well, in South Africa, it is happening. Government-funded chairs like the one that I hold (the Department of Science and Technology and the National Research Foundation Chair in Development Education) are created as an "epistemological watch." Centers are being created, and institutes are being set up to look at, from an African view, what actually happened. The South African Constitution has *ubuntu* ("I am because we are") ingrained into its basis. The rage among Africans is captured in the speech by former President Thabo Mbeki on launching the Constitution of South Africa in 1996:

I am born of the peoples of the Continent of Africa. The pain of the violent conflicts which the people of Liberia, Somalia, the Sudan, Burundi, and Algeria are experiencing is a pain that I also bear. The dismal shame of poverty and suffering and the human degradation of my Continent is a blight that we share. The blight on our happiness that derives from this and from our drift to the periphery of the ordering of human affairs leaves us in a persistent shadow of despair. … The thing we have done today (with the adoption of the South African Constitution) says that Africa reaffirms that she is continuing her rise from the ashes. (Mbeki, 1996)

CONCLUSION

What about going beyond the rage? How can we transform the public spaces, the classrooms, the policies that guide us all in the twenty-first century? I will outline several points.

The first one is integration. Integration is known as the panacea of all countries bedevilled by marginalization going forward. But if it is done within affirmative action strategies between women and men, between blacks and whites, the situation ends up inadvertently serving to couch "in-groups" and rendering them invisible and safely stowed away in their fairly conservative positions of privilege, reinforcing what Carol Lee Bacchi (1996) refers to as "the power of the insiders." This makes the unproblematized institutional cultures and processes remain the "unmarked standard," representing the universal, while women fumble along, constantly on the defensive, eternally the ones who need to explain themselves. Once inside the institution, the category (be it "woman" or "black") sticks as a label, and is used at whim by the insiders either as proof of benevolence, or as a demonstration of congenital incapacity of the "Other." Whichever way one looks at it, there is often a negative ascription that preempts the conversion of the opportunity availed by women's access into institutions being translated into institutional tools or turned into opportunities for the institution to reflect and arrive at a more advanced understanding as to the tenets of its previous policies.

The second point is the tensions between transformation and reform. Sometimes a good philosophy such as *ubuntu*, or even reconciliation, sounds and feels right. But like humanism, a good philosophy is only the beginning. On the other hand, it is proper to want to change. The only problem is that it is about change in structure without change in ideology. We have to grasp the concept of "transformation." It is transformation that demands that both the philosophy *and* structure be changed. It goes into the constitutive rules by which systems are built.

Third, we have to renegotiate space and relationships. How? We have to realize that deep historical wounds will not be healed by simply putting children into one space, or inviting people to come together to engage in dialogue to solve problems. Relationships must to be renegotiated. Renegotiation requires trying to understanding each other at a level we call "metaphysical." The metaphysics of a culture—at once its way of making sense of the world and its rationalization of its basic cultural structures (i.e., that which is normally taken for granted by the members of that culture)—is ignored in the present cultures we are living in. It needs to be brought out into the open when it is dysfunctional and needs to be transformed, and when it is necessary to renegotiate relationships with people from other cultures who come to the table with a different metaphysic. Taking the South African situation, it is clear that the Western metaphysics deriving from European history, with all its eccentricities, is accepted as the norm, while mumblings continue about how other cultures are marginalized. The marginal cultures should be given a space to express themselves *without duress* in public institutions and engage in changing the constitutive rules of the game.

Fourth, we need to be putting content to culture. Culture can be seen as the template shaping values, behavior, and consciousness within a human society from generation to generation. It is the totality of socially transmitted behavior patterns, arts, beliefs, institutions, and all other products of human work and thought: "a precipitate of history." But this does not help us very much when we would like to apply this in recommending actions on equality and equity of use of public spaces and institutions. We have to break this down and name the substantive elements (e.g., knowledge, food, history, arts, dance, and rituals). From here we can go into discussions (e.g., cultural justice, cultural injustice, and cognitive justice).

Cultural injustice occurs when people are forced by coercion or persuasion to submit to the burdensome condition of suspending—or permanently surrendering—what they naturally take for granted. This means that in reality, the subjugated person has no linguistic or cultural "default drive"—that critical minimum of ways, customs, manners, gestures, and postures that facilitate uninhibited, un-self-conscious action (Kwenda, 2003). Cultural justice means that the burden of constant self-consciousness is shared, or at the very least recognized, and where possible rewarded. The sharing part is important because it is only in the mutual vulnerability that this entails that the meaning of intimacy and reciprocity in community can be discovered.

It is in this sharing that, on the one hand, cultural difference is transcended and, on the other, cultural arrogance, by which is meant that disposition to see in other cultures not simply difference, but deficiency, is overcome. The cultural work that is entailed in constructing functional tolerance therefore goes beyond providing equal opportunities in, say, education, to the unclogging of hearts filled with resentment.

REFERENCES

Bacchi, Carol. 1996. The Political Use of Categories. In Carol Bacchi (ed.), *The Politics of Affirmative Action* (pp. 1–14). London: Sage Publications.

Berger, Peter L., and Thomas Luckmann. 1967. *The Social Construction of Reality: A Treatise in the Sociology of Knowledge*. London: Penguin.

Bergesen, Albert. 1994. Turning the World Systems Theory on its Head. In Mike Featherstone (ed.), *Global Culture: Nationalism, Globalization and Modernity* (pp. 67–81). London: Sage.

Best, Steven, and Douglas Kellner. 1994. *Postmodern Theory.* London: MacMillan Books.

Boon, Mike. 1996. *The African Way: The Power of Interactive Leadership.* Johannesburg: Zebra Press.

Debourou, Djibril M. 1996. The Case of Benin. In Association for the Development of African Education (ed.), *Formulating Educational Policy: Lessons and Experiences from Sub-Saharan Africa* (pp. 39–61). Paris: IIEP.

Ekins, Paul. 1992. *A New World Order. Grassroots Movements for Global Change.* London: Routledge.

Fägerlind, Ingemar, and Lawrence J. Saha. 1989. *Education and National Development. A Comparative Perspective.* Oxford. Pergamon Press.

Fobih, Dominic Lwaku, Albert K. Koomson, and Ebenezer F. Godwyll. 1996. The Case of Ghana. In Association for the Development of African Education (ed.), *Formulating Educational Policy: Lessons and Experiences from Sub-Saharan Africa* (pp. 63–84). Paris: IIEP.

Foucault, Michel. 1994. Human Nature: Justice Versus Power. In Fons Elders (ed.), *Reflexive Water: The Basic Concerns of Mankind* (pp. 135–97). London: Souvenir Press.

Fromm, Erich. 1975. *The Art of Loving*. London: Unwin Books.

Fundanga, Caleb M. 1996. Practical Effects of Economic and Political Conditionality in Recipient Administration. In Kjell Havnevik and Brian van Arkadie (eds.), *Domination or Dialogue? Experiences and Prospects for African Development Cooperation* (pp. 89–97). Uppsala: Nordiska Afrikainstitutet.

Galtung, Johan. 1996. *Peace by Peaceful Means: Peace, Conflict, Development and Civilization.* London: Sage Publications.

Giddens, Anthony. 1995. *The Consequences of Modernity*. Cambridge: Polity Press.

Harcourt, Wendy. 1994. Introduction. In Wendy Harcourt (ed.), *Feminist Perspectives on Sustainable Human Development* (pp. 1–8). London: Zed Books.

Havnevik, Kjell, and Brian van Arkadie. 1996. Introduction. In Kjell Havnevik and Brian van Arkadie (eds.), *Domination or Dialogue? Experiences and Prospects for African Development Cooperation* (pp. 13–23). Uppsala: Nordiska Afrikainstitutet.

Henderson, Hazel. 1996. *Creating Alternative Futures: The End of Economics.* New York: Kumarian Press.

Huntington, Samuel P. 1996. *The Clash of Civilizations and the Remaking of World Order.* New York: Simon & Schuster.

Kamano, Joseph P. 1996. The Case of Guinea. In Association for the Development of African Education (ed.), *Formulating Educational Policy: Lessons and Experiences from Sub-Saharan Africa* (pp. 85–102). Paris: IIEP.

Ki-Zerbo, Joseph. 1996. Notes from personal interview with Catherine A. Odora Hoppers, Amman, Jordan.

Kwenda, Chirevo V. 2003. Cultural Justice: The Pathway to Reconciliation and Social Cohesion. In David Chidester, Phillip Dexter, and Wilmot James (eds.), *What Holds Us Together: Social Cohesion in South Africa* (pp. 67–80). Pretoria: Human Sciences Research Council.

Lengerman, Patricia M., and Jill Niebrugge-Brantley. 1988. Contemporary Feminist Theory. In George Ritzer (ed.), *Sociological Theory*, 2nd edition. (pp. 430–43). New York: Alfred A. Knopf.

Lewin, Keith, Angela Little, and Christopher Colclough. 1982. Adjusting to the 1980s: Taking Stock of Educational Expenditures. In *Financing of Educational Development* (pp. 13–38). Proceedings from an International Seminar in Mont Sainte Marie, Quebec. Ottawa: IDRC.

Loxley, John, and David Seddon. 1994 (December). Stranglehold on Africa. *Review of African Political Economy*, vol. 21, no. 62, pp. 485–93.

Mbeki, Thabo. 1996. I am an African. Speech made on behalf of the African National Congress in Cape Town, on the occasion of the passing of the new Constitution of South Africa, May 8.

McNeely, Connie L. 1995. *Constructing the Nation State: International Organizations and Prescriptive Action.* London: Greenwood Press.

Meadows, Donella. 2000. Untitled. In Frederick Franck, Janis Roze, and Richard Connolly (eds.), *What Does It Mean To Be Human? Reverence for Life Reaffirmed by Responses from Around the World* (pp. 67–69). New York: Circumstantial Productions, St. Martin's Press.

Miller, Errol. 1991. *Men at Risk.* Kingston: Jamaica Publishing House.

Mkandawire, Thandika. 1996. Economic Policy-Making and the Consolidation of Democratic Institutions in Africa. In Kjell Havnevik and Brian van Arkadie (eds.), *Domination or Dialogue? Experiences and Prospects for African Development Cooperation.* Uppsala: Nordiska Afrikainstitutet.

Mohan, Giles. 1994 (December). Manufacturing Consensus: Geo-Political Knowledge and Policy Based Lending. *Review of African Political Economy*, vol. 21, no 62, pp. 525–35.

Odora, Catherine A. 1993. *Educating African Girls in a Context of Patriarchy and Transformation. A Theoretical and Conceptual Analysis.* Doctoral dissertation, Institute of International Education, Stockholm University.

Odora Hoppers, Catherine A. 1998a. The NQF, Equity, Redress and Development. A Human Centered Perspective. Keynote address to the CEPD/University of Witwatersrand conference on Reconstruction, Development and the National Qualifications Framework. Johannesburg: Center for Education Policy Development.

_____. 1998b. Structural Violence as a Constraint to African Policy Formulation in the 1990s. Repositioning Education in International Relations. Presentation at seminar, Institute of International Education, Stockholm University.

Olukoshi, Adebayo. 1996. The Impact of Recent Reform Efforts on the African State. In Kjell Havnevik and Brian van Arkadie (eds.), *Domination or Dialogue? Experiences and Prospects for African Development Cooperation* (pp. 48–70). Uppsala: Nordiska Afrikainstitutet.

Paulston, Rolland G., and Martin Liebman. 1993. Invitation to Post-Modern Reflection on Critical Social Cartography. Paper presented at the Comparative and International Education Society Annual Conference, Kingston, Jamaica, March.

Pieterse, Jan N. 1991. Dilemmas of Development Discourse: the Crisis of Developmentalism and the Comparative Method. *Development and Change*, vol. 22, no. 1, pp. 5–29.

Rivière, Philippe. 1999. How the United States Spies on Us All. *Le Monde Diplomatique*, January, pp. 2–3.

Roddick, Anita. 2001. *Take It Personally: How Globalization Affects You and the Powerful Ways to Challenge It.* London: Harper Collins.

Rust, Val. 1991. Post-Modernism and Its Comparative Education Implications. *Comparative Education Review*, vol. 35, no. 4, pp. 610–26.

Samoff, Joel. 1992a. The Intellectual/Financial Complex of Foreign Aid. *Review of African Political Economy*, no. 53, pp. 60–87.

———. 1992b. Defining What Is and What Is Not an Issue: An Analysis of Assistance Agency Africa Education Sector Studies. Stockholm: SIDA.

South Commission. 1990. *The Challenge to the South*. Report of the South Commission. Oxford: Oxford University Press.

wa Irumba, Katebalirwe Amooti. 1996. The Case of Uganda. *Formulating Educational Policy: Lessons and Experiences from Sub-Saharan Africa* (pp. 141-164). Association for the Development of African Education. Paris. IIEP.

wa Thiong'o, Ngugi. 1981. *Education for a National Culture*. Harare: Zimbabwe Publishing House.

NOTE

1. These sections draw from Odora Hoppers (1998b).

Chapter Eight

Studying Globalization: The Vertical Case Study Approach

Lesley Bartlett and Frances Vavrus

What new methodological approaches are required to examine globalization and education? How can scholars trace the global circulation of educational policies and the ways they are remade in practice? In this chapter, we outline one promising methodological approach, the vertical case study (VCS). We call this approach a "vertical case study" due to our initial conceptualization of it (Bartlett and Vavrus, forthcoming; Vavrus and Bartlett, 2009). Despite its name, the VCS approach incorporates vertical, horizontal, and transversal elements of analysis because studies of how global policies, processes, and discourses manifest and are transformed in local contexts must examine the processes, sets of relations, articulations, and networks that stretch across space and time and connect scales, places, and actors.

In this chapter, we first describe the conceptual framework that informs our methodological approach followed by a discussion of the three "axes" of the VCS: the vertical, horizontal, and transversal. To ground this discussion, we draw on a collaborative research project to exemplify the contribution of a VCS approach to studies of globalization and education, and we conclude by briefly describing future avenues for VCSs of global education policy and practice in the field of international and comparative education.

CONCEPTUAL AND METHODOLOGICAL FRAMEWORKS

Central to our work has been Anna Tsing's theorization of "global connections" (2005, p. 1). As Tsing writes, seemingly global and universalizing systems such as capitalism and democracy operate in specific material and social contexts. These systems "can only be charged and enacted in the sticky materiality of practical encounters" (p. 3). These so-called global forces, she contends, are themselves "congeries" of local-global interactions. To illustrate the study of global connections, Tsing introduces the metaphor of friction. She argues that friction is produced through continuous social interaction among actors at various levels and is required to "keep global power in motion," though it may just as easily "slow things down" (p. 6). This metaphor encapsulates "the awkward, unequal, unstable, and creative qualities of interconnection across difference" (p. 6). Global encounters, when conceptualized in this way, often result in new and unanticipated cultural and political forms that exclude as well as enable.

Understanding the impact of globalization on education, then, requires simultaneous attention to multiple levels, including (at least) international, national, and local ones, and careful study of flows (and frictions) of influence, ideas, and actions through these levels. Qualitative research on education must consider the profound changes in the global economy and (inter)national politics that make the national and international levels of analysis as important as the local. The growing interconnections between national economies and international financial institutions, and between national educational systems and global organizations that fund and evaluate their operations, are some of the most important issues for scholars of education today.

VCSs examine these interconnections by de-centering the nation-state from its privileged position as *the* fundamental entity in comparative research and relocating it as one of several important units of analysis. As Marginson and Mollis (2001) write, "Governance remains national in form, and nation-states continue to be central players in a globalizing world, but partly as local agents of global forces, [as] the nation-state now operates within global economic constraints" (p. 601). Thus, multilevel research that situates the nation-state within a world marked by global agencies and agendas is essential. Yet the national-global relationship is only one part of a VCS because the local-national and the local-global connections are equally significant. The goal of VCSs is to develop a thorough understanding of the particular at each level and to analyze how these understandings produce similar and different interpretations of the policy, problem, or phenomenon under study.

This reconceptualization of globalization parallels other conceptual developments that have influenced our methodological approach, including sociocultural studies of policy, actor network theory, reconceptualizations of space, and "policyscapes," as outlined in the following.

Sociocultural Studies of Education Policy

In its approach to the study of global education policy, the VCS draws from sociocultural studies of "policy as practice" (Levinson and Sutton, 2001; Shore and Wright, 1997). While some approaches to policy studies adopt an instrumentalist stance to investigate "what works," a sociocultural approach understands policy as a deeply political process of cultural production engaged in and shaped by social actors in disparate locations who exert incongruent amounts of influence. These actors differ in their authority to "(1) define what is problematic in education; (2) shape interpretations and means of how problems should be resolved; and (3) determine to what vision of the future change efforts should be directed" (Hamann and Rosen, 2011, p. 462). These three points highlight how sociocultural approaches to education policy attend to the political contestations that shape the policy cycle.

A sociocultural approach, then, requires attention to both policy formation and policy implementation as cultural and social processes. Policy formation results in "a normative cultural discourse with positive and negative sanctions, that is, a set of statements about how things should or must be done, with corresponding inducements or punishments. ... Policy thus (a) defines reality, (b) orders behavior, and (sometimes) (c) allocates resources accordingly" (Levinson, Sutton, and Winstead, 2009, p. 770). Policy implementation occurs through a complex process of *appropriation,* during which social actors interpret and selectively implement policies, thereby adapting ideas and discourses developed in a different place and potentially at a different historical moment "into their own schemes of interest, motivation, and action" in accordance with their own symbolic, material, and institutional constraints (Levinson, Sutton, and Winstead, 2009, p. 782). This notion of policy appropriation as cultural and social production is founded upon practice theory (e.g., Bourdieu, 1977, 1990), which is known for arguing against structure/agency dichotomies in favor of attention to the moment when both are mutually constituted through social practice (Levinson, Sutton, and Winstead,

2009). Thus, rather than reproducing a structure/agency divide, as some have argued (Robertson, 2012), the approach we are proposing examines how structures are culturally produced in the "friction" of social practice.

Actor Network Theory

The emphasis on policy flows and enactments within sociocultural approaches to policy can be further enhanced by concepts derived from actor network theory. Networks are "assemblages" of dynamic actors and resources that can "move educational practices across space and time" (Nespor, 2003, p. 369; Ong and Collier, 2004). As developed by Latour (2005) and others, actor network theory considers how, within networks, people and objects get invited, excluded, and enrolled, a moment in which they accept (at least temporarily) the interests and agenda as set by focal actors; how linkages are established (or fail to "take"), shift, and dissolve; and how social acts curtail or facilitate future actions. Koyama (2011) notes, "The strength of the theory lies in its insistence on following the ongoing processes 'made up of uncertain, fragile, controversial, and ever-shifting ties' (Latour, 2005, p. 28) rather than attempting to fit the actors and their activities into bounded categories, geographical sites, or groups of analysis" (p. 705).

Importantly, and quite controversially, Actor Network Theory (ANT) emphasizes the role played by non-human actors, which, in effect, dissolves binaries by focusing on *interactions* among actors within a network rather than on their location (local, national, global) within it. From this perspective, people, objects, and texts can become vested and act, and ANT traces how human and non-human actors become "enrolled" in and are then "accountable" to networks, and how both are "produced by particular interactions with one another" (Fenwick and Edwards, 2010, p. 8).

Thus, the VCS approach incorporates sociocultural studies of policy and ANT in its conceptual framework. It is grounded in practice theory as applied to the study of policy in examining how its formation and implementation are socially and culturally produced in the "friction" of encounters (Tsing, 2005), and it endeavors to trace spatially non-contiguous assemblages of actors. Our approach actively seeks to avoid the dilemma suggested by Robertson of equating the global "to the macro, and structural," making it "a social force that the local (or micro) must face" and "pitting structures (as global/macro) against agents (as local/micro)" (2012, p. 8). The approach takes heed of an insight developed by de Sousa Santos, Nunes and Meneses (2007) that the "global" is always a "local." They contend, and we concur, that globalizing, universalist accounts of social "truths," such as policies, operate as "globalized localisms" that have acquired hegemonic status through the authority of specific knowledge systems, regimes of power, or funding agencies, but they are not the sole truth.[1] In addition, the VCS approach acknowledges that "global institutions," like the World Bank, are nonetheless "local" spaces constructed through the shifting cultural production of human (and non-human) actors through social practices (see, e.g., Goldman, 2006; Li, 2007). In this way, the distinction made in the VCS approach between micro-, meso-, and macro-levels is not a reification of dichotomies but rather a metaphorical reminder to conduct research across concatenations of sites, including international and bilateral development organizations, national and regional ministries of education, and community-based classrooms.

Multi-sited Ethnography and the Spatial Turn

The emphasis within both sociocultural studies of policy and ANT on process and negotiation requires multi-sited methodologies. While techniques for engaging multiple field sites have existed for quite some time and were used intensively by urban anthropologists in the 1960s and those working transnationally in the 1990s, multi-sited ethnography has been most coherently codified in the work of George Marcus (1995, 1998). Multi-sited ethnography was spurred by recognition of not only the flow of people, goods, and ideas across space but also the interconnectedness across dispersed locations (Coleman and von Hellermann, 2011). In addition, it addresses the necessity of examining what Marcus calls "distributed knowledge systems" and "active knowledge making," or the multiple and spatially diffuse sources of knowledge and ways of knowing among those in our ethnographic studies (2011, pp. 23–25).

More precisely, this shift in qualitative research results from a reconceptualization of space as socially produced, "the product of interrelations ... constituted through interactions ... always under construction" (Massey, 2005, p. 9; see also de Certeau, 1984). This "spatial turn" requires a rethinking of the global/local antinomy (e.g., Kearney, 1995), moving away from the tendency to look at how global structures shape local practices and toward a recognition that seemingly universalizing systems, which include policy regimes, "can only be charged and enacted in the sticky materiality of practical encounters" (Tsing, 2005, p. 3). At the same time, this shift also triggers what Feldman (2011, p. 377) calls "the decomposition of ethnographic location," particularly at a time when the idea of the "culture" or "social group" as a unit of study has been heavily critiqued. As such, multi-sited ethnography within a VCS approach is necessitated by the ways that globalization and transnationalism "challenge ethnographic methods of inquiry and units of analysis by destabilizing the embeddedness of social relations in particular communities and places" (Falzon, 2009, p. 2). This rethinking of space and of the local/global has prompted a proliferation of concepts, each with methodological implications. Here we focus on one in particular—scapes—and its employment in Carney's concept of policyscapes.

Policyscapes

Scholars in comparative and international education have struggled with the implications of "the spatial turn" for studies of global educational policy. Carney makes a significant contribution to these efforts through his development of the concept of "policyscape." Drawing on anthropologist Arjun Appadurai's concept of an ideoscape, which Appadurai employs (alongside mediascapes) to signal the chains of images intended to intensify or contest state power (1990, 1996), Carney defines a policyscape as an "educational ideoscape ... that might capture some essential elements of globalization as a phenomenon (object and process) and provide a tool with which to explore the spread of policy ideas and pedagogical practice across different national school systems" (2009, p. 68). Carney argues that global flows of policies are reshaping the state; as a result, the state has been "dislodged from its national context and sucked into the disjunctive forces and imaginative regimes of different global 'scapes,' developmental agencies, and their vested interests" while continuing to "mediate the terms on which new regimes and technologies can be received" (2012, p. 4). From the perspective of policyscapes, comparative education researchers are able to "retain the state as an important object for analysis without being beholden to it" (2012, p. 4). The value of the VCS is that it specifically promotes attention to state-level actors while tracing how their actions may be circumscribed or motivated by historical factors as well as actions and pressures emanating from other actors, such as grassroots political activists or donors with a particular agenda. Thus, the vertical, horizontal, and transversal axes of the VCS approach lend themselves to studying policyscapes across disparate sites.

THE "AXES" OF THE VERTICAL CASE STUDY

Drawing specifically on the conceptual and methodological innovations outlined in the previous section, the VCS approach unfolds along three "axes"—the vertical, the horizontal, and the transversal. First, this approach insists on simultaneous attention to and across micro-, meso-, and macro- levels, or spatial scales, which constitute the *verticality* of comparison. Too often qualitative work reifies social, political, and economic processes as "forces" or "systems" with explanatory power. There has been a tendency to take the macro for granted and focus exclusively on a single-site locality rather than carefully exploring how changes in national and international institutions, discourses, and policies are influencing social practice at the school level. In contrast, we aver that attention to the ways global processes are shaped by and in turn influence social action in various locales is essential. "The local" cannot be divorced from national and transnational forces but neither can it be conceptualized as determined by these forces.

In addition, the VCS approach also recognizes that space itself is socially produced (Massey, 2005), and every "level" is an instance of the "local." In other words, the World Bank or one country's ministry of education are also "local" contexts, with their own complex social, cultural, and material relations. However, as shown in work by de Sousa Santos and colleagues (2007), the World Bank's "local" often becomes globalized and loses any sense of the cultural or historical specificity of norms and values. This perspective runs counter to the explanation of globalization provided by the strand of institutionalist theory known in comparative education as world culture theory (Baker and LeTendre, 2005; Meyer, Boli, Thomas, and Ramirez, 1997). Chabbott (2009), for example, explains in her book on the history of the World Conference on Education for All that the standardization of "appropriate development goals" and the means for achieving them was accomplished by "the work of both international development organizations and international development professionals who articulate and carry packages of 'correct' principles [and] 'appropriate' policies" (p. 2). Yet the social location of these early development professionals quickly becomes obscured in world culture theory as the focus shifts to the norms and priorities of the organizations themselves and to the "global environment." This approach to analyzing globalization provides many useful insights, but our concern is with its obfuscation of the relations of power that elevate certain local views of the world to the level of the global. As Kathryn Anderson-Levitt (2012, p. 441) explains,

> Most anthropologists define culture as the making of meaning, with an emphasis on the process itself as contested. It follows that world culture is locally produced in social interaction, and that meanings are then reconstructed in the global/local nexus. Power matters, particularly the hidden power to make resources for meaning making widely available, and to make them attractive and scientifically persuasive. How actors succeed in claiming particular ideas as global and how the locals strategically respond are questions where anthropologists can contribute to understanding the global/local nexus and the exercise of power within the world polity.

Discussions of "world culture" too often fail to consider the role of social interactions and power in the processes of establishing and maintaining such norms across locations. An analysis that compares these multiple "locals" and problematizes the uptake of certain discourses, processes, and policies and the enrollment in networks is critical to the VCS approach.

One example of how this vertical dimension can be developed comes from the work of Meg Gardinier (2012), who used a VCS approach to explore why national policy-makers in

Albania took up certain international models of citizenship education in their reforms and how Albanian teachers appropriated these models to fit with their understanding of the local schooling context. She examined these actors' multiple sources of knowledge about democratic citizenship and the process by which citizenship education projects were taken up and negotiated in post-communist Albania. She concluded:

> although national policy-makers aimed to modernize the Albanian education system by infusing international models into national policies, teachers strategically interpreted and adapted these foreign models to reflect their experience with the political context of schools, their pedagogical and subject knowledge, and their familiar forms of teaching practice. The resulting process of hybrid localization and enactment has significant implications for the outcomes of educational reform in Albania and other democratizing countries. (2012, p. 1)

This example reveals the value of looking at social actors working at international, national, regional, and more local levels.

Second, the *horizontal* dimension of the VCS approach emphasizes the importance of comparing how similar policies unfold in distinct locations that are socially produced and "simultaneously and complexly connected" (Tsing, 2005, p. 6). The horizontal element takes two primary forms. First, scholars might trace people, policies, or practices across sites. For example, Laura Valdiviezo's (2009) work on how teachers understand and implement bilingual intercultural education in Cuzco, Peru, examined the professional development they received in Cuzco and then followed teachers to schools in locations around the province. Alternately, the "horizontal" element may prompt a series of comparative case studies of how a similar phenomenon manifests across different locations. This type of horizontal comparison juxtaposes cases that follow the same logic to address topics of common concern. For example, in her study of language ideologies, policies, and practices in Lebanon, Zeena Zakharia (2009) conducted surveys of administrators, teachers, and students across ten schools in greater Beirut, and then conducted ethnographic research at three of those ten to consider how religious ideologies and socioeconomic factors influenced language policies and practices. Furthermore, at each of the three schools she selected two focal students, and then did fieldwork at school and at home regarding their language practices.

Third, the VCS emphasizes the importance of *transversal* comparison, that is, of historically situating the processes or sets of relations under consideration and tracing the creative appropriation of educational policies and practices across time and space. The transversal element reminds us to study *across and through* levels to explore how globalizing processes intersect and interconnect people and policies that come into focus at different scales. The VCS approach expands the locations of research while showing how actors are related through specific historical contingencies that connect disparate social sites and social actors. In this way, transversal analysis enables one to show how "the specificity of place is not linked to a place-based identity, for places are *traversed* by unequal relations of power and struggles to contest these relations" (Mahon and Keil, 2009, p. 4).

One particularly insightful example of this analytical process comes from Christina Kwauk's research on international sport for development through a VCS of its uptake in the Pacific island nation of Samoa. She traces the longstanding geo-political relations between Samoa and Australia and New Zealand, whose development agencies promote the "healthy body/healthy nation" narrative but whose sports authorities simultaneously create alternative pathways to economic growth for young Samoan athletes who leave the island and send home remittances. These athletes traverse vast spatial and social distances as sport "not only becomes a 'free ticket' overseas in the minds of many Samoans, but [also sets] in motion new pathways of productivity and practices of development" (Kwauk, 2013, p. 9). This brief example and the ones previously mentioned illustrate the various axes of VCSs. In the following section, we offer an extended example to exemplify the value of VCSs in globalization and education.

VERTICAL CASE STUDIES OF GLOBAL EDUCATION POLICY-AS-PRACTICE: LEARNER-CENTERED PEDAGOGY IN TANZANIA

We draw on a collaborative research project that examined how secondary school teachers in northern Tanzania understood and implemented learner-centered pedagogy (LCP). It involved graduate students from our own institutions and faculty members at Mwenge University College of Education in northern Tanzania (Vavrus and Bartlett, 2012).[2] The research was guided by two key questions: (1) How do teachers educated in teacher-centered pedagogy understand, interpret, and implement learner-centered approaches to teaching? (2) What are the material and ideological constraints teachers identify as obstacles to pedagogical change?

The first step in the research process was the analysis of documents to ascertain the genesis of learner-centered policy—where it originated, how it developed, and how it was adopted as "best pedagogical practice" among international educational development organizations. We also examined national educational policy shifts in Tanzania since 1967, when the country adopted a socialist policy known as Education for Self-Reliance, and reports of World Bank–funded educational initiatives in Tanzania. In addition, we reviewed current secondary school curricula and the 2010 national exams for O-level students, which contributed to "vertical" and "transversal" perspectives.

The next step was the development of the horizontal axis by conducting structured observations, interviews, and focus groups in six focal, private, secondary schools in two regions of northern Tanzania. We interviewed school heads from each school, and twenty-three of the approximately thirty-five teachers from these schools agreed to participate in our study. From our research team, we assigned two or three researchers to work at each school for a period of five weeks.

A systematic and comprehensive analysis of this entire project has been offered elsewhere (Vavrus and Bartlett, 2013). Here, instead, we seek to use elements from the larger study to exemplify the value of the VCS approach in three principal areas—the transversal, the vertical, and the horizontal—beginning with the transversal as this may be the least obvious facet of the approach.

Learner-Centered Pedagogy as Localism: Transversal Comparisons

It is important to examine, transversally, the ways in which LCP, a specific approach to teaching and learning popularized in the temporal and cultural context of the United States and the United Kingdom in the 1970s (Cuban, 1993; Ravitch, 1983), has been taken up, simplified, and spread globally. In so doing, LCP "globalized" very particular understandings of teaching and learning that rely upon culturally specific notions of individualism, competition, cooperation, and authority, and presume certain material conditions in schools and classrooms (Tabulawa, 1997). As such, LCP becomes a "globalized localism," that is, it has "globalized" particular understandings of teaching and learning that arose in specific cultural contexts; these understandings assume certain material conditions for teachers while obscuring the pedagogy's cultural, historical, and material specificity as it is taken up by policy-makers, teacher educators, and teachers in very distinct contexts (see also Vavrus and Bartlett, 2012).

Tanzania also provides a compelling case for the exploration of how the "global education-al visions" that Carney (2012, p. 2) describes are enacted in policy. An analysis regarding Tanzania's history as a socialist state that nevertheless sought to embrace the non-aligned "Third World" movement throughout the Cold War and its more recent turn toward neoliber-alism suggests different historical contingencies that bear on the appropriation of educational policy today. Document analysis and interviews with key informants in our study make it possible to track the sedimentation of this globalized pedagogical discourse in national poli-cies and curricula in Tanzania as it settles somewhat uneasily on top of the nationalist socialist discourse of education for self-reliance.

A brief review of Tanzanian education policies from 1995 to 2010 shows that these poli-cies display relative stability through a "common set of linguistic codes" (Carney, 2012, p. 10). Whereas the 1995 *Education and Training Policy* still contained traces of Nyerere's socialist goal of primary schooling teaching children to "respect and enrich our common cultural background ... national unity, identity, ethic, and pride" and to prepare them "for the world of work" (1995, p. 5), any vestigial notion of children working for the good of the collective disappeared by 2000–2001, when new national primary, secondary, and teacher education policies were implemented. These policies begin with explicit references to the 1990 Education For All conference in Jomtien that set targeted global educational goals, the 1995 World Social Summit in Copenhagen, and the 2000 Millennium Development Summit as global initiatives shaping Tanzania's policy priorities because it is now part of the global development and education community.

The momentum for LCP in Tanzania has increased alongside international pressure to expand secondary schooling in sub-Saharan Africa. For instance, the Secondary Education in Africa initiative, which was developed by the World Bank's Africa Region in 2002, makes a strong economic argument for investing in this sector if African youth are to compete in a "technology driven global economy" ("At the crossroads," 2007, p. 13). This economy pur-portedly demands students who, during secondary school, "acquire analytic and problem solving skills and most important have the motivation and the competence for further learning and skill acquisition [and] active participation in rapidly changing increasingly democratic societies" (2007, p. 17). In Tanzania, which has had, for decades, one of the lowest secondary school enrollment rates on the continent, a new discourse of secondary education expansion for the knowledge economy began to arise in the early 2000s. It was enacted in policy with the Secondary Education Development Programme, which ran from 2004 to 2009, and continues in Secondary Education Development Programme II, which is intended to last from 2010 to 2015.[3]

These examples add further weight to Carney's contention that the current policyscape is constituted, in part, through "learning processes," which are comprised of "learner-centered pedagogy, classroom democracy, and active learning through which teachers are restyled as facilitators of learning and students as independent learners" (2009, p. 68).[4] Clearly, the policyscape concept contributes an insightful and productive way of conceptualizing global-ization in the study of policy. Yet, as Steiner-Khamsi (2010) suggests, one would expect such convergence in the analysis of policy talk. The value of qualitative approaches for the study of educational policy derives from their ability to move beyond the professed aims of policy to examine how policies are made and contested at various levels by a more diverse range of policy actors.

Vertical Assemblages

A careful analysis of vertical assemblages is also important to the type of analysis we propose. Vertical assemblages are temporary, shifting alliances or networks of people, objects, and ideas; researchers examine how assemblages are amassed, organized, challenged, and defended (Koyama, 2010). An actor-network approach to policy-as-practice, then, seeks to trace "the specific materializing processes through which policymaking actually works to animate educational knowledge, identities, and practices" (Fenwick and Edwards, 2010, p. 710).

The value of tracing vertical assemblages in our study may be illustrated by contrasting the impact of curriculum developers and assessment developers working at the national level on teachers' pedagogical decisions. Our research in Tanzania revealed that, while the national curriculum was heavily influenced by donor support and donor pressure, the more independent national assessment unit was not similarly enrolled in the LCP network. Reflecting on his experiences in the 1990s, one Tanzanian scholar wrote that "[n]early all curriculum integration projects based at the Ministry of Education and Culture or TIE [Tanzania Institute of Education, which develops curricula and teaching materials] are run by donor funds, without which they will stop. ... The donor pressure on what should be included in the content is tremendous" (Mbunda, 1997, p. 183, as cited in Brock-Utne, 2000, p. 128).

Such influence, in part, explains the appearance of LCP in Tanzanian curricula. Yet the National Examination Council of Tanzania continued to devise high-stakes exams that captured rote memorization more than critical thinking. Because the tests have serious consequences for students, for teachers who may receive "motivation" money if their students perform well, and for schools (especially private schools) whose existence may depend on the high scores that attract new families and their tuition fees, the tests paradoxically encourage methods that emphasize the memorization of factual information rather than LCP approaches. This tendency is compounded by the breadth of the exams, which cover four years of information for seven or more subjects, making the acquisition of both core knowledge and higher-order thinking skills a great challenge (Shuyler and Vavrus, 2010). The Tanzanian teachers in our study made clear that they struggle with implementing a competency-based curriculum when the high-stakes, national exams continue to emphasize the recall of facts and when their students may not have the skills in English to fully grasp what is being asked of them.

Such analyses of vertical assemblages demonstrate that it is not sufficient to examine how LCP is produced and incorporated at the national level; one must also consider how various actors, including school heads and teachers, appropriate it across multiple sites.

The Value of Horizontal Comparisons

In addition to transversal and vertical analysis, horizontal comparisons are an important component in the VCS approach. In our study, we included six high schools in two adjacent regions in Tanzania to demonstrate the significant impact of transnational institutions and social movements on the material conditions of "local" schools and on the organizational dynamics within them. For instance, teachers at the school funded by an American non-profit organization enjoyed extensive professional development in LCP, a life skills program for students, a sizable library with materials for developing inquiry-based projects, and relative material wealth as reflected in the availability of books, handouts, paper, photocopiers, and internet access. These factors influenced the shape and tenor of the appropriation of LCP at that school, as observed by the research team and reported by its teachers.

In contrast, the Catholic and Lutheran schools presented a markedly different context within which to develop the more egalitarian relations between teachers and students that are implicit in LCP. For example, one teacher at a Catholic school complained that there were constraints on teachers organizing debates among students on topics of concern and interest to students, such as prostitution or HIV/AIDS. She gave the following account describing when she took her female students to debate male pupils at a rural seminary:

> And they said, "These boys are priests, we cannot discuss such." And that was the end of that topic. And I wanted somebody to tell me: those are boys, they are priests, yes, but who are they going to minister to? People who are prostitutes and … these are ills that are affecting the society. … We have to train them to talk about these things openly. They're going to be leaders, and they'll have to talk about prostitution at one time or another one, and AIDS and what, you can't avoid it. And the people just said, "Mmm-hmm" [negative sound], and nobody really wanted to commit.

In religiously affiliated schools, teachers' appropriations of the educational policies promoted by international institutions and embedded in national curricula were heavily influenced by religious notions of propriety, including gender norms.

More broadly, the horizontal comparison across these six high schools demonstrates how different material and ideological contexts affect the appropriation of LCP within one country. According to the Tanzanian teachers who participated in the study, LCP is simply more difficult to implement in schools with overcrowded classrooms, few books to share among many students, limited poster board for making teaching aids, and even notebook paper to enhance group or pair work. For instance, at Dunia Secondary School, teachers explained in a focus group discussion that the shortage of textbooks required them to spend class time drawing diagrams and figures on the board for students to copy. As one teacher noted:

> Maybe I will comment on the same idea he's given about resources. We have an idea of improvising, but it is something that has not been implemented fully. Resources are very few, but I just want to give you an example. Maybe you have a topic, for example in biology. In the teaching process as a teacher, the students have a textbook and the students see the pictures in the textbook, but you only have five textbooks for a class of 70 students. It becomes difficult because you have to draw the picture so that the students can see the lesson.

In the case of private, church-affiliated schools like Dunia, school heads relied almost exclusively on student tuition to cover expenses and often increased the number of students to generate revenue even though the purchasing of teaching and learning materials did not keep pace. The stretching of resources has implications for the pedagogical methods that teachers are likely to use when textbooks are limited and class sizes large. Teachers frequently used the term "spoon feeding" to describe the primary method of instruction because of these constraints. As the horizontal comparison revealed, the shortages of resources, more severe in some schools than in others, made "spoon feeding" more likely and learner-centered teaching more of a challenge.

Moreover, because LCP relies extensively on dialogue, and because Tanzanian education policy mandates the use of English at the secondary level, LCP is difficult to implement in schools or classrooms where students and teachers have a limited command of English, if the teachers actually enforce this national language policy in their classrooms. At the school funded by the U.S. organization, for instance, there were a number of foreign staff members who spoke only English, not Kiswahili, and a steady stream of U.S. volunteers to work with the students to enhance their language skills. This institutional context also seemed to foster the use of more learner-centered methods in the classroom than in the other schools. The differences in material resources and knowledge of English matter greatly for the high-stakes national exams that, as previously mentioned, create an intense pressure for teachers to "cover the syllabus" and "teach to the test." Because the national exams are entirely in English (with the exception of the Kiswahili language test), the differences in language use across these school sites are potentially quite significant and indicate how national policies, influenced by international organizations, are differentially appropriated in practice. This study, then, shows scholars of globalization and education how globalized localisms such as LCP, which emerge in specific material and cultural contexts, get taken up, made universalist, spread, and then remade as they are again localized in distinct material, sociopolitical, and cultural contexts.

CONCLUSIONS AND FUTURE DIRECTIONS

These brief examples from our larger collaborative research project illustrate the transversal, vertical, and horizontal axes of comparison that constitute the VCS approach. We believe it offers much to contemporary efforts in educational studies to reconceptualize "the nature of locality" in the face of globalization. The VCS uses multi-sited ethnography to trace the appropriation of policy in various phases, across space and time, and by diverse actors in distinct assemblages. In this way, the approach allows us to examine how the appropriation of policies contributes to the continued cultural production of policyscapes. Moreover, this project of exploring the interconnectivity of global educational ideoscapes and local educational practice provides a way to forestall "forced acts of coherence and closure" (Carney, 2012, p. 12) and to add conceptual and methodological tools for studying global educational policy formation and implementation.

The VCS provides a particularly important analytical approach to the study of global educational policy because it incorporates a transverse analysis of how actors, including non-human actors like policies and national exams, operate at different levels or scales and become enrolled in and accountable to networks that span space and time. Actors creatively appropriate elements of policy, shaped by their own motives and interests as well as their institutional constraints and social commitments. Such an approach can be fruitfully engaged to examine how policyscapes, such as the push for "quality" education with its attendant regimes of student and teacher assessment, policies to care for "vulnerable children," or the current emphasis among donors on early grade reading pedagogies, are differentially appropriated over time and space.

Such an approach may well require methodological shifts in our field. Lone researchers could fruitfully engage in the sort of multi-sited ethnography we have detailed here. However, as Marcus (2011) warns, participant-researcher relationships in multi-sited ethnographies may need to be considerably reconfigured, implying a new set of norms surrounding ethnographic knowledge production that brings together a broader range of actors and scales in a single study. There is noteworthy potential in the joint planning and conduct of comparative ethnography, in which a team of researchers would examine how a specific policyscape, such as teacher assessment policy, is appropriated in distinct locations. This appealing avenue of research unleashes significant (but, as we have learned, not unproblematic) opportunities for collaboration with scholars living and working in distinct material, social, and cultural conditions (see Vavrus and Bartlett, 2013). Such partnerships may help to diversify knowledge production and ways of knowing in the field by expanding analysis across multiple researchers and multiple scales simultaneously.

REFERENCES

Anderson-Levitt, Kathryn. 2012. Complicating the Concept of Culture. *Comparative Education*, vol. 48, no. 4, pp. 441–54.

Appadurai, Arjun. 1990. Disjuncture and Difference in the Global Cultural Economy. *Public Culture*, vol. 2, no. 2, pp. 1–24.

_____. 1996. *Modernity at Large: Cultural Dimensions of Globalization*. Minneapolis and London: University of Minnesota Press.

At the crossroads: Choices for Secondary Education in sub-Saharan Africa (2007, 5 February). SEIA Synthesis Report: Executive Summary. Unpublished report.

Baker, David P., and Gerald K. LeTendre. 2005. *National Difference, Global Similarities: World Culture and the Future of Schooling*. Stanford: Stanford University Press.

Bartlett, Lesley, and Frances Vavrus. Forthcoming. Transversing the Vertical Case Study: A Methodological Approach to Studies of Educational Policy as Practice. *Anthropology and Education Quarterly*.

Bourdieu, Pierre. 1977. *Outline of a Theory of Practice*. Cambridge: Cambridge University Press.

_____. 1990. *The Logic of Practice*. Stanford: Stanford University Press.

Brock-Utne, Birgit. 2000. *Whose Education for All? The Recolonization of the African Mind*. New York: Falmer Press.

Carney, Stephen. 2009. Negotiating Policy in an Age of Globalization: Exploring Educational "Policyscapes" in Denmark, Nepal, and China. *Comparative Education Review*, vol. 53, no. 1, pp. 63–88.

_____. 2012. Imagining Globalization: Educational Policyscapes. In Gita Steiner-Khamsi and Florian Waldow (eds.), *World Yearbook of Education 2012*: *Policy Borrowing and Lending* (pp. 339–53). New York: Routledge.

Chabbott, Colette. 2009. *Constructing Education for Development: International Organizations and Education for All*. New York and London: Routledge.

Coleman, Simon, and Pauline von Hellermann. 2011. *Multi-Sited Ethnography: Problems and Possibilities in the Translocation of Research Methods*. New York: Routledge.

Cuban, Larry. 1993. *How Teachers Taught: Constancy and Change in American Classrooms, 1890-1990*, 2nd edition. New York: Teachers College Press.

de Certeau, Michel. 1984. *The Practice of Everyday Life*, trans. Steven Rendall. Berkeley: University of California Press.

de Sousa Santos, Boaventura, João A. Nunes, and Maria P. Meneses. 2007. Introduction: Opening up the Canon of Knowledge and Recognition of Difference. In Boaventura de Sousa Santos (ed.), *Another Knowledge is Possible: Beyond Northern Epistemologies* (pp. xix–lxii). London: Verso.

Falzon, Mark-Anthony. 2009. Introduction: Multi-Sited Ethnography: Theory, Praxis and Locality in Contemporary Research. *Multi-Sited Ethnography*. Surrey: Ashgate.

Feldman, Gregory. 2011. If Ethnography is More than Participant-Observation, then Relations are More than Connections: The Case for Nonlocal Ethnography in a World of Apparatuses. Anthropological Theory, vol. 11, no. 4 , pp. 375–95.

Fenwick, Tara, and Richard Edwards. 2010. *Actor-Network Theory in Education*. New York: Routledge.

Gardinier, Meg. 2012. From Global Projects to Classroom Practice: The Localization of Democratic Citizenship Education in Post-Communist Albania. Doctoral dissertation, School of Education, Cornell University.

Goldman, Michael. 2006. *Imperial Nature: The World Bank and Struggles for Social Justice in the Age of Globalizations*. New Haven: Yale University Press.

Hamann, Ted, and Lisa Rosen. 2011. What Makes the Anthropology of Educational Policy Implementation "Anthropological"? In Bradley Levinson and Mica Pollock (eds.), *A Companion to the Anthropology of Education* (pp. 461–77). New York: Wiley Blackwell.

Kearney, Michael. 1995. The Local and the Global: The Anthropology of Globalization and Transnationalism. *Annual Review of Anthropology*, vol. 24, pp. 547–65.

Koyama, Jill. 2010. *Making Failure Pay: For-Profit Tutoring, High-Stakes Testing, and Public Schools*. Chicago: The University of Chicago Press.

_____. 2011. Generating, Comparing, Manipulating, Categorizing, Reporting, and Sometimes Fabricating Data to Comply with No Child Left Behind Mandates. *Journal of Education Policy*, vol. 26, no. 5, pp. 701–20.

Kwauk, Christina T. 2013. "No Longer Just a Pastime": Sport for Development in Times of Change. ASAO Working Session: Contemporary Sporting Formations in Oceania. Doctoral dissertation, University of Minnesota.

Latour, Bruno. 2005. *Reassembling the Social: An Introduction to Actor-Network Theory*. Oxford: Oxford University Press.

Levinson, Bradley A.U., and Margaret Sutton. 2001. Introduction: Policy as/in Practice: A Sociocultural Approach to the Study of Educational Policy. In Margaret Sutton and Bradley Levinson (eds.), *Policy as Practice: Toward a Comparative Sociocultural Analysis of Educational Policy* (pp. 1–24). Westport, CT: Ablex.

Levinson, Bradley A.U., Margaret Sutton, and Teresa Winstead. 2009. Education Policy as a Practice of Power: Theoretical Tools, Ethnographic Methods, Democratic Options. *Educational Policy*, vol. 23, pp. 767–95.

Li, Tania Murray. 2007. *The Will to Improve: Governmentality, Development, and the Practice of Politics*. Durham, NC: Duke University Press.

Mahon, Rianne, and Roger Keil (eds.). 2009. *Leviathan Undone: Towards a Political Economy of Scale.* Vancouver: University of British Columbia Press.

Marcus, George. 1995. Ethnography in/of the World System: The Emergence of Multi-Sited Ethnography. *Annual Review of Anthropology*, vol. 24, pp. 95–117.

_____. 1998. *Ethnography through Thick and Thin.* Princeton: Princeton University Press.

_____. 2011. Multi-Sited Ethnography: Five or Six Things I Know About It Now. In Simon Coleman and Pauline von Hellermann (eds.), *Multi-Sited Ethnography: Problems and Possibilities in the Translocation of Research Methods* (pp. 16–34). New York: Routledge.

Marginson, Simon, and Marcela Mollis. 2001. "The Door Opens and the Tiger Leaps": Theories and Reflexivities of Comparative Education for a Global Millennium. *Comparative Education Review*, vol. 45, no. 4, pp. 581–615.

Massey, Doreen. 2005. *For Space.* London: Sage.

Meyer, John W., John Boli, George Thomas, and Francisco O. Ramirez. 1997. World Society and the Nation-State. *American Journal of Sociology*, vol. 103, pp. 144–81.

Nespor, Jan. 2003. Educational Scale-Making. *Pedagogy, Culture, and Society*, vol. 12, no. 3, pp. 309–26.

Nyerere. 1995.

Ong, Aihwa and Stephen Collier. 2004. *Global Assemblages: Technology, Politics, and Ethics as Anthropological Problems.* Malden, MA: Wiley-Blackwell.

Ravitch, Diane. 1983. *The Troubled Crusade: American Education, 1945-1980.* New York: Basic Books, Inc., Publishers.

Robertson, Susan. 2012. Researching Global Education Policy: Angles In/On/Out .... In Antoni Verger, Mario Novelli and Hulya Kosar Altinyelken (eds.), *Global Education Policy and International Development: New Agendas, Issues and Practices* (pp. 33–51). New York: Continuum Publishers.

Shore, Cris, and Susan Wright. 1997. *Anthropology of Policy: Critical Perspectives on Governance and Power.* London and New York: Routledge.

Shuyler, Ashley, and Frances Vavrus. 2010. Global Competition and Higher Education in Tanzania. In Laura Portnoi, Val Rust, and Sylvia Bagley (eds.), *Higher Education, Policy, and the Global Competition Phenomenon* (pp. 177–90). New York: Macmillan.

Steiner-Khamsi, Gita. 2010. The Politics and Economics of Comparison. *Comparative Education Review* , vol. 54 , no. 3, pp. 323–42.

Tabulawa, Richard. 1997. Pedagogical Classroom Practice and the Social Context: The Case of Botswana. *International Journal of Educational Development*, vol. 17, no. 2, pp. 189–204.

Tsing, Anna Lowenhaupt. 2005. *Friction: An Ethnography of Global Connections.* Princeton: Princeton University Press.

Valdiviezo, Laura. 2009. Bilingual Intercultural Education in Indigenous Schools: An Ethnography of Teacher Interpretations of Government Policy. *International Journal of Bilingual Education and Bilingualism*, vol. 12, no. 1, pp. 61–79.

Vavrus, Frances, and Lesley Bartlett (eds.). 2009. *Critical Approaches to Comparative Education: Vertical Case Studies from Africa, Europe, the Middle East, and the Americas.* New York: Palgrave Macmillan.

_____, and Lesley Bartlett. 2012. Comparative Pedagogies and Epistemological Diversity: Social and Materials Contexts of Teaching in Tanzania. *Comparative Education Review*, vol. 56, no. 4, pp. 634–58.

_____, and Lesley Bartlett. 2013. *Teaching in Tension: International Pedagogies, National Policies, and Teachers' Practices in Tanzania.* Rotterdam: Sense Publishers.

Vavrus, Frances, Matthew Thomas, and Lesley Bartlett. 2011. *Ensuring Quality by Attending to Inquiry: Learner-Centered Pedagogy in Sub-Saharan Africa.* Addis Ababa: UNESCO-International Institute for Capacity Building in Africa.

Zakharia, Zeena. 2009. Positioning Arabic in Schools: Language Policy, National Identity, and Development in Contemporary Lebanon. In Frances Vavrus and Lesley Bartlett (eds.), *Critical Approaches to Comparative Education: Vertical Case Studies from Africa, Europe, the Middle East, and the Americas* (pp. 215–31). New York: Palgrave Macmillan.

NOTES

1. For an extended analysis of globalized localism and localized globalism, see Vavrus and Bartlett (2012).

2. See Vavrus and Bartlett (2012, 2013) for a list of the members of the research team. The "we" in this description of the project refers to the collaborative research by this team and not our work alone.

3. For an elaborated analysis of this policy history, see Bartlett and Vavrus, forthcoming.

4. See Vavrus, Thomas, and Bartlett (2011) for further examples of LCP as taken up in education policy in sub-Saharan Africa.

Part II

Globalization Impacts in Various Educational Sectors

Chapter Nine

Globalization Responses from European and Australian University Sectors

Jan Currie and Lesley Vidovich

Despite the global financial crisis of 2008 and the need to regulate markets, the neoliberal agenda of globalization remains as a powerful force in reforming higher education worldwide. For example, countries across the globe continue to re-engineer their universities to try to compete in the rankings of international league tables. They strive to be "world class" even though the top one hundred universities are dominated by two English-speaking countries, the United States and the United Kingdom. More and more, institutions are run as business enterprises in a managerial fashion and are pressured to generate new forms of income. Increasingly, they are also held accountable for their responsiveness to economic and social needs, especially regarding their contribution to regional and national competitiveness in the global economy.

Another major impact on universities is the use of the Internet and online education. Harden (2013) argues that higher education is at a tipping point. New interactive Web technology is creating a global marketplace where courses from numerous universities are available on a single website. It will be difficult for universities around the world to compete with the United States as it has developed many of these sites first. Its premier universities such as the Massachusetts Institute of Technology and Harvard are creating online education ventures such as edX with their courses known as massive open online courses (MOOCs). This will broaden access to education, which Harden suggests is "equal in significance to the invention of the printing press, the public library or the public school" (2013, p. 61).

Friedman (2013) warns that the MOOCs revolution will create a more competency-based world where universities will have to move from a "model of 'time served' to a model of 'stuff learned'" (p. A23). A blended model of teaching may develop where students combine online lectures with teacher-led classroom experience. He concludes, "The world of MOOCs is creating a competition that will force every professor to improve his or her pedagogy or face an online competitor" (p. A23).

There will be winners and losers among universities in this global marketplace of higher education. How higher education policy-makers at the national and institutional levels respond to these trends depends upon a range of inter-related factors. Among these are the political economy of the particular country and its position in the global economy. Linked factors are the degree to which policy-makers want their universities to join the competition and the pressure that they place on their universities to do so. Other factors include national culture and the structural features of the particular higher education system; for example, how autonomous are universities within a national system and how much power does the national government have to insist on certain accountability regimes. At the institutional level, cultural and structural factors are also important—along with the university's world ranking—in determining its responses.

This chapter looks at how higher education policy-makers in Europe are positioning the region in this global marketplace and describes how policy-makers in three countries (Australia, the Netherlands, and France) have responded to the neoliberal model of "best practice" in the university sector that is sweeping the world. These three countries are on a continuum from Australia, the most compliant, to France, the most resistant, in adopting this neoliberal model. We argue that the historical traditions and political economy of these nations influence how higher education policy-makers respond to the dominant neoliberal model. The neoliberal model has its origin in Anglo-American countries and is actively promulgated through supranational organizations, such as the Organization for Economic Cooperation and Development (OECD) and the World Bank (Rizvi and Lingard, 2010). France, with traditions different from those of the United States and the United Kingdom, has adopted some neoliberal economic reforms but has resisted others, whereas Australia and the Netherlands have tried to emulate the Anglo-American leading universities.

For example, despite OECD urgings to jettison the election system in French universities and to apply more modern managerial systems, the French higher education system has preserved its semi-collegial forms of governance and has an election process for choosing the president and representative councils at each university. In contrast, the Netherlands and Australia have moved closer to the managerial university model that is common in the United States. Australia has aggressively adopted the concept of "world class" university and is striving to move its universities up the international league tables. The Netherlands has also put greater emphasis on research. It rewards those universities that produce more research publications and patents. France has been more reluctant to move in this direction.

Before discussing specific regional and country responses to globalization, we examine the global phenomenon of university rankings and performance assessments. We conclude by raising issues about future global trends in higher education policies and practices and the need to continue researching context-specific difference in how institutions, nations, and regions respond to these trends.

GLOBALIZATION, UNIVERSITY RANKINGS, AND PERFORMANCE ASSESSMENTS

The fundamental force underpinning neoliberal globalization is the privatization of the economy and the squeeze on public spending (Currie, 2005). This movement to shift substantial resources from the public sector to the private sector began simultaneously in the United States with the Reagan government and in the United Kingdom with the Thatcher government. It then spread to other Anglo-derived countries, and later more globally. In higher education, governments have reduced relative funding for universities and have forced them to become more entrepreneurial and corporate in nature (Marginson and Considine, 2000) with acceleration toward privatization. However, these trends have not been universal. For example, many European countries such as Norway and France resisted the trend toward privatization of the university sector (Currie, DeAngelis, de Boer, Huisman and Lacotte, 2003).

While the image of globalization is often of homogenization based on the American model, it is not an inexorable process that sweeps all nations down the same path. Globalization creates a space that is not completely constructed; there is an uncertainty with it and often contradictory meanings and trends. Despite the increasing interconnectedness of different jurisdictions forged by international organizations such as OECD, higher education policies and practices often take on different "shades" in specific localized contexts (Rizvi and Lingard, 2010). This is a consequence of their different historical traditions, cultures, and deeply embedded public policy structures and processes. Recently, Owen (2011), writing in the context of the United States, remarked on the growing idolatry of market forces and the re-engineering of traditionally open intellectual and social spaces of the university to spaces of control and regulation. He argued that for U.S. universities, the post-9/11 era has created a strange hybrid of neoliberalism and the security state, a condition where free-market laissez-faire economy and increased state control collide. Thus, the impact of globalization is complex and likely to vary across both place and time.

Global university rankings are often based on the *Shanghai Jiao Tong Institute of Higher Education*—now known as the *Academic Ranking of World Universities (ARWU)*—and *Times Higher Education* models.[1] These rankings produce the most followed league tables and provide a powerful impetus for individual universities to become global actors. Attwood (2009) observed, "Governments are swayed by [rankings], universities fall out over them and vice-chancellors [presidents] have even lost their jobs because of them." At the national level in many countries, the drive for more universities to achieve "world class" status has translated into new policies on research assessment. However, not all countries have chosen to implement research assessment exercises. One interesting example is mainland China, which gave its universities greater autonomy and provided a few selected universities with additional funding to compete more effectively internationally. In contrast, the Hong Kong Special Administrative Region (Yang, Vidovich, and Currie, 2007) followed its previous colonial master in instituting a research assessment process very similar to the U.K. model.

It appears that many policy-makers around the world have identified research assessment exercises as a necessary force to make their universities more competitive in international rankings. However, as Altbach (2006) noted, "the fact is that essentially all of the measures used to assess quality and construct rankings enhance the stature of the large universities in the major English-speaking centres of science and scholarship and especially in the United States and the United Kingdom" (p. 3). In a similar vein, Marginson (2006) observed, "the model global university is English speaking and science oriented" (p. 27). This limits the number of universities that can truly compete to be "world class" and points to the unequal playing field in the university rankings game.

In looking at the three countries in this chapter and comparing those with the United States and the United Kingdom (see Table 9.1), it is clear that Australian, Dutch, and French universities are in a challenging race. It appears that the Netherlands (population 16.7 million) and Australia (22.9 million) are remaining competitive in these world rankings, especially for being two countries with much smaller populations than the United States (312.8 million). France (63.6 million) has done reasonably well; however, for a country almost equal in size to the United Kingdom (63.6 million), it is lagging in the world university rankings. For branding purposes, universities tend to quote the ranking that best portrays their strengths and enhances their reputation.

To counter these global rankings based mainly on research publications, the Centre for Higher Education Development in Germany developed the CHE Excellence Ranking, which is exclusively about disciplines and does not create a league table of European universities. It gathers survey data on students' views about study programs and combines this with research strengths and internationalization of teaching staff and students. More recently, the European

Table 9.1. *THE* and *ARWU* 2012 World University Rankings: Top One Hundred and Three Hundred Universities

Country	*THE* Top 100	*ARWU* Top 100	*THE* Top 300	*ARWU* Top 300
United States	47	53	94	119
United Kingdom	10	9	39	30
Netherlands	7	2	13	10
Australia	6	5	10	9
France	4	3	10	13

ARWU = Academic Ranking of World Universities; THE = Times Higher Education.

Commission asked the Center for Higher Education Policy Studies at the University of Twente in the Netherlands to create a European Classification of Higher Education Institutions, known as the U-Map, Lifelong Learning Project. They extended the measures beyond research and included these five indicators: teaching and learning, research, student profile, knowledge exchange, and international presence. One of the results was to indicate the diversity of universities in Europe.

Australia is considering creating a local version of the U-Map as an antidote to research-focused rankings imposed by outside agencies (Trounson, 2013). This will enable universities to highlight their strengths in other areas such as teaching or community service—an interesting case of policy borrowing from Europe to Australia.

As indicated earlier, one of the major organizations that influence higher education policy trends worldwide is the OECD. It is moving into the area of rankings with a different emphasis. It wants to measure and compare student learning outcomes across universities around the globe. It is conducting a feasibility study for the Assessment of Higher Education Learning Outcomes (AHELO) to determine whether it is practically and scientifically possible to assess what university students know and can do when they graduate. It aims to evaluate student performance across a range of different cultures, languages, and types of institutions (OECD, 2013). It is considering generic skills (e.g., critical thinking, problem solving, and communication) and discipline-specific skills in economics and engineering. It will also include a contextual questionnaire to be able to link performance data with student backgrounds and learning environments. The feasibility study has involved twenty-three thousand students and 248 institutions in seventeen countries.

The OECD claims that a full scale AHELO would be a "low stakes, voluntary international comparative assessment" (OECD, 2013) for fostering improvement and that it will report at the institutional level and not allow national comparisons or provide league tables. However, given that universities are increasingly competing for the "best and the brightest" students from around the globe, it is not hard to imagine that with publication of performance data, the construction of league tables by others would not be precluded, especially on the rationale that they can inform "customer" choices in higher education. At this point in 2013, the future of AHELO is uncertain. The final report of the feasibility study is imminent and then "OECD countries will decide whether to delve deeper into the subject as well as set up steps toward conducting a full-scale AHELO" (OECD, 2013).

Any study of globalization and higher education must seek not only to identify commonalities in higher education policy directions across national boundaries, but also the ways in which particular local contexts mitigate against wholesale or simplistic adoption of macro trends that serve selective interests. Although many universities have actively sought to engage with these globalization trends, others have subverted or opposed these policy directives. To pursue these issues, we now turn to how policy-makers in particular regions and countries have responded to the global trends, with an emphasis on the policy discourses of increasing university autonomy concurrent with new forms of accountability in research and teaching and learning that together are creating policy dissonance and tensions within universities and systems of higher education.

NATIONAL AND REGIONAL CONTEXTS

Political Economies of Australia, the Netherlands, and France

Gross domestic products per capita (GDP, derived from purchasing power parity) rankings in 2011 placed all three countries among the top thirty-five nations in the world: the Netherlands (seventeenth, $42,000), Australia (twenty-first, $40,800), and France (thirty-fifth, $35,000). France is more social democratic in its political orientation in 2013 with a higher level of public sector expenditure per gross domestic product than the Netherlands or Australia (CIA World Factbook, 2013). All three countries have introduced tuition fees, with France the lowest, the Netherlands in between, and Australia the highest.

Australia can be described as an advanced market economy and was the best economic performer in the OECD during the global financial crisis. The Netherlands is also a market economy that is highly industrialized with a small, mechanized agricultural sector. It went from twenty-six years of economic growth with a surplus to a deficit in 2009. As a result of the global financial crisis and the European euro crisis, it introduced austerity measures to reduce its deficit. France is a mixed economy with a commitment to capitalism but also to maintaining social equality through tax policies and social welfare spending to reduce income disparity. It recently introduced a much higher tax on incomes over U.S. $1.3 million, with the consequence that a few of its richest citizens have opted to leave the country, one being the French actor, Gérard Depardieu, who was given Russian citizenship by President Putin to avoid the high taxes of France's socialist-led government.

All three countries (Australia, the Netherlands, and France) alternate between right- and left-leaning governments and sometimes form coalitions across the right and left to deliver middle-of-the-road governments. Currently in 2013, Australia and France have left-leaning governments and the Netherlands has a right-leaning centrist government led by the People's Party for Freedom and Democracy in coalition with the Labor Party. Australia has a minority Labor government in coalition with the Greens and Independents. France elected a socialist president after many years of economic neoliberal Gaullist (right-wing) governments. In a sense, these three countries could be said to be moving toward the "Third Way," which is between the dogmas of free-market capitalism with reduced government spending and big-government regulation with higher welfare spending.

In Europe, another globalizing force is operating to bring greater economic and cultural integration into the region. Hence, the next section discusses Europe's globalizing strategy of creating a European Higher Education Area.

European Higher Education Area

To create Europe as a globally competitive knowledge economy, two agendas were developed based on the Bologna Declaration (1999) and the Lisbon strategy for growth and jobs adopted in 2000 and re-launched in 2005. The Bologna Declaration committed an initial set of twenty-nine signatories to six objectives, aiming to establish a European Higher Education Area by

2010. These countries would adopt uniform degree structures, align their national quality assurance agencies, develop a credit transfer system, and encourage staff and student mobility, among other things. The Lisbon strategy had two targets to be reached by 2010: total (public and private) investment of 3 percent of Europe's gross domestic product in research and development and an increase in Europe's overall employment rate. Kwiek (2009) argues that an indirect impact of globalization on European universities is "the delinking of the nation-state and public universities" (p. 184). Robertson (2009) noted a similar decline in the influence of the nation-state. She quoted Viviane Reding, member of the European Commission responsible for Education and Culture, who laid out the bases in her speech, "Making the EU a Prominent Figure in the World Education Market." Reding said, "We see that national governments acting alone cannot meet the challenges of globalization, new technologies and of the single market" (Robertson, 2009, p. 75).

As a result of the focus on the regionalization of Europe and a decline in the concept of a welfare state, there has been reduced funding of public universities. Consequently, nation-states have made their universities more autonomous and reliant on third stream (private sector) income. According to Kwiek (2009), public universities have to become more self-reliant and self-supported and not look to the nation-state for total funding. This augurs in changes in governance, research, accountability regimes, and student mobility. Universities are given greater autonomy and increased governance responsibilities while national governments have responsibility for the strategic orientation of the system as a whole. Research has also shifted from being the responsibility of the individual researcher to teams and global networks (European Commission, 2006).

The Bologna Follow-Up Group adopted an agreed set of European standards and guidelines for quality assurance. This means that quality assurance agencies in each nation submit themselves to a cycle of reviews. Erasmus, Socrates, and Jean Monnet programs were introduced to increase cooperation and mobility across Europe. Erasmus started in 1987 and is the most successful student exchange program in the world. Each year more than 230,000 students study abroad. Socrates began in 1994 with the aim of strengthening the European dimension of education at all levels. The Jean Monnet program stimulates teaching and research on European integration in universities and establishes special chairs and centers of excellence in Europe and across the world. All of these programs were rolled into the Lifelong Learning Program after 2007. In addition, a Europass was created so that each individual would have a learning and working ID designed to encourage mobility and lifelong learning in an enlarged Europe (European Commission, 2005). It would individually encode the student's record of learning and workplace experiences.

"Culturally the goal is to create a European citizen with a European sensibility and a sense of responsibility to a bigger political entity—Europe" (Robertson, 2009, p. 69). Kwiek (2009) describes this new European citizen as one who is not bound up in the nation but an "individual with an individuated 'knowledge portfolio' of education, skills and competencies" (p. 107). This new pan-European educational space, where there is free movement of knowledge, is being built to create the lifelong learner. Even though there is an attempt to create an integrated Europe, the nation-states persist and continue to compete in the higher education stakes. The current financial crisis has shaken and even threatened eventually to destroy the European Union and its currency, the euro. Although this has not happened, fault lines are still apparent within Europe despite desperate reform efforts.

The Bologna process has achieved greater "harmonization" among European universities and most have moved toward a 3-2-3 structure of three-year undergraduate baccalaureates, two-year masters programs, and three-year doctoral programs. The Erasmus program has enabled greater mobility of students among European universities but not achieved yet the percentage that was projected. Along with harmonization, there is also competition among nations and within nations as each university strives to be "world class." Globalization creates these contradictions, integration, and contestation simultaneously. This next section will look briefly at some of the reforms that have emerged over the last decade with a goal of enhancing how selected national systems of higher education compete in this global marketplace.

NATIONAL HIGHER EDUCATION SYSTEMS AND CHANGE

This section focuses on the responses to globalization pressures in the university sectors of three countries (Australia, the Netherlands, and France) with particular attention to recent changes in the 2000s.

Australia

The 2000s have witnessed rapid acceleration of federal government steerage of Australia's thrity-nine public universities with the stated goal of enhancing the country's positioning in the global knowledge economy. A key turning point in tightening the federal government's control was the election of a Labor government in 2007 on a platform of an "Education Revolution." It immediately established two major reviews (Bradley, 2008; Cutler, 2008) to focus on raising the quality of higher education and research. The government's response to the reviews' recommendations, *Transforming Australia's Higher Education System*, highlighted that new higher education policies were "essential to enable Australia to participate fully, and benefit from, the global knowledge economy" (Department of Education, Employment, Workplace Relations and Social Inclusion, 2009, p. 5).

A centerpiece of the reforms was a new and very powerful national regulator, the Tertiary Education Quality and Standards Agency. It began operation in 2012 evaluating the performance of higher education providers against a Higher Education Standards Framework. The agency monitors standards in the five domains of qualifications, teaching and learning, information, research, and the providers themselves (Tertiary Education Quality and Standards Agency, 2012). The power of this regulator is reflected in its potential to de-register universities if their performance does not meet threshold standards and to allocate financial resources based on performance at the margin.

OECD (2008) made reference to the Australian government's longstanding use of funding to forge policy implementation in higher education. It is clear that this strategy of financial "sticks and carrots" continues to prevail. Over the last decade in the Australian university sector, institutional autonomy has been further marginalized in favor of accountability to enhance the quality of institutional outcomes for national competitive advantage in the global arena. The federal government used its increasing power to steer research and teaching-learning in the Australian university sector.

In research, the Australian government established its Excellence in Research in Australia (ERA) policy in 2009, with the goal of enhancing its quality and international competitiveness. To date, there have been two ERA assessment exercises flowing from this policy, in 2010 and 2012. In the first, journals were ranked within discipline clusters on a scale extending from "world class" to "below international standard" to provide a de facto measure of the quality of a publication. The ERA, and its central feature of journal ranking, was hotly debated within the academic community. Criticisms revolved around its methodological weaknesses, its time-consuming nature, its distortion of research activity, and its marginalization of locally relevant research, especially in the social sciences (see Currie and Vidovich, 2014, for more detail). Much lobbying from institutions and academics ensued about the positioning of particular journals in the rankings as well as the weaknesses of the assessment system as a whole. Subsequently in the 2012 ERA, the controversial journal rankings were dropped and the criteria for research assessment, arguably, became even less transparent. For example, initial policy intentions were to include "research impact" in the ERA assessments such that research quality was in part defined by its usefulness to the community in the short term. However, the impact dimension was dropped due to difficulties of measurement, although trials have continued.

While the initial 2010 ERA had no funding implications for universities, the 2012 ERA saw the beginning of research performance funding allocated to universities on the basis of these assessments. One of the goals of the ERA was to further concentrate research funding in Australian higher education and increase the likelihood of some Australian universities moving up the ranks in international league tables. As such, the ERA further entrenches hierarchy within the Australian university sector.

In teaching and learning, Australian government policy is even less settled than it is in research, although not for lack of trying. Bradley's review (2008, p. xxii) recommended the development of "indicators and instruments to assess and compare learning outcomes" along with the articulation of standards for different disciplines, as well as teaching-learning performance funding for universities. Although the proposed financial rewards for performance were limited, they symbolized the new priority that quality teaching-learning was to be given. However, by early in the second decade of the 2000s, there was a backing off from proposed performance funding for teaching-learning, although university performance data were being published on MyUniversity (2013). This is a government website with the stated goal of providing customer choices about the performance of all Australian universities.

It would seem that one of the primary reasons for removal of incentive funding for teaching-learning performance was the difficulty in measuring student learning outcomes in a way that would permit comparisons as the basis for allocation of funds. In their haste to put assessment of teaching-learning quality on the agenda, policy-makers initially decided to employ the Collegiate Learning Assessment (CLA) generic skills test for graduates from the United States. However, with headlines in the *Australian Higher Education Supplement* such as "US Test of Skills a Poor Fit Here" (Lane, 2010, p. 25), reflecting wider negative sentiments across the sector, the government planned to develop an adapted Australian version of the CLA to measure student learning outcomes.

At the time of writing in early 2013, the CLA seems to have been shelved, although a formal announcement about a mechanism to measure learning outcomes is not yet evident. It is possible that the OECD's AHELO project (with its third and final report on feasibility studies due in the first half of 2013) may be used to fill the breach, enabling both international and national comparisons (see earlier section on Globalization, University Rankings, and Performance Assessments). Despite difficulties in instrumentation, the Australian government's intention is clearly to enhance the accountability of universities for producing high-quality student learning outcomes to prepare them for contributing to Australia's success in a global knowledge economy.

Overall, the major thrust of the Australian government's higher education policy, in response to accelerating globalization in the 2000s, has been to tighten regulation of the university sector with the guiding principle of enhancing quality in research and teaching-learning, where measurable. In this, the concept of quality has been constructed as accountability for achieving internationally competitive or "world class" outcomes from research and teaching-learning. The concept of standards has now permeated higher education policies, although there appears to be some confusion about whether it is minimum/threshold standards or aspirational standards that are most important to Australia's international positioning.

Questions remain, such as who should be setting and monitoring the standards (i.e., is the new regulatory authority, Tertiary Education Quality and Standards Agency, an appropriate body) and are these standards measurable in valid and reliable ways? In research and teaching-learning, the sector has witnessed successful discrediting of the mechanisms initially put in place to measure performance and allocate funding. It seems that the government's intention to regulate universities has outstripped its ability to create instruments to measure performance accurately. The policy changes that have occurred suggest policy-on-the-run creating greater confusion and concern across the sector.

With performance funding attached and increasing visibility of performance reporting, these assessments become more high-stakes for universities, as the higher education sector is further differentiating. The general trend, then, has been a shift in the locus of ultimate control of higher education from within universities to the federal government and to the market. This has been accompanied by the increasing use of funding levers to embed national policies rapidly throughout the sector. The irony, however, is that with the setting of narrowly pre-scribed, ill-fitting performance indicators, Australian government policy may well be under-mining the creativity and innovations that are deemed to be at the heart of a global knowledge society of the twenty-first century.

The Netherlands

During the last three decades, the Dutch government moved to position its universities in the vanguard of knowledge economies—"to be among the top-5 most competitive economies in the world" (Veerman Committee, 2010, p. 8). As described recently by a report from the Dutch Ministry of Education, Culture and Science (2011), "the government is striving for a higher education system with international allure, world-class research that attracts scientific top talent and reinforcement of the international position of the business community" (p. 1). To enable universities to gain this international allure, the government first initiated reform toward greater autonomy of Dutch universities (thirteen universities plus thirty-nine universities of applied sciences) in its *Higher Education: Autonomy and Quality* White Paper in 1985.

De Boer and Goedegebuure (2007) noted that giving universities greater autonomy marked a shift from an interventionary to a facilitatory state. This shift unfolded through several reforms in different areas, such as university governance, quality assurance, and further strengthening of institutional autonomy. One of these reforms was known as the 1997 Modernization of University Governance. It empowered leadership at the top and middle levels of the universities by granting the Central Executive Board (consisting of the rector plus two non-academics from outside of the university) additional powers. The rector was still a professor from within the university but was no longer elected by staff and students. Members of the Executive Board were appointed by a Supervisory Board, a newly established board made up of lay members appointed by the Minister of Education.

Representative councils of staff and students were retained but lost considerable power and were, generally speaking, reduced to advising the executive in terms of the strategic directions of the university. It is important to note that decision-making may have been somewhat different within universities and not as top down as the reforms suggested. A national evaluation demonstrated that university leaders and managers did not necessarily sideline their internal constituencies and these changes did not entirely lead to the death of collegiality

(Huisman, de Boer, and Goedegebuure, 2005). Academics still controlled important teaching and research decisions.

At the same time, New Public Management became the narrative for Dutch universities. Universities were to "act as societal entrepreneurs [and become] corporate organizations, prompt in responding to the needs of the economy and the labor market" (Leišyte, 2007, p. 117). In the first decade of the 2000s, there was a continued pursuit of deregulation. Policies were introduced to further strengthen institutional autonomy and to align them closer to the market (*Strategic Plan Education and Research of 2000 and 2004*; Dutch abbreviation "HOOP"). Leišyte (2007) noted that in exchange for increased institutional autonomy, more accountability was regarded as necessary. Accountability came in a variety of ways, such as quality assurance mechanisms for teaching and research and performance-based reporting requirements.

In recent years, the Dutch government has struggled to balance substantial institutional autonomy with its responsibility for the performance of the system as a whole. It could be described as returning to the interventionary state to some extent. Two developments are worth mentioning.

First, in response to persistent complaints about the administrative burden due to increased accountability requirements, changes in quality assurance took place. The Dutch-Flemish Accreditation Organisation (NVAO) was established soon after a 2003 treaty between Flanders and the Netherlands. It was based on both governments instituting the Bologna process to instil a culture of quality in their higher education systems. NVAO assesses learning outcomes at program levels, reviews institutional quality assurance systems, and engages in audits of internal quality assessments of universities.

An example of one area that NVAO is assessing is the degree of internationalization of a university. Internationalization, according to NVAO, is the process by which a university moves from being a workplace steeped in a national or regional identity to a multinational and multicultural working environment. For example, NVAO assesses whether there are changes in subject content that include an international context, whether academics publish in English and collaborate successfully with partner institutions in Europe and overseas, and whether graduates realize international and intercultural learning outcomes.

Second, there has been an ongoing debate about differentiation and profiling. Profiling is a process whereby institutions identify distinctive characteristics to enhance system diversity. Governments can then classify institutions and use performance-based funding to reward excellence in university research and teaching. Klumpp, de Boer, and Vossensteyn (2011) describe how a nexus may develop between differentiation, strategic profiling of universities, and excellence. They note that even though the Dutch government prescribes a binary system with universities and universities of applied sciences, there has been a blurring of the boundaries between the two. In this regard, the Dutch system of higher education appears to be moving ever so slightly toward a more unitary system and adopting some aspects of the more hierarchical higher education systems of the United States and United Kingdom, even though at this stage the universities in particular remain more egalitarian.

In contrast to the unitary systems, where the divide between research universities and applied universities has disappeared, most European systems created binary systems at the expense of vertical diversity or more hierarchical systems (Beerkens-Soo and Vossensteyn, 2009). Within a European-style binary system, there is not as much differentiation among the research universities and a more egalitarian model was developed where universities were funded in a similar way. To develop a profile of world class universities, countries have begun to fund universities differently and have veered toward greater differentiation within a unitary system and one of the policy tools used is profiling.

In 2009, ex-minister Plasterk commissioned a review of the Dutch higher education system led by Cees Veerman, former Minister of Agriculture. The Veerman Report (Veerman Committee, 2010), known as "Differentiating in Triplicate" or "Future-Proofing Higher Education," concluded that Dutch higher education was not ready for the future. The commission said that the current system was not flexible enough to meet the rapidly changing demands of students and employers. The dropout rate was too high, and highly gifted students were not being challenged enough. It recommended that institutions specialize more, focus on their strengths, and phase out weak programs and disciplines.

To this end, the Dutch Ministry of Education, Culture and Science responded to the Veerman Report with its *Quality in Diversity Report* (2011). It identified a fundamental change in the financing of Dutch higher education where a growing proportion of higher education funding will be earmarked for quality and profiling. It also wanted more programs for excellent students and expanded the scope for tuition fee differentiation with a view to creating more expensive, excellent tracks. It recommended greater clustering of research programs, more programs that met the demands of the labor market, and finally more collaboration in the golden triangle of knowledge institutions, the business community, and government.

Based on the Veerman Report and the resulting discussions, the government introduced a system of performance-based contracting between the government and individual institutions, known as "contractualization." Even though the contract is related to only some parts of teaching and concerns a small part of the overall budget of an institution, it is seen as a clear break with the previous steering from a distance mode. In 2013, the Ministry of Education initiated negotiations directly with universities, which were seen as the first stage toward much greater differentiation within the higher education system. Some academics are questioning whether the current profiling of institutions and the resulting contractualization are at odds with institutional autonomy (for which lump sum budgeting is a more appropriate method). They are concerned that this is a not-so-subtle way of gaining more control of institutions. Time will tell if the Dutch system of higher education will resemble that of the United States with its unitary system, where there is no differentiation between technical and comprehensive institutions, and where there is greater differentiation within a vertical hierarchy of universities.

France

In contrast to the Australian and Dutch universities, some limited autonomy came to French universities only recently with the passage in 2007 of Libertés et Responsabilités des Universités legislation. It took effect gradually over five years and was not fully implemented until January 1, 2012. This act gave France's eighty universities considerable budgetary autonomy and an increase in the power of university management to recruit staff and liaise with industry for additional funding. (The act did not cover three overseas universities that are expected to gain budgetary autonomy by 2013.)

Deficits in university budgets soon emerged because the funding was not increased enough to match rising student and staff numbers. There were also problems of budgetary competence because university presidents were still elected by staff and students and not on the basis of their managerial abilities (Rey-Lefebvre, 2012). In 2013, nineteen universities were in deficit and forty of the eighty were in a perilous state. The President of Montepellier-3, Anne Fraisse, commented, "At this price, better that we return to our chains" (Rey-Lefebvre, 2012, p. 9). She noted a lack of forty to forty-five million euros to pay existing salaries. According to Radier (2012), university budgets in France have stagnated during the last five years (2007 to 2012), partly due to the economic crisis during this period. Consequently, autonomy has not been met with universal acclaim during this period of austerity. Several authors have critiqued the university reforms, questioning why these changes are taking place now (Beaud, Caillé, Encrenz, Gauchet and Vatin, 2010) and whether they will create the elites that France needs (Garçon, 2011).

Along with greater autonomy, universities agreed to introduce teaching evaluations in 2008. However, the *Syndicat* (union of university teachers) was against the evaluation of teachers per se, arguing that this would impinge academic freedom. In the end, the union agreed to the evaluation of courses but not teachers (Blanc, 2013). A new reform bill is set to be debated in parliament in May 2013 that will change the evaluation of universities again. It will replace the highly criticized Evaluation Agency for Research and Higher Education by a newly created High Council of Research and Higher Education Evaluation that will allow institutions to perform the evaluations themselves at the request of the universities.

Just as students are having more say about their education with the ability to evaluate teaching in French universities, they are being asked to pay higher tuition fees than previously but still at a relatively low level compared with Anglo-Saxon countries. The higher fees contradict the French value of equality. Radier (2012) points out that "the greatest weakness of the French system is that it is becoming more unequal" (p. 82). Although the state still provides about 90 percent of higher education funding, institutions have been allowed to charge tuition fees, and these are beginning to vary by type of institution. Some of the universities are almost free whereas others charge as much as fifteen thousand euros for a master's degree, with the average close to five hundred U.S. dollars (Guinochet, 2012).

On another front, France is trying to catch up with technological changes that are sweeping higher education systems around the world. Minister of Education Genevieve Fioraso realizes that France is behind in the Internet battle with only 3 percent of French university courses online. She launched "FUN," France université numérique, with the goal of putting 20 percent of French courses on the Internet in five years (Gabizon, 2013). She urged universities to teach differently without moving to virtual universities as she feels that face-to-face contact is still essential. Another of her goals is to increase the number of international students studying in France from their current enrollment of about 10 percent. Currently, most of these students are from Francophone Africa and are non-fee paying. The minister hopes to increase the intake of international fee-paying students by offering some courses in English. This move to allow courses to be taught in English in 2013 has been met with considerable opposition (Hagège, 2013). It is seen as against the very essence of receiving a French education and another step in giving into neoliberalism and letting the market determine education policy.

CONCLUDING COMMENTS

Clearly, the pressures and challenges of globalization and their impact on higher education are here to stay. However, their effects are neither uniform nor inevitable and, where conducive political economic and cultural conditions prevail, they can be mediated and changed. These global forces appear to penetrate universities in the guise of public sector reforms (quality assurance and evaluation programs) and reduced government funding, accompanied by greater university autonomy in some contexts.

While there is growing evidence of policies travelling across higher education sectors in different jurisdictions in a global knowledge era (Ozga and Jones, 2006), there are also significant variations in response to globalization across different regional, national, and local contexts. The three countries considered here can be represented at different points on a continuum of responses to globalization, and its ideological barrow of neoliberalism, from Australia and the Netherlands closest to the Anglo-Saxon model to France veering away from it ever so slightly.

We would argue that, in an era of accelerating globalization, it is more important than ever to conduct fine-grained international comparative research in higher education that fore-grounds context-specific differences. In addition to providing more nuanced understandings of globalization processes and possibly developing typologies of responses to globalizing pressures across different jurisdictions, such research can provide the basis for critically informed policy learning (Vidovich, 2013).

Although we focused more on research and the competition to move up in international league tables and less on how teaching has changed, it is evident that there is also increased competition among universities around the globe for the "best and the brightest" students and resulting changes in their curriculum (de Wit, 2009). World rankings are also shifting toward more emphasis on teaching and attracting international students as staff and students become more mobile. In *The Great Brain Race*, Wildavsky (2010) documented how international competition for the top talent is transforming the world of higher education with much greater mobility of students and staff, creating a new global meritocracy. With a greatly augmented flow of international students, internationalizing the curriculum has also risen as a policy priority. Thus, there is a close nexus between international university league tables, striving for "world class" status, and policy reforms in research and teaching-learning. Europe har-monized its degree structure so that it could better compete for international talent. Australia was ahead of Europe in recruiting paying international students; however, to stay competitive it continues to alter its curriculum offerings and is delivering more of its courses online.

For European universities, Robertson identified two concerns that came together which universities could help to create: a single market and a European citizen. Is the "European" citizen any different from the global citizen? How will national citizenship goals blend with the idea of global citizenship, or will there be contradictions? Many universities around the world identify the global citizen as one of their goals in their mission statements. It is certainly a goal found in almost all Australian universities and in the slightly different guise of the international citizen in Dutch universities. Will the Internet and staff and student mobility help to create this global/international citizen within most universities worldwide? It is clear that MOOCs are rapidly transforming universities and the profession of teaching, just as the printing press did in spreading access to knowledge. There were unintended consequences of the printing press as it doomed Latin as a unifying language in Europe and entrenched national language differences. What will be the unintended consequences of virtual universities? Who will have access to this virtual world, and how will students get credentialed? These are questions still to be solved as the intensification of globalization in higher education reaches new heights.

Acknowledgments

This chapter has benefited from Australian Research Council funding and the excellent editing of Paul Snider. It draws on work by Harry de Boer and Jeroen Huisman on the higher education system in the Netherlands. In addition, Harry de Boer reviewed the Dutch section and Richard DeAngelis reviewed the French section and provided us with recent material for each country.

REFERENCES

Altbach, Philip G. 2006. The Dilemmas of Ranking. *International Higher Education*, vol. 42, Winter, pp. 2–3.

Attwood, Rebecca. 2009. Redrawing Ranking Rules for Clarity, Reliability and Sense. *Times Higher Education*, December 10. http://www.timeshighereducation.co.uk/news/redrawing-ranking-rules-for-clarity-reliability-and-sense/409501.article

Beaud, Olivier, Alain Caillé, Pierre Encrenaz, Marcel Gauchet, and François Vatin. 2010. *Refonder L'Université*. Paris: La Découverte.

Beerkens-Soo, Maarja, and Hans Vossensteyn. 2009 (November). Higher Education Issues and Trends from an International Perspective. Report on the Veerman Commission. Center for Higher Education Policy Study, University of Twente, The Netherlands.

Blanc, Quentin. 2013. Les Étudiants Pourraient Noter les Professeurs à l'Université, *Le Figaro*, 21 janvier, p. 15.

Bologna Declaration. European Ministers of Education. 1999. http://www.bolognabergen2005.no/Docs/00Main_doc/990719BOLOGNA_DECLARATION.pdf

Bradley, Denise. 2008. *Review of Australian Higher Education*. Canberra: Commonwealth of Australia.

CIA World Factbook. 2013. https://www.cia.gov/library/publications/the-world-factbook/index/nl.html

Currie, Jan. 2005. Privatization and Commercialization: Two Globalizing Practices Affecting Australian Universities. In Akira Arimoto, Futao Huang, and Keiko Yokoyama (eds.), *Globalization and Higher Education* (pp. 23–38). Research Institute for Higher Education: Hiroshima University, Japan.

_____. Richard DeAngelis, Harry de Boer, Jeroen Huisman, and Claude Lacotte. 2003. *Globalizing Practices and University Responses: European and Anglo-American Differences*. Westport: Praeger.

_____, Lesley Vidovich. 2014. Aspiring to "World Class" Universities in Australia: A Global Trend with Intended and Unintended Consequences. In Roberta M. Bassett and Alma Maldonado-Maldonado (eds.), *The Forefront of International Higher Education: A Festschrift in Honour of Philip G. Altbach*. New York: Springer.

Cutler, Terry. 2008. *Venturous Australia: Building Strength in Innovation*. Melbourne: Cutler & Company.

De Boer, Harry F., and Leo Goedegebuure. 2007. "Modern" Governance and Codes of Conduct in Dutch Higher Education, *Higher Education Research and Development*, vol. 26, no. 1, pp. 45–55.

De Wit, Hans. 2009. *Internationalisation, Teaching and Learning and Strategic Partnerships*. Keynote address at Internationalising Learning and Teaching in Academic Settings Conference, Sydney University, December 10, 2009.

Department of Education, Employment, Workplace Relations and Social Inclusion. 2009. *Transforming Australia's Higher Education System*. Canberra: Australian Government. http://www.innovation.gov.au/HigherEducation/Documents/TransformingAusHigherED.pdf

Dutch Ministry of Education, Culture and Science. 2011 (August). *Quality in Diversity*. The Netherlands.

European Commission. 2005. *Toward a European Qualifications Framework for Lifelong Learning*. Commission Staff Working Document, SEC (2005) 957. Brussels: European Commission.

_____. 2006. *Delivering on the Modernisation Agenda for Universities. Education, Research and Innovation*. (COM (2006) 208 final.) Brussels: European Commission.

Friedman, Thomas. 2013. The Professors' Big Stage. *The New York Times*, March 5, p. A23.

Gabizon, Cécilia. 2013. Les Universitiés Françaises se Lancent dans la Bataille du Numérique. *Le Figaro*, 14 janvier, p. 16.

Garçon, François. 2011. *Enquête sur la Formation des Élites*. Paris: Perrin.

Guinochet, Fanny. 2012. Le Vrai Prix des Études. *Challenges*, no 311, 6 septembre, pp. 62–66.

Hagège, Claude. 2013. Refusons le Sabordage du Français. *Le Monde*, 26 avril, p. 18.

Harden, Nathan. 2013. The End of the University as We Know It. *The American Interest*, vol. 8, no. 3, January/February, pp. 55–62.

Huisman, Jeroen, Harry de Boer, and Leo Goedegebuure. 2005. The Perception of Participation in Executive Governance Structures in Dutch Universities. *Tertiary Education and Management*, vol. 12, October, pp. 227–39.

Klumpp, Matthias, Harry de Boer, and Hans Vossensteyn. 2011 (June 24). On Differentiation, Profiling and Excellence: A Comparative Outline Regarding Connections between University Profiles and Excellence Concepts. Paper presented at the CHER Conference, University of Reykjavik, Iceland.

Kwiek, Marek. 2009. Globalisation: Re-reading Its Impact on the Nation-state, the University and Educational Policies in Europe. In Maarten Simons, Mark Olssen, and Michael A. Peters (eds.), *Re-Reading Education Policies: A Handbook Studying the Policy Agenda of the 21st Century* (pp. 184–204). Rotterdam: Sense Publishers.

Lane, Bernard. 2010. US Test of Skills a Poor Fit Here. *The Australian Higher Education Supplement*, December 1, p. 25.

Leišyte, Lindvika. 2007. University Governance and Academic Research: Case Studies of Research Units in Dutch and English Universities, Ph.D. Thesis, University of Twente, The Netherlands.

Marginson, Simon. 2006. Rankings Ripe for Misleading, *The Australian*, 6 December, pp. 26–27.

_____ and Mark Considine. 2000. *The Enterprise University: Power, Governance and Reinvention in Australia*. Cambridge: Cambridge University Press.

My University Website. 2013. Australian Government. http://content.myuniversity.gov.au/sites/MyUniversity/pages/aboutpostgraduateresearch#Discipline

Organization for Economic Cooperation and Development (OECD). 2008. *Tertiary Education for a Knowledge Society*. Paris: OECD.

_____. 2013.*Testing Student and University Performance Globally: OECD's AHELO*. http://www.oecd.org/education/skills-beyond-school/testingstudentanduniversityperformancegloballyoecdsahelo.htm

Owen, Graham. 2011. After the Flood: Disaster Capitalism and the Symbolic Restructuring of Intellectual Space. *Culture and Organization*, vol. 17, no. 2, pp. 123–37.

Ozga, Jenny, and Robert Jones. 2006. Travelling and Embedded Policy: The Case of Knowledge Transfer. *Journal of Education Policy*, vol. 21, no. 1, pp. 1–17.

Radier, Véronique. 2012. Universités: Peuvent Mieux Faire. *Le Nouvel Observateur*, 1 novembre, p. 82.

Rey-Lefebvre, Isabelle. 2012. Des Universitiés s'Alarment de la Dégradation de leur Budget, *Le Monde*, 16 novembre, p. 9.

Rizvi, Fazal, and Bob Lingard. 2010. *Globalizing Education Policy*. London: Routledge.

Robertson, Susan. 2009. Europe, Competitiveness and Higher Education: An Evolving Project. In Roger Dale and Susan Robertson (eds.), *Globalisation and Europeanisation in Education,* (pp. 65–84). Oxford: Symposium Books.

Tertiary Education Quality and Standards Agency. 2012. Higher Education Standards Framework. Australian Government. http://www.teqsa.gov.au/about-teqsa

Trounson, Andrew. 2013. Profile Tool Will Highlight Weakness, *Australian Higher Education Supplement*, February 13, p. 19.

Veerman Committee. 2010. Committee on the Future Sustainability of Dutch Higher Education System, *Threefold Differentiation for the Sake of Quality and Diversity in Higher Education*, House of Representatives 31288, no. 96, April.

Vidovich, Lesley. 2013. Balancing Quality and Equity in Higher Education Policy Agendas: Global-local Tensions. In Paul Axelrod, Roopa Desai Trilokekar, Theresa Shanahan, and Richard Wellen (eds.), *Policy Formation in Post-Secondary Education: Issues and Prospects in Turbulent Times.* Montreal: McGill-Queen's University Press.

Wildavsky, Ben. 2010. *The Great Brain Race: How Global Universities are Reshaping the World.* Princeton: Princeton University Press.

Yang, Rui, Lesley Vidovich, and Jan Currie. 2007. University Accountability Practices in Mainland China and Hong Kong: A Comparative Analysis. *Asian Journal of University Education*, vol. 2, no. 1, pp. 1–21.

NOTE

1. *Academic Ranking of World Universities* published by Shanghai Jiao Tong University, China, uses six indicators, including alumni and staff winning Nobel Prizes and Fields Medals, highly cited researchers, articles published in *Nature* and *Science*, articles indexed in Science Citation Index, and per capita performance with respect to institution size. *Times Higher Education* World University Rankings includes thirteen separate indicators under five categories: teaching (30 percent), research (30 percent), citations (research impact) (32.5 percent), international mix (5 percent), and industry income (2.5 percent).

Chapter Ten

Globalization of the Community College Model: Paradox of the Local and the Global Revisited

Rosalind Latiner Raby

Since the early 1990s, traditional four-year universities were criticized as being unable to meet the needs of a changing global economy and as such "the existence of a recognized alternative to traditional universities [is] indispensable" (Cerych, 1993, p. 5). Today, students are achieving secondary education in increasing numbers (Organization of Economic Cooperation and Development, 2012; UN Education Science and Cultural Organization, 2012), and even with massification policies, entrance to the traditional university is still highly competitive and cannot serve all the students who want a university education. Options exist with a higher education institution that offers a more advanced curriculum than secondary school and that serves as a lower-cost option for adult learners, displaced workers, lifelong learners, and non-traditional learners. These institutions are known by several names including colleges of further education (FE), community colleges, polytechnics, regional colleges, regional technical institutes (Terciarios), technical colleges, and technical and further education colleges (TAFEs) (Raby and Valeau, 2012). Although they exist in an amorphous field (Kintzer, 1998), community college global counterparts are a unified category because they share noted commonalities and thus can be compared (Raby and Valeau, 2009, Wiseman, Chase-Mayoral, Janis, and Sachdev, 2012).

Community college global counterparts have roots in several Western European institutions, were applied in a unique form in Canada and the U.S., and then re-invented globally. Although many variations existed in the early 1970s (Organization of Economic Cooperation and Development, 1971), a self-promotion campaign designed by Canadian and U.S. community colleges, which were actively engaged in international expansion in the 1980s, marketed an image of the community college as the most emulated system in the world (Raby and Valeau, 2012). It is in this context that community colleges are believed to permeate the world. Since Raby (2000), there have been three major publications on community college global counterparts (Elsner, Boggs, and Irwin, 2008; Raby and Valeau, 2009; Wiseman, Chase-Mayoral, Janis, and Sachdev, 2012). These volumes include case studies and empirical research largely written by authors from the countries under study. The new generation of research shows that globalization has complex repercussions that, while largely unidirectional, can involve multiple countries.

Proliferation of community college global counterparts across time and space is directly linked to cultural, economic, and philosophical globalization processes. Globalization, in this chapter, creates a condition whereby community colleges have permeated the world, but in doing so affects both universality of experience as well as localized applications. For at least two decades, there has been a global need to address issues related to labor and technology training, accessibility for the mass populace, and the "intransigence of university-dominated systems" (Kintzer, 1998, p. 1). Such education, it is argued, continues to provide opportunities that lead to employment, economic development, and prosperity, and can contribute toward improved social conditions (Biden, 2011; Wiseman, Chase-Mayoral, Janis, and Sachdev, 2012). This chapter explores the effect that globalization has on the growth of community college global counterparts since 2000 and explores ramifications caused by the local and global dialectic.

U.S. COMMUNITY COLLEGE CHARACTERISTICS

The U.S. community college is a publicly supported two-year institution, accredited to grant short-cycle certificates, award an associate's degree as the highest degree, prepare non-certificated graduates for mid-level labor markets, and enable students to transfer to a university to complete a bachelor's degree. In addition to academic, workforce development, and skills training, colleges also offer noncredit courses in English for recent immigrants (which also support their acculturation processes), remedial education, and community enrichment programs that directly benefit the local community. Open admission allows all students to enroll regardless of educational attainment or socioeconomic status. As such, the student population mirrors the multicultural and multiethnic mixture of the local community. Kintzer (1998) identified internal traits of streamlined governance, flexible requirements, output of educational opportunities, open access, and local community connections that are found, with some variation, in all community college global counterparts.

GLOBALIZATION AND COMMUNITY COLLEGE GLOBAL COUNTERPARTS

Examination of community college global counterparts reveals the effects of globalization on localized interpretations of similar policy as well as on similar institutional design. McLaren (1999, citing San Juan, Jr., 1998) discerns the global and the local as "mutually constitutive parts of a contradictory social whole" (p. 10). In this context, neither an external push for sameness nor an internal drive to maintain difference takes priority. As similar policies, ideals, programs, and structures traverse from country to country, community college global counterparts share common characteristics. However, it is the localized application that endows the uniqueness of each model. Thus, like two sides of the same coin, on one side exists the formation of the similar and accentuation of universality of experience derived from development of new systems, structures, and modalities that combine economic, political, and cultural characteristics. On the other side of the coin, globalization simultaneously heightens localized connections that accentuate singularity of experience.

Globalization to Promote a Realm of Sameness

Globalization, as promoting homogenization, affects two trajectories: one that influences the U.S. model through adoption of global values for global citizenship and the other that promotes the U.S. prototype abroad through globalized educational programs. In both, globalization emphasizes universal reference and the "compression of the world" (Robertson, 1992, p. 8) in which homogenization results from economic and philosophical flows that create a shared construct. It is this shared construct that influences social practice and social institutions.

Global Values for Global Citizenship

Global values effect change in curriculum with an explicit aim to better prepare students for global citizenship. This global identity reinforces knowledge and awareness that distances individuals from constraints of ethnicity/nationalism to view human experience in more universal terms (Schattle, 2009). Since 2000, associations that serve U.S. community colleges, such as the American Association of Community Colleges, the Association of International Educators, and the Institute of International Education, contribute to the development of similar global values by celebrating similarities to create a sense of community amidst diversity (Raby, 2007). Sameness is also perpetuated indirectly when the characteristics identified for global citizenship are those that mirror values found in Western countries.

Global Educational Programs

Since the 1980s, Canadian and U.S. community college international development programs reinforced a sameness by duplicating a tangential aim of community colleges to prepare skills that service a flexible global economic workforce. International development programs are bilateral and cooperative agreements in which a U.S. or Canadian community college provide English as a second language, technical, vocational, occupational, language, and knowledge transfer to other countries. Many of these programs provide resource development in relevant disciplines and technologies, training, consultation, educational services, and professional development. While some international development programs are initiated from non-U.S. countries (Oliver, et al., 2009; World Federation of Colleges and Polytechnics [WFCP], 2013), most programs originate from Canada and the United States (Hartenstine, 2013). International development programs are not imposed on another country, but rather result from personal and educational exchanges. In some cases, in-bound flows occur in which a Canadian or U.S. host community college receives visits from ministries, educators, Fulbright scholars, and local entrepreneurs from other countries. In the last decade, outbound flows allow Canadian and U.S. colleges to develop familiarization tours to visit counterparts in other countries with the purpose of initiating future bilateral contracts via education programs, sister-city agreements, and local international business centers (Raby, 2012).

For the past fifteen years, two rationales—privatization and humanitarian—have explained college engagement in development programs and the proliferation of sameness around the world. In the privatization rationale, the host college receives payment for their expertise in training, curriculum delivery, and management style (Schugurensky and Higgins, 1996). Revenue earning has been a driving force behind many of the programs, such as the Southern Alberta Institute of Technology (SAIT Polytechnic) revenue-generating, energy training program (Nixon, 2011). In the humanitarian rationale, the host college provides assistance as a means to "apply our ideals, our sense of decency and our humanitarian impulse to the repair of the world, [as] investment in development is indeed investment in prevention" (Koltai, 1993, p. 2). Current examples include creating a "college of the people" in the Dominican Republic (Halder, 2008) and democracy building efforts through the U.S. Agency for International Development Scholarships for its Education and Economic Development Program (California Colleges for International Education, 2010). Both rationales maintain that the absence of a community college global counterpart is linked to the educational under-preparation of the adult population, which translates to high levels of un- and underemployment (Castro and Garcia, 2003; Wiseman et al., 2012). As such, the benefits that accrue to a local population through a community college global counterpart justifies the homogenization in which an educational prototype is adopted from one country to another.

A manifestation of globalization that results in the institutionalization of sameness is the branch college abroad. The driving force to establish a branch college ranges from a privatization to a humanitarian rationale. Early examples—American College in Singapore (1988) and Los Angeles-Tokyo Community College (1996)—showed how socioeconomic adjustments were difficult to overcome and ultimately led to their demise (Yamano and Hawkins, 1996). Current branch campuses include the New York-Chile Branch campus (Li, 2010), Houston Community College District campuses in Qatar and Brazil (Spangler and Tyler, 2011), Montgomery College campus in India, and Lone Star College campuses in Indonesia and Kazakhstan (Hartenstine, 2013). Since these campuses are so new, their impact and challenges have yet to be fully assessed.

Homogenization Resulting from Economic and Philosophical Flows

Globalization heightens interdependence between societies that result in what Robertson (1992, p. 8) refers to as the "global system of societies." This system allows the transporting and adopting of similar economic and philosophical flows. Global connectivity shows how greatly the world influences local capital and labor markets, communications, demographic flows, energy, environment, health, and popular culture. Education drives this connectivity through adoption of specific programs that support the type of knowledge that all adults need in a globalized economy. One such adoption is open access, which is a cornerstone of many community college global counterparts. Open access is purposefully marketed abroad and embraced by those who view it as desirable and hence readily adaptable.

Economically, globalization links education to national productivity and to jobs needed by the global economy. Community college global counterparts fill this void by targeting nontraditional audiences to meet the changing demands of the global economy (Jephcote and Raby, 2012; Spangler and Tyler, 2011). Today, low-cost work-related training and associate's degrees are offered in the Caribbean (Morris, 2012) and in Brazil (WFCP, 2013). Social advancement in the workplace is a primary reason why students attend Indian community colleges (Xavier and Valeau, 2009) and why women in particular attend Japanese junior colleges (Anazi and Paik, 2012).

Philosophically, globalization imparts ideals that education can provide skills that will result in individual socioeconomic mobility. This philosophy continues despite evidence that "the process of globalization is often accompanied by efforts at dedemocratization" (McLaren, 1999, p. 11). In an attempt to counter societal inequities, community college global counterparts maintain open access and low tuition to assist students who cannot afford university tuition, have an academic background that is lacking, or who are denied access due to minority status. In particular, developing countries adopt community college global counterpart designs to allow entrance for previously restricted populations.

Globalization flows facilitate diffusion of the U.S.-style education. A three-part construct to understand these flows was defined in Raby and Tarrow (1996) and expanded by Raby in the earlier edition of the book (2000). In *full acceptance* of the model, the concept of open access and adoption of specific curricula are transplanted from one country to another, as exemplified by Indian community college duplication of U.S. community colleges (Xavier and Valeau, 2009), Collège Universitaire Régional (Senegal) model on French polytechnics (Gueye and Sene, 2009), and Chinese vocational education model on German vocational education (Barabasch, Huang, and Lawson, 2009). While full acceptance is rare, authors still explore the steps needed to realize this transference (Lee and Young, 2003). In *modified acceptance*, singular characteristics are adopted, such as U.S.-style English as a second language curriculum in Lebanon (Al-Kafaat Foundation, 2012), U.S.-inspired social renovation in Vietnam (Ba Lam and Huy Vi, 2009), and Australian TAFE configurations of bachelor's degrees for emerging occupational fields in the United States (Raby and Valeau, 2009). In *modified rejection*, elements of what was originally borrowed are drastically changed, such as unification of Israel's regional colleges with universities (Dadividovich and Iram, 2009) and the evolution of privatization and servicing of women in Japan's junior colleges (Anzai and Paik, 2012; Yamano and Hawkins, 1996).

Localization Impact on Differentiation of Institutional Design

The impact of localization creates individualized responses that define the local as a significant actor in the globalization process. Thus, "unlike the promoting of globalization for sameness, the advent of the local cannot be ignored" (Eagleton, 1996, quoted in McLaren, 1999, p. 11). Emphasizing the role of the local in the context of globalization correlates to what Eskow (1998) refers to as global paradox: when the polity and economy grow larger, the needs of the local become more manifest. Steiner-Khamsi and Quist (2000) define this as a recontextualization wherein local realities are defined in unique ways. Thus, just as there are examples of globalization interdependency that are built and sustained through international development programs, there are also examples where community college global counterparts emerge as a response to local needs (Raby and Valeau, 2009; Wiseman, et al., 2012).

Maintaining Local Identities

The needs of the local environment influence the development of educational programs offered by community college global counterparts. The localized application is what endows the uniqueness of each institution. Local connections are made between a college, local universities, local governments, and local/global industries. The local is reinforced through personal exchanges (student, faculty, staff, etc.), through social media (individual or programmatic), and through dissemination within the international scholarly community. This global flow of information is translated into unique educational programs that specifically service local communities. For example, the associate's degree program at several Hong Kong community colleges is grounded in local economic needs that result in different colleges in the region offering different educational programs (Lee and Young, 2003). The new Japanese junior college curriculum now offers other classes that are different from those of a few years ago as a response to changing local workforce needs (Anzai and Park, 2012). It is inevitable that in a globalized economy, the autonomy of a local community college global counterpart can clash with international universities that define accreditation or with global businesses which define credentialization as a criterion for hiring. In this context, not only can there be an elimination of the local voice, but the external design can create weakened programmatic relevancy and insecure future job placement that diminishes the impact the local college can have on its local population. Nonetheless, despite these potential clashes, there are numerous case studies (Raby and Valeau, 2009; Wiseman, et al., 2012) that profile how local colleges are successfully taking control of their destinies despite globalization influences.

Localization Policies

Localization influences stem from various contexts. In some countries, centralized govern-ment policy defines degrees and credentials that the community college provides, such as in some Latin American countries (Castro and Garcia, 2003) and Vietnam (Ba Lam and Huy Vi, 2009). The Brazilian government (through the Coordenação de Aperfeiçoamento de Pessoal de Nível Superior) is establishing a protocol for the training of 4,500 Brazilian students over the next three years (WFCP, 2013). Non-profit organizations that are grounded in serving local populations also have an imprint on the design of institutions that provide new access for post-secondary education, such as the Aga Khan Humanities Project in Tajikistan (Hamon, 2009) and the Indian Center for Research and Development of Community Education (Xavier and Valeau, 2009). Finally, local economic needs continue to mandate training as not only a response to compete and survive in a market that is globally driven, but also to specifically address the goal to build a local educated populace.

Localization Distinctions

Localization manifests itself in specific distinctions that exist between community college global counterparts in terms of geographical location, institutional name, and structure.

Geographic variations are manifested in different institutional types linked to geographic regions. In addition, publications about these institutions are found mostly in area-specific journals. For example, one type of a community college global counterpart—TAFE col-leges—are largely found in Australia, while another type—FE—is largely found in Great Britain (Raby and Valeau, 2012). Even technical education has a geographic presence largely within western Europe. Only community colleges are present in countries on all continents.

Institutional names vary widely: fifty names define institutions in this field (Raby and Valeau, 2012). In addition to specific institutional names (higher colleges of technology, junior colleges, university colleges), there are descriptive terms that highlight academic level (secondary, post-secondary, pre-baccalaureate), length of study (short cycle, short-term, two-year, and three-year), type of study (post-compulsory, tertiary, non-university), and context of curriculum (lifelong education, transfer education, vocational education). There is no single descriptor that crosses all community college global counterparts. Moreover, as these institu-tions proliferate, there are significantly more name variations today than there were a decade or two ago.

Structural variation includes some counterparts being part of a secondary education sys-tem, but most being post-secondary. Some offer only vocational-technical training, while most offer a multi-focus curriculum. Some allow transfer to university, while others do not. As noted, the length of study varies with institutional type. There remain distinct organizational patterns in which institutions are managed nationally in Germany, regionally in Israel, by states in the United States, by individual districts in Norway, and by secondary school systems in Indonesia. Accreditation is defined by the Ministry of Higher Education in Turkey (Aypay, 2008), the ministries of education in Brazil and Japan (Castro and Garcia, 2003; Japan Minis-try of Education, Culture, Sports, Science and Technology, 2005), the ministries for vocation-al education in Benin and Cote d'Ivoire (Sawadogo, 2008), or the Ministry of Labor and Employment in Brazil (Castro and Garcia, 2003). Most are publicly funded, yet for some, "public" means "belongs to the public" and not funding from public sources (Epperson, 2010, p. 115).

ROLE OF COMMUNITY COLLEGE GLOBAL COUNTERPARTS IN HIGHER EDUCATION ACCESS

The belief that educational access contributes to developing human capacity is the foundation for the development of almost all community college global counterparts. Access is seen in two interrelated ways: enrollment patterns (or who benefits simply by getting into the institution) and completion patterns that illustrate how a completed educational program contributes to future individual mobility.

Enrollment Patterns

There is typically no restriction on who enrolls in a community college global counterpart. As such, enrollment numbers are exceptionally strong and, in many countries, 33 to 59 percent of all higher educational students attend community college global counterparts (Raby and Valeau, 2012). By sheer numbers, the impact on higher educational access is undeniable. For some institutions, access specifically allows entry for students who cannot get into traditional universities due to low test scores or personal finances, such as U.S. community colleges, junior colleges in Iran, Hong Kong community colleges, and the collèges universitaires régionaux in Senegal. For some institutions, access allows entry for students who were shut out of higher education for other reasons, such as age or social class, such as Indian community colleges, British FE, and Taiwan junior colleges. Admission to those who are otherwise denied access not only allows these groups to envision their own future but also provides these groups with the skills that otherwise would not be available without a higher level of education.

Local Access

Community college global counterparts are purposefully placed in remote, rural, or urban poor areas with the intent to make them accessible to local students. This is seen in Scottish FEs (Lowe and Gayle, 2007), Japanese junior colleges (Anzai and Paik, 2012), and Ugandan community education centers (Mugimu and Cullinane, 2011). Curricular changes adopted by particular colleges intersect local resources and local needs, often with the goal to build contexts for local sustainability (Quint-Rapoport, 2006). In some colleges, this takes the form of connecting indigenous languages instruction to sustainable business. In Taiwan community colleges, local sustainability is part of what is called a grassroots social action curriculum that is designed specifically to allow the local community to have more control over their lives (Chen and Wang, 2009).

Non-Traditional Student Composition

Community college global counterparts not only attract, but enroll large percentages of students from working and lower classes; students who balance study, work, and family; and students from non-dominant ethnic, racial, and gender groups. In Turkey, 80 percent of students at Vocational Schools of Higher Education are low-income students (Aypay, 2008, p. 143). The mandates of Senegal Regional University Center (Gueye and Sene, 2009) and Brazil *Centro Federal de Tecnología* (Castro and Garcia, 2003) are to serve non-typical higher education students for whom university was not accessible. At the same time, enrollment opportunities can reinforce inequality because community colleges are less valued than universities (Marmolejo, 2010). However, a diametrical contrast is exemplified in Cyprus where the English Preparatory School, which is a community college global counterpart, in North

Cyprus is the choice of last resort for Turkish mainlanders, but is also the school of choice for Turkish Cypriot students (Kusch, Pema, Onurkan, and Akhmadeeva, 2009).

Gender, as a non-traditional demographic, is included in many mission statements indicating an intent for equal access (Raby and Valeau, 2009) and can be a means to enhance women's educational opportunities by changing stereotypes that contribute to societal inequalities (Yonemura, 2012). Despite mission verbiage, existing gender inequities are still reflected in composition and in curriculum. Both faculty and student compositions are reinforced through a self-selecting process as is seen in Uzbekistan (Tursunova and Azizova, 2009) and in Uganda (Mugimu and Cullinane, 2011). Curriculum reinforces gender stereotypes by focusing on a skill set that is gender-defined as is currently seen in Uganda (Mugimu and Cullinane, 2011) and a decade ago in Japan (Japan Ministry of Education, Culture, Sports, Science and Technology, 2005). However, there is also evidence that these institutions do enhance educational opportunity, job attainment, and thereby social mobility. The self-selecting process has positive outcomes, such as in Wales FE that attract lower-income women ages twenty-four to forty who were initially disengaged from learning and then given an opportunity to re-enter higher education (Jephcote, 2011). The gender-specific curriculum in contemporary Japan provides workforce skills that were previously denied to women (Anzai and Paik, 2012). Finally, as a catalyst for social change, institutional policies reinforce entrepreneurial practices in Senegal (Gueye and Sene, 2009) and build small business sustainability in India (Cook, 1996) to improve women's mobility.

Completion Patterns

There is a link between finishing a college program, employment, and social mobility. The goals for completion vary as some community college global counterpart college programs are terminal, and as such, success results in certificates or associate's degrees that are designed to open specific job opportunities (Spangler and Tyler, 2011; Wolf, 2009). Other educational programs award credits that permit transfer to obtain a bachelor's degree that provides alternative opportunities to access jobs requiring a bachelor's degree. There are still other programs that facilitate a reverse transfer in which university students choose to attend the community college global counterpart to prepare for a different educational path (Raby and Valeau, 2009). Each of these choices provides the possibility of social mobility.

Because most community college global counterparts have multiple missions, transfer into higher institutions is not their sole purpose. There are as many institutions that offer transfer options (vocational schools of higher education in Turkey, pre-university centers in Singapore, and Indian community colleges) as there are institutions where there is no option for students to transfer between institutional types (Russian institutes of technology, French upper-level specialized colleges, university colleges in Senegal). Moreover, where the transfer option exists, far fewer students actually transfer to universities. In the United States, less than 25 percent transfer annually, in Japan the annual transfer rate is less than 11 percent, and in Israel and some parts of China and Korea, the transfer rate is even less (Raby and Valeau, 2012). These low percentages are not indicative of a lack of success. It remains an elitist argument that the only recognized social mobility is achieved via a transfer option that leads to a bachelor's degree. Success, therefore, is any program that improves educational outcomes, enhances workforce preparedness, and closes achievement gaps for historically underrepresented students,

Access and Workplace Training

Most community college global counterparts offer an associate-level degree. Because jobs requiring an associate degree are the fastest-growing job group in the global economy (Wolf, 2009), community college global counterpart education, no matter the length or terminal nature, provides a potential to gain employment that leads to social and professional advancements. Lower-level skills that were once provided by secondary schools, such as those provided by technical and vocational education and training schools, or vocational education and technology schools, are not enough to secure modern day employment. Instead, higher-level skills required by high demand occupations and, increasingly, those with an academic foundation are now necessary to educate students for life rather than for a single job. For example, the mission to produce graduates with vocational and life skill competencies is found in Japanese technical colleges, HKU Space Community College (Hong Kong), and New Zealand polytechnics.

Access and Human Capital

Community college global counterparts emphasize education to build human capital, which then is believed to be a key element for increasing individual mobility in their jobs, earning potentials, and status in their local community. In the United States, a wide range of research shows that the benefits of attending community college include not only earning gains, but also much broader gains, such as improvement of job prospects, physical and mental health, and even a reduction of crime (Mullin, 2011). European research also shows that community college global counterparts not only contribute to growth in participation by women, ethnic minorities and immigrants, and to some extent those in the working class (Scott, 2009), but that despite existing external and internal barriers, there is substantial success of these groups toward completion (Schofield and Dismore, 2010). Additional international research shows that completion in the United Arab Emirates higher colleges of technology (Kamali, 2008) and in Jamaican community colleges (Morris, 2012) specifically impacts non-academic skills that lead to community building. As such, community college global counterparts do offer life-transforming educational opportunities, and any education, be it short-term, certificate-based, degree-based, or transfer-based, has direct connections to advancing social mobility.

REPERCUSSIONS OF GLOBALIZATION

There are five repercussions that were defined in the original edition of this chapter (Raby, 2000), and which still result from globalization: (1) financial, (2) academic, (3) cultural, (4) applied, and (5) philosophical. Strydom and Lategon (1998) suggest that these repercussions heighten "disadvantage(s) to whom the community college model should serve" (p. 98). Yet, while these disadvantages still occur, definitive positive social change does result that, in turn, perpetuates the allure of these institutions.

On the *financial* level, substantial difficulties exist in executing these institutions in economically strained periods. Low budgets impact faculty salary, student-faculty ratio, student support services, and facilities maintenance, which affect student achievement (Jephcote, 2011). The changing global economy undermines efforts such that "wherever short-cycle colleges are found, financing is the primary dilemma" (Ishumi, 1998, p. 163; also see Marmolejo, 2010), which in turn complicates efforts to maintain open access. The 2008 global economic crisis raised living costs, which altered accessibility for students who attended community college global counterparts in Japan, Britain, and New Zealand, while increased student tuition in many U.S. states actually eliminated open access for thousands of students (Sutin, Derrico, Valeau and Raby, 2011). In California, however, despite over eight hundred million dollars in budget cuts since 2008-09, student enrollment continues to increase. As such, despite low funding, community college global counterparts continue to service the non-traditional and provide an appeal for future educational access.

On the *academic* level, it is difficult to define standards that are acceptable both locally and globally. Difficulty exists in maintaining academic autonomy in a system that incorporates ties to local universities for accreditation and local industries for professionalization. In Turkey, vocational schools of higher education are part of the university system (Aypay, 2008). O.P. Jindal Community College (India) is affiliated with India Gandhi National Open University (Fischer, 2011), and Al-Balqa Applied University (Jordan) supervises all functions of local community colleges (Meeham, 2012). These relationships do speak to a lack of self-determination. Nonetheless, they also are evidence of local interests in which quick changes can be made to bridge the gap between academia, technical training, and specific community needs. This is seen in Japanese junior colleges that changed their curriculum to respond to new work needs (Anzai and Paik, 2012) as well as in Nunavut Arctic community colleges which designed new curriculum for workforce sustainability (Gaviria, 2012).

On the *cultural* level, local and culture-bound sociopolitical, economic, and environmental issues can counter basic tenets of the community college ideal. When international development programs implement new institutional initiatives, cultural intolerance can arise from strained relationships between indigenous staff, partners abroad, and local financial backers, all of whom have their own, oftentimes conflicting, agendas. Values that predominantly reflect mainstream Western culture, by default, make them a feature of Westernization and that diminishes individual (local) initiatives. The questions of who controls what is defined as knowledge, what gets taught and acted upon in a global culture, therefore, are of extreme importance (Raby and Valeau, 2012).

On the *applied* level, community colleges provide students with training and retraining for jobs that contribute to the economic well-being of a country. Actualization of socioeconomic reform, however, depends upon the type of education exported (technical/vocational, personal development, professional, or academic), the type of student targeted, the relationship of the type of education to the college's mission, and what students actually do with this education (i.e., transfer to a university, work, or drop out). Thus, when colleges are cost-ineffective and have out-of-date courses, it ensures a status of graduates that is not equal to those with a university education as shown in studies from Israel (Davidovitch and Iram, 2009), Mexico (Gregorutti, 2012), and Lebanon, where 27 percent of the officially unemployed held intermediate diplomas from community colleges (Meehan, 2012).

Finally, on the *philosophical* level, many community college global counterparts pride themselves as a significant form of "community education in the context of redressing inequalities" (Ural, 1998, p. 199). Research evidences that even though future pay and status may be low, community college global counterparts nonetheless do increase access for underprivileged youth in Venezuela (Castro and Garcia, 2003), open opportunities in Poland and Canada (Butler, et al., 2008), enhance employment opportunities for women in Japan (Anzai and Paik, 2012), and provide access with site offices and satellite centers in Barbados and Jamaica (Morris, 2012). Most importantly, as a result of globalization, many assert that as this ideal is realized in the United States (Mullin, 2011), it can also be realized in their own country (Castro and Garcia, 2003; Yonemura, 2012).

Consequences of globalization also can reinforce linguistic and cultural inequities that are often connected with Westernization by mandating curricular changes and even the adoption of institutional form. As the global collides with the local, it hinders attempts to maintain cultural identity and autonomy. Exporting U.S. features is complicated by the ethics of aid, trade, and neocolonialism that maintain non-academic ulterior motives. The more community college global counterparts stress values and norms that reflect predominantly mainstream Western culture, the greater the potential to diminish local initiatives. Nonetheless, the potential for reform that results from an introduction of a community college global counterpart to a society neutralizes these concerns (Raby and Valeau, 2009; Wiseman, et al., 2012). As such, community college global counterparts continue to grow in popularity and students who attend these institutions do so in increasing numbers. In this context *any* job is better than unemployment and *any* education allows an ability to become socially mobile, no matter how small the impact (Castro and Garcia, 2003). The popularity of these institutions intensifies because they satisfy a basic education that serves a societal void. Future development and support of these institutions persists because they are (1) less expensive and more accessible than universities, (2) adaptable to providing a job-oriented, as well as transferable, curriculum that addresses varying interests of the community, and (3) able to meet the demands of emerging local population needs.

CONCLUSION

Most of the trends written about in the earlier edition of this chapter (Raby, 2000) continue today. The existence of community college global counterparts continues to impact social change at both global and local levels. The process of introducing a community college model into a society continues to encourage local educational change. This change does provide access for those defined as non-traditional, can help career/personal advancement as students complete required programs, and can impact the local economy by introducing a newly trained and globally prepared workforce. Global links are cultivated by global mobility, sharing of curriculum, and imitation of institutional forms. These relationships are dynamic and establish bonds between individuals on campus, the local neighborhood, and the global community.

Globalization influences on community college global counterparts remain complex. International development programs, primarily from Canada and the United States, continue to build symbiotic relationships that are maintained as an institution in one country is "more likely to act as consulting members of teams interested in the knowledge and technology that other nations produce" (Kintzer, 1998, p. 2). The imprint of globalization on local communities has not only followed a similar pattern, but has become institutionalized in that these counterparts continue to reappear in similar form in different countries. This is not a standardization of form, but a similar response to external and local need for change. Seen in this way, it is possible that just the process of introducing a community college model into a society (whether intentional or not) results in local social change.

Despite the popularity of community college global counterparts, implications for developing countries interested in creating, revising, or endorsing characteristics are clear. Today, it is still critical to highlight community college ideals as well as to understand their realities. Reverberations from globalization can force countries to abandon a basic tenet of the community college, that of open access. Nonetheless, this education, while expanding opportunity, still can perpetuate low status and the inequalities that result. As such, it is important to note that the variations of each community college global counterpart are in themselves a reaction to a globalization process as each country is attempting to integrate an ideal into its own context.

In the new millennium, the politics of borrowing evidences that the United States is not the sole owner of flow patterns and transmission of ideas to nations around the world, and that globalization does not support solely U.S.-centric interests. The suggested homogenization in which a single form is adopted across boundaries has not occurred, as recent research shows that unique strands specific to each counterpart continue to define the field. In fact, it is the local variability that remains a critical element in not only the diversity of these institutions, but their growing appeal. In this context, the dialectic between global and local influences on social change shows the strength of the local roots that are an inherent component in these unique institutional constructs (Raby and Valeau, 2012). As such, localized applications may have had far more merit than originally intended.

Research from the past decade shows that globalization flows are effectively transmitted when both philosophical ideals and economic limitations are understood. Reverberations from globalization can force an abandonment of the basic and most emulated tenet of the community college, that of open access. Globalization can also use that open access to facilitate continued inequalities. It is in this context that the imprint of the community college global counterpart has not diminished and has instead become ingrained in post-secondary educational structures.

REFERENCES

Al-Kafaàt Foundation. 2012. English Language Program Broadens Education Advancement Opportunities. Report on Nassau Community College (NCC) in New York and Al-Kafaàt Foundation Vocational Technical School in Lebanon. http://www.hedprogram.org/impact/success/2012-SS-Nassau-AlKafaat.cfm

Anzai, Shinobu, and Chie Matsuzawa Paik. 2012. Factors Influencing Japanese Women to Choose Two-Year Colleges in Japan. *Community College Journal of Research and Practice*, vol. 36, no. 8, pp. 614–25.

Aypay, Ahmet. 2008. The Vocational and Technical Schools of Higher Education in Turkey. In Paul A. Elsner, George R. Boggs, and Judith T. Irwin (eds.), *Global Development of Community Colleges, and Further Education Programs* (pp. 137–49). Washington, DC: Community College Press.

Ba Lam, Dang, and Nguyen Huy Vi. 2009. The Development of the Community College Model in Vietnam in the Time of Country's Renovation and International Integration. In Rosalind Latiner Raby and Edward J. Valeau (eds.), *Community College Models: Globalization and Higher Education Reform* (pp. 91–117). Dordrecht: Springer Publishers.

Barabasch, Antje, Sui Huang, and Robert Lawson. 2009. Planned Policy Transfer: The Impact of the German Model on Chinese Vocational Education. *Compare: A Journal of Comparative and International Education*, vol. 39, no. 1, pp. 5–20.

Biden, Jill. 2009. American Community Colleges: A Global Model for Higher Education. Remarks made to the Opening Ceremony of the 2009 World Conference on Higher Education, Paris, July 5, 2009. http://www.unesco.org/education/wche/speeches/jill-biden-speech-2009WCHE.pdf

Butler, Norman L., Catherine Smith, Barry Davidson, Tyrone Tanner, William Allan Kritsonis. 2008. Polish Post-Secondary Vocational Schools vs. Canadian Community Colleges: A Comparison of Information Accessibility and Accountability Submission. *Lamar University Electronic Journal of Student Research*. Spring. (ED502177) http://www.eric.ed.gov/PDFS/ED502177.pdf

California Colleges for International Education. 2010. *Annual Report*. http://ccieworld.org/reports.htm

Castro, Claudio de Moura, and Norma M. Garcia (eds.) 2003. *Community Colleges: A Model for Latin America?* Washington, DC: Inter-American Development Bank.

Cerych, Ladislav. 1993. The Return to Europe: Issues in Post-Community Higher Education. In Arthur Levine (ed.), *Higher Learning in America: 1980-2000* (pp. 5–27). Baltimore: The John Hopkins University Press.

Chen, Amy Shi-min, and Wei-ni Wang. 2009. From Education To Grassroots Learning: Towards A Civil Society Through Community Colleges In Taiwan. In Rosalind Latiner Raby and Edward J. Valeau (eds.), *Community College Models: Globalization and Higher Education Reform* (pp. 51–71). Dordrecht: Springer Publishers.

Cook, Jean. 1996. Community Self-Help International Development Projects: A Humanistic Perspective. In Rosalind Latiner Raby and Norma Tarrow (eds.), *Dimensions of the Community College: International, Intercultural, and Multicultural Perspectives* (pp. 37–53). New York: Garland Publishing.

Davidovitch, Nitza, and Yaacov Iram. 2009. College-University Dialogue: From Confrontation to Cooperation. In Rosalind Latiner Raby and Edward J. Valeau (eds.), *Community College Models: Globalization and Higher Education Reform* (pp. 373–401). Dordrecht: Springer Publishers.

Eagleton, Terry. 1996. *The Illusions of Postmodernism*. Oxford: Blackwell.

Elsner, Paul A., George R. Boggs, and Judith T. Irwin (eds.). 2008. *Global Development of Community Colleges, Technical Colleges, and Further Education Programs.* Washington, DC: Community College Press of the American Association of Community Colleges.

Epperson, Cynthia K. 2010. An Analysis of the Community College Concept in the Socialist Republic of Viet Nam. Unpublished Ph.D. dissertation, University of Missouri, St. Louis.

Eskow, Steven. 1998. World Community College: Has Its Time Come? *Community College Times*, Nov. 31.

Fischer, Karin. 2011. U.S. Promotes Ties Between American Community Colleges and India. *Chronicle of Higher Education.* August 28. http://chronicle.com/article/US-Promotes-Ties-Between/128807/?sid=cc&utm_source=cc&utm_medium=en

Gaviria, Patricia. 2012. Indigenous Rights and Advanced Capitalism in Community Colleges: The Case of Nunavut Arctic College. In Alexander W. Wiseman, Audree Chase-Mayoral, Thomas Janis, and Anuradha Sachdev (eds.), *Community Colleges Worldwide: Investigating the Global Phenomenon* (pp. 99–129). Bingley, U.K.: Emerald Publishing.

Gregorutti, Gustavo. 2012. The Mexican Idea of Two-Year University Degrees: A Model of Opportunities and Challenges. In Alexander W. Wiseman, Audree Chase-Mayoral, Thomas Janis, and Anuradha Sachdev (eds.), *Community Colleges Worldwide: Investigating the Global Phenomenon* (pp. 49–71). Bingley, U.K.: Emerald Publishing.

Gueye, Barrel, and Ibra Sene. 2009. A Critical Approach to the Community College Model in the Global Order: The *College Universitaire Régional* of Bambey (Senegal) as a Case Study. In Rosalind Latiner Raby and Edward Valeau (eds.), *Community College Models: Globalization and Higher Education Reform* (pp. 235–53). Dordrecht: Springer Publishers.

Halder, John. 2008. Three Styles of Community College Development: India, the Dominican Republic, and Georgia. In Paul A. Elsner, George R. Boggs, and Judith T. Irwin (eds.), *Global Development of Community Colleges, and Further Education Programs* (pp. 269–77). Washington, DC: Community College Press.

Hamon, M. Max. 2009. A Liberal Arts Interdisciplinary Curriculum in Tajikistan. In Rosalind Latiner Raby and Edward J. Valeau (eds.), *Community College Models: Globalization and Higher Education Reform* (pp. 569–89). Dordrecht: Springer Publishers.

Hartenstine, Mary Beth. 2013. Community College Global Partnerships Bring Local Benefits. *IIE Network*, Spring. http://www.nxtbook.com/naylor/IIEB/IIEB0113/index.php?startid=40

Ishumi, Abel G.M. 1988. Vocational Training as an Educational and Development Strategy: Conceptual and Practical Issues. *International Journal of Educational Development*, vol. 8, no. 3, pp. 163–74.

Japan Ministry of Education, Culture, Sports, Science and Technology. 2005. Higher Education. http://www.mext.go.jp/english/org/f_formal_22.htm

Jephcote, Martin. 2011. The Unintended Consequences of Funding Policies on Student Achievement at Colleges of Further Education in Wales and England. In Seward Sutin, Daniel Derrico, Edward Valeau, and Rosalind Latiner Raby (eds.), *Increasing Effectiveness of the Community College Financial Model: A Global Perspective for the Global Economy* (pp. 265–75). New York: Palgrave Macmillan Publishers.

_____ and Rosalind Latiner Raby. 2012. A Comparative View of Colleges of Further Education (UK) and Community Colleges (US): Maintaining Access in an Era of Financial Constraint. *Research in Post-Compulsory Education*, vol. 17, no. 3, pp. 349–66.

Kamali, Tayeb. 2008. Case Study: The Higher Colleges of Technology in the UAE. In Paul A. Elsner, George R. Boggs, and Judith T. Irwin (eds.), *Global Development of Community Colleges, and Further Education Programs* (pp. 161–75). Washington, DC: Community College Press.

Kintzer, Frederick. 1998. Community Colleges Go International: Short-Cycle Education around the World. *Leadership Abstracts World Wide Web Edition*, vol. 11, no. 6, pp. 1–4.

Koltai, Leslie. 1993. Are There Challenges and Opportunities for American Community Colleges on the International Scene? Keynote Address at the Comparative and International Education Society Western Region Conference, Los Angeles, California, November 5–6.

Kusch, Jim, Eriola Pema, Gulen Onurkan, and Liliya Akhmadeeva. 2009. The Community College at the Crossroads. In Rosalind Latiner Raby and Edward J. Valeau (eds.), *Community College Models: Globalization and Higher Education Reform* (pp. 417–37). Dordrecht: Springer Publishers.

Lee, Eddy W.C., and Enoch C.M. Young. 2003. Pioneering the Community College Movement in Hong Kong. *International Journal of Lifelong Education*, vol. 22, no. 2, pp. 147–58.

Li, Sophia. 2010. Chile's First Community College Remakes Technical Education's Image. *Chronicle of Higher Education*, November 7. http://chronicle.com/article/Chiles-First-Community/125272/?sid=cc&utm_source=cc&utm_medium=en

Lowe, Janet and Vernon Gayle. 2007. Exploring the Work/Life/Study Balance: The Experience of Higher Education Students in a Scottish Further Education College. *Journal of Further and Higher Education*, vol. 31, no. 3, pp. 225–39.

McLaren, Peter. 1999. Introduction: Traumatizing Capital: Oppositional Pedagogies in the Age of Consent. In Manuel Castells, Ramón Flecha, Paulo Freire, Henry Giroux, Donald Macedo, and Paul Willis (eds.), *Critical Education in the New Information Age* (pp. 1–36). Boulder: Rowman & Littlefield.

Marmolejo, Francisco. 2010. Two Year Colleges: Second-Class Citizens in the World of Higher Education. *Chronicle of Higher Education*. August 18. http://chronicle.com/blogs/worldwise/2-year-colleges-second-class-citizens-in-the-world-of-higher-education/26305

Meehan, Mark W. 2012. Islam, Modernity, and the Liminal Space Between: A Vertical Case Study of the Institute of Traditional Islamic Art and Architecture in Amman, Jordan. Unpublished Dissertation, Department of Educational Administration, Higher Education Leadership, College of Education, University of South Carolina.

Morris, Camille. 2012. Community College Model in Anglophone Caribbean: Relevance and Future. Presentation at the Comparative and International Education Society (CIES) National Conference, San Juan, Puerto Rico, April 22–27.

Mugimu, Christopher, and Jeanna Cullinane. 2011. Financing Community Polytechnics in Uganda. In Stewart Sutin, Daniel Derrico, Edward Valeau, and Rosalind Latiner Raby (eds.), *Increasing Effectiveness of the Community College Financial Model: A Global Perspective for the Global Economy* (pp. 175–85). New York: Palgrave Macmillan Publishers.

Mullin, Christopher. 2011. The Road Ahead: A Look at Trends in the Educational Attainment of Community College Students. American Association of Community Colleges. http://www.aacc.nche.edu/Publications/Briefs/Pages/pb09292011.aspx

Nixon, Gordon. 2011. Revenue Generation Through Training a Global Energy Workforce. In Stewart Sutin, Daniel Derrico, Edward Valeau, and Rosalind Latiner Raby (eds.), *Increasing Effectiveness of the Community College Financial Model: A Global Perspective for the Global Economy* (pp. 225–41). New York: Palgrave Macmillan.

Oliver, Diane, Pham Xuan Thanh, Paul A. Elsner, Nguyen Thi Thanh Phuong, and Do Quoc Trung. 2009. Globalization of Higher Education and Community Colleges in Vietnam. In Rosalind Latiner Raby and Edward J. Valeau (eds.), *Community College Models: Globalization and Higher Education Reform* (pp. 197–219). Dordrecht: Springer Publishers.

Organization for Economic Cooperation and Development. 1971. Short Cycle Education: Search for Identity. Paris: OECD.

_____. 2012. *Education at A Glance 2012: OECD Indicators.* Paris: OECD Publishing. http://dx.doi.org/10.1787/eag-2012-en

Quint-Rapoport, Mia. 2006. The NGO-ization of Community Colleges: One (More) Manifestation of Globalization. *College Quarterly*, vol. 9, no. 1, pp. 2–12.

Raby, Rosalind Latiner. 2000. Globalization of the Community College Model: Paradox of the Local and the Global. In Nelly P. Stromquist and Karen Monkman (eds.), *Globalization and Education: Integration and Contestation Across Cultures* (pp. 149–73). New York: Rowman & Littlefield.

_____. 2007. Community College International Education: Looking Back to Forecast the Future. In Edward Valeau and Rosalind Latiner Raby (eds.), *International Reform Efforts and Challenges in Community Colleges* (pp. 3–14). San Francisco: Jossey-Bass.

_____. 2012. Global Engagement at US Community Colleges. Global Engagement: New Modalities. *International Briefs for Higher Educational Leaders*, no. 2 (pp. 9–11). Washington, DC: American Council on Education (ACE) and The Boston College Center for International Higher Education.

_____ and Norma Tarrow (eds.). 1996. *Dimensions of the Community College: International, Intercultural, and Multicultural Perspectives*. New York: Garland Publishing.

_____ and Edward Valeau (eds.). 2009. *Community College Models: Globalization and Higher Education Reform*. Dordrecht: Springer Publishers.

_____, and Edward Valeau. 2012. Educational Borrowing and the Emergence of Community College Global Counterparts. In Alexander W. Wiseman, Audree Chase-Mayoral, Thomas Janis, and Anuradha Sachdev (eds.), *Community Colleges Worldwide: Investigating the Global Phenomenon* (pp. 19–49). Bingley, U.K.: Emerald Publishing.

Robertson, Roland. 1992. *Globalization Social Theory and Global Culture*. London: Sage.

San Juan, Jr., Epifanio. 1998. *Beyond Postcolonial Theory*. New York: St. Martin's.

Sawadogo, Geremie. 2008. Community Colleges and Further Education in French West Africa. In Paul A. Elsner, George R. Boggs, and Judith T. Irwin (eds.), *Global Development of Community Colleges, and Further Education Programs* (pp. 9–18). Washington, DC: Community College Press.

Schattle, Hans. 2009. Global Citizenship in Theory and Practice. In Ross Lewin (ed.), *The Handbook of Practice and Research in Study Abroad: Higher Education and the Quest for Global Citizenship* (pp. 3–20). New York: Routledge.

Schofield, Cathy, and Harriet Dismore. 2010. Predictors of Retention and Achievement of Higher Education Students Within a Further Education Context. *Journal of Further and Higher Education*, vol. 34, no. 2, pp. 207–21.

Schugurensky, Daniel, and Kathy Higgins. 1996. From Aid to Trade: New Trends in International Education in Canada. In Rosalind Latiner Raby and Norma Tarrow (eds.), *Dimensions of the Community College: International, Intercultural and Multicultural Perspectives* (pp. 53–79). New York: Garland Publishing.

Scott, Peter. 2009. Access in Higher Education in Europe and North America: Trends and Developments. Paper prepared for the UNESCO Forum on Higher Education in the Europe Region: Access, Values, Quality and Competitiveness, 21–24 May, Bucharest, Romania.

Spangler, Mary S., and Art Tyler, Jr. 2011. A Houston-Doha Partnership: Leveraging Local Assets to Create a Global Enterprise. *International Educator*, vol. 20, no. 4, pp. 54–57.

Steiner-Khamsi, Gita, and Hubert O. Quist. 2000. The Politics of Educational Borrowing: Re-opening the Case of Achimota of British Ghana. *Comparative Education Review*, vol. 44, no. 3, pp. 272–99.

Strydom, A. H. (Kalie), and Laetus O.K. Lategan (eds.). 1998. *Introducing Community Colleges to South Africa*. Bloemfontein: University of the Free State Publications.

Sutin, Stewart, Daniel Derrico, Edward Valeau, and Rosalind Latiner Raby (eds.). 2011. *Increasing Effectiveness of the Community College Financial Model: A Global Perspective for the Global Economy*. New York: Palgrave Macmillan Publishers.

Tursunova, Zulfiya, and Nodira Azizova. 2009. Building a Knowledge-Based Society: The Role of Colleges in Uzbekistan. In Rosalind Latiner Raby and Edward J. Valeau (eds.), *Community College Models: Globalization and Higher Education Reform* (pp. 545–61). Dordrecht: Springer Publishers.

UN Education Science and Cultural Organization. 2012. *EFA Global Monitoring Report 2012. Youth and Skills: Putting Education to Work*. Paris: UNESCO. http://www.unesdoc.unesco.org/images/0021/002180/218003e.pdf.

Ural, Ipek. 1998. International Community College Models: A South African Perspective. In A.H. (Kalie) Strydom and Laetus O.K. Lategan (eds.), *Introducing Community Colleges to South Africa* (pp. 106–19). Bloemfontein: University of the Free State Publications.

Wiseman, Alexander W., Audree Chase-Mayoral, Thomas Janis, and Anuradha Sachdev. 2012. Community Colleges: Where Are They (Not?). In Alexander W. Wiseman, Audree Chase-Mayoral, Thomas Janis, and Anuradha Sachdev (eds.). *Community Colleges Worldwide: Investigating the Global Phenomenon* (pp. 3–19). Bingley, U.K.: Emerald Publishing.

Wolf, Laurence. 2009. Challenges and Opportunities for Post-Secondary Education and Training in Barbados, Bahamas, Guyana, Jamaica, and Trinidad and Tobago. In Rosalind Latiner Raby and Edward J. Valeau (eds.), *Community College Models: Globalization and Higher Education Reform* (pp. 173–97). Dordrecht: Springer Publishers.

World Federation of Colleges and Polytechnics (WFCP). 2013. CCISP Establishes Training Protocol for Brazilian Students with CONIF and CAPES. June 23, 2013. http://wfcp.org/category/news/

Xavier, Alphonse, S.J., and Edward Valeau. 2009. Indian Community College System: Democratic Response to Globalization. In Rosalind Latiner Raby and Edward J. Valeau (eds.), *Community College Models: Globalization and Higher Education Reform* (pp. 79–91). Dordrecht: Springer Publishers.

Yamano, Tina, and John N. Hawkins. 1996. Assessing the Relevance of American Community College Models in Japan. In Rosalind Latiner Raby and Norma Tarrow (eds.), *Dimensions of the Community College: International, Intercultural and Multicultural Perspectives* (pp. 259–73). New York: Garland Publishing.

Yonemura, Akemi. 2012. Implications of the Community College Model in Ethiopia. In Alexander W. Wiseman, Audree Chase-Mayoral, Thomas Janis, and Anuradha Sachdev (eds.), *Community Colleges Worldwide: Investigating the Global Phenomenon* (pp. 213–44). Bingley, U.K.: Emerald Publishing.

Chapter Eleven

Growing Up in the Great Recession: Revisiting the Restructuring of Gender, Schooling, and Work

Peter Kelly and Jane Kenway

I work 3 jobs—I am not lazy.
I stand for what I believe in—I am not cowardly.
I am very pissed off. I must take three loans to afford a decent education.
I have always believed in the American Dream, but the 1% have stolen that.
I AM THE 99%. [1]

In this chapter, we revisit our earlier work on many of the globalizing material and discursive forces that were restructuring local and global labor markets during the 1990s and that were changing the nature of work (Kelly and Kenway, 2001; Kenway and Kelly, 2000). We also revisit the forms of vocational education and training (VET) deemed capable of preparing young people to transition into these labor markets, and the gendered dimensions of these processes of restructuring and transition. A return to these concerns enables us to consider that in the precarious, globalized labor markets of the early twenty-first century, the self, if it wants to be employable, must think about, act on, and perform itself as an enterprise (Kelly, 2013). This "ethically slanted maxim for the conduct of a life" (Weber, 2002) has particular consequences for the ways in which the youthful self, often narrowly imagined as being in transition, can know itself, both in being, and in becoming. We will illustrate the limits and possibilities of the self as enterprise, and the work that the self must do on the self to secure that enterprise via reference to the social enterprise–based VET programs that the U.K. celebrity chef Jamie Oliver deployed in sometimes successful, often times unsuccessful, attempts to transform the lives of the young people most marginalized from, and by, education and training systems and labor markets (Kelly and Harrison, 2009). We conclude with a preliminary discussion of what it means for the self as enterprise to grow up, to be, and to become somebody, in the context of the Great Recession and an Age of Austerity in the aftermath of the 2008-09 global financial crisis (GFC).

ECONOMIES OF SIGNS AND SPACES AND THE RESTRUCTURING OF GENDER, WORK, AND EDUCATION

Globalization underlies many of the changing relationships between economic and cultural influences, place, institutions, and personal relationships and identities. In this sense, restructuring is a local expression of global trends and forces. Four important processes of restructuring are key components of the ways in which globalization has been impacting on the lived experiences of VET in Australian schools. These intersecting and overlapping processes consist of (1) the restructuring of the labor market, (2) the associated restructuring of the family and of transitions from childhood to adulthood, (3) the restructuring of schooling and the transitions from school to work, and (4) the restructuring of locality.

We base our arguments on the work of British sociologists Giddens (1991, 1994), Lash and Urry (1994), and Urry (1995), as well as the complementary feminist research of Massey (1994) and Walby (1997). Their work provides a conceptual framework that allows for a multi-layered analysis of large-scale economic and cultural shifts and influences, their social and cultural manifestations in place and space, their implications for identity and biography, and the role of gender and other axes of power, such as class and ethnicity, in these processes.

Giddens (1994), for example, addresses what he calls the "altered context of political life" and argues that there are three processes at work in this altered context: (1) the reorganization of space and time, (2) the move to a "post-traditional social order," and (3) the increasing centrality in our lives of "social reflexivity." He also argues that these are associated with changes in broad structures of feeling—with a generalized sense of tension and emotional and moral disquiet. Urry (1995) is concerned with the "sociology of place" and with exploring the ways in which place and its dynamic articulations with wider global forces shape the ways local people live and change their lives, pointing to the social and cultural issues associated with the restructuring of local economies and public services and the localization of the global. Although his concern has been with place, he is now also interested in that which flows through and influences place; for instance, the flow of tourists, workers, information, and screen images. His focus on cultural constructions of place and the ways in which place and identity intersect provide for a space wherein memories and traditions often collide with the present.

Giddens (1994) identified the emergence of a "post traditional order" during the second half of the twentieth century. This order is a result of the many challenges to traditional ways of doing things, organizing our lives, and interacting with nature. This post-traditional order emerges as a consequence of a range of factors, including the declining influence of traditional agencies of socialization (the church, the family, and the school) and the rise of other significant influences (the media, popular culture); new scientific and technical knowledge and its applications to nature and our bodies; new social movements and their challenges to convention and habit; the clash of values brought about by the rise of global differences; and the spread of different cultures around the globe. As a result of the changing nature of tradition, the late twentieth and early twenty-first century can be characterized as "a runaway world of dislocation and uncertainty," a world of "manufactured uncertainty" (Giddens, 1994, pp. 93–95). In this world we now often have to decide upon many of the things that once were taken for granted or regarded as simply natural. Feminist work on globalization has been particularly conscious of the "uneven and fractured" (Bakker, 1996, p. 19) process of both globalization and identity formation within the webs of power that constitute what Grewal and Kaplan (1994) call "scattered hegemonies." This feminist literature identifies the geography of gender and explores the changing gendered discourses, identities, and relations of local-cultural space/places, pointing to place-based variations in the construction and reconstruction of gender. Studies of the changing economic base of place assist us to see how gender has been reshaped accordingly (Bagguley, et al., 1990). This literature has also examined the ways in which changing economic forms and regional policies are differentiated by locality and by gender, and how such changes brought about changes in gender relations at work and home and in the overall gender order of the locality (Kenway, Kraak, and Hickey Moody, 2006; Walby, 1997).

Following Giddens (1991, pp. 187–201), we argue that the altered context of political life has provided "new mechanisms for self identity." Narratives of self are shaped by the rapidly changing circumstances of social life on a local, national, and global scale, and by associated new forms of fragmentation and integration, thereby bringing about an array of new choices in relation to education, work, family, and leisure. While freedom from old constraints offers more apparent choice and autonomy, it also generates new uncertainties and fragmentations in relation to gender, family, work, knowledge, and authority—Who am I? Whom do I believe? What is my place in this world, my future? Will I survive? How? Central to the biographical project of identity formation, then, are issues of risk, trust, and ontological security. In this context Giddens (1991, p. 203) argues that individuals must resolve many "dilemmas of the self" and these are particularly consequential at key points or "fateful moments."

These ideas prompted us initially to consider how space and time are being reorganized in young people's lives and the implications of such reorganization for socially and spatially situated young people. The notion of the increasing centrality of social reflexivity helped us to (1) explore the knowledge that schools draw on to understand social and economic change and to assist young people to deal with it, and (2) see the significance of certain knowledge and authority in VET and the ways in which these connected with the gendered biographies of young women and men.

We were particularly interested in the ways in which young people construct their narratives of self-identity in particular times and places; how they deal with increased choice and autonomy; the dilemmas of the self that they addressed; their fateful moments; and the ways in which risk, trust, and ontological security were inscribed in their lives and the survival values that they and their peers and communities drew on to sustain themselves. Young men and women experienced these matters differently, some experienced more risk and uncertainty than others, and had different ways of maximizing choice, minimizing risk, and searching for certainty in their distinctive localities.

THE ALTERED CONTEXTS OF EDUCATIONAL LIFE

Four significant restructuring dynamics to the altered context of educational life have been important in our research.

The Restructuring of Gender and Work

In Australia, the country we know best, as in other advanced Western economies, a feature of globalizing labor processes and labor markets is what Bakker (1996, p. 7) calls the "gender paradox of restructuring." This paradox involves the "contradictory effects of the dual process of gender erosion and intensification," and demonstrates that arguments about the feminization of restructured globalized/local labor markets are inadequate. These transformations destabilize class and gender identities and relationships to the extent that masculinity and femininity are being reconceived in a post-traditional social order. These identity processes are, indeed, being de-traditionalized and re-traditionalized at the same time.

These processes have particular implications for the broad structures of feeling associated with masculinity. Indeed, in the schools we have studied, we found a generalized sense of tension and emotional disquiet about boys' education and, more subtly, about masculine identity (Kenway, Watkins, and Tregenza, 1998). There has always been a strong historical identification between masculinity, potency, and paid work. Our research into masculinity demonstrated that as males lose power in one sphere they try to regain it in another; they search for new ways of expressing it in order to reclaim their sense of manhood (Kenway and Fitzclarence, 1997; Kenway and Willis, 1995). Changes in employment may have contributed to the rise of gender fundamentalism. Mac an Ghaill (1996), for example, demonstrated that during the 1980s to 1990s new hierarchies between high and low status vocational fields were developing in the United Kingdom. The emerging high status technological and commercial subject areas such as business studies, technology, and computer studies were providing some young men with what he calls an "ascending and modernizing version of working class masculinity" with an associated disposition toward an instrumental, rationalized, forward planning of career and life options.

We found that the themes of de-traditionalization and re-traditionalization apply differently to young women. Many girls adopt what might be called a non-traditional approach to work. They expect to do paid work *and* to share household work. Further, the feminist movement had led many to hope for work in the core labor market. For those who gain such work, this is often non-traditional in the terms of the history of women's work. But in the context of the intensified masculine core, it takes on many traditional elements. Further, due to overwork, many women contract out much of their household and caring work. This, too, is non-traditional for them but in the creation of a new home service class, it re-traditionalizes class relations between women. With regard to VET, our research indicated that girls who undertake vocational education programs tend to be clustered in programs associated with retail, hospitality, service, and administration work. Many in our research expressed a keen interest in hospitality (Kenway amd Kelly, 2000; see also Teese, Davies, Charlton, and Polesel, 1995). Indeed, Adkins (1995, 1997) has argued that hospitality and tourism represent both de-traditionalizing and re-traditionalizing moments for women and men, particularly in the context of family relations.

Restructuring the Family and the Transitions from Childhood to Adulthood

Significant changes in family forms have been taking place since the 1970s: dual parent, sole parent, divorced, blended, de facto, serial, and same-sex family groupings. In addition, changing patterns of work and unemployment impacted household dynamics. Different patterns beyond the traditional family and the traditional use of household space can be identified, including young people in work and parents not; mothers in work and not fathers; parents never home due to overwork in one or multiple jobs; parents often away on increasing travel associated with jobs; parents at home all the time due to outworking, or an office at home; telecommuting; and possibly all the family at home all the time when there is no paid work at all (Bakker, 1996; Brodie, 1995; Delhi, 1998; Edwards and Magarey, 1995). In our research, we met young people across this range including those who do not live at home and those who bring in the family income while at school.

These transformations impact traditional transitions from childhood to adulthood—a theme developed in the youth studies literature (Kelly, 2006, 2007). One aspect of traditional transitions has been the move into the paid labor market as paid employment is often seen to mark the onset of adulthood. Young people's patterns of work have been de-traditionalizing this transition process. More young people today are in part-time work while at school. More are unemployed, underemployed, or in multiple jobs. More are staying at home longer or they are part of the working poor, living independently. Changing patterns of independence and dependence between parents and children increase the potential for stress and tension in households (Sweet, 1995).

Restructuring Schools and the Transitions from School to Work

Australian education systems during the 1990s, as a consequence of processes of globalization, have been characterized by processes of de- and re-centralizing the institutions of the state. On the de-centralizing side of this agenda are changes to school management processes, funding on a per capita basis, and the inter-school competition that arose from both. On the re-centralizing side are curriculum and market ideologies. VET for school students is part of this dynamic (Kenway, Tragenza, and Watkins, 1997).

VET has been centralized through the reflexively ordered National Training Reform Agenda (Kenway and Willis, 1995). These processes mirror what Giddens (1994) calls "burgeoning institutional reflexivity." Over time and in various ways, an avalanche of reports led to VET curricula that promote workplace competencies, enterprise education, and new apprenticeship and traineeship schemes. While such documents appeared to represent a sense of certainty in the field, in fact "radical doubt" (Giddens, 1994) about their effects has led to their constant revision (see Kelly, 1999; Kenway, 1999). At the same time, VET in schools has been decentralized through other imperatives that cluster around the master narrative of the market. These imperatives include school/industry partnerships and the introduction of the training market with its stress on a level playing field between public and private providers and user choice and user fees. Schools now compete for clients (students and industry partners for work placement).

These shifts have generated new gender and power issues for schools, teachers, and students. In the field of VET, entrepreneurial male teachers appear to be taking over from more pastoral female teachers. Networking with local business and industry and local service organizations such as the Rotary Club seem easier for some male teachers. Some schools have become private providers and are making demands that certain of their teachers retrain. Such demands are usually made on those teachers whose subjects attract lower student numbers. New vocational agendas require the reorganization of students' use of space and time. VET students in schools are now dispersed across quite complicated multi-credentialing and multi-site arrangements. The institutional reflexivity and manufactured uncertainty (Giddens, 1994) that characterizes the emergence of VET policy and practices, and the de- and re-traditionalizing of class and gender identities that emerge in a post-traditional social order have affected profoundly the schools in our study. These processes have unsettled some traditional understandings of schooling, education, and young people for teachers in our schools. Many teachers face significant difficulties keeping up to date with the reflexively monitored VET system and have had to rely on expert advice to assist them.

Restructuring Locality

Our research found that an appreciation of the changing economic base of place and the associated sociology and culture of place is vital to understanding the directions of VET in schools and in considering the suitability of schools' approaches. All the patterns noted previously were manifested differently in different localities. Each had its particular patterns with regard to the labor market, the family, school-to-work patterns, and gender and class relations and identities.

The localities we have studied include places we identified as depressed, traditional rural; entrepreneurial/tourist rural; provincial manufacturing cities in decline; inner-city localities empty of most possibilities of employment except in some service industries; and a post-Fordist boom city. Each of these localities has been differently affected by the localization of the global order of work. Many have also been affected by processes of national, state, and local government restructuring with regard to the privatization and downsizing of public services. Industry restructuring, the demise of the public sector, and reductions in public services have had a severe impact on people's capacity to find and travel to work. Most of the localities at the time of our study had high levels of unemployment, youth unemployment, and working poor. Indeed, in some of these places, social welfare benefits were an important part of local economies. These localities were of special concern due to the economic and social difficulties and associated cultural changes they were experiencing. School students there had to contend with particular problems because of the instability and uncertainty of their locations and required specific educational interventions.

At that time many regional economies in Australia were exploring various forms of renewal and restructuring (McKinsey and Company, 1994). This was the case in the localities where we were doing our research. They each had particular responses to globalizing processes and had mobilized their resources in particular ways. In our research, localities' economic restructuring had often led to the displacement of manufacturing in regional areas. However, restructuring had also led to the *manufacturing of place* by local government councils. The marketing of place, industry, tourism, and hospitality had developed as part of a locality's growth strategy. Local councils had taken on the job not only of developing regional economic plans but also of promoting the region to prospective industries (employers) and residents. They were now in the business of branding the local; of giving it an image, a personality. This was done through such things as the use of glossy brochures and stickers and posters.

For example, we did some of our research in the Geelong region of the Australian state of Victoria. Here the City of Greater Geelong had just re-badged itself as a great place to live through the slogan "Geelong: Smart Move." In brochures, posters, and booklets, much was made of Geelong's waterfront and its proximity to natural attractions (nearby beaches and mountains). Colorful flags still line the entrance to the city and, at that time, incentives were made available to potential homebuyers including free membership of the Geelong Australian Rules Football Club (the Cats). One of the city's main industries and employers was the U.S.-based multinational car manufacturing company Ford. Decisions made at a distance constantly threatened the future of this company in the town (and still do). The locals were urged to buy Ford via the slogan "Ford: Live it."

Two of our other research schools were in the western suburbs of the city of Melbourne, a region historically reliant on the employment opportunities offered by large-scale manufacturing enterprises. It is to these parts of Melbourne that successive waves of post-war unskilled migrant labor had been attracted. Consequently this region boasts an incredible diversity of ethnic, religious, and language groups. These groups have generated extensive community networks during the post-war boom years and in the last three decades of industrial decline. One young Maltese Australian woman in our study boasted of, and also lamented, her connection to a large family network of uncles, aunts, and seventy-eight cousins.

In this region the same processes of *manufacturing place* were occurring. The brochures and Websites developed by various local and regional government agencies emphasized the lifestyle benefits of multicultural diversity as the economy attempted to restructure and build on its industrial (iron) age infrastructure. In a promotional brochure, the Western Region Economic Development Organization positioned itself as a "facilitator of change within the region—a promoter of the region's competitive benefits of world class infrastructure (Australia's best port, best road system, and best airport) within a dynamic, multicultural living environment." The Western Region Economic Development Organization indicated that it and its "stakeholder groups in local government and the private sector have repositioned the region to emerge once again as one of the powerhouses of Australia's economy."

One of these stakeholders, the City of Maribynong, argued in its 1996/97 Annual Report that the city "is the cultural, business and retail center of Melbourne's western region. The west is Australia's premier industrial zone." Industrial land was claimed to be "10 times less expensive than in Sydney and 56 times less expensive than in Osaka"; "60% of all industrial land sales in Victoria last year were in Melbourne's west"; "41% of all Victoria's exports are from the west"; "Over the next four years there will be $7 billion worth of projects in Melbourne's west."

This accessibility to various important nodes in transport networks figured prominently in the region's promotional material. It appeared that if you intended to promote the region for its manufacturing industrial base, then you had to be able to demonstrate its connections to transport networks that can move manufactured products into global markets. This process was different from promoting an information-age economy because in that context one needed only to demonstrate access to information networks. In the context of three decades of de-industrialization, there was an attempt to reposition the region as an industrial zone that had access to global transport networks (for export/import activities), and which compared favorably to other industrial zones in global manufacturing economies/markets.

One final example from our earlier study illustrates many of the processes of transformation and restructuring that we are discussing here. This rural locality was a one-industry town: the dairy industry and the local dairy factory, which we called Corbetts, is the major player in the local economy. What we saw in this area were the ways in which the nature of both business organization and dairy production were changing. Corbetts was originally a farmers' cooperative, embedded in the community. It had strong connections to the locality but these connections were changing during the time of our research. Previously Corbetts' manager had been a "big man" in the community: he belonged to local-service organizations. In its new guise, Corbetts became a public company, joined up with other similar companies, and was managed from a distance with global as well as local markets in mind. In order to be competitive in these new spaces, and to win and maintain a distant, trusting customer base, it needed to conform to internationally recognized quality assurance practices.

Here we saw the global in the local in very direct ways. A leading local employer now operated at arm's length from the local schools and did not even have work placement for students due to the particular management, work, health, and safety practices necessary to meet international standards. The path from school and farm to factory and back to the farm for local boys had been disrupted. Family connections into the factory no longer counted for employment purposes. Certain hygiene and quality control practices required new forms of work skills and expertise. In the context of globalizing markets and best practices, dairy production and the processing and manufacturing of dairy products was being transformed by new production technologies and products; by processes of rationalization at the company level and at the farm level (larger farms, larger herds, new milking technologies); by new herd gene technologies that had increased farm output; and by a movement into global food-products markets. What we observed here was the way in which the locality was opened up and restructured by regional/global markets and networks and flows (Lash and Urry, 1994). The industry and the economic base of the region were increasingly regulated by processes and flows quite distant from the places where students at the local school lived and might have hoped to gain a job and build a life.

Geography is always gendered, as gender relations in this region and era of change demonstrated. Indeed, these relations reflected the deeply gendered patterns of behavior in rural areas that Dempsey (1990, 1992) elaborated in the early 1990s. Many of the boys subscribed to traditional masculinities associated with farming and mechanics and sport. Farms are passed down from fathers to sons, but boys "backed up" with a trade qualification—just in case. The work chances of the young women in this place were limited by the local labor markets that were both very restricted and highly gendered. There were limited jobs for girls, and most jobs were poorly paid. Typically, the girls had two types of response: absorption in local cultures of femininity, or migration out of the town. Some girls planned to stay in the district and take whatever casual jobs were available. They celebrated their locality. They constructed their femininity in much the same ways that their mothers did in relation to particular understandings of home, community building, and women's rural roles. They also became involved in the informal and reproductive economy of activities such as childcare (babysitting). We got the sense in talking to these young women that they were preparing to become guardians of the local moral order. Already they were constructing the city as a dangerous space of drugs and crime and in contrast the rural was imagined as safe. The girls who looked to migrate from the area had a deficit view of their locality, and sometimes a fantasy view of elsewhere. For some of these young women, the city was imagined as alien, unsafe, and so their ambitions were a little more limited, and extended no farther than a neighboring provincial city.

WORKING IN *JAMIE'S KITCHEN*: CULTIVATING THE SELF AS ENTERPRISE

As we might say, with more than a little understatement, much has happened since we explored these ideas and concerns in the first edition of this book. We can leave aside our own personal trajectories, and the lives that the young women and men in our research have gone on to live. We can also acknowledge that much of what we say next privileges a rather WEIRD (*W*estern, *e*ducated, *i*ndustrialized, *r*ich, *d*emocratic) view of the world. However, during the last decade, places, regions, nations, and the globe have been reshaped, often dramatically, and with much hurt, pain, and suffering for the most vulnerable and marginalized by such things as the following: the dot.com bubble of the turn of the century; the attacks on New York, Washington, and in Pennsylvania on 9/11, and in Madrid, London (7/7), Mumbai, Baghdad, Peshawar, and too many other places since; the apparently never-ending U.S.-led war-on-terror, and manifestations of that war in Iraq and Afghanistan, at Abu Ghraib, at Guantanamo, and in black-sites in the strangest places around the world (e.g., Libya and Syria); the GFC of 2008-09; young people's involvement in protests and revolutions such as Iran's short-lived Green Revolution of 2009, the so-called Arab Spring, the Spanish *Indignados*, the Greek Indignant Citizens Movement, the global Occupy movement (We are the 99%), leading up to, during, and subsequent to 2011—the year *Time* magazine called "The Year of the Protestor" (*Time Magazine*, 2011); and the emergence of the Great Recession and government austerity programs in many European Union and Organization for Economic Cooperation and Development economies as the echoes of the GFC are re-imagined as being about sovereign debt crises.

In recent work (Kelly, 2013; Kelly and Harrison, 2009), we have argued that twenty-first century, twenty-four/seven, flexible capitalism creates new demands for those who work, and for those who want to work, to imagine themselves as an enterprise. In what follows we will sketch an approach to imagining the limits and the possibilities of the self as enterprise. We will illustrate these limits and possibilities with reference to the sorts of vocational education and training that U.K. celebrity chef Jamie Oliver offers to marginalized young people. A VET regime designed to make up young people as the passionate, enterprising persons best equipped to secure a form of parlous redemption, even salvation, in the precarious, globalized labor markets of the twenty-first century.

In *The Culture of the New Capitalism*, Richard Sennett (2006) identifies three key, unfolding processes shaping the emergence of what he calls "flexible capitalism." It is worth stressing that the changes Sennett describes are complex; they unfold unevenly and with a variety of consequences (intended and unintended); they may look different and impact differently in different configurations of time/space/place—such as in different organizations (large/small, startup/established), or in different towns, cities, regions, nations, or free-trade communities. However, this framework enables us to discuss changes in twenty-first century work regimes that foreground the powerful demands for flexibility, both at the level of the organization, and at the level of the self.

The first of the processes Sennett (2006, pp. 37–47) identifies is the "shift from managerial to share holder power" in many, mostly larger, organizations. Sennett locates the energizing moment for this shift in the 1970 breakdown of the Bretton Woods agreement, and the subsequent freeing of vast amounts of capital to find optimal returns anywhere around the globe. Takeovers, mergers, acquisitions, and buyouts became the playthings of increasingly mobile capital. All enabled by the frenzied activity of wealth holders seeking wealth creation, and facilitated by the demands, not always successful, for the interests of fluid, mobile, digitized capital to be accorded more currency/value than those of more territorially fixed players such as nation-states and flesh-and-blood workers (Beck, 2000). For Sennett, this explosion in the volume and circulation of capital, and the emergence of sophisticated investment instruments/practices, means that managers and executive officers in many large organizations are confronted by investors who have become active judges: "a turning point in such participation occurred when pension funds, controlling vast quantities of capital, began actively pressuring management. The increasing sophistication of financial instruments like the leveraged buyout meant that the investors could make or break corporations while its management stood by helplessly" (page 39).

This globalized circulation/flow of often predatory capital, always on the lookout for bigger, better, faster returns on its risk activity, ushered in the second process that Sennett identifies as energizing the flexibilization of capitalism. Citing Bennett Harrison's notion of impatient capital, Sennett (2006, pp. 39–40) argues that "empowered investors" in greatly enhanced, globalized circuits of capital demanded short-term rather than long-term results: "whereas in 1965 American pension funds held stocks on an average for 46 months, by 2000 much in the portfolios of these institutional investors turned over on an average of 3.8 months." In these emerging investment markets, share/stock prices, rather than dividends or earnings ratios, became the favored measures/indicators of return or potential return. As Sennett indicates, there is little new in money chasing money. However, organizations have had to transform their institutional processes, practices, and structures to satisfy the fetishization of the short term by impatient, globalized, digitized capital: "Enormous pressure was put on companies to look beautiful in the eyes of the passing voyeur; institutional beauty consisted in demonstrating signs of internal change and flexibility, appearing to be a dynamic company, even if the once-stable company had worked perfectly well" (Sennett, 2006, pp. 40–41). In Sennett's understanding of flexible capitalism this is a profound change, and a continuing driver of change: the re-engineering, re-working, re-invention of the organization—and, we would add, of the self—that accompanies the myriad, complex demands for flexibility, nimbleness, and innovation signals a highly consequential break from the steel hard shell/iron cage of the Weberian bureaucracy. And the possibility of thinking or acting otherwise in twenty-first century capitalism is indeed limited: what might be the possibilities for, and the consequences of, risking the indifference or wrath of impatient, globalized capital?

The third driver of this post-bureaucratic, flexible capitalism is, for Sennett, the information, communication, and transportation revolutions of the last three decades that have transformed the nature of all productive activities—service-based, manufacturing, agricultural, and mining. Under the unfolding, sometimes uneven, influence of the global development and deployment of these technologies, twenty-first century work looks different and is imagined and regulated in different ways. It can be undertaken by microprocessor-governed machines and hardware that displace humans on a massive scale. It can be organized within organizational architecture that, ideally, looks less like a pyramid, is flatter with less layers, and that constantly strives for real time rather than lag time in processes of command and control, but also of innovation and development. The promise of these technologies is forms of flexibility, nimbleness, responsiveness, and creativity that appeal—for however short a term—to impatient capital. These forces are felt not only at the organizational level, at the level of being an attractive object of mobile, digital, impatient capital. They are highly consequential for the individual, the self, that constantly encounters these *norms* of economic activity, and must make choices, fashion a self, practice his/her freedom in the spaces structured by these demands and expectations: How flexible are you? How flexible are you prepared to be/become? In summary, then, Sennett (1998, p. 59) argues that these:

> are the forces bending people to change: reinvention of bureaucracy, flexible specialization of production, concentration without centralization. In the revolt against routine, the appearance of the new freedom is deceptive. Time in institutions and for individuals has been unchained from the iron cage of the past, but subjected to new, top-down controls and surveillance. The time of flexibility is the time of a new power. Flexibility begets disorder, but not freedom from restraint.

Over one hundred years ago, in *The Protestant Ethic and the "Spirit" of Capitalism*, Max Weber (2002) explored the particular virtues that should be seen as attaching to work (hard work, done well, was its own reward), and the influence that certain Protestant sects had on articulating these virtues, and a so-called spirit of capitalism. The precarious, globalized labor markets of twenty-first century flexible capitalism demand particular forms of personhood, and demand processes of education and training capable of producing such persons. In this sense it is useful to think of these demands as being demands that the self, if it wants to be employable, must think about, act on, and perform itself as an enterprise. Drawing on Weber's legacy, and the work of Zygmunt Bauman (2004) and Michel Foucault (2000a, b), we can argue that twenty-first century, flexible capitalism is energized by a spirit that sees in the cultivation of the self—as an ongoing, never ending enterprise—an "ethically slanted maxim for the conduct of a life" (Weber, 2002). The cultivation, conduct, and regulation of the self is a never-ending project shaped by an ethic of enterprise that promises to support, facilitate, and energize this project. This spirit is analyzable as an institutionally structured, individualized entrepreneurialism; a structured series of incitements to manage the life course as an entrepreneurial do-it-yourself project. This is a project that requires us to know and govern ourselves in ways that facilitate the pursuit of this calling.

The self as enterprise is required to think of itself, imagine the work that it should do on itself within a widespread, embracing set of normative terms that seek to position the self as entrepreneurial, active, autonomous, prudential, risk-aware, choice-making, and responsible (Kelly, 2006). The self as an enterprise is a self that is capable of continuing to engage in both the enterprise of the self and in the enterprises of production and consumption. This self is required to develop a certain self-awareness, a particular self-understanding, a type, form, and level of reflexivity that equips it to exercise a well-regulated autonomy. This form of selfhood should also have the capacity to exercise, on a continual, ongoing basis, practices of freedom that require the exercise of choice, and acceptance of the responsibilities for the consequences of choices made, or not made, especially in relation to what it means to be a worker in the globalized, risky labor markets of the WEIRD economies. In this sense, we all, as individual entrepreneurs of our own biographies and portfolios of choice and achievement, carry an increasingly onerous burden. Individualization processes increasingly locate the self as the space/site in which the tensions, risks, contradictions, paradoxes, ambiguities, and ambivalences of globalized, rationalized capitalism are to be resolved and managed, or not (see also Kelly and Harrison, 2009).

At first glance, the self as enterprise does not have a gender, an ethnic background, a particular age, or a specific geographic location. However, on closer inspection, it becomes clear that gender neutrality assumes masculinity; that "no ethnic background" assumes "whiteness"; that "no age barrier" means a productive, enterprising adulthood that runs from the mid-twenties to the mid-forties; and that "no place" in effect means a cosmopolitan, post-industrial urban geography that makes enterprise understandable, thinkable, possible. The particular character of the self as enterprise can be diverse and can accommodate an array of possibilities. What it means to be entrepreneurial, active, autonomous, prudential, risk-aware, choice-making, and responsible can be relatively open. However, the expectations and norms of the self as enterprise take on particular limits and possibilities in different labor markets. Participation in these labor markets is not about unlimited possibilities but rather suggestions, incitements, and demands to imagine and practice the self in ways that conform, more or less, to the norms that give shape to these fields. You want to work here? These are the expectations! [2]

The lessons of the self as enterprise in *Jamie's Kitchen* are difficult to learn, even imagine, for many marginalized young people who have had little success in the education, training, and work environments that demand that they/we can develop and perform this form of personhood. These lessons and these difficulties were made very apparent in two reality television shows in the last decade: *Jamie's Kitchen* (aired in the United Kingdom in 2000 and in Australia in 2003) and *Jamie's Kitchen Australia* (aired over thirteen weeks in 2006) (Smith, 2006).

In the original series, celebrity chef Jamie Oliver took fifteen unemployed young Londoners and tried to turn them into trainee chefs who had the capacity to work in his new London restaurant called, appropriately, Fifteen. The original series was followed by *Jamie's Kitchen Australia* which tracked the opening of the Fifteen franchise in Melbourne. Since the initial television series there have been larger, yearly, cohorts of trainees, and in 2004 the Fifteen Foundation was established as a for-profit social enterprise. The Fifteen Foundation had opened restaurants in Cornwall, Amsterdam, and Melbourne. In these endeavors, the Foundation claimed to be "driving forward our dream of building Fifteen into a global social enterprise brand inspiring young people all over the world." As a social enterprise, the Foundation claimed that it "exists to inspire disadvantaged young people to believe that they can create for themselves great careers in the restaurant industry" (Fifteen Foundation,[3] 2007).

We argued in *Working in Jamie's Kitchen* (Kelly and Harrison, 2009) that throughout both series we see and hear about an apparent lack of passion, energy, excitement, and entrepreneurial flair in the young people making the first steps in trying to become employed. The possibility of self-transformation, of being somebody different, of doing something different within the space of a year is held out to these young people. And this possibility is something that can be realized if they embrace food in the ways that Oliver imagines it. We also see an emphasis on the individual as the figure who must recognize their deficits and lacks, who must understand themselves as being an agent who can transform their own life and circumstances through their own efforts.

These understandings are mapped out in a document titled *What's Right With These Young People*, where the Fifteen Foundation aims to inform potential franchisees "about what goes on with our young people during their time with us" (Fifteen Foundation, 2005). In this document, the Foundation states that: "Fifteen exists to reach out to young people who are disregarded in society—the focus all too often is on what's wrong with them." Embedded in this discourse are references to social understandings of the type of young person that Fifteen targets—understandings that are often negative and that attach themselves to a variety of problem behaviors, histories, and relationships. As a consequence of these issues, many of the trainees show "low self esteem, self defeating patterns of behaviour, and social networks that serve to keep them locked into poverty and underachievement."

The widespread critique of what is wrong with young people in these circumstances—by schools, businesses and managers, and state and nongovernment authorities and agencies—is something the Foundation is explicit about. The Foundation suggests that new opportunities, new responsibilities, and new relationships will provide the possibility for young people to transform themselves: "This involves a unique encounter with food and Jamie's inspiring approach to cooking and service. But Fifteen is so much more than a chef training project. Food and cooking are the means to the end. The purpose is personal transformation for each young person."

In this sense, the Foundation positions certain understandings of food, its production, preparation, presentation, and consumption, as a technology of self-transformation (Foucault, 2000b). The purpose is not so much to train chefs, but to utilize food, cooking, and the work environment of a commercial kitchen that thinks about, prepares, and presents food in particular ways, as a means to transform the opportunities, choices, and self-understandings of young people previously at risk of living and leading *wasted lives* (Bauman, 2004).

In analyzing the forms that the self and self-knowledge have taken at different times, Foucault (2000b, pp. 87–88) argued that the sorts of studies that he undertook were guided by the concept of *technologies of the self*: those "procedures, which no doubt exist in every civilization, suggested or prescribed to individuals in order to determine their identity, maintain it, or transform it in terms of a certain number of ends, through relations of mastery or self knowledge." For Foucault, an analysis of these technologies of the self could be guided by questions of the following type: "What should one do with oneself? What work should be carried out on the self? How should one 'govern oneself' by performing actions in which one is oneself the objective of those actions, the domain in which they are brought to bear, the instrument they employ, and the subject that acts?"

From this perspective we can analyze passion, and the characteristics it assumes in *Jamie's Kitchen*, and in the training of marginalized young people as a powerful technology of self-transformation. In this setting passion is analyzable along the following three axes.

First, passion emerges from and frames particular forms of knowledge and ways of knowing the self, VET, paid work, the restaurant industry, and food. So, marginalized young people are understood in certain ways, and as requiring certain processes and practices to be put in place to enable a passion to emerge or develop from an initial sense of self that is anything but passionate (at least in relation to the ends that the training program has in mind). In the time and spaces spanned by the original series, the emergence of a vision to develop Fifteen as a global social enterprise brand, and the Australian series, *truths* about how to achieve this vision have been reflexively reformulated to produce, for example, different ways of understanding the entering behaviors of these young people. Early in the first series, we get a sense that trainees ought to enter the program with evident, pre-existing, and substantial levels of passion. Passion in this time/space is largely seen as intrinsic. It is something you bring with you (King, 2005). Later it is re-imagined as something that has to be developed and nurtured.

Knowledge here also has as its objects the sorts of understandings of food that Jamie Oliver is famous for (Smith, 2006). Food, understood in these ways, is something to get passionate about. It can excite the passions. It can be produced, prepared, presented, and consumed with passion. Because food is understood in these ways, the work that goes on in a restaurant kitchen is also something to be passionate about.

Second, passion is produced, regulated, and managed within relations of power that emerge from and give shape to particular fields of possibilities. In these spaces, military metaphors are often used to identify *command and control* structures that are understood as being vital to the task of preparing and presenting substantial amounts of food, *to order*, and on time (Bourdain, 2000; Buford, 2006; Caddwalladr, 2007). Sovereignty resides in the capacity to order someone to do something, and to the required consistency and quality. Throughout both series, in kitchens and in off-the-job training spaces, we witness the exercise of sovereignty by head chefs, trainers, and teachers at the same time as we witness trainees resisting, or choosing to conform to, these demands. The aim of the exercise of sovereignty is to establish the field and its limits, in which appropriate forms of passion might emerge. Sovereign power cannot *will* passion into existence, but it might establish the conditions in which it emerges or is uncovered.

In this training environment, disciplinary power takes a form that requires trainees to submit to the often menial, mundane tasks of cleaning, of maintaining a work place/space and its utensils. It also involves learning, repeating, and mastering the mechanics of food preparation. At one level this cleaning, sweeping, tidying, dicing, slicing treadmill seeks to develop essential skills. At another it also promises to develop new forms of self-awareness: as individuals who can discipline themselves, can conform to the demands of rationalized clock time, and can become passionate about doing these things well through a sense that they have a purpose, and that this purpose contributes to a larger project that can deliver feelings and understandings of self-worth, competence, and ability. Again, discipline cannot *will* passion into existence, but these forms and relations of power promise to produce a skill, knowledge, and attitude base from which passion might be uncovered or emerge.

Third, passion seeks to produce certain practices of the self. These practices take their shape from the field of possibilities structured by the relationships between knowledge and relations of power outlined previously. In *Jamie's Kitchen* and in the Fifteen program, these practices of the self include such things as attendance requirements at college and work placements; the mundane, menial tasks of cleaning; learning how to correctly prepare and present ingredients so that dishes can be cooked, assembled, and presented for consumption— the seemingly endless practice of diverse skills and techniques that are vital to food preparation in the chaotic context of commercial kitchens; tasting and testing of foods in ways that develop new vocabularies, understandings, and orientations to food and its possibilities; shopping and sourcing expeditions to develop and practice skills necessary to knowing food as having different origins, qualities, and possibilities in terms of preparation, and as ingredients for particular dishes; and team-building excursions to test the limits of the self, to locate the self in different fields where different understandings of the self, and of others, and of a team might be encouraged to form and emerge.[4]

As we demonstrated in *Working in Jamie's Kitchen* (Kelly and Harrison, 2009), many of the most marginalized young people have great difficulty in conforming to the demands that the self should imagine and think about itself as an enterprise in the education and training systems, and globalized labor markets of a more flexible capitalism. Their marginalization bears testament to this inability to conform. We want to finish this discussion with a hint of what the future may hold for many young people as these demands to imagine the self as enterprise take on new dimensions in the aftermath of the GFC.

GROWING UP IN THE GREAT RECESSION

The unfolding effects of what some are calling the Great Recession in Europe and the United States, and the emergence of sovereign debt crises and significant austerity programs in many European Union/Organization of Economic Cooperation and Development economies represents a largely successful framing of responses to the downstream effects of the GFC as being principally about state debt levels. In this discourse, those that depend most on state-provided services, payments, and programs will be the ones to carry the greatest burden of government austerity measures. In early 2011, the then Governor of the Bank of England, Mervyn King, claimed that those made unemployed or who have had their benefits cut as a consequence of the GFC, recession, and austerity "had every reason to be resentful and voice their protest." He suggested that the billions spent bailing out the banks and the need for public spending cuts were the fault of the financial services sector: "The price of this financial crisis is being borne by people who absolutely did not cause it" (Inman, 2011).

During the so-called Year of the Protester (*Time Magazine*, 2011), we witnessed how many young people around the world had begun both to experience what some of these consequences might be and to give voice to much of their anxiety, uncertainty, and anger about their experience of these consequences. In some contexts, record high levels of youth unemployment and precarious employment, student debt accompanying increased costs for higher education, housing costs that lock many out of home ownership, and the challenges for young people's physical and mental well-being are reshaping young people's sense of self and of their chances for meaningful participation in relationships and settings that have traditionally identified someone as an adult, as a citizen. These concerns are well captured by the many hundreds, even thousands of contributions from young people to a Tumblr page called *We Are the 99%*.

We want to present, in addition to the opening quote, another example from these posts, which are usually accompanied by an image chosen by the young person to represent themselves or their situation. The posts illustrate some of the issues that we have discussed so far, and point towards the work that might be done in what some are calling the "lost decade" to come. One young woman, as she peers at the camera, half-hidden by a note pad she is holding, posted:

> I CAN'T FIND MY FUTURE.
> I looked in college.
> I found debt.
> I looked to my parents.
> I found debt and heartbreak.
> I looked at my friends.
> I found grief and sorrow.
> I looked at the land.

I found MY COMMONS DESTROYED, MY LAKES AND RIVERS AND SOIL AND TREES
AND BEES AND WORMS DESTROYED.
I looked at my fellow humans.
I found disease, debt, sorrow, dissonance, hate, greed, misery, AND NO ONE CARES ANY-
MORE.
well. I CARE. an awful lot.
I'M TAKING MY FUTURE BACK.
(IT'S MINE)
I AM THE 99%.[5]

What we see in these and the thousands of similar posts, and in a variety of other spaces, is a powerful questioning of many of the markers of adulthood that have framed young people's identity, their sense of self, both in *being*, and in *becoming*: *becoming* an adult, *becoming* a citizen, *becoming* independent, *becoming* autonomous, *becoming* mature, *becoming* responsible (Kelly, 2006, 2007, 2011). These markers frame accounts of what it is to be an aspirational, enterprising young person who has a prudential eye to the future: to *their* future as adults with some sort of investment in an education, a career, relationships, consumption, housing, possibly parenting.

We are the 99% represents, in this sense, an attempt to re-imagine what it means to be a person who is connected to others in various spheres of life. Of course not everyone who might qualify will imagine themselves as being a member of the 99%, but the material concerns of those who do are able to be reframed via the networking that is promised by social media. That is, we can imagine ourselves as being part of this thing called the 99% because social media enables us to imagine that such a thing exists, or exists as imagined by those who come to identify themselves in this way.

One danger, as we saw at different times over the last three years, is that in carrying out these experiments, the traditional institutions and apparatuses of democratic and/or oppressive regimes will use the various strategies, tactics, and forces at their disposal to suppress, discredit, and/or disperse these emerging "cultures of democracy" (Gaonkar, 2007; Taylor, 2007), and the people (young and old) who are involved in the making of them. And in mobilizing these forces, these institutions will protect and promote some interests, and not others.

Despite these dangers, we can argue that these cultures of democracy are cultures in which young people's aspirations and concerns with education, work, debt, and relationships will continue to shape their social imaginary, their sense of engagement, and their participation in those aspects of life that give a concrete character to that thing we call democracy. There is much research and work to be done in support of these endeavors.

REFERENCES

Adkins, Lisa. 1995. *Gendered Work: Sexuality, Family and the Labor Market.* Buckingham, UK: Open University Press.

———. 1997. Community and Economy: The Retraditionalisation of Gender. Paper presented at "Transformations: Thinking through Feminism," Institute for Women's Studies, University of Lancaster (July 17–19).

Bagguley, Paul, Jane Mark-Lawson, Don Shapiro, John Urry, Sylvia Walby, and Alan Warde. 1990. *Restructuring: Place, Class and Gender.* London: Sage.

Bakker, Isabella (ed.). 1996. *Rethinking Restructuring: Gender and Change in Canada.* Toronto: University of Toronto Press.

Bauman, Zygmunt. 2004. *Wasted Lives: Modernity and its Outcasts.* Cambridge: Polity.

Beck, Ulrich. 2000. *The Brave New World of Work.* Cambridge: Polity.

Bourdain, Anthony. 2000. *Kitchen Confidential: Adventures in the Culinary Underbelly.* London: Bloomsbury Publishing.

Brodie, Janine. 1995. *Politics on the Margins: Restructuring and the Canadian Women's Movement.* Halifax: Fernwood Publishing.

Buford, Bill. 2006 *Heat*. London: Jonathan Cape, Random House.

Caddwalladr, Carole. 2007. Ramsay's Kitchen Queen. *The Guardian Weekly*, Sunday, April 29. http://observer.guardian.co.uk/foodmonthly/story/0,,2065123,co.html

Delhi, Kari. 1998. Nurturing Globalisation. International symposium on *Gender, Education and Globalization*. Paper presented at the American Education Research Association (AERA) Conference, San Diego.

Dempsey, Ken. 1990. *Smalltown: A Study of Social Inequality, Cohesion and Belonging*. Melbourne: Oxford University Press.

———. 1992. *A Man's Town: Inequality between Women and Men in Rural Australia*. Melbourne: Oxford University Press.

Edwards, Anne, and Susan Magarey. 1995. *Women in a Restructuring Australia: Work and Welfare*. St. Leonards, New South Wales: Allen and Unwin.

Fifteen Foundation. 2005. *What's Right with These Young People*. London: Fifteen Foundation.

———. 2007. Fifteen Foundation. http://www.fifteenrestaurant.com

Foucault, Michel. 2000a. The Ethics of the Concern of the Self as a Practice of Freedom. In Paul Rabinow (ed.), *Michel Foucault Ethics, Subjectivity and Truth* (pp. 281–302). London: Penguin.

———. 2000b. Technologies of the Self. In Paul Rabinow (ed.), *Michel Foucault Ethics, Subjectivity and Truth* (pp. 223–52). London: Penguin.

Gaonkar, Dilip Parameshwar. 2007. On Cultures of Democracy. *Public Culture*, vol. 19, no. 1, pp. 1–22.

Giddens, Anthony. 1991. *Modernity and Self Identity: Self and Society in the Late Modern Age*. Cambridge: Polity Press.

———. 1994. *Beyond Left and Right: The Future of Radical Politics*. Stanford: Stanford University Press.

Grewal, Inderpal, and Caren Kaplan. 1994. *Scattered Hegemonies: Postmodernity and Transnational Feminist Practice*. Minneapolis: University of Minnesota Press.

Inman, Phillip. 2011. Bank of England Governor Blames Spending Cuts on Bank Bailouts. *The Guardian*. http://www.guardian.co.uk/business/2011/mar/01/mervyn-king-blames-banks-cuts

Kelly, Peter. 1999. Wild and Tame Zones: Regulating the Transitions of Youth at Risk. *Journal of Youth Studies*, vol. 2, no. 2, pp. 193–211.

———. 2006. The Entrepreneurial Self and Youth at-Risk: Exploring the Horizons of Identity in the 21st Century. *Journal of Youth Studies*, vol. 9, no. 1, pp. 17–32.

———. 2007. Governing Individualized Risk Biographies: New Class Intellectuals and the Problem of Youth at-Risk. *British Journal of Sociology of Education*, vol. 28, no. 1, pp. 39–53.

———. 2011. *Breath* and the Truths of Youth at-Risk: Allegory and the Social Scientific Imagination. *Journal of Youth Studies*, vol. 14, no. 4, pp. 431–47.

———. 2013. *The Self as Enterprise: Foucault and the "Spirit" of 21st Century Capitalism*. Farnam, UK: Gower.

———, and Lyn Harrison. 2009. *Working in Jamie's Kitchen: Salvation, Passion and Young Workers*. Basingstoke, UK: Palgrave Macmillan.

———, and Jane Kenway. 2001. Youth Transitions in the Network Society. *British Journal of Sociology of Education*, vol. 22, no. 1, pp. 19–34.

Kenway, Jane. 1999. In and Out of Place: Girls, Localities and Work. Paper presented at the annual conference of the Network of Women in Further Education, Northern Sydney, Institute of TAFE, Sydney.

——— and Lindsay Fitzclarence. 1997. Masculinity, Violence and Schooling Challenging Poisonous Pedagogies. *Gender and Education*, Special Issue on Boys' Education, vol. 9, no. 1, pp. 117–33.

———, and Peter Kelly. 2000. Local/global Labour Markets and the Restructuring of Gender, Schooling and Work. In Nelly P. Stromquist and Karen Monkman (eds.), *Globalization and Education: Integration and Contestation across Cultures* (pp. 173–97). Lanham: Rowman & Littlefield.

———, and Sue Willis. 1995. *Critical Visions: Policy and Curriculum Rewriting the Future of Education, Gender and Work*. Canberra: Australian Government Publishing Service.

———, Anna Kraack, and Anna Hickey Moodey. 2006. *Masculinity beyond the Metropolis*. Basingstoke, UK: Palgrave Macmillan.

———, Karen Tregenza, and Peter Watkins (eds.). 1997. Vocational Education Today: Topical Issues. Deakin Centre for Education and Change, Geelong, Victoria.

———, Peter Watkins, and Karen Tregenza. 1998. Vocational Education Policies: Are Boys at Risk? In Sheena Erskine and Maggie Wilson (eds.), *Gender Issues in International Education* (pp. 71–91). New York: Garland.

King, Debra. 2005. In Pursuit of Passion: A Frame Analysis of the Popular Management Literature. Paper presented at the Australian Sociology Association annual conference, December 5–8, Hobart, Australia.

Lash, Scott, and John Urry. 1994. *Economies of Signs and Space*. London: Sage.

Mac an Ghaill, Mairtin. 1996. What about the Boys?: Schooling, Class and Crisis Masculinity. *Sociological Review*, vol. 44, no. 3, pp. 381–97.

Massey, Doreen. 1994. *Space, Place and Gender*. Cambridge: Polity Press.

McKinsey and Company. 1994. *Lead Local, Compete Global: Unlocking the Growth Potential of Australia's Regions*. Sydney: McKinsey and Co.

Sennett, Richard. 1998. *The Corrosion of Character: The Personal Consequences of Work in the New Capitalism*. New York: Norton & Co.

———. 2006. *The Culture of the New Capitalism*. New Haven: Yale University Press.

Smith, Gilly. 2006. *Jamie Oliver: Turning Up the Heat.* Sydney: Pan Macmillan Australia.

Sweet, Richard. 1995. All of Their Talents? Policies and Programs for Fragmented and Interrupted Transitions. Dusseldorp Skills Forum, October, Melbourne.

Taylor, Charles. 2007. Cultures of Democracy and Citizen Efficacy. *Public Culture*, vol. 19, no. 1, pp. 117–50.

Teese, Richard, Merryn Davies, Margaret Charlton, and John Polesel. 1995. *Who Wins at School? Boys and Girls in Australian Secondary Education.* Melbourne: Department of Education Policy and Management, The University of Melbourne.

Time Magazine. 2011. Person of the Year: The Protester, December 14.

Urry, John. 1995. *Consuming Places.* London: Routledge.

Walby, Silvia. 1997. *Gender Transformations.* London: Routledge.

Weber, Max. 2002. *The Protestant Ethic and the " Spirit " of Capitalism: And Other Writings.* London: Penguin.

NOTES

1. One of the thousands of comments posted by young people to the We are the 99% Tumblr page: http://wearethe99percent.tumblr.com/post/12835134546/i-work-3-jobs-i-am-not-lazy-i-stand-for-what-i

2. This discussion draws on Kelly, 2013, pp. 7–16, 71–94.

3. The Melbourne franchise of Fifteen closed at the end of 2010. The Fifteen Foundation is now called the Jamie Oliver Foundation.

4. This discussion draws on Kelly and Harrison, 2009, pp. 1–25, 79–87, 141–65.

5. http://wearethe99percent.tumblr.com/post/20116769441/i-can-t-find-my-future-i-looked-in-college-i

Chapter Twelve

Globalization, Adult Education, and Development

Shirley Walters

The processes of globalization over the past twenty-five years continue to reconfigure the international and local contexts in which the practices and policies of adult education are debated and redesigned. They impact on adult education in many contradictory ways. Adult education as used here refers to informal, non-formal, or formal education for adults that is most often integral to social processes. It encompasses (1) educational strategies that help people to survive the harsh conditions in which they live (including education relating to basic needs such as health care, nutrition, family planning, and literacy); (2) skilling for the informal sector of the economy; (3) skilling for the formal labor market, including training for unemployed workers and re-skilling people already engaged in the labor market at all levels; and (4) political and cultural education that addresses civic and social justice issues (Wolpe, 1994), encouraging people to participate actively in civil society through political parties, trade unions, social movements, and cultural organizations (Walters, 2008).

GLOBALIZATION AND DEVELOPMENT

Globalization—a short-hand term for describing the global capitalist economy—impacts on every level of society. It not only reflects processes in which social relations are linked at the economic level, but it also permeates political, social, cultural, and environmental spheres and everyday life. Adult education is deeply implicated in the economic and ideological contestations of the day.

Wallerstein, an eminent sociologist, historical social scientist, and world systems analyst, persuasively argues that we are in the middle of a deep structural crisis. There has been a fundamental shift in capitalist development conditions, resulting in a struggle for successor economic and political systems, which he presents as alternative "choices." He argues that we can "choose" collectively a new stable system that essentially resembles the present system in some basic characteristics—a system that is hierarchical, exploitative, and polarizing. Alternatively, we can "choose" collectively a radically different form of system, one that has never previously existed—a system that is relatively democratic and relatively egalitarian (Wallerstein, 2009).

He urges us to try to analyze the emerging strategies that the two major "camps"—one which he refers to as the camp of the "spirit of Davos" (represented by the International

Monetary Fund and the World Bank, among others) and the camp of the "spirit of Porto Alegre" (represented by social movements and social justice activists)—are developing and which orient our political choices accordingly. He argues that there are several different strands within the two camps that make the situation confusing intellectually, morally, and politically and, therefore, unpredictable and uncertain.

There are echoes between Wallerstein's analysis and those of other perspectives of globalization (e.g., Arruda, 1996; Development Alternatives with Women for a New Era, 1997; Gindin, 1998). One is the "competitive globalization" (reflected in the "spirit of Davos"), the hegemonic form that has the accumulation of capital as its internal logic. It is top-down in its approach to development; it is shaped by the corporate interests of transnational corporations and the geopolitical interests of the rich and powerful corporations and countries. The other is "cooperative globalization" (reflected in the "spirit of Porto Alegre"), which has the accumulation of human capacities as its internal logic and human development as its primary motivating force. It has a bottom-up approach to development that is shaped by the basic needs of the planet's inhabitants and by citizen action. The proponents of this perspective argue that it is imperative for the very survival of the planet to find development alternatives to the neoliberal, competitive, and environmentally destructive economic and sociopolitical policies and practices that are dominating the world (Wallerstein, 2009).

Debates about globalization are also, therefore, debates about development. They highlight the fault lines that run through the literature, debates, and the practices of adult education that were present at the Sixth International Conference on Adult Education (CONFINTEA VI) in Belem, Brazil, in 2009. This is the UN Educational, Scientific and Cultural Organization–sponsored conference that occurs every twelve years in order to take stock of progress made in adult learning and education (UN Educational, Scientific and Cultural Organization Institute for Lifelong Learning [UIL], 2010).

CONFINTEA VI showed that globally and locally, the social and economic impact of globalization has been uneven and contradictory between countries of the Global North and of the Global South. New lines of inequality have been created, "between 'core' and 'periphery,' between insiders and outsiders of contemporary society" (Walters and Cooper, 2011, p. 29). These are to be seen across all three fundamental inequalities of the world: gender, class, and ethnicity.

The financial turmoil of the past few years has further exacerbated levels of poverty, inequality, and security, as have the climatic, environmental, and political crises (Walters and Cooper, 2011, p. 29). As Mohanty (2012) elaborates, "[G]lobalization has come to represent the interests of corporations and the free market, rather than self-determination and freedom from political, cultural and economic domination for all the world's peoples" (p. viii).

Neoliberal policies entrench these inequalities at regional and local levels such that adult education, lifelong learning, and work cannot be discussed outside broader socioeconomic and political contexts (Walters and Cooper, 2011). It is widely accepted, for example, that globalization has been a driving factor in the commodification of learning, transforming it into a possession that can be traded in the marketplace. Learning has become an individualized and increasingly expensive possession. This inevitably widens the gap between the rich and the poor: those with substantial education who are able to pursue opportunities for lifelong learning and those with little or inadequate formal education, who cannot afford further education.

In the past twenty years, lifelong learning has become a key strategy of regions such as the European Union, where it is closely tied to the drive for economic competitiveness. At the same time, research has shown (Livingstone and Sawchuk, 2004) that shifts in the global economy have not actually resulted in an increasing demand for skills and knowledge, but that there is an underutilization of knowledge and skills, rather than a real skills shortage. The nature of capitalism, which is to maximize profit and the accumulation of wealth, must per force continually drive down the costs of production and of labor, which is achieved through underutilizing skilled labor and creating a surplus labor force. This deskilling process has been termed "learning as dispossession," where people are stripped not only of their identity, but also of the very understanding of their own exploitation (Mojab, 2009, p. 14). In such scenarios, workers may develop a sense of worthlessness and come to believe in their own inferiority, thus colluding in their own exploitation.

Similarly, despite claims in the literature on the knowledge economy and learning organizations, that new forms of knowledge are being recognized, and that new spaces are being created for informal learning, the reality is that much work has been devalued—especially work in informal and survival economies—and been rendered "invisible," together with the knowledge and skills embedded in them (Walters and Cooper, 2011). Simultaneously, the world has witnessed historic people's revolutions in Tunisia, Egypt, Libya, and elsewhere against autocratic rulers, occupations, and neoliberal economic policies. Social movements are responding in many parts of the world to environmental degradation and social, cultural, and economic issues.

Drawing inspiration from other traditions, such as the popular education legacy of Brazilian educator/philosopher Paulo Freire, and as a counterpoint to "competitive globalization," several movements of adult educators, community organizers, and social justice activists are involved in organizing and educating from below. They are defining development differently and are experimenting with new "pedagogies of possibility" (Manicom and Walters, 2012).

SOME TRENDS AND ISSUES FOR ADULT EDUCATION

What's in a Name: Adult Education, Adult Learning, or Lifelong Learning?

The Hamburg Declaration on Adult Learning (UN Educational, Scientific and Cultural Organization Institute for Education, 1997, p. 1) defines adult education as follows:

> Adult education denotes the entire body of ongoing learning processes, formal or otherwise, whereby people regarded as adults by the society to which they belong, develop their abilities, enrich their knowledge, and improve their technical or professional qualifications or turn them in a new direction to meet their own needs and those of their society.

Adult education has a history that includes the development of a professional field of practice, the professional development of adult educators, and state-sponsored systems of adult education delivery. It has had professional associations that have bound practitioners together as both discursive and professional communities. It has, however, always been on the sidelines, or the junior partner, in the broader education field, struggling to be recognized alongside educators and vast state systems that support children's education.

In the past twenty years, the discourses of "adult learning" and "lifelong learning" have catapulted into prominence; the CONFINTEA V conference in 1997 already was referring to "adult learning" in its declaration, rather than to adult education. The 2009 Belem Framework for Action (UIL, 2009) foregrounds "adult learning and education" in the context of lifelong learning. Lifelong learning is understood as a philosophy, a conceptual framework, and an organizing principle that binds all forms and levels of education and learning, with "adult learning and education" an essential part.

The increased traction that the concept of adult learning has gained over adult education is significant as it emphasizes the embeddedness of adult learning in the political, social, cultural, and economic fabric of society, whereas adult education is still often associated with personal development for the middle classes and basic education for the poor (Walters, 2008). The shift in discourse to adult learning reflects the rapidly increasing influence of information and communication technologies on adult education and adult learning processes worldwide. There are several popular adult educators who are unhappy with this shift for at least two reasons. Firstly it is a shift to individualization of learning and a way of letting governments "off the hook" to support an institutionalized system of adult education.

Changed conceptions of time and space enable different learning and teaching possibilities. "Globalisation has expanded, offering a vast array of opportunities to some, but also creating new challenges, demands and barriers for others" (UIL, 2010, p. 55). Online courses and easy access to information and knowledge on the worldwide Web enable individuals to take control of their own learning, although equally the populations of many poorer countries, or of poor communities in relatively wealthy countries, are excluded from these technologies. There are, however, positive developments in the use of mobile technologies for learning. With the ubiquitous use of mobile phones throughout the world, this offers new possibilities for the spread of learning opportunities for many more people.

In the discourse of adult learning, learning rather than teaching is being accentuated, with a shift to the needs of learners. Individuals are required to take responsibility for their own learning, with the educator playing different roles. As the state retreats from responsibility for education and training provision, the onus is on individuals to engage in lifelong learning to keep abreast of developments in the marketplace and achieve global economic competitiveness. Continuing professional development and skills training have gained ascendancy over demands of social movements for adult and lifelong learning aimed at social justice, redress, and equity.

In South Africa, a range of terms has been used to describe adult education, including "continuing education," "nonformal education," and "popular education," each with its own history and meanings. In the past twenty years, there has been the adoption within government of the term "adult basic education" to denote "the second chance to learn" provision by the state, business, and not-for-profit organizations and to distinguish it from skills training for work. It includes adult education up until the equivalent of nine years of schooling and is strongly linked to formalizing processes within the field.

The debates and redesign of adult education policies in South Africa since the early 1990s manifest the competing needs for economic development and simultaneous achievement of redress and equity for black women and men excluded from the education and training system by apartheid. However, in practice, the state has not funded adult basic education adequately and the area of workplace training has been left largely to the private sector and the market. The South African National Qualifications Framework has attempted to address the competing needs by integrating adult learning with other forms and levels of learning, to create paths for lifelong learning.

Regardless of terminology, however, CONFINTEA VI (UIL, 2010) noted that:

> The role and place of adult learning and education in lifelong learning continues to be underplayed. At the same time, policy domains outside of education have failed to recognise and integrate the distinctive contributions that adult learning and education can offer for broader economic, social and human development. The field of adult learning and education remains fragmented. Advocacy efforts are dissipated across a number of fronts, and political credibility is

diluted precisely because the very disparate nature of adult learning and education prevents their close identification with any one social policy arena. (p. 45)

Moreover, the conference report noted that "new social and educational challenges have emerged alongside existing problems, some of which have worsened in the interim, nationally, regionally, and globally. Crucially, the expectation that we would rebuild and reinforce adult learning and education in the wake of CONFINTEA V has not been met" (UIL, 2010, p. 45).

National Qualification Frameworks

In the last twenty-five years, the phenomenon of national qualifications frameworks (NQFs) has arisen as a direct consequence of some aspects of globalization. As of 2013, it is estimated that there are about 142 NQFs worldwide. NQFs attempt to "manage" the complex relations between education, training, and work. Their initial emergence was informed by perceptions of fundamental changes in the global economy, which had implications for the traditional divide between education and training and for the formal recognition of workplace and life experience (Illeris, 2003, p. 167). These views complemented the views of business and government, which saw qualifications frameworks as a means to make education more relevant to the workplace and as a steering mechanism by which the state could achieve social objectives such as educational reform and equity.

Chakroun (2010) describes NQFs as classifiers that specify the relationship and the horizontal and vertical continuum between different forms of qualifications. But in most cases, as Chakroun explains, NQFs go beyond the role of classifiers and provide "visions" that aim to redefine the way qualifications relate to one another and how they are applied and valued in societies. For example, to assist with the achievement of lifelong learning, they can make it easier to validate prior learning and to put value on learning programs that allow for credit accumulation and transfer.

In many cases, they are seen as drivers of reform, most often in vocational education and training. While the "early starter" countries like Australia, the United Kingdom, and New Zealand emphasised vocational education and training, increasingly NQFs are aiming to bring all provision (i.e., basic, further and higher education, plus vocational education and training) into one system. South Africa was one of the first to do this. Adult learning and education are integral to NQFs.

Chakroun states that there are two broad policy arguments and rationales put forward in favor of an NQF, namely, internal systemic policy reform and external international recognition of qualifications in a globalized labor market. However, several authors have argued that irrespective of their increasing appeal, NQFs are not necessarily good policy practice, especially in a developing country context. Their key argument is that NQFs may achieve little if they are not fit for the purpose, whether from support for economic development to personal learning careers, and if they are not part of a wider national strategy. NQFs and their value are, rightly, contested.

A significant change in the global environment has been the development of "second and third generation" qualifications frameworks (Deij, 2009). The global phenomenon of formal national, regional, and transnational qualifications frameworks effectively means that no country or region can ignore them for a variety of reasons, ranging from lifelong learning to good governance and international trade. NQFs are an attempt at finding a mechanism to describe and compare complex education and training systems transnationally, perhaps in a way similar to the way that macro-economic indicators are used to compare national economies (Walters and Isaacs, forthcoming). However, as Walters and Isaacs (forthcoming) point out, NQFs raise very real questions of comparability and of developing models that articulate very different forms of learning. They argue that the best way to address such challenges is through research-driven policy that informs the political and organizational shape of the NQF.

NQFs are concerned with bringing multi-faceted, diverse, pedagogical, political, and organizational interests into relationship with one another in order to build coherence in a complex system, and as such they will always be contested. They are articulated with national and globalized discursive practices and will reflect these. They are important and strategic mechanisms for the "governing of knowledge." Reflecting on the experience of the South African NQF, they can provide an opportunity to address, in a modest but important manner, aspects of lifelong learning in ways that contribute to greater equity and social justice (Walters and Isaacs, forthcoming).

NQFs can therefore contribute to how a society manages the relations between education, training, and work by finding common ground between distinct forms of learning and their articulation with workplace practices in the interests of the public good. It can be argued that this can best be done through a strong, research-driven, collaborative approach to NQF development that seeks means of portability, ways of enabling boundary crossings through building relational agency, of improving quality and relevance, and of understanding better, different forms and sites of learning.

Learning and Work

The global economy has significantly reshaped the nature of work and reconfigured ways of working. New and diverse forms of work are ever increasing, and non-standard forms of work are becoming the norm in many sectors. Global communication technologies, in particular, have had a profound impact on how we understand work, resulting in increased flexibility of work in relation to time and space, with the lines between work and personal life becoming more fluid. The casualization of work has blurred the distinction between employment and unemployment, while diminishing opportunities for formal employment have led to burgeoning growth in the informal sector, particularly in countries in the Global South, which has challenged traditional notions of paid and unpaid work (Walters and Cooper, 2011).

As the international division of labor is reshaped by global forces, different segments of the labor market—corresponding with different lifelong learning relations and capacities—articulate in increasingly complex ways. Sawchuk and Kempf's (2009) research describes the system of guest workers in Canada and sets out a useful political economy of guest workers in the Americas over the past two hundred years. Their particular focus is on agricultural guest workers, but they describe how the guest worker systems are expanding in places like Canada from agriculture to the hospitality industry, to transport, to light manufacturing.

Guest workers live in what elsewhere may be called free trade zones, where they are employed on contracts of six weeks to eight months and work six to seven days a week, ten to twelve hours per day; where they have no rights to health and safety or freedom of movement; and where they face unceremonious cancellations of contracts with few avenues of appeal. As Sawchuk and Kempf (2009) say, "guest workers' experiences in North America offer perhaps the closest contemporary approximation to the initial system of chattel slavery which affected Africa so badly" (p. 156). According to Sawchuk and Kempf (2009), these peripheral transnational labor markets are "increasingly central to the labor and learning of the [twenty-first] century" (p. 164). They have close resonances with the notorious migrant labor systems in South Africa, which have existed for centuries—and which continue in various forms today. Despite "the broader pedagogy of guest work life" (Sawchuk and Kempf, 2009, p. 160) being one of isolation, alienation, and exploitation, a dense fabric of intercultural learning surrounds guest workers that cuts across family, communities, and borders, and that manages to generate cultures of solidarity and struggle.

Bhattacharjee (2009) is the international organizer for Jobs with Justice, for migrant workers in India. She reflects on how migration is seldom an individual choice but rather a forced necessity; the migrants are economic and political refugees. She believes that the conditions of migrants are an excellent barometer of what is going wrong in the world, arguing that issues must be dealt with at the local level in order to challenge the social relations underpinning globalization:

> [W]orkplace struggles have to be fought "from the inside out"; those at the heart of the system of exploitation, but on the periphery of the international labor market in terms of social power— migrant workers, contract workers, women workers—have to lead in forging new ways of organizing towards a more just and fair system of work." (Bhattacharjee, 2009, as cited in Walters and Cooper, 2011, p. 36)

This requires rich informal, political education. Bhattacharjee emphasizes that there is a need not simply to research work and learning "as it is," but "to research ways in which we can learn to work and learn differently" (as quoted in Walters and Cooper, 2011, p. 36).

Forrester and Li (2009) argue that workplace learning largely ignores the processes of workers' learning in production and in their unions and therefore does not acknowledge the knowledge that they develop on the job. Employee skills development in the United Kingdom tends to focus on short-term interests to increase productivity and competitiveness, as is seen globally more and more, marginalizing workers' learning needs and knowledge.

Forrester and Li describe the establishment and training of fifteen thousand workplace union learning representatives (ULRs) in the United Kingdom in the late 1990s. Their role was to develop learning agreements with employers and help to create workplace-learning centers that particularly targeted young people and women. Despite the ULRs experiencing numerous difficulties, the authors concluded that the ULR model provides rich possibilities for more transformative learning within the workplace. First, the ULRs can contest the dominant training discourses and constraints of work-based learning. Second, they can act as catalysts for change by developing a learning culture in their organizations. Finally, they can raise wider issues of workplace control, design, and democracy. Forrester and Li argue that this offers an expanded understanding of union learning, foregrounding pathways of worker and union learning not always recognized or prioritized by British trade unions, and pointing to the interdependence of "union learning" and work-based learning.

In their paper, Walters and Cooper (2011) demonstrate that relationships of power and politics are central to understanding work and lifelong learning in a number of ways. First, the previous examples show that there are enduring social inequalities that impact on education and training, learning, and knowledge. Second, a more inclusive understanding of work needs to be developed that reduces the polarization between a globalized, capitalist economy on the one hand and a low-skills labor market and an informal/survivalist economy on the other. "Majority" work must be made visible and the value of such work in the reproduction of society acknowledged through deliberately constructed research agendas. Third, dominant, hegemonic conceptions and hierarchies of knowledge need to be challenged and the importance of people's knowledge and indigenous knowledge systems recognized and valued.

Finally, the authors make the cogent argument that the global capitalist economy is not totally determining, but may be challenged by social forces at regional and local levels. As they say, "The dominant views of lifelong learning need to be turned inside out if the Belem

Framework [the document emanating from CONFINTEA VI] is to make a difference in the majority world" (Walters and Cooper, 2011, p. 37).

Everyday Learning and Education

The relation between everyday learning and education (defining the latter as organized learning) is one of the most fundamental questions in educational discourse. Larsson (1997) states that "adult education … must be understood as something that can change the results or the character of everyday learning" (p. 255). It is becoming increasingly accepted that skills learned in the home, in the community, or in the course of work can be recognized toward further educational qualifications or for employment. In South Africa, this is termed recognition of prior learning and has become a priority focus of the South African Qualifications Authority, which is the oversight body for the South African National Qualifications Framework.

Recognition of prior learning has been particularly important for poorly educated women entering or returning to work after raising children, and there has been an explosion of access courses to facilitate entry into higher education. It is mainly women who have used these, so it is important to question what knowledge is being accredited by whom, as gender and Eurocentric biases are built into assessment practices internationally. Key questions are: whose knowledge is affirmed, how is that knowledge constructed, and does it challenge the subordination of marginalized sectors? As Walters and Cooper (2011) point out, "[w]hose knowledge counts is very much a question of who is doing the counting" (p. 33).

A critical stance on the affirmation of everyday knowledge is adopted by many people concerned with marginalized knowledges. The debates around the relationships between everyday knowledge and disciplinary knowledge can be ferocious, and have been referred to as "knowledge wars" (Fenwick, 2010). These "wars" have been sustained over centuries and continue to run through debates on adult education and development.

Morrison and Vaioletti (2011) discuss key issues raised by indigenous peoples during CONFINTEA VI and argue for the importance not only of affirming indigenous knowledge, but also suggest how the people can and should be involved in design, implementation, and monitoring of adult education programs. Schmelkes (2011) proposes the importance of intercultural education in Latin America, not only among indigenous people, but among whole populations, "to be a guiding philosophy in general and adult education in particular" (p. 103).

In many instances, indigenous knowledge affirms human and environmentally sustainable values. The resurgence of the arguments for the valorization of indigenous knowledge from indigenous people around the world, which has strong echoes in the women's movements, is an important critique of the human capital paradigm. These arguments emphasize that humanity must work toward a renewed consciousness for future human existence rather than being dominated by narrow economic imperatives. Cooperative global movements are furthering these perspectives.

The essential role that social movements play in the production of knowledge and in informal and non-formal adult learning processes has been highlighted by several writers (e.g., Eyerman and Jamison, 1991; Welton, 1997). Torres (2011) points to the ways in which social movements are challenging neoliberalism and how popular education has become a tool of empowerment for social movements.

Social movements are considered carriers of historical projects of importance to all people. They address universal questions such as the relations between men and women through women's movements and nascent men's movements, between nature and people through environmental movements, and between master and slave through liberation and civil rights movements. In their search for knowledge through their actions in these movements, people produce culture and new knowledge. A social movement can therefore be characterized by its cognitive praxis.

Globally, the majority of people manifestly engage with learning for their own purposes and interests to meet a social, economic, political, or technical need. The significant role of not-for-profit organizations as expressions of the relationship between local action and globally significant social movements on the one hand, and between local communities and governments on the other, has been critical both to adult education and to building civil society.

In the past two decades, international and UN conferences on such topics as adult education, housing, women, and the environment are have all been excellent examples of global organizing by social movements and not-for-profit organizations, which ensure that citizen's voices are heard by governments. These efforts, among others, have been used to highlight the critical importance of developing a global civil society in order to engage with global governance structures and globalizing economic forces.

At the workplace, there are also examples of international solidarity developing among workers in order to connect their very local struggles to the global struggles against capitalist domination. Marshall (1997), for example, describes how steelworkers in Canada and Chile developed joint strategies to ensure that employers did not play Canadian workers off against Chilean workers. They consciously developed strategies to engage in the global economy to negotiate with employers more effectively, demonstrating how forms of cooperative globalization can be established by workers within a rampantly competitive environment.

Participation: Problems and Possibilities

A central theme in adult education is that of participation, relating to systemic, substantive, cultural, or personal dimensions. Questions about participation are posed in different ways in the literature as to the form, purpose, interests, beneficiaries, possibilities, and constraints. Participation at the interpersonal, classroom, organizational, and broader societal levels often addresses issues of power relations. These can be in relation to ethnicity, social class, gender, age, physical ability, or geography.

A session during CONFINTEA VI explored ways "to combat the social and economic risks of continued inequalities in access to and participation in adult learning, particularly in relation to the exclusion of women, rural populations, older adults, migrants, indigenous populations, ethnic and linguistic minorities, and people with disabilities" (UIL, 2010, p. 15).

The debates about participation, and the forms it takes, are essential aspects of adult education. Feminist popular education, in particular, unpicks what participation means and how to maximize it through the ways facilitators work. In a recent book by Manicom and Walters (2012), feminist popular educators detail the importance of creating safe, accessible learning spaces to enable full participation of all participants. They highlight the importance of deepening dialogue through the politics of voicing and listening. They demonstrate the ways in which the organizational, pedagogical, and political are intertwined with one another. Participation at its root holds questions about vision and social purpose.

SOCIAL PURPOSES OF ADULT EDUCATION

CONFINTEA VI declared, "Adult learning and education should be embedded in the broader vision and wider perspectives of sustainable development which will encompass cultural, political, economic, and social issues. There should also be a dynamic and binding relationship between sustainable economic development and sustainable human development" (UIL, 2010, p. 33).

As explained earlier, "competitive globalization" requires adult education and training to be concerned primarily with economic development, with developing human capital that will contribute to productive labor and economic competitiveness. "Cooperative globalization" is concerned with human values and the development of human capacities. Adult learning is central to the missions of both, but their social purposes and underlying logics are very different.

These different notions of globalization have different understandings of democracy and different views of people's participation in society. Democracy within the competitive framework is limited to representative forms while full, participatory democracy is the goal within the cooperative framework. But globalization challenges understandings of democracy, as democracy has been closely related to nation-states. A central arena of development and contestation is therefore the future of democracy and citizenship.

Clearly, the notion of citizenship is a site of struggle where global and local interests try to influence its meaning within specific contexts. In a context where discourses of the market and business have become increasingly hegemonic, all educational institutions have an important role to play in ensuring that people—particularly poor, marginalized people, including women—are supported in their attainment of active citizenship.

The Mumbai Statement on Lifelong Learning, Active Citizenship, and the Reform of Higher Education (UN Educational, Scientific and Cultural Organization, 1998) captures succinctly some of the critical concerns. It states:

> We see the purpose of lifelong learning as democratic citizenship, recognizing that democratic citizenship depends on such factors as effective economic development, attention to the demands of the least powerful in our societies, and on the impact of industrial processes on the caring capacity of our common home, the planet. The notion of citizenship is important in terms of connecting individuals and groups to the structures of social, political and economic activity in both local and global contexts. Democratic citizenship highlights the importance of women and men as agents of history in all aspects of their lives. (p. 1)

Thus the notion of citizenship is undergoing radical redefinition, under pressure from globalizing economies on the one hand and social movements of environmentalists and feminists on the other. In addition, feminism in modern society challenges the masculine structures of the state, the market, and civil society. In effect, feminist discussions about citizenship challenge men to accept a duty to act against the patriarchal order (in which women are second-class citizens) and to act for a society of equal citizenship.

Although the literature on lifelong learning is often presented as gender neutral (Ferris and Walters, 2012) and concerned mainly with vocational and individualistic goals of adults (Jarvis, 2009), there is growing recognition of the importance of feminist perspectives (Preece, 2009). Manicom and Walters (2012) observe that,

> in the context of globalization, we are increasingly understanding learning as ubiquitous and perpetual, and knowledge as something produced, not discovered; we are also witnessing an explosion of interest in pedagogy across diverse sites of practice, disciplines and fields of scholarship, including feminist scholarship and activism. … This "pedagogical turn" promises a reinvigoration of the domain of feminist popular education. (p. 4)

Stromquist (2013) emphasizes the critical importance of gender in building stable democracies. She argues that women need more than just inclusion; they need "fair recognition" and "gender justice." One of the models of gender justice posed by Goetz (2007, cited in Strom-quist, 2013, p. 2) is based on positive freedoms that empower women to protect their political, civil, social, and economic rights. Adult education has an essential role to play in gender justice: in restructuring understandings of gender norms, restructuring gender practices, and transforming the social relations of gender (Stromquist, 2013).

Yet Stromquist stresses that CONFINTEA VI paid little attention to the real problems and needs of women in education, in contrast to the strong goals and actions from CONFINTEA V, in 1997. She argues that, because those who are marginalized in society have the least leverage in transforming government policy, those who do have leverage need to collectively resolve to fight for the rights of women to adult education, in the name of democracy and social justice.

Ferris and Walters (2012) suggest that the advent of the HIV and AIDS pandemic can help re-think and refine pedagogical approaches within a lifelong learning paradigm that might enrich lifelong learning practices more generally. While both children and adults are affected, women are most susceptible and this compounds the inequalities that they experience. They argue that HIV and AIDS is about people, not simply about the virus, therefore an approach to HIV and AIDS education must include the economic, social, psychological, spiritual, and cultural dimensions of people's lives.

Further, the impact of the pervasive trauma and grief within HIV and AIDS-saturated environments can be likened to other environments of violence, trauma, and grief. These may be related to other diseases, substance abuse, poverty, discrimination, and migration, and are often exacerbated in times of war, economic, political, or climatic turbulence or uncertainty. Given the global uncertainties, they state that it is fair to assume that trauma and grief are widespread and therefore should not be ignored by educators as they design and facilitate interventions. Indeed, learning within these contexts cannot ignore *any* aspect of people's lives, individually or collectively.

Similarly, Horsman (1999, 2009) highlights the centrality of violence in many societies around the world, its impact on learning, and how essential it is to acknowledge this when designing and facilitating learning. Where violence is endemic for the majority of the population, educators and learners need to understand how to work with trauma (their own or others) if they are to overcome the enormous barriers to successful learning which violence of all kinds can cause.

Moreover, because violence is so pervasive generally in society today, Horsman proposes that educators should assume all learners have experienced some form or another of violence and build this into their programs. Humanistic pedagogical approaches are needed that create respectful, peaceful environments, where people can learn in community, developing curiosity and understanding about their own and others' struggles. Through this they can begin to experience success, increased self-esteem, and greater connection with others, which can help the processes of healing (Horsman, 2009).

Lifelong learning should consist of day-to-day practices that include males and females, children and adults across generations; that recognize the importance of sustainable liveli-hoods (life-wide learning); and work with deeply personal issues relating to death and sexual relations. They need to tap into the cultural, spiritual, and intimate aspects of people's lives (life-deep learning) and lead to self- and social transformation. Interventions are needed that are systemic—aimed at changing policy—and individual.

Environmental concerns challenge the dominant paradigm of citizenship in two ways: they expand its sphere beyond the nation-state to the global level and vice versa, and they expand it beyond the present generation and require us to consider the intergenerational dimension of our sociability and our moral and citizenship duties. Environmental and ecological changes, which may seem divorced from work, in fact will have a significant impact on the future of work (Beck, 2000). The 2009 Bonn Declaration reaffirmed that:

> Through education and lifelong learning, it is possible to achieve economic and social justice, food security, ecological integrity, sustainable livelihoods, respect for all life forms and essential values that foster social cohesion, democracy and collective action. Gender equality, with special reference to the participation of women and girl children in education, is critical for enabling development and sustainability. (UN Educational, Scientific and Cultural Organization, 2009, p. 1)

However, this would entail not only expanding education and lifelong learning opportunities, but also ensuring the quality and relevance of these programs to develop core skills or capabilities for sustainability. State structures and institutions like NQFs need to enable integration across education and training and interconnectedness for planetary sustainability. The quote from Paul Belanger's address to CONFINTEA VI, that "[t]he planet will not survive unless it becomes a learning planet" (UIL, 2010, p. 84), expands understandings of the interconnectedness of all life forms and the necessity for an environmentally sustainable and socially just future.

Adult and lifelong learning for active citizenship requires all educators to work collaboratively across regions in order to take on the pedagogical and political challenges of creating alternatives that can build on the positive aspects of globalization. Wallerstein (2009) urges engagement in serious intellectual debate about the parameters of the kind of world-system we want and the strategies of transition. He also urges us to build, in the Gramscian sense, alternatives in order to learn sensible and sustainable modes of production. Educators and learners are implicated as they need to engage, along with other activists, with issues such as those described by Arruda (1996, p. 30): "We are seeking to connect critically the micro with the macro and, in the search for a vision of the world which will be both utopic and viable, point to a horizon of a cooperative globalization, built by individuals and societies that have become active and conscious subjects, personally and collectively, of their own development."

The struggle over economic, political, and social priorities becomes a crucial curriculum issue for learners and educators. Adult learning for active citizenship is therefore both about pedagogy and politics. Active citizens need to come to understand in a profound way what it means to think, feel, and act both globally and locally on an everyday basis.

There is a deep division between those who are oriented to the "spirit of Davos" and those to the "spirit of Porto Alegre." However, the stakes are so high for planetary survival that the imperative to move from these polarities to a place where citizens can develop new, workable visions of the future is key to understanding the mission of adult education and development now and into the future. The potential of adult learning for development will be fully realized only through such collective struggles that span national and regional boundaries.

Finally, to quote from the chairperson of the International Council for Adult Education's keynote address to CONFINTEA VI:

> For today's citizen, being able to continue learning, no matter where you live on the planet, is not an unnecessary hobby reserved for a privileged minority. To learn is to increase one's autonomy; it is to enjoy that necessary freedom to question and know more; it is to gain one's self-esteem and consequently the esteem of others; it is to enable each citizen to bolster his or her sense of personal efficiency; it is to experience the joy of learning. The right to learn is not a luxury but a source of inner energy that, in our present societies, has become socially necessary to continue building ourselves and our communities. We all have the right to experience the full potential of human intelligence. We all have the right to learn how to be, to evolve and to live together. To be able to

co-pilot our lives through all the transitions that await us is a perfectly legitimate aspiration. Lifelong learning can only be lifelong and life-wide if it is also life-deep. This is the deeper meaning of adult education and that is why lifelong learning has become a fundamental right. (UIL, 2010, p. 80)

REFERENCES

Arruda, Marcos. 1996. Globalization and Civil Society: Rethinking Cooperativism in the Context of Active Citizenship. Rio de Janeiro: Institute of Alternative Policies for the Southern Cone of Latin America, unpublished manuscript.

Beck, Ulrich. 2000. *The Brave New World of Work*. Oxford: Blackwell Publishers Ltd.

Bhattacharjee, Anannya. 2009.Migration and Organizing: Between Periphery and Centre. In Linda Cooper and Shirley Walters (eds.), *Learning/Work: Turning Work and Lifelong Learning Inside Out* (pp. 142–53). Cape Town: HSRC Press.

Chakroun, Borhène. 2010. National Qualification Frameworks: From Policy Borrowing to Policy Learning. *European Journal of Education*, vol. 45, no. 2, pp. 199–216.

Development Alternatives with Women for a New Era. 1997. From "There Is No Alternative" to "There Must Be an Alternative." University of Western Cape, Bellville, Cape Town.

Deij, Arjen. 2009. Towards a Common Understanding of the Development Stages of National Qualification Frameworks. European Training Foundation (ETF) unpublished working paper on NQF developments. Turin, Italy.

Eyerman, Ron, and Andrew Jamison. 1991. *Social Movements: A Cognitive Approach*. Philadelphia: Pennsylvania State University Press.

Fenwick, Tara J. 2010. Let the River Run: Knowledge Wars and Educational Futures in Globalized Spaces. UWC's Vice Chancellor's Annual Julius Nyerere Lecture on Lifelong Learning, University of the Western Cape, Bellville.

Ferris, Heather, and Shirley Walters. 2012. Heartfelt Pedagogy in the Time of HIV and AIDS. In Linzi Manicom and Shirley Walters (eds.), *Feminist Popular Education in Transnational Debates: Building Pedagogies of Possibility* (pp. 75–91). New York: Palgrave MacMillan.

Forrester, Keith, and Hsun-Chi Li.2009. Learning, Practice and Democracy: Exploring Union Learning. In Linda Cooper and Shirley Walters (eds.), *Learning/Work: Turning Work and Lifelong Learning Inside Out* (pp. 309–21). Cape Town: HSRC Press.

Gindin, Sam. 1998. Socialism "With Sober Senses": Developing Workers' Capacities. *The Socialist Register* (U.K.), vol. 34, pp. 75–101.

Horsman, Jenny. 1999. *Too Scared to Learn: Women, Violence and Education.* Toronto: McGilligan Books.

———. 2009. *Women, Work and Learning: The Impact of Violence.* Pretoria: SAQA.

Illeris, Knud. 2003. Workplace Learning and Learning Theory. *Journal of Workplace Learning*, vol. 15, no. 4, pp. 167–78.

Jarvis, Peter (ed.). 2009. *The Routledge International Handbook of Lifelong Learning.* London: Routledge.

Larsson, Staffan. 1997. The Meaning of Lifelong Learning. In Shirley Walters (ed.), *Globalization, Adult Education and Training: Impacts and Issues* (pp. 250–61). London: Zed.

Livingstone, David, and Peter Sawchuk. 2004. *Hidden Knowledge: Organized Labor in the Information Age.* Toronto: Broadview Press.

Manicom, Linzi, and Shirley Walters. 2012. Introduction: Feminist Popular Education: Pedagogies, Politics, and Possibilities. In Linzi Manicom and Shirley Walters (eds.), *Feminist Popular Education in Transnational Debates: Building Pedagogies of Possibility* (pp. 1–24). New York: Palgrave MacMillan.

Marshall, Judith. 1997. Globalization from Below: The Trade Union Connections. In Shirley Walters (ed.), *Globalization, Adult Education and Training: Impacts and Issues* (pp. 56–67). London: Zed.

Mohanty, Chandra Talpade. 2012. Foreword. In Linzi Manicom and Shirley Walters (eds.), *Feminist Popular Education in Transnational Debates: Building Pedagogies of Possibility* (pp. vii–x). New York: Palgrave MacMillan.

Mojab, Shahrzad. 2009. Turning Work and Lifelong Learning Inside Out: A Marxist–Feminist Attempt. In Linda Cooper and Shirley Walters (eds.), *Learning/Work: Turning Work and Lifelong Learning Inside Out* (pp. 4–15). Cape Town: HSRC Press.

Morrison, Sandra L., and Timote M. Vaioleti. 2011. Inclusion of Indigenous Peoples in CONFINTEA VI and Follow-up Processes. *International Review of Education: CONFINTEA VI Follow-up*, vol. 57, nos. 1–2, pp. 69–88.

Preece, Julia. 2009. *Lifelong Learning and Development: A Southern Perspective.* Studies in International Education Research. London and New York: Continuum/Bloomsbury Academic.

Sawchuk, Peter H., and Arlo Kempf. 2009. Peripheralization, Exploitation and Lifelong Learning in Canadian Guest Worker Programmes. In Linda Cooper and Shirley Walters (eds.), *Learning/Work: Turning Work and Lifelong Learning Inside Out* (pp. 154–66). Cape Town: HSRC Press.

Schmelkes, Sylvia. 2011. Adult Education and Indigenous Peoples in Latin America. *International Review of Education: CONFINTEA VI Follow-up*, vol. 57, nos. 1–2, pp. 89–106.

Stromquist, Nelly P. 2013. Adult Education for Women for Social Transformation: Reviving the Promise, Continuing the Struggle. In Tom Nesbit and Michael R. Welton (eds.), *Adult Education and Learning in a Precarious Age: The Hamburg Declaration Revisited* (pp. 29–38). San Francisco: Jossey-Bass.

Torres, Carlos Alberto. 2011. Dancing on the Deck of the Titanic? Adult Education, the Nation-State and New Social Movements. *International Review of Education: CONFINTEA VI Follow-up*, vol. 57, nos. 1–2, pp. 39–56.

UN Educational, Scientific and Cultural Organization Institute for Education. 1997. The Hamburg Declaration. The Agenda for the Future. Document adopted at CONFINTEA V. Fifth International Conference on Adult Education. Hamburg: UIE. http://www.unesco.org/education/uie/confintea/pdf/con5eng.pdf.

UN Educational, Scientific and Cultural Organization Institute for Lifelong Learning. 1998 (April). The Mumbai Statement on Lifelong Learning, Active Citizenship, and the Reform of Higher Education. Hamburg: UIL.

_____. 2009. Bonn Declaration, World Conference on Education for Sustainable Development. Bonn, Germany.

_____. 2010. CONFINTEA VI. Sixth International Conference on Adult Education, Final Report. http://www.unesco.org/en/confinteavi.

Wallerstein, Immanuel. 2009 (November). Crisis of the Capitalist System: Where Do We Go from Here? The Harold Wolpe Memorial Lecture. Harold Wolpe Trust, Cape Town:

Walters, Shirley. 2008. Draft South African National Report on the Development and State of the Art of Adult Learning and Education. Country report for CONFINTEA VI, University of Western Cape, Bellville.

_____ and Linda Cooper. 2011. Learning/Work: Turning Work and Lifelong Learning Inside Out. *International Review of Education: CONFINTEA VI Follow-up*, vol. 57, nos. 1–2, pp. 27–38.

Walters, Shirley, and Samuel B. A. Isaacs. Forthcoming. National Qualifications Frameworks Governing Knowledge: Insights from South Africa. In Tara Fenwick, Eric Mangez, and Jenny Ozga (eds.), *World Yearbook of Education 2014: Governing Knowledge: Comparison, Knowledge-based Technologies and Expertise in the Regulation of Education*. Oxford: Routledge.

Welton, Michael R. 1997. In Defense of Civil Society: Canadian Adult Education in Neo-Conservative Times. In Shirley Walters (ed.), *Globalization, Adult Education and Training: Impacts and Issues* (pp. 27–38). London: Zed.

Wolpe, AnnMarie. 1994. *Adult Education and Women's Needs*. Bellville, South Africa: CACE Publications.

Part III

National Case Studies of Globalization Impacts

Chapter Thirteen

Globalization in Japan: Education Policy and Curriculum

Lynne Parmenter

The purpose of this chapter is to provide an overview of some of the ways that globalization is interpreted, negotiated, and appropriated in school and higher education policies and curricula in Japan. As the third largest economy in the world, a Confucian heritage country in which education is highly valued, and a country in which tensions between appeal to cultural homogeneity and recognition of the implications of internationalization are readily apparent, Japan is an interesting case study of globalization and education.

The chapter begins with a brief discussion of theories of globalization and education that are salient to subsequent discussion of the case in Japan. It goes on to provide an overview of education policy-making and implementation of education policy in Japan, describing some of the main structures and processes of education policy development and enactment that impact the ways globalization is mediated and negotiated in Japan. This is followed by a more detailed analysis of globalization as it is manifested in the content of policies and curricula at various levels in education. Separate sections on school education (age six to eighteen) and higher education (age eighteen plus) contain analysis of several key policies, curricula, and initiatives, examining the ways in which globalization is portrayed, used, negotiated, appropriated, and incorporated into educational policies and practices. Finally, a section on emerging themes and issues draws together the threads of analysis and discusses implications for future globalization and education in Japan.

GLOBALIZATION AND EDUCATION POLICY

Since the first edition of this book was published, literature on globalization and education has burgeoned. The purpose of this section is not to provide an overview of this literature, but to identify some of the themes that are central to discussion of the situation in Japan. Four main themes are considered: the move from anti-globalization to diverse globalizations, the global-national issue, the development of global competence and competitiveness through education, and the development of global citizenship through education. The first two deal mainly with the scope, definition, and conceptualization of globalization, while the second two focus on the ways education policy translates globalization into practice in schools and universities.

From Anti-Globalization to Diverse Globalizations

The discourse of "anti-globalization" has weakened over the past decade. Mertes (2010, p. 77) describes the anti-globalization movement as "a misnomer for the wide-ranging and, at times, splintered social movements that principally grew in response to the imposition of neoliberal economic policies beginning in the late 1970s." He asserts that most activists within the anti-globalization movement did not actually oppose all forms of globalization, and that it is more accurate to speak of "alternative globalization" than "anti-globalization."

This argument applies equally to education, where the dual targets of "anti-globalization" have been neoliberal economic policies as applied to education, together with the perceived threat of attack on cultural and societal values through globalization construed as "Westernization" or "Americanization." This perceived threat and the need to protect traditional culture, whatever that means, are still explicitly voiced occasionally in national education policies, but much less so than in the 1990s. At the same time, although the "threat" of globalization is usually no longer openly expressed as such in policies, it is still apparent implicitly as an undercurrent in policy and curriculum documents (Phan, 2013, p. 170). This is very clear in Japan, as will be discussed later.

That said, it seems that the inevitability of globalization is now generally accepted, and the emphasis has moved from "anti-globalization" to "diverse globalizations," or different ways of appropriating and managing globalization, a path which Held and McGrew (2002, p. 134) advocated over a decade ago. By reframing the discourse from "alternatives to globalization" (e.g., Kang, 1998) to "alternative globalizations" (e.g., Ribeiro, 2009), those who initially took a stance against globalization, or who were on the periphery experiencing the negative effects of economic globalization, have claimed a voice in the discourse and opened up new perspectives and a new discourse of diverse globalizations.

The Global/National Issue

Connected to the move from anti-globalization to diverse globalizations is the changing relationship between the national and the global. Education policies and national curricula have traditionally been used as a key vehicle for creating and maintaining national identity, national unity, and patriotism in most countries of the world (Hobsbawm, 1992, p. 91), and globalization was initially seen by many ministries of education or equivalent as a serious threat to this role.

As globalization has become a more familiar concept, however, it has become clear that it is not simply a larger territorial sphere that will engulf and supersede the nation, but that the relationship between national and global is more complex, and both cause changes in the other. This concept of the more complex interlinking of national and global is explained by Sassen (2007, p. 79), who argues that "the global—whether an institution, a process, a discursive practice, or an imaginary—simultaneously transcends the exclusive framing of national states yet partly inhabits national territories."

Along similar lines, but through empirical data obtained from group interviews with 250 high school and middle school students in the United States, Mitchell and Parker (2008) found that young people do not conceptualize the world in terms of the same nation/globe binary spatial assumptions as their parents' generation. This shift in conceptualizing the relationship of national and global is still under-researched and needs to be examined empirically in other countries and contexts. If it proves to be widespread, however, it would be highly significant for discussions of globalization and education.

Development of Global Competence and Competitiveness Through Education

Globalization obviously impacts and is mediated by all areas and levels of education, from national and transnational policy-making, norms, and assessment regimes to the content of curriculum, teaching practices, and the identities of students in classrooms (Rizvi and Lingard, 2010). One of the better researched areas of globalization and education has been the impact of international rankings on education policy-making. At the school level, Program for International Student Assessment (PISA) is the best known example of international rankings and is an interesting example of how a transnational organization such as the Organization for Economic Cooperation and Development gains influence in different ways over national education reforms in both its member and non-member countries (e.g., Bieber and Martens, 2011). This is applicable to Japan, as discussed later in this chapter.

At the higher education level, the rhetoric of world-class universities and the impact of world rankings have been well documented internationally (Hazelkorn, 2011; Salmi, 2009) and are widely debated in Japan (Ishikawa, 2009). Underpinning this phenomenon is institutional and/or governmental subscription to a global discourse of neoliberal education reform which includes competition, performativity, and knowledge capitalism (Ng, 2012, p. 446). In many countries, neoliberal reforms aimed at higher education have also changed systems of government funding of universities, introduced new control mechanisms such as quality assurance and research and teaching assessment exercises, and revised the relationship between government control and institutional management (Harland, 2009, p. 513). This has been true in Japan, especially affecting national universities (Kaneko, 2012).

The widespread acceptance of the value or inevitability of the neoliberal discourse of education, regardless of the personal beliefs of those constructing or implementing it, also facilitates the globalization of education in the form of regional policies and frameworks spreading beyond their intended sphere of influence. The clearest examples are probably European initiatives. For example, as Moutsios (2012, p. 3) points out, the European Higher Education Area now covers forty-seven countries (twenty-seven European Union members and twenty non-European Union countries in Europe and Central Asia). However, an additional twenty-three countries are participating in the Bologna Process with observer status, including Japan, and other countries are participating in selected actions of the Process. Moutsios (2012) highlights the lack of resistance to this particular form of globalization of education, stating that:

> What is noteworthy in this transnational policy making process is the widespread consensus with which it is carried through. ... There is hardly any questioning of the goals of the policy network by those taking part in it; the concern is instead about the irregular or slow pace of implementation. (p. 21)

The general acceptance of the value or inevitability of international frameworks, policies, and standards, which extends in some cases to active seeking of the same, impacts the way they are used. For example, the Common European Framework of Reference for Languages, which was never intended to be used beyond Europe when it was created, is being adopted for use at various levels of education in many countries of the world, from China to Kazakhstan to New Zealand (Byram and Parmenter, 2012). What is notable, however, is that the 260-page document, which devotes the majority of its pages to theories and implementation of plurilingalism and action-based learning for the purpose of developing autonomous, intercultural competent citizens, is most often reduced to several pages of descriptors, used to assess language compe- tence on a scale of A1 to C2.This is true in Japan as elsewhere, where the Common European

Framework of Reference for Languages has been appropriated by universities (Nagai and O'Dwyer, 2011) and by the Ministry of Education (Monkasho, 2013) for neoliberal-friendly purposes of ensuring transparency and aligning to globally transferable attainment levels and targets, rather than for the intended purpose defined previously.

At the same time, governments, schools, and universities aim to make their graduates "globally competent" and "globally competitive" through curriculum and other initiatives. While such aims are still much easier to find in visions and mission statements than in empirical results, they are becoming the focus of increasing attention and action. The concepts of being "globally competent" or "globally competitive" are still difficult to define, although some initial attempts have been made. For example, Boix Mansilla and Jackson (2011) define global competence in the following way:

> Students demonstrate global competence through awareness and curiosity about how the world works—informed by disciplinary and interdisciplinary insights. Specifically, globally competent students are able to perform the following four competences:
>
> 1. Investigate the world beyond their immediate environment, framing significant problems and conducting well-crafted and age-appropriate research.
> 2. Recognize perspectives, others' and their own, articulating and explaining such perspectives thoughtfully and respectfully.
> 3. Communicate ideas effectively with diverse audiences, bridging geographic, linguistic, ideological, and cultural barriers.
> 4. Take action to improve conditions, viewing themselves as players in the world and participating reflectively. (p. 11)

The importance of this notion is recognized by individuals as well as by institutions and governments, as students in many parts of the world start to "shop" globally for an education that will in turn facilitate a global career (Dickmann and Baruch, 2011).

Development of Global Citizenship Through Education

Another related strand of research and practice in the field of globalization and education has been global citizenship education. As Andreotti (2011) points out,

> the different meanings attributed to "global citizenship education" depend on contextually situated assumptions about globalisation, citizenship and education that prompt questions about boundaries, flows, power relations, belonging, rights, responsibilities, otherness, interdependence, as well as social reproduction and/or contestation. (p. 307)

The question she then poses, "Where is one speaking from as a 'global citizen' or a 'global educator'?" is key to understanding different conceptualizations of global citizenship education.

Global citizenship education clearly overlaps significantly with the development of global competence, in that both are concerned with the issue of educating children and young people to participate fully in a globalized world, but global citizenship education tends to focus more on the individual and the individual's place in society, centered more on questions of self and others in the world and less on global competitiveness (Pashby, 2011). The two are certainly not mutually exclusive, as the majority of areas covered, including knowledge and competences to be included, are shared. However, global citizenship education tends to be more firmly based in citizenship education aims such as building a global civic culture (Boulding, 1988), working toward global social justice by addressing inequalities that exist and may be aggravated by globalization (e.g., Unterhalter and Carpentier, 2010), and addressing political, social, and cultural aspects of identity and citizenship in a globalized world (Osler and Vincent, 2002). These issues of how education should contribute to students' development of how they see themselves in the world and how they should contribute as citizens in the world are highly pertinent to analysis of education and globalization in Japan.

PROCESSES OF EDUCATION POLICY-MAKING AND IMPLEMENTATION IN JAPAN

Since the establishment of a ministry of education in 1871 and compulsory elementary school education in 1872, Japan has developed a highly centralized education system, with a range of mechanisms employed to ensure that central policy reaches every teacher and student in every classroom in Japan, and that every child has access to the same curriculum. Some of the key features of this system are explained briefly in this section, together with the implications of the system for discussion of globalization and education in Japan.

Policy and Curriculum Reform System

Perhaps the most significant feature of education policy in Japan is the entrenched system of policy and curriculum reform, which ensures that all reform is considered, debated, and negotiated for many years before it is actually enacted. This is particularly true at school level, where the cycle of curriculum reform typically takes about eight years from the forming of committees by the Central Council for Education to discuss reform to enactment of policy in schools through the Courses of Study.

Simultaneously, education policy and curriculum reform in Japan are very much based on incrementalism, defined by Birkland (2011, p. 256) as "a model of decision making in which policy change is accomplished through small, incremental steps that allow decision makers to adjust policies as they learn from their successes and failures." In Japan, for example, introducing foreign language activities in the Course of Study as a requirement to the last two years of elementary school (ages ten to twelve) for just over twenty-six hours a year (one forty-five-minute class per week for thirty-five weeks) from 2011 was a major reform that involved years of debate not only in governmental committees and academic circles, but also across the national media.

This combination of incrementalism and lengthy policy process in a highly centralized system guarantees stability and coherence, and means that teachers are not subjected to constantly changing policies depending on the whims of specific governments or individuals, as in some other countries. At the same time, it makes it difficult for education policies and curricula to respond to rapid changes in society, even as these same policies and curricula state that this is what schools, universities, and students should be doing. For example, in the introduction to a policy document that was one of the key reference documents for the latest curriculum reforms in Japan, published in 2001, the minister of education at the time stated that one of the three key educational problems in Japan was that, "Science is developing rapidly, the economy and society are globalizing, and society is changing rapidly due to the information age and so on, but the existing education system lags behind the progress of time and society" (Machimura, 2001, para. 4). Still, education reform processes were not changed, and the incremental curriculum reforms that followed were implemented ten years later.

In relation to globalization and education, what this means is that the process of policy and curriculum reform is not necessarily conducive to dealing with the demands and requirements of education in a rapidly changing world, and some of the assumptions upon which policies and curricula are based may be in conflict with some of the recommendations in policy regarding education and globalization.

Courses of Study and Textbook Authorization

The main means through which the Ministry of Education, Culture, Sports, Science, and Technology (hereafter referred to by its Japanese abbreviation "Monkasho") ensures that policy and curriculum reform is implemented as intended in schools is through the Courses of Study and textbook authorization.

The Courses of Study (Monkasho, n.d.), published for every subject and curriculum area at every level of education, provide detailed specification of aims and content of each subject and curriculum area, down to the level of which *kanji* (Chinese characters) children should learn in which year at elementary school. Teachers do not usually read these Courses of Study directly, but there is also a textbook authorization system. As well as detailing aims and content, the Courses of Study all include notes for "creation of teaching plans and treatment of content." Textbook publishers must adhere to these notes and to the aims and content in preparing textbooks, which then have to be authorized before they can be used in schools. Education is very heavily dominated by textbooks, and it would be very unusual to observe a subject-based class in a Japanese school that did not use a textbook. Textbooks, too, are prepared over a four-year cycle and are used for four years.

The implication of this situation is that textbook publishers self-censor to avoid including anything that may not pass authorization, and also avoid any potentially controversial content, any material that may date quickly, and most material related to living people. This, combined with the fact that most teachers use only the textbook and companion teacher's manual for their classes, means that students have few opportunities to consider current or controversial events or trends, although such content is not explicitly prohibited or excluded from the curriculum.

Reliance on textbooks (based on educational aims and content specified four to twelve years earlier), combined with conservative textbook content, has obvious implications for students' knowledge of the world, and for the development of competences and of how they learn to see themselves in the world.

GLOBALIZATION AND SCHOOL EDUCATION

As described previously, the processes of school-level educational policy reform and curriculum implementation in Japan are not particularly conducive to dealing with rapid change in society. However, in their content, educational policies and curricula do engage with globalization, and this section explores the ways in which globalization is portrayed, appropriated, and managed in some of the key policy and curriculum documents.

The two documents chosen as case studies for analysis here are the Courses of Study (*gakushuu shidou youryou*) for elementary and junior high school and the explanatory documents accompanying them, published in 2008, and the draft document of the Central Education Council Basic Plan for Promoting Education Committee (*Chuuou Kyouiku Shingikai Kyouiku Shinkou Kihon Keikaku Bukai*) (2013), made available on the Monkasho website in March 2013. These documents are different in nature, as the first represents the "distilled" version of policy, after it was negotiated for many years and approved as the official version of education curriculum in all state schools, while the second is an initial draft of a document intended to stimulate debate and reform regarding the direction, form, and content of education over the next decade and beyond. Together, they provide a snapshot of ways in which globalization is interpreted and portrayed in education policy in Japan.

Courses of Study are produced for all areas of the curriculum at kindergarten, elementary school, junior high school, and senior high school, and are accompanied by explanatory documents, which are all available in Japanese from the Monkasho website (Monkasho, n.d.). As explained previously, these Courses of Study are detailed and have to be followed by schools and textbook publishers. For each level of education, the first section of the Course of Study is entitled General Provisions Section, and the explanatory document of the General Provisions Section for elementary, junior high, and senior high school begins as follows:

> In the [twenty-first] century, the importance of new knowledge, information and technology as a foundation for politics, economics, culture and activities in all spheres of society is increasing dramatically, and we are in what is known as the "knowledge-based society." This kind of knowledge-based society, combined with globalization, accelerates international competition in human resources and knowledge itself in the form of ideas and so on, while augmenting the need for international cooperation and coexistence with different cultures and civilizations. In this context, the fostering of "power to live," which stresses harmony of solid academic ability, a rich heart and a healthy body, is increasingly important. (Monkasho, 2008a)

The appeal to the global context, the identification of the changing nature and power of knowledge, and the delineation of global competition and global coexistence and collaboration as important aspects of society thus take pride of place at the very beginning of the Course of Study explanations, at all levels of school education.

This is followed by further use of the global context, this time to selectively use findings of PISA to justify gaps or weaknesses in the Japanese education system. An explanation is given to the effect that PISA and other international studies have found that Japanese children have problems with test questions that require thinking, judgment, or expression and those that require application of knowledge. It is also stated that the distribution of results on reading questions is widening and this is due to issues with learning motivation, study habits, everyday routines, and home study environment, and that there are issues with self-confidence, anxiety about the future, and physical strength (Monkasho, 2008a). As in many other countries, external (international) "evidence" is being used to justify the implementation of national government priorities. In exactly the same way as Rautalin and Alasuutari (2009) argue occurs in Finland, the validity of PISA results and their relevance for national reform are presented as beyond question in Japan, and PISA is used to justify the Monkasho agenda for reform.

Despite the opening rhetoric about living in an era of globalization, there is little direct reference to the development of global competence or global citizenship in the main body of the Courses of Study. The basic vision of the "ideal" person coming out of the Japanese education system is seen in the aim of moral education, which is implemented across the curriculum, throughout school life, and out into families and the community, as many schools send home guidelines for parents on what their children should do and how they should behave, for example, in the holidays. The ideal is as follows:

> Moral education … aims to foster … having a rich heart, respecting traditions and culture and loving the ancestors who developed these, aiming to create new individualized culture, respecting the public spirit, striving to develop a democratic society and state, respecting other countries, and developing Japanese people who autonomously contribute to the peace and development of international society and to protection of the environment as they create the future. (Monkasho, 2008b, p. 1)

Three pertinent points prevalent throughout the school curriculum in Japan are evident in this extract. The first is the emphasis on traditions, culture, and respect for ancestors, which is emphasized more strongly in these Courses of Study than in previous versions, reflecting a concern for strengthening national identity and national pride in Japanese schools. This concern of the government is partly a response to the perceived threat of globalization to national identity, as discussed in the first part of this chapter, and there is as yet no recognition in government education policy documents that the younger generation may be more comfortable with multiple local, national, and global identities than the traditional dichotomy between national and global spheres suggests.

The second point is related. Throughout the Courses of Study, as in this extract, the aim of education is to develop "Japanese people," and the only recognition of the fact that an increasing number of children in Japanese schools have one or two non-Japanese parents is in a brief section on how to deal with children who have returned or migrated from other countries, which states that "appropriate guidance should be given to children who have returned from abroad or similar,[1] so that they adapt to school life and their experiences of life overseas are used" (Monkasho, 2008b, p. 4). As the vast majority of non-Japanese or half-Japanese children in Japan were born and have always lived in Japan, this is not relevant to most, but the assumption that the population of Japanese schools is homogenously "pure" Japanese still underpins policy and curriculum. This assumption, as well as negating the lived experience of many teachers and children in Japanese schools, constrains the way Monkasho can approach globalization and education, as the tension between discourses of globalization, diversity, and change and those of nationalism, homogeneity, and tradition have not been addressed and are ignored in policy and curriculum. The territorial dichotomy of national and global still seems to exist in the minds of policy and curriculum makers, and the interlinking discussed earlier in this chapter is not yet recognized.

The third point relates to the phrase regarding the peace and development of international society. Although this may seem vague, it is a genuine and passionately held shared belief among the majority of teachers in Japan that education should promote peace at all levels, from interpersonal to global. Peace education is embedded throughout the curriculum from elementary to senior high school, and this is an area in which students often do learn about the world, and are encouraged to develop a strong sense of their own responsibility as global citizens. It is also notable that global peace is about the only area in which students are encouraged to see themselves directly in the world sphere, not necessarily through the lens of the nation. At the same time, many of the skills, values, and behaviors that students are encouraged to develop at classroom, school, local, and national levels in Japan (e.g., in the previous extract, development of democratic society, respect for others) are actually easily extendable beyond the nation. In this way, even though there is little explicit emphasis on global competence and global citizenship in the Courses of Study, the knowledge (to some extent), competences, values, and behaviors that students learn transfer quite readily.

The Courses of Study provide a distilled and carefully moderated interpretation of globalization and its implications for education, but the imperative of dealing with globalization is much more obvious in the draft document of the Central Education Council Basic Plan for Promoting Education Committee (*Chuuou Kyouiku Shingikai Kyouiku Shinkou Kihon Keikaku Bukai*) (2013). Here, the overall message is one of crisis, expressed very clearly in the preface to the 113-page document (2013, p. 2), as follows:

> The whole world is changing rapidly through the development of globalization, but our country, which faces severe problems of deindustrialization and decrease in the working population, is in an extremely critical situation, and the occurrence of the Great East Japan Earthquake has only

exacerbated and accelerated this. These movements throw up major questions regarding how society, which has until now been predicated on material wealth, should be, and how people should live.

The theme of crisis in the global context is repeated again and again, with reference to Japan's economy being eclipsed by BRIC (Brazil, Russia, India, and China) countries (p. 3), rates of progression to university being below the Organization for Economic Cooperation and Development average (p. 12), and so on.

As Giddens (2002, p. 34) points out, one aspect of globalization is the dominance of manufactured risks rather than natural hazards. In Japan, where the Basic Plan for Promoting Education Committee was established shortly after the huge earthquake, tsunami, and nuclear disaster of March 2011, the combination of natural and manufactured risks is reflected in this document by a real sense of crisis, and a notion that radical change rather than incrementalism is required to overcome the current situation. Whether this will translate to practice in risk-averse Japanese policy-making processes is doubtful, but the four key directions for education identified in the report are (1) cultivation of the ability to cope with rapid societal change and live independently and actively; (2) cultivation of people who can realize the future through leadership and innovation in global society; (3) construction of a learning safety net, providing access to educational opportunities for everyone; and (4) creation of dynamic, close-knit communities (Central Education Council Basic Plan for Promoting Education Committee, 2013, p. 16). Manufacturing crisis and fear of global failure are clear reactions to global competitiveness, and the solutions provided in this draft are to develop global competence and to strengthen citizenship and community.

At the same time, these issues regarding assumptions of homogeneity in Japanese schools and ways of dealing with migration as an aspect of globalization are still brushed under the carpet. While it is recognized as part of a section on education for children with special needs that an increasing number of Japanese children spend part of their childhood outside Japan and there are issues with non-Japanese children in Japan not attending school, the measures proposed to deal with this are still the superficial, short-term measures of Japanese language education for those whose level of Japanese is below the grade level, accompanied by guidance on adaptation to Japanese study habits (Central Education Council Basic Plan for Promoting Education Committee, 2013, pp. 51–52). In 2012, 1.23 percent of the population of Japan was non-Japanese, and a further 2.1 percent of children born in Japan had one non-Japanese parent, but recognition of multiple identities and diversity is not addressed. The children who are different are still the problem, and assimilation is still the answer. Even as globalization is recognized and engagement in global society exhorted, fundamental assumptions about Japanese society as culturally homogenous are beyond violation, it seems. It remains to be seen how far the gap between assumptions of homogeneity and realities of increasing diversity has to widen before the government addresses this issue. In the meantime, teachers, schools, and local communities respond in their own ways to their own situations and contexts.

GLOBALIZATION AND HIGHER EDUCATION

As in many other countries, the impact of neoliberal globalization on higher education in Japan has been substantial, reflecting Gopinathan and Lee's (2011) statement that:

> in general, educational institutions, including schools and universities, are having to comply with the public management principles of doing more with less and enhanced managerial efficiency to

maximize the value for money; in particular public money, invested in the education sector as influenced by the rise of neo-liberalism and economic rationalism. (p. 291)

This has been particularly true in the national universities. In 2003, under a neoliberal government, the National University Corporation Law (Law 122, http://law.e-gov.go.jp/htmldata/H15/H15HO112.html) was passed, directly affecting over one hundred universities, affiliated junior colleges, and research institutes in Japan, including many of the top-ranked universities. This law redefined national universities as independent legal entities, no longer under direct control as part of the government, but as autonomous institutions under contract to the government.

As Kaneko (2009, p. 61) describes, this means that university budgets are no longer so tightly controlled by the government, facilities are no longer the property of the government, and faculty members and administrators are no longer government employees. It also means that the market forces become more powerful in university governance, and accountability and performance become part of the contract between government and university. As Yonezawa (2007) emphasizes, public higher education is being "industrialised" (p. 128), and:

> If we treat higher education as a growing industry in the knowledge-based global economy, the policy and governance issue of higher education should be treated as industrial and labour related policies. This approach sometimes conflicts with the traditional idea and image of higher education. ... The image of university as an ivory tower still works as an idealistic image of the university system, for example, in Japan. (Yonezawa 2007, p. 126)

This discord between the image of universities and the harsh realities of global neoliberal reforms has been significantly magnified in Japan by national demographics. There are many more private universities than national universities in Japan, and they were subject to market logic long before 2003, as Goodman (2010) describes:

> The rhetoric of the market and de-regulation (kiseikanwa)—spurred in particular by the belief that de-regulation was the best means to re-stimulate the faltering economy—led to a 31 per cent increase in the number of four-year universities in Japan between 1992 and 2004 as more and more organizations entered the sector. (pp. 69–70)

Goodman goes on to explain how, during the same period, the population of eighteen-year-olds in Japan decreased by 31 percent, and how the rise in supply and fall in demand mean that there is now effectively a university place for everyone who wants one in Japan.

This availability of "universal higher education" has exacerbated the effects of neoliberal policies, intensifying market competition and leading to credential inflation (Kariya, 2011). It has also increased differentiation between the "top" universities, which are still highly competitive to enter and which are under huge pressure to achieve excellence and retain their market lead, and the lower-level universities, which are rapidly diversifying as they struggle to survive (Kitagawa and Oba, 2009).

Globalization has impacted higher education in Japan not only through structural reform of the system, but also in terms of the form and content of educational provision. Higher education in Japan is much more diverse than school education and considerably less constrained by central policy. The tensions that exist at the school policy level between being open to globalization on the one hand and trying to promote nationalism and preserve the myth of homogeneity on the other are far less apparent at the higher education level, where universities are encouraged by government to be increasingly engaged in globalization processes and networks.

The primary focus of concern and effort is internationalization, with a particular focus on attracting international students to Japan and developing Japanese higher education as a regional hub. At the institutional level, due to the demographics described previously, some of the less prestigious universities are heavily dependent on international students for their survival (Yonezawa, Akiba, and Hirouchi, 2009, p. 126). In most cases, however, financial incentives do not play a large part in internationalization initiatives, unlike in some other countries. In a survey of four-year universities in Japan conducted by Tohoku University in 2007-2008, to which 624 university leaders (82.5 percent) responded, only 2.6 percent of university leaders stated that they would only implement internationalization if it was financially beneficial, compared to 18.6 percent saying they would implement internationalization if it was not a financial burden, 45.3 percent responding that they would implement internationalization under the expectations of nonmonetary returns, and 32 percent saying that internationalization itself has significance, so there is no expectation of financial return (Yonezawa, Akiba, and Hirouchi, 2009, p. 137). Taken within the context described previously of increasing pressure to cut costs and ensure financial efficiency, this finding raises a contradiction in consideration of globalization of higher education in Japan, and relates to Jones and de Wit's (2012) conclusion on the globalization of internationalization, namely that, "there is a need for more reflection on the 'why' question, the rationales for internationalization" (p. 50).

One example of an initiative that provides some insights into the "why" is the "Global 30" initiative. Aimed at recruiting three hundred thousand international students by 2020 (or thirty ten-thousands, using the Japanese system of counting, hence Global 30), thirteen of the top universities in Japan have started offering courses in English at undergraduate and graduate levels. The initiative saw 21,429 international students in Global 30 programs in 2011, so there is still some way to go (Monkasho, 2008c). The purpose of the initiative is not economic profit, as international students pay the same tuition fees as Japanese students in universities in Japan, and the government and participating universities subsidize Global 30 students. Rather, the aim seems to be twofold. First, related to the previous discussion, as Burgess, Gibson, Klaphake, and Selzer (2010) point out: "Given the low birth rate in Japan, more international students are vital if Japan's universities are to survive and its research centres are to remain competitive" (p. 469).

Second, on a slightly more ambitious note than mere fight for survival, it can be argued that the selection of the top universities to spearhead this project was intended to raise the international profile of Japanese universities, to attract the best students to Japan, and to establish Japan as a regional education "hub." It is no coincidence that the Global 30 universities are also those that can be found in the world university rankings. The aim is clearly to develop an elite group of universities that receive additional funding for research and educational innovation such as participation in the Global 30 project, and will represent Japanese higher education in the global sphere. This is significant in terms of the impact of globalization of higher education, in that it represents the phenomenon of global rankings as scopic systems, as explained by Robertson (2012):

> Scopic systems in higher education are also forms of power in that they simultaneously frame education problems, offer a desired re/solution, project outward with considerable global spatial extension, reinforce new social practices over time because of further rounds of data gathering and projection, and tap into emotions (shame, pride) that change behavior—deep inside national territorial states and institutions. (p. 243)

This indeed is what is happening as the top universities in Japan are propelled down the path of global rankings and global competitiveness. At the same time, although it is only a very small minority of universities in Japan that are currently engaged globally in this way, the fact that they project outward globally and the fact that they are elite means that the process also impacts on the whole national system. Ishikawa (2009) analyzes the perceived threat to fundamental values of education in Japan:

> The global rankings demonstrate the existing reality of a global hierarchy in higher education in a plain, explicit and blatant manner. ... The notion of elite education is something that the Japanese education system cast off in the nation's post-World War II transition to democratic society. (p. 166)

The hierarchy of universities in Japan has never disappeared, so it cannot be argued convincingly that global rankings and suchlike threaten the reality of the higher education system in Japan. What they do threaten is the discourse of equality—equality of opportunity and equality of provision—as institutions and even the government abandon the post-war cherished idea of equality in and through education, and switch to a discourse of competition and elitism.

Around the same time as the Global 30 initiative was launched, Monkasho asked the Central Education Council to make recommendations for the medium- and long-term future of university education. In January 2011, the Central Education Council produced a report entitled, "Graduate Education in Globalized Society: Enabling Graduates to be Active in Diverse Fields in the World" (Central Education Council, 2011). This report proposes a series of strategies designed to bring graduate education in Japan in line with international norms and standards, including increasing the numbers of Ph.D. students (historically, many universities in Japan have offered doctoral level courses but did not grant Ph.D. degrees in humanities and social sciences), greater transparency and the transcending of national boundaries to promote collaborative education through double degrees, and so on (Central Education Council, 2011, pp. 55–61). This commitment to the process of alignment with international standards should be seen within the context of Japan's participation in the first Bologna Policy Forum, where representatives from fifteen countries joined representatives of the (then) forty-six countries in the European Higher Education Area to discuss global academic mobility, knowledge-sharing, and cooperation. The one-page statement issued by the Bologna Policy Forum (2009) included the following paragraph: "We are convinced that fair recognition of studies and qualifications is a key element for promoting mobility and we will therefore establish dialogue on recognition policies and explore the implications of the various qualifications frameworks in order to further mutual recognition of qualifications."

These proposed reforms to the higher education system are not unique to Japan, of course, but illustrate well how standardization to "global standards" is perceived to be necessary to assure the quality and compatibility of nationally recognized qualifications. Through such measures, and through internationalization, the response to globalization in higher education in Japan is to attain full integration into the global education sphere, thereby raising the global competitiveness of its universities and the global competence of Japanese students.

THEMES, ISSUES, AND DIRECTIONS

While the previous discussion is partial, it raises several key themes relevant to globalization and education in Japan. First, at the school level, tensions between increasingly tenuous assumptions about cultural homogeneity constrain educational policies and curricula, and cause tensions in how globalization is perceived and portrayed in the Courses of Study and other documents. Linked to this is the tension between national and global, which is still evident in policies and curricula, although it may be less true in the minds of young people themselves. Until these two issues are addressed rather than ignored, the gap between policy and the reality faced by teachers and students in classrooms and in their everyday lives will continue to widen. While the rhetoric of crisis emphasizes the need to respond proactively to globalization, the content of some of the strategies proposed fails to recognize some of the key assumptions that need to change for this to happen.

Another point at the school level is the gap between policy structures/processes and the content expounded in the policies themselves. While the discourse is about adaptability to change in global society, creativity, and autonomy, the structures and processes ensure that change is minimal, opportunity for creativity on the part of teachers or students is limited, and autonomy is carefully controlled. Neither end of the continuum is completely good or bad for education, of course, but this does provide an example of how globalization is managed, appropriated, and negotiated through both discourse and structures.

In higher education, the message is more coherent, and policies and initiatives to transcend national boundaries and engage in the global education sphere have progressed from the level of promoting international exchange at the individual level to large-scale strategies such as Global 30, and the reform of higher education systems, qualifications, and programs. There is relatively little resistance to these measures from higher education institutions, although the wider issues of neoliberal globalization of higher education combined with national demographics do present significant challenges and affect the survival of universities and the jobs and salaries of those who work in them.

The effects of engagement on the development of global competence and global citizenship among school and university students in Japan, and on the global competitiveness and recognition of Japanese universities, are still unclear and remain to be seen.

REFERENCES

Andreotti, Vanessa. 2011. The Political Economy of Global Citizenship Education. *Globalisation, Societies and Education*, vol. 9, no. 3-4, pp. 307–10.

Bieber, Tonia, and Kerstin Martens. 2011. The OECD PISA Study as a Soft Power in Education? Lessons from Switzerland and the U.S. *European Journal of Education*, vol. 46, no. 1, pp. 101–16.

Birkland, Thomas. 2011. *An Introduction to the Policy Process*, 3rd edition. Armonk, NY: M.E. Sharpe.

Boix Mansilla, Veronica, and Anthony Jackson. 2011. *Educating for Global Competence: Preparing our Youth to Engage the World*. New York: Asia Society.

Bologna Policy Forum. 2009. Statement by the Bologna Policy Forum 2009. http://www.ond.vlaanderen.be/hogeronderwijs/bologna/forum/Bologna_Policy_Forum_Statement_29April2009.pdf

Boulding, Elise. 1988. *Building a Global Civic Culture: Education for an Interdependent World*. Syracuse, NY: Syracuse University Press.

Burgess, Chris, Ian Gibson, Jay Klaphake, and Mark Selzer. 2010. The "Global 30" Project and Japanese Higher Education Reform: An Example of a "Closing In" or an "Opening Up"? *Globalisation, Societies and Education*, vol. 8, no. 4, pp. 461–75.

Byram, Michael, and Lynne Parmenter (eds.). 2012. *The Common European Framework of Reference: The Globalization of Language Education Policy*. Bristol: Multilingual Matters.

Central Education Council. 2011. Guroobaruka shakai no daigakuin kyouiku: Sekai no tayouna bunya de daigakuin shuuryousha ga katsuyaku suru tame ni: Toushin. [Graduate education in globalized society: Enabling graduates to be active in diverse fields in the world – Report.] http://www.mext.go.jp/component/b_menu/shingi/toushin/__icsFiles/afieldfile/2011/03/04/1301932_01.pdf

Central Education Council Basic Plan for Promoting Education Committee. 2013. Dai2ki kyouiku shinkou kihon keikaku ni tsuite (toushin (soan)) [On the second phase basic plan for promoting education (report (preliminary draft))]. http://www.mext.go.jp/b_menu/shingi/chukyo/chukyo9/shiryo/__icsFiles/afieldfile/2013/03/19/1332164_3_2.pdf

Dickmann, Michael, and Yehuda Baruch. 2011. *Global Careers*. London: Routledge.

Giddens, Anthony. 2002. *Runaway World: How Globalization is Reshaping our Lives*. London: Profile Books.

Goodman, Roger. 2010. The Rapid Redrawing of Boundaries in Japanese Higher Education. *Japan Forum*, vol. 22, no. 1–2, pp. 65–87.

Gopinathan, S., and Michael Lee. 2011. Challenging and Co-opting Globalization: Singapore's Strategies in Higher Education. *Journal of Higher Education Policy and Management*, vol. 33, no. 3, pp. 287–99.

Harland, Tony. 2009. The University, Neoliberal Reform and the Liberal Educational Ideal. In Malcolm Tight, Ka Ho Mok, Jeroen Huisman, and Christopher Morphew (eds.), *The Routledge International Handbook of Higher Education* (pp. 511–21). New York: Routledge.

Hazelkorn, Ellen. 2011. *Rankings and the Reshaping of Higher Education: The Battle for World-Class Excellence.* Basingstoke: Palgrave Macmillan.

Held, David, and Anthony McGrew. 2002. *Globalization/Anti-globalization.* Cambridge: Polity.

Hobsbawm, Eric. 1992. *Nations and Nationalism since 1780: Programme, Myth, Reality*, 2nd edition. Cambridge: Cambridge University Press.

Ishikawa, Mayumi. 2009. University Rankings, Global Models, and Emerging Hegemony: Critical Analysis from Japan. *Journal of Studies in International Education*, vol. 13, no. 2, pp. 159–73.

Jones, Elspeth, and Hans de Wit. 2012. Globalization of Internationalization: Thematic and Regional Reflections on a Traditional Concept. *AUDEM: The International Journal of Higher Education and Democracy*, vol. 3, no. 1, pp. 35–54.

Kaneko, Motohisa. 2009. Incorporation of National Universities in Japan: Design, Implementation and Consequences. *Asia Pacific Education Review*, vol. 10, no. 1, pp. 59–67.

_____. 2012. Incorporation of National Universities in Japan: An Evaluation Six Years on. In Hans Schuetze, William Bruneau, and Garnet Grosjean (eds.), *University Governance and Reform: Policy, Fads, and Experience in International Perspective* (pp. 179–95). New York: Palgrave Macmillan.

Kang, Liu. 1998. Is There an Alternative to (Capitalist) Globalization? The Debate about Modernity in China. In Frederic Jameson, and Masao Miyoshi (eds.), *The Cultures of Globalization* (pp. 164–88). Durham, NC: Duke University Press.

Kariya, Takehiko. 2011. Credential Inflation and Employment in "Universal" Higher Education: Enrolment, Expansion and (In)equity via Privatisation in Japan. *Journal of Education and Work*, vol. 24, no. 1–2, pp. 69–94.

Kitagawa, Fumi, and Jun Oba. 2009. Managing Differentiation of Higher Education System in Japan: Connecting Excellence and Diversity. *Higher Education*, vol. 59, no. 4, pp. 507–24.

Machimura, Nobutaka. 2001. 21-seiki kyouiku seiki puran (kihonteki kangaekata) [21st century education renewal plan (basic way of thinking)]. http://www.mext.go.jp/a_menu/shougai/21plan/p0.htm

Mertes, Tom. 2010. Anti-Globalization Movements: From Critiques to Alternatives. In Bryan Turner (ed.), *The Routledge International Handbook of Globalization Studies* (pp. 77–95). Abingdon: Routledge.

Mitchell, Katharyne, and Walter Parker. 2008. I Pledge Allegiance to... Flexible Citizenship and Shifting Scales of Belonging. *Teachers College Record*, vol. 110, no. 4, pp. 775–804.

Monkasho. n.d. Shingakushuu shidouyouryou (honbun, kaisetsu, shiryoutou) [New Courses of Study (main text, explanations, materials etc.)]. http://www.mext.go.jp/a_menu/shotou/new-cs/youryou/index.htm

_____. 2008a. Shougakkou gakushuu shidou youryou kaisetsu: Sousokuhen. [Elementary school Course of Study explanation: General Provisions section]. http://www.mext.go.jp/component/a_menu/education/micro_detail/__icsFiles/afieldfile/2009/06/16/1234931_001.pdf

_____. 2008b. Shougakkou gakushuu shidou youryou. [Elementary school Course of Study]. http://www.mext.go.jp/component/a_menu/education/micro_detail/__icsFiles/afieldfile/2010/11/29/syo.pdf

_____. 2008c. "Ryuugakusei 30-man nin keikaku" kosshi [Essentials of the "Plan for 300,000 international students]. http://www.uni.international.mext.go.jp/ja-JP/documents/international_students_plan_jp.pdf

_____. 2013. Kakuchuu/koutou gakkou no gaikokugo kyouiku ni okeru "CAN-DO risuto" no katachi de no gakushuu toutatsu mokuhyou settei no tame no tebiki [Handbook for establishing learning attainment targets in the form of "can-do lists" in foreign language education in each junior and senior high school]. http://www.mext.go.jp/a_menu/kokusai/gaikokugo/__icsFiles/afieldfile/2013/05/08/1332306_4.pdf

Moutsios, Stavros. 2012. Academic Autonomy and the Bologna Process. Working Papers on University Reform, EPOKE, Department of Education, Aarhus University, Denmark. http://edu.au.dk/fileadmin/www.dpu.dk/forskningsprogrammer/epoke/WP_19.pdf

Ng, Shun Wing. 2012. Rethinking the Mission of Internationalization of Higher Education in the Asia-Pacific Region. *Compare: A Journal of Comparative and International Education*, vol. 42, no. 3, pp. 439-459.

Nagai, Nobuko, and Fergus O'Dwyer. 2011. The Actual and Potential Impacts of the CEFR on Language Education in Japan. *Synergies Europe*, no. 6, pp. 141–52.

Osler, Audrey, and Kerry Vincent. 2002. *Citizenship and the Challenge of Global Education.* Stoke-on-Trent: Trentham Books.

Pashby, Karen. 2011. Cultivating Global Citizens: Planting New Seeds or Pruning the Perennials? Looking for the Citizen-Subject in Global Citizenship Education Theory. *Globalisation, Societies and Education*, vol. 9, no. 3–4, pp. 427–42.

Phan, Le Ha. 2013. Issues Surrounding English, the Internationalization of Higher Education and National Cultural Identity in Asia: A Focus on Japan. *Critical Studies in Education*, vol. 54, no. 2, pp. 160–75.

Rautalin, Marjaana, and Pertti Alasuutari. 2009. The Uses of the National PISA Results by Finnish Officials in Central Government. *Journal of Education Policy*, vol. 24, no. 5, pp. 539–56.

Ribeiro, Gustavo. 2009. Non-hegemonic Globalizations: Alter-native Transnational Processes and Agents. *Anthropological Theory*, vol. 9, no. 3, pp. 297–329.

Rizvi, Fazal, and Bob Lingard. 2010. *Globalizing Education Policy.* London: Routledge.

Robertson, Susan. 2012. World-class Higher Education (for Whom?). *Prospects*, vol. 42, no. 3, pp. 237–45.

Salmi, Jamil. 2009. *The Challenge of Establishing World-class Universities*. Washington, DC: The World Bank.

Sassen, Saskia. 2007. The Places and Spaces of the Global: An Expanded Analytic Terrain. In David Held and Anthony McGrew (eds.), *Globalization Theory: Approaches and Controversies* (pp.79–105). Cambridge: Polity.

Unterhalter, Elaine, and Vincent Carpentier (eds.). 2010. *Global Inequalities and Higher Education: Whose Interests are We Serving?* Basingstoke: Palgrave Macmillan.

Yonezawa, Akiyoshi. 2007. Strategies for the Emerging Global Higher Education Market in East Asia: A Comparative Study of Singapore, Malaysia and Japan. *Globalisation, Societies and Education*, vol. 5, no. 1, pp. 125–36.

Yonezawa, Akiyoshi, Hiroko Akiba, and Daisuke Hirouchi. 2009. Japanese University Leaders' Perceptions of Internationalization: The Role of Government in Review and Support. *Journal of Studies in International Education*, vol. 13, no. 2, pp. 125–42.

NOTE

1. In this extract, "or similar" is a translation of "tou" which means "and so on, or similar, etc." In this case, it refers mainly to non-Japanese immigrants in addition to Japanese returnees, but this is not specified in the Japanese original.

Chapter Fourteen

Global Encounters of the Universal and the Particular in Educational Policies in Mexico 1988–2006

Rosa Nidia Buenfil

KEY FEATURES OF GLOBALISM IN EDUCATION AND INTERNATIONAL AGENCIES

To some extent, interconnectedness among nations is not new, nor is the influence international agencies exercise upon particular countries. One can trace back to the 1960s, for instance, the inclusion of the Multinational Project of Educational Technology Transference in the overall developmental strategy sponsored by the Organization of American States and the Inter-American Development Bank whose influence in Latin America cannot be overlooked (Chaves, 1962; Davis, 1950; Organization of American States, 1966). UN Educational, Scientific and Cultural Organization (UNESCO) reports (1965, 1968, 1971, and later), and Organization for Economic Cooperation and Development (OECD) reports (1971 and 1993) can be considered the ancestors of what today is viewed as the globalization of educational policies.

The 1990 world conference on Education For All in Jomtien, Thailand (UNESCO, 1994), the two key meetings hosted by CEPAL-UNESCO (on "Education and Knowledge: Axis for Productive Transformation with Equity" [1992] and the *V Meeting of the Intergovernmental PPEALC Commission* [UNESCO, 1993]), *La Globalización Incrementa la Pobreza en el Mundo?* (World Bank, 2000), and the *Education For All Global Monitoring Report* (UNESCO, 2004)—these are the new versions of old global connections. Those were links by which academic trends, financial agreements, exchange of scholars, and administrative strategies from international agencies became visible to the Latin American region, and which fifty years ago would have been conceptualized as an outcome of domination and dependency.

Perhaps what distinguishes contemporary globalization from the connections in the 1960s is, on the one hand, that they take place in a world politically, economically, and culturally reorganized (i.e., from east and west to north and south). On the other hand, today we are more aware of what is happening elsewhere given the overarching presence of digital technology and media, the increasing visibility of previously unnoticed "minorities" emerging today in the political arena, and the conflictive encounter among opposing tendencies.

It is argued here that globalization is not so much a tendency toward homogenization and universalism, but a mutual contamination and clash between universalism and particularism, homogenization and heterogeneity. However, the tendency toward homogeneity cannot be overlooked, as there are some educational features that can be verified throughout the world; for example, an expansion of the school system and a demand for schooling as well as acceptance of a general model of schooling.

Some have said that a global narrative of educational progress has emerged and functions as an educational ideology (Fiala and Lanford, 1987) contributing to the globalizing process. Policies of restriction and adjustment in universities both in industrialized and in "Third World" countries and the internal measures permeated by the marketing they dictate are increasing. The tendency to impose a thinning of financial support for public schools can be linked to a neoliberal design and a global procedure. Our focus of interest, Mexico, receives influence directly from international agencies such as the World Bank, OECD, UNESCO, and from Latin American organizations such as the UNESCO Regional Office for Latin America and the Caribbean (OREALC) and the UN Economic Commission for Latin America (CE-PAL). However, the recommendations proposed by these agencies are given different meanings, resignified[1] in their implementation in each particular site.

CONCEPTUAL ASSUMPTIONS INFORMING THIS ANALYSIS

Before the analysis of the traces of globalization in a Mexican educational policy is presented, the context of discussion will be sketched. In the literature specializing in education, relationships between globalization and capitalism, globalization's historical tendency and presumed necessity, the notions of universalization and homogeneity, and the links between globalization and a promising or catastrophic horizon, are frequently found. Even from a progressive culture-oriented perspective, economic issues are often put forward (McLaren and Gutierrez, 1997). While some describe globalization as a historical tendency involving the universalization of the market economy, others emphasize how naive it is to believe that globalization guarantees a better distribution of wealth in the world economy, as in the end it is a hierarchical market system organized by just one pole of the world capitalist structure, involving the prevalence of a central point of view. Still others see it as a means to produce such educational innovations, holding that through them students would develop world cognitive maps for better understanding everyday local events (Perlmutter, 1991).

Mexican literature on the relationship between education and globalization has been reviewed (Buenfil, 2000) and more recent discussion continues to show two extremes: either catastrophic or productive (Perez-Ordaz, 2008). Any review could be quite lengthy because of the great quantity of writing that has been produced covering the debates on related topics as integration versus fragmentation, centralization versus decentralization, juxtaposition versus syncretization, etc., especially as new aspects have been detected (Popkewitz and Rizvi, 2009). However, it is time to set some analytical grounds for their examination.

The widely dispersed meanings of *globalization* (Buenfil, 1998, 2000) can be analyzed through, on the one hand, a genealogical effort, tracing how it had become a key signifier in the late 1980s and remains so in the first decades of the twenty-first century; as a process of worldwide interconnections it can be found much earlier. The works by Wallerstein (1989), Braudel (1991), and McLuhan and Powers (1989) began a proliferation of writing on the subject. Considering this and the fact that globalization has distinct significations in many different disciplinary approaches, political views, economic perspectives, and long- or short-term historical considerations, what we have is a wide dispersion of meanings. On the other hand, in an organizing gesture this area of dispersion has been grouped into a *family resemblance* (Wittgenstein, 1963) through the aggregation of three sets:

1. The polarization of two discursive fields where the meaning of "globalization" has been temporarily fixed either as a good value or as an evil threat; yet—despite these opposing perspectives—they share the view of an intrinsic connection between globalization, modernity, and neo-liberal capitalism.

2. Globalization is seen as a necessary universal homogeneous process involving the real exploitation of the planet as a single entity that organizes production, the market, and competitiveness, and whose effects are global economic, military, cultural, and political formations.

3. Globalization is dissociated from a universal necessary tendency of history and from impending cultural, economic, ethical, or political imperialization (i.e., the ruling of a single homogeneous view over the planet [not even if it were non-capitalist]) and understood rather as interconnectedness. This third position implies (a) assuming our existential situation as a multi-directed conditioning of the universal and the particular, the homogeneous and the heterogeneous; and as the product of the interaction of opposite tendencies such as fragmentation and integration, centralization and decentralization; (b) the production of syncretic and hybrid economic, cultural, educational and political schema bringing about positions against foundationalist nostalgia for a mythical uncontaminated identity; and (c) the existence of conflict, generated by the interconnectedness and contact of the diverse, as our planet has unequal development in each realm and geopolitical area. Tension, encounter, friction, clash, and conflict are part of globalization and this can hardly be overlooked or concealed by wishful Enlightenment thinking. Instead of leading to a pessimistic outlook, this challenges us to invent different forms of plural utopias that are not to be taken a priori as new transcendental universals.

Once a problematization of the meanings of globalization has been sketched, other theoretical considerations will be introduced concerning the imbrications and mutual contamination of the universal and the particular.

The Universal and the Particular Cannot be Thought of Apart from Each Other

From here two ideas can be derived: globalization cannot be understood as mere homogenization of the planet under a universal direction, and global educational policies that are already an outcome of the contact between universalism and particularism, are resignified when they reach the particular sites of educational practices and agents. The universal is frequently understood as "something common to all particulars," but one seldom asks oneself how these universals came to be: they either derive from a metaphysical entity or they are a social agreement. From Rousseau's *Social Contract* onward, universal values have been increasingly interrogated; the relationship between universality and particularity has become an issue and can no longer be taken for granted. Today many consider them to be an outcome of negotiations historically and geographically situated and no longer transcendental a priori. This should not be misunderstood as "the abyss of relativism," as foundationalists call it (Habermas, 1989).

The lack of an ultimate positive foundation[2] of morals, science, the community, and so on, does not amount to saying that "anything goes."[3] The relationalist position[4] to be sustained here holds rather that all foundations, including "our universal values," are historically established, therefore, context-dependent, which means on the contrary that there is no a-temporal essence but all universal values once were particular values that came to reach some universality. They have to be defined in each specific context (be it within a wider or a narrower scope), and in our world these contexts are heterogeneous and unequal.[5] They may of course, expand their area of influence as long as they both persuade and articulate other particulars, and dominate other particulars imposing on them their particularity as "the universal" (thus, implying, of course, political relations).

Accordingly, if one understands globalization as mere universalization then one must, at least, account for the construction of a particular as the universal. Universalization cannot be understood apart from its counterpart (i.e., the presence of particulars), and each "application" of the universalized value will be "contaminated," so to speak, both by the particular context of its source and the particular context of each implementation.

GLOBAL EDUCATIONAL TRENDS AND NATIONAL POLICIES

In Mexico, global educational policies can be traced throughout the whole schooling system: from the basic level to higher education. One topic in old and even recent discussion concerns the links and distance between strategies and their means as drawn up in policies and "what really happens in schools." To put the extreme view, some are convinced that policies are discourses that remain at a general level and never have contact with what "really happens in the classroom." Therefore, one should study the particularity of local actions in the classroom. Others would argue that policies determine, as an overarching apparatus, all corners of educational practices. Therefore, one should study the goals and strategies of state apparatuses and see how they affect specific institutions. The position held in this chapter is that no matter where one starts the search, one has to look for the circulation of some meanings throughout different levels as causality is never fixed nor is it unidirectional, but rather characterized by a "multi-way" mobile conditioning.

Consider Giddens' approach to this issue:

> People live in circumstances in which disembedded institutions, linking local practices with globalized social relations, organize major aspects of day-to-day life. Globalization articulates in a most dramatic way this conflation of presence and absence through its systemic interlocking of the local and the global. (Giddens, 1990, p. 79)

In the last decade of the twentieth century, research was produced linking the classroom with national policies and global neoliberalism (McLaren and Gutierrez, 1997). Educational reforms were also studied as specific forms of governing practices, namely, "the administration of the soul" (Popkewitz, 1991, p. 7), and "neoliberalism" (including the dismantling of the welfare state) that occurred well before Thatcher in Great Britain or Reagan in the United States (Popkewitz, 1991, 2000). Popkewitz therefore objects to one current association between globalization and neoliberalism and the fact that the discursive representation of time has not scrutinized the Western narrative of progress enabling the management and surveillance of "the Third World" in the guise of some notion of "development." Further, discourses of and about neoliberalism re-inscribe the state/civil society distinction that was undermined with the construction of the liberal welfare state itself (Popkewitz, 2000).

A book edited by Popkewitz and Rizvi (2009) addresses globalization and education, exploring them from a variety of theoretical positions and geopolitical locations, and concentrating on educational aspects that range from the institution to the schoolteacher, from the global imaginaries to the teaching and learning practices, from basic education to higher education. However, these coauthors share the drive to denaturalize some fixations (e.g., globalization is the homogenization of educational systems under the rule of Western neoliberal views beginning in the 1990s), and pursue several common objectives dealing with (1) the historicity of globalization; (2) political and cultural differentiation, social inclusion and exclusion; (3) economic, cultural, and political interconnectedness; (4) schooling, pedagogical practices, and research; and (5) social location and research (Popkewitz and Rizvi, 2009, pp. 2–3). In all cases, the authors place emphasis on the circulation of the signifiers incarnating international recommendations and their displacement throughout different levels or social strata as they become national policies.

Let us focus now on some examples of research carried out in Mexico that illustrate how globalization travels throughout different social scopes, as it moves from the international recommendation, to the national policy, to the school-specific program (curriculum and syllabi), and finally to the classroom. Some examples will be discussed in reference to the specific features of how these national policies take—or retrieve[6]—from international agreements, especially two key items of global recommendations within a Mexican national policy: *Modernización Educativa* (Educational Modernization; Secretaría de Educación Pública [SEP], 1989).

Research conducted by Medina (1996) puts forward the similarities between the World Bank recommendations and the Mexican reform. Two critical items of this reform are also analyzed: how the revaluation of the teachers' role is disseminated across different educational actors (López Ramírez, 1998), and how educational quality is resignified in its implementation (López Nájera, 2009), both authors showing the political and discursive movements of *Modernización Educativa* through time and space, from its beginning in the late 1980s to recent actualizations in 2006, and its displacement from the international level to the national policy, to a state program, and then to a local proposal.

Conditions of Production of the *Modernización Educativa* Discourse

Modernización Educativa is the name given to a Mexican educational policy in force from 1988 to 1996, although modernization as a trend had been fostered much earlier, in the 1930s by national policies, and in the 1960s by international agencies such as the International Monetary Fund, World Trade Organization, the World Bank, and the Inter-American Development Bank for the whole continent and particularly for Latin America.

In the 1980s, the Mexican government adopted "social liberalism" (a euphemism for neoliberalism[7]) as the philosophical axis for this reform, thereby subordinating education to administrative and economic views (e.g., education as investment), economic needs (e.g., schooling as a depot for the unemployed), and rate of progress (e.g., education paced as training), thus inscribing on education a managerial administration (productivity over teaching and results over process). Neoliberalism in Mexico has been articulated with a traditional moral and institutional conservatism, and with the contingent effects of a political reform.

Although neoliberalism entails the thinning of the state (i.e., the reduction of the institutional apparatus) and the opening of "social participation," in Mexico it is the conservative forces who are better organized and have the means to occupy those spaces deserted by state control. Conservatives include the Roman Catholic Church through its different affiliations (the political ecclesiastic hierarchy, civilian associations headed by religious interests, and the majority of "parents' associations"), the *Partido Acción Nacional*, and religiously based private interests, among others. At the same time, both nationalist and pro-U.S. entrepreneurial associations, either secular or pro-religious, have increased the number of private schools at all levels of education, the competitiveness of which has become increasingly strong and legitimized because they meet a demand that the official system cannot.

The point here is that globalization emerges as a nodal signifier in *Modernización Educativa* in a peculiar articulation with neoliberalism and neoconservatism. It interlaces the various threads of educational policies and the Mexican context, temporarily fixing the meaning of this educational reform and permeating diverse official measures to actualize it. Thus, from curricula to "incentives" for schoolteachers, from school administration to finance, from programs to textbooks, this meaning circulates acquiring specific features at each level yet keeping the promise of a future of "a more competitive national integration into the new world concert."

The System of Significations of *Modernización Educativa*

The three main documents where this policy is condensed are the *Programa Nacional para la Modernización Educativa* (National Program for Educational Modernization; SEP, 1989), the *Acuerdo Nacional para la Modernización de la Educación Básica* (National Agreement for the Modernization of Basic Education; SEP, 1992), and *Ley General de Educación* (General Education Law; SEP, 1993). The 1992 *Acuerdo* (Agreement) does not present any substantial change if compared with the original 1989 *Programa*, but the political insertion of the *Acuerdo* as an agreement allegedly achieved as the product of consensus introduced some strategic difference between them (i.e., there was a "consultation" with schoolteachers and their proposals were said to have been incorporated in the *Acuerdo*).[8]

Within this context, the meaning of *Modernización Educativa* is displayed in values (e.g., "quality," "equity," "productivity"), institutions, rituals, and budgets orientating educational courses of action and incarnating their values. The Programa is structured in ten chapters, the first of which displays the values and rationale for this policy. Before the first chapter, the text of the president's speech introduces the program, beginning with a review of the history of the Mexican school system. This review operates as a device to link the new program with the nationalist value, with the idea of a process whose almost natural course or logical consequence is *Modernización Educativa*. The main proposals of the policy document are organized in the other nine chapters devoted to school levels (primary, secondary, and higher education) and to specific areas such as schoolteacher qualifications, adult education, training schemes, open education, and educational evaluation. A final chapter is devoted to premises, equipment, and building maintenance.

The first chapter condenses the orientation of the reform. After establishing links between the policy and the Mexican Constitution, reinforcing them with a reference to the Mexican Revolution, the *Programa* seems to be sufficiently legitimized in advance. However, it stresses seven challenges or goals, among which decentralization occupies a key position, and later proposes decentralization as policy in items and sub-items where the model and its goals and civic values are presented. Quality, coverage (of the demand for schooling), and decentralization are the strategic axes of this reform. Five key items are said to guarantee the much-needed quality: content, teaching and learning methods, teacher qualifications and in-service training, links between school levels, and links with science and technology. Each chapter starts with a diagnosis of the then current schooling system covering basic schooling; schoolteachers' qualifications and in-service training; adult education; occupational training; secondary education; higher education; graduate studies; and scientific, humanistic, and technological research, indicating its main failures, and consequently establishing the main challenges for the plan (SEP, 1989). The *Acuerdo* (SEP, 1992) puts forward the following deficiencies: insufficient coverage and quality, lack of articulation among school levels, high proportion of repetition in primary and high school, excessive concentration of administration, and poor teacher conditions. The orientation to be stressed by the new policy follows from this diagnosis. The similarities between these two documents of the Mexican reform, in terms of values, strategies, orientation, and ways to legitimize the program, are remarkable.

One can see in both the *Programa* and the *Acuerdo* that globalization operates as the *cause* of *Modernización Educativa*, but also as the *consequence* that this reform will bring about. Globalization is signified as the *goal* of the policy but also as that which confers meaning to other discrete components of the general program (e.g., basic competencies, didactic material, content and methods, curricula and syllabi). It is constructed as a *means* to achieve a further end (i.e., the insertion of Mexico in the international market) and also as an *end* in itself. And in reading the different chapters of both official documents, one can observe how globalization circulates throughout the different items involved in the general strategy.

The World Bank and the *Acuerdo*: Is It Mere Coincidence?

Some of the specific items stressed in the Mexican educational policy are almost a literal translation of international recommendations: widening access, redistributing places, and improving quality; enhancing pertinence and relevance, level integration, and teachers' conditions; and promoting administrative de-concentration.

The official documents offer the solutions: quality; equity; reform of plans and syllabi; integration of the former kindergarten, primary, and secondary into a "basic cycle"; administrative decentralization; and the revaluing of schoolteachers (Buenfil, 1996). In the following, I present some relevant examples, using a compilation created by Medina in her research (1996, p. 52 ff):

The World Bank maintains that:

> Education is the cornerstone of economic growth and social development as well as one of the main means of people's welfare. Primary teaching is the basis; therefore there are three fields where it is necessary to introduce improvements: the teaching environment, teacher training and motivation, and the administration of educational systems. (1990, p. 2)

Modernización Educativa proposes:

> More resources, more effective teaching time, and adequate programs; better text books and teachers properly stimulated might have poor effects on educational quality and access if they cannot get beyond the obstacles and inefficiency of centralism and excessive bureaucracy damaging the national educational system. This is why it is important that the other axis of our strategy is the reorganization of the national educational system. (SEP, 1992, p. 7)

No sophisticated analysis is needed to see the similarity between these two pieces: the emphasis on the environment in the former is translated into teaching time, programs, textbooks; improvement in teaching motivation and training is translated into teachers properly stimulated (which in the Mexican document occupies one of the five central positions); and improvement in the administration of educational systems is translated into "overtaking centralism and excessive bureaucracy and [engaging in] the general re-organization of the national educational system."

Another example. The World Bank states:

> Research undertaken in diverse countries has shown that the amount of time devoted to academic studies is systematically related to learning levels in children at school. In general, the more time teachers devote to actual teaching, the more the children learn. ... Three factors determine the annual number of hours dedicated to study any subject at school: the duration of the school year in hours, the proportion of these hours assigned to the subject and the amount of time lost due to school stoppage, absence of teachers or students, and other interruptions. (1990, p. 21)

The Mexican educational policy echoes:

> It is of great importance to rectify an evident tendency in recent years to reduce the number of effective class-days in the school year. As a first step, beginning with the next school term, an increase of at least ten percent in effective school days will be encouraged, and this can be achieved [strictly following the official school calendar]. (SEP, 1992, p. 7)

More examples of this "translation" of key World Bank aspects retrieved by the Mexican policy are provided by Medina (1996) who compared the 1990 World Bank document and the 1992 Mexican *Acuerdo* in an accurate localization of paragraphs: motivation toward teacher's qualification improvement (SEP, 1992, pp. 8, 22; World Bank, 1990, pp. 5, 26–30); and opportunities for professional advancement (SEP, 1992, p. 20; World Bank 1990, p. 28). Even the timing for updating teachers' guides shows a surprising similarity between the two documents.

This may sound quite reasonable—until one becomes aware that contemporary conditions for Mexican schoolteachers are overlooked, as many of these "non-effective days" are used for teacher training, in-service seminars, or simply as a break in an exhausting double shift school job. This shows the clash between global homogeneity and particularity.

Dissemination of the Meaning of *Modernización Educativa*

While in previous pages one could witness the similarity between international educational recommendations and the literal text of the Mexican *Modernización Educativa,* this does not amount to seeing globalism as pure homogenization.

Focusing now on the items "schoolteacher's role" and "quality," and showing one side of heterogeneity in a global process, let us turn to analyze how this Mexican policy is resignified and its meanings proliferate at the point of its implementation. The proliferation and iterability (alteration in repetition) of meanings of these items proposed both in the *Programa* and the *Acuerdo* are conceptualized as dissemination (Derrida, 1981).

The question of schoolteachers occupies one of the central positions of the *Acuerdo*, and one of its three main proposals (decentralization; reformulation of school content, teaching material, and syllabi; and the revaluation of the schoolteacher's role). The latter is in turn unfolded into another six points: (1) basic qualifications, (2) in-service programs, (3) wages (equal to three and four minimum wages), (4) housing, (5) *carrera magisterial* (involving a new promotion system[9] that takes into account qualifications, productivity, etc.), and (6) social recognition and acknowledgment of the teachers' work.

In his research, López Ramírez (1998) deals with four main groups of protagonists in this policy: the Ministry of Education (SEP) and its administrators, the dominant teacher's (white union [SNTE]), the dissident leftist union (CNTE), and classroom teachers. Taking one item for this exercise, the "revaluation of the schoolteachers' role," he shows how in each site the policy is disseminated and adopted. He explains that despite its importance as a nodal point articulating the whole discursive edifice, "the teachers' role" meaning is resignified at each level of appropriation and implementation. In the words of then President of Mexico Carlos Salinas, "We need to forge the right mechanisms for the acknowledgment of their work; we must strengthen their role, reconcile their sense of service, and improve their living conditions" (SEP, 1989, p. xii). The following strategy was proposed: a system conferring awards, prizes, distinctions, honors, and economic incentives to schoolteachers' productivity and achievement.

The (conservative teachers union) SNTE understood the "revaluation of the schoolteach-ers' role" as an opportunity to revitalize the historic heritage of schoolteachers; to rescue and strengthen the "tradition of the Normal school"[10]; and to link these two aspects to solve their problems of immobility (lack of promotion) and isolation, thus improving their economic and labor conditions (López Ramírez, 1998, p. 152). CNTE resignified this nodal point as mere demagogy and a failed attempt. In their view, this was just a government product that would not achieve or recuperate the highly valued image the schoolteachers had lost (López Ramírez, 1998, p. 137).

Finally, the classroom teachers, confessing they had not studied the reform, resignified the "revaluation of the schoolteacher's role" as a policy that proved incapable of resolving their labor and economic conditions. They supported their opinion citing daily experience. One teacher said:

> The *Programa Modernizador* states that a critical and self-reflective teacher is needed but both the society and the pupils no longer respect us. We have lost today our human values. ... They used to respect us, support from the government used to arrive, but today it is no longer like that. We could fail a pupil [in an exam] but with the new evaluation forms we have to pass them all. (López Ramírez, 1998, p. 137)

Following López Ramírez's research on the dissemination of several nodal points of the *Modernización Educativa*, it can be said that this educational policy is resignified by the protagonists according to their position:

> SEP administrators: reproduce it, legitimizing and magnifying it. SNTE unionists: introduce nu-ances supplementing, criticizing and deconstructing it. CNTE unionists: antagonize it, fissuring, negating, criticizing and deconstructing it. Classroom teachers: fissure it, antagonizing, decon-structing, disseminating, threatening, and, paradoxically, reproducing it. (López Ramírez, 1998, p. 154)

Further research needs to be done to examine in a systematic way what we have already observed (i.e., how the "revaluation of the schoolteachers' role" is also resignified as a "com-pulsory way to study and update their skills," a way to "bargain with certificates and diplo-mas," to "simulate," to "produce low academic quality pupils," as well as the opposite: a way to improve the schoolteachers' qualifications and living conditions, especially of those who, following the new rules, aim to succeed in their trajectory of *carrera magisterial*). Further research also needs to be conducted to understand how, apart from schoolteachers, other schooling practices (e.g., teaching and learning, new curricula, etc.) are permeated by this global view and yet disseminated and resignified in educational policies.

A last example concerns the resignifications of "educational quality," its displacements along international recommendations, the national policy of educational modernization (com-mented previously), and the appropriations made at the state level and in actual local use. The sources of this signifier and how later it travels along different geopolitical scales are analyzed by López Nájera (2009).

Although "educational quality" is not a novel signifier in the field, in the last decade of the twentieth century and the first decade of the twenty-first it has gained centrality and has become a structuring function of educational policies and reforms.

To give "quality" meaning, international agencies, drawing from educational research during the decade from 1980 to 1990 in different parts of the world, began to produce recommendations for increasing children's educational performance at the elementary level especially for the developing countries. The World Bank (1990 and 1994) identified one hundred research reports studying the factors that determine educational performance. However, only eighteen documents written in the past twenty years specifically included productive functions and provided a more objective basis for the study of these relationships than those that use other statistical techniques or qualitative analysis (World Bank, 1994). [11]

According to UNESCO-OREALC (1992), publications dealing with quality in education were preponderant in Latin America during the 1990s, and thus there exists a substantial accumulation of data. In addition, the Education For All document, *The Quality Imperative*, states that "in the eighties, studies regarding the factors that determine effective teaching began to produce more coherent results" (UNESCO/Education For All, 2004, p. 43).

As López Nájera (2009) shows, during the 1980s they identified those factors that were considered to be determinant in improving student learning, such as professionalization of teachers, access to preschool education, increase of teaching hours, discipline as a condition for learning, specific methods for students with different needs, and the possession of textbooks (among others).

The deficiencies and weaknesses of educational systems in developing countries were represented in different ways by international organizations. The World Bank (1994) identified low performance and high rates of grade repetition, limitations in teacher performance (i.e., that "students who enter teaching have a low academic profile and low socioeconomic status"), inefficiency in organizing the time spent on teaching, the use of traditional methodology by teachers for all types of students in any situation, and their incapacity to maintain discipline in class. Quantitative indicators and data gathered by the ministers of education (e.g., number of students served, number of students graduated, number of students failed, etc.) were taken as proof of the World Bank's assertions. According to this agency, it was necessary to begin to place greater emphasis on qualitative processes and indicators that would provide information regarding elements that would help identify the variables for effective learning.

As López Najera (2009) asserts, UNESCO-OREALC associated those critical conditions with elementary education, especially those concerning the inequality with which education reached children: "The disparity of conditions in which children of different social groups go to school ... requires greater resources and efforts in order to close the gap between their own culture and the school culture" (UNESCO-OREALC, 1992, p. 32). Along with the drive toward equity to reach the populations most affected by poverty, UNESCO-OREALC also concentrated on coverage and "the expansion of the systems ... contents, and processes of the educational experience, information [that] shows how and how much students learn" (1992, p. 25). In the face of a lack of policies that would effectively reach populations characterized as "vulnerable," OREALC initiated a compensatory scheme of focalization involving programs and assigning resources for indigenous communities or outlying urban areas. The agency complemented quantitative indicators with more qualitative variables.

For its part, UNESCO, in *Education For All: The Quality Imperative* (2004), also presented a general view of instability where national policies are rebuked for focusing for decades on the quantitative aspect of education without taking into account factors that impact educational performance. For Education For All, the insufficient allocation of economic resources to the sector (presumably ameliorated by the external aid that this agency coordinated), the lack of organization for effective use of time in the classroom, as well as the unreliability of data provided by information systems in the poorer countries, were all identified as factors that produce a situation that must be overcome.

As López Nájera (2009) emphasizes, this critical situation prompted the need for specialists in education to carry out research in order to "detect" the variables that could improve educational performance, that is, those not focused primarily on quantifying the number of students, schools, books, etc., but rather those that would show how books helped students learn more, or how teachers could modify the ways they interacted with children so that they responded more adequately. These academic pieces provided the elements that came to represent educational quality. This helps explain the extensive output during the 1980s and 1990s, gathered and condensed by the organizations into their own universalized idea of educational quality.[12]

The variety of meanings involved in the emergence of the signifier "quality" in this phase would then meet the contextual particularities of implementation. However, one can clearly observe the displacements and transference of the meanings used by the international agencies to local implementations, operating as frames of reference to the proposals in Mexican educational policy.

A major part of the elements proposed in the documents of the World Bank (1994), UNESCO-OREALC (1992), and *Education For All* (UNESCO, 2004) were adopted in the documents that regulate national educational policy in Mexico. The purpose now is to show the political and discursive movements involved in the circulation (displacements) of the signifier "quality" along the national educational discourse. In the *Acuerdo Nacional para la Modernización de la Educación Básica* (SEP, 1992), it is declared that "there is a clear consensus on the need to transform the educational system. This social demand, widespread both across the country's geography as well as among sectors of society, *is for quality education*" (SEP, 1992, p. 55, emphasis added).

Further, the *Acuerdo* describes as especially critical the working conditions of teachers and the centralized organization of the educational system, as well as "deficiencies" in the curricula and study programs at the time. Thus, this agreement proposes to remedy the deficiencies in the educational sector through policies for the training of teachers, decentralization, and changes in curricular content (as mentioned previously).

This emphasis on quality initially inscribed in the 1989 reform has prevailed in policies undertaken by subsequent administrations. The *Programa de Desarrollo Educativo 1995-2000* (Program for Educational Development) declared of educational quality that "This subject is so vast that it permeates the entire Program" (SEP, 1995, p. 30). Quality, the Program for Educational Development document said, is inextricably bonded with coverage (p. 30), with management (i.e., margins of autonomy, institutional support, and normative regulation) (p. 43), with the number of teaching hours (p. 54), with assessment and evaluation (p. 55), and with teacher education (p. 57), and centralized organization is responsible for the inadequate attention to the specific needs of regions and of the country's diverse social groups.

In the case of the *Programa Nacional de Educación 2001–2006* (National Education Program 2001–2006; SEP, 2001), educational quality is again associated with the need for greater equality among the most impoverished and marginalized populations in the educational process—migrant, indigenous, and marginalized children. Following the course initiated by the 1992 *Acuerdo*, the National Education Program also establishes the need to promote more effective management, emphasized especially in the dynamic of social participation in the school. In addition, the program establishes that, "in the scenario that is taking shape, it will be necessary to open an extensive debate regarding the role of new technologies ... tending toward the definition of a national policy that will allow for orienting the potentialities of new technologies to the benefit of education and national development" (SEP, 2001, p. 36); this explicitly proposes the need to discuss and incorporate the new information and communication technologies to satisfy the demands of the twenty-first century.

In the 1990s, educational improvement was associated with "equality," which was strongly tied to quality, as is evidenced by the following quote: "The challenge for elementary education continues to be coverage, but *along with quality*. ... Coverage and *quality* are intimately linked. Both merge to achieve greater equality" (SEP, 1995, p. 30, emphasis added). In the same manner, the National Education Program considers the challenge of quality along with equality, although in this document the need to switch educational objectives from universal coverage to quality is more strongly emphasized:

> For decades, ... efforts were concentrated on accelerated construction of schools, massive production of free textbooks and training or preparation of teachers .... Today, [there is] an opportunity to concentrate national efforts on *improving the quality of services* and differentiated attention toward vulnerable groups. (SEP, 2001, p. 111, emphasis added)

The deficiencies and critical situation of the educational system presented in the previous section—as well as the end of the goal of universal coverage due to its supposed recent completion—constitute conditions that favor the interpretation of a new horizon of fulfillment. As López Nájera (2009) has indicated, during the past two decades the idea has been forming that educational quality is good, beneficial, and desirable, and that it will compensate all our insufficiencies, rectify errors of the past, and improve elementary education (adding kindergarten to primary and secondary education, the law established "basic education").

At a more restricted geopolitical level but still within the frame of a national policy, in the state of Oaxaca, the signifier "quality" is also structuring educational policies as can be observed in the *Programa Cubano-Oaxaqueño de Mejoramiento de la Calidad Educativa en Oaxaca* (Cuban-Oaxacan Program for the Improvement of Education in Oaxaca), conducted by an international team. "Quality" structures the whole idea of achievement and is associated with quantitative and qualitative indicators related to school management, teacher education and practices, teaching methods, syllabi, content, material and human resources, the pupils' activities inside and outside the schools, parents' participation and assessment, community collaboration, and with the continuous evaluation of all these. Here one can observe the imprint of the international agencies' meaning of quality but also the term's resignification through its contact with the Cuban consultants and their own intellectual horizon as well as with the contextual conditions of Oaxaca as one of the poorest states in the Mexican Republic.

Furthermore, again in Oaxaca at a more restricted local level, in a freelance project conducted by schoolteachers in search of better programs for the marginalized indigenous population in Oaxaca (a state of many specific ethnic cultures), the signifier "quality" is associated merely with the possibility of being visible in the broader context. Here, the signifier "quality" appears only in the first paragraphs of their principal document; it is associated with a desire for progress for the people and is invoked no more in the lines of the text.

In the previous paragraphs, traveling along different geopolitical contexts, one can observe the different meanings acquired by the signifier "educational quality," which show simultaneously the traces of international agencies, the national appropriations, the state resignifications, and the more local ones. It is possible to appreciate the displacement of the signifier and its meanings, the partial fixations as well as the movements that alter these meanings, the geopolitical continuities, and the transformations resulting from the political use of the signifier in each context. However, in three of the four contexts described, this signifier keeps a central, structuring position that in each case provides the core parameters of a promise of fulfillment.

THE INTERNATIONAL MEETS THE LOCAL: CENTRALITY AND DISSEMINATION OF THE GLOBAL

To interweave the threads of the argument, some points will be restated. Global recommendations in education involving some uniformization of neoliberal criteria, measures, values, and strategies are well known in both industrialized and poor countries. However, their very implementation in each particular site produces a resignification or reinterpretation. The encounter between the global policy and the specific conditions of each actualization brings to the fore the complex tension between universality and particularity when one conceptualizes globalization and then produces an interpretation of its effects on education.

The old existence of international agencies producing educational recommendations has been mentioned. In the 1960s, more attention was given to the impact certain agencies, particularly the Organization of American States and the World Bank, were having in Latin American countries. The traces of that (in)famous trend on educational technology fostered in the 1960s, when learning seemed guaranteed by organizing teaching through behavioral objectives, can still be found in some contemporary curricula. [13]

We have witnessed the increasing presence of UNESCO from the 1960s through its regional office (OREALC) and the *Proyecto Principal de Educación en América Latina y el Caribe* project, as well as of OECD, the World Bank, and the Inter-American Development Bank in the past decade. The different conditions in which the links between international and national, "central and peripheral," "advanced and developing" countries were observed in the 1960s today cannot be overlooked. The economic interdependence, the raising of minority voices, the end of the Cold War, the noticeable environmental decay, the exponential increase and centrality of a digital culture, and the increasing presence of critical perspectives and intellectual trends undermining our enlightened faith in progress, are among the most evident conditions that show this transformation. However, and even considering these differences, a tendency toward an intense asymmetric interconnection on a planetary scope must be acknowledged.

The previous discussion demonstrates that even if the term globalization has recently come to be used with frequency, the tendency toward internationalization is not new. The position assumed here associates globalization neither with a universal, necessary tendency of history nor with a cultural, economic, ethical, or impending political imperialization (i.e., the ruling of a single homogeneous view over the planet [even if non-capitalist]). Rather, drawing upon arguments by Giddens (1990), Robertson (1990), Perlmutter (1991), and Kwame and Gates (1997), globalization understood as interconnectedness was subscribed: interpenetration of economic tendencies, contact of cultural diversity, intertwining of many traditions, and interdependence of political trends. This means acknowledging our everyday life as a multidirected conditioning of the universal and the particular, the homogeneous and the heterogeneous; understanding that opposite tendencies such as fragmentation and integration, centralization and de-centralization contaminate and interact with each other.

This interaction produces syncretic and hybrid economic, cultural, educational, and political schemas conflicting with assorted fundamentalist positions that foster a mythical pure and uncontaminated identity, and showing its political character as our planet has unequal development in each realm and geopolitical area. Tension, encounter, friction, clash, and conflict are part of the process and wishful enlightenment thinking will not eliminate it. The implementation of a Mexican educational policy could be understood through these notions.

In analyzing the impact of *Modernización Educativa* on teachers' identity (Medina, 1996), the "revaluation of the schoolteachers' role" (López Ramírez, 1998), and the displacements of the signifier "quality" (López Nájera, 2009) in Mexico, some political and discursive movements were rendered visible. The hegemony of these nodal points structuring the program and temporarily fixing its meaning was achieved through the circulation of signifiers such as teacher education or educational quality along different geopolitical scales (international, national, and local) and different subject positions (authority of the Ministry of Education, white unionist, dissident unionist, classroom schoolteacher). This shows the way in which syncretic and hybrid cultural and educational meanings are produced, how resignifications take place, and why they are not merely linguistic operations of a politically neutral character, but rather they are embedded in power relations. The dissemination (Derrida, 1981) and proliferation of meanings permitted us to grasp the effects of discursive-political relationships whereby words, ideas, and values incarnated in other meaningful practices such as institutional spaces, budgetary appointments, the designation and removal of key functionaries, etc., are included and excluded, and involve political forces interacting in regard to moral, civic, and epistemic contents.

This analytical exercise also enabled our understanding, as López Nájera states, of how educational policies in their regulatory function display a grand, all-encompassing project where all the expectations of what can be achieved in the educational sector may be deposited, showing the radically ambiguous and empty character of the signifier chosen for this purpose, for although in different projects and documents the intent is to offer a positive idea of the variables and indicators that are posited when speaking about quality, or teacher identity, the exaltation of the sense of fulfillment above and beyond any specific content has made it possible to situate itself as the core idea of policies and programs in the sector. And this is neither pure demagogy nor a minor issue, but the very task of policies and reforms as cultural theses, regulatory practices, and ideological functions; that is, they embody a particular political, cultural, and social feature.

Beyond the ethical and political value of including particular views in any global recommendation, value that may or may not be considered by "universal" policy-makers in international agencies, there is another dimension where the encounter between universality and particularity operates. This dimension has been the axis of this chapter. It refers to the particularity (local) overflowing and contaminating the universal (global). This particularity is derived from the specific instantiations of the reform and cannot be anticipated by policy designers as it operates precisely in the actualization or implementation of educational policies, and in so doing, it produces a surplus of meaning, an excess of signification. This surplus is a discursive space for ethical and political intervention.

REFERENCES

Arditi, Benjamín. 1996. *The Underside of Difference*. Working Papers. No. 12. Essex: Centre for Theoretical Studies in the Humanities and the Social Science.

Bernstein, Richard. 1983. *Beyond Objectivism and Relativism: Science, Hermeneutics and Praxis.* Oxford: Basil Blackwell.

Braudel, Fernand. 1991. *Escritos sobre la Historia*. Mexico: Fondo de Cultura Económica.

Buenfil, Rosa Nidia. 1997. Education in a Postmodern Horizon: Voices from Latin America. *British Educational Research Journal*, vol. 23, no. 1, pp. 97–107.

_____. 1998. Globalización: Significante Nodal en la Modernización Educativa. *Cuadernos Pedagógicos*, nos. 26–27, pp. 135–52.

_____. 2000. Globalization, Education and Discourse Political Analysis: Ambiguity and Accountability in Research. *International Journal of Qualitative Studies in Education*, vol. 13, no. 1, pp. 1–24.

CEPAL-UNESCO. 1992. *Educación y Conocimiento: Eje de la Transformación Productiva con Equidad*. Santiago, Chile: CEPAL-UNESCO.

_____. 1997. *Séptima conferencia regional sobre la integración de la mujer en el desarrollo económico y social de América Latina y el Caribe*. Santiago, Chile: CEPAL.

Chaves, Fernando. 1962. *La Educación Cooperativa en América Latina*. Washington, DC: OAS.

Davis, Harold Eugene. 1950. *Social Science Trends in Latin America.* Washington, DC: American University Press.

Derrida, Jacques. 1981. *Dissemination.* Chicago: The University of Chicago Press.

Fiala, Robert, and Audri Gordon Lanford. 1987. Educational Ideology and the World Educational Revolution, 1950–1970. *Comparative Education Review*, vol. 31, no. 3, pp. 315–32.

Giddens, Anthony. 1990. *The Consequences of Modernity.* Cambridge: Polity Press.

Habermas, Jurgen. 1989. *El Discurso Filosófico de la Modernidad.* Buenos Aires: Taurus.

Kwame, Anthony, and Henry Gates. 1997. *The Dictionary of Global Culture.* New York: Alfred A. Knopf.

López Nájera, Itzel. 2009. *La Calidad Educativa entre lo Global y lo Local. El Peregrinaje de un Significante de Plenitud* (Educational Quality between the Global and the Local: The Journey of a Signifier of Fulfillment). (M.S. thesis). México: DIE-Cinvestav-IPN.

López Ramírez, José. 1998. *Modernización Educativa. Resignificaciones por Cuatro Protagonistas* (Educational Modernization: Resignifications for Four Protagonists). (M.S. thesis). México: DIE-Cinvestav-IPN.

McLaren, Peter, and Kris Gutiérrez. 1997. Global Politics and Local Antagonisms: Research and Practice as Dissent and Possibility. In Peter McLaren, *Revolutionary Multiculturalism: Pedagogies of Dissent for the New Millennium* (pp. 192–222). Boulder: Westview Press.

McLuhan, Marshall, and Bruce Powers. 1989. *The Global Village* Oxford: Oxford University Press.

Marchart, Oliver. 2007. *Post-Foundational Political Thought: Political Difference in Nancy, Lefort, Badiou and Laclau.* Edinburgh: Edinburgh University Press.

Margolis, Joseph. 1991. *The Truth about Relativism.* Oxford: Blackwell.

Medina, Patricia. 1996. *Impacto de la Modernización Educativa en la Identidad de los Maestros de Primaria.* México: Universidad Pedagógica Nacional.

Organization of American States. 1966. *Yearbook of Educational, Scientific and Cultural Development in Latin America.* Washington, DC: OAS.

Organization of Economic Cooperation and Development. 1971. *Educational Policies for the 1970s Conferences on Policies for Educational Growth.* Paris: OECD.

_____. 1993. *Education at a Glance. Indicators.* Paris: OECD.

Pan American Union. 1968. *The Alliance for Progress and Latin American Development Prospects: A Five-Year Review 1961-1965.* Baltimore: Johns Hopkins Press (for Organization of American States).

Perlmutter, Howard. 1991. On the Rocky Road to the First Global Civilization. *Human Relations*, vol. 44, no. 9, pp. 897–920.

Pérez-Ordaz, Angélica. 2008. El Desafío: ¿Educación vs. Globalización? *Casa del Tiempo*, vol. 1, no. 5–6. http://www.difusioncultural.uam.mx/casadeltiempo/05_iv_mar_2008/

Popkewitz, Thomas. 1991. *A Political Sociology of Educational Reform: Power/Knowledge in Teaching, Teacher Education and Research.* New York: Teachers College Press.

_____. 2000. Reform as the Social Administration of the Child: Globalization of Knowledge and Power. In Nicholas Burbules and Carlos Alberto Torres (eds.), *Globalization and Education: Critical Perspectives* (pp. 157–86). New York: Routledge.

_____ and Fazal Rizvi (eds.). 2009. *Globalization and the Study of Education.* (National Society for the Study of Education Yearbook, Vol. 108, No. 2). Malden, MA: Wiley-Blackwell.

Robertson, Roland. 1990. Mapping the Global Condition. In Mike Featherstone (ed.), *Global Culture: Nationalism, Globalization and Modernity* (pp. 15–30). London: Sage.

Rorty, Richard. 1989. *Contingency, Irony and Solidarity.* Cambridge: Cambridge University Press.

Secretaría de Educación Pública. 1989. *Programa de Modernización Educativa.* México: Secretaría de Educación Pública.

_____. 1992. *Acuerdo Nacional para la Modernización de la Educación Básica.* México: Secretaría de Educación Pública.

_____. 1993. *Ley General de Educación.* México: Secretaría de Educación Pública.

_____. 1995. *Programa de Desarrollo Educativo. 1995-2000.* México: Secretaría de Educación Pública.

_____. 2001. *Programa Nacional de Educación, 2001-2006.* México: Secretaría de Educación Pública.

UNESCO. 1965. *Actas de la Conferencia General.* Paris: UNESCO.

_____. 1968. *Education, Human Resources and Development in Latin America.* New York: UNESCO-ECLA.

_____. 1971. *World Survey of Education.* Paris: UNESCO.

_____. 1991. *United Nations Program for Development.* Paris: UNESCO.

_____. 1992. *Measuring the Quality of Education: Why, How and For What?* Santiago de Chile: UNESCO.

_____. 1993. *V Reunión del Comité Intergubernamental.* Santiago de Chile: Proyecto Principal de Educación en América Latina y el Caribe (PPEALC)-Ministerio de Cultura y Educación de la Nación.

_____. 1994. *Educación para Todos: Finalidad y Contexto. Monografía 1. Conferencia Mundial sobre Educación para Todos* (Jomtien, Thailand). Paris: UNESCO.

_____. 2004. *Global Monitoring Report 2005. Education For All: The Quality Imperative.* Paris: UNESCO.

UNESCO/EFA. 2004. *Education for All.* Paris: UNESCO.

UNESCO-OREALC (Schiefelbein, E. [ed.]). 1992. *La Calidad de la Educación en América Latina: Problemas y Posibilidades*, Edición preliminar. Paris: UNESCO.

Wallerstein, Immanuel. 1989. *El Capitalismo Tardío.* México: Siglo XXI.

Wittgenstein, Ludwig. 1963. *Philosophical Investigations.* Oxford: Basil Blackwell.

World Bank. 1990. *Educación Primaria: Documento de Política del Banco Mundial*. Washington, DC: World Bank.
_____. 1994. *Improving the Quality of Primary Education in Latin America and the Caribbean: Toward the 21st Century*, Washington, D.C.: World Bank.
_____. 2000. *¿La Globalización Incrementa la Pobreza en el Mundo?* http://www.bancomundial.org/temas/globalizacion/cuestiones2.htm

NOTES

1. Resignification should be understood here as an operation by means of which a different meaning (signification) is attached to a signifier. It does not imply that the first signification is truer than the second, only that there can be differences in meaning attached the same word. The point is to determine whether there are differences when the term "quality" is inscribed within a context of a UNESCO document, in the context of an official Mexican law, or in the context of a freelance educational proposal issued by schoolteachers.

2. I agree with Bernstein (1983), Margolis (1991), and Rorty (1989), among others, on the idea that relativism is a false problem posed by foundationalists.

3. Or, as Habermas (1989) bitterly accused "postmodernists" of doing, that the difference between repression and emancipation is blurred.

4. This has an obvious family resemblance to post-foundationalism (Arditi, 1996; Marchart, 2007).

5. For a lost Third World village, allopathic vaccination may be quite progressive and liberating while for a neighboring village the very same allopathic vaccination could become a repressive and colonizing practice (if their normal medicine is homeopathy or naturist). There is no privileged position from which our "senior brother" will pre-define how this allopathic vaccination will be appropriated in each particular site. (More examples appear in Buenfil, 1997.)

6. I will use the verb *retrieve* to mean that a word is recovered, rescued, recuperated, or taken from one discursive context and inscribed in a different one. For instance, the signifier "quality" can be retrieved from a global recommendation (e.g., UNESCO) and inscribed in a local program (e.g., the *Programa Cubano-Oaxaqueño de Mejoramiento de la Calidad Educativa en Oaxaca*, as shown in the third section of this chapter).

7. Neoliberalism will be treated as the contemporary logic borrowed from economics by other social fields, including education, particularly the marketing strategies now pervading educational policies.

8. Following the 1989 *Programa de la Modernización Educativa*, there was a consultation with teachers about the document, and later (1992) the *Acuerdo Nacional para la Modernización Educativa* was issued, both edited by the Ministry of Education. There are some modifications and specifications in the latter, but some analysts assert that the *Acuerdo* had already been written before the consultation, that the consultation had been a farce, and that its "results" had been "oriented" beforehand. The official group, on their part, claimed they could show the insertion of the consultation results in the *Acuerdo*. In my view, this proves neither that the consultation could have been manipulated, nor the opposite. As we can see, this is not a matter of "true or false" but rather of how this process took place.

9. There is a strong coincidence in the way in which this point is developed in the *Acuerdo* and the way that the World Bank recommends (SEP, 1992, pp. 5, 28ff).

10. The *Normalist* tradition refers to the high academic and professional value that teacher education used to have since the time it was created, emulating the French *École Normale* and, later, the *École Normale Superieure*. This tradition was preserved up to the Mexican Revolution and the first half of the twentieth century.

11. In the reduction from one hundred to twenty reports a first politico-discursive operation is already visible: what is included and what excluded as productive, meaningful and relevant for their purposes. Why does the qualitative approach hegemonize in those contexts? The particularity of these twenty reports comes to be a universal approach that will represent the World Bank's position.

12. As López Nájera shows, this set of deficiencies represented in the disorganization of time in the classroom, in the scarce preparation of teachers, and in the ineffectiveness of the "developing" countries' systems for gathering information, make up an overall critical situation, and make up a chain of equivalencies that summarizes the need to change focus: it is no longer enough for children to enter and leave school; what now must be assured is that these children actually learn in their passage through it.

13. The complex process through which an international educational recommendation is produced, how consensus is reached, and how the political forces involved negotiate before the agreement is issued was not elaborated here. Therefore, the particular is also strongly operating already in this scenario, not only when the "universal" international trend reaches the "particular" site of its implementation as a policy or as a reform.

Chapter Fifteen

The Impacts of Globalization on Education in Malaysia

Molly N.N. Lee

A quick review of the *Malaysia Education Blueprint, 2013-2025* (Ministry of Education, 2012) and the *National Higher Education Strategic Plan Beyond 2020* (Ministry of Higher Education, 2007) shows that many of the recent educational reforms that have taken place or are planned to take place in the near future are very much influenced by the global trends in educational changes that are occurring throughout the world. Educational changes do not occur in a void, nor do education policies materialize out of thin air. There is always a particular ideological and political climate and a social and economic context that together influence the shape and timing of education policies as well as their outcomes (Taylor, Rizvi, Lingard, and Henry, 1997).

Much that has been written about educational reforms in Malaysia tends to focus on socioeconomic and political forces internal to the country (Jasbir and Mukherjee, 1993; Morshidi, 2010; Santhiram, 1997). However, educational changes are only partially conditioned by internal forces. As some commentators point out, we should "move away from social change conceived as the internal development of societies to focusing on changes as the outcomes of struggles between the members of a figuration of interdependent and competing nation-states" (Featherstone and Lash, 1995, p. 2). We should also consider the influence of global trends on educational changes that have occurred in a particular country. As Archer (1991) notes, global processes are now partly constitutive of local realities, so the local contexts cannot be completely understood in strictly local terms. But this does not mean these global trends offer a sufficient explanation for local policies either. Global trends provide a source of policy borrowing and a backdrop of policy choices. However, they are adapted to and blended with local conditions and options in a fluid and contingent policy process (Christie, 1996).

GLOBAL INFLUENCES

Many of the educational changes in Malaysia have been very much influenced by globalization, which "refers to all those processes by which the peoples of the world are incorporated into a single world society, global society" (Albrow, 1990, p. 9). Globalization can be viewed as a multidimensional process that unfolds in realms such as the global economy, global politics, global communications, and worldwide cultural standardization and hybridization

(Pieterse, 1995). The revolution in global communications, together with multinational invest-ment, has given huge impetus to cultural globalization. The globalization of culture has been alluded to by many writers (Featherstone, 1990; Robertson, 1992; Waters, 1995), including a UN Educational, Scientific and Cultural Organization report that notes, "More generally, the same forces—trade, transport and communications—which are driving the globalization of science and technology are also driving the globalization of culture and are now reinforced by the relaxation of global political tensions" (UN Educational, Scientific and Cultural Organization, 1991, pp. 60–70).

What have made the globalization process feasible were, of course, the communication and information revolutions, combined with an increased mobility of people, money, services, goods, and images (Appaduria, 1990). Likewise, Malaysia has been incorporated into the world capitalist economy, affected by technological changes and assimilated into the global culture within which education operates.

According to Davies and Guppy (1997), there are two sets of arguments that use globaliza-tion as a conceptual framework for comprehending pan-national changes in education: one is "economic globalization" and the other is "global rationalization." The economic globaliza-tion perspective focuses on the ascendancy of the global marketplace in shaping educational reform. The opening up of world markets and the relatively free movement of capital and technology offer great potential for economic growth. However, the effects of globalization on a country's development potential depend critically on its educational or human resource capacity (Stewart, 1996). New market demands for better quality products and high technolo-gy jobs require a very skilled labor force, and rapidly changing tastes result in flexible and specialized production and greater worker responsibility.

Therefore, schools must adjust to this economic restructuring by making changes in the goals and content of the learning process. Ilon (1994) notes that such changes would increase the need for a global curriculum, that is, "a curriculum emphasizing information gathering, manipulation, management, and creation" (p. 99). Furthermore, this economic transformation would also require curricula that concentrate on "consumer relations, problem solving, entre-preneurialism, and cross-cultural multi-skilling" (Davies and Guppy, 1997, p. 439). A more recent document produced by a group of American information technology companies advo-cates the need to develop twenty-first century skills to ensure economic competitiveness. Besides learning a list of core subjects and global issues, the students should also learn (1) learning and innovative skills and (2) life and career skills, as well as (3) information, media, and technology skills (Partnership for 21st Century Skills, 2008). Basically, the need for change in education is largely cast in economic terms and particularly in relation to the preparation of a workforce and competition with other countries.

On the other hand, global rationalization stresses the idea of a system of world culture. According to Meyer (1980), the world system is not simply a collection of nation-states engaged in economic exchange, but also an overarching social system of institutional rules and structural properties. These rules define the parameters within which nations operate and strongly influence the behavior of nations. At the same time, the behavior of nations helps shape the institutional structure and pushes its evolution in new directions. Indeed, a central feature of the institutional perspective is its emphasis on evolving world cultural imperatives, as compliance with them is an important source of legitimacy and resources. Examples of how world cultural norms have evolved over time can be seen in the practice of schooling, environ-mentalism, human rights, women's rights, and other transnational social movements. Accord-ing to this line of argument, the institutionalization of schools into rationalized bureaucratic forms is very much part of the world culture. Empirical studies have shown that there is a continual worldwide convergence of education systems and curricula. Not only are subjects such as mathematics, science, and social studies standard, but the number of classroom hours devoted to each is almost identical across nation-states (Benavot, Cha, Kamens, Meyer and Wong, 1991; Kamens, Meyer, and Benavot 1996). Similarly, educational reforms such as multicultural education, skill-centered curriculum, and standardized testing that have crossed national boundaries are very much part of the globalization process (Davies and Guppy, 1997).

Both economic globalization and global rationalization seem to point to processes of institutional convergence, but does it mean that all education systems are going to be very similar because of increasing global influences? No doubt, in recent years, national education systems may have become more porous, and educational reforms across nations may bear remarkable similarity because there has been much policy "borrowing," "transfer," or "copying," which "leads to universalising tendencies in educational reform" (Haplin, 1994, p. 204). As Ball (1998) observes, "National policy making is inevitably a process of bricolage: a matter of borrowing and copying bits and pieces of ideas from elsewhere, drawing upon and amending locally tried and tested approaches, cannibalizing theories, research, trends and fashions and not infrequently flailing around for anything at all that looks as though it might work" (p. 126).

However, this does not mean that there is a full-scale globalization of education and that the world has become more uniform and homogenized through a technological, commercial, and cultural synchronization emanating from the West. Rather, what we can observe is a plurality of national responses to the global forces. According to Pieterse (1995), globalization is a process of hybridization that gives rise to unique responses from different nation-states to global trends originating from various metropolitan centers, which are not necessarily located in the West.

Cultural theorists are divided as to whether globalization means cultural standardization or increasing diversity. The most plausible deduction seems to be that it means both at the same time. This double movement produces cultural homogenization and, at the same time, a wide range of cultural hybrids and mixes (Green, 1997). Similarly, educational reforms are shaped by a complex interaction of local and global forces. It would be a mistake to view global influences simply as impositions on local contexts, as this would overlook the agency of local actors as well as different forms that adaptation to local context brings (Christie, 1996). Usually, policy ideas are received and interpreted differently within different national and cultural contexts. Therefore, in our attempts to understand education changes and policies, we need to examine how policy ideas are being "recontextualized" in specific national settings thus give rise to local variations of generic policies (Ball, 1998).

IMPACTS ON NATIONAL CONTEXT

Malaysia is a middle-income country in southeast Asia with a multi-ethnic population of 28.3 million. In 2011, the Malaysian economy was the third largest in southeast Asia and ranked thirtieth in the economies of the world, with a gross domestic product per capita of U.S.$9,801 and a growth rate of 5.1 percent (Department of Statistics, Malaysia, 2012). Malaysia has transformed itself from a producer of primary products to a multi-sector economy based on services (48 percent), industries (40 percent), and agriculture (12 percent). Malaysia is a prominent supplier of tin, palm oil, and rubber. It is also one of the world's largest exporters of semi-conductor components and devices, electrical goods, solar panels, and information and communication technology (ICT) products.

The accelerating pace of globalization of the economy has been at the base of Malaysia's economic growth over the past three decades. The Malaysian economy interfaced with the global economy in what has been described as the "international division of labor." Multinational corporations from advanced countries went in search of political stable offshore production sites and cheap labor in third world countries, and in return they offered mass employment to the host countries. As a result of concerted effort to attract foreign direct investments by offering the comparative advantages of lower wages, the prohibition of unionization among a new industrial labor force, sound physical and social infrastructure, low fiscal tax, and other incentives, the Malaysian economy became integrated with the globalization of industrial production (Khoo, 2000). A major measure taken by Malaysia to promote manufactured exports was the establishment of Free Trade Zones from 1971 onward. Nearly three-quarters of the Free Trade Zone firms are foreign-owned,[1] accounting for more than 90 percent of the total direct employment within the Free Trade Zones (Ariff, 1991). Much of the foreign direct investment is in the electrical and electronic products, rubber products, and textile and wood products industries. Demands for these products come from export markets such as the United States, Singapore, Japan, and the People's Republic of China.

In the early 1980s, Malaysia ventured into a heavy industrialization drive based on the production of steel, automobiles, motorcycle engines, and cement. This heavy industrialization program was a combined effort of state investment (represented by HICOM, the Heavy Industries Corporation of Malaysia), "East Asian technology" (sourced from Japanese and South Korean firms through joint ventures), and indigenous management (Machado, 1994). That major shift in the industrialization program was a response to meet the challenges of the competitive global trading environment at that time. The national strategies then were to increase the supply of skilled workers and upgrade technological capacity. During that period, the emphasis was to develop high value-added, capital-intensive, and export industries producing more varied, better-designed, and competitive products that meet the demand of global markets. The Seventh Malaysia Plan (1996–2000) states, " In meeting the challenges arising from increased globalization and continued tightness in the labor market, priority will continue to be accorded to improving the competitiveness of industries through increases in productivity, research and development as well as the provision of adequate supporting infrastructure" (Malaysia, 1996, p. 263).

However, after the 2008 global financial crisis, Malaysia is taking steps to readjust its economic strategies in the face of slow recovery of the global economy. Malaysia can no longer rely on low labor cost as a comparative advantage for there are other very competitive countries in this respect such as Vietnam, Bangladesh, Cambodia, and others in the region. The Tenth Malaysia Plan (2011–2015) states, "today's globalized economy, with regional production networks and greater regional integration, creates competitive pressures for greater specialization" (Malaysia, 2011, p. 14). Therefore, Malaysia is making a shift toward higher value-added and knowledge-intensive activities and hopes to move from a middle-income country to a high-income country through specialization. Malaysia has identified eleven National Key Economic Areas[2] for further development in terms of "having a critical mass and ecosystem of firms and talent to drive economies of scale" (Malaysia, 2011, p. 14). Instead of relying on export-oriented growth strategy, Malaysia aims to promote domestic demand to become a major driver of growth mainly by energizing the private sector. At the same time, Malaysia hopes to diversify export markets by making stronger inroads into emerging markets in Asia and the Gulf States including China and India, which are two rapidly growing economies in the region. Furthermore, economic growth during the Tenth Plan period will be driven by significant increases in productivity rather than by high capital and labor inputs, as well as by efficiency gains from removing distortions within the economy.

Global forces do not operate only in the economic sphere, nor do they originate only from the West. As discussed in the previous section, cultural globalization is occurring at the same time as economic globalization, and religion is very much a critical ingredient of cultural globalization (Robertson, 1991). In recent decades, one has witnessed the spread of Islamic resurgence in many Muslim countries,[3] including Malaysia. The intellectual characteristics of this global trend are the fervent belief that society should be organized on the bases of Islamic religion, advocacy of greater political freedom, and a general aversion to Western civilization (Chandra, 1987). These characteristics are quite evident as reflected by the political uprisings in the "Arab Spring" countries and the number of terrorist attacks against Western powers such as the September 11 (2001) and the Bali bombing incidents (2002). The spread of Islamic revivalism has been attributed to various factors by different scholars.[4] According to Turner (1991), the fundamentalist revival in Islam is an example of the relativizing effect of globalization. He maintains that Western modernization in either its capitalistic or Marxist forms failed to deliver either material benefits or a coherent system of meanings to the Islamic world. Indeed, rapid industrialization and urbanization appeared to offer only stark inequality between the populace and the politically dominant elite. Islamic revivalism in various Muslim countries marks a rejection of Western modernization and secularism. In the context of Malaysia, the intra-ethnic group conflict among the Malays has resulted in the use of Islam as a political ideology both to maintain the status quo and to demand fundamental change in the political system.[5] Islam has become both an agent and a symbol of the many rapid social changes now occurring in Malaysia.

The manifestation of the Islamic influences takes place at two levels: the individual and the organization. At the individual level, there is the rapid diffusion of what is regarded as Islamic attire[6] and a decline in social communication between the sexes among a significant portion of the Muslim population, the widespread use of Islamic forms of greetings,[7] an overt concern about Muslim dietary rules,[8] and strict adherence to religious duties[9] (Chandra, 1987, pp. 2–5). The Malaysian government launched its Islamization program in 1982 by promoting Islamic values such as diligence, hard work, discipline, sincerity, honesty, respect, and loyalty in public administration (Mauzy and Milne, 1983) and by setting up Islamic institutions such as an Islamic university and an Islamic banking system in 1983, an Islamic Foundation devoted to social welfare, and an Islamic insurance scheme. The increased government intervention in Islamic affairs is an indication of the government's desire to increase its legitimacy among Muslims, as well as the impact of the spread of Islamic revivalism throughout the world. This Islamic movement in turn has its influence on what is being taught in schools, resulting in an emphasis on the teaching of moral values throughout the whole curriculum.

IMPACTS ON EDUCATION

What we have discussed so far are the changes that globalization has brought to the economic and social contexts of Malaysia. Now we shall examine, in greater detail, how these changes have influenced the education system at both the school level and the tertiary level.

School Level

The Ministry of Education has recently released the *Malaysia Education Blueprint, 2013-2025*, which is the outcome of a comprehensive review of the Malaysian education system that involved experts from international organizations such as the UN Educational, Scientific and Cultural Organization , the Organization for Economic Cooperation and Development, and the World Bank (Ministry of Education, 2012). The comprehensive review was made in the context of rising international education standards, the Malaysian government's aspiration of better preparation of Malaysia's children for the needs of the twenty-first century, and increased public and parental expectations of education policy. The *Blueprint* reported the performance of Malaysian students against international standards, refined the goals of the Malaysian education system, and suggested educational reforms to achieve these goals. Each of these educational aspects will be analyzed to show how the interaction of international influences and local realities are being played out in the new set of education policies in accordance with the *Education Blueprint*.

According to Carnoy (herein), globalization has produced an increased emphasis on educational measurements and comparisons of school outcomes across countries and within countries. International benchmarking of education systems and international assessment of student performances has been pushed by international organizations such as the International Association for Evaluation of Educational Achievement, the Organization for Economic Cooperation and Development, and the World Bank. Over the past two decades, international student assessments, such as the Program for International Student Assessment (PISA) and the Trends in International Mathematics and Science Study (TIMSS), have emerged as a means of directly comparing the quality of educational outcomes across different countries. Malaysia participated in TIMSS since 1999 and recently in 2009+ PISA. The results from both these international assessments were discouraging. The longitudinal TIMSS study shows that Malaysia's student performance is declining in absolute terms. In 1999, the average student score was higher than the international average both in mathematics and science. But by 2007, Malaysia's student performance had slipped below international average in both mathematics and science. The test results in 2007 show that 18 percent and 20 percent of Malaysia's students failed to meet the minimum proficiency levels in mathematics and science, which is a two- to fourfold increase when compared to 7 percent and 5 percent, respectively, in 2003. Similarly, in the 2009+ PISA, Malaysia ranked among the bottom third of the seventy-four participating countries. Almost 60 percent of the fifteen-year-old Malaysian students failed to meet the minimum proficiency level in mathematics, while 44 percent and 43 percent, respectively, did not meet the minimum proficiency in reading and science (Ministry of Education, 2012). These poor performances in international assessments have spurred the Ministry of Education to revamp the whole education system by revisiting its educational goals and transforming its delivery system.

Like many other countries, the national educational philosophy for Malaysia stresses the holistic development of the individual: intellectually, spiritually, emotionally, and physically. Looking ahead, the *Education Blueprint* draws on lessons from other high-performing education systems and develops a refined articulation of the specific skills and attributes that students would need to thrive in tomorrow's economy and globalized world. The list of student aspirations includes knowledge, thinking skills, leadership skills, bilingual proficiency, ethics and spirituality, and national identity. It is interesting to note that the Malaysian education system places emphasis on ethics and spirituality, national identity, and bilingual proficiency. Being a Muslim country, the school system stresses the teaching of values and religious education. Muslim students have to take Islamic studies, and non-Muslim students have to take moral education. In addition, the Malaysian schools emphasize the teaching of language and noble values across the curriculum. Examples of such noble values are compassion, self-reliance, humility, honesty, diligence, cooperation, love, and justice. The penetration of Islamic influence in schools can be further seen in the teaching of Islamic science[10] and the study of Islamic civilizations in the subject of history.

Another controversial issue is the role of English in the school curriculum. One of the major reforms in the 1970s was the conversion of all English-medium schools in Malaysia into Malay-medium. Since then, English has been taught in schools as a second language. As expected, there has been a general decline in the standard of English in the country, which is now causing great concern among political leaders and employers in the commercial sectors. With the globalization of the economy, the importance of English as an international language of trade and the transfer of scientific knowledge and technical know-how cannot be further ignored. In 2003, after more than thirty years of using the Malay language as the medium of instruction for all subjects in schools, the Malaysian government implemented a policy that made English the medium of instruction for mathematics and sciences. The objective of this policy is to produce a new generation of students who are scientifically and technologically knowledgeable and fluent in English. However, the policy was short-lived, for in 2009 the Malaysian government, under great political pressure, made a U-turn and reverted back to using the Malay language to teach these two subjects. The U-turn is not well-received by many stakeholders, especially among middle-class parents, and now there is plan to make English a compulsory subject to be passed in the Sijil Pelajaran Malaysia[11] examination. The "bilingual proficiency" stated in the *Education Blueprint* is a political compromise of national priority in using the national language as the medium of instruction and the global imperative of acquiring English proficiency among the Malaysian work force.

As Malaysia is a multi-ethnic society, multicultural education is an important aspect of policy-making. There are different approaches to the task of constructing multicultural education (Lynch, 1986). The possible policies that can be pursued by governments range from assimilation of minority groups into the values and social norms of the majority group, to the integration of different groups until the divisive aspects of each group have been whittled away and a new culture has been created, to cultural pluralism that recognizes the cultural and social diversity of different ethnic groups but seeks to create a political and economic unity from them (Watson, 1980). Malaysia has opted for the integration approach. Education is seen as a means of redressing the ethnic imbalances and of creating a sense of national unity among the diverse ethnic groups. Ever since independence in 1957, education policies have been concerned with how to bring about racial harmony and national identity in a national system of education and how to raise the economic status of the indigenous Bumiputeras.

To address these student aspirations and to prepare the nation to perform at the international level, it is imperative that the Malaysia education system be transformed so as to provide equal access to quality education, to reduce achievement gaps (rural-urban, socioeconomic, gender), to give children shared values and experiences by embracing diversity, and to maximize student outcomes within the current budget. The *Education Blueprint* (Ministry of Education, 2012, pp. 15–16) recommended eleven "shifts" to transform the Malaysian education system:

1. Provide equal access to quality education of an international standard;
2. Ensure every child is proficient in Bahasa Malaysia and English language;
3. Develop values-driven Malaysians;
4. Transform teaching into the profession of choice;
5. Ensure high-performing school leaders in every school;
6. Empower JPNs,[12] PPDs,[13] and schools to customize solutions based on needs;
7. Leverage ICT to scale-up quality learning across Malaysia;
8. Transform ministry delivery capabilities and capacity;

9. Partner with parents, community, and private sector at scale;
10. Maximize student outcomes for every Malaysian Ringgit [Malaysian currency];
11. Increase transparency for direct public accountability.

Some of these shifts in education policies will be examined with special reference to the global influence on the educational settings in Malaysia. To improve the quality of education, Malaysia will continue to benchmark the learning of languages, mathematics, and science to international standards. Furthermore, it will launch a new Secondary Curriculum and revise the Primary Curriculum in 2017. It will also revamp the national examinations and assessments to increase focus on testing higher-order thinking skills by 2016. It will increase access to preschool education and provide better teaching and physical resources to students with special needs. There will also be a move from six to eleven years of compulsory schooling.

As in many advanced countries, Malaysia is striving toward an all-graduate teaching force. The Ministry of Education has upgraded the Teacher Training Colleges into Teacher Training Institutes that offer degree programs to pre-service teachers. The ministry is also collaborating with many of the local universities including the Open universities to offer degree programs to in-service teachers. The ministry plans to implement competency-based and performance-based career progression among Malaysian teachers by 2016. The professionalization of the Malaysian teaching force is hoped to be achieved through Continuing Professional Development from 2013 onwards with greater emphasis on school-based training.

One current global trend in education reform is the decentralization of national education systems. The growing interest in decentralization arises from the realization that many education systems, particularly those in the third world, have expanded rapidly, making it increasingly difficult to plan and administer all education activities effectively and efficiently from the center. Under the quality and efficiency rationales, decentralization can be a means of increasing effectiveness by moving control over the schools closer to the parents and communities, and making education more responsive to local problems and needs. In the context of Malaysia, State Education Departments and District Education Departments were established for the central ministry to delegate power to the state level and for the State Education Departments to deconcentrate routine tasks to the district level (Lee, 2006). The *Education Blueprint* recommends that these State Education Departments and District Education Departments be empowered to customize solutions to local needs. It further suggests that school-based management be encouraged so that schools have the autonomy to practice operational flexibility in budget allocation and curriculum implementation as well as making decisions on personnel matters.

Malaysia, like many countries in the region, has invested heavily in the use of ICT in schools since 1999 under the Smart School Initiative. Unlike other countries, Malaysia does not rely on a single specialized agency or a particular division of the Ministry of Education to implement its ICT in education programs. Instead, the Malaysian government rolled out a nationwide initiative known as the Smart School Initiative, which is based on strategic public-private partnerships involving various stakeholders including ministry, industry, community, and parents. The initiative involves the use of ICT in the teaching-learning process as well as in the management and administration of schools. It entails the capacity development of teachers, administrators, and technicians in using ICT effectively in their daily practices (Ministry of Education, 2011). The *Education Blueprint* recommends that the Ministry provide Internet access and virtual learning environments via 1BestariNet[14] for all ten thousand Malaysian schools by 2013.

Higher Education

In studying the globalizing practices in Anglo-Pacific and North American universities, Currie (1998) identifies a few interesting trends, which include a shift from elite to mass higher education, the privatization of higher education, the practice of corporate managerialism, and the spread of transnational education. Not surprisingly, the impacts of all these trends are found in Malaysia. Higher education in Malaysia may have started with a single university, the University of Malaya in 1962, but as of 2007, there are in existence 20 public universities, 36 private universities and university colleges, 21 polytechnics, 37 community colleges, and 485 private colleges (Ministry of Higher Education, 2007). The rapid expansion of higher education has been fueled by strong social demand for higher education, seen as the main avenue for social mobility and social justice, facilitated by the democratization of secondary education, and the growing affluence of the Malaysian society. In 2003, the enrollment at tertiary level for the cohort of seventeen- to twenty-three-year-olds was 979,745 students, or 29 percent of the age cohort. This number was expected to increase to 1,480,600 students or 40 percent in 2010, and by 2020 this number will further increase to 2,078,900 or 50 percent of the cohort (Ministry of Higher Education, 2007). However, the actual tertiary student enrollment was only 1,103,963 in 2010 (Malaysia, 2011), which is about 30 percent of the age cohort, showing that the projection has fallen short by 10 percent. The developed countries in the Asia-Pacific region such as Republic of Korea, Australia, and Japan have high gross enrollment ratios over 50 percent. These comparative figures show that Malaysia still has to increase participation in higher education in accordance with its National Higher Education Strategic Plan.

The rapid expansion of higher education and the rising unit cost have caused tremendous fiscal strains on many governments, which therefore have to seek other sources of funding and restructure their higher education systems. The restructuring of higher education in many countries involves the privatization of higher education, the corporatization of public universities, the implementation of student fees, and the formation of strategic partnerships between public and private sectors in the provision of higher education. While private higher education has been a long tradition in countries such as the United States, Japan, South Korea, Indonesia, and Philippines, it is a relatively new phenomenon in Malaysia. With the deregulation of higher education in the mid-1990s, there was a sharp increase of new private universities and colleges. In 1995, there was not a single private university in the country but, by the year 2008, there are a total of 36 private universities and university colleges and 485 private colleges. In 2011, about 50 percent of the students enrolled in higher education were enrolled in private institutions (Malaysia, 2011). Generally, it can be seen that in the newly established private sectors, the governments liberalize and deregulate education policies to allow private higher education to be established to absorb the increasing demand that cannot be met by the public sector due to budgetary constraints.

Besides the privatization of higher education in Malaysia, the public universities are being corporatized. The corporatization of public universities is a move to allow them to operate like business organizations by charging student fees, seeking research grants and consultancies, franchising education programs, renting out university facilities, and investing in other business ventures. As higher education systems expand, they become more bureaucratic and regulated so as to ensure consistency of treatment in various areas pertaining to the governance and management of higher education institutions. Many public and private universities in Malaysia have adopted "corporate managerialism" in their attempts to improve their accountability, efficiency, and productivity. Management techniques from the corporate sector such as mission statements, strategic planning, total quality management, ISO certification, rightsizing, and benchmarking are being institutionalized in higher education institutions (Lee, 2004).

In general, the relationship between the state and higher education institutions is constantly being redefined with the state demanding more accountability and higher education institutions insisting on more autonomy (Neave, 2001). The trend is an increase in institutional autonomy in return for more accountability. In the context of Malaysia, the institutional autonomy of private universities and corporatized public universities has increased in terms of governance structure, academic matters, financial management, staff management, leadership appointment, and student intake. At the same time, higher education institutions in Malaysia are increasingly being subjected to public accountability. Malaysian universities are subjected to more internal and external control. In 2007, the Malaysian Qualifications Agency, which was a merger of the National Accreditation Board (LAN)[15] and the Quality Assurance Division of the Ministry of Higher Education (QAD),[16] was established for quality assurance of higher education in both the public and private sectors. The Malaysian Qualifications Agency accredits higher education programs and carries out institutional audits, as well as rates higher education institutions in Malaysia.

The liberalization of higher education in the Asia-Pacific region has also resulted in a wide range of innovative public-private partnerships (Lee and Neubauer, 2009). Examples of public-private partnerships in Malaysia include local governments partnering with private companies to set up state universities, public universities franchising their education programs to private higher education institutions, public universities partnering with private companies to engage in market-related activities such as the setting up of industrial parks and incubators, and the practice of outsourcing to private companies to provide various student services.

The internationalization of higher education is another global trend that involves cross-border higher education and internationalizing the curriculum for domestic students. Cross-border higher education is defined as the movement of people, knowledge, programs, providers, and curriculum across national or regional jurisdictional borders (Knight, 2006). The higher education sector not only supported globalization, but also became globalized in the process. The cross-border mobility of students, programs, institutions, and teachers helped in globalizing higher education. The private sector, cross-border providers, and technology-based modes of delivery changed the landscape of higher education and made it a marketable service across countries (Varghese, 2011).

Malaysia strives to be an international hub for education. Currently, various efforts are undertaken to obtain international recognition for higher education programs in Malaysia. A national higher education global network has been strengthened through various memoranda of understanding and memoranda of agreement between local and foreign universities. International collaboration has been strengthened with the establishment of four research chairs in Malay studies at foreign universities. Regional and international research centers such as the Institute of Malaysia and International Studies and the Institute of Occidental Studies in the National University of Malaysia, the Asia-Europe Institute in the University of Malaya, as well as the Institute of East Asia Studies in the University of Malaysia Sarawak have been established to promote economic research and research on languages, and national and regional cultures. The enrollment of international students in Malaysian higher education institutions has increased significantly from 18,242 students in 2001 to 40,525 in 2005, forming 4.19 percent of the overall total student enrollment. In 2011, the number increased to ninety thousand and the government hopes to attract two hundred thousand students by 2020 (Chi, 2011). To attract more international students to study in Malaysia, the government has set up Malaysia Education Promotion Centres in Dubai, Beijing, Jakarta, and Ho Chi Minh City.

The emergence of foreign-linked programs reflects a growing trend of cross-border higher education. In most cases, the curricula used in the cross-border higher education programs are usually imported directly from the foreign institutions, although some institutions do try to adapt some of the curricula to local context. Education is increasingly becoming commodified. In Australia, cross-border higher education now exceeds wheat as an export earner. In the global context, boundaries around how, where, and under whose authorities education is carried out and certified become less clear as universities and technical and other education colleges internationalize their campuses, curricula, and teaching staffs. As some commentators astutely ask, "How can governments define their educational purposes and keep track of what is happening in their education systems, given the tangle of institutional links now being created across regions and countries, and given the problems of regulating the borderless frontiers of cyberspace?" (Taylor, et al., 1997, p. 74). With the expansion of cross-border higher education, the Malaysian government is faced with the same dilemma. To control the quality foreign higher education providers, the Malaysian government only allows a small number of foreign branch campuses to be set up in the country. To assure the quality of higher education, the Malaysia Qualification Agency was established to accredit higher education programs as well as carry out academic audit on higher education institutions.

CONCLUSION

In this chapter, I have argued that an examination of the global forces impinging on education systems is just as essential as an examination of the global economy would be to an understanding of the dynamics of economic development in any one country. In analyzing the impacts of globalization on education, one notices two concurrent but opposing streams: one is homogenization and the other is particularization. While we can identify certain global trends in educational reforms across nations, we should not assume that there is total convergence of education policies in all education systems. In fact, the impact of globalization on the policies as well as content and process of education should take into account the sociopolitical and economic context of each nation. What usually emerges is a hybrid of local variations of education policy ideas that may have originated from various metropolitan centers.

The Malaysian case study shows that many of the educational changes that have occurred are very much influenced by global trends as well as the internal dynamics of social, economic, and political forces. The international benchmarking of student performances in TIMSS and PISA has resulted in a comprehensive review by the Malaysian government of its education system. The outcome of this review is the *Malaysia Education Blueprint*, which outlines the national educational goals and the strategies to transform the education system in order to achieve these goals. The Malaysian education system places great emphasis on ethics and spirituality, national identity, and bilingual proficiency. To improve the education system, the *Education Blueprint* suggests eleven "shifts," which include revising the school curricula, increasing access to preschool education, providing better resources to special education, and implementing eleven years of compulsory schooling. The teaching force will be upgraded and professionalized. The management and administration of the school system will be decentralized to the state, district, and school levels. Teachers and education administrators will be trained to use ICT effectively in carrying out their responsibilities. At the higher education level, Malaysia has rapidly expanded its private higher education, corporatized its public universities, and strived to become the regional hub of education.

Many of the educational changes that have occurred in Malaysia are the results of interaction between global challenge and national response. Whether an ideological belief gets political commitment in a particular setting depends on the interplay of conflict and compromise among diverse interests. Moreover, the translation of policy ideas into actual practice also depends on a whole host of factors such as feasibility, resource constraints, bureaucratic routines, time, and the personalities of key actors in the implementation process. How ideas get translated into policies and practices depends greatly on the local settings, and, very often, what may at first appear to be similar policies may end up as quite different practices.

REFERENCES

Albrow, Martin. 1990. Introduction. In Martin Albrow and Elizabeth King (eds.), *Globalization, Knowledge and Society* (pp. 3–13). London: Sage.

Appaduria, Arjun. 1990. Disjuncture and Difference in Global Cultural Economy. In Mike Featherstone (ed.), *Global Culture: Nationalism, Globalization and Modernity* (pp. 295–310). London: Sage.

Archer, Margaret. 1991. Sociology of One World: Unity and Diversity. *International Sociology*, vol. 6, no. 2, pp. 131–47.

Ariff, Mohamed. 1991. *The Malaysian Economy: Pacific Connections*. Singapore: Oxford University Press.

Ball, Stephen. 1998. Big Policies/Small World: An Introduction to International Perspectives in Educational Policy. *Comparative Education*, vol. 34, no. 2, pp. 119–30.

Benavot, Aaron, Yun-Kyung Cha, David Kamens, John W. Meyer, and Suk-Ying Wong. 1991. Knowledge for the Masses: World Models and National Curricula, 1920-1986. *American Sociological Review*, vol. 56, no. 1, pp. 85–100.

Chandra, Muzaffar. 1987. *Islamic Resurgence in Malaysia*. Kuala Lumpur: Fajar Bakti.

Chi, Melissa. 2011. Government Aims to Attract 200,000 International Students by 2020. *Malaysian Insider*, September 13. http://www.themalaysianinsider.com/malaysia/article/government-aims-to-attract-200000-international-students-by-2020

Christie, Pam. 1996. Globalization and the Curriculum: Proposals for the Integration of Education and Training in South Africa. *International Journal of Educational Development*, vol. 16, no. 4, pp. 407–16.

Currie, Jan. 1998. Globalizing Practices and the Professoriate in Anglo-Pacific and North American Universities. *Comparative Education Review*, vol. 42, no. 4, pp. 435–59.

Davies, Scott, and Neil Guppy. 1997. Globalization and Educational Reforms in Anglo-American Democracies. *Comparative Education Review*, vol. 41, no. 4, pp. 435–59.

Department of Statistics, Malaysia. 2012. *Malaysia @ a Glance*. http://www.statistics.gov.my/portal/index.php?option=com_content&view=article&id=472&Itemid=96&lang=en

Featherstone, Mike (ed.). 1990. *Global Culture: Nationalism, Globalization and Modernity*. London: Sage.

_____, and Scott Lash. 1995. Globalization, Modernity and the Spatialization of Social Theory: An Introduction. In Mike Featherstone, Scott Lash, and Ronald Robertson (eds.), *Global Modernities* (pp. 1–24). London: Sage.

Green, Andy. 1997. *Education, Globalization and the Nation State*. New York: St. Martin's.

Haplin, David. 1994. Practices and Prospects in Educational Policy Research. In David Haplin and Barry Troyna (eds.), *Researching Educational Policy: Ethical and Methodological Issues* (pp. 198–206). London: Falmer Press.

Ilon, Lynn. 1994. Structural Adjustment and Education: Adapting to a Growing Global Market. *International Journal of Educational Development*, vol. 14, no. 2, pp. 95–108.

Jasbir, Singh, and Hena Mukherjee. 1993. Education and National Integration in Malaysia: Stocktaking Thirty Years after Independence. *International Journal of Educational Development*, vol. 13, no. 2, pp. 89–102.

Kamens, David, John W. Meyer, and Aaron Benavot. 1996. Worldwide Patterns in Academic Secondary Education Curricula. *Comparative Education Review*, vol. 40, no. 2, pp. 116–38.

Khoo, Boo Teik. 2000. Economic Nationalism and Its Discontents: Malaysian Political Economy after July 1997. In Richard Robison, Mark Beeson, Kanishka Jayasuriya, and Hyuk Rae Kim (eds.), *Politics and Markets in the Wake of the Asian Crisis* (pp. 212–37). London: Routledge.

Knight, Jane. 2006. *Higher Education Crossing Borders: A Guide to the Implications of the General Agreement on Trade in Service (GATS) for Cross-border Education*. Paris: COL/UNESCO.

Lee, Molly N.N. 2004. *Restructuring Higher Education in Malaysia*. Monograph Series No. 4/2004. Penang: School of Educational Studies, Universiti Sains Malaysia.

_____. 2006. Centralized Decentralization in Malaysian Education. In Christopher Bjork (ed.), *Educational Decentralization: Asian Experiences and Conceptual Contributions* (pp. 149–58). Dordrecht: Springer.

_____, and Deane E. Neubauer. 2009. Redefining Public and Private in Asia Pacific Higher Education. In Terrance W. Bigalke and Deane E. Neubauer (eds.), *Higher Education in Asia/Pacific: Quality and the Public Good* (pp. 33–47). New York: Palgrave Macmillan.

Lynch, James. 1986. *Multicultural Education: Principles and Practices*. London: Routledge and Keagan Paul.

s Motor Vehicle Industry: National Industrial Policies and Japanese
omo (ed.), *Japan and Malaysian Development: In the Shadow of the*
dge.
-2000. Kuala Lumpur: Percetakan Nasional Malaysia Bhd.
5. Kuala Lumpur: Percetakan Nasional Malaysia Bhd.
. The Mahathir Administration in Malaysia: Discipline through Islam.

the Authority of the Nation-State. In Albert Bergesen (ed.), *Studies of*
lew York: Academic Press.
inds towards Making All Schools Smart. Kuala Lumpur: Educational
on.
2013-2025: Preliminary Report. Kuala Lumpur: Ministry of Education.
tional Higher Education Strategic Plan Beyond 2020. Kuala Lumpur:

; Directions of Malaysia's Higher Education: University Autonomy in
r Education, vol. 59, no. 4, pp. 461–73.
in Higher Education: An Extension into the Modern Use of Analogues.
uy Neave (eds.), *Higher Education and the Nation State: The Interna-*
. 13–75). Oxford: Pergamon.
21st Century Skills, Education and Competitiveness: A Resource and
orage/documents/21st_century_skills_education_and_competitiveness_

oridization. In Mike Featherstone, Scott Lash, and Ronald Robertson
ondon: Sage.
Paradigm: Thinking Globally. In David G. Bromley (ed.), *Religion and*
ins in Theory and Research (pp. 207–24). Greenwich, CT: JAI Press.
nd Global Culture. London: Sage.
rials for National Integration in Malaysia: Match or Mismatch? *Asia*
2, pp. 7–20.
Education. *International Journal of Educational Development*, vol. 16,

id Miriam Henry. 1997. *Educational Policy and the Politics of Change*.

London: Routledge.
Turner, Byran S. 1991. Politics and Culture in Islamic Globalism. In Ronald Robertson and William R. Garrett (eds.), *Religion and Global Order* (pp. 161–82). New York: Paragon.
UN Educational, Scientific and Cultural Organization. 1991. *World Education Report*. Paris: UNESCO.
Varghese, N.V. 2011. *Globalization and Cross-border Higher Education: Challenges in the Development of Higher Education in Commonwealth Countries*. Paris: UNESCO IIEP.
Waters, Malcom. 1995. *Globalization*. London: Routledge.
Watson, Keith. 1980. Education and Cultural Pluralism in Southeast Asia: With Special Reference to Peninsular Malaysia. *Comparative Education*, vol. 16, no. 2, pp. 139–203.

NOTES

1. Most of these foreign-owned firms are from Singapore, Japan, the United Kingdom, and the United States (Ariff, 1991).

2. The eleven focus sectors in the National Key Economic Areas are education; agriculture; communication content and infrastructure; palm oil; health care; wholesale and retail; electrical and electronics; oil, gas, and energy; business services; greater Kuala Lumpur/Klang Valley; financial services; and tourism (Economic Transformation Program, 2013).

3. Examples of such countries are Saudi Arabia, Egypt, Morocco, Pakistan, Afghanistan, Libya, Iran, Iraq, Syria, and Indonesia.

4. See Ayoob (1981), Chandra (1987), Lyon (1979), and Nagata (1984).

5. The two main political parties in this religious conflict are the United Malays National Organisation and Parti Islam Se-Malaysia.

6. Muslim females are supposed to cover their heads when appearing in public by wearing the *tudung*, and Muslim males are supposed to grow beards as their way of emulating the Prophet and his companions.

7. Islamic greetings mean the use of Islamic terminology, usually Arabic, in daily speech.

8. Muslim dietary rules include not only the avoidance of pork but also the avoidance of meat from animals that are not slaughtered in the manner prescribed by the religion.

9. Religious duties involve saying daily prayers, fasting in the month of Ramadhan, paying Zakat (Islamic tax), and performing the *haj* (pilgrimage to Mecca).

Malaysia strives to be an international hub for education.

what it is doing - international recognition through partnership - research , Malaysian Education Promotion Centres

what are its challenges? opportunities?

W S O T

Chapter Sixteen

The Consequences of Global Mass Education: Schooling, Work, and Well-being in EFA-era Malawi

Nancy Kendall and Rachel Silver

Over the past century, there has been a notable global effort to expand access to schooling. The shape, scope, and consequences of this enlargement have differed regionally—from a rapid opening up of higher education in the United States in the post–World War II era, to the more recent accelerated growth of basic educational opportunity across much of southern and eastern Africa. This chapter examines the impact of the mass education initiative launched at the 1990 World Conference on Education for All (WCEFA) on one particular country, Malawi.

The 1990 Education For All (EFA) Declaration, signed by over 150 countries, was justified in terms of the expected expansion and democratization of the economic and social benefits that have historically accrued to school graduates, and of the power of schooling to foment sustainable individual, national, and global development. Indeed, EFA-sensitive mass schooling policies implemented since 1990 have generally increased overall enrollment in schools, and improved (though not equalized) school access for groups historically marginalized by gender, race, ethnicity, class, caste, rurality, language, and special needs. There is growing evidence, however, that these massified schooling opportunities have only occasionally expanded and much less equalized economic and social benefits in the twenty-first century, even as they demand significant state and family resources (Kendall, 2007). We argue in this chapter that the failure of mass schooling to democratize economic and social opportunity reflects in part the concurrent implementation of global economic and political policies that reshaped the types of services and labor opportunities available to most EFA-era graduates, particularly in countries whose economies are heavily indebted to international development organizations (IDOs), private banks, and other global capitalist actors.

This chapter asks how students, parents, teachers, and community and national leaders in Malawi make sense of the failure of mass primary schooling (promulgated as the core component of EFA) to improve their lives. It considers what their responses might reveal about the nature and workings of global development models in the twenty-first century, and about the reconfigurations of sociocultural, economic, and political relations that have resulted from them. We explore these questions by examining how participants in a geographically diverse range of Malawian primary schools make meaning of their schooling experiences and of their and their peers' post-school lives. In so doing, we bring into dialogue people's educational and life experiences with global discourses about the purposes and intended outcomes of mass schooling today.

Malawi is a particularly fruitful place through which to examine the late twentieth and early twenty-first century schooling massification project, as it has been at the forefront of adopting the global development policy package of which EFA is a part. While Malawi's global position, geographic and resource realities, and historical relations shape the particulars of this case study, we believe, and other researchers' work has indicated (e.g., Bajaj, 2010; Serpell, 1993; Vavrus, 2006) that by analyzing the increasingly fraught relationships among formal schooling, economic opportunity, and social status, the story that we tell here can inform our understanding of the consequences of EFA around the world, particularly in sub-Saharan Africa.

ANALYTIC TOOLS

Some anthropologists have characterized contemporary globalization as a reconceptualization of the relationships among individual, national, and global prospering through the lens of cultural, economic, and political neoliberalism. From this perspective, globalization represents a new model of international development; as Edelman and Haugerud (2005) argue, "development debates fuse with those on globalization—especially globalization as 'free-market' or neoliberal economic policies" (p. 3).

An anthropological approach to examining globalization and/as neoliberalism neither assumes a stable and unitary meaning to these terms, nor focuses primarily on economic systems or models. Instead, anthropologists have played a key role in showing the diverse ways that people and institutions around the world respond to the discourses, policies, and practices that constitute these subjects in their globalizing forms. Anthropologists have theorized globalization, neoliberalism, and development as generative fields of meaning-making in the twenty-first century (e.g., Edelman and Haugerud, 2005; Ferguson, 2006; Ong, 2006). Through their attention to the circulation of power as a central component of lived experiences, anthropological approaches are able to shed new light on how people understand and are affected by the broad policy and discursive shifts that have signified the expansion of neoliberal globalization. This expansion has most often taken the nationalized economic form of structural adjustment policies (SAPs) in poor countries, now implemented through poverty reduction strategy papers (PRSPs).[1]

SAPs, which have been applied in more than three-quarters of Latin American countries and more than two-thirds of African countries, consist of a bundle of policies designed to "adjust" the macroeconomic environment of countries. Common core elements of SAPs include lowering trade barriers, floating (i.e., devaluing) a country's currency, moving toward models of "export-driven growth," privatizing state companies and services, and cutting government expenditures, including by shrinking the civil service and either limiting access to or introducing user fees for public social services such as schooling.

While there are cogent debates about the successes and failures of SAPs and their successors, PRSPs, to restructure and improve countries' macroeconomic climates, there is little debate—even by their promulgators—about the increased social and economic inequities these policies have generated (e.g., Easterly, 2000), the stagnation of formal labor employment opportunities, and the increase in unstable, more extractive forms of informal or low-waged (often agricultural) labor in many of the poorest countries (Little and Dolan, 2005; Vavrus, 2006).

We engage Foucauldian notions of governmentality and of power as shifting, diffuse, and negotiated (Foucault, Burchell, Gordon, and Miller, 1991) to examine the consequences of EFA and SAPs in Malawi. The realities of people's daily lives are nested and bound up in systems of power that visibly and invisibly structure what is easily imagined or enacted, and we draw on critical researchers who have worked to explicate these systems (e.g., Ferguson, 2006). We employ an anthropology of policy lens (Shore, Wright, and Peró, 2011; Sutton and Levinson, 2000), informed by the work of critical and poststructural education theorists (e.g., Apple, 2013; Vavrus, 2006), to explicate both the scope and types of power that official policy may wield and generate, as well as the centrality of the meaning that people make of discourses, policies, and daily practices in fully understanding the consequences of global engagement in a policy field. As Vavrus (2006) notes, "What most ethnographic studies of policy share, then, is an emphasis on relations of power, on cultural practices that affect policy interpretations, and on sustained [researcher] engagement" (p. 119).

THE GLOBAL EXPANSION OF BASIC EDUCATION

As a significant literature has now documented, from the 1980s to the 2000s SAPs generally contracted state funding for social services, including education, even as the proportion of state resources sent abroad as development loan interest payments expanded. These effects have been particularly pronounced in sub-Saharan African countries pressured to adopt SAP measures, where, on average, per capita incomes declined, education spending dropped significantly between 1986 and 1996, and debt as a share of GDP rose from 58 percent in 1988 to 70 percent in 1996 (Naiman and Watkins, 1999).

It was in this environment that the World Bank, the UN Children's Fund, and the UN Educational, Scientific and Cultural Organization (UNESCO) co-hosted the WCEFA in 1990. The original mandate of the resulting Declaration on EFA aimed to provide educational opportunities for all children and adults through formal, informal, and non-formal settings. In setting priorities for overseas development assistance, however, many IDOs narrowed the definition of EFA from the right of every individual (adult and child) to a quality education (formal or non-formal) to policies and programs that supported free, quality, compulsory, and largely state-organized formal primary schooling for all children (Mundy, 2006).

This narrowing reflected the World Bank's strong and growing support for public investment in primary schooling, particularly for girls. This position was informed by a series of rates-of-return studies that indicated that state investment in (girls') schooling provided extremely high public returns (e.g., Psacharopoulos, 1987), and captured the World Bank's understanding of schooling as an investment in human capital. For United Nations organizations like UNESCO, which framed their interest in educational expansion in human rights terms, assuring that each child had the right to access government-supported schooling opportunities was a relatively comfortable "first step" in achieving the broader rights agenda that drove their participation in the WCEFA.

Despite the promises by many low-income countries to rapidly expand school access, and those made by wealthy countries to bankroll such expansion, there was relatively little change in educational opportunity directly following the WCEFA (Mundy, 2006). In fact, Malawi was one of the first countries in the world to adopt an EFA policy when the government introduced free primary education (FPE) in 1994.

As has proven to be the case for many subsequent EFA adopters in the region (e.g., Kenya, Tanzania, and Uganda), Malawi's FPE policies were introduced as part of what we here refer to as a global policy package. This global policy package consisted of three key aspects: FPE, political democratization (linked in various ways with discourses of good governance and decentralization), and SAPs. As has been argued previously (Kendall, 2007; Odora-Hoppers, this volume), the "global package" conceptualization is particularly useful in understanding mass education as a key aspect of a powerful new global development model whose core component is the neoliberalization of state-economy-society relations.

EDUCATIONAL GLOBALIZATION THROUGH THE LENS OF THE GLOBAL POLICY PACKAGE

Because EFA travels together with structural adjustment measures and governance reforms, schooling outcomes are fundamentally delimited by how these policies together reshape economic, political, and social institutions and fabrics (Kendall, 2007; Vavrus, 2006). This means, in turn, that arenas as diverse as school systems, state services, food security, global capital movement, labor markets, and the (re)constitution of social, political, and economic modes of survival and thriving become analytically salient, if not essential, in understanding how people make sense of what it means to be educated, what it means to have a "bright future," and what rights, responsibilities, and spaces of belonging can be found in families, communities, states, and the world.

IDOs have claimed since the 1980s that if countries adopted the global policy package—that is, if they invested in their human capital, "freed" their economies to be disciplined by global markets, and democratized their political systems—they would attract international investment and fuel economic growth and job creation. Thus, government investment in mass schooling was central to creating an investment climate that would lure transnational capital to newly productive economic hubs—poor countries with investment-friendly laws, relative physical security, and well-trained and cheap labor.

Contrary to IDOs' expectations, however, there is extensive documentation of the failure of SAPs to achieve their stated economic growth goals in countries like Malawi, a growing literature about how SAPs have often intensified economic and social inequities (including age and gender inequities), and devastating analyses of the extractive realities of global capital in Africa (Ferguson, 2006). Indeed, in contrast to IDO theories of what is attractive to potential investors, global capital has avoided states that have more fully adopted the global package and has largely flowed to countries marked by poverty, political violence, and instability. Global capital in Africa often invests in mineral extraction in destabilized countries, where international corporations can establish their own security systems and extract resources with little oversight by governments and few responsibilities to citizens (Ferguson, 2006; Reno, 1998). Common targets of investment have included Angola, the Democratic Republic of Congo, and Nigeria. More recently, sub-Saharan Africa has been the target of widespread land sales, described as follows by a pro-land investment business Website urging increased "investment" in Africa:

> Two-thirds of the targeted farmland is located in Africa, especially in sub-Saharan Africa. In Africa, reported large-scale acquisitions of farmland amount to 4.8% of Africa's total agricultural area—equivalent to the area of Kenya. Most of the targeted countries are poor with weak land governance, have high yield gaps and good accessibility. (How We Made It in Africa, 2013)

Malawi, for better or worse, has neither easily extractable mineral resources nor abundant farmland to target. Since the global policy package was faithfully adopted in 1994 by Malawi's first democratically elected, multiparty president, Dr. Bakili Muluzi, Malawi's economy and people's livelihoods have been volatile. There have been three significant food shortages, accompanied by wild spikes in maize (the staple food) prices; the national economy has become increasingly dependent on tobacco exports; the rural poor are increasingly adopting insecure, "multiplex" (Bryceson, 2002) livelihood approaches; the country has experienced limited yet deeply extractive engagements with global capital; and most people have remained desperately poor. The failure of SAPs to positively impact people's livelihoods might be best summarized by Lea and Hanmer's (2009) pithy statement that "by 2007 GDP per capita [in Malawi] had regained its level achieved in 1979."

In the following sections, we explore the disconnects between what the government and IDOs promised from FPE, what parents and students expected from FPE, and the socioeconomic realities of contemporary Malawi. We examine these disconnections through the meaning that people make of becoming educated, the connections that people trace between schooling and survival, and the implications of these disjunctures for mass education in the twenty-first century.

FPE and State Sovereignty

The consequences of FPE policies on state sovereignty and people's well-being provide a picture of educational globalization in economically dependent countries that runs contrary to the often rosy ideals promulgated by IDOs and many researchers and theorists supportive of global neoliberalization. As Ferguson notes, this may be one of the reasons that so many compendia on globalization largely ignore Africa. However, we agree with him that "a review of recent scholarship on the political economy of Africa suggests that a continent that is widely understood to be simply backward or excluded vis-à-vis the newly emergent forms of global society may in fact reveal key features of how the 'global' works today, and how it might work in the future" (Ferguson, 2006, p. 48).

In 1994, Malawi transitioned to multiparty democracy from a thirty-year dictatorship under Dr. Hastings Kamuzu Banda. The end of the Cold War brought an abrupt termination of financial support to Banda from the West, and in a few short years, a nascent civil society movement for democracy gained strength. IDOs began calling for a rapid transition to multiparty democracy, a freeing of the state-controlled economy to global market forces, and an expansion of civil rights and opportunities for economic and political advancement, including through schooling.

In 1994, Malawians voted in Dr. Bakili Muluzi as president, and he rapidly implemented the global policy package almost wholesale. Among other measures, Muluzi adopted FPE, cut the size and salaries of the civil service, rolled back rural extension services, privatized state corporations (including the agricultural markets, transportation systems, and education sector), floated the currency, expanded small business licenses, allowed smallholder farmers to grow tobacco, removed state subsidies for basic food and agricultural inputs, stripped village heads of their historical responsibilities as local judges, opened up the radio airwaves, claimed that democracy would bring absolute freedom, and allowed civil society organizations to promulgate child rights messages (Kendall, 2007). By the early 2000s, he began decentralizing government social sectors, including education.

Odora-Hoppers (this volume) demonstrates how current forms of globalization (here signified by the global policy package) have generally increased the power and penetration of IDOs into previously sovereign arenas of state governance, including education and financial policy-making. Both Kendall and Silver found this dynamic in their research with the Ministry of Education in Malawi, conducted in 2001 and 2012; in exchange for relatively small (but desperately needed) amounts of money to fund schooling efforts, IDOs gained an increasingly powerful seat at the policy-making table. IDOs were able to leverage these small resources because they amounted to almost the entirety of the country's education development budget. In the late 1990s, IDOs began to discursively and practically permeate Malawi's official policy-making arenas: they forced the government to allow IDO-selected civil society representatives to attend policy meetings, placed IDO contractors in ministry offices, and publicly divvied up management of development efforts in the education sector among themselves. As Mkandawire (2010) has noted, these relations and policy-making practices, which have accompanied structural adjustment measures in many countries, significantly blur lines of sovereignty, democratic decision-making, and financial accountability, and raise important questions about the government's power to shape children's educational experiences and outcomes.

While transformations in governmental and international relations are key consequences of globalized neoliberalism, we turn our attention in this chapter to the lesser-studied question of the consequences of the global policy package on people's everyday experiences with their schools, communities, markets, and governments. Our analysis draws on over six years of ethnographic research conducted in southern, central, and northern Malawi between 2000 and 2012. Our research designs were shaped by Bartlett and Vavrus' (herein) concept of vertical ethnography and Reinhold's concept of "studying through" (1994, pp. 477–79) policyscapes. In all of our work, research activities focused on participant understandings of the purposes and outcomes of schooling and included interviews and group conversations with students, teachers, parents, and community leaders; observations of school and community practices; and document analyses.

Educational Policy in the EFA Era

From the missionary era through 1994, schooling in Malawi was constrained to a minority of the population; primary schooling never reached 60 percent net enrollment rate (NER), and secondary schooling never reached more than 5 percent NER. There were significant differences in enrollment rates across communities, regions, and groups, caused by colonial educational relations and Banda's own political and religious biases (Kendall, 2007).

Before the 1990s, those who gained a Malawian secondary school degree were virtually guaranteed employment in the country's civil service. Those who completed a primary degree often gained social status in their communities, in part because of their literacy and numeracy skills, and in part through access to lower-level civil service positions. Schooling at each level was designed to "weed out" the majority of learners, creating an elite-generating institution that was nationally and regionally recognized: educated, male Malawian workers were prized in South African mines, for example, and until the late 1980s, the Malawian government actively coordinated these labor opportunities and worker travel.

In 1994, Muluzi declared immediate FPE. In a period of about six months, school attendance rose an astronomic 50 percent (UNESCO, 2004). According to UNESCO (2004, p. 3), "net enrollments prior to FPE had been 58% for girls, increasing to 73% by 1996; and 58% also for boys … increasing to 68% by 1996." While FPE opened the school doors to many more children (particularly girls), the financial burdens on the state (which began spending up to 27 percent of the annual state budget on schooling) and on families (who were estimated by the World Bank [2004] to still be providing 80 percent of public schooling costs through, for instance, books, supplies, construction materials, and volunteer labor) were extreme. IDOs provided some additional resources to support FPE, but they never reached the levels promised at the WCEFA.

Primary schools after the 1994 declaration of FPE (hereafter, EFA-era schools) are commonly described by international and government actors as being of very low quality, as evident in the low scores that Malawian children achieve on national and international tests of basic skills and the system's low rate of efficiency in graduating students (World Bank, 2004). This situation led one prominent Malawian academic to ask the following of governmental and nongovernmental policy-makers attending a meeting about educational quality:

> At policy level, we need to think about what constitutes a school: Why should we force our children to go to schools that are empty? Is that seriously what we want our schools to be? To me, it begs the question, what has happened to our society? What has happened to our communities? … *Because I don't see seriously how we can encourage people to go to school where the environment is so poor.* (Emphasis added.)

These common national and international approaches to conceptualizing school quality maintain the central understanding of schooling as an institution charged with (efficiently) producing "capitalized" children. We found in our research that, with the exception of widespread agreement on the desire for schools to teach people to read and write, IDO and governmental discourses of quality largely missed students' and parents' desires for and concerns about EFA-era schools. Government and IDO conceptualizations of EFA-era schools tend to reproduce discourses of sector-specific, international standards and expertise (for example, in assessment or early grade reading) as techno-rational solutions to improving schooling. In contrast, parents and teachers talked about teachers' declining social and economic status, the increasing futility of schooling for children's likely futures, particularly the expanding numbers of educated children who could not find employment, and restricted access to secondary schooling and the opportunities it was viewed as offering. Parents and teachers were speaking, in other words, about the social significance and economic power of being an educated person, and about the fraying linkages between schooling and a "bright future." Parents' and students' concerns about school experiences and outcomes point to the need for analyses of the sociocultural and political economic relations that impact links between school certification, formal (particularly public sector) labor opportunities, the social meanings of being an "educated person," and people's survival and well-being.

IDOs' Engagement with EFA-Era Schooling

Most adults with whom Kendall spoke in 2001 said that their understanding of and response to FPE was constituted by two contradictory narratives: what the Muluzi government had said that FPE would do (democratize economic, social, and political opportunity, and represent the state's full investment in all Malawians, no matter their region, ethnicity, gender, or religion), and the reality of deeply underfunded primary schools that remained academically oriented and test-driven, even as schooling was increasingly delinked from economic opportunities in domestic and regional labor markets.

The concerns of parents, teachers, and students about FPE can in many cases be traced to the global policy package and its implementation in Malawi. For example, there are remarkably low levels of resources available to each child in a Malawian school: Southern and Eastern Africa Consortium for Monitoring Educational Quality (2011) claims that the government's *goal* is to increase spending to U.S.\$6.58 per pupil per year by 2014, while the World Bank estimates spending per primary pupil at around U.S.\$10. Given current levels of spending, an increase in resources seems an evident prerequisite to improving children's experiences in schools. But Malawi, whose borders were determined by colonial negotiations and not concerns for sovereign sustainability, does not have the internal resources to increase FPE funding for all of its citizens, and the international community, despite its promises at WCE-

FA, has not provided this funding. IDOs have argued instead that the government needs to improve system efficiency and planning, and have tied funding to planning conditionalities.

IDOs' roles in shaping the daily realities of FPE are further complicated by the effects of SAPs and decentralization policies on the socioeconomic landscape in which EFA-era schools function. For example, World Bank restrictions on the size of the civil service and on the salaries that teachers could receive meant that teachers could not be trained and hired as they had been during the pre-FPE years. Thus, though not targeted at the education sector, civil service conditionalities have played a key role in the decline in teachers' status and salaries over the past twenty years. Similarly, within the education sector, IDO funding foci and conditionalities have determined and delimited what opportunities exist for Malawian students. In the decade following FPE, most IDOs refused to provide significant funding for secondary or tertiary education, arguing that such investment favored the country's elite. This created a politically untenable secondary school bottleneck in the country, which was only partially resolved when Muluzi unilaterally declared that existing Distance Education Centers would become Community Day Secondary Schools. Even with this expansion, secondary NER remained at under 30 percent, while primary NER approached 97 percent in 2010 (UNESCO, 2012).

SAPs also significantly impacted families' capacities to support schools, especially in rural areas. For example, the combined effects of the removal of food and agricultural subsidies and price controls, privatization of the agricultural market system, increased population pressures, drought, and AIDS stripped many rural families of any safety net that they had previously accumulated and made it much more difficult for them to recover from a year of bad rains (Robson, Ansell, van Blerk, Chipeta and Hadju, 2007), even as the financial burden of primary schooling was only partially alleviated by FPE and the costs of secondary schooling skyrocketed.

These examples are indicative of the power of people's daily experiences and evaluations of FPE to inform our understanding of the consequences of the global policy package—and thus of global neoliberalism—on people's lives and on the capacity of mass education to equalize or democratize social, economic, and political relations.

Imagined Possibilities and Foreseeable Futures: Delinking FPE from Socioeconomic Mobility

In Malawi, as in many other poor countries that have rapidly massified educational access over the past decades, there is an active negotiation occurring between the majority of students and parents and the global elite who are responsible for official education policy-making. These negotiations concern the purposes, meanings, and consequences of mass schooling in an era of global adjustments to employment and survival options. Data on employment in Malawi is notoriously bad (Castel, Phiri, and Stampini, 2010), but it appears that even as educational enrollment exploded, Malawi's formal labor sector shrank. Intra- and international labor movement patterns have also shifted, as low-salary or short-term labor opportunities have expanded in tobacco-growing areas and across the Mozambican border, and longer-term contract labor opportunities in South Africa have declined: Bryceson and Fonseca (2006) found that only informal, irregular labor opportunities and agricultural opportunities grew during the EFA era in Malawi.

Certainly, there have been elites created in the new Malawian economy, but as many students, teachers, and parents wryly noted, most new elites have not gained their status through schooling. Just the opposite, in fact: as one teacher trainee said, "Money now talks too much. These [tobacco] farmers have even openly laughed at us, saying 'you are educated but you are dressed in rags.' The children hear this and they look at us to say, 'Ah-ah, why should I come to school when there are uneducated millionaires?'"

This trend is not unique to Malawi, and it has posed a tremendous challenge to the "schooling for formal employment" discourse that predominated during the Malawian government's introduction of FPE. Indeed, as primary and secondary levels of school certification, formal labor opportunities, and socioeconomic status become delinked in communities around the world, international and governmental discourses concerning the purposes of schooling and the expectations that people and governments should have for schooling have likewise shifted. IDOs now explain that mass education is "necessary but not sufficient" for national development, and that the reason it is not achieving intended outcomes is because of low quality. This argument maintains the ideological purity of the neoliberal rationalization for investment in schooling, even as the contortions required to argue for continued state and family educational investment grow more complex. It is worth quoting a rather typical World Bank report (2007) on educational reform (this one on the Middle East and North Africa, or MENA):

> Education is a necessary but not sufficient condition for economic growth. Research on the MENA region supports this view. Per capita economic growth in the region over the past 20 years has been relatively low despite the improvements in educational attainment. Ironically, higher economic growth corresponded to low levels of education attainment in the 1960s and 1970s. ... One explanation is that the quality of instruction in the region is too low for schooling to contribute to growth and productivity. Another is that it is the *relative* rather than the *absolute* level of educational outcomes that explains the tenuous link between education and economic growth in MENA. Foreign direct investment, for example, would gravitate to those countries that have better education outcomes, all other factors being equal. ... Finally, the weak relationship between education outcomes and economic growth may also be related to the high levels of public sector employment, and low numbers of dynamic and internationally competitive economic sectors. (pp. 6–7)

In the new global development parlance, unemployment is a significant problem, but government employment is an even bigger one. Indeed, government officials increasingly tell Malawians that they should not expect the government to generate jobs for them. Instead, they should appreciate the government's investment in them through FPE, and they should expect and want to work for themselves after graduation.

For the most part, however, parents and students do not buy these arguments. They both continue to link schooling to desires for formal employment and to push back on elites' arguments that schooling can contribute meaningfully to the new (entrepreneurial) paths to success that both the global policy package and the Malawian government are promulgating. This conflict—between majority beliefs about what schooling should do, and elite discourses proclaiming a new ideal for schooling outcomes—is central to understanding the roles that schooling is and is not playing in improving people's lives. More importantly, it is essential to understanding the sense that people make of themselves, their communities, their government, and the global economies and societies in which they function and to which they aspire. In the following sections, we explore this sense-making in greater detail, seeking to explain how diverse actors understand the purposes of EFA-era schooling in Malawi.

EDUCATION, INDEPENDENCE, AND CARE: PARENT, STUDENT, AND LOCAL LEADER DISCOURSES ABOUT THE PURPOSES OF SCHOOLING

Schooling's continued importance is evident in conversations with students and parents. For most of them, school represents an investment toward a bright future in which people are independent, employed, and able to support others. Each end goal—independence, employment, and the capacity to support dependents—was entwined and linked explicitly to schooling in our conversations with students, teachers, and parents.

In interviews and focus group discussions in 2012, young students linked independence specifically to the ability to take care of oneself, one's family, and one's community. Silver had the following conversation with a group of rural Standard 4 boys:

> Silver: … Many people said that you come to school because you want to be independent; what does it mean to be independent?
> Student A: It means to be on your own and be able to support yourself.
> Student B: It means that you can be able to be on your own to support yourself and be able to support your parents.
> Student C: It is important to be independent because you are able to assist those who cannot assist themselves, like orphans.
> Student D: People rely on you; you become reliable so that in future people can rely on you.

Students consistently linked independence to a particular *type* of (stable) job after school completion, primarily in the civil service. With stunning regularity, learners in diverse schools answered what they wanted to be when they grew up: nurse, teacher, doctor, police, soldier, driver, and clerk. Just as students (and their parents) consistently linked schooling to care through the medium of (largely public sector) formal employment, parents also clearly articulated that independence meant financial security—the ability to rely on oneself because one had a steady paycheck. As one mother explained:

> When they [parents] say that the child should have a bright future, they mean that the child goes through secondary education, completes secondary, then goes through university and is able to secure a good job which will assist the child to be independent—not to rely on anybody else, so the parents should be able to say that, "If I die, I can die peacefully, because I know that my child will not have any problems. She is secure in life."

A "bright future" was also linked by interviewees to changes in urban locations and consumer relations. According to one nongovernmental organization (NGO) employee, "I think [students] have expectations that whenever they finish their education they will be able to find jobs and live comfortable lives unlike the life they are living."

Students, parents, teachers, and NGO staff members all said that students desired urban lives marked by access to commodities like packaged foods, business clothing, cars, and computers, and to services like electricity, piped water, television, dependable transportation, and health care. This vision of the good life closely mirrors research from around the region indicating that schooling is viewed as the mechanism through which to attain a form of "modernity" that is at odds with most rural citizens' own daily experiences, and that in important ways ruptures children's engagement with natal rural homes (Serpell, 1993; Stambach, 2000).

What it means to be successful in life, according to interviewees, is therefore very much bound to securing formal sector employment and then using that job to enable self-reliance and family care. The linkages made in the previous quotation are assumed: if you go to school and work hard, you will proceed in your schooling; if you proceed through formal education, you will get a stable job; and, finally, if you get a job, you will have a "bright future." It is not surprising that parents and students so consistently viewed this path as the desired outcome of schooling: this is the educational path to success that was forged through the elitist missionary, colonial, and post-colonial school systems in Malawi; it is the path that Muluzi initially claimed FPE would provide to all; and it is a path that many people around the world desire for themselves and their families. In EFA-era Malawi, however, each link in this assumed chain fails for the majority of children and their families.

Elite Discourses about the Purposes of FPE

In contrast to students, parents, and many teachers, policy-makers, head teachers, NGO staff, and other educated community members commonly framed the purposes of schooling in terms that shifted responsibility for self-care and survival to the individual—a shift that speaks directly to Foucauldian models of neoliberal governmentality and that appeared to undermine historically rooted and majoritarian-supported tropes that tied independence gained through individual employment to support and care for others. Silver had the following conversation with a head teacher of one rural school:

> Silver: I hear students and teachers talk very often about wanting to be independent. When you say independent, what do you mean exactly?
> Head: When we say someone is independent we are talking about somebody who actually has got enough knowledge and that one can perform his or her duties knowledgeably. … It might not mean that someone has to be employed, but when he is doing some business—when he is doing some farming—he should actually be able to transact whatever he is doing—the activities. He should have records or whatever and see whether he or she is actually excelling in life, you see?

For the head teacher, independence implied the generation of sufficient income to support oneself, and the possession of knowledge relevant to succeed in self-identified ventures, like small businesses or farming. The idea of becoming formally employed, and thus independent and able to take care of others so prevalent in students' and parents' narratives, is noticeably absent here. A policy-maker echoed this elite narrative, further linking individual income generation directly with national development:

> Learners having gone through the system should be able to generate their own income. Because when you look at the structure of education in Malawi, not everybody will have access to secondary education. The majority of the learners only go as far as primary, so for those that go as far—primary education should be an end in itself. It should … enable the beneficiaries to earn a meaningful life, they should be able to contribute to national development through economic activities like farming, engaging in small scale businesses and what.

Government and international education planners and policy-makers were often well-aware that parents' and students' goals for schooling were tied to stable, formal employment. They were also well aware that, in part because of the civil service retrenchment that occurred because of SAPs, these positions were not available to most children, especially the children of the rural poor. Their response was to tell people that they could and should not expect employment after primary, secondary, or even university, unless it was self-generated.

The efforts by educated and policy elites to reframe the purposes of schooling often sidestepped three central concerns that parents, students, and teachers raised to contest elite narratives and the new expectations they espoused. First, students, parents, and teachers argued that schools were not meant to teach the skills promulgated in the new elite narratives.

Students, parents, and teachers commonly talked about schools as institutions tasked with promoting one particular "modern" outcome: formal employment. As such, schools were not appropriate places in which to try to teach children skills (like farming and small business) that they could just as easily or better learn from family members or in informal settings. Many interviewees felt that farmers could and should learn from the government about how to improve their practices, but this learning should be hands-on and offered by agricultural extension workers who knew farmers and the land. People regularly mentioned agricultural extension models that had provided such support during the Banda era as good examples of such education; these programs were drastically cut in response to the global policy package. Teachers, through their very profession and its associated personal history of schooling, not farming, showed themselves to be inappropriate educators on these subjects. More importantly, however, schooling was meant to free people from farming; the notion that one would go to secondary school and return to farming was widely viewed as ludicrous; indeed, people who completed schooling and were "just farming" or "just sitting" were regularly referred to as failures or fools.

Second, parents and students pushed back against the assumption that FPE was "free" for rural families and should therefore be pursued for the intrinsic benefits of knowledge. Parents and students volunteered their time and labor, as well as provided financial resources to their schools, even though there were increasing opportunity costs to keeping older children in school. Indeed, given the lowering value of school certification and the rising costs of keeping children in school, students were more inclined to seize the rare economic opportunities that presented themselves, often leaving school to engage in "ganyu" (piecework).

Parents' capacity to keep children in school was also complicated by social changes that had accompanied the global policy package, including the norming of "child rights" and political democracy not as "Ufulu weni weni," or real freedom, but as "chite chili chose chomukufuna," or freedom to do anything. These messages were largely translated to mean that children did not have to listen to their parents or teachers, and that adults did not have to listen to each other (Kendall, 2007). Thus, if even a young child said they did not want to attend school, some parents threw up their hands and declared, "With democracy, there is nothing I can do."

Third, many (though certainly not all) students and parents contested the ideological basis of the new elite framing of schooling and its purposes. They argued that people wanted to help develop the country, but that the government had a key role to play in such development. The newer agricultural and labor opportunities that policy-makers described were, as people knew from experience, likely to be tied to self-generated, irregular, export-oriented, often risky, and often highly mobile (e.g., crossing national borders) opportunities that were deeply classed and gendered. They were not likely to be tied to formal schooling. People wanted to go to school, however, and people wanted to work—to better their own lives and to catalyze their country's development. Shouldn't the government, therefore, be responsible for assuring that the quality of life associated with previous formal, urban, wage labor opportunities was available to more Malawians? This mode of contestation pushed back directly against the claim by many policy-makers that rural citizens were failing to understand the labor opportunities that awaited them: people did understand them, but they felt that they were not the answer to their own or the country's development. They contested the government's and IDOs' claim that, once the state provided FPE, security, well-being, and opportunities for survival were each individual's personal responsibility.

In sum, IDO staff, NGO workers, academics, government employees, and the highly educated—that is, informants employed in the formal sector themselves—were the most likely to decry people's narrow focus on gaining formal employment through schooling, and to push for people to reconceptualize schooling's purpose as the broader acquisition of knowledge, either for its own sake or to provide individuals with the tools needed to become self-sufficient. Many adults and youth contested this reconceptualization, laying claim to their right to the economic and social benefits that previously accrued to formal school graduates and to stability in a form of post-schooling employment that would grant them independence and allow them to support others.[2]

VOTING WITH THEIR FEET: THE IMPLICATIONS OF EFA-ERA DISJUNCTURES ON GIRLS' AND BOYS' SCHOOLING PRACTICES

The new elite framing of schooling and its purposes was highly contested by many, but certainly not all, of the students and parents with whom we spoke. Patterns of contestation were gendered and classed in ways that deserve more attention. We argue that these patterns illuminate what happens to schooling in an era of neoliberal globalization. We move from the meaning stakeholders make around schooling's purposes to the impacts of economic and political adjustment on school-goers. We explore who stays in school and who leaves, the relationship between school-going and elite socioeconomic status, and the implications of these new patterns for national and global efforts to increase individual survival and thriving, socioeconomic equity, and state development.

Malawian schools teach to the Primary School Leaving Certificate exam, whose main goal is to sort out who can and cannot continue to secondary school, and who will therefore potentially have access to the formal employment opportunities that, while limited, still represent a payoff that largely accrues only to those with secondary or tertiary degrees (Castel, Phiri, and Stampini, 2010). Yet, Malawi's new elites are largely tobacco farmers and business entrepreneurs—that is, those who can take advantage of the new agricultural and informal labor paths to economic well-being opened up by SAPs. These paths of social mobility are not equally accessible to all, nor are they consistently linked to school achievement or certification. Tobacco farming occurs mostly in the northern and central regions; much of this land is controlled through patrilineages, and tobacco farming itself is deeply masculinized in terms of control of the resources gained through its cultivation (Prowse, 2009). Girls (and boys whose families do not control fertile land), therefore, have little access to tobacco wealth opportunities.

Effective entrepreneurial activities were viewed by interviewees as requiring at least two types of capital—financial and social networks—neither of which is primarily derived through formal education, and neither of which is equally distributed in communities. In a seven hundred-family study conducted in the central region in 2009, Kendall found that, in general, boys from slightly better-off families were much more likely than girls and very poor boys to be able to access these forms of capital. As other studies of the gendered nature of entrepreneurialism have also indicated, girls from wealthier families who could access such capital often explained that they still preferred to stay in school because many entrepreneurial activities were viewed as male activities, and girls faced social and physical dangers in pursuing them as unmarried women. In contrast, boys from very poor families, especially orphaned boys living with their grandmothers, did not face social opprobrium for entrepreneurial activities, but reported that they were often unable to access capital and relied on piecemeal labor to acquire a daily meal: they could not participate in more remunerative activities that required longer gestational periods.

Given these realities, it is not surprising that in the school in which Kendall's 2009 study took place, girls and a subset of high-achieving, very poor boys made up the majority of students who regularly attended classes in the upper primary grades. Wealthier boys were largely opting out of school if and when they could pursue other moneymaking opportunities. Girls and boys who stayed in school usually said they did so in the slim hope that they would have the chance to continue on to secondary school and university, and then into a job. Academically lower-performing girls were more likely to say that they did not expect to be selected for secondary school, but that primary school constituted a valued protective space in which they were not yet expected to fully take on adult roles. As a focus group of low-performing grade eight girls said, they understood how unlikely it was that they would continue their schooling, but the only other options they saw available to secure their survival were to get a boyfriend, get married, or have a child (which in this area would allow them access to land); become a nun; or farm with their parents. Very poor boys saw their only alternative to school as eking out a living through food crop farming and piecework manual labor. These shifting patterns of retention and attendance in the upper grades of primary school were mirrored to a lesser extent in shifts in enrollment and attendance in the lower grades.

Though most parents viewed enrolling all young children in school as commonsense, some parents resisted or fully devolved decision-making about whether to attend school to their child. The scarcity of seats at the secondary school level, coupled with soaring secondary school graduate unemployment rates, made the job of convincing reluctant parents and students difficult. According to one deputy head teacher, "We encourage parents to send their children to school so that they become independent financially or economically in the future. I have heard from some parents that it is a bit difficult, because these days learners will see form four [grade 12] leavers who don't have jobs, who are just idling around or staying—remaining at home and they [learners] become discouraged."

Schooling and Social Status

Indeed, this shift in attitudes toward schooling pointed toward a broader change in people's conceptualizations of social status and power. While during the colonial and Banda era social status was often tied to being educated, this link was being rapidly weakened by the lack of economic power wielded by the rural educated since the implementation of the global policy package. Research participants spoke of the increasing numbers of secondary school completers remaining around the villages, lacking work and "just sitting." One village head explained in 2012: "Those who can afford to do business, they indulge in businesses. But most of the students, they just indulge in piecework, like going to another person's farm and digging for payment, something like that. Others they just stay home and do nothing. They go to bed, wake up early, just wait at home, then go back to sleep because they have nothing to do." A parent described children as saying: "So and so was able to graduate from school, but he is not able to secure a job, so why should I bother myself instead of going to play or do my own things? Why should I go to school if anything I will end up like that person graduating but doing nothing?"

Bajaj (2010) notes similar trends in Zambia and writes about the re-categorization of (primarily male) school-leavers who cannot find employment as "loafers." We similarly found that, while education leaders spoke of schooling as making students more flexible in their capacity to pursue diverse, global livelihood strategies, in practice, secondary schooling was viewed as making people less locally flexible; no longer appropriate farmers, those who were not able to secure formal labor were being recast as a generation that "just sits." In contrast, uneducated people who made money through tobacco farming or entrepreneurial activities were described as playing increasingly powerful social roles in extended families and communities and were described by peers as having made a smart choice to leave school. Many interviewees said there has been an important shift in social status, from what they described as the "traditionally" valued characteristics of education, comportment, and lineage, to the new value of money. They argued that "money is now king," and that the power associated with having money had become a paramount consideration in social status and extended family functioning, even as new modes of wealth creation were delinking personal independence from care for others.

To summarize, the purposes of education for Malawian youth, parents, and teachers are multiple, but they are largely framed in terms of schooling for a "bright future," which includes independence, self-reliance, and the ability to care for family through (ideally urban) formal wage labor. The outcomes of EFA-era schooling—and particularly people's access to a "bright future" through schooling—are systematically differentiated by class, gender, social networks, and geographic status. These differentiated outcomes are affecting who enters school, who stays in school, and how much support children receive for school from families and peers. Though it has never been the case that FPE included all children equally (Kadzamira and Rose, 2001), our research indicates that inequitable patterns of school engagement may be expanding and hardening in ways that respond to growing economic and social inequities in Malawi and around the world. These patterns reflect the individual and familial calculuses that fuel the "feminization" of education and low-wage industrial labor around the world (Sassen, 2000), and explain the number of countries and communities in sub-Saharan Africa in which enrollment rates in primary school are actually declining. As early as 1998, Bredie and Beharry noted that low educational quality was an incomplete explanation for these declines; they called for an analysis of private rates of return and pointed to the consequences of broader economic relations on families' school decision-making processes.

CONCLUSIONS AND FUTURES

As elucidated previously, in Malawi, students attended school to access a bright future marked by economic independence through formal employment and care for others. Yet, since the introduction of FPE, neither formal sector employment nor secondary school opportunities expanded to match the expectations of primary school students and their parents.

While the path to economic and social status through schooling grew increasingly tenuous, students, parents, and teachers saw increasing wealth (and inequality) being created by means *outside* of the traditional trajectory suggested by FPE. One Malawian scholar explained the draw that tobacco farms in northern Malawi have had for many learners, as kids "see millionaires" made rich from their business ventures. She explained: "Like in Kasungu, Lilongwe, Ntchisi, you know Mchinji—*people are illiterate, but they are farmers; they are rich*" (emphasis ours). That is, wealthy Malawians like these farmers offer disconfirming evidence to students that wealth and success require formal schooling. Similarly, students talked about male peers who dropped out of school, traveled to Mozambique, and came back to display highly visible new forms of wealth.

Finally, many male students spent their free time watching video shows; these images of great material wealth from abroad—wealth that remains, for the most part, out of the reach of the youth now exposed to them—were increasing, just as access to formal employment and steady salaries in Malawi were, proportionately, on the wane. Ferguson (2006, p. 21) theorizes this phenomenon more broadly:

"Globalization" has not brought a global consumer culture within the reach of most Africans, and still less has it imposed a homogenization of lifestyles with a global norm. Rather, it has brought an increasingly acute awareness of the semiotic and material goods of the global rich, even as economic pauperization and the loss of faith in the promises of development have made the chances of actually attaining such goods seem more remote than ever.

Elite stakeholders (policy-makers and development organizations included) have responded to the patent failure of FPE and the global policy package to improve people's post-school economic and social well-being in two ways. First, they have blamed the quality of the educational product being offered by the state and doubled down on techno-rational interventions. Second, they have argued that people should invest in formal schooling for its value in better preparing people for informal sector work, whether as a farmer or entrepreneur. These framings, themselves reflective of a broader global shift toward neoliberal forms of state-society relations (Harvey, 2005), fundamentally aim to transform the messages that students and their parents take away about what they should expect from EFA-era schools, from their governments, and from themselves. It is a framing that many students and parents ridiculed, particularly as related to the claim that schools are appropriate spaces for learning how to be farmers or entrepreneurs. FPE was less and less an honored path to independence, and increasingly instead a last hope for those whose social networks and status provided no better options.

As financial opportunity and social status is delinked from educational opportunity, real and important changes are occurring in who attends school and for how long, and the purposes to which people feel schooling should be put. These new patterns are deeply classed and gendered, and they should serve as the basis for the next ten years of research and thinking about schooling's role in shaping economic, political, and social outcomes in Malawi and globally.

EFA garnered support from a vast range of global actors and institutions, representing nearly the full spectrum of ideological stances. For all of these actors, the data that we have about the economic, social, and political consequences of poor people attending EFA-era schools should raise important ethical questions. What does it mean to encourage very poor families to invest in educating their children when their hopes and aspirations for their children's betterment through schooling are tied to shrinking (and increasingly insecure) formal labor opportunities? What does it mean when schooling draws 27 percent of the government's funding and leads to both the dwindling of other social services and increased government dependence on IDOs? What are the ethical implications of having increasingly higher levels of schooling become "necessary but not sufficient" to even have a chance for desired economic, social, and geographic mobility in many places in the world? How do new discourses of the "educated entrepreneur" engage traditions of independence-in-order-to-care-for-others? And what are the implications of allowing IDOs and governments to delink mass schooling from the cultivation of "bright futures," which consistently include economic security, social status, the ability to consume "modern" amenities and products, and the capacity to care for dependents?

FPE, in its daily practices and lived outcomes, has begun to hollow out the links between schooling and a "bright future"—links that are, fundamentally, about the role that Malawians consistently say they expect their government and each other to play in assuring their economic survival and well-being (National Democratic Institute, 1996, 2012). Schools are achieving gender parity just as (and, we would argue, because) they fail to meet most school-goers' expectations. While no longer regularly linked to elite opportunities, EFA-era schools continue to be test-driven and therefore to teach most children that they are school failures. FPE also teaches people that their government is a failure: its investment in FPE was accompanied by a concomitant withdrawal in many other areas of people's lives (including agricultural and veterinary extension services, providing markets for produce and livestock, and subsidizing basic food and agricultural products). Yet, FPE is not affording access to a bright future for the majority of its populace.

This chapter casts a harsh light on the role that mass schooling is playing in shaping relations among the Malawian state, its people, and the international development community. It offers insight into globalization processes that, without necessary intent (see Ferguson, 2006), have negatively impacted many Malawians and their material basis for survival, and in which an unmet global financial commitment to mass schooling plays a key role in downgrading the state's sovereignty and capacity to provide services and opportunities to its populace. These shifts have their mirrors and shadows in many places and for many people around the world, and they raise key questions about the purposes and consequences of mass schooling for the global majority and their governments. If schooling teaches most children about their personal failures and responsibility to secure their own survival in an increasingly insecure world, what consequences is it likely to have on global relations of power and on people's survival strategies? If secondary or tertiary schooling is necessary but not sufficient to thrive in the global knowledge economy, when does investment in FPE become a boondoggle for most of the world's poor children, families, and states? Conversely, what formal and informal educational opportunities might address these issues? For example, structural adjustment measures have created a new Malawian elite—the "uneducated, millionaire tobacco farmer." What role might he play in transforming global relations of power, and how might agricultural extension practices raise his awareness about tobacco's effects on land productivity, the health effects of the pesticides used to grow it, the gendered dynamics of tobacco sales and family food productivity, the changing global landscape for smoking and its implications for future tobacco sales, and the rising tide of HIV infections that currently accompany seasonal tobacco payouts? What roles might be played by non-school educational institutions, such as initiation camps, which have been cast as retrograde and sexually dangerous by most government and IDO actors, but to which Malawian NGOs have long pointed in terms of their potential power to teach girls and boys new and different messages about what it means to be an educated Malawian woman or man? Are there opportunities for state, nongovernmental, and community actors to claim new educational spaces, for different global ends? And if there are, what support might such educational efforts gain from a global community that has proven incapable of fulfilling its promises to support the expansion of a formal school model that many Malawians feel is ill-suited to improving their lives?

Similarly, we might ask how policy reforms in other arenas might transform FPE outcomes. For example, what effects are land ownership laws having on women's capacity to accumulate wealth through farming? In turn, how does this affect their children's education? As AIDS continues its terrible march and the Malawian populace continues to grow and get younger, are there new village-based, state- and internationally-supported caregiving careers that will open up and transform the value of educational certification? Might changes in migration policies create new, easier, and less gender-segregated paths to capital accumulation? How might climate change and its resulting water and food shortages be better managed globally, so that Malawian families' survival is not so regularly threatened?

We ask these questions in an attempt to move EFA's universal rights agenda forward by identifying trends in people's lived experiences of the global policy package, linking them to global relations of power, and suggesting necessary critical conversations about them. Educated elites' focus on techno-rational solutions to low educational quality, and on the "backwards" mindset of people who expect schooling to lead to stable employment, limits our collective capacity to recognize and address the global structural inequities that shape FPE and that are reflected in people's consistent pushing back on the claim that there is no governmental or global responsibility to support Malawians' efforts to achieve "bright futures" through schooling. This resistance should remind us that EFA is not simply a technology to increase human capital; it is fundamentally a negotiation about who is responsible for people's well-being in the current era of globalization. As Ferguson (2006) reminds us, "to take seriously African experiences of the global requires that any discussion of 'globalization' and 'new world orders' must first of all be a discussion of social relations of membership, responsibility, and inequality on a truly planetary scale" (p. 23). The global policy package offered one particular vision of how mass education would transform relations among individual capacity, national development, and global capital. It is failing. We may examine its failures in terms of the new models of power, belonging, and well-being that are being promulgated in EFA-era schools, in an effort to (re)claim schooling for purposes and outcomes that better address people's desires for basic security and well-being, but equally for their desire to gain independence through care for each other. These can, and we argue should, be the building blocks for new models of global educational practices that lead to "bright futures."

Acknowledgments

Kendall gratefully acknowledges financial support from FLAS, Fulbright-Hays, Fulbright, Spencer Foundation, TAG Foundation, and the Wenner-Gren Foundation. Silver's funding was made possible by Save the Children's SUPER Fellowship program.

REFERENCES

Apple, Michael. 2013. *Can Education Change Society?* New York: Routledge.

Bajaj, Monisha. 2010. Intergenerational Perspectives on Education and Employment in the Zambian Copperbelt. *Comparative Education Review*, vol. 54, no. 2, pp. 175–97.

Bredie, Joseph, and Girindre Beharry. 1998. School Enrollment Decline in Sub-Saharan Africa: Beyond the Supply Constraint. Washington, DC: The World Bank.

Bryceson, Deborah. 2002. Multiplex Livelihoods in Rural Africa: Recasting the Terms and Conditions of Gainful Employment. *The Journal of Modern African Studies*, vol. 40, no. 1, pp. 1–28.

_____ and Jodie Fonseca. 2006. Risking Death for Survival: Peasant Responses to Hunger and HIV/AIDS in Malawi. *World Development*, vol. 34, no. 9, pp. 1654–66.

Castel, Vincent, Martha Phiri, and Marco Stampini. 2010. Education and Employment in Malawi. *Working Paper Series* 110. Belvedere, Tunisia: African Development Bank Group.

Easterly, William. 2000. The Effect of IMF and World Bank Programs on Poverty.

Edelman, Marc and Angelique Haugerud (eds.). 2005. *Anthropology of Development and Globalization: From Classical Political Economy to Contemporary Neoliberalism*. Malden, MA: Blackwell Publishing.

Ferguson, James. 2006. *Global Shadows: Africa in the Neoliberal World Order*. Durham, NH: Duke University Press.

Foucault, Michel, Graham Burchell, Colin Gordon, and Peter Miller. 1991. *The Foucault Effect: Studies in Governmentality*. Chicago: University of Chicago Press.

Harvey, David. 2005. *A Brief History of Neoliberalism*. Oxford: Oxford University Press.

How We Made It In Africa. 2013. http://www.howwemadeitinafrica.com/

Kadzamira, Esme, and Pauline Rose. 2001. *Educational Policy Choice and Policy Practice in Malawi: Dilemmas and Disjunctures*. IDS Working Paper 124. Brighton: University of Sussex Institute of Development Studies.

Kendall, Nancy. 2007. Education for All Meets Political Democratization: Free Primary Education and the Neoliberalization of the Malawian School and State. *Comparative Education Review*, vol. 51, no. 3, pp. 281–305.

Lea, Nicholas, and Lucia Hanmer. 2009. Constraints to Growth in Malawi. Policy Research Working Paper 5097. Washington, DC: The World Bank.

Little, Peter, and Catherine Dolan. (2005). Nontraditional Commodities and Structural Adjustment in Africa. In Marc Edelman and Angelique Haugerud (eds.), *The Anthropology of Development and Globalization* (pp. 206–15). Malden, MA: Blackwell Publishing.

Mkandawire, Thandika. 2010. Aid, Accountability, and Democracy in Africa. *Social Research*, vol. 77, no. 4, pp. 1149–82.

Mundy, Karen. 2006. Education for All and the New Development Compact. *Review of Education*, vol. 52, pp. 23–48.

Naiman, Robert, and Neil Watkins. 1999. A Survey of the Impacts of IMF Structural Adjustment in Africa. Washington, DC: Center for Economic and Policy Research.

National Democratic Institute. 1996. Can You Call Yourself A Farmer if You Don't Go to The Garden? Washington, DC: NDI.

_____. 2012. No Voice, No Power: Malawians Share Their Concerns About Citizen Participation in Government. Washington, DC: NDI.

Ong, Aihwa. 2006. *Neoliberalism as Exception: Mutations in Citizenship and Sovereignty*. Durham: Duke University Press.

Prowse, Martin. 2009. Becoming a Bwana and Burley Tobacco in the Central Region of Malawi. Journal of Modern African Studies, vol. 47, no. 4, pp. 575–602.

Psacharopoulos, George (ed.). 1987. *Economics of Education: Research and Studies*. Oxford: Pergamon Press.

Reinhold, Sue. 1994. Local Conflict and Ideological Struggle: "Positive Images" and Section 28. Unpublished doctoral thesis. University of Sussex, U.K.

Reno, William. 1998. *Warlord Politics and African States.* Boulder: Lynne Rienner.

Robson, Elspeth, Nicola Ansell, Lorraine van Blerk, Lucy Chipeta, and Flora Hadju. 2007. AIDS and Food Insecurity: 'New Variant Famine' in Malawi? *Malawi Medical Journal*, vol. 19, no. 4, pp. 136–37.

Sassen, Saskia. 2000. Women's Burden: Counter-Geographies of Globalization and the Feminization of Survival. *Journal of International Affairs*, vol. 53, no. 2, pp. 503–24.

Serpell, Robert. 1993. *The Significance of Schooling: Life-journeys in an African Society.* Cambridge: Cambridge University Press.

Shore, Cris, Susan Wright, and Davide Peró (eds.). 2011. *Policy Worlds: Anthropology and the Analysis of Contemporary Power.* New York: Berghahn Books.

Southern and Eastern Africa Consortium for Monitoring Educational Quality. 2011. *Quality of Primary School Inputs in Malawi*. Policy Brief No. 2. SACMEQ.

Stambach, Amy. 2000. *Lessons from Mount Kilimanjaro: Schooling, Community, and Gender in East Africa.* New York: Routledge.

Sutton, Margaret, and Bradley Levinson (eds.) 2000. *Policy as Practice: Toward a Comparative Sociocultural Analysis of Educational Policy*. Stamford, CT: Ablex Publishing.

UN Educational, Scientific and Cultural Organization. 2004. Education for All Global Monitoring Report 2003/4. Gender and Education for All: The Leap to Equality: The introduction of free primary education in sub-Saharan Africa. http://unesdoc.unesco.org/images/0014/001469/146914e.pdf

_____. 2012. *Malawi*. Paris: Institute for Statistics.

Vavrus, Frances. 2006. Adjusting Inequality: Education and Structural Adjustment Policies in Tanzania. In Benjamin Piper, Sarah-Dryden-Peterson, and Young-Suk Kim, eds., *International Education for the Millennium: Toward Access, Equity, and Quality*. Cambridge, MA: Harvard Education Press.

World Bank. 2004. *Cost, Financing, and School Effectiveness of Education in Malawi: A Future of Limited Choices and Endless Opportunities*. Africa Region Human Development Working Paper Series. Washington, DC: World Bank.

_____. 2007. *The Road Not Traveled: Education Reform in the Middle East and North Africa*. Executive Summary, MENA Development Report. Washington, DC: The World Bank.

NOTES

1. PRSPs have formally succeeded SAPs as the mechanism structuring IDOs' formal involvement in macroeconomic policy in Malawi. There are numerous debates about the conceptual underpinnings of the two approaches (e.g., is the differentiation of growth versus equity approaches meaningful?), and about the practical implications of the two mechanisms (e.g., do PRSPs sound a lot like SAPs because of undue IDO influence in the PRSP process, or because SAPs are good economic practice?), which we cannot review here. Many researchers have argued, however, that the structural adjustments that have occurred in countries like Malawi during the PRSP era are remarkably similar to those that occurred during the SAP era, and that it is more helpful to see PRSPs as a continuation of the SAP process than as a break. We would agree. For example, the 2012 floating of the Malawi Kwacha parallels the policy decisions (and resultant poverty-increasing outcomes for the middle class and the poor) that occurred during the 1994 devaluation.

2. Of course, very few people saw schooling in entirely black and white terms; interviewees also identified education's significance for knowledge's sake, as a moralizing process, as a method of fostering good manners, and as necessary for national (economic) development.

Chapter Seventeen

Globalization and Education in Post-Apartheid South Africa: The Narrowing of Education's Purpose

Salim Vally and Carol Anne Spreen

Almost twenty years since the first democratic elections, the promise of a post-apartheid era of prosperity linked to globalization and international competitiveness has been deeply disappointing for most South Africans. Inequality, unemployment, and poverty remain pervasive and seemingly intractable since the advent of democratic rule in 1994. The official average national unemployment rate according to the latest statistics is 25.2 percent (Statistics South Africa, 2013), although the more accurate expanded rate[1] of unemployment is 35.9 percent (Posel, Casale, and Vermaak, 2013). South Africa is also a country that evinces the highest level of inequality in the world with a Gini coefficient of 0.63 (UNDP, 2013). The massacre of thirty-four mineworkers[2] by police at Marikana in August 2012, reminiscent of the Sharpeville massacre in 1960, together with frequent protests around the lack of municipal services, highlight the deep pathologies that continue in South Africa and underline the failure of an export-led, macroeconomic policy to address unemployment, inequality, and poverty, exacerbated by the adverse effects of globalization in South Africa.

In this chapter, we wish to show how skills development has been promoted as one of the major interventions expected to address the racialized economic imbalances inherited from the apartheid era and examine how it relates education to economic rationales and success in international competition. While we briefly highlight and discuss only a few of these policies and initiatives—the National Qualification Framework (NQF) and Outcomes-Based Education, the Further Education and Training (FET) Policy and the Skills Development Strategy, we firmly believe human capital logic permeated all the major post-1994 educational reforms to the detriment of addressing inequality and building a socially just education system. This chapter ends with an examination of higher education under coroporate globalization including the privilidging of disciplines which have a purchase in the marketplace.

Instead of engaging with the structural failures of the South African economy, the dominant discourse blames the education and training system for its inability to address the demands of the local and the global economy and for the lack of skills among the workforce necessary for higher levels of economic growth. The "lack of skills" discourse has achieved the status of mantra and drowned out virtually all other conceptions of education's social role and purposes and forecloses any meaningful discussion about the complexities of the relationship between education systems, the demands of global capitalist labor markets, and society. In a situation of mass unemployment and inequality, this pre-emptive discourse is seductive, playing, as it does, into the anxieties and ambitions of both parents and young people. Sears' (2003) commentary about the consequences of underemployment in Canada is certainly pertinent too for South Africa:

> Students facing a dismal market are likely to be more sympathetic to the idea that education should provide them with competitive advantages. Parents may have some sympathy for [this discourse] as they seek out opportunities for their children to succeed. … Vocationalism is a central means by which education is being reoriented towards the market. The goal of lean schooling is to teach students how to realize themselves through the market, both by marketing themselves and meeting their needs through the market. (p. 78)

This seemingly common-sense approach embraces human capital logic and places the burden of responsibility squarely on individuals and their "deficits" while obscuring the real structural obstacles to procuring decent and remunerative employment. In effect, therefore, the underlying premise of the dominant global discourse is characterized by a strong concentration on the relationship between education and skills development on the one hand and the economy on the other. The "transition from school to work" problem is then simplistically reduced to inadequate career planning and the lack of "entrepreneurial skills" (Sears, 2003, p. 80).

In a related article on the World Bank's Education Strategy 2020, we show how the World Bank "views education as a means of accumulating human capital to increase economic growth, labor productivity and technological skills for the labor market" (Vally and Spreen, 2012, pp. 195–96). The article describes how education and training is transformed into a panacea for economic performance as it is assumed that investment in human capital and technology will automatically increase productivity and skills. The World Bank's Education Strategy 2020 promotes the need for an "agile" workforce—a current preoccupation of transnational corporations that require mobile productive workers to be distributed at short notice to temporary employment without the burden on the employers to carry the cost of training. In the concept note produced by the World Bank, we read that globalization and new information technologies "are pressuring countries to become more productive and competitive, a challenge that translates into a call for a more highly skilled and more agile workforce. As a result, education systems face increased challenges to equip post-school graduates with knowledge and skills relevant to a rapidly changing context" (World Bank, 2010, p. 2).

In South Africa, too, despite contestation, the language around skills development remains largely hostage to the power of corporate conceptions of global skills and knowledge. It fails to relate such a discourse to an alternate conception of the economy—a conception not dominated by the power of global corporate regimes and their interests. At the behest of globalization, education is increasingly being molded toward fulfilling economic goals in order to produce skilled workers to bolster the competitive edge of South Africa within the globalized economy. The articulation of this goal with present macroeconomic imperatives such as privatization and the reliance on market mechanisms has resulted in education being increasingly commodified and transformed into a service rather than a right or a common good. Consequently, social justice policies declared in formal education policies have been sacrificed.

Three critical influences on the post-apartheid government's skills development policies since 1994 are economic competitiveness, premised on the assumptions of global capitalist integration; the necessity to redress racial inequality through employment equity measures at the workplace; and technological changes to production. The political transition to a post-apartheid dispensation in South Africa presented new challenges to the various social actors due to globalization and the pressure to integrate with the rest of the world economy. Through corporatist structures and struggles on the ground, these policies were translated into practice. In this context, the issue of skills development through interventions in the "supply-side" (i.e., education institutions) is deemed to be "ideologically neutral." Such interventions leave relatively untouched social relations and the "demand side."

The particular transition—a process of "negotiated compromise" that left intact the power of the economic elite, albeit through new configurations of power sharing, and the nature of the present state—has had an impact on the policy choices made by the government. For South African big business and international capital, the negotiated settlement or political denouement between the dominant liberation movement and the apartheid government was necessary to open up market opportunities, a context aptly described by the late revolutionary South African scholar Neville Alexander (2013) in the following way:

> Capital is amoral. Ardent as well as "reluctant" racists of yesteryear have all become convinced "non-racialists" bound to all South Africans under the "united colours of capitalism" in an egregious atmosphere of Rainbow nationalism. The same class of people, often the very same individuals, who funded Verwoerd, Vorster and Botha are funding the present regime. The latter has facilitated the expansion of South African capital into the African hinterland in ways of which the likes of Cecil John Rhodes or Ernest Oppenheimer could only dream. (p. 34)

Today in South Africa the interests of mining, manufacturing, and agricultural capital shape the character of the state and its policies and are themselves complicit in erecting the structural barriers to high-quality education for the working class and the poor. Corporate culpability in acquiescing to the racial imbalances entrenched by the apartheid legacy remains unacknowledged. Globalization has deepened and extended these inequalities, through, for instance, business's ability to relocate to centers of cheaper labor in the world, the replacement of workers by technologies, the low levels of training investment in occupational skills following sea-changes in technological innovation, and the absence of a protective and supportive environment for workers. In addition, in some approaches to the issue of skills and knowledge as related to labor markets, much of the "advice" proffered to government by multilateral organizations such as the World Bank and the International Monetary Fund did not lend itself to important contextual and historical factors (Vally and Motala, 2013).

The reality is that low-paid and insecure jobs, low levels of investment in skills acquisition, unsatisfactory conditions of work, and the specter of unemployment are an inherent part of capitalist development, and blaming the poor themselves provides no greater understanding of the underlying causalities or any useful explanations. "Supply side" skills development explanations provide no solution to the problematic of the relationship between the lack of resources even to pursue the possibility of employment, the effects of low wages on demand, or the form and quality of work available. Focusing on interventions on the supply side alone avoids any recognition of the causal factors affecting demand.

This chapter is also aimed at stripping away the glib assumptions behind the global market-oriented macroeconomic policy and "supply-side" discourse as it relates to education policy. Emphasis will be placed on how attempts at international competitive advantage and the skills-orientation have shaped education policy and practice and resulted in genuflection toward redistribution and redress instead of effectively narrowing inequalities. Early analysis of education policy by Chisholm and Fuller (1996) demonstrated how the international and local political economy as well as the outcomes of specifically education-based social struggles shaped the narrowing of post-apartheid educational policy founded on individualistic investment in human capital. The democratic process itself has been frustrated under globalization.

It is not our intention to go through these debates but to give concrete examples of the often incoherent adoption and emulation of education policies (such as outcomes-based education) from the developed Western world predominantly in order to foster international competitiveness in a globalized economy (Spreen, 2001).

We further demonstrate the articulation between the "global" and the "local" is a complex interplay influenced by political, socioeconomic, and cultural forces and interests, and identify how many of these currently adopted post-apartheid education policies directly relate to global trends and have had the effect of undermining social justice in education (Christie, 1997). The global trend has relegated many educational institutions to a corporate model where survival of the fittest, a culture of competitiveness, and individualism are the dominant hallmarks. Where knowledge is commodified and marketized and often where courses and subjects that do not have an edge in the marketplace are being phased-out.

OUTCOMES-BASED EDUCATION AND ECONOMIC DEVELOPMENT

The resolute endeavor to compete in the global marketplace permeated most socioeconomic initiatives undertaken by the South African state. Education policy documents were not immune from this desire and are replete with exhortations to mold learners and institutions into this instrumental role. The neoliberal macroeconomic policy Growth Employment and Redistribution, introduced in 1996, displaced the Keynesian Reconstruction and Development Plan and resuscitated human capital theory, highlighting education and training as a key determinant of long-term economic performance and income redistribution. As in other countries during the 1990s, Growth Employment and Redistribution emphasized the marketization of education, public-private partnerships, efficiency, and accountability. These policies viewed the education and training system as a vehicle to improve productivity of the workforce and hence the competitiveness of the South African economy, while simultaneously providing rhetorical support for redistribution and redressing historical imbalances. It has been shown elsewhere that these two goals did not complement each other (Spreen and Vally, 2006; Chisholm, 2004; Motala, Vally, and Spreen, 2010).

With the advent of the NQF and the adoption of the principle of outcomes-based education (OBE), the new education policy for primary and secondary schools, Curriculum 2005 (C2005), was hailed as the centerpiece for the transformation of teaching and learning in South Africa. Launched amid great fanfare in late March 1997, the C2005 framework was promoted in the mass media as "an end to apartheid education," "liberation through a new kind of learning," "teaching for the real world," "education into the [twenty-first] century," and so on. There were also exaggerated claims made for OBE, namely that it would provide a panacea for South Africa's economic development (Department of Education, 1996). OBE was introduced in South Africa through the trade unions to address the "post-apartheid" challenge of ensuring the requisite knowledge, values, and skills base (Spreen, 2001) that would, in turn, "provide the conditions for greater social justice, equity and development" and align the curriculum to the "global competitive challenge," explained as providing the "platform for developing knowledge, skills and competencies for innovation, social development and economic growth for the [twenty-first] century" (Curriculum Review Committee, 2000).

The introduction of OBE in South Africa can be mapped to the global rise of competency debates with its emphasis on data-driven, evidence-based accountability measures of educational quality (Spreen, 2001). The emphasis of OBE on skills-orientated mastery of predetermined benchmarks had wide appeal for the goals of integrating education in training in South Africa. Reflecting this global skills-orientation, South African policy-makers borrowed broad vocational and occupational outcomes-based frameworks from Australia and the United States (see, for instance, Jansen, 2004; Spreen, 2004). The curriculum mirrored the curriculum statements and the organization of learning areas similar to those promoted in Canada's Common Curriculum. It also established accreditation schemes for transfer of credits based on Scotland's vocational and technical standards and created a version of an NQF that relied heavily on the New Zealand NQF (Spreen, 2001).

In many ways, OBE served to reinforce South Africa's buy-in to an elaborate global educational monitoring system put in place to hold schools and teachers accountable for delivering "quality schools" with "high achievement" regardless of public investiture in education and governmental services to address broad social inequalities (Spreen and Vally, 2010). Elsewhere Steiner-Khamsi, Silova, and Johnson (2006) describe the international resonance of OBE as "signposts of a new neo-liberal era in education reform that epitomized the language of public accountability, effectiveness and market regulation" (Steiner-Khamsi, Silova, and Johnson, 2006, p. 221). They argue that the global OBE movement has generally been part of a larger "new public administration reform that emphasizes data-driven or evidence-based accountability and panoptic surveillance of system performance that is consistent with Foucault's observations of the modern state" (Steiner-Khamsi, Silova, and Johnson, 2006, p. 222).

In many ways, focusing on OBE, which was introduced as an incredibly complex and grandiose curricular approach, resulted in the neglect of all other aims of education and helped create a climate where the only things that mattered were those that could be measured. Early critiques of OBE took issue with the fact that the jargon, complexity, and structures proposed created a "maze" that only experts could find their way through (Chisholm, Motala, and Vally, 2003). More recently, others have described how this confusion has only been compounded by the various new iterations and changes in the curriculum over time (Spreen and Vally, 2010). A review of the 2009 report commissioned by the Minister of Basic Education describes how the "wide-ranging policy confusion and inadequate support of teachers by the education authorities have bedeviled the implementation of the revised OBE school curriculum" (Pretorius, 2009). In these earlier critiques, the point was well made that "instrumental outcomes might be appropriate for technical subjects but not for more creative or affective learning. In many subjects the desired outcomes were inherent in the process of learning itself" (Chisholm, Motala, and Vally, 2003, p. 377). While some curriculum theorists have argued that a more precise technical and scientific approach to educational delivery was needed, specifically employing better time management and discipline in schools and the classrooms (Taylor, Vinjevold, and Muller, 2003), others suggested OBE required "more time and a more accurate intervention" (Curriculum Review Committee, 2000). We argue quite differently that continuation of the narrowed instrumental and technical approach to teaching and learning has ignored the main problem of addressing the achievement gap, that is, structural inequality and the impact of poverty on learners.

By focusing on outcomes, the more fundamental issue of the purpose of education is avoided. Rather than reducing disparities and inequalities, the curriculum has had a greater chance of being implemented successfully and better serving learners in well-resourced schools, with more qualified teachers catering to better-prepared students. While the provision of short-term technical skills in the classroom is possible and yielded some immediate results, many of the benefits of these interventions waned over time. A policy emphasizing curriculum reform and its related normative outcomes either ignores or downplays the real conditions in classrooms (often violent, overcrowded, and lacking in basic material resources) under which teachers work and students are expected to learn.

While most children in South Africa face a plethora of social problems, including hunger, poverty, HIV/AIDS, and violence (particularly among those children who live in rural areas and urban townships), specific conditions pertinent to the South African reality—issues of racism, sexism, the challenges of transition, regional disparities, etc.—were phrased in the curriculum in a bland and decontextualized manner. Official statistics show the extent of poverty, with over twelve million children (two-thirds of the total number of children) living in poverty-stricken households and an estimated 20 percent of children having lost one or both parents (Meintjes and Hall, 2009, pp. 77–78). Criticism aimed at teachers and schools that avoids examining these socioeconomic issues ignores the fault lines. The reality is that the single factor that more than any other determines a school's performance is its intake of students, which reflects the context and conditions that surround the children who go there. Generally, a school that is situated in a poor community will struggle, while one that is based in a more affluent area will prosper.

Elsewhere we have argued that outcomes-based education was "imported" without attention to structural factors such as classroom space and resources, pervasive poverty, and local contextual factors—for example, teacher familiarity with OBE, work pressure, parental involvement and language instruction support, and school collegiality (Spreen, 2001; Spreen and Vally, 2010). Many teachers have suggested that OBE is too time-consuming and requires "too many resources and teaching experiences that they simply do not have" (Spreen and Vally, 2010, p. 51). School-based researchers document a range of barriers to teaching in rural South African schools—including class size, shortage of teachers, lack of teaching and learning materials, poor infrastructure, and lack of parental involvement (see Kunene, 2009; Nelson Mandela Institute, 2005; Ramadiro, 2005; Spreen and Vally 2010). From the outset, OBE has had many critics, but even these were overshadowed by its false promises—the silver bullet of OBE to kill the old system and usher in economic and social transformation. Instead of addressing the local context of schooling and important infrastructural issues like building and resourcing libraries and creating reading and literacy programs, the focus of post-apartheid curriculum reform was on large-scale technocratic approaches to teaching and learning, rather than social transformation.

While an argument can be made for borrowing from other countries, much of the transference of the new curriculum was selective and from countries very different from South Africa. One cannot learn how to read effectively without access to libraries with a range of literature and books to read for pleasure. A blind spot obscuring the reality of an unconscionable situation with only 7 percent of schools having libraries (narrowly defined by the Department of Education as schools that have spaces that are stocked with books) and similar provision for laboratories (see National Education Report Card in Pendlebury, Lake, and Smith, 2009). For the greater number of schools in South Africa, not only are there are no libraries, but there are few books *in the classroom*, no books suitable to the bilingual challenge in schools, and very few laboratories, computers, or educational resources to support new ways of teaching and learning.

In contrast, countries such as Brazil, where the social dynamics and inequalities are similar to South Africa, were ignored. Worth noting is that the adoption and implementation of OBE marked a dramatic departure from earlier policy proposals, displacing initiatives that had currency with the democratic movement up through the early 1990s. During the struggle against apartheid, a rich legacy of alternative education ideas and vital education social movements came into being. The latter included People's Education influenced by the ideas of Paulo Freire and grounded in the South African reality (Motala and Vally, 2002), Workers

Education (Cooper, Andrew, Grossman, and Vally, 2002), and Education with Production (Rensburg, 2001).

A curriculum model employed by Paulo Freire while he was secretary of education of the Workers' Party administration in the Brazilian city of Sao Paulo has much to offer and would not have encountered much of the present criticisms leveled at the new curriculum and OBE. Unlike the top-down imposition of policy in South Africa, in Sao Paulo, teachers played a critical role in curriculum reform and curriculum became the centerpiece for a strategy of emancipation (Torres, 1994). Brazilian educational reforms also involved the active participation of the community at large and the contribution of social movements, respected the specific dynamics in each school, used the Freirean methodology of action-reflection in the curriculum and included a model of continuing teacher training, and employed critical analysis of the curriculum in practice. By contrast, in South Africa, the mass democratic movement was marginalized from the education policy and school reform process. The present narrow, reductive, and instrumentalist notion of education at the behest of corporate globalization is in sharp contrast to these traditions of the mass democratic movement. Yet as South Africa approaches the end of the second decade of democracy, those in grassroots organizations are increasingly returning to liberatory traditions that embraced a critical and purposeful education that recognized the importance of human needs, not human capital.

Increasingly, those trying to grapple with the seemingly intractable nature of the education crisis believe that educational reforms in South Africa have floundered because they have not always attended to issues in which the social class context of schooling helps determine redistributive patterns in society. Moreover, the focus of C2005 and OBE has been on individual disadvantage abstracted from its broader social context. The importance of community engagement, participation, and social mobilization through resurgent social challenge and public protest in moving toward achieving equitable outcomes needs once again to be revisited. Community based organizations, nongovernmental organizations, trade unions, social movements, and worker and community colleges have always been extremely important educational agents with a vast array of foci, whether health, environmental, agricultural, basic human rights issues, or simply education for leisure. The tremendous contributions of these organizations and movements to social change and development are well-known (Vally, Motala, and Ramadiro, 2009), especially in communities experiencing great difficulties particularly when the state withdraws financial support. The demise of the community-based organizations and nongovernmental organizations has been of serious concern. Vital civil society organizations involved with community education and development were severely weakened in the past two decades with donor funding shifting from the mass democratic movement to the African National Congress government. There is a need to resuscitate these organizations and to support those that have managed to survive to continue their invaluable contributions to building democracy and critical citizenship. This requires greater public awareness and community engagement, not one which turns back the tide in favor of socially conservative and reductive approaches to schooling. In a participatory democracy, education has an obligation to contribute to a sense of citizenship worthy of its name. Public activity will produce the energy necessary to revive the ideas, strategies, and passions which informed the struggles against apartheid education and reinvent spaces for teaching and learning that support social change.

Yet, the dilemma remains how to situate social development initiatives within an export-oriented and market-dependent macroeconomic framework—a framework that is inimical to the social justice policies propounded in formal policy texts. In the following section, we bring these issues to light by discussing the education and training strategies and the discourse on the skills shortage. These strategies rarely refer to what could be arguably the sine qua non of foundational skills formation: literacy and numeracy. We acknowledge that skills are important for South Africa's developmental needs but not for the fickleness of the international market economy alone. This should be abundantly clear given the current global economic and financial meltdown.

GLOBAL COMPETITIVENESS, THE KNOWLEDGE ECONOMY, AND THE "SKILLS SHORTAGE"

The uncritical acceptance of human capital logic wherein there is a direct relationship between education and the economy is most pronounced in the FET and Skills Development policies. South Africa's initial conception of FET was expressed through the Education Green and White Papers (Department of Education, 1997, 1998) and the FET Act (Department of Education, 1998).

Despite the marriage of human capital theory assumptions with notions of redress in South Africa's earlier FET policy, there was a clear danger that individual and institutional redress would be undermined. The race to create global skills and international competencies deemed necessary for the global knowledge economy ignores local learning needs and particular historical education environments. Like almost all aspects of South Africa's society, education and training are inextricably bound up with the history of colonialism, apartheid, and the particular form of racial capitalism that developed in South Africa. This historical context has shaped the nature and extent of such provision for different social classes and social groups in South Africa (Badroodien, 2004, p. 21).

This history is located within a framework of serving the interests of a global capitalist market economy driven by the desire to maximize profits (Chisholm, cited in Badroodien, 2004) but also to ensure that impoverished black youth in the rural areas develop the skills and knowledge to prosper there, and not migrate to the cities (Badroodien, 2004). The system inherited by the first democratic government had evolved primarily out of a technical training system that had, in turn, emerged in the first quarter of the twentieth century as a response to the extraction of metals and minerals and the development of the apartheid state (Badroodien, 2004; Motala, Vally, and Spreen, 2010). Importantly, skills development and vocational education provision were originally shaped according to the prevailing system of apprenticeships and the kind of jobs that were available for various workers in a racially constituted labor market. This sector in particular has been preoccupied with racialized and gendered social conceptions related to a "salvation paradigm" of the white working-class poor, emphasizing its contribution to regulate and sort poor white, African, and colored urban male and female workers "to take their rightful place in society" (Baatjes, Baduza, and Sibiya, 2013, p. 105).

Though small, this dual system (parallel learning on the job and in formal educational institutions) was effective at providing the skills needed in the economy and in the public sector, with the bulk of training occurring in state-owned enterprises, large corporations, and municipalities (Wedekind, 2013). With the recession of the mid-1970s, and political and economic pressure to broaden the skills base and create a black middle class, the system slowly opened up to young people of other color groups but became increasingly disconnected from the work-based apprenticeship system (Chisholm, 1983). By the time the first democratic elections were held in 1994, the FET system consisted of more than 150 institutions with very uneven quality, delivering a dated curriculum, and producing fewer and fewer qualified artisans (Wedekind, 2013).

These earlier policies must be read in conjunction with the current Skills Development Act, which aims to establish a new system to control and direct the provision of education and training and to guide the implementation of the NQF within the economic sphere. These areas are seen to be crucial to the knowledge economy. There is a danger that the urgency around globally competitive skills will allow employers and macroeconomic policies to determine the content of the curriculum and what is valued as knowledge. Furthermore, private providers have greater capacity to engage in competitive bidding and are likely to offer training only to those learners who have the ability to pay.

In this way, global competition has had profound implications for the newly revised technical vocational education and training (TVET) policy and practice. The renewed importance of TVET came into sharp focus in the last decade as radical changes in the global economic system, combined with scientific and technological innovation and transfer, demanded new (largely formal) ways of preparing youth and adults for the labor market. In South Africa, this view of vocational education is now more prominently attached to increasing supply-side human capital for the economy, as well as addressing increasing unemployment among the youth (Department of Higher Education and Training, 2012; National Planning Commission, 2011). Current programs and institutional initiatives around vocational education are shifting rapidly in ways that try to build a closer connection between skills and competencies for youth employment and the provision of strongly regulated institutional pathways from school to work.

Internationally, TVET has also recently resurfaced within the discourse of the World Bank and other international agencies such as the UN Educational, Scientific and Cultural Organization (UNESCO). For example, the UNESCO *2012 Global Monitoring Report* revealingly titled, "Putting Education to Work," focuses on skills as a solution to "reduce unemployment, inequality and poverty, and to promote economic growth" (UNESCO, 2012, p. 202). The report is infused with language from the realm of business, exhorting youth to develop entrepreneurial skills and "investing in skills which pays dividends" (p. 203). The report is particularly laudatory of South Africa's policy framework relating to youth skills development: "At least eight policies present priorities for skills development. They include the National Development Plan, the Accelerated and Shared Growth Initiative, the new Growth Path, the National Skills Development Strategy, the National Youth Policy, and Strategic Plans for the Department of Labour, Basic Education, and Higher Education and Training" (UNESCO, 2012, p. 208). Under this view, investment in TVET is seen as a key part of the success of emerging economies.

The importance of TVET is underscored in current national education policies related to the FET sector, the National Skills Development Strategy (Department of Higher Education and Training, 2010, 2011), and most recently, in the Green Paper on Post-school Education and Training (Department of Higher Education and Training, 2012). The key public institutions for vocational education are the fifty FET colleges that accommodate four hundred thousand students and are staffed by sixteen thousand educators (Department of Higher Education and Training, 2013).

Strategies for addressing job creation and reducing unemployment have been central to government's stated priorities. The vocational education system, centered on the colleges, and the Sector Education and Training Authorities have been the focus of the strategy. In March 2013, the president signed the Further Education and Training Colleges Amendment Act into law. This marked the latest stage in a series of reforms to the South African technical, vocational, and occupational education and training system. These reforms have introduced major changes to the institutional landscape, the qualifications, the curriculum, and the demographics of the system. While the reforms have been premised on a notion of making the post-schooling system more responsive to the needs of the labor market, and to a lesser extent the wider developmental agenda of the state, there have been a range of countervailing forces at play that have made the reform process contested and the outcomes uncertain. According to Wedekind (2013):

> One of the striking features of reforms in the FET College system is the continuity of the discourse *employed* to justify the reforms. ... The FET system has consistently been viewed as a vehicle for solving critical social problems and specifically for addressing a crisis in employment. Across the fifteen years under discussion ... policy texts and commentators have focused on the need for colleges to be responsive to the needs of the employer, and for colleges to produce learners who are employable. As new policies have been developed, they lament the same problems in the colleges: poor quality, lack of articulation, poor alignment with economic priorities and poor linkages with industry. (p. 91)

As in other countries, the response in South Africa has been reorienting its TVET system in order to serve business and industry interests, and to transfer responsibility for TVET policy and practice from education to labor market needs (Baatjes, Baduza, and Sibiya, 2013). Baatjes and others suggest, "the modernisation of the skills development regime in South Africa is driven by human capital theory that advocates infinite re-skilling and perpetual and rigorous training programmes as the solution to economic problems" (Baatjes, Baduza, and Sibiya, 2013, pp. 112–13). Investment in the education of individuals is therefore seen as the solution to all the structural problems of the economy. According to these authors:

> The role of vocational education is being framed within a context of: (a) an increase in the levels of "formal" unemployment above 25%; (b) a call for an 8-9% economic growth requirement set as the target for creating employment; (c) an acknowledgement of perpetual crises in education marked by fiscal constraints, teacher strikes and student unrest; (d) relentless socio-economic struggles of the poor manifested in service delivery protests; and (e) South Africa as the society that evinces the greatest level of inequality in the world. (Baatjes, Baduza, and Sibiya, 2013, p. 101)

However, the current expansion of TVET comes at a time when there are not enough jobs available in the economy *for anyone*, including those with university degrees or with substantial qualifications through vocational education and training. Moreover, the increasing joblessness and underemployment among graduates is now being explained as a failure of the education system, including a lack of proper work-based learning or relevant curricula that do not provide the proper skills required by the labor market.

Despite the clear lack of jobs available in the economy to absorb "skilled" workers, over the next fifteen years the South African government has planned to increase enrollment in vocational education from four hundred thousand to four million students (Department of Higher Education and Training, 2012). And, while there has been a great push to expand vocational education in hopes that it will address the stubbornly high unemployment rate, there remains significant resistance from young people to participate in vocational education due to its failure to produce employment, as well as its traditional association with low-wage jobs and inferior academic status.

With the rapid expansion of TVET (increasingly provided by and aligned with industrial needs), scholars have warned against the narrowing orientation of vocational education as technical training that, among others, teaches and produces skills that limit the type of employment possible to youth (Baatjes, Baduza, and Sibiya, 2013; Vally and Motala, 2013). A more nuanced understanding of education for employability needs to be developed—including "socially useful" employment. Adult educators need to understand the learning and teaching experience in more complex ways than is usually associated with projects that aim to enhance employability such as industry partnerships or work experience programmes (McGrath, et al., 2010). For example, "employability skill sets" need to be differentiated between those required to access work, those required to do the work, those required to function in the workplace, and those required to progress (Wedekind, 2013).

In their critique of adult education programs, Baatjes et al. (2013) refer to Collins' notion that human capital–induced tradition of adult education, which is now most prevalent in vocational education and undermines the prospects of achieving an emancipatory, critical practice of adult education (Collins, 1991, p. 16). At the heart of this critique is a concern about the deskilling effects of educators brought about by an uncritical embrace of technicist formulations and training models and the reduction of educators as mere facilitators of learning and training or "corporate drones." Elsewhere, Baatjes and Hamilton (2012) have highlighted the problem of warehousing of thousands of South African youth in narrowly constructed training programs, particularly from the working class who, despite earning certificates and requisite skills, struggle to make their way into employment in the formal labor market. These youth, like their counterparts in countries such as Portugal, Spain, Greece, and Italy where youth unemployment is estimated as high as 52 percent, require a progressive and democratic vocational education system that affords them training, dignity, adequate remuneration, and socially useful employment (McKinsey Center for Government, 2012, p. 11).

While we are, for various reasons, critical of the narrow utilitarian purposes and technicist views of human capital theory and its attendant deficit, we are not arguing that education and training have no role to play in economic development. Rather, the motivation for education and training must come from an approach to economic and social development which recognizes the interrelatedness of society and the economy where human needs dominate (Walters, 1997). Education and training cannot be the panacea for economic performance and it certainly should not be used to conceal the intrinsic weakness of the economic structure and unequal ways in which employment is distributed. Baatjes et al. (2013) explain, "In more recent times, educators in vocational education have been recast as 'training entrepreneurs' or 'service providers' whilst students have been reframed as 'customers.' Given the critical turn to market-driven vocational education, the urgency to retrieve, renew and advance education as a vocation has become imperative" (p. 114). These authors propose a transformation for adult education which "arms adult educators with the ability to create and exercise a more holistic and democratic practice" (Baatjes, Baduza, and Sibiya, 2013, p. 114). Their focus on building a transformative pedagogy of vocational education is important, particularly in South Africa, because of the lack of robust debate about a philosophical orientation toward vocational education in post-school education.

Similarly, we suggest that education and training strategies need to confront a number of critical issues. First, a nation's competitive advantage in the global economy is often based on workers' disadvantage. The kind of training that would foster more democratic forms of work organization and address developmental issues will not necessarily be the same as that which would increase competitiveness. Second, the concept of "social development" is not adequately explained in the education and training discourse. Where it is referred to, it is linked to "economic growth." This fits into the macroeconomic conception that growth leads automatically to increased well-being of the population. This notion prioritizes skills, which boost productivity and competitiveness, but undervalues or neglects those developmental skills necessary to sustain significant numbers of people outside the formal economy. These are the very skills that make the country not only materially but also culturally prosperous. It is questionable whether industry-led apprenticeships will adequately address this issue. It has been suggested that skills can be developed in a variety of environments and that other training programs should coexist with apprenticeships (Vally and Motala, 2013). Also, trainees are paid well below prevailing industry rates. Companies might well be prepared to support school leavers and young workers while they go through apprenticeships, but once they qualify and are entitled to higher wages they are likely to be retrenched.

Without a fundamental restructuring of the South African economy, there can be no meaningful skills development agenda. While the efforts of government through various policies to encourage artisanal training and vocational education can be useful, these must be articulated within an economic structure that is far more equitable and democratic, allowing for a wider range of economic activities which are not constrained by the needs of a dominant global economy driven by the logic of its accumulation path. This is crucial for the progressive alternative approaches that seek to make sense of the skills development question within a rapidly changing landscape of political and economic development in South Africa. It is little wonder then that over the past two decades education and training through human capital and instrumental learning oriented to narrow economic interests inculcates a particular philosophical orientation significantly shaping and affecting the views and purpose of education. Higher education, like schooling and TVET, has also been narrowed to meet the interests of the global knowledge economy (see Baatjes, Spreen, and Vally, 2012).

HIGHER EDUCATION AND THE KNOWLEDGE ECONOMY

Elsewhere we have discussed how the changing nature of the South African state (from apartheid to neoliberalism) has created a particular relationship with higher education based on the states orientation to the global economy (Baatjes, Spreen, and Vally, 2012). The neoliberal transformation in higher education can be viewed directly through the mergers of academic institutions, user fees, budgetary cutbacks, and the introduction of new funding formulas. These measure should be seen against the backdrop of the competition between public and private institutions. Higher education in South Africa, despite nominally being transformed, continues stratification and exclusion. Reconfiguring the tertiary landscape—a consequence of the racial imaginations of the erstwhile apartheid regime—has not resulted in a substantially reformed system. In Baatjes et al. (2012, p. 140), we argue that "the result of the efforts of the post-apartheid bureaucrats and managers has, in fact, been the elaboration of a differentiated system, one that in the contemporary case, is designed to address market-driven skills and economic demands, global competition, and cost-effiency through increased privatization, often at the cost of equity and including."

Beginning with the merger process initiatied in the late 1990s, the number of higher education institutions was reduced from thirty-six to twenty-one and the number of colleges from 120 to 50 (Council on Higher Education, 2007, p. 22). Teacher training colleges were closed down and a few were incorporated into universities. The rationalization process primarily involved historically "white" insitutions absorbing and reconfiguring formerly "black" institutions. Together with the introduction of particular form of knowledge production discussed subsequently, universities also adopted a corporate culture as the appropriate form of management and leadership. As in other countries, the adoption of the "corporate-modeled, profit-protocol university" (Williams, 2001, p. 21) in South Africa, with its "focus on productivity and endowments fosters an understanding of transformation that is in total opposition to the role that universities are meant to play in addressing the wide range of socio-ceonomic problems in South African society" (Baatjes, Spreen, and Vally, 2012, p. 149).

The views of Manuel Castells on the knowledge-based economy and the information society have been especially influential in South Africa, particularly the impact of these on the socioeconomic and cultural dimensions of higher education (Castells and Cardoso, 2006). Neville Alexander addresses Castells' adoption of the "knowledge economy" in relation to academic transformations that are now taking place in higher education worldwide and its implications for teaching and scholarship, the privileging of the STEM (science, technology, engineering, and mathematics) disciplines relative to liberal arts and human sciences, and the privatization of the public education sector.

> [T]he third capitalist industrial revolution has brought about a symbiotic, mutually reinforcing, relationship between university researchers, especially in the STEM disciplines, and trans-national corporations that are heavily dependent on the knowledge produced in the relevant research centres. … In order to maintain international competitiveness, these corporations push for governments to design national systems of innovation. One consequence, privatization, touches the entire educational spectrum. The FET sector (including vocational education and other post-secondary schools) increasingly finds itself inhabiting and operating within a privatized world [that functions with a view] towards attracting corporate sponsorships and a client base (student as consumer) to replace dwindling state funding. (Alexander, 2014, p. 63)

There have been many debates about the managerial or corporatized university across all institutions of higher learning in South Africa since the late 1990s. Universities increasingly have to raise their own funding, most often from the private sector and in the process modify curriculum and programs to meet rapidly changing market needs (Baatjes, Spreen, and Vally, 2012). In the process, long established departments (most notably within the humanities and social sciences) that fail to cater specifically to market needs are culled. While previously, TVET would have served as a lever almost exclusively for the disadvantaged, there are now higher education courses designed with specific niche training needs in mind, and entry for disadvantaged students in these sectors is determined by ever increasing fiscal and qualification barriers (Baatjes, Spreen, and Vally, 2012).

Alexander (2014) speaks to the importance of countering an education system that reproduces economic and social inequality:

> Instead of human beings trying to see what is common among people and individuals, the tendency is strengthened to view people as potential clients and exploitable entities which can be instrumentalised for one's own personal benefit or for that of one's in-group. Difference, instead of constituting a bridge towards understanding the intrinsic value of diversity—biological, cultural and political—becomes a springboard for xenophobic stereotyping and latent social conflict. To put it differently, the emphasis which is, justifiably, placed on the STEM disciplines in the context of the systemically determined desire to be innovative and to remain competitive runs the danger of throwing out the baby of humanity with the bathwater of "irrelevant" subjects and knowledge. The emphasis that is, consequently, put on the quantifiability of outcomes and of knowledge itself simply sweeps away all nuance, all understanding of complexity and contradiction and creates the illusion of a simple, linear universe in which, once anything has a number, it is in some sense "valuable." This is not a mere issue of curricular adaptation; it requires a complete rethink of the meaning of the curriculum in both its global commonalities and its regional, national and local peculiarities. It requires a rethinking of the relationship between tradition and modernity if we in the economic South are not simply to become economode photocopies of the "advanced" North. (Alexander, 2013a, p. 66)

If higher education and TVET are thought to be an essential component of the knowledge economy with unprecedented leverage then, as Alexander argues, it should be used precisely in order to narrow this gap. He asks, "is it morally and politically defensible to use public revenues, dispensed via government and universities, to maximise profits for corporate entities which appropriate such profits for their shareholders? ... In the face of the global reality that more than two-thirds of humanity are excluded from these circuits, this is culpable naivety at best and intellectual dishonesty at worst" (Alexander, 2014, p. 64).

Civil society or, more precisely, the majority of South Africans excluded from accessing higher education institutions, in some sense is one of the main constituencies to which any university or post-secondary system, especially in the South, has to be accountable.

CONCLUSION: GLOBALIZATION FROM BELOW

One of our concerns has been the role of educational institutions as democratic sites of learning in educating citizens and encouraging a commitment to social change and increasing levels of social equality. In the South African context, there is a strong tradition of university academics and post-graduate students working closely with civil society, understood as the ensemble of people's organizations and grassroots structures, including trade unions, civic, faith-based and sports associations, student bodies, rural and women's groups, and many others. Discussing the social justice aims of education, Alexander refers to the work of Martha Nussbaum who has spoken out "against the commodification and vulgarisation of knowledge through the assault on the liberal arts curricula" and suggests that universities, instead of educating and training clients and service providers, ought to have as their main objective the education of global citizens (Alexander, 2014, p. 65). According to Nussbaum (2010), global citizenship

> requires a lot of factual knowledge and students might get this without a humanistic education— for example, from absorbing the facts in standardized textbooks. ... Responsible citizenship requires, however, a lot more: the ability to assess historical evidence, to use and think critically about economic principles, to assess accounts of social justice, to speak a foreign language, to appreciate the complexities of the major world religions. ... World history and economic understanding ... must be humanistic and critical if they are to be at all useful in forming intelligent global citizens, and they must be taught alongside the study of religion and of philosophical theories of justice. Only then will they supply a useful foundation for the public debates that we must have if we are to cooperate in solving major human problems. (pp. 93–94)

The philosophical orientation toward any educational sub-sector determines not only the meaning and purpose of that system, but also shapes the curricula and pedagogy in relation to beliefs about its learners. Engagement with alternative forms of education become necessary and urgent at a time when current instrumentalist notions of education are ostensibly tied to a role in addressing poverty, inequality, and unemployment without reference to the complexities of deeply rooted economic systems underpinned by the ideology of neoliberal globalization and the wide-spread failures of free-market economic systems (Anderson, Brown, and Rushbrook, 2008; Brown, Lauder, and Ashton, 2010). According to Wedekind (2013), these realities require us to engage more rigorously with liberatory forms of education that offer much better and broader learning outcomes than the dominant mechanistic and technicist perspectives that drive the different sub-systems of education in South Africa.

Progressive educators should play a key role in building education institutions and pedagogical practices linked to a vision of a society that embraces social justice, economic equality, and sustainable development. The larger project of progressive education is framed as education that fosters fundamental democratic learning principles and the preparation of students for active citizenship. Vocational education in particular should therefore not limit the aspirations of students to narrow technicist skills and credentials but rather increase their range of social and occupational possibilities. The broader goals of education in a democratic society must support all citizens with the opportunities for intellectual growth, personal enrichment, and social improvement. Education should therefore also oppose the reproductive and anti-democratic outcomes of narrowly conceived occupational education by responding to the needs of students rather than those of industry. As Baatjes et al. (2013) suggest, "In fact, democratic vocational education should foster intellectual capability in students to change an industrial infrastructure, rather than having their lives and work determined by labour force requirements" (p. 115).

Finally, we concur with Henry (1999) that at the international level it is more possible today to imagine alliances between social groups battered by the vagaries of the world market. In fact, globalization itself, through new technologies and the worldwide flow of ideas and information, provides opportunities to find a common language with which to confront the various destructive aspects of capitalism. We need globalization from below through unions, women's movements, and other global alliances and networks in order to produce an alternative praxis to corporate globalization.

REFERENCES

Alexander, Neville. 2014. Implications of the University's Third Mission, with Special Reference to South Africa. In Salim Vally and Enver Motala (eds.), *Education, the Economy and Society* (pp. 59–67). Pretoria: UNISA Press.

_____. 2013. South Africa Today: The Moral Responsibility of Intellectuals. In Hanif Vally and Maureen Issacson (eds.), *Enough is a Feast: A Tribute to Neville Alexander, 22 October 1936-27 August 2012*. Johannesburg: Foundation for Human Rights.

Anderson, Damon, Mike Brown, and Peter Rushbrook. 2008. Vocational Education and Training. In Griff Foley (ed.), *Dimensions of Adult Learning: Adult Education and Training in a Global Era* (pp. 234–50). Berkshire: Open University Press.

Baatjes, Britt, and Sherri Hamilton. 2012. Blade's Paper Fails to Make the Cut. http://mg.co.za/article/2012-01-20-blades-paper-fails-to-make-the-cut/

Baatjes, Ivor, Uthando Baduza,and Anthony Tolika Sibiya. 2013. Building a Transformative Pedagogy in Vocational Education in South Africa. In Salim Vally and Enver Motala (eds.), *Education, the Economy and Society* (pp. 96–120). Pretoria: UNISA Press.

Baatjes, Ivor, Carol Anne Spreen, and Salim Vally. 2012. The Broken Promise of Neoliberal Restructuring of South African Higher Education. In Brian Pusser, Simon Marginson, and Imanol Odorika (eds.), *Universities and the Public Sphere: Knowledge Creation and State Building in the Era of Globalization* (pp. 139–59). New York: Routledge.

Badroodien, Azeem. 2004. Technical and Vocational Education Provision in South Africa from 1920 to 1970. In Simon McGrath, Azeem Badroodien, Andre Kraak, and Lorna Unwin (eds.), *Shifting Understanding of Skills in South Africa—Overcoming the Historical Imprint of a Low Skills Regime* (pp. 20-45). Cape Town: HSRC Press.

Bond, Patrick. 2012. World Bank's Jim Kim Goes to Joburg—But Will He Miss Maikana and Medupi? *Counterpunch*, September 5. http://www.counterpunch.org/2012/09/05/world-banks-jim-yong-kim-comes-to-south-africa/

Brown, Phillip, Hugh Lauder, and David Ashton. 2010. *The Global Auction: The Broken Promises of Education, Jobs, and Incomes*. Oxford: Oxford University Press.

Castells, Manuel, and Fernando Henrique Cardoso (eds.). 2006. *The Network Society: From Knowledge to Policy*. Baltimore: Center for Transatlantic Relations, Paul H. Nitze School of Advanced International Studies, Johns Hopkins University.

Chisholm, Linda. 1983. Redefining Skills: Black Education in South Africa in the 1980s. *Comparative Education*, vol. 19, no. 3, pp. 357–71.

_____ (ed.). 2004. *Changing Class: Education and Social Change in Post-Apartheid South Africa*. London and Cape Town: ZED and HSRC.

_____and Bruce Fuller. 1996. Remember People's Education? Shifting Alliances, State-building and South Africa's Narrowing Policy Agenda. *Journal of Education Policy*, vol. 11, no. 6, pp. 693–716.

_____, Shireen Motala, and Salim Vally (eds.). 2003. *South African Education Policy Review 1993-2000*. Johannesburg: Heinemann Press.

Christie, Pam. 1997. Global Trends in Local Contexts: A South African Perspective on Competence Debates. *Discourse: Studies in the Cultural Politics of Education*, vol. 18, no. 1, pp. 55–69.

Cooper, Linda, Sally Andrew, Jonathan Grossman, and Salim Vally. 2002. Schools of Labour and Labour's Schools: Worker Education Under Apartheid. In Peter Kallaway (ed.), *The History of Education Under Apartheid* (pp. 111–33). London: Peter Lang.

Collins, Michael. 1991. *Adult Education as Vocation*. London: Routledge

Council on Higher Education. 2007. *Review of Higher Education in South Africa: Selected Themes*. Pretoria, South Africa: CHE.

Curriculum Review Committee. 2000. A South African Curriculum for the Twenty-First Century. May 31. *Revised National Curriculum Statement*. Pretoria: Government Printer.

Department of Education. 1996. *The South African Schools Act*. Pretoria: Government Printer.

_____. 1997. *Education White Paper 3: A Programme for the Transformation of Higher Education*. Government Printer: Pretoria.

_____. 1998. *Green Paper on Further Education and Training: Preparing for the Twenty-First Century through Education, Training and Work*. Pretoria: Government Printer.

Department of Higher Education and Training. 2010. *National Skills Development Strategy II*. Pretoria: Government Printer.

_____. 2012. *Green Paper for Post-school Education and Training*. Pretoria: Government Printer.

_____. 2011. *Nationals Skills Development Strategy III*. Pretoria: Government Printer.

_____. 2013. Statistics on Post-School Education and Training. Pretoria: Government Printer.

Henry, Miriam. 1999. Working With/Against Globalization in Education. *Journal of Education Policy*, vo. 14, no. 1, pp. 85–97.

Jansen, Jonathan. 2004. Importing Outcomes-Based Education into South Africa: Policy Borrowing in a Post-Communist World. In David Phillips and Kimberly Ochs (eds.), *Educational Policy Borrowing: Historical Perspectives* (pp. 199–220). Oxford: Symposium Books.

Kunene, Angeline. 2009. Learner-Centeredness in Practice: Reflections from a Curriculum Education Specialist. In Katherine Pithouse, Claudia Mitchell, and Relebohile Moletsane (eds.), *Making Connections: Self-Study and Social Action* (pp. 139–52). New York: Peter Lang.

McGrath, Simon, Seamus Needham, Joy Papier, Volker Wedekind, and Trish van der Merwe. 2010. Employability in the College Sector: A Comparative Study of England and South Africa. *Final Report of the Learning to Support Employability Project*. Nottingham: School of Education, University of Nottingham .

McKinsey Center for Government. 2012. Education to Employment: Designing a System that Works. http://mckinseyonsociety.com/education-to-employment/report/

Meintjes, Helen and Katherine Hall. 2009. Demography of South Africa's Children. In Shirley Pendlebury, Lori Lake, and Charmaine Smith. (eds.), *South African Child Gauge 2008/2009* (pp. 71–78). Cape Town: Children's Institute/University of Cape Town.

Motala, Enver, Salim Vally, and Carol Anne Spreen. 2010. Reconstituting Power and Privilege or Transforming Education and Training? In Brij Maharaj, Ashwin Desai, and Patrick Bond (eds.), *Zuma's Own Goal: Losing South Africa's "War on Poverty"* (pp. 241–260). Trenton, NJ: Africa World Press and The Red Sea Press.

Motala, Shireen, and Salim Vally. 2002. People's Education: From People's Power to Tirisano. In Peter Kallaway (ed.), *The History of Education Under Apartheid, 1948-1994* (pp. 174–94). Maskew Miller Longman: Cape Town.

Nelson Mandela Institute. 2005. *Emerging Voices: A Report on Education in South African Rural Communities*. Cape Town: HSRC Press.

National Planning Commission. 2011. *National Development Plan: Vision for 2030*. Pretoria: Government Printer.

Nussbaum, Martha. 2010. *Not for Profit. Why Democracy Needs the Humanities*. Princeton, NJ: Princeton University Press.

Pendlebury, Shirley, Lori Lake, and Charmaine Smith. 2009. *South African Child Gauge 2008/2009*. Cape Town: Children's Institute, University of Cape Town.

Posel, Dorrit, Daniela Casale, and Calire Vermaak. 2013. What is South Africa's "Real" Unemployment Rate? Politics web. http://www.politicsweb.co.za/politicsweb/view/politicsweb/

Pretorius, Cornia. 2009. "Flawed" Tender for Textbooks. *Mail & Guardian*, December 4 http://mg.co.za/article/2009-12-04-flawed-tender-for-textbooks

Ramadiro, Brian. 2005. Community-Based Research Study on the Right to Basic Education: Results of a Snapshot Survey: Durban Roodeport Deep (DRD) and Rondebult (2003-5). Johannesburg: Education Policy Unit, University of the Witwatersrand.

Rensburg, Patrick van. 2001. *Making Education Work: The What, Why and How of Education with Production*. Gaborone and Johannesburg: Foundation for Education with Production International; and Uppsala: Dag Hammarskjöld Foundation.

Sears, Alan. 2003. *Retooling the Mind Factory—Education in a Lean State*. Aurora, Ontario: Garamond Press.

Spreen, Carol Anne. 2001. *Globalization and Educational Policy Borrowing: Mapping Outcomes-Based Education in South Africa*. Ph.D. Dissertation, Teachers College, Columbia University.

_____. 2004. The Vanishing Origins of OBE: Agency and Resistance to Educational Transfer in South Africa. In David Phillips and Kimberly Ochs (eds.), *Historical Perspectives on Policy Borrowing and Lending* (pp. 221–36). Oxford: Oxford University Press.

_____, and Salim Vally. 2006. Education Policy, Inequality and Rights in Post-Apartheid South Africa. *International Journal of Educational Development*, vol. 26, no. 4, pp. 352–62.

_____, and Salim Vally. 2010. Outcomes-Based Education and Its (Dis)contents: Learner Centered Pedagogy and the Education Crisis in South Africa. *Southern African Review of Education*, vol. 16, no. 1, pp. 39–58.

Statistics South Africa. 2013. Quarterly Labour Force Survey (QLFS), 1st Quarter 2013. http://www.statssa.gov.za/publications/statsabout.asp?PPN=P0211&SCH=4701

Steiner-Khamsi, Gita, Iveta Silova, and Eric M. Johnson. 2006. Neoliberalism Liberally Applied: Educational Policy Borrowing in Central Asia. In Jenny Ozga, Terry Seddon, and Thomas S. Popkewitz (eds.), *World Yearbook of Education 2006: Education, Research and Policy: Steering the Knowledge-Based Economy* (pp. 217–45). New York: Routledge.

Taylor, Nick, Penny Vinjevold, and Johann Muller. 2003. *Getting Schools Working: Research and Systemic School Reform in South Africa.* Cape Town: Pearson Education South Africa.

Torres, Carlos Alberto. 1994. Paulo Freire as Secretary of Education in the Municipality of São Paulo. *Comparative Education Review*, vol. 38, no. 2, pp. 181–214.

UNDP, 2013. *Human Development Report 2013: The Rise of the South: Human Progress in a Diverse World*. New York: UNDP.

UN Educational, Scientific and Cultural Organization. 2012. *Education For All Global Monitoring Report: Youth and Skills, Putting Education to Work.* Paris: UNESCO.

Vally, Salim, and Enver Motala. (eds.). 2013. *Education, the Economy and Society.* Pretoria: UNISA Press.

_____, and Brian Ramadiro. 2009. From "Abjectivity" to Subjectivity: Education Research and Resistance in South Africa. In David Hill and Ellen Rosskam (eds.), *The Developing World and State Education: Neoliberal Depredation and Egalitarian Alternatives* (pp. 179–96). New York: Routledge Press.

_____, and Carol Anne Spreen. 2012. The World Bank and Human Rights: Dichotomizing Rights and Responsibilities. In Steven Klees, Nelly P. Stromquist, and Joel Samoff (eds.), *The World Bank and Education: Critiques and Alternatives* (pp. 173–87). Boston: Sense Publishers.

Walters, Shirley. 1997. *Globalization, Adult Education and Training.* London: ZED books.

Wedekind, Volker. 2013. FET Colleges, Employability, Responsiveness, and the Role of Education. In Salim Vally and Enver Motala (eds.), *Education, the Economy and Society.* Pretoria: UNISA Press.

Williams, Jeffrey. 2001. Franchising the University. In Henry Giroux and Kostas Myrsiades (eds.), *Beyond the Corporate University: Culture and Pedagogy in the New Millennium* (pp. 15–28). New York: Rowman and Littlefield.

World Bank. 2010. Concept Note for the World Bank Education Strategy 2020. Washington, DC: World Bank.

NOTES

1. The official or "narrow" rate of unemployment excludes all individuals who report during the census that they do want work but have not taken "active" steps to search for work in the previous month. At the end of 2012, there were approximately 3.1 million non-searching unemployed and 4.5 million searching (official) employed. The strict (official) rate of unemployment was 24.9 percent but alternative estimates consider it to be 35.9 percent.

2. On August 16, 2012, an elite special unit of the South African Police Services opened fire on striking miners at the Marikana platinum mine operated by the Lonmin company. The mine is near the town of Rustenburg, one hour's drive from Johannesburg. Thirty-four miners were killed and seventy-eight injured. It is worth noting that the World Bank's International Finance Corporation provided Lonmin with a $150 million loan in 2007 (Bond, 2012).

Chapter Eighteen

"Still Hanging off the Edge": An Australian Case Study of Gender, Universities, and Globalization

Jill Blackmore

For over twenty years, globalization has been the justification for the radical transformation of education in most Western capitalist states. Through a raft of policies, education has been more tightly linked to the economy on the assumption that economic growth leads to social well-being generally. Universities are now considered to be central to knowledge economies, lifelong learning, and innovation. While universities have always been internationally networked through communities of scholars, their position as key sites of knowledge production, legitimation, and dissemination is now being challenged by the democratization of knowledge with the internet, open access publication, and digital economies. Kelsey (1995) saw universities early in the 1990s as the primary sites of critique of the ideologies of liberal market theory and alternative ideas. But they were also an obvious target for "radical market oriented restructuring" (Kelsey, 1995, p. 58). Recent evidence suggests that decades of corporatization have reduced this critical capacity and universities are now viewed in more instrumental ways as servicing national economies (Barnett, 2011). Corporatization involves transforming universities into a business by mobilizing processes, discourses, and practices of marketization, managerialism, and privatization (Ball, 2012; Blackmore and Sachs, 2007). In 2014, universities are complex multinational organizations embedded in global market relations as academic capitalism has escalated and intensified (Slaughter and Leslie, 1997). The purpose of universities and the role of academics are under challenge. Both struggle with competing value systems with regard to their use value in terms of internationalization and commercialization and their roles with regard to informing critical intellectual debate and providing a public service (Marginson, 2011).

This chapter demonstrates the impact on gender equity during two phases of restructuring in Australian higher education. The first structural adjustment occurred during the late 1980s into the 1990s, and the second is occurring with the transitioning to a new knowledge economy in the decades marked by 9/11 and the global financial crisis. It argues that in the geographically "marginal" Anglophone nation states (Australia and New Zealand), women are at greatest risk with globalized restructuring. Despite the gender-free language associated with discourses of globalization and education reform, the policies they justify have changed the very nature of the state and its relation to the individual, households, and community. Any major restructuring of the economy and organizations such as universities is gendered because labor markets, perceptions of use-value and hierarchies of knowledge, the relationship between public and private lives, and the division of labor ingrained in educational work are socially and historically constituted in gendered ways. Gender restructuring occurs because institutionalized discourses, practices, policy legacies, and sedimented power relations come into play to protect established interests and ideas of who we are and how we work (Blackmore and Sachs, 2007).

NEOLIBERALISM AND STRUCTURAL ADJUSTMENT

Globalization is often described as the changes brought about by the speeding up of transnational engagement arising from globalized markets seeking cheaper labor and new consumers, the emergence of new information and communication technologies, and the unprecedented and uneven flows of students, refugees, workers, migrants, and tourists. While disputably not a new phenomenon, globalization was initially as much an ideology as an *awareness* of the possibilities of, and arising from, new markets, ideas, and technologies—a "reality in the making." Some saw globalization putting the nation-state at risk, if not rendering it irrelevant. Others saw globalization offering greater democratic possibilities in terms of governance and the strengthening of transnational organizations promoting global citizenship and agreements on human rights (Held, McGrew, Goldblatt, and Perraton, 1999). Most recently, the subversive and democratizing capacities of the Internet and mobile technologies have been made evident by the Arab Spring uprisings.

There has been an ongoing transnational (and often bipartisan) policy convergence in the Anglophone nation-states since the 1980s underpinned by the dominance of the ideologies of neoliberalism (Ong, 2007). Globalization discourses during the 1980s promoted powerful mythologies about level playing fields, borderlessness, and freely flowing markets. The neoliberal policy orthodoxy of structural adjustment was developed by U.S. right-wing economic think tanks and prescribed for developing nation-states by international financial bodies such as the Organization for Economic Cooperation and Development (OECD) (Pande and Ford, 2011), and the International Monetary Fund. Structural adjustment policies prescribed reducing public expenditure by shrinking state welfarism, deregulating financial and labor markets, and privatizing the provision of education, health, and welfare.

The context involved new regional alliances and trading blocs emerging in response to globalization. Structural adjustment policies were voluntarily adopted with bipartisan support during the 1990s in Australia and New Zealand as well as South Africa (Kelsey, 1995), whereas the United Kingdom and United States undertook milder "self-adjustment" measures (Carnoy, 1995). Australia and New Zealand, marginalized politically and economically as well as geographically, were "on the edge" of the North American Free Trade Agreement (NAFTA), European Union, and Association of South East Asian Nations (ASEAN). Both were increasingly vulnerable to international exigencies and U.S. domination; both within/outside dominant Western cultural, political, and economic enclaves; both with their own colonial and imperialist histories in relation to their own indigenous populations, postcolonial relations with neighborhood states; and both subject to European and American economic and cultural colonization. The post-1945 welfare states of the United Kingdom, Australia, and New Zealand moved away from state provision in education, health, and welfare to one of state subsidization of the "targeted" needy or post-welfarism with significant equity effects with costs flowing onto individuals and families.

NEW KNOWLEDGE ECONOMIES

Policy borrowing has intensified due to mobile actors and policies of international bodies such as the OECD, the International Monetary Fund, and the World Bank at the same time global rankings have taken on heightened value in higher education (e.g., Times Higher Education) (Marginson, 2011). The millennium discourse has been about how universities are central to knowledge economies and that academic work has to be harnessed to promote innovation and application (Department of Education, Employment and Workplace Relations, 2009). While initial political responses to globalization had been toward unifying governance in the 1990s, the risks associated with global economic interdependence have emerged post-millennium and with the global financial crisis of 2008, destabilizing old political alliances and changing relationships between developing and developed economies. Trade and labor flows are becoming more multilateral, particularly with the relative weakening of the Western economies such as the United States, the United Kingdom, and the European Union.

Neoliberal policies premised upon individual choice are being refueled by the aspirations of emergent Asian and Middle Eastern middle classes, whereas privatization of provision offers solutions to governments in developing nations unable to meet demand. Whereas Western dominance of the international education market intensified after the 1990s as a source of funding domestic students and regional economies, there has been a radical shift with the rise of Asian economies post-2000. No longer can Western universities assume as they did a decade ago that they provide the brain-power of knowledge economies and Asia the labor-power of industrialization in a unilateral flow of ideas and labor (Brown, Lauder, and Ashton, 2011). China, India, Singapore, and Indonesia now actively produce their own graduates by investing in technology and the massification of schooling and higher education. Asian graduates will compete in professional as well as unskilled global labor markets. Massive open online courses (MOOCs) offered by elite universities undermine local markets. Even then, post-2000, the insecurity of global labor markets and rising costs have made it questionable as to the extent higher education is capable of fulfilling the promise of secure employment for graduates (Brown, Lauder, and Ashton, 2011). In this fluid, contested, and changing context, some argue that the traditional liberal arts university is now under threat (Barnett, 2011).

FEMINIST CRITIQUES

Feminists were initially skeptical about the usefulness of the concept of globalization theoretically and its universalizing discourses given their concerns about the situatededness of women's experiences (Blackmore, 1999, 2000). When the state withdrew its services under structural adjustment policies, women and girls lost government protection and funds, and many assumed greater responsibility for the care of the aged, young, and sick, while in many developing nation-states women and girls were withdrawn from education (Unterhalter, 2007). Transnational global policy bodies now recognize the inequitable gender effects of structural adjustment policies, indicated by a policy shift encapsulated in the UN Millennium Development Goals (2000), which has made female participation in education a priority (Unterhalter, 2007). The OECD and World Bank now view gender equity as producing national economic and social benefits and as indicative of national "stability" (e.g., the Gender Development Index).

Women experience a number of paradoxes arising from responses to the above. Education policies continue to mobilize neoliberal market discourses of choice that assume a generic gender-, race-, and class-neutral self-maximizing individual. But evidence shows that women with equivalent credentials continue to receive lower wages in the market, even within a year of exiting university. In Australia, the gender gap increased with heightened employment insecurity as it did in most nation states (Graduate Careers Australia, 2012). The promise of choice through the massification of education where women are now the majority of students in most nations has also been a time of rising religious intolerance and fundamentalism (Nussbaum, 2010). Many women participated in the Arab Spring uprisings, only to find themselves oppressed by newly elected governments that mandated traditional gender roles (e.g., Egypt, Tunisia). Religious fundamentalism is often articulated as anti-Western cultural, social, and economic imperialism. Defending culture is equated with traditional gender relations premised upon inequality. In Western nations, neoliberalism and the rise of religious fundamentalism have produced a tension between socially conservative ideologies of female subservience and democratic notions of citizenship rights, the latter often conflated into neoliberal market ideologies of choice.

Collectively, these have led to an escalation of fear as a motivating political factor, often leading to social fragmentation rather than social cohesion. Education in particular is a site where this generalized anxiety is expressed through intensified competitive individualism in the twenty-first century and attacks on women and girls seeking to access education (Blackmore, 2010). Yet women now participate in higher rates than men in undergraduate higher education in the Anglophone and many Asian and Middle Eastern countries, although not necessarily in executive leadership where decisions are made about what counts (Sobehart, 2006). Findlow (2013) argues, for example, that, "higher education is being conceptualised as part of a neoliberal 'feminist' social change project in the post-imperial context of the Arab Gulf" (p. 112).

CORPORATIZING HIGHER EDUCATION

Institutionally, there has been a shift from semi-bureaucratic to corporate governance generally in the United Kingdom, Australia, and New Zealand (Blackmore, 2011; Olssen, Codd, and O'Neill, 2004). The corporatization strategies "retooling" education and the public sector generally during the 1990s have included privatization, marketization, and the commodification of educational work of teaching and research, directed by new forms of "hybrid" managerialism, linked to strong accountability regimes, of performance management, quality assurance, and research assessment (Besley, 2009; Blackmore, 2009b; Morley, 2003). Corporatization has changed the value and practices of teaching and research, how we define quality and the distribution of rewards as universities have become more porous to the wider world. Corporatization was the product of ideologies of New Public Administration being imposed in higher education during the 1980s in the United Kingdom, New Zealand, and Australia. The New Public Administration argued that private sector management practices were more efficient and effective than public sector bureaucracies. In Australia, under the unified national system created after 1989 with the imposition of new managerialism, executive prerogative was asserted (Blackmore, 2011). While "self-governing" universities are said to have increased institutional autonomy, they have become even more accountable to government for outcomes and efficiencies to be achieved through enterprise bargaining, with ongoing demands for continuing improvement and productivity gains with less resources. Devolution of governance by the state facilitated the shift from state regulation (and full provision) to state supervision of an increasingly privatized and deregulated system. At the same time, the state has steered (safely) from a distance while reducing education expenditure, effectively downloading the financial crisis of the state down the line.

During the 1990s, marketization was accompanied by new modes of devolved governance. New managerialism downloaded responsibility onto individual academics, universities, and students for outcomes justified by discourses of "responsibilization" (Beck, 1994). Those at the interface of customer "delivery of service" were considered to know how best to use resources. In reality, it meant individual units (academics, departments, and universities) competed with each other while expected to do more with less. This principle of subsidiarity tapped into and aligned with discourses of marketization—self-help, self-interest, and self-promotion—themes evident in discourses of mutual responsibility of the unemployed and those on welfare. Less government and individual voluntarism were key elements of Reaganomics, Thatcherism, Blair's Third Way, Howardism in Australia, and most recently the U.K. Coalition's notion of the Great Society. All idealize the traditional family in ways that ignore or subsume women's interests as being synonymous with that of the family unit.

While the 1990s corporatization saw markets penetrate the structures, processes, discourses, and practices of the academy during the 1990s, the 2000s have been marked by a blurring of the boundaries between the university and the private and public sectors through a push for partnerships, commercialization, and innovation to address the needs of knowledge-based economies and redistribute the costs of higher education (Gordon and Whitchurch, 2010). Universities have become more networked locally and internationally with a range of public and private agencies and providers, with universities increasingly subcontracting out services.

Actors also use state resources to enable interstitial organizations to emerge that bring the corporate sector inside the university, to develop new networks that mediate between the private and public sectors, and to expand managerial capacity to supervise new flows of external resources, investment in research infrastructure for the New Economy, and investment in infrastructure to market institutions, products, and services to students (Slaughter and Rhoades, 2004, p. 1).

In the twenty-first century, universities are now transnational corporate enterprises. Higher education as a global market is also under considerable pressure due to its massification, intensified competition for international students with new Asian providers, and the rise of online provision with MOOCs. Elite universities in the United States and in Australia are capturing global markets through MOOCs while retaining their distinctiveness of excellence through the few students paying for face-to-face interaction. Whereas the welfare state previously disciplined the market within its national boundaries, in a globalized context the corporate state now mediates transnational market relations in education and increasingly steers and regulates a wider range of public and private education providers from a distance through policy and contractualism while being disciplined by international markets and global policy fields such as the OECD (Rizvi and Lingard, 2010). Comparison is now the new mode of governance of universities and individuals, achieved through rankings and regimes designed and determined outside the field of higher education (Blackmore, 2009b; Marginson, 2010). While the welfare state was against markets, the post-welfare contractualist state and market increasingly coincide, even to the detriment of its citizenry.

More generally, the post-war relationship between public sector employment and the notion of a public university is dissolving. Universities in this context are seen both as an export industry (international education) for the creation of wealth based on new knowledge and as central to skill formation in post-Fordist workplaces..Underlying both is an instrumental approach to the role of the academy. Academic work has also been radically redefined as the globalized university is opened up to international markets, requiring them to be more adaptive to different cultural environments, flexible in terms of time, efficient in use of resources, entrepreneurial in attracting new projects, and mobile in terms of travel. In Australian universities, the market re/creates new academic and student identities, emphasizing the individualistic and competitive over collegial relationships, redefining students as clients in contractual rather than pedagogical relationships, and re-positioning efficiency over equity (Olssen, et al., 2004). Corporatization has challenged the very nature and function of the university. Universities operate within pseudo or managed markets, and deal with issues around the public good education services that are thought not appropriately governed through the market (Marginson, 2012).

REDEFINING EQUITY

This market-led recovery has led to a shift in values and in ethos of the academy that has had significant gendered impacts. The welfare state had invested in free higher education as a social, cultural, public good that particularly benefited women during 1974 to 1988. Labor, traditionally claiming the territory of social justice, struggled in 1988 with the efficiency/ equity tension brought about by corporate managerialism emerging in the 1980s. Labor resolved this tension in higher education during this time by arguing (based on human capital theory) that both individuals and the state benefit from higher education, and therefore individuals must contribute in the form of a deferred tax. The losers during the 1990s were mature age women and working class males; the winners were middle-class school leavers.

Equity increasingly came to be perceived as inefficient and a cost against public sector reform. On the one hand, the state seeks to privatize educational costs and reduce state educational expenditure, while on the other the state seeks to control educational outputs to improve economic productivity (Rizvi and Lingard, 2010). Student contributions have increased based on the argument that individuals receive significant private benefits as part of the wider trend for educational costs to be privatized. Australian families, as in the United States, spend the most in the OECD on education (OECD, 2009). Under the conservative Howard government (1996–2006), privatization intensified with moves to full fees in postgraduate courses, which impacted the social sciences and humanities most, already affected by a shrinking public sector as a source of students and research income. Master of business administration degrees, the area of greatest expansion, tended to be financed by employers or international students, the latter now funding the expansion of domestic places. Fees have risen as government funding has reduced, further escalating student/staff ratios during the 2000s. In Australia as elsewhere, women again bear the burden of increased teaching loads as they constitute over 55 percent of staff (most of them on contract) at and below lecturer level (Australian Bureau of Statistics, 2012).

Bakker (1994) refers to "markets as institutions imbued with structural power relations and those have an asymmetrical gender dimension to them" (p. 3). Markets work at multiple levels—individual, institutional, national. Although markets claim to recognize and reward quality and merit, it is reputation and performativity (being seen to perform in particular ways) that often counts (Ball, 2000). For individuals, markets are "social settings that foster specific types of personal development and penalize others" (Bakker, 1994, p. 4). Markets rely on and produce knowledge hierarchies about what counts around immediate impact, relevance, and use-value. In order to succeed in market-driven systems, individuals and institutions have to be mobile and flexible (Metcalfe and Slaughter, 2008). Gender is critical to be able to capitalize on the opportunities of the corporate university and become an internationally strategic academic (Riegraf, Aulenbacher, Kirsch-Auwater, and Muller, 2010).

GENDER EQUITY STRATEGIC POLICY

As policy shifted from the supply side to demand-driven in university sectors, Australian universities have sought to reposition themselves within/against multiple, often but not necessarily, contradictory external pressures for equity and productivity (Blackmore, Brennan, and Zipin, 2011). The reliance of the second wave of the women's movement in Australia (as in New Zealand and Scandinavia) and feminist policy activism within social democratic governments through the femocrats for equity reform since the 1970s has made state-driven gender equity strategies vulnerable in the restructuring process as governance has shifted from bureaucratic to corporate governance (Blackmore, 2011). The move to a post-welfare state had serious repercussions for equity policy, how it was produced, and who was responsible for its enactment.

The new managerialism in universities promoted a range of different structures, practices, and valuings (Deem, 2003). The specialist equity units, personnel, and policies developed under the equal opportunity and affirmative action legislation were relocated within human resource management and domesticated. Devolution of responsibility down to the smallest unit meant responsibility for equity shifted onto individual managers, largely untrained in, and many uncommitted to, equity work. The mainstreaming and downstreaming of equity either diluted the specialist expertise of equity personnel and policy units, or meant the adoption of only those equity objectives that had immediate benefits for corporate ends (Blackmore and Sachs, 2007).

Equity became marginal, if not absent, in the range of reports restructuring higher education in Australia after the Equity and Diversity Framework (National Board of Education, Employment and Training, 1996). In Australia, the neoconservatism of the Howard federal coalition government (1996–2006) further weakened equity provision, curtailing policy activism, downsizing, and downgrading equity infrastructure. The newly created Equal Opportunity in the Workplace Agency moved from strong monitoring mechanisms to weak self-reporting of equity outcomes by large employers such as universities. Recognition of long-term discrimination of group difference for women and indigenous Australians was collapsed into an individualized discourse of diversity that treats all differences as equal and diversity as "a problem" to be managed (Bacchi, 1999). Notions of "group" disadvantage as a basis for citizenship claims upon the state have been increasingly supplanted by individual "consumer" demands upon a market state through discourses of choice.

Feminism also experienced backlash gender politics during the 1990s, with equity discourses in education shifting away from girls and women to a crisis of masculinity, focused on boys' underachievement in schooling and male underrepresentation in higher education. Gender studies supplanted women's studies, and courses and units focused on masculinity increased (Davis and Laker, 2011). Equality was assumed given the numerical feminization of the student body and academic workforce globally (UN Educational, Scientific and Cultural Organization, 2009). Bell (2010) argues that this obfuscated a horizontal gender division of labor with women largely in the lower levels of the academy, and a vertical segmentation based on an uneven distribution of women across the disciplines, being concentrated in public service industries of health, education, management and commerce, and creative arts. Equity policies, while existing, were therefore symbolic as they did not systematically inform practice or become central to individual universities' strategic plans, decision-making, or institutional performance indicators, although some universities have profiled equity as a form of market distinction (Blackmore and Sachs, 2007).

When the Bradley, Noonan, Nugent, and Scales' (2008) *Review of Australian Higher Education* put equity back on the agenda, the focus was to increase to 20 percent of all students the participation of non-traditional higher education users (working class, rural, and indigenous families) by 2015 in the Higher Education Participation and Partnership Program, with no mention of gender. Again, this increased pressure on regional and newer universities that catered to more academically diverse cohorts of students requiring greater pastoral care and inclusive pedagogies (Walker, 2006). Any intensification of teaching impacts most on women contracted in at the lower levels, thus making tenure and a research pathway doubly difficult.

Targeted gender equity policies continue to focus on women's lack of participation in specific disciplines such as engineering and their ongoing underrepresentation at the professorial level. While women constituted over 55 percent of students in Australian universities in 2010, they continue to be underrepresented in the "hard" sciences. For academics, marginal improvements have occurred at associate and full professorial level (increasing from 13 to 18 percent between 2002 and 2008 [Australian Bureau of Statistics, 2012]). Again the discourse is about the needs of knowledge economies not being met by the ageing academic workforce rather than social justice. Within the discourse of knowledge economies, the lack of women in the upper echelons of the academy internationally is seen to be "wasted talent" (Bexley, James, and Arkoudis, 2011). For feminists internationally, the equity agenda for women in academia and leadership generally in Australia is seen to have stalled if not regressed (Husu and Morley, 2000).

REGULATED DEREGULATION AND GLOBALIZED HIERARCHIES

The game has again changed. Post-2010, the Australian international education market is under threat due to a high Australian dollar, a competitive international education market with the United Kingdom and United States ramping up activities in Asia, and elite Asian universities entering the market as well as growing their own skilled workforce (Gribble and Blackmore, 2012). Australian higher education is, with the emergence of new knowledge economies, under significant pressure in terms of its role in the production of employable "global workers" and professionals (Brown, Lauder, and Ashton, 2011).

Differentiation

The response of universities has been to ratchet up the processes of corporatization, to be more responsive and relevant, to source new funds in partnerships and networks with industry and government, to focus on quality and excellence to be distinctive in the market, and for executives to better manage *and* direct teaching and research. Collectively, the strategies of corporatization have more tightly coupled higher education to national economic priorities while deregulating, de-professionalizing, and casualizing academic labor that is increasingly numerically feminized; at the same time, institutions seek greater flexibility to adjust to volatile market demands (Blackmore, 2010; Hey and Bradford, 2004; Reay, 2000). The speeding up and intensification of the processes of corporatization together with reduced funding, institutional compacts, a focus on the application rather than discovery aspects of knowledge production, the rise of new learning technologies, together with new disciplinary regimes of research assessment and quality assurance, has encouraged greater differentiation between universities.

In a demand-driven sector, units and courses that are not popular with students, or required through professional accreditation, are cut. So while access for women students and participation in universities has improved, there has been little attention to the question as to the role and function of the university in terms of curriculum and research other than its immediate use value. Client-focused curriculum provision, as well as student-centered consumption-driven evaluation systems, encourages giving students "what they want" based on "immediate use value" rather than thinking about curriculum development based on professional and academic judgment (Blackmore, 2009a). This utilitarian turn has led to the demise of some "pure" foundational disciplines (e.g., anthropology, history) altogether in some universities and significant retrenchments on even the elite campuses. Some Australian universities have pushed strongly toward interdisciplinarity, embedding individual sociologists, historians, anthropologists, and philosophers in research and teaching units that tend to be focused on the health or material sciences. The driving force devaluing the humanities and social sciences is their perceived lack of use value and capacity to produce income and the focus of new managerialism is on perceived student or industry demand (itself often constructed by policy).

Academic De-professionalization and Managerial Professionalization

Corporate managerialism during the 1990s increasingly produced a bifurcation between line management and academics, with power resting increasingly with managers over strategies, course content, research priorities, and academic appointment processes. By the 2000s, line management had arguably become the core work of universities with a proliferation of new layers of management and managers of research, online learning, community engagement, internationalization, and quality assurance, with more administrators than academics in many Australian universities (Blackmore and Sachs, 2007). Universities have become more porous to externally determined arrangements and priorities; internally, this has produced a blurring of professional and academic roles as multiple career pathways are emerging through partnerships, contract research, and shared curriculum (Gordon and Whitchurch, 2010). New modes of knowledge production and dissemination emerge with the new forms of expertise required by the Internet (e.g., instructional design for e-learning, Web management, and research management).

New managerialism has also led to a shift from more collegiate and quasi-democratic (although still patriarchal and bureaucratic) systems of university governance to "quasi-market managerial practices" and a shift in the locus of influence from academics to management as evident in the declining power and reduced role of Academic Boards, the academic body governing quality (Blackmore, 2011; Rowlands, 2011). Most academics have little say in strategic planning forums, and U.S. and Australian studies cite that the majority of academics see university decision-making as being undemocratic, more bureaucratic, centralized, and hierarchical (Rowlands, 2011). Academic boards now undertake the symbolic work of quality assurance reacting to regulatory mechanisms introduced during the 2000s such as the Tertiary Education Quality and Standards, a national body that mandates adherence to the Australian Qualifications Framework. University councils similarly have been legislated in 1990 and again since 2010 to be less representative of the academic and student community and more of corporate business (Rowlands, 2011).

For academics, on the one hand, the scope, scale, and depth of their work has increased. Academics are now expected to teach, research, do service in the university and community, form partnerships, market and promote courses, mentor colleagues and students, inform policy and practice, produce high-quality research outputs, source funds for their research, develop international collaborations, teach online and off campus, and disseminate research in the media and for practitioners. This creates new possibilities for the entrepreneurial academic. But these possibilities are limited for scholars in the lower ranks of the academic workforce and particularly for those who have family responsibilities. Sessional/contract/lecturers and contract researchers pick up where tenured academics can do no more to deal with large classes, administrative work, and planning, often without commensurate recognition or opportunities.

Academics refer to a sense of the undermining of esteem accorded to the traditional academic core work of research and teaching, resulting in a sense of deskilling and de-professionalization (Shapper and Mayson, 2005). The changing role of the professor is indicative of this shift in that the professor's job has expanded at the same time its esteem value has reduced as the professoriate has become marginal to decision-making. Recruitment into the professoriate is increasingly based on commercial expedience, through partnerships or managerial position, and not based on research record. Salary gaps are emerging between those taking the traditional academic research route and professors brought in from non-academic positions or in management roles, with individual bargaining creating a gender gap (Altbach, Reisberg, Yudkevich, Androuschack, and Pacheco, 2012). Such recruitment practices mean that many executive managers do not have prior university, research, or teaching experience, and often lack understanding as to the implications for practice of policies. At the same time, academics are increasingly expected to align their research with national, university, and faculty priority areas. Performance management and appraisal, together with standardized student evaluation systems upon which academics are judged, increasingly produce a self-managing "strategic" academic (Bansel and Davies, 2010; Blackmore and Sachs, 2007). Being strategic requires greater compliance to organizational norms and strategic imperatives that marginalizes those with counter-hegemonic stances, particularly those in the social sciences and humanities that are often considered to be overly "critical," ignoring how researching the social, political, and organizational is what they do.

Disciplining Academics

As in New Zealand, the imposition of private industry management practices through public sector reform has been performance-based with the new contractualism. There is now explicit use of contracts in all relations in university life including performance agreements between universities and governments, between faculties and their university, and between individual academics and management. Strategic planning links all levels: from national policies through to the CEOs down to faculties, then to schools/departments and individual performance plans of academics. Performance management systems lead to increased reporting and accounting mechanisms to facilitate the state and university management to steer from a distance through strategic plans, competitive bidding, financial contracts, and quantifiable performance outcomes (Baird, 2011; Strathern, 2000).

Quality is now seen to be critical to international performance and what makes a university distinctive. On the one hand, the Australian higher education sector needs to be seen to be high quality to attract students. On the other, individual universities need to be ranked as of "world excellence" as the scale of comparison has gone, and accountability regimes are going, "global." In Australia, the Bradley et al. (2008) review led to a new regulatory body, the Tertiary Education Quality and Standards Authority. The Tertiary Education Quality and Standards Authority requires that all university courses meet the accreditation requirements of the Australian Qualifications Framework and undertake regular quality assurance reviews required to retain the status of a university. The Australian Qualifications Framework standardizes academic work and regulates academic pedagogies while at the same time these are expected to meet rising expectations to deliver to the market; and this regulation impacts on academic work through student evaluation of teaching (Blackmore, 2009a). This outcomes orientation and emphasis on performativity continues to skew the focus away from the core work of teaching and research and more onto recording, accounting, and measurement (Blackmore and Sachs, 2007).

In research, the focus has shifted from rewarding quantity to rewarding quality. The pressure to publish in particular ways (international refereed journals) and in particular forums (international conferences) has also intensified. The notion of what constitutes research has been reconstituted through new management practices of research assessment and formulaic funding mechanisms premised upon metrics. In Australia, the push to measure research output to get value for government investment has been ratcheted up through frequent policy shifts. After 1987, research quantums awarded points to individual academics (and their institutions) according to their productivity (measured by income earned in competitive bidding plus publication output). After the 1989 structural reforms that introduced managerialization and marketization into a unified and massified sector, universities sought to develop research cultures and increase research capacity over the past two decades. In Post's (2010) research assessment with the Excellence in Research in Australia, the policy focus moved from quantity of research output to quality, and onto developing concentrations of research foci within specific universities. This has led to a re-differentiation between research-intensive, research and teaching, and teaching-intensive universities. University financial systems under development during the 1990s to take on private sector market activities with offshore investment and individual faculties and centers have now amplified to take on entrepreneurial work with industry, increasing the numbers of financial and legal personnel appointed to manage research and contractual relations (Besley, 2009). This had inherent biases, given that older universities have stronger research cultures and are well established in science, engineering, and medical areas that bring in the highest research income (input), areas where women are underrepresented. Increasingly, the push has been to make the academic practices of the physical sciences the norm. Social sciences, humanities, and creative arts have increasingly moved toward measuring outputs through citations and building teams. Often this devalues practitioner-based research that informs professional practice (the focus of humanities, education, and health). As humanities research investment has dried up, the pressure has been to push for other sources of funding through partnerships.

Testing quality in the student-centered university has led to student charters and generic student evaluations of teaching that are more about accountability than improving quality (Blackmore, 2009a). Academics are accountable to a wider range of external audiences—students, executives, supervisors, research bodies, ethics committees, industry sponsors, and research partners and internally to align with university strategic plans. Their response is to practice new forms of self-regulation in terms of what research they do and how they do research and teach, narrowing understandings of what constitutes a good academic (Bansel and Davies, 2010). Audit cultures not only intensify academic labor and divert energy away from the core work of teaching and research, but they also require compliance to corporate norms and images of managerial action. In this sense, being strategic for an academic means getting the money—compromising and aligning oneself with university priorities. Being a manager means adhering to strategic plans and key performance indicators. Being critical for both managers and academics of one's university is seen to be disloyal and, in some cases, open for disciplinary action.

These factors have a number of implications for both equity and quality, as women academics, concentrated in the lower echelons, usually teach more than male academics, or tend to be concentrated in the faculties (humanities, social sciences, arts) or newer universities that have lower research funding inputs, no medical or engineering faculties, fewer marketable products, or research that has no immediate use-value. Discourses about excellence promoted through global university rankings tend to consolidate well-established hierarchies of elite universities (Dever and Morrison, 2009). Competitive national grant schemes premised upon science models of research in turn consolidate old knowledge hierarchies that privilege science and technology and selective student recruitment. In turn, this has the wider effect of exacerbating disciplinary and institutional differences.

Gender is central to how the managed education market works differentially in terms of what is valued, and images of academic or entrepreneurial leadership (Bakker, 1994). Multiple studies in Europe, the United States, and Australia indicate that academic women continue to be disadvantaged in demand-driven markets with the persistence of white male dominance of research leadership (Brooks and Mackinnon, 2000; Glazer-Raymo, 2008, in the United States; Riegraf, et al., 2010, in Europe). This has gendered implications about what research gets done (and funded), who gets to do research, and what knowledge gets valued. The accounting mechanisms tend to privilege older institutions and the "hard" disciplines where women are not well represented (Deem and Ozga, 1997, for the United Kingdom; Glazer-Raymo, 2008, for the United States; Riegraf, et al., 2010, for Europe; Sobehart, 2006, for cross national case studies). In Australia, for example, women gained only 20 percent of the prestigious professorial and laureate fellowships in 2010 and the majority are in science (Australian Research Council, 2011). The quality discourse also captures many women academics' desire for quality teaching and "perfectionism" and exacerbates their guilt when they cannot achieve it due to overwork. Women academics talk about "being good" by complying with all the accountabilities yet are unable to "do good" by retaining the quality of content and pedagogy (Acker and Feuerverger, 1997; Blackmore and Sachs, 2007; Morley, 2000).

These studies point to accumulated disadvantage due to organizational practices as the gap between the proportion of female Ph.D. students "in the line" (55 percent of doctoral students are female) and women at full professorial level (18 percent) remains wide (Dever and Morrison, 2009). The expectations at all levels of the academy require increased workload and time that conflicts with a work-life balance (Diezmann and Grieshaber, 2010; Jos, 2011). Add to this subtle practices of exclusion from networks and external resources and a lack of transparency and questioning of what counts as academic merit and authority (Riegraf, et al., 2010). At the same time, accountability can also facilitate equity by making the processes of promotion and funding allocation transparent and putting the quality of teaching on the agenda. Both can lead to greater recognition of women academics as has been the case of the Australian Institute of Teaching and Learning awards and funds to research teaching. But this potential has been undermined by the difficult conditions of work with larger classes, more academically and culturally diverse student cohorts requiring more pastoral care, and more reporting and recording.

E-learning: The Latest Technological Fix

With the massification of higher education, technology has often been posited as a solution to widen participation and provision. New learning technologies, as did distance education previously, have opened up new possibilities for many students unable to physically attend university due to location or work. The trend in the 1990s was toward "generic" and well-packaged international courses delivered online (McWilliam and Taylor, 1998), designed by universities' commercial arms that developed training units and workplace-based courses for industry, the public sector, and unions. These have progressed from the underlying behaviorism of instructional design and student management systems to an emergent industry of e-learning or blended learning.

Multimodal learning also offers a range of pedagogical approaches for off- and online learning, and facilitates greater flexibility for students both learning and earning. In the era of MOOCs, online learning is now seen to be critical in attracting and retaining students. E-learning requires different academic pedagogies using different learning technologies, reconfigured learning spaces, and online management systems as well as significant investment in infrastructure and technical support and professional development. But technology has exacerbated, not lessened, the intensification of labor, as multimodal pedagogies are time-consuming, require continual professional learning about fast-changing technologies, and lead to escalating response times, thus raising expectations for exceptional performances as teachers. Mobile technologies also result in little to no down time for academics, invading their leisure and home time. Information management systems have allowed administrative work to be downloaded onto academics, ranging from organizing class lists to inputting results and monitoring casual staff.

The emergence of MOOCs as context-free floating signifiers of elitism has led executives to consider the potential affordances for greater efficiencies, where online units developed by elite universities are accredited by other universities. MOOCs dispense with the need for the teacher, providing only minimal interactivity due to their massive enrollments, in which assessment is reduced to standardized assessment through multiple choice tests and self-paced computer-assisted learning. Again, the pedagogical potential is exaggerated. While equity is created by providing mass access to high-tech online learning or what Janet Newson (1994) calls "echnopedagogy," MOOCs tend to produce context-free units, and commodify curriculum into "consumable bites" for multiple audiences, thus reducing student/teacher interaction. Increasingly, the on-campus experience will be what enables universities to claim distinctiveness. The danger is that of an impoverished curriculum for the masses and retaining the experience of "being" on campus for the elite students and universities.

Those who teach, predominantly women in casual and senior lecturer positions and below, are therefore entrapped by either intensified work facilitating the highly desirable face-to-face pedagogies or reduced professional input into online courses developed as packages from multiple institutions. Meanwhile teaching gets substantively harder as the capacity to attract, retain, and pass students determines key performance indicators, course requirements (e.g., advanced standing, length of courses, etc.) have been decreased, and international students and diverse academic abilities of students require greater language skill support (Deem and Ozga, 1997). Interactivity is now viewed as key, with a focus on providing the blend of modes of learning personalized for each student.

Flexibility and Marketization

In Australia, academic labor markets have been restructured by federal policies favoring "flexibility." The post-1987 move to decentralized enterprise bargaining removed many of the protections of a centralized wage bargaining system as it relied on the power of unions to negotiate in individual workplaces. Unregulated intake and the push for massification and widening participation since 2010 means universities seek increasing flexibility while at the same time push for greater research and industry partnerships. Industrial agreements have also facilitated the employer prerogative in determining hours and work conditions; as pay raises are contingent on productivity gains, this can mean "trading off" of extended time for availability across the day and year for family leave (Pocock, 2011).

Institutional flexibility is contingent on individual flexibility and the casualization of academic work, which is now exceptionally high in some universities and in some courses (more than 60 percent in some instances). The majority of the increasingly large cohort of teaching-only and research-only staff on contract and "soft funds" are women (Coates, Dobson, Goedegebuure, and Meek, 2009). Women academics at the lower level of the tenured academic hierarchy do much of the teaching and therefore bear the brunt of student, managerial, and institutional surveillance, through performance appraisal, customer satisfaction surveys, and student charters as well as organization of casual staff. Women also tend to make up the majority of the invisible class of "research staff" (research assistants, administrative and clerical staff, etc.) who are without career paths, do not have access to teaching, and are reliant upon "soft" research funds arising out of their academic employers' capacity to win grants (Australian Bureau of Statistics, 2012; Reay, 2000). Even at higher levels of executive management, women tend not to bargain as well and individualized contracts lead to greater gender gaps in wages (Altbach, et al., 2012; Riegraf, et al., 2010). In Australia, there is a widening gender pay gap as top-level university managers, mostly men, receive considerably higher salaries as executive managers than the top professors, exacerbating a growing gender divide between academics and management, as well as between high flying researchers and teachers. Even then academic salaries are reducing relative to other professions. Generally "as salaries in the higher education sector fall relative to other professional occupations, there may be a greater feminization of certain sectors of the academic profession" (Deem and Ozga, 1997, p. 34). Performance-based management and the intensification of work and rising expectations for quality in teaching and research have together built-in discriminatory practices because women with familial responsibilities for care cannot put in the same hours (Pocock, 2011). The conflict between work and home has increased as have the hours required to achieve promotion.

The expansion and intensification of academic labor has ripple effects upward to middle management where many female academics have moved into administration as heads of schools and deans. For individual women, the entrepreneurial university of the twenty-first century offers opportunities as leaders. Women in the newly corporatized university of the 1990s were often positioned as "change agents" either by management or as a political stance, being both insiders and outsiders of male-dominated cultures, where they undertook the emotional management work of systems in crisis, but often as the colluded self (Blackmore and Sachs, 2007). Middle managers juggled competing demands of accountability upward for efficiency and downward by resource-starved and overworked academics. Personally, they experienced isolation and stress (Blackmore, Brennan, and Zipin, 2011). Such academics refer to a sense of dissonance between academic and management value systems, a sense of colluding with something they do not agree with (Davies and Bansel, 2007). Many female academics express a strong sense of ambivalence about whether they are empowered or exploited by the postmodern entrepreneurial university, although all agree they are overworked and undervalued (Blackmore, Brennan, and Zipin, 2011; Blackmore and Sachs, 2007; Riegraf, et al., 2010).

At the same time, the new work order demands a driven worker who is adaptable, mobile, flexible in use of time and interests, and also in alignment with corporate expectations. The expectation is that academics be culturally flexible and globally mobile workers, able to travel or to work "online" from home. Flexibility and mobility currently work against the career patterns of women academics, who enter later and who generally have family responsibilities (Jos, 2011). It reflects the dual processes of the re-privatization of work with the privatization of educational costs of the institution (e.g., use of car between multiple campuses, use of home office) and the invasion of private time by home/work (Brodie, 1996).

THE FUTURE OF GENDER EQUITY IN THE ENTREPRENEURIAL UNIVERSITY?

A number of paradoxes emerge within the audit culture. Universities are being told they must be more client-driven, yet research or publications written for non-academic professional journals and practitioners do not "count." Indeed what counts in research is narrowing, with a focus on metrics and citations and what is measurable in research assessment. While universities are being encouraged toward greater interdisciplinarity for "problem-solving," research assessment reasserts the old disciplinary hierarchies. Emphasis on the immediate and applied, and consultancies with policy-makers has exacerbated the tendency to favor quantitative over qualitative research (science, math, engineering, medicine, information technology, and management), male-dominated disciplines, and those more able to attract private sector funding, sponsorships, and partnerships. The female-dominated humanities, social sciences, education, and nursing disciplines with their interdisciplinary, community, and professional service orientation or practitioner research approaches have less scope for measurable, immediate commercial application. As Lyotard (1984) argued: "the key question is not whether it is true, but whether it is saleable. … Universities are all about creating skills and no longer ideals" (p. 48). Increasingly, the norm in terms of academic practice is the "hard" sciences: working in research teams, metrics, and application. A focus on partnerships also jeopardizes academic independence and being critical public intellectuals. Feminist research and scholarship is considered to be too critical, irrelevant, and subjected to government and industry censorship.

While competition, confrontation, and the "macho" management styles of the 1990s were producing more workplace stress and less productivity, the transnational environment exerts new pressures and conditions that favor particular forms of entrepreneurial masculinity linked to science and technology, flexibility, and mobility (Connell, Wood, and Crawford, 2005). The shift to more overtly competitive cultures has a significant effect on how women view their possibilities as "culture is a key site in which issues of power and identity are enmeshed and in which male power is reproduced" (Deem and Ozga, 1997, p. 26). Even when women do get into leadership, the dominant institutional norms and practices place increased pressure on women to behave in particular ways to gain credibility (Blackmore and Sachs, 2007). Rarely mentioned is the lack of ethnic and racial diversity within executive leadership that fails to mirror the diversity of student and national populations (Dill, 2009; Heward, Taylor, and Vickers, 1997). Executive appointments and indeed leadership appointments generally tend to produce "homosociability"—selecting people who "best fit" current organizational needs and who are "people like us," which often produces gender, racial, and ethnic homogeneity as well as similar belief systems and ways of working (Ahmed, 2012; Blackmore, Barty, and Thomson, 2006).

Conservative social commentators argued in Australia that equal opportunity policies had succeeded given women's overrepresentation in tertiary education as students and academics. This discourse emerged as the language practices in education have become market-oriented with learners positioned as consumers and courses packaged into modules. Neoliberal discourses significantly alter how individuals relate to others and society—away from notions of citizenship, obligation, and community to notions of being self-interested competitors. The trend to marketize teaching and research in close partnerships and sponsorship arrangements has ethical and political implications. Whereas the welfare state, while still patriarchal, had provided some spaces for feminist activism within itself and publically funded universities, the post-welfare state and entrepreneurial universities judge women's claims according only to whether they benefit the economy.

Universities, previously strategic sites for feminist political activism, are now employed in the service of the nation-state and the economy, putting prior modes of counter-hegemonic engagement at risk. Despite feminist ambivalence about their location in the academy as a privileged elite, as feminists they have welcomed increased participation of more socioeconomically and culturally diverse student groups, but to their own cost as equity work is time and energy consuming. In Australia, feminist lobbyists and human rights activists have changed their strategies, appealing to international bodies such as the UN Children's Fund to bring national governments into line on gender equity. Even within a liberal perspective, feminists argue that universities will be more productive and creative if they continue to value their traditional functions of pedagogy, research, and collegiality; if universities are more inclusive of cultural difference as a result of internationalization; and if public good is gained from universities being good corporate citizens (Nussbaum, 2010). Feminists have called upon quality assurance processes to demand transparency in institutional practices, arguing that equity is one measure of quality. And universities should take seriously their role of critical intellectualism, as there are few alternative forums for debate.

Contemporary life in the academy is fraught with ambiguities and tensions between long-held values, often more discursive than real for many women, of academic freedom, intellectual independence, and collegiality with entrepreneurial, competitive, and contractual values. In liberal Western states, on the one hand, there is the call for new forms of leadership in a culturally diverse and inclusive workplace that promises opportunities and spaces for individual women. On the other hand, well-established modes of gender/power relations take on new forms through the processes of restructuring with the emergence of the flexible, mobile, and entrepreneurial academics. Entrepreneurialism has reinvigorated images of masculinist leadership, one in which there is the enduring image of men in leadership, with only nine out of thirty-eight Australian vice chancellors female in 2013. The entrepreneurial university produces new transnational professional elites and knowledge workers, but also provides greater opportunities for transnational masculinities with more mobility and less domestic responsibility (Connell, et al., 2005). More generally, the entrepreneurial university realizes only restricted spaces for the collective voice with a weakening basis of claims for gender equity other than those that align with organizational missions and in universities that have less of a liberal humanist disposition. In Australia, education is increasingly viewed in policy more as a positional rather than a public good; that is, one in which individuals rather than the public gain the most benefits from investment in education because it provides comparative advantage to them as individuals. If the liberal comprehensive university is under threat, so too is its sense of its commitment to the public good broadly defined as social, political and cultural as well as economic well-being for all.

REFERENCES

Acker, Sandra, and Grace Feuerverger. 1997. Enough is Never Enough: Women's Work in the Academe. In Catherine Marshall (ed.), *Feminist Critical Policy Analysis*, Vol. 2 (pp. 122–40). London: Falmer Press.

Ahmed, Sarah. 2012. *On Being Included. Racism and Diversity in Institutional Life.* North Carolina: Duke University Press.

Altbach, Phillip, Liz Reisberg, Maria Yudkevich, Gregory Androuschack, and Ivan F. Pacheco (eds.). 2012. *Paying the Professoriate. A Global Comparison of Compensations and Contracts.* New York: Routledge.

Australian Bureau of Statistics. 2012. *Australian Yearbook 2012.* Canberra: Commonwealth Government Printing Service.

Australian Research Council. 2011. *Selection Report and Funding Outcomes for 2011.* National Competitive Grants Program. http://www.arc.gov.au/ncgp/dp/DP12_selrpt.htm

Bacchi, Carol. 1999. *Women, Policy, Politics: The Construction of Policy Problems.* Thousand Oaks, California: Sage.

Baird, Jeanette. 2011. Accountability in Australia. More Power to Government and Market. In Bjorn Stensaker and Lee Harvey (eds.), *Accountability in Higher Education: Global Perspectives on Trust and Power* (pp. 25–48). London: Routledge.

Bakker, Irene. 1994. *The Strategic Silence: Gender and Economic Policy.* London: Zed Books/North-South Institute.

Ball, Stephen J. 2000. Performativities and Fabrications in the Education Economy: Towards the Performative Society? *Australian Educational Researcher,* vol. 27, no. 2, pp. 1–24.

_____. 2012. *Global Education Inc.: New Policy Networks and the Neo-liberal Imaginary.* London: Routledge.

Bansel, Peter, and Bronwyn Davies. 2010. Through a Love of What Neoliberalism Puts at Risk. In Jill Blackmore, Marie Brennan, and Lew Zipin (eds.), *Re-Positioning University Governance and Academic Work* (pp. 133–46). Rotterdam: Sense Publishers.

Barnett, Ronald 2011. *Being a University.* Oxford: Routledge.

Beck, Ulrich. 1994. *The Risk Society.* Oxford: Polity.

Bell, Sharon. 2010. Women in Science: The Persistence of Gender in Australia. *Higher Education Management and Policy,* vol. 22, no. 1, pp. 47–48.

Besley, Tina (ed.). 2009. *Assessing Quality in Educational Research.* Rotterdam: Sense Publishers.

Bexley, Emmeline, Richard James, and Sophie Arkoudis. 2011. *The Australian Academic Profession in Transition: Addressing the Challenge of Reconceptualising Academic Work and Regenerating the Academic Workforce.* Canberra: Department of Education, Employment and Workplace Relations.

Blackmore, Jill. 1999. Globalisation/Localisation: Strategic Dilemmas for State Feminism and Gender Equity Policy. Special Issue on Globalization and Education. *Journal of Education Policy,* vol. 14, no. 1, pp. 33–54.

_____. 2000. Globalization: A Useful Concept for Feminists Rethinking Theory and Strategies in Education. In Nicholas Burbules and Carlos Torres (eds.), *Globalization and Education Issues: Critical Perspectives* (pp. 133–56). New York: Routledge.

_____. 2009a. Academic Pedagogies, Quality Logics and Performative Universities: Evaluating Teaching and What Students Want. *Studies in Higher Education,* vol. 34, no. 8, pp. 857–72.

_____. 2009b. Feeling the Quality and Weight of Research Accountability in Australian Universities. In Tina Besley (ed.), *Assessing Quality in Educational Research* (pp. 225–42). Rotterdam: Sense Publishers.

_____. 2010. Educational Organizations and Gender in Times of Uncertainty. In Michael Apple, Stephen J. Ball, and Luis Armando Gandin (eds.), *Routledge International Handbook of the Sociology of Education* (pp. 306–17). New York: Routledge.

_____. 2011. Bureaucratic, Corporate/Market and Network Governance: Shifting Spaces for Gender Equity in Education. *Gender, Work and Organization,* vol. 18, no. 5, pp. 433–66.

_____ and Judyth Sachs. 2007. *Performing and Reforming Leaders: Gender, Educational Restructuring and Organizational Change.* New York: SUNY Press.

_____, Karen Barty, and Pat Thomson. 2006. Principal Selection: Homosociability, the Search for Security and the Production of Normalised Principal Identities. *Educational Management, Administration and Leadership,* vol. 34, no. 3, pp. 297–317.

_____, Marie Brennan, and Lew Zipin (eds.). 2011. *Re-Positioning University Governance and Academic Work.* Rotterdam: Sense Publishers.

Bradley, Denise, Peter Noonan, Helen Nugent, and Bill Scales. 2008. *Review of Australian Higher Education: Final report.* Canberra: Commonwealth of Australia.

Brodie, Janine. 1996. New State Forms, New Political Spaces. In Robert Boyer and Daniel Drache (eds.), *State Against Markets: The Limits of Globalization* (pp. 383–98). New York: Routledge.

Brooks, Ann, and Alison Mackinnon (eds.). 2000. *Gender and the Restructured University.* Buckingham: Open University Press.

Brown, Phil, Hugh Lauder, and David Ashton. 2011. *The Global Auction: The Broken Promises of Education, Jobs and Incomes.* Oxford: Oxford University Press.

Carnoy, Martin. 1995. Structural Adjustment and the Changing Face of Education. *International Labour Review,* vol. 134, no. 6, pp. 653–73.

Coates, Hamish, Ian Dobson, Leo Goedegebuure, and Lynne Meek. 2009. Australia's Casual Approach to its Academic Teaching Force. *People and Place,* vol. 17, no. 4, pp. 47–48.

Connell, Raewyn, Julian Wood, and June Crawford. 2005. Global Connections of Intellectual Workers. *International Sociology,* vol. 20, no. 1, pp. 5–26.

Davies, Bronwyn, and Peter Bansel. 2007. Governmentality and Academic Work: Shaping the Hearts and Minds of Academic Workers. *Journal of Curriculum Theorizing,* vol. 23, no. 2, pp. 9–26.

Davis, Tracy, and Jason Laker. 2011. Introduction. In Jason Laker and Tracy Davis (eds.), *Masculinities in Higher Education: Theoretical and Practical Considerations* (pp. xi–xiv). New York: Routledge.

Deem, Rosemary. 2003. Gender, Organizational Cultures and the Practices of Manager-Academics in UK Universities. *Gender Work and Organization,* vol. 10, no. 2, pp. 239–59.

_____ and Jenny Ozga. 1997. Women Managing for Diversity in a Postmodern World. In Catherine Marshall (ed.), *Feminist Critical Policy Analysis,* Vol. 2 (pp. 25–40). London: Falmer Press.

Department of Education, Employment and Workplace Relations. 2009. *Transforming Australia's Higher Education System.* Canberra: Department of Education, Employment and Workplace Relations. http://www.deewr.gov.au/highereducation/Pages/TransformingAustraliasHESystem.aspx

Dever, Maryanne, and Zoe Morrison. 2009. Women, Research Performance and Research Context. *Tertiary Education and Management,* vol. 15, no. 1, pp. 49–62.

Diezmann, Carmel M., and Susan J. Grieshaber. 2010. *The Australian Story: Catalysts and Inhibitors in the Achievement of New Women Professors.* Melbourne: Higher Education Research and Development Society of Australasia Conference Proceedings.

Dill, Bonnie Thornton. 2009. Intersections, Identities and Inequalities in Higher Education. In Bonnie Thornton Dill, and Ruth Enid Zambrana (eds.), *Emerging Intersections: Race, Class, and Gender in Theory, Policy, and Practice* (pp. 229–52). New Brunswick, NJ: Rutgers University Press.

Findlow, Sally. 2013. Higher Education and Feminism in the Arab Gulf. *British Journal of Sociology of Education,* vol. 34, no. 1, pp. 112–31.

Glazer-Raymo, Judith (ed.). 2008. *Unfinished Business: New and Continuing Gender Challenges in Higher Education.* Baltimore: Johns Hopkins.

Gordon, George, and Celia Whitchurch. 2010. *Academic and Professional Identities in Higher Education.* London: Routledge.

Graduate Careers Australia. 2012. *GradStats.* http://www.graduatecareers.com.au/research/researchreports/gradstats/

Gribble, Cate, and Jill Blackmore. 2012. Re-positioning Australia's International Education in Global Knowledge Economies: Implications of Shifts in Skilled Migration Policies for Universities. *Journal of Higher Education Policy and Management,* vol. 34, no. 4, pp. 341–54.

Held, David, Anthony McGrew, David Goldblatt, and Jonathan Perraton (eds.). 1999. *Global Transformations: Politics, Economics and Culture.* Cambridge: Polity Press.

Heward, Christine, Paul Taylor, and Rhiannon Vickers. 1997. Gender, Race and Career Success in the Academic Profession. *Journal of Further and Higher Education,* vol. 21, no. 2, pp. 205–18.

Hey, Valerie, and Simon Bradford. 2004. The Return of the Repressed? The Gender Politics of Emergent Forms of Professionalism in Education. *Journal of Education Policy,* vol. 19, no. 6, pp. 691–713.

Husu, Lisa, and Louise Morley. 2000. Academe and Gender: What Has and Has Not Changed? *Higher Education in Europe,* vol. 25, no. 2, pp. 2–4.

Jos, Helke. 2011. Transnational Academic Mobility and Gender. *Globalisation, Societies and Education,* vol. 9, no. 2, pp. 183–209.

Kelsey, Jane. 1995. *The New Zealand Experiment: A World Model of Structural Adjustment?* Wellington: Bridgit Wlliams.

Lyotard, Jean-Francois. 1984. *The Postmodern Condition: A Report on Knowledge.* Manchester: Manchester University Press.

Marginson, Simon. 2010. How Universities Have been Positioned as Teams in a Knowledge Economy World Cup. In Jill Blackmore, Marie Brennan, and Lew Zipin (eds.), *Re-Positioning University Governance and Academic Work* (pp. 17–33). Rotterdam: Sense Publishers.

––––––. 2011. Higher Education and Public Good. *Higher Education Quarterly,* vol. 65, no. 4, pp. 411–33.

––––––. 2012. The Impossibility of Capitalist Markets in Higher Education Published online by *Journal of Education Policy* 30 November. http://dx.doi.org/10.1080/02680939.2012.747109

McWilliam, Erica, and Paul Taylor. 1998. Teacher Im/material: Challenging the New Pedagogies of Instructional Design. *Educational Researcher,* vol. 27, no. 8, pp. 29–35.

Metcalfe, Amy, and Sheila Slaughter. 2008. The Differential Effects of Academic Capitalism on Women in the Academy. In Judith Glazer-Raymo (ed.), *Unfinished Agendas: New and Continuing Gender Challenges in Higher Education* (pp. 80–111). Baltimore: John Hopkins University Press.

Morley, Louise. 2003. *Quality and Power in Higher Education.* London: McGraw Hill.

––––––. 2000. The Micropolitics of Gender in the Learning Society. *Higher Education in Europe.* DOI: 10.1080/03797720050115490

National Board of Education, Employment and Training. 1996. *Equality, Diversity and Excellence: Advancing the National Higher Education Equity Framework.* Canberra: National Board of Education, Employment and Training.

Newson, Janet. 1994. "Technopedagogy": A Critical Evaluation of the Effects on Academic Staff of Computerised Instructional Technologies in Higher Education. *Higher Education Policy,* vol. 7, no. 2, pp. 37–40.

Nussbaum, Martha. 2010. *Not for Profit: The Case for the Humanities.* Boston: Harvard University Press.

Olssen, Mark, John Codd, and Anne-Marie O'Neill. 2004. *Education Policy: Globalisation, Citizenship, and Democracy.* London: Sage.

Ong, Aihwa. 2007. Neoliberalism as a Mobile Technology. *Transactions of the Institute of British Geographers,* vol. 32, pp. 3–8.

Organization for Economic Cooperation and Development. 2009. *Higher Education to 2030.* Paris: OECD.

Pande, Rohini, and Deanna Ford. 2011. *Gender Quotas and Female Leadership.* World Bank. http://wdronline.worldbank.org/worldbank/a/c.html/world_development_report_2012/background_papers_notes/WB.978-0-8213-8810-5.references.sec2

Pocock, Barbara. 2011. *Doing Things Differently: Case Studies of Work-Life Innovation in Six Australian Workplaces.* Adelaide: Centre for Work and Life, University of South Australia.

Post. 2010.

Reay, Diane. 2000. "Dim Dross": Marginalized Women both Inside and Outside the Academy. *Women's Studies International Forum,* vol. 23, no. 1 (Jan.-Feb.), pp. 13–21.

Riegraf, Birgit, Brigitte Aulenbacher, Edit Kirsch-Auwarter, and Ursula Muller. 2010. *Gender Change in Academia.* Berlin: Verlag.

Rizvi, Fazal, and Bob Lingard. 2010. *Globalising Education Policy.* London: Routledge.

Rowlands, Julie. 2011 (October). Academic Boards: Less Intellectual and More Academic Capital in Higher Education Governance? *Studies in Higher Education*, iFirst Article, pp. 1–16. doi.org/10.1080/03075079.2011.619655

Shapper, Jan, and Susan Mayson. 2005. Managerialism, Internationalization, Taylorization and the Deskilling of Academic Work: Evidence from an Australian University. In Peter Ninnes and Meeri Hellstén (eds.), *Internationalizing Higher Education* (pp. 181–97). New York: Springer-Verlag.

Slaughter, Sheila, and Gary Rhoades. 2004. *Academic Capitalism and the New Economy.* Baltimore: Johns Hopkins.

———, and Larry L. Leslie. 1997. *Academic Capitalism: Politics, Policies, and the Entrepreneurial University.* Baltimore, MD: Johns-Hopkins.

Sobehart, Helen (ed.). 2006. *Women Leading Education across the Continents.* London: Rowman and Littlefield.

Strathern, Maralyn (ed.). 2000. *Audit Cultures: Anthropological Studies in Accountability, Ethics and the Academy.* London: Routledge.

UN Educational, Scientific and Cultural Organization. 2009. *Global Education Digest.* Paris: UNESCO.

Unterhalter, Elaine. 2007. *Gender, Schooling and Global Social Justice.* London: Routledge.

Walker, Melanie. 2006. *Higher Education Pedagogies.* Buckingham: Open University Press.

Index

About the Editors and Contributors

Monisha Bajaj is associate professor of International and Multicultural Education in the School of Education at the University of San Francisco, United States. Her research and teaching interests focus on peace and human rights education, social inequalities and schooling, and educational innovation in the Global South. She is the editor of the *Encyclopedia of Peace Education* and is the author of a teacher-training manual for the UN Educational, Scientific and Cultural Organization on human rights education as well as *Schooling for Social Change: The Rise and Impact of Human Rights Education in India*, which received the Jackie Kirk Outstanding Book Prize of the Comparative and International Education Society in 2012.

Lesley Bartlett is associate professor in the Department of International and Transcultural Studies at Teachers College, Columbia University, United States. Her research and teaching interests include studies in literacy and multilingualism; migration, development, and education; and sociocultural studies of teaching and learning. Her publications include *The Word and the World: The Cultural Politics of Literacy in Brazil*, *Additive Schooling in Subtractive Times* (with Ofelia Garcia), *Teaching in Tension* (edited with Frances Vavrus), and *Refugees, Immigrants and Education in the Global South* (edited with Ameena Ghaffar-Kucher).

Jill Blackmore is Alfred Deakin professor in the Faculty of Arts and Education, and director of the Center for Research in Educational Futures and Innovation, at Deakin University, Australia. Her research interests include, from a feminist perspective, globalization, education policy and governance in universities, educational leadership and redesign, and teachers' and academics' work. Recent publications include *Performing and Reforming Leaders: Gender, Educational Restructuring and Organisational Change* (with Judyth Sachs), *Repositioning the University: Changing Governance and Academic Work* (co-edited with M. Brennan and L. Zipin), and *Mobile Teachers and Curriculum in International Schooling* (co-edited with R. Arber and A. Vongalis-Macrow).

Rosa Nidia Buenfil is professor at the Department of Educational Research, Center of Research and Advanced Studies of the National Polytechnic Institute, Mexico. Her two main research interests are the political and discursive analysis of educational reforms in Mexican history, and contemporary theoretical debates (poststructuralism, globalization, territoriality, cosmopolitics). Recent publications include: Politics, Global Territories and Educational Spaces, in Popkewitz, and Rizvi's *Globalization and the Study of Education*; The Debate on

Subjectivity Does Not End, in Peters and De Alba's *Subjects in Process*; and Subjectivation, Democracy and Cosmopolitics in *World Journal of Education*.

Martin Carnoy is Vida Jacks professor of Education and Economics at Stanford University, United States. He writes on the underlying political economy of educational policy. Much of his work is comparative and international and investigates the impact of global economic and social change on educational systems. Examples of this are his books *Sustaining the New Economy: Work, Family and Community in the Information Age*; *Cuba's Academic Advantage*; and *The Low Achievement Trap*. His latest book compares higher educational expansion, financing, and quality in Brazil, China, India, and Russia—*University Expansion in a Changing Global Economy*.

Jan Currie is emeritus professor in the School of Education, Murdoch University, Australia, and works part-time in the Pay Equity Unit of the Department of Commerce in the Western Australian State Government. She has written extensively on globalization and its impact on higher education and on the gendered nature of universities. She co-edited *Universities and Globalization* and co-authored *Gendered Universities in Globalized Economies*: *Globalizing Practices and University Responses*, and *Academic Freedom in Hong Kong*. Her most recent publications are on pay equity audits in Australian and Swedish universities.

Noel Gough is Foundation professor of Outdoor and Environmental Education in the Faculty of Education, La Trobe University, Melbourne, Australia. Previously he held senior academic appointments at the University of Canberra and Deakin University, and has also held visiting fellowships at universities in Canada, South Africa, and the United Kingdom. His teaching, scholarship, and publications focus on educational philosophy and theory, curriculum inquiry, and poststructuralist research methodologies, with particular reference to environmental education, science education, internationalization, and globalization.

Catherine A. Odora Hoppers holds a South African Research chair in Development Education at the University of South Africa. She has been a distinguished professional at the Human Sciences Research Council and an associate professor at the University of Pretoria. She is also the recipient of honorary doctorates from Orebro University (Sweden) and Nelson Mandela Metropolitan University (South Africa). She is a member of the Academy of Science of South Africa and a fellow of the African Academy of Sciences.

Peter Kelly has published extensively on young people, the practice of youth studies, social theory, and globalization. He recently held a chair in Childhood and Youth Studies at Edge Hill University, United Kingdom and is currently Deputy Head of School (Research and Innovation), School of Education, RMIT (Australia). His current research interests include a critical engagement with young people and new cultures of democracy in the context of the Great Recession, austerity, and the aftermath of the global financial crisis. His books include *Working in Jamie's Kitchen: Salvation, Passion and Young Workers* (co-authored with Lyn Harrison) and *The Self as Enterprise: Foucault and the "Spirit" of 21st Century Capitalism*.

Nancy Kendall is associate professor of Educational Policy Studies at the University of Wisconsin-Madison, United States. Kendall conducts comparative ethnographic research on global constructions of international development education policy and their intersections with children's and families' daily lives. Research projects have included Education For All, gender and schooling, and political democratization and educational governance. She is the author of *The Sex Education Debates* and has published in journals including *CICE*, *Compare*, *Comparative Education Review*, *International Journal of Educational Development*, and *Sexuality Research and Social Policy*.

Jane Kenway is a professorial fellow of the Australian Research Council, member of the Australian Academy of Social Sciences, and professor, Education Faculty, Monash University, Australia. Her research focuses on the politics of educational change in the context of wider social, cultural, and political change. Her recent joint authored books are *Haunting the Knowledge Economy*, *Masculinity Beyond the Metropolis*, and *Consuming Children: Education-Advertising-Entertainment*. Her most recent jointly edited book is *Globalising the Research Imagination*. Her current Australian Research Council team research project is *Elite Independent Schools in Globalising Circumstances: A Multi-sited Global Ethnography*.

Molly N.N. Lee is the former program specialist in higher education at UN Educational, Scientific and Cultural Organization Asia and the Pacific Regional Bureau for Education in Bangkok. Previously, she has been a professor of Education in Universiti Sains Malaysia, Penang, Malaysia. Her professional expertise is in higher education, teacher education, information and communication technologies in education, and education for sustainable development. Her recent academic publications include Management of Research and Innovation in Malaysia, Globalizing Practices in Asian Universities, Centralized Decentralization in Malaysian Education, Teacher Education in Malaysia: Current Issues and Future Prospects, The Impact of Globalization on Education in Malaysia, Case Studies of National and Regional Implementation Schemes Related to the Use of ICT in Education: The Case of Malaysia, and others.

Caroline Manion holds a Ph.D. from the Ontario Institute for Studies in Education, University of Toronto (OISE, UT), Canada, with a specialization in comparative, international, and development education. She is currently an instructor in the Department of Leadership, Higher and Adult Education and the Comparative, International and Development Education collaborative degree program at OISE, UT. Her research interests include global governance and educational multilateralism, gender equity and social justice, education for social transformation, social movements and civil society, development ethics, feminist transnationalism, postcolonial theory, and sociology of religion.

Kathryn Moeller is assistant professor in Educational Policy Studies and an affiliate of the Department of Gender and Women's Studies at the University of Wisconsin-Madison, United States. Her areas of research specialization in education include gender, poverty, development, globalization, and corporations in the field of education, which she analyzes using critical social theories and ethnographic methodologies. Her current research examines the influence of U.S. transnational corporations on the practices, policies, and institutions in the field of gender, education, and development. She has a publication in *International Journal of Educational Development* and a forthcoming publication in Feminist Studies.

Karen Monkman is professor at DePaul University, United States. Her research interests encompass equity, lived experience, and policy, and focus on education as it relates to gender and globalization. Recent publications on globalization include a co-edited thematic section and co-authored section introduction in *Handbook of Social Justice in Education* (with Pauline

Lipman). Gender-related work on policy can be found in *Theory and Research in Education*, and *Research in Comparative and International Education*; and on transformative education and female genital cutting in *Women's Studies International Forum*, and other publications.

Karen Mundy is professor and associate dean of research at the Ontario Institute for Studies in Education, University of Toronto, Canada. Her research interests include the global politics of Education For All, educational policy and reform in sub-Saharan Africa, the role of civil society organizations in educational change, and global citizenship education. She has published five books and more than four dozen articles and book chapters, including most recently an edited volume entitled *Public Private Partnerships in Education: New Actors and Modes of Governance in a Globalizing World*. She has worked with foundations, international organizations, and nongovernmental organizations.

Lynne Parmenter is associate dean of the Graduate School of Education at Nazarbayev University, Astana, Kazakhstan. She previously lived and worked in Japan for seventeen years, teaching at schools and then working as an associate professor at Fukushima University and as a professor at Waseda University. She is interested in global citizenship education, intercultural education, language education, teacher education, and education policy and curriculum, and has received funding for projects in these areas in Japan, the United Kingdom, and Kazakhstan. Recent publications include *The Common European Framework of Reference: The Globalisation of Language Education Policy*, co-edited with Michael Byram.

Rosalind Latiner Raby is senior lecturer in the Educational Leadership and Policy Studies Department of the College of Education, California State University, Northridge, United States. She also serves as the Director of California Colleges for International Education, a non-profit consortium whose membership includes eighty-four California community colleges. Since 1984, she has advanced community college internationalization as well as research on community college global counterparts.

Rachel Silver is a graduate student in educational policy studies and anthropology at the University of Wisconsin-Madison, United States. Her research focuses on gendered constructions and experiences of global educational development policy in East and Southeast Africa. She is co-author of *Educated for Change?: Muslim Refugee Women in the West* (with Patricia Buck), an ethnographic exploration of Somali refugee women's schooling experiences in Kenya's Dadaab refugee camps and one US-based site of secondary resettlement.

Carol Anne Spreen is associate professor in the Department of Leadership, Foundations and Policy at the University of Virginia, United States, and visiting professor at the University of Johannesburg, South Africa. Her scholarship and policy work focus on issues of education rights, school reform, and educational equity. Her current research centers on teacher's lives and work in rural South African schools, and using participatory/action research to study the long-term impact of poverty and inequality on educational access and outcomes.

Nelly P. Stromquist is professor of international education policy in the College of Education at the University of Maryland, United States. She specializes in issues related to international development education and gender, which she examines from a critical sociology perspective. Her research interests focus on the dynamics among educational policies and practices, gender relations, and social change. Her most recent books include co-editing *The World Bank and*